D1736665

THE OXFORD HANDBOOK OF

ECOCRITICISM

THE OXFORD HANDBOOK OF

ECOCRITICISM

Edited by

GREG GARRARD

OXFORD

UNIVERSITY PRESS

OXFORD
UNIVERSITY PRESS

Oxford University Press is a department of the University of Oxford.
It furthers the University's objective of excellence in research, scholarship,
and education by publishing worldwide.

Oxford   New York
Auckland   Cape Town   Dar es Salaam   Hong Kong   Karachi
Kuala Lumpur   Madrid   Melbourne   Mexico City   Nairobi
New Delhi   Shanghai   Taipei   Toronto

With offices in
Argentina   Austria   Brazil   Chile   Czech Republic   France   Greece
Guatemala   Hungary   Italy   Japan   Poland   Portugal   Singapore
South Korea   Switzerland   Thailand   Turkey   Ukraine   Vietnam

Oxford is a registered trademark of Oxford University Press
in the UK and certain other countries.

Published in the United States of America by
Oxford University Press
198 Madison Avenue, New York, NY 10016

Library of Congress Cataloging-in-Publication Data

The Oxford handbook of ecocriticism / edited by Greg Garrard.
pages cm
Includes bibliographical references and index.
ISBN 978-0-19-974292-9 (acid-free paper)   1. Ecocriticism.   2. Ecology in literature.
3. Philosophy of nature in literature.   4. Conservation of natural resources in literature.
I. Garrard, Greg, editor of compilation.
PN98.E36O94 2014
809'.93355—dc23
2013013891

1 3 5 7 9 8 6 4 2
Printed in the United States of America
on acid-free paper

CONTENTS

Preface   ix
CHERYLL GLOTFELTY

Introduction   1
GREG GARRARD

PART I HISTORY

1. Being Green in Late Medieval English Literature   27
   GILLIAN RUDD

2. Shadows of the Renaissance   40
   ROBERT N. WATSON

3. Romanticism and Ecocriticism   60
   KATE RIGBY

4. Cholera, Kipling, and Tropical India   80
   UPAMANYU PABLO MUKHERJEE

5. Ecocriticism and Modernism   98
   ANNE RAINE

6. W. E. B. Du Bois at the Grand Canyon: Nature, History,
   and Race in *Darkwater*   118
   JOHN CLABORN

7. Pataphysics and Postmodern Ecocriticism: A Prospectus   132
   ADAM DICKINSON

PART II THEORY

8. Ecocriticism and the Politics of Representation   155
   CHERYL LOUSLEY

9. Cosmovisions: Environmental Justice, Transnational American
   Studies, and Indigenous Literature   172
   JONI ADAMSON

10. Feminist Science Studies and Ecocriticism: Aesthetics and
    Entanglement in the Deep Sea   188
    STACY ALAIMO

11. Mediating Climate Change: Ecocriticism, Science Studies,
    and *The Hungry Tide*   205
    ADAM TREXLER

12. Ecocriticism, Posthumanism, and the Biological Idea of Culture   225
    HELENA FEDER

13. Ferality Tales   241
    GREG GARRARD

14. Biosemiotic Criticism   260
    TIMO MARAN

15. Phenomenology   276
    TIMOTHY CLARK

16. Deconstruction and/as Ecology   291
    TIMOTHY MORTON

17. Queer Life? Ecocriticism after the Fire   305
    CATRIONA SANDILANDS

18. Postcolonialism   320
    ELIZABETH DELOUGHREY

19. Extinctions: Chronicles of Vanishing Fauna in the Colonial and
    Postcolonial Caribbean   341
    LIZABETH PARAVISINI-GEBERT

PART III GENRE

20. Ecocritical Approaches to Literary Form and Genre: Urgency,
    Depth, Provisionality, Temporality   361
    RICHARD KERRIDGE

21. Are You Serious? A Modest Proposal for Environmental Humor   377
    MICHAEL P. BRANCH

22. Is American Nature Writing Dead? 391
   DANIEL J. PHILIPPON

23. Environmental Writing for Children: A Selected Reconnaissance of
   Heritages, Emphases, Horizons 408
   LAWRENCE BUELL

24. The Contemporary English Novel and its Challenges to Ecocriticism 423
   ASTRID BRACKE

25. "A Music Numerous as Space": Cognitive Environment and the
   House that Lyric Builds 440
   SHARON LATTIG

26. Rethinking Eco-Film Studies 459
   DAVID INGRAM

27. Green Banjo: The Ecoformalism of Old-Time Music 475
   SCOTT KNICKERBOCKER

28. Media Moralia: Reflections on Damaged Environments
   and Digital Life 487
   ANDREW McMURRY

29. Talking about Climate Change: The Ecological Crisis
   and Narrative Form 502
   URSULA KLUWICK

PART IV THE VIEWS FROM HERE

30. Ecocriticism in Japan 519
   YUKI MASAMI

31. Engaging with *Prakriti*: A Survey of Ecocritical Praxis in India 527
   SWARNALATHA RANGARAJAN

32. Chinese Ecocriticism in the Last Ten Years 537
   QINGQI WEI

33. German Ecocriticism: An Overview 547
   AXEL GOODBODY

34. Barrier Beach 560
   ROB NIXON

Index 567

PREFACE

In 1980 population biologist Paul Ehrlich and economist Julian L. Simon made a wager. Ehrlich, in his best-selling book *The Population Bomb* (1968), forecast that the exponentially growing human population coupled with increasingly resource-consumptive lifestyles of the affluent would outstrip natural resources, resulting in widespread famine in the 1970s and 1980s and resource shortages on a global scale. Simon, author of *The Ultimate Resource* (1981), countered that human ingenuity, technological innovation, and market forces would keep pace with environmental problems, averting catastrophe perhaps indefinitely. The bet concerned whether the prices of five different commodity metals would increase or decrease in ten years. Prices fell during the decade, and Simon won the first round of a continuing debate between environmental doomsayers and those whose hope lies in *homo sapiens technologicus*. Simon's victory notwithstanding, the specter of environmental catastrophe persists, and although cornucopians and environmental jeremiahs disagree, ultimately both positions share faith in the human potential to create a better world, cornucopians through innovation within the framework of the existing social order, jeremiahs through changes in policy and culture. Ecocriticism emerged as a movement among literary scholars in the early 1990s, born of an awareness of environmental crisis and a desire to be part of the solution.

The Oxford Handbook of Ecocriticism marks the coming-of-age of this movement. The 2013 projected publication date of this volume coincides with the twenty-first anniversary of the major professional organization in this field, the Association for the Study of Literature and Environment (ASLE). Founded in the US in 1992, ASLE began with fifty-four members, most of whom shared a scholarly interest in American nature writing, a tradition that had until then received negligible attention from literary critics. By 2012 ASLE's membership topped one thousand, with nine international affiliate organizations—in the UK and Ireland, Canada, India (two groups), Japan, Korea, Taiwan, Australia and New Zealand, and Europe. As David Mazel's *A Century of Early Ecocriticism* documents, writers and scholars have long been interested in the relationship between literature and the environment. The consolidation of these concerns in the late twentieth century under the rubric of ecocriticism created a community of scholars whose conversations and collaborations have accelerated the rhizomatic spread of this field to the point where a guidebook is needed to navigate the terrain.

The proliferation of anthologies of ecocriticism is one measure of the astonishing growth of environmental literary studies, and the specific topics of these volumes as well as their places of publication map the diversification of the field.[1] Between 1990 and 1995, seven critical anthologies were published on literature and environment, most of which investigated the representation of nature, wilderness, or environment in literary works. In the next five years, 1996 to 2000, eighteen ecocriticism anthologies appeared, broadening the purview to include urban environments, ecofeminist perspectives, rhetorical studies, and international audiences (with books published in Japanese, Korean, German, and French). Between 2001 and 2005, twenty-three ecocritical anthologies were published, further widening the reach "beyond nature writing"—as one book was entitled—with titles on environmental justice, theater, ecolinguistics, children's literature, and animal studies. The years 2006 to 2010 brought to print thirty-three ecocritical anthologies and marked the rise of postcolonial ecocritical studies, queer ecology, transatlantic conversations, toxic discourse, studies of visual media, and an expanding international reach in subject and place of publication to include China, India, Australia, the Caribbean, Finland, Spain, and Latin America. In just two years, 2011 and 2012, twenty anthologies have been published or are forthcoming, continuing the earlier interest in animals, and also including the posthuman, naturecultures, material ecocriticism, introductory anthologies for classroom use, and titles from or about Korea, Italy, Turkey, and Norway, in addition to the perennially productive United States and United Kingdom.

It is inaccurate to say, as some have claimed, that early ecocritics were hostile to literary theory. After all, what is ecocriticism if not an effort to bring environmental considerations into the discourse of literary criticism and theory? *The Ecocriticism Reader* (1996), edited by Cheryll Glotfelty and Harold Fromm, frequently cited as a foundational anthology in this field, opened with a substantial section on ecotheory. Regardless of ecocriticism's early stance toward theory, one of the most striking aspects of the *Oxford Handbook of Ecocriticism* as a state-of-the-field collection is how theoretical the field has become, heavily influenced by continental philosophy and thinkers such as Gaston Bachelard, Roland Barthes, Ulrich Beck, Guy Debord, Gilles Deleuze and Félix Guattari, Jacques Derrida, Michel Foucault, Sigmund Freud, David Harvey, Martin Heidegger, Edmund Husserl, Wolfgang Iser, Fredric Jameson, Jacques Lacan, Ernesto Laclau and Chantal Mouffe, Bruno Latour, Karl Marx, Maurice Merleau-Ponty, Edward Said, Ferdinand de Saussure, Gayatri Spivak, Raymond Williams, and Slavoj Žižek, among others cited by the contributors to this volume. These sources help ecocritics to theorize connections between literature, the environment, and, for example, the nature of language, textuality, perception of space, construction of difference, species boundaries, social class, power, risk, ideology, agency, human psychology, epistemology, and ontology.

Equally noteworthy in contemporary ecocriticism is that a handful of recent theorists (several are contributors to this volume) are cited with great frequency, raising questions and piloting approaches that are shaping the discourse of ecocriticism in the twenty-first century: Stacy Alaimo, Lawrence Buell, Donna Haraway, Ursula Heise, Timothy Morton, Catriona Sandilands, Rob Nixon, Val Plumwood, and Cary Wolfe. Taken together, this new canon of theorists suggests that emerging directions in ecocriticism include interrogating conceptions of the human to take fuller account of embodiment, materiality, trans-corporeality, contingency, hybridity, animality, queerness, and technology. Race, class, and gender stand out as important ecocritical categories in current practice, inflecting work in postcolonial ecocriticism, environmental justice, and globalization studies. The nature of Nature continues to preoccupy ecocritics, with increasing emphasis on breaking down the nature-culture binary, critiquing the conceit of a nature separate from the human realm. Indeed, the growth of ecocriticism parallels the rising awareness of the "end of nature," as Bill McKibben's 1989 book on climate change was so memorably titled. We live in the age of the Anthropocene, in which humans are a major force influencing the land, water, and weather of the Earth. That human-wrought changes are damaging the life support systems of the planet lends urgency to any project that may help us better understand culture as reflector and shaper of people's attitudes and actions.

The *Oxford Handbook of Ecocriticism* joins more than three hundred other titles in fourteen subjects covered by the Oxford Handbook series. The series is rapidly expanding and is now online. In 2012 the Literature subject area had twenty-one titles, with strengths in Shakespeare, early modern, modern, and American topics. This volume on ecocriticism is one of the first volumes in the series devoted to criticism and theory. The thirty-plus essays featured in *The Oxford Handbook of Ecocriticism*, authored by a mix of established leaders and newer scholars, together offer a critical overview of major historical periods, theoretical approaches, topics, genres, and geographies. In commissioning essays, editor Greg Garrard has struck a fine balance between critical overviews of major areas of inquiry and experimental forays into new territory. Readers will welcome fresh approaches to ecocritically well-studied periods such as romanticism and the nineteenth-century as well as ventures into less-studied periods, such as the medieval and the postmodern. You will find essays representing lively theoretical arenas, such as postcolonial ecocriticism, environmental justice, and feminist science studies, and essays venturing into new realms such as biosemiotics and pataphysics. In addition to essays that make new arguments about nature-oriented genres—for example, Daniel J. Philippon's "Is American Nature Writing Dead?"—are pioneering treatments of genres that have been heretofore all but ignored by ecocritics, genres such as humor, old-time music, children's literature, and digital media. Finally, in a selective update of Patrick D. Murphy's *The Literature of Nature: An International Sourcebook* (1998), *The Oxford Handbook of Ecocriticism* concludes with reports on ecocritical activity and research in India, China, Japan, and Germany, and a coda by one of the most eloquent of contemporary environmental critics, South African writer Rob Nixon.

If population was regarded by many as the most pressing environmental issue of the 1970s and 1980s, the dominant environmental issue looming over this collection like a big, dark cloud is climate change. Many essays mention climate change, and two explicitly focus on it. Adam Trexler, whose essay considers how fiction mediates climate change, found more than two hundred works of fiction about anthropogenic global warming, published in the last thirty years. Ursula Kluwick examines how climate change science is communicated to the public via nonfiction narrative forms such as the documentary, popular science books, and climate change manuals. However, despite keen attention to climate change, compared with early work in this field ecocriticism as practiced today focuses less on specific environmental issues and more on questions of environmentality and the nature of the human.

After twenty-one years of concerted effort, what have ecocritics achieved? Ecocriticism has changed the landscape of literary studies, moving from the margins into the mainstream. Virtually all major academic journals in literary studies publish ecocriticism, and many have devoted special issues to the topic. Ecocriticism has attracted the best and brightest minds in the discipline, the editor of the *Oxford Handbook* being a prime example. Ecocriticism has given literary scholars, most of whom are teachers, a meaningful role to play in addressing the most pressing issue of our time—the degraded environment. But has ecocriticism made a difference? It is too early to tell. The field is yet young. By the geological clock twenty-one years is infinitesimal. Even in the timescale of human evolution, two decades is scarcely one generation. It takes time for ideas to reach a tipping point. It takes even more time for culture to change. Meanwhile, the work goes on at a prodigious pace. Were he alive today, poet Allen Ginsberg might howl:

> I saw the best minds of my generation obsessed by
> theory, burning ecocritical brainy,
> chaining themselves to the computer screens at dawn
> looking for a climate fix.

Cheryll Glotfelty

NOTE

1. This paragraph and the final paragraph are adapted from Cheryll Glotfelty, "Why Anthologize Ecocriticism? Questioning Audience, Purpose, Publisher, and Cost," a paper delivered at the conference of the Association for the Study of Literature and Environment, Bloomington, Indiana, June 2011.

LIST OF CONTRIBUTORS

Joni Adamson is professor of english and environmental humanities at Arizona State University, where she is a Senior Sustainability Scholar. She is the author of *American Indian Literature, Environmental Justice, and Ecocriticism* (2001) and co-editor of *American Studies, Ecocriticism and Citizenship* (2013). Her co-edited volume, *Keywords for Environmental Studies* is forthcoming.

Stacy Alaimo is professor of english at the University of Texas at Arlington. Her publications include *Undomesticated Ground: Recasting Nature as Feminist Space* (2000), *Material Feminisms* (edited with Susan Hekman, 2008) and *Bodily Natures: Science, Environment, and the Material Self* (2010), which received the ASLE Award for Ecocriticism. She is currently writing about sea creatures, science, and aesthetics.

Astrid Bracke teaches at the Radboud University Nijmegen (the Netherlands) and has published in *English Studies* and *ISLE*. Her current research examines the development of the new British nature writing since 2000, its depiction of contemporary natural landscapes, and particularly how ecocriticism can engage with these.

Michael P. Branch is professor of literature and environment at the University of Nevada, Reno. He has published many books and articles on environmental literature and is also a humorist and essayist whose work appears often in journals and magazines. His "Rants from the Hill" essays appear monthly in High Country News online.

Lawrence Buell is Powell M. Cabot Research Professor of American Literature at Harvard University and author of several ecocritical books including most recently *The Future of Environmental Criticism* (2005). His contribution to this volume is related to a book-in-progress on the aesthetics, ethics, and politics of environmental memory.

John Claborn completed his PhD at the University of Illinois in 2012. His research has been published in *English Language Notes*, *ISLE*, *Modern Fiction Studies*, and *Studies in American Jewish Literature*. Claborn teaches at the University of Illinois and is working on a book manuscript called *Ecology of the Color Line: Race and Nature in American Literature, 1895-1941*.

Timothy Clark is professor of english at the University of Durham and a specialist in the fields of modern literary theory and continental philosophy, Romanticism, and ecocriticism. He has published many articles in literary and philosophical journals and published seven monographs, including *The Cambridge Introduction to Literature and the Environment* (2011).

Elizabeth DeLoughrey is an associate professor of english at the University of California, Los Angeles. She is the author of *Routes and Roots: Navigating Caribbean and Pacific Island Literatures* (2007) and co-editor of the collections *Caribbean Literature and the Environment: Between Nature and Culture* (2005) and *Postcolonial Ecologies: Literatures of the Environment* (2011).

Adam Dickinson is an associate professor in the English Department at Brock University in St. Catharines, Ontario, Canada. He is the co-editor (with Madhur Anand) of *Regreen: New Canadian Ecological Poetry*. He also has recent work in *ISLE: Interdisciplinary Studies in Literature and Environment*.

Helena Feder is associate professor of literature and environment at East Carolina University. She has published articles in *Women's Studies, Green Letters, Interdisciplinary Studies in Literature and Environment*, and the *Journal of Ecocriticism*. Her book, *Ecocriticism and the Idea of Culture* is forthcoming from Ashgate Press.

Greg Garrard is Sustainability Professor at the University of British Columbia. He is the author of *Ecocriticism* (2004, 2011 2nd edition) as well as numerous essays on animal studies and environmental criticism. He has recently edited *Teaching Ecocriticism and Green Cultural Studies* (2011) and become co-editor of *Green Letters: Studies in Ecocriticism*, the journal of the Association for the Study of Literature and the Environment (UKI).

Cheryll Glotfelty is professor of literature and environment at the University of Nevada, Reno. She is the co-editor of *The Bioregional Imagination: Literature, Ecology, and Place* (2012) and *The Ecocriticism Reader: Landmarks in Literary Ecology* (1996) and editor of *Literary Nevada: Writings from the Silver State* (2008).

Axel Goodbody is professor of German studies and European culture at the University of Bath. A past president of the European Association for the Study of Literature, Culture and Environment, he is associate editor of the online journal *Ecozon@*. Recent publications include the edited volume *Ecocritical Theory: New European Approaches* and an essay on "Frame Analysis and the Literature of Climate Change."

David Ingram is a lecturer in Screen Media at Brunel University, London. He is the author of *Green Screen: Environmentalism and Hollywood Cinema* (2000) and *The Jukebox in the Garden: Ecocriticism and American Popular Music Since 1960* (2010), as well as several articles on film and music. He is a member of the Advisory Board of the Association for the Study of Literature and the Environment-UKI.

Richard Kerridge is co-ordinator of Research and Postgraduate Studies at Bath Spa University and founding Chair of the Association for the Study of Literature and the Environment (United Kingdom and Ireland). He has recently completed *Beginning Ecocriticism* and has published ecocritical essays on a wide variety of topics. His nature writing has been published in *BBC Wildlife*, *Granta*, and *Poetry Review* and has twice received the *BBC Wildlife* Award for Nature Writing. Currently he is writing a memoir about British reptiles and amphibians.

Ursula Kluwick is lecturer in english literature at the University of Berne. She is the author of *Exploring Magic Realism in Salman Rushdie's Fiction* (2011), and she is currently working on a monograph dealing with the representation of water in Victorian literature.

Scott Knickerbocker is an assistant professor of english and environmental studies at The College of Idaho. He is the author of *Ecopoetics: The Language of Nature, the Nature of Language* (2012) and various journal articles and chapters for edited collections, most recently on Hemingway. Scott plays banjo in the Hokum Hi-Flyers, an old-time string band based in Boise, Idaho.

Sharon Lattig teaches at the University of Connecticut. Her research in the fields of lyric poetry, ecocriticism, and cognitive poetics has appeared in *Intertexts, Challenging the Boundaries* and *Contemporary Stylistics*. In 2009 and 2010, she taught at Universität Osnabrück as a Fulbright Scholar. Her doctorate is from The CUNY Graduate Center.

Cheryl Lousley is assistant professor of english and interdisciplinary studies at Lakehead University, Canada. Her research is published in *Canadian Literature, Environmental Philosophy, Canadian Poetry, Essays on Canadian Writing, Interdisciplinary Studies in Literature and Environment*, and elsewhere. She edits the Environmental Humanities book series with Wilfrid Laurier University Press.

Timo Maran is a Senior Research Fellow at the Department of Semiotics, University of Tartu, Estonia. His publications include *Mimikri semiootika* [Semiotics of mimicry] (2008), *Readings in Zoosemiotics* (ed., with D. Martinelli and A. Turovski, 2011), *Semiotics in the Wild* (ed., with K. Lindström, R. Magnus, and M. Toennessen, 2012).

Yuki Masami is professor at Kanazawa University, Japan, where she teaches environmental literature and EFL. Yuki's recent works include *Mizu no oto no kioku* [Remembering the Sound of Water: Essays in Ecocriticism] (2010) and *Tabi no houe* [The Hearth of Contemporary Japanese Women Writers: Ecocritical Approaches to Literary Foodscapes] (2012).

Andrew McMurry is associate professor of english literature at the University of Waterloo, where he teaches environmental rhetoric, nineteenth century fiction and new media theory. He is the author of *Environmental Renaissance: Emerson, Thoreau, and the Systems of Nature* (2003) and various articles on ecocriticism, many of them on the Critical Ecologies stream of the online journal *Electronic Book Review.*

Timothy Morton is Rita Shea Guffey Chair of English at Rice University. He is the author of *Hyperobjects: Philosophy and Ecology after the End of the World* (2013), *Realist Magic: Objects, Ontology, Causality* (2013), *The Ecological Thought* (2010), and *Ecology without Nature* (2007).

Upamanyu Pablo Mukherjee is a reader at the Department of English and Comparative Literary Studies at Warwick University. He is the author of three monographs: *Crime and Empire* (2003), *Postcolonial Environments* (2010), and *Natural Disasters and Empire* (2013). He has also edited a special issue of the *Yearbook of English* on "Victorian World Literatures" (2011) and published widely in scholarly journals and edited collections.

Rob Nixon is the Rachel Carson Professor of English at the University of Wisconsin. He is the author of four books, including *Slow Violence and the Environmentalism of the Poor* (2011), which received an American Book Award and three other prizes. Nixon has written for the *New York Times*, the *New Yorker*, and elsewhere.

Lizabeth Paravisini-Gebert is professor of Caribbean culture and literature at Vassar College. She is the author of a number of books, including *Literatures of the Caribbean* (2008), and numerous articles and literary translations. She is currently working on a book entitled *Endangered Species: The Environment and the Discourse of the Caribbean Nation.*

Daniel J. Philippon is associate professor of english at the University of Minnesota, Twin Cities. He is the editor of *Our Neck of the Woods: Exploring Minnesota's Wild Places* (2009), among other books, and is a past president of the Association for the Study of Literature and Environment (ASLE).

Anne Raine is associate professor of english at the University of Ottawa. She has published on Willa Cather, Gertrude Stein, Marianne Moore, and W. E. B. Du Bois, and is completing a book on how female modernists from Stein to Zora Neale Hurston negotiated the divide between the professionalizing sciences and the feminized field of "nature work."

Swarnalatha Rangarajan is associate professor of english at the Department of Humanities and Social Sciences, Indian Institute of Technology Madras. She is the founding editor of the *Indian Journal of Ecocriticism* (IJE) and is currently working on a book project titled, *Ecocriticism of the Global South.*

Kate Rigby FAHA is professor of environmental humanities in the School of English, Communications and Performance Studies at Monash University. She is the author of *Topographies of the Sacred: The Poetics of Place in European Romanticism* (2004), and co-editor (with Axel Goodbody) of *Ecocritical Theory: New European Approaches* (2011).

Gillian Rudd is a reader at Liverpool University. Her publications include *Greenery: Ecocritical Readings of Late Medieval English Literature* (2007); articles on mice (*YES* 36:1, 2006), clouds (*Essays and Studies 2008: Literature and Science*), flowers (*The Oxford Handbook to Medieval Literature*, OUP, 2010), various pieces on *Sir Gawain and the Green Knight*, and "Animalia," a paper colloquium for *Studies in the Age of Chaucer* 34 (2012).

Catriona (Cate) Sandilands is a professor in the Faculty of Environmental Studies at York University (Canada) and the author of numerous articles and chapters on environmental literatures, cultural studies, and queer and feminist ecologies. She is co-editor of *Queer Ecologies: Sex, Nature, Politics, Desire* (2010).

Adam Trexler is an independent scholar, cyclist and environmental activist based in Oregon. He is the author, with Adeline Johns-Putra, of a survey of climate change literature and criticism in *WIREs Climate Change*.

Robert N. Watson is distinguished professor of english, associate Dean of humanities, and holds the Neikirk Chair for Educational Innovation at UCLA. His most recent book, *Back to Nature,* won the Dietz prize for the year's best book in early modern studies and the ASLE prize for the best book of ecocriticism.

Qingqi Wei is an associate professor of english in Nanjing Normal University, China. His publications include "Wei An (1960–1999): A Storyteller of Mother Earth," *ISLE* (Winter 2008) and "Ecocritics' Responsibility: An Interview with Scott Slovic on His *Going away to Think*," *Foreign Literary Studies* 31 (2009), and dozens of articles in Chinese. He is also the translator of a number of English novels.

THE OXFORD HANDBOOK OF

ECOCRITICISM

INTRODUCTION

GREG GARRARD

SEVENTEEN years ago Jennifer Wallace wrote a piece for the *Times Higher Education Supplement* introducing ecocriticism to British academia. An environmental activist nicknamed "Swampy" had recently become famous for constructing and inhabiting tunnels underneath woodlands threatened with road-building projects. According to Wallace, ecocritics such as Jonathan Bate and James McKusick were "Swampy's Smart Set"—the high-brow cultural arm of the environmental movement. The frame of reference of the article is explicitly Romantic: ecocriticism is understood to confront Marxists and New Historicists over the meaning and significance of British Romanticism. Marilyn Butler is quoted speaking of the new movement with patrician curiosity and indulgence. Wallace says Butler

> is a little uncertain about the parameters or the point of ecocriticism. "What is it? Who are they?" she wonders. Much of it seems to her to be old-fashioned and nostalgic writing about nature under a new, trendy name. But on the other hand, she is intrigued by the latest interest in science and man's dependence on his environment. (Wallace 1997)

Bate's responses to some degree confirm Butler's anxieties: he asserts that ecocriticism is an anti-Enlightenment counter-revolution inspired by British Romanticism and American wilderness writing. Jay Parini's 1995 *New York Times Magazine* article "The Greening of the Humanities" depicts ecocritical pioneers who share the values and ambitions of their British counterparts, but are healthier with deeper tans: "Magnificent specimens of the human animal" in fact (Parini 1995).

Perhaps it is something to warrant a stereotype. If so, the sturdy sandal-wearing backpacker/literary critic laboring to reverse the Enlightenment disenchantment of the world might seem tolerably flattering. This figure is, though, representative only of what Lawrence Buell, one of Parini's original "specimens," has taught us to see as "first-wave" ecocriticism: inclined to celebrate nature rather than querying "nature" as a concept; keen to derive inspiration as directly as possible from environmental activism; and willing to defer in matters of truth to the natural sciences, especially ecology. "Second-wave" ecocriticism is too diverse and diffuse to summarize, let alone stereotype, but its connections with political environmentalism and ecological science are, on the whole, more complex and ambivalent. As Buell observes, for second-wave critics, "The discourses of science and literature must be read both with and against each other" (Buell 2005, 19). As contributions to this volume suggest, queer, deconstructionist, and postcolonial varieties of ecocriticism are, at times, sharply critical of environmentalism: its metaphysics, its gender and racial politics, and its troubling relationship with colonial and neocolonial histories.

Even the metaphor of first and second wave is considered problematic. Buell himself cautions that it is not "a tidy, distinct succession" and observes that "Most currents set in motion by early ecocriticism continue to run strong, and most forms of second-wave revisionism involve building on as well as quarreling with precursors" (17). (Indeed, many second-wave critics wear Tevas for hiking just like their predecessors.) In a critique of both Buell's *The Future of Environmental Criticism* and my *Ecocriticism* (Routledge 2004, 2011 2nd edition), Greta Gaard has pointed out that ecofeminism and feminisms of color arguably predate both the ecocritical origin and the putative first wave of feminism without featuring prominently in either history. As a result, she argues, "feminists and ecocritics utilizing feminism's 'wave' metaphor will inadvertently erase the history of ecological feminism and feminisms of color from both feminism and ecocriticism alike" (Gaard 2010, 646). In their authoritative introduction to *Postcolonial Ecologies,* Elizabeth DeLoughrey and George Handley likewise "call attention to an implicit production of a singular American ecocritical genealogy that, like all histories, might be reconfigured in broader, more rhizomatic, terms" (DeLoughrey and Handley 2011, 15). Just as there were surely pallid, clean-shaven agoraphobes at the early conferences organized by the Association for the Study of Literature and the Environment (ASLE), there were essays with "second-wave" interests such as environmental justice in Cheryl Glotfelty and Harold Fromm's pioneering anthology *The Ecocriticism Reader.*

All such cautions notwithstanding, Buell is right to point out that "First-wave ecocritical calls for greater scientistic literacy tend to presuppose a bedrock "human" condition, to commend the scientific method's ability to describe natural laws, and to look to science as a corrective to critical subjectivism and cultural relativism" (18). By contrast, as several essays in this collection will show, ecocriticism is better characterized today as a critique of what Michel Foucault dubbed "bio-power," or "the entry of life into history, that is, the entry of phenomena peculiar to the life of the human species into the order of knowledge and power, into the sphere of political techniques" (141–142). Of course, as Foucault admits, biology and history had always been interwoven, but in the course of the eighteenth century the relationship was consciously integrated in techniques of political power for the first time. While for Foucault, the sole organism of interest is the human animal, and the institutions of bio-power the prison, the asylum and the sex clinic, ecocritics have extended his analysis far beyond our own species. As a result, the techniques and institutions of bio-power subjected to critique have come to include the *environmental surveillance* practiced and required by environmental organizations themselves. Timothy Luke's *Ecocritique*, an early example of the Foucauldian approach, characterized the work of the Worldwatch

Institute, which publishes reports on the "state of the world," in terms of disciplinary "geopower":

> As biological life is refracted through economic, political and technological exis-
> tence, "the facts of life" pass into fields of control for disciplines of ecoknowledge and
> spheres of intervention for their management as geopower at various institutional
> sites. (Luke 1997, 91)

In 1997, Luke's skeptical approach was somewhat heterodox; now it is the norm. The second part of this volume, "Theory," attests to the prevalence of Foucauldian ecocriticism
and to the proliferation and diversification that is still going on.

Summaries and generalizations of any kind are risky, as we have seen. Nevertheless,
we might encapsulate the mission of the environmental humanities, of which ecocriticism is a key part,[1] in chiasmic terms as the *historicization of ecology* and the *ecologiza-
tion of history*. As the Foucauldian approach emphasizes, ecology and environmentalism
are themselves the outcomes of specific institutional and political histories, which continue to inform, constrain, and deform both fields of endeavor today. It is necessary
to historicize ecology, as well as learning from it. At the same time, the environmental humanities challenge the anthropocentrism or "human racism" of traditional historical narratives, including histories of literature. Ecocriticism now reaches back long
before Romanticism—into medieval British literature in the historical organization of
the first part of this volume. Here, more patently than elsewhere, the desire to represent
the mainstream of ecocritical work has won out over the sort of "rhizomic" approach
recommended by Handley and DeLoughrey: "history" is restricted to Anglo-American
literary history, although Claborn and Mukherjee's essays demonstrates that that
restricted economy itself has always been exposed to its racial "others."

From seeking a return to nature identified with Romantic poets, wilderness prophets
and Native Americans, ecocritics have turned more consistently to the critical historicization of "nature" outlined in the first section of the Handbook, and theoretical reflection on what Donna Haraway has dubbed "naturecultures" in the second. Moreover,
the emphasis on nature writing and Romantic poetry, which was never total even
in first-wave criticism, has been supplemented in more recent work by extremely
wide-ranging cultural analysis. In the third section, on "Genre," my bias favors novelty over norm, with chapters on such genres as climate change fiction, environmental
humor and old-time country music outnumbering those on more familiar topics like
nature writing and eco-film.

It seems unlikely that any literary critic, even at Cambridge, could now ask of
ecocritics "who are they?" The question "what do they want?" is more difficult
to answer today than it was in 1997. The more important and interesting question,
now and in the future, is *where* are they? Postcolonial critics such as Mukherjee,
DeLoughrey, Nixon, and Paravisini-Gebert disrupt the canonical and theoretical
constructs of first-wave ecocriticism, but their institutional locations are at the center
of Anglo-American academia. Hence the inclusion in the Handbook of a series of

surveys of ecocritical work in what we might call, with conscious irony, ecocriticism's "emerging markets": Japan, China, India, and Germany. The traffic in ideas and publications, including postcolonial ones, has until recently flowed from the old and neo-colonial "centers" to the "periphery." ASLE, an organization founded and based in the United States, requires no national modifier, unlike later affiliates like ASLE-Korea and ASLE-UK and Ireland. The European Association for the Study of Literature, Culture and the Environment (EASLCE), while pleased to affiliate with ASLE, chose its name as a conscious declaration of independence. ASLE itself is acutely aware of the problem and keen to address it.

Starting with Japan, the first non-Anglophone country to embrace ecocriticism, the Handbook presents a series of "Views From Here" surveying ecocriticism in non-Anglophone academies. Along with important recent collections (Oppermann 2011, Estok and Kim 2013), these surveys contribute to the gradual overturning of Anglo-American dominance, which many ecocritics see as intellectually limiting and politically problematic. So the structure of the Handbook recalls a spiral: from a mainly British literary history in the first section out through postcolonial and other theoretical challenges to the diversity of genres and non-Anglophone vantage points that increasingly characterize the field. It is a structure that replicates the center/periphery organization of ecocriticism to date in order ultimately to subvert it.

Such self-conscious organization also, inevitably, draws attention to the problems of coverage highlighted by Gaard. It is unfortunate that academic reviewers often attack writers and editors for what they leave out rather than addressing what they have chosen to include (what I have called the Argument from Absence [Garrard 2012a, 220–221]), despite the obvious fact that absence is inherently infinite. The scale of the Handbook might lead a reader to the erroneous conclusion that it pretends to be comprehensive, when in fact it seeks only to be reasonably inclusive. Individual essays, too, are more often exemplary than synoptic. Rather than attempt an impossible all-round defense against flanking maneuvres by wily critics of absence, I commissioned scholars whose work interested me and worked energetically with them as editor to ensure a range of rigorous and distinctive viewpoints. Since "coverage" is a lie, the Handbook makes no pretense to it.

The commissions for most of the essays were generalized rather than specific, so the recurrent *topoi*, as well as the lacunae, of the Handbook are largely fortuitous. Climate change turned out to be a concern of numerous contributors, including Lousley, Clark, Morton, Trexler, Kerridge, Kluwick, Philippon, and Bracke. Interest in issues of colonialism and postcolonialism went beyond the authors commissioned to write on it specifically, encompassing DeLoughrey, Paravisini-Gebert, Nixon, Mukherjee, Trexler, and Rangarajan. My own essay deliberately explores the borderland ecocriticism shares, mainly amicably, with critical animal studies, but Feder, Buell, Watson, Rigby, and Sandilands chose to venture there too. Furthermore, ecocriticism has always encouraged stylistic and formal experimentation in scholarly work, so I was pleased to include essays by Dickinson, Branch, Morton, McMurry, and Nixon that did not pay heed too slavishly to academic conventions.

It is notable that, although the roster includes several authors who have made important contributions to ecofeminism, only Stacy Alaimo has chosen to engage directly with it. Then again, neither have any authors discussed deep ecology, perhaps because both it and ecofeminism have become part of the tacit knowledge base of ecocriticism. One of the major forms ecofeminism now takes is "intersectional analysis," which claims that justice for oppressed groups—originally women in ecofeminism, but now many other human identity groups are included—coincides both theoretically and in practice with environmentalist objectives. The plausibility of such claims tends to be inversely proportional to the rhetorical emphasis with which they are made, and so I have chosen not to include intersectional work of the most ambitious kind. Nevertheless, essays by Adamson, Claborn, Sandilands, Philippon, Rangarajan, and Nixon showcase subtle and persuasive forms of intersectional analysis.

The succeeding sections briefly introduce each of the essays in context. The *Oxford Handbook of Ecocriticism* seeks to witness—not encompass, let alone exhaust—the diversity of contemporary ecocriticism. Its heft is a symptom not of hubris, but of the desire and opportunity to celebrate the field widely and generously. If nothing else, it is a weighty book to ballast us intellectually against the storms that environmentalists see in our future.

HISTORY

In Jonathan Bate's *Romantic Ecology* (1991), it is a claim about history that sparks an ecocritical insurgency. Responding to Alan Liu's claim that there is "no nature except as it is constituted by acts of political definition made possible by particular forms of government," Bate states that "It is profoundly unhelpful to say '*There is no nature*' at a time when our most urgent need is to address and redress the consequences of human civilization's insatiable desire to consume the products of the earth" (Bate 1991, 56). Yet the alternative to Liu's overweening, anthropocentric "history" is not the ahistorical Nature of Wordsworthian Romanticism, but a more nuanced sense of the tessellation of both key terms. It is true that what we call "nature" is often a forgotten or pastoralized remnant of human culture, but equally there can be no exclusively human history in the first place—just as all evolution is coevolution, all history is environmental. That said, when ecocritics rummage in the literary archive, they tend not to draw on the work of environmental historians, with its strongly empiricist bias. As several contributions to this section will demonstrate, they tend rather to the "history of ideas" approach in the tradition of Lynn White's 1967 essay "The Historic Roots of our Ecologic Crisis" (White Jr. 1996), Carolyn Merchant's ecofeminist *The Death of Nature* (1983) and Max Oelschlaeger's *The Idea of Wilderness* (1991). What is contested in such historical work is the *intellectual or aesthetic genealogy* of either environmental crisis or the movements that seek to address it.

Thus Rudd's essay, which plumbs the greatest historical depths in the collection, appeals to the common humanity of both premodern author and contemporary reader, but delights in a multiplicity of perspective. Looking back at the remote world of medieval England one perceives continuity and discontinuity, which Rudd organizes around the word and the color "green." This simple conceit makes possible an engaging and original re-reading of a canonical text, *Sir Gawain and the Green Knight*, but also challenges the assumptions and assertions of environmentalist texts such as White and Merchant that recruit the Middle Ages for their arguments. Rudd cunningly admits the anti-Paganism of the Green Knight poem, but then also points out how such a reading serves more modern Romantic purposes. "Green" in this medieval poem signifies a moment of choice or change—not merely inconstancy—that might still resonate.

Robert Watson's 2006 study *Back to Nature* is among the most eloquent and illuminating works of ecocriticism, so it is with particular pleasure that we publish an extension of that analysis. Planetary environmental crisis may be recent, but according to Watson, its origins lie primarily in the European Renaissance. What Merchant claimed was a decisive shift away from a feminine "organic" to a masculine "mechanistic" cosmos in the early modern period is reconceptualized by Watson in terms of a radically revised relationship between words and things: where material things were seen by medieval Christians as supervening harmfully between man and the Word of God, Renaissance thinkers and artists began to worry that words were coming between man and the ultimate reality: things. Humans are still seen as fallen creatures, but from animal plenitude not divine grace.

The genius of Watson's approach is that it views environmentalism, sympathetically but still critically, as beholden to epistemological anxieties that, far from being part of the human condition, are quite recent and historically contingent. Ironically, the desire to go "back to nature" (seen as ideally pure, untainted physical reality) is, for Watson, a fundamentally anti-ecological one, as he explains in his essay in this volume:

> Making nature an antidote for the complexity of our cognitive ecosystems involves a denial of the indispensable complexity of nature. Ecocritics must instead make vivid, as Shakespearean drama often does, the beautiful patterns of our interdependences.

Watson analyses *A Midsummer Night's Dream* alongside several examples of Renaissance painting, making this essay also a contribution to the new field of visual ecocriticism (Braddock and Irmscher 2009). Crucially for Watson, ecocriticism is primarily a work of *comprehension* not *activism*; it acknowledges the urgency of the crisis without being determined by it. Like Lynn White Jr., Watson considers Christianity a key influence on our modern cultures of nature, but he distinguishes more carefully than White's famous essay between Catholic and Protestant art and epistemology.

Watson writes of the Renaissance with the breadth of reference of the ideal Renaissance scholar. Kate Rigby's work is similarly magisterial thanks to her deep engagement with both British and German Romanticism. She comprehends Romanticism as a European movement, initially fortuitous but later on quite self-conscious, as well as an "enduring dimension of eurowestern modernity." It makes sense, then, to discuss Romanticism as a set of historical texts and authors, sprawling yet bounded in time, and also as a revolutionary worldview that transcends any such local, contingent habitation.

Rigby's particular innovation here is to ally Romantic proto-environmentalism with contemporary postequilibrium ecology, as distinct from the Augustan notion of the "balance of nature" that inspired early twentieth-century ecologists (Kricher 2009) and late twentieth-century ecocritics. Her essay highlights the complexity and ambivalence of Romantic constructions of animals: they are at once Other and brother. Perhaps most surprising is the diversity Rigby finds in Romantic neo-Paganism, from the anti-Semitic forms later adopted by some Nazis through sexually liberating, ecstatically embodied varieties to Heine's critique of compensatory fantasies of nature as leisure space. Ironically the Romantics have, in some accounts, been taken to exemplify exactly these kinds of fantasies.

The center of gravity of "history," thus far, lies somewhere in the North Sea—between the British Isles, the Netherlands of Watson's Renaissance and Rigby's "Jena Romantics." Pablo Mukherjee's postcolonial analysis of discourses of the "diseased tropics" draws it far to the south and east to India, site of one of the most culturally and ecologically significant colonial enterprises. Mukherjee diagnoses a severe case of ambivalence in colonial literary treatments of cholera, in which colonizers were portrayed as at once the superior "gifted race" whose destiny it was to dominate the subcontinent, and as peculiarly liable to succumb to tropical diseases. This is a critique of imperial bio-power of the kind discussed earlier in the introduction, which considers cholera in discursive rather than biogeographical terms. At the same time, though, it retains a strongly materialist interest in the way that colonizers blamed the tropics for their diseases whilst ignoring the role of their own networks in spreading them. Besides throwing light on specific colonial anxieties, Mukherjee does vital work in drawing attention to "how the discursive and practical detection, production, circulation and containment of diseases contribute to specific imaginings and conceptualizations of environments." Pathogens and parasites are of immense evolutionary and ecological significance (Dunn 2011), but have received almost no attention in ecocriticism. If Mukherjee's piece is positioned in the Handbook so as to exemplify the British "Victorian" era, it also highlights the conceptual instability and incipient globality of that phase.

Since ecocritical studies of Modernism have been scarce up to now, I have chosen two essays to represent this pivotal moment in the history of Western art. Anne Raine seeks in some measure to reconcile ecocriticism and Modernism, in spite of the overtly "Promethean" hostility to nature of spokesmen like Wyndham Lewis. Like Rigby, Raine emphasizes the diversity contained within her ostensible cultural moment, and discusses diasporic Modernism as well as the canonical "men of 1914." In addition to recuperative readings that show how accepted ecocritical terms of value can be applied to Modernists, Raine explores a revisionist alternative in which Modernist writers are seen as usefully questioning the concept of nature. In the latter respect, Raine sees Modernism as anticipating aspects of second-wave ecocriticism that are, to borrow Kate Soper's term, "nature-sceptical" (Soper 1995). Taken together with Rigby's argument in the previous essay, Raine's essay suggests an intriguing possibility: as well as historicizing ecocriticism, such readings might help us to historicize ecology itself. Both authors contend that the metaphorics of the natural sciences might usefully be characterized as Augustan, Romantic or Modernist. As such they exemplify the process of "reading both with and against" science endorsed by Buell.

John Claborn's contribution on African American Modernism is a continuation of research that yielded one of the most remarkable ecocritical essays I have read: an extraordinarily detailed piece on William Attaway that draws extensively on environmental history (Claborn 2009). In the analysis published here, Claborn accepts the argument of Paul Outka's superb critique of the white American conservationist rhetoric of wilderness in *Race and Nature* (2008), but then shows how African American author W. E. B. Du Bois too enjoyed the sublimity of sites such as the Grand Canyon. What was distinctive in his case, though, was the juxtaposition of wilderness experience and the cosmopolitanism of Paris as remarkably similar liberatory spaces for African Americans. Claborn concludes that "By juxtaposing this social expression of racial community in Paris with nature's mixing of colors at the Grand Canyon, Du Bois naturalizes integration and internationalizes a vision of democracy across the color line." It is a conclusion that enriches and productively complicates arguments about the racialization of wilderness, and demonstrates that the widely attested African American ambivalence towards American landscapes could still motivate enthusiastic expression. In particular, Claborn's delightful portrait of white tourists intruding on Du Bois's romantic reverie in Scotland implies that the enforced "doubleness" of the black subject can represents a highly sophisticated form of admiration for wild nature rather than always a painfully compromised one.

The last chapter in "History," so to speak, ought perhaps to be postmodernism, but the experimental protocol outlined here by poet Adam Dickinson eludes any such classification. Although as an exercise in pataphysics, or the "science of imaginary solutions," Dickinson's essay is in a tradition that long predates both ecocriticism and postmodernism, it is presented as a prospectus for a project at the intersection of these movements. Dickinson's project, a continuation of the work presented in *The Polymers* (2013), includes aspects of both modernist procedural writing and postmodernist self-experimentation, but extends these into the "synthesis of science and wonder" of ecocriticism. As a pataphysician, Dickinson seeks to draw attention to poetic practices in science at the same time that he imports scientific procedures into poetry. In principle, then, it takes ecocriticism beyond the narcissism of narrative scholarship into unexplored realms of criticism as itself a *poetic experiment* in an unusually strong sense. Dickinson promises to treat his own body as a symbiotic organism: simultaneously an "interior semiotic surface" preserving signs of his activities and proclivities, and a potentially toxic "downstream" site of unwilling disposal. Dickinson is interested, scientifically and poetically, not only in how we "write the environment" but in how the "environment writes us."

THEORY

Buell's wave metaphor and Kate Soper's distinction between "nature endorsing" and "nature skeptical" perspectives are both useful ways to characterize the history and development of ecocriticism, but I tend to think in terms of centripetal and centrifu-gal forces. The emphasis on place and dwelling—notably in bioregionalism and much ecocritical pedagogy—impels us to hunker down in our locale, or as Gary Snyder urges in "For the Children," one of his schmaltzier poems: "*stay together / learn the flowers / go light*." The characteristic centripetal posture is a huddle, the protectiveness of which is hard to dissociate from defensive, exclusionary parochialism. National parks exem-plify centripetal environmentalism: they provide necessary protection for endangered species and vulnerable ecosystems, but may also sustain (though until recently sel-dom memorialized) the colonial translocations and expulsions of indigenous people required to endow them as pure wilderness spaces. Yosemite in the United States and Kruger in South Africa are two examples.

Centrifugal ecocriticism, by contrast, is fascinated by hybrid spaces, cosmopolitan identities and naturecultural ironies, such as the unanticipated biodiversity of horribly polluted landscapes such as the exclusion zone around the Chernobyl nuclear accident site (Weisman 2008) and the Rocky Mountain Arsenal, a Superfund site that has been dubbed America's "most ironic nature park" (Cronon 1996). The decentering effect of centrifugal criticism has been accelerated in recent years by the subversive energies introduced by encounters with deconstruction and queer theory. If centripetal ecocriti-cism tended to rely on popularized versions of ecology to validate its intuitions, cen-trifugal approaches informed by the sceptical perspectives of science studies and animal studies have ironically been forced into more rigorous and detailed engagements with biological science than heretofore. So the gyre described by this section circles out from questions of politics, science and culture (human and non-human) towards still more radical questioning of logocentrism, ethnocentrism, and heteronormativity.

Back in the 1990s when Theory was identified primarily with anthropocentric, impen-etrable French philosophers, ecocriticism was pleased to constitute itself as anti-Theory. While a few still see it that way, there is now a relaxed acceptance that theoretical reason-ing and philosophical reflection are modes of understanding as indispensable as per-sonal experiences and close readings of cultural texts. A deicidal reconfiguration of the theoretical pantheon has been required, though: out, for most critics, went psychoana-lysts such as Jacques Lacan and Julia Kristeva and in came phenomenologists and sys-tems theorists. Figures from before the age of High Theory such as Raymond Williams and Martin Heidegger were revalued (Goodbody and Rigby 2011). The biophobic side of Foucault developed by Judith Butler is now being supplanted by a materialist concep-tion of discourse that admits nonhuman agencies. Diverse as these perspectives are, the essays in this section suggest that the presiding figures today are the French anthropolo-gist of science, Bruno Latour, and the American biologist-turned-critic Donna Haraway.

Cheryl Lousley's essay heads up this section because it incisively accounts for the importance for ecocriticism of Latour and Haraway in the course of a reading of Canadian author Douglas Coupland's *JPod* (2007) and a critical revaluation of the founding text of modern environmentalism, Rachel Carson's *Silent Spring* (1962). The argument of postmodern relativists and scientific realists, which was too often a ster-ile tussle between straw men, is superseded by what Lousley characterizes, following Haraway, as "'modest' methods of developing truth claims without disavowing their embeddedness in mechanisms and relations of power." After all, as Latour observes with evident anguish in his lecture "Why Has Critique Run Out of Steam?," sophisticated sociological questioning of scientific truth claims seems indistinguishable from politically-motivated undermining of, for example, climate science. As a result, he suggests,

> entire Ph.D. programs are still running to make sure that good American kids are learning the hard way that facts are made up, that there is no such thing as natural, unmediated, unbiased access to truth, that we are always prisoners of language, that we always speak from a particular standpoint, and so on, while dangerous extremists are using the very same argument of social construction to destroy hard-won evidence that could save our lives. (Latour 2004b, 227)

For Latour, though, "reconnecting scientific objects with their aura, their crown, their web of associations" (237)—their *politics,* in a generous sense—is understood to enrich, not impoverish, their claim to reality and significance. The vital contribution of *Silent Spring,* as Lousley shows, was to contextualize scientific knowledge of the environmental impact of organic pesticides in such a way that they became politically visible, debatable and, ultimately, actionable. In this way, DDT and the organisms it afflicted were thereby welcomed into what Latour calls the social "collective" as salient *intra-actors.*

Lousley's essay also points up the indebtedness of much ecocritical theory to what we might call the "materialist Foucault." While there is much in his work that conduces to postmodern relativism, it is also possible to read Foucault as agnostic regarding the possible autonomy and agency of subjects constituted by the epistemic regimes that are his primary interest. As Lousley explains, "Foucault suggests that power not only operates on a pre-formed object—on a juvenile delinquent, or crop pests, for example—but is also at work in constituting this object as a unit of analysis, that there is such a thing as agricultural pests amenable to chemical management." Inspired in part by Foucault, Haraway, and Latour too are interested in these enabling conditions, but they also attest to the reality that, once elicited by scientific discursive practices that invite them into the collective, both human and nonhuman agents, delinquents and pests, remain quarrelsome and unpredictable. Lousley's biopolitical analysis contrasts with the "reconnection with nature" of centripetal ecocriticism, in which reconnecting was separable from and antecedent to engagement in environmental politics. As she says, "We should be suspicious of the *ease* with which a middle-class North American might 're-connect' with nature via a walk with an iPod in the woods as compared to the *difficulty* of, say, gathering knowledge about and re-organizing coltan mining and electronics manufacturing." It may inherit from Foucault something of a monomania about *power* as opposed to other axes of social psychology (could there not be compassion/knowledge systems as well as power/knowledge ones?), but Lousley's essay also conveys the full force and significance of Latour's rhetorical question: "*What term other than ecology would allow us to welcome nonhumans into politics?*" (Latour 2004a, 226; italics appear in original).

Latour's work is also significant for ecocritics whose concerns center on environmental justice, as Joni Adamson's essay shows. If we accept what he calls the "modernist constitution," which distinguishes categorically between a unitary "nature" and multiple, human-only cultures, we condemn anthropology to condescending multiculturalism. As Latour caustically observes, we then have but one request for indigenous Others: " 'Thanks to nature, I know in advance, without needing to hear what you have to say, who you are; but tell me anyway what representations you have made of the world and of yourselves—it would be so interesting to compare your visions to the equally factitious ones of your neighbors'" (210–211). In reality, as Adamson shows, contemporary indigenous politics and literature assume, like Latour, nonhuman membership of the collective: both the Universal Declaration of the Rights of Mother Earth, framed at a conference hosted by the Bolivian president Evo Morales, and such classic environmental justice texts as Leslie Marmon Silko's *Almanac of the Dead* endorse an inclusive Latourian "cosmopolitics." Far from perpetuating the myth of the Ecological Indian, as I claimed in *Ecocriticism* (2004; 2011 2nd edition), indigenous activists and texts themselves contest idealizations of pre-Columbian civilizations as peaceful and environmentally benign, while also affirming that indigenous knowledge can play a positive role in the negotiation of sustainable multinatural, multicultural collectives. Indeed, Adamson cites Annette Kolodny's research on the nineteenth-century Penobscot writer Joseph Nicolar in support of her view that indigenous peoples have been articulating cosmovisions more multiple and inclusive than those of the nation-state for hundreds of years. According to my reading of Kolodny, by contrast, indigenous leaders such as Nicolar and, indeed, Morales, have seen political opportunity in Euro-American idealisations like the Ecological Indian (Garrard 2010, 6–7). It may be that our positions differ only in the cynicism with which they read the same evidence, however.

Latour and Haraway also provide a point of departure for Stacy Alaimo, whose work as both author and editor exemplifies the sustained and productive encounter of ecocriticism, feminism and science studies (Alaimo 2010, Alaimo and Hekman 2008). In this essay, though, she takes feminist ecocriticism beyond its familiar boundaries into the remote and necessarily mediated space of the deep oceans. As Alaimo states:

> The ocean eludes the feminist, environmentalist, and environmental justice models of ordinary experts, embodied or situated knowers, domestic carbon footprint analysts, and trans-corporeal subjects who take science into their own hands and conceive of environmentalism as a scientifically mediated but also immediate sort of practice.

At the same time, though, Alaimo criticizes the *denial* of entanglement of human and nonhuman agencies in popular representations of the deep seas. In TV documentaries and glossy coffee table books, the creatures of the abyss are reductively framed either as weird specimens of scientific study and classification or as objects of purely aesthetic attention: "Even as the ocean is being emptied of its life through massive industrial extractions that the quaint term 'fishing' cannot begin to suggest, there is no shortage of films, television programs, coffee table books, and web sites replete with stunning photos of ocean creatures." In some ways these representations conform to definitions of "ecoporn" adumbrated by feminists and ecocritics, yet Alaimo also insists that viewing deep-sea photography should be seen as an emotional and political entanglement that begins to constitute a crucial new collectivity.

Climate change is a more obviously controversial site of scientific, artistic, and political entanglement than the abyssopelagic zone. Adam Trexler, who has reviewed climate change literature with Adeline Johns-Putra (Trexler and Johns-Putra 2011), shows how recalcitrant anthropogenic global warming is to fictional representation, thereby anticipating Richard Kerridge's essay in this collection. Whether or not one agrees with his characterization of the struggle of ecocriticism with questions of realism, Trexler argues persuasively that ecocritics could learn from science studies how mediation, whether by scientists or novelists, can elicit things rather than obscuring them:

> The things that emerge from this process [of research] are neither merely material, real, independent of human beings; nor are they pure intellection, constructed by the will of scientists, ideology, or discourse. Categorically, they are "hybrids', 'half object and half subject', resisting human agency and producing human knowledge at the same time.

Trexler's account answers the criticism that talk of the "agency" of things in science studies misleadingly implies choice and intention, and recalls Latour's insistence that we read "thing" as both a physical object and in the Nordic sense of a gathering or parliament like the Icelandic *Althing*. He goes on to apply Latourian theory to Amitav Ghosh's *The Hungry Tide* (2004) in a way that, in effect, construes it as fictional scientific ethnography. Both literature and science "mangle" together material and human agencies, as Trexler demonstrates in a brilliant, sustained analysis of Ghosh's representation of Pilar's binoculars. Trexler shares with Alaimo the optimistic conviction that encounters with artworks *constitute* meaningful entanglements rather than merely reporting them at one or more removes. He seems ultimately to admire *The Hungry Tide* not in spite of its unwillingness to represent climate change directly, but in some way because of it.

Whereas Lousley, Adamson, Alaimo and Trexler's Latourian perspective articulates a radically decentring notion of multinaturalism, the next three essays consider the implications of extending multiculturalism beyond the human species. The first, by Helen Feder, introduces two types of "posthumanist": one allied to an Internet movement preoccupied with renouncing humanity by technological means; the other concerned philosophically to overcome "humanity" in an idealised and anthropocentric sense. Dismissing the first group as geeks deludedly seeking disembodiment, Feder astutely evaluates the arguments and evidence in favor of a posthuman sense of "culture." The implications are sometimes startling: elephant communities whose encounters with people have become increasingly violent, perhaps as a result of the psychological, demographic and cultural disruptions caused by ivory poaching, are said by biologist Gay Bradshaw to be "resisting colonialism." While neither Feder nor the theorists and scientists surveyed in her essay dispute the uniqueness of symbolic communication in human culture, she demonstrates that there is no non-circular argument for restricting our conception of culture to our species alone. The encounter of science studies, critical animal studies and ecocriticism exemplified by Feder and Alaimo's contributions seems one of the most potentially productive in the field today.

The relationship between animal rights and environmentalist politics was characterized by Mark Sagoff in 1984 as a "bad marriage, quick divorce" (Sagoff 1984). T. C. Boyle's novel *When the Killing's Done* (2011) powerfully fictionalizes both the tensions and the congruences between movements to protect animals and to restore ecosystems. At one remove from such conflicts between activists, my essay concentrates on feral dogs in order to bring into focus the conceptual differences between ecocriticism and critical animal studies. Adopting from cartography the metaphor of "triangulation," the essay uses the insights of evolutionary biology and ethology as well as fictional representations in order to locate and comprehend the figure of the feral animal more securely. The empiricism of my approach contrasts with the scepticism more generally typical of critical animal studies; it seeks to show that interdisciplinary study can yield deeper, more reliable knowledge of the collectives we inhabit than posthumanistic theorization can yield by itself.

Although Latour is a French scholar, the authors collected here are all based in North America where science studies is prominent. Timo Maran, by contrast, represents a well-established school of thought that is not only European, but quite specifically (if not exclusively) Baltic in origin. The theory of biosemiotics he discusses shares with Feder the idea that semiosis is a fundamental property of life, but takes it beyond mammalian societies to the cellular level. According to Maran, what are usually seen as "material" or biochemical processes such as DNA transcription, cellular exchange and sensory activity are better seen as semiotic or communicative activities. The key biosemiotic concept of autopoeisis, or self-organization, furthermore coincides with the Latourian emphasis on nonhuman intra-actants. Thanks to its rich history of interdisciplinary research, though, biosemiotics also contributes such seminal concepts as semiotic filtering, or "translation" between systems, and the semiotic regulation of ecological processes. As Maran states, "human cultural and semiotic activities cannot be treated as a semiotic island in the vast ocean of unsemiotic void." As we will see, Timothy Morton wants to show how the boundary between words and world deconstructs itself, but where his work bounces energetically between concepts, biosemiotics adopts more cautious procedures from biology: it distinguishes between analogical and homological processes, and it adopts typological gradations of semiosis. The notion of "interpretation" developed by biosemiotics is therefore both universalizing—no hermeneutic is categorically reserved for humans—and discriminating. In part, the difference is due to Morton's reliance on a poststructuralist interpretation of Saussurean semiotics, whereas Maran deploys a more sophisticated Piercean structure. The latter acknowledges the existence of iconic and indexical signs in which the relationship between sign and object is non-arbitrary. By contrast, the poststructuralist Saussurean framework is inherently anthropocentric: it conceptualizes the signifier in verbal terms and the signified in mentalistic ones, and it considers the relationship between them a matter of labile social convention. The growing familiarity of ecocritics with the work of Estonian and Finnish biosemioticians is therefore a welcome development.

In this as in other fields of research, many Anglo-American ecocritics (the present author included) are hampered by functional monolingualism. Timothy Clark's fluency in German as well as English informs both his *Cambridge Introduction to Literature and the Environment* (2010) and the essay published here. Phenomenology has influenced the development of ecocriticism, especially the work of Maurice Merleau-Ponty as refracted through David Abram's popular *The Spell of the Sensuous* (2006). Well versed as he is in this tradition, Clark considers that the climate crisis exposes severe limitations in what is known as "eco-phenomenology," in particular its idealization of the body or "Flesh" as an agent of political change. Clark contrasts Abram's neo-animism unfavorably with Gernot Böhme's "Nature politics," a formulation, founded in but not limited to aesthetic responses, that has much in common with the kind of democratization discussed by Lousley. We might say, in fact, that Abram's is a primitivistic "poetics of authenticity" and Böhme's is a "poetics of responsibility" (Garrard 2004; 2011 2nd edition). Clark concludes his essay with a series of challenges to ecophenomenology, including animals, gender and globality, and a manifesto for its reconstruction.

The next essay is by another British Timothy with a deconstructive bent: Timothy Morton, probably the most influential theorist of ecocriticism today. His *Ecology without Nature* (2007), *The Ecological Thought* (2010, and *Hyperobjects* (2013) have had a seismic impact, especially at the postgraduate level. While his arguments extend the posthumanism of predecessors like Haraway, it is his inimitable *style* that innervates or irritates, according to taste: he excels in wild generalizations, vivid illustrations, and memorably comic, gnomic utterances. "Deconstruction and/as Ecology" exemplifies the phenomenological conception of a "world" using Tolkien's *The Lord of the Rings*, and takes Bilbo Baggins's song "The Road Goes Ever On and On" to anticipate Jacques Derrida's concept of *différance*. Yet Morton describes the film adaptations of Tolkien as "a worldwide Olympics of death, unto eternity, may the best elf win." Disciplinary gaps between literary criticism and microbiology, say, or ecology and evolutionary biology are not so much bridged as exuberantly transgressed: a computer program is like DNA/RNA transcription, which is like Nature, which in turn is like a self-referential postmodernist poem. Like Clark, Morton insists on the deconstructive radicalism of ecology, which he thinks has too little affected the environmental criticism supposedly derived from it. He work embodies an appealingly extravagant confidence in *reading* as both a scientific and humanistic practice, as well as the author's confidence in the accuracy and relevance of examples drawn from fields such as mathematics and genetics. Morton's ambition has injected much-needed vim into ecocritical theory.

Catriona Sandilands's *The Good-Natured Feminist* (1999) is an authoritative revaluation of the rich, diverse tradition of ecofeminism. Ever since its publication the author has been a leading light in the movement to integrate the insights of queer theory and ecocriticism. Here, Sandilands considers the significance of "queer animals"—homosexual creatures, primarily, but also others such as intersexed individuals that do not conform to an ideal heterosexual dyad of male and female. It is clear that queer organisms are queerer than we can suppose, even given broad liberal definitions of sexual diversity, but Sandilands cautions against using them simply to legitimate stigmatized human sexual behaviors and identities. She quotes Karen Barad as saying that, "in an important sense…there are no "acts against nature"…only 'acts of nature'," a statement that simultaneously affirms queer identities in the face of homophobia and contradicts the ethical basis of popular environmentalism. The notion of "symbiogenesis" she discusses decenters humanity from its position of privilege, but perhaps also relativizes human moral responsibility for environmental change.

Sandilands is grimly fascinated, as I am, by Lee Edelman's *No Future* (2004), an uncompromisingly radical work of queer theory (Garrard 2012b) that critiques the figure of the Child as both source and imagined destination of heteronormative politics. Edelman proposes that queers accept the identification with the death drive proposed for them by hegemonic culture, and "[f]uck the social order and the Child in whose name we're collectively terrorized' (Edelman 2004, 29). While Sandilands is far more cautious than I am about recruiting this argument in service of Malthusian objections to overpopulation—not least because Edelman attempts to distinguish between the Child and actual children—she does see ecocritical uses for its aggressive anti-naturalism. She goes on to weave a sympathetic reading of Canadian novelist Jane Rule's *After the Fire* (1989) through with fascinating material on the vital role of fire in postequilibrium ecology in order to demonstrate, without reductive simplification, "affinities between social and ecological transformation."

The last two essays in this section represent the spiral out from an Anglo-American "center" that continues with the "Views from Here." The Latourian essays with which we began were developing a distinctive posthumanist and materialist theoretical framework, whereas the later contributions are hybrids of ecocriticism and existing fields of philosophy and literary theory: phenomenology, deconstruction, and queer theory. Of these encounters, the scope is greatest where ecocriticism meets research on globalization and postcolonialism, as the authorial and editorial work of Elizabeth DeLoughrey has amply demonstrated (DeLoughrey 2009, DeLoughrey and Handley 2011). As with critical animal studies, there are points of tension as well as overlap: postcolonial critics contest both the moral universalism of environmental charities and the epistemic universalism of environmental science. Where the concept of globalization preferred by ecocritics such as Ursula Heise allows for the emergence of new configurations of economic and political power, postcolonialism insists on the continuing importance of colonial and neocolonial circuits. Of all the theories included in this section, postcolonial ecocriticism is the least concerned about anthropocentrism because it is so profoundly keyed to movements for human emancipation. As such, DeLoughrey draws powerful— indeed painful—attention to the proper ambivalence of scholars from the United States (though the point applies elsewhere, if less pointedly) given that it is a point of origin for both ecocriticism and imperial military power. DeLoughrey reminds us of the colossal human and environmental cost of militarization, primarily that of the United States in her account but also including, in Africa and Asia especially, the appalling impact of probably the most destructive machine in history: the mass-produced AK47. Her postcolonial critique shapes her response to the representation of what she calls "wars of light"—atomic testing, primarily—in Pacific Island literature.

If DeLoughrey's primary points of reference lie in postcolonial theory, Lizabeth Paravisini-Gebert makes greater use of environmental history. Since the Caribbean islands have suffered environmental ruination as a consequence of colonialism, their literatures conduce to postcolonial ecocriticism. Paravisini-Gebert explains how dozens of species were driven to extinction on land and sea because of hunting and conversion of habitats to plantations, and expresses support for belated conservation efforts in the region. Her discussion of early modern accounts of the Caribbean notes their surprising attention to loss of biodiversity, and it also frames her discussion of a more complex and ambivalent extinction event: the deliberate extirpation of the Haitian Creole pig and the later reintroduction of a similar breed. Her conclusion offers a neat summary of the central claim of postcolonial ecocriticism: "The Caribbean's path to environmental justice reveals... that environmental problems are a manifestation of other, larger problems endemic to culture, society, and economic structures in colonized societies struggling to continue to exist in a globalized world." Thanks to this hybrid critical practice, ecocriticism is increasingly reading further afield than Europe and North America. In the process, though, it may be relinquishing the concern for the more-than-human world that was, in the beginning, its most distinctive ethical position.

GENRE

All literary critical movements demand revision of the canon. Feminism, postcolonialism, and critical race studies (though not Marxism, curiously) have transformed the curriculum in Anglophone universities. What was unusual about ecocriticism in the 1990s was that it called for a revaluation of genres as well as a shuffling of preferred authors. In Lawrence Buell's seminal *The Environmental Imagination* (1996), Henry David Thoreau presided over a canon of American nature writers then little known outside the Western Literature Association. Ecocritics ever since have tended to work on nonfiction and poetry, and fiction and drama less often, an order of priority unfamiliar to other critical schools. However, as this section attests, it is a situation that is changing: "environmental nonfiction" is preferred over nature writing, and we research an increasingly wide range of the authors and texts.

The section begins with a contribution from Richard Kerridge, our most reliable navigator of questions of genre. He shows in detail why, as Trexler has already suggested, climate change poses a particular challenge for existing literary genres, but he also expresses a hope, nursed presumably by many scholars but seldom openly acknowledged, that ecocritical criteria of value might extend beyond academic criticism to influence cultural debate more widely. At the moment, outside academia the reverse is true: overtly environmentalist artworks risk negatively evaluation for their "political agenda," while environmental criteria are rarely applied to any other artefacts at all. Kerridge's innovation here is to point out that ecocritical criteria are *contradictory*, which commits the critic to difficult judgments in every case. Kerridge honestly confronts the dilemma of activism and scholarly detachment, but he also pleads, like Mike Branch's essay, for the extension of the emotional range of ecocriticism into absurdity, comedy and profound grief. He points out that, while *ontologically* posthumanism criticizes assumptions of human uniqueness, *ethically* we need to amplify our sense of human responsibility, not attenuate it. Kerridge concludes with an inclusive, practical list of genres and the aspects of environmental crisis they might help to address.

It was, appropriately enough, a comedian from chilly Scotland who said "Global warming? About f***ing time." There is no shortage of popular environmental comedy, but almost no recognition of it in academic circles. Mike Branch rectifies the situation in his delightfully funny "Are You Serious?," which explains why ecocritics need to lighten up a bit. As motoring journalist and demagogue Jeremy Clarkson has shown with his incessant attacks on George Monbiot, the stereotype of the miserable, self-righteous environmentalist who knits his own tofu continues to have comedy value. It is also, of course, a stigmatizing and marginalizing strategy to which the proper response is, as Branch shows, to poke fun right back. It helps that Branch is no mean comic writer himself, as well as thoroughly knowledgeable about comic masterpieces of American literature such as Henry Thoreau's *Walden* and Edward Abbey's *Desert Solitaire*. Luckily, he knows how lethal explication is to humor, as do I. So read the essay.

Having briefly attracted the scholarly attention of ecocritics, is nature writing now dead? It has certainly taken some severe pummeling, notably in Dana Phillips in *The Truth of Ecology* (2003) and Timothy Morton's *Ecology without Nature*. So is it time to move on? As Dan Philippon acknowledges, nature writing is frequently portrayed as something second or third wave ecocriticism needs to get *past*, like some humiliating adolescent fad. Whilst he admits the force of some of these critiques, Philippon reasserts the countercultural value of nature writing—especially in the United States—and demonstrates its adaptability to issues like climate change and food miles. In fact many ecocritics cut their teeth on environmental nonfiction and continue to love it through all vicissitudes. Writers themselves are responsive to critical suspicion of nature writing in its rhapsodic and jeremiadic forms, and seek paths beyond them. Philippon's careful assessment of contemporary American "motherhood environmentalists" Sandra Steingraber, Amy Seidl, and Barbara Kingsolver is a sterling example of the sort of critical judgment Kerridge calls for, as well as a stout defense of the continuing importance of environmental nonfiction.

The association of childhood with nature is a key construct of Romantic ecology after Rousseau, and children's literature is saturated with anthropomorphic animals. In his contribution to the Handbook Lawrence Buell, the Dean of American ecocriticism, brings to bear on this key genre the seemingly effortless eloquence and insight that are his trademarks. Buell accepts that ostensibly environmental or animal-centered fictions can easily be read as allegorical—"a bad boy story in animal drag" like *The Tale of Peter Rabbit*. But, as he points out, there are counter-allegorical elements in children's stories that prevent us dismissing them as crudely anthropomorphic projections of exclusively human concerns. Richard Adams's *Watership Down*, he tells us, combines an allegorical quest narrative with quite detailed attention to "lapine natural history." Even if the Romantic construct of the natural child was idealized, it is demonstrable that childhood experience of in the outdoors is formative for most environmentalists, while the converse risk of "nature deficit disorder" in children brought up mainly indoors (Louv 2008) is, as Buell recognizes, more speculative but at least plausible. Just as environmental nonfiction has adapted in response to changing concerns, children's literature has shifted from the Carson-era environmentalism of Dr. Seuss's *The Lorax* (1971) to such contemporary examples as S. Terrell French's *Operation Redwood* (2010), which betray the influence of the environmental justice movement.

Few works of children's literature are as overtly environmental as Seuss's and French's books, and the same is true of literary fiction for adults. Ecocritical analysis has tended to fixate on the relatively straightforward examples: Don DeLillo's *White Noise* (1985); Margaret Atwood's *Oryx and Crake* (2003); Cormac McCarthy's *The Road* (2006); Amitav Ghosh's *The Hungry Tide*. Astrid Bracke's essay takes issue with this narrow canon, and models a critical practice that can shed light on a much wider array of novels. Thanks to dominant, anthropomorphic modes of characterization, novels may be less well suited than other literary genres to challenging anthropocentrism. Yet Bracke's analysis elicits ecocritical significance from texts with no obvious environmental dimension, such as John McGregor's haunting *If Nobody Speaks of Remarkable Things* (2002), a novel set on the day Princess Diana died and populated by a cast of near-anonymous characters. Bracke's close readings dedicate minute attention to punctuation and narrative architecture, thereby showing how formal elements (not just environmental "content") of a novel can be integrated into an ecocritical reading. Bracke is even prepared to defend Ian McEwan's *Solar* (2010), which I and some other ecocritics found disappointing (Garrard 2013), for its salutary anti-apocalyptic and anti-doctrinaire attitude. The essay concludes by recommending a diagnostic rather than evaluative approach to environmental criticism.

If novels have received relatively short shrift from ecocritics, poetry has been hailed from the outset. Scholars have sought to assess how ecocentric various poets and poems are, or have made more or less tenuous claims about how poetic form might itself be seen as "ecological." Lattig's analysis is of the latter sort, but is conducted more carefully than most. It draws on cognitive poetics, a branch of literary theory well founded in scientific psychology. Lattig's framework recalls biosemiotics: the key concept of *affordance*, defined by Lattig as "what the environment offers the organism for its use as determined by both the environment and the animal cognizing it," is cognate with Jakob von Üexküll's foundational concept of *Umwelt*. But Lattig also shares Bracke's minute attentiveness to literary form, as for example in her illuminating account of how a line ending in Emily Dickinson's poetry functions as the boundary of positive affordance: "It marks the limits of the terrain in which one is at home while simultaneously exposing one to the ambiguity of the undefined, or the vague, afforded by the use of, for example, enjambment." It is worth noting that, where Morton sees meaning as always haunted and disrupted by non-meaning (the "dark side"), Lattig shows how occlusion deepens perception as a beckoning absence. Such formal analysis is necessarily remote from environmental politics; it operates at the point where poetry, illuminated by science, becomes perception restructured by action: "As lyric poetry imagines the word as an enactor or creator of a world and as a constructed image of a world, its spatial sense may be seen to inhere in the lexical interplay of perceived and enacted space."

It is when ecocritics develop scientifically informed reading practices, not just ecologically motivated ones, that they depart most decisively from their predecessors in the era of High Theory. In David Ingram's essay, we move beyond the written word for the first time in this section of the Handbook, but we also see the old psychoanalytic paradigm in film criticism contrasted with a cognitivist theory similar to Lattig's. Where Morton reconciles—at least rhetorically—contemporary science and the Old Gods of poststructuralism, Ingram considers that Marxist and deconstructive approaches deserve to be supplanted by biocultural ones. He is scornful of assumptions made about an abstract being known as "the subject," whose responses may or may not resemble those of actual cinema audiences, and he criticizes film critics who assert implausibly direct relationships between formal and technical aspects of movies and their ideological valence. Ingram's empirical bias suggests a response to Kerridge's anxiety about the split between concern and inaction on climate change: if we tried to *find out* why the split exists, the answers might be quite different to the speculations of ecocritics.

It sometimes seems that ecocritics' interest in art forms is in inverse proportion to their popularity outside universities. Ingram has helped to rectify this unfortunate bias with *Green Screen* (2004), his critical survey of Hollywood cinema and environmentalism, and a book on popular music, *The Jukebox in the Garden* (2010). Ecocritical treatments of music are few and far between (though see *Green Letters: Studies in Ecocriticism* 15:1), hence the inclusion here of Scott Knickerbocker's essay on "The Ecology of Country and Old-Time Music." It is not just the medium that is relatively unfamiliar territory for ecocriticism; Knickerbocker's analysis also confronts the association of country music with the predominantly anti-environmental "red" states in the United States. These are also, by the way, the most fervently Christian parts of the country— a vast constituency largely ignored by ecocritics. It is especially important, then, that Knickerbocker teases out the vestiges of conservative environmentalism, and conveys the pleasures and possibilities of the participatory, anti-commercial vibe of old-time music. More surprising still is the analogy he proposes between old-time music and modernist art, in that "it formally enacts ecological ways of knowing,... reiterates natural processes, and...envelops its musicians in an aural environment often coextensive with an outdoor environment." However plausible the reader finds such a close relationship between artistic form and ecology, there is no doubt of the recuperative value of the analysis, and the hints it provides of new coalitions for environmentalism.

Andrew McMurry's—what shall we call it?—*torrential* piece on digital media provides a startling contrast in topic and tone from Knickerbocker. McMurry takes Morton's airy prose and pours thousands of kilojoules of energy into it. His essay joins in the crucial work of opening ecocritical discussion on digital media, as yet only just begun, while at the same time confronting the daft assumption that more familiar media, our books and music and fine art, are not already digital. The essay is a paean to our species as a "killer ape," as well as—jarringly at times—a critique of human "arrogance;" it plots humanity's desperate course into the future, self-monitoring ever more frenetically as we crash and burn. Yet we have, as McMurry acknowledges, no alternative habitations than semioscapes, be they digital or analogue. Perhaps we have merely to choose between an environmentalist narrative of moral or epistemological decline and a more optimistic posthumanist endorsement of adaptation and continuity; we have been cyborg primates ever since the invention of the atlatl, if not before. For McMurry, even if there is faint hope in the digital "gaming" of environmental solutions, we have still to insist on the priority, in the last analysis, of biophysical reality.

This section concludes as it began: with an essay on climate change. It matters not only because of the geographical and temporal scale of the problem, but because the climate crisis faces us with such a glaring misalignment of discourse and behavior and concerted political action. Kluwick helpfully draws on Mike Hulme's analysis, in *Why We Disagree about Climate Change* (2009), of climate change as a "wicked" problem that is intrinsically difficult, if not impossible, to "solve" as such. Like many of the essays here, she honors the science of climatology while resisting scientification, and identifies a variety of barriers to action beyond the "splitting" identified by Kerridge. Kluwick's analysis of popular representations of climate change, such as Al Gore's *An Inconvenient Truth* (2006), finds in them a marked ambivalence about individual agency: we are all encouraged to "do our bit," but the measures proposed are obviously pitifully inadequate to the scale of the problem described. Like Ingram, Kluwick concludes that we have too little information on how readers and audiences actually react to know how to make environmental communication more effective.

Despite including both genres of longstanding interest to ecocritics, such as poetry and environmental nonfiction, alongside less familiar ones, this section has inevitably left out others of importance: theatrical drama, advertising, news media, online social networks and genre fiction such as Gothic and romance. Like the pieces collected in the final section, the intention is not to encompass diversity; rather to hint at how much further it extends.

Views from Here

The spread of organizations linked to ASLE gives some indication of the growth of interest internationally in ecocriticism. ASLE-Japan was the earliest, but there are now affiliated academic associations in India, Korea, Taiwan, Canada, Australia/New Zealand, and the United Kingdom and Ireland. The European Association for the Study of Literature, Culture and Environment roughly encompasses the European Union, although unlike the European Union it does not exclude Turkey. EASLCE's excellent work emphasizes the challenges that need to be met as ecocriticism internationalizes: addressing the predominance of English; identifying and promoting primary texts and theoretical models from non-Anglophone cultures; ensuring translation both from and, more importantly, into English of key texts; and strengthening institutional and personal research links that both include and exceed the Anglophone academy.

In several countries, Scott Slovic, ASLE founder member and editor of *Interdisciplinary Studies in Literature and Environment*, has been instrumental, along with other scholars such as Lawrence Buell, Ursula Heise, Patrick Murphy, and Terry Gifford, in both spreading the word about ecocriticism and encouraging the exploration of native literatures. Slovic's energy and passion for ecocriticism seem inexhaustible. Yet, as Yuki and Goodbody's surveys indicate, ecocriticism mainly spread through departments of American literature in Japan and Germany, and the leading exponents of ecocriticism as applied to German literature are *Auslandsgermanisten*, scholars based outside Germany like Goodbody himself (including Kate Rigby and Timothy Clark in this volume). German ecocritics are still more likely to be Americanists, including Catrin Gersdorf, Hubert Zapf, and Sylvia Mayer. More striking yet is the predominance of Anglo-American theoretical models: while France continues to be an important source of philosophical inspiration (though not ecocritical research) thanks to Bruno Latour, non-Anglophone theory is limited in this volume to DeLoughrey's adaptation of Martiniquan Édouard Glissant's ideas and, as already noted, Timo Maran's Baltic biosemiotics.

Yuki's account outlines a three-stage process by which ecocriticism becomes established: dissemination of American ideas and texts; comparison of these with local counterparts; and what we might call either nationalization or naturalization. In Japan, though, as she also shows, all three stages emerged in quick succession and continue to overlap. Such globalization has sometimes taken ironic forms, as when the American ecocritical ideal of dwelling in bioregions was conveyed by cosmopolitan means to East Asia. What has too seldom occurred is a fourth stage of "writing back," in which Japanese, German, Baltic or Indian authors begin to exercise a corresponding influence over Anglophone critics. These surveys are intended to facilitate exactly this development.

Swarnalatha Rangarajan shares Yuki's optimism about ecocriticism in Asia. While she acknowledges the huge difficulties facing India, both those of colonial and more recent origin, she prefers to stress native resources of hope. In this survey, these are predominantly from India's Hindu and aboriginal traditions rather than the Muslim, Christian or secular ones (the Tamil tradition she discusses is pre-Islamic). Her account intriguingly combines theoretical positions that have been seen as antithetical: ecophilosophical ideas associated with deep ecology, and postcolonialism. Rangarajan also points out the extraordinary richness of Anglophone Indian literature for ecocriticism, with authors like Arundhati Roy, Indra Sinha, Mahasweta Devi, and Amitav Ghosh to draw upon.

Qingqi Wei picks out ecocentric traditions in Chinese history similar to those Rangarajan finds in the ancient Indian concept of *Prakriti*, but also identifies affinities between canonical American nature writers and Chinese authors. According to Wei's survey, Lu Shuyuan takes spiritual resistance to modernization to be central to the ecocritical mission, while Zeng Fanren sees Taoism as anticipating ecology—albeit after "adaptation." At the same time, Wei acknowledges the current limitations of Chinese ecocriticism, including a relative lack of attention to Chinese-language texts and the necessity of acknowledging the exceptionally long history of transformations of the Chinese landscape. China brings to sharp focus the dilemmas of both environmentalism and ecocriticism today: its government has acted to limit population growth (a contribution to slowing climate change that vastly outweighs the Kyoto Protocol in importance), acknowledged the ecological risks to the country and made huge investments in renewable energy. At the same time, though, Chinese ecocritics are doing their research at a time of unprecedented, unconstrained—probably unconstrainable—economic and industrial growth.

Our last survey by Axel Goodbody addresses the history and politics of environmentalism in Germany as a factor informing relative lack of interest in ecocriticism there. Specifically, Nazi flirtations with ecological ideas have cast a long shadow. Yet, as Goodbody shows, there are numerous German texts and philosophers (not just Martin Heidegger!) who ought to be of interest to ecocritics, even if they have not always identified themselves as environmentalists. Two strands of German ecocritical theory are discussed in more detail: the work of Hartmut and Gernot Böhme, and the school of cultural ecology led by Hubert Zapf.

The Handbook concludes with a superb reflective essay by Rob Nixon, whose book *Slow Violence* (2011) is an instant classic of postcolonial ecocriticism. "Barrier Beach" is an exemplary piece of narrative scholarship that combines personal reminiscence with literary analysis, phenomenology and political critique of the spatial organization of South African *apartheid*. Its discussion of African American relationships to wilderness recalls Claborn's surprising conclusions about black Modernism, while its lightly worn understanding of the intersections of boundaries in nature with those among and between human beings harks back to Adamson, Sandilands and the postcolonial essays in the Handbook. Nixon's prose is enviable in its own right, but more important is its devastating combination of penetrating insight and effortless readability, which has the potential to take ecocriticism outside academia where, as Kerridge observes, it urgently needs to be. Nixon ends the Handbook on an upbeat note, but it is hard-won; lived as well as known; and far from utopian.

It ought to leave us with a painful question: who has heard of the environmental humanities, let alone ecocriticism? A glimpse in the *Times Higher* and *New York Times Magazine* is afforded us every decade or so, perhaps. Ecocritics are not alone as academics seeking a wider audience, but we have better reason than most to consider it a priority. Dissensus is energizing intellectually but may well be fatal politically. A worthy counterpart to this Handbook, which seeks to witness the breadth and diversity of ecocriticism, might be a consensus statement—as brief as the time and attention span of politicians is restricted—that explains what we do and why it matters. We can give good answers to the questions "Who are they?" and "What do they want?" We have come a long way, and we should be proud to show it.

NOTE

1. The environmental humanities disciplines include ecocriticism, environmental history, and environmental philosophy. Ecotheology might also be considered one of the environmental humanities.

WORKS CITED

Alaimo, Stacy. 2010. *Bodily Natures: Science, Environment, and the Material Self.* Bloomington: Indiana University Press.

Alaimo, Stacy, and Susan Hekman. 2008. *Material Feminisms.* Bloomington, IN.: Indiana University Press.

Bate, Jonathan. 1991. *Romantic Ecology: Wordsworth and the Environmental Tradition.* London: Routledge.

Braddock, Alan C., and Christoph Irmscher. 2009. *A Keener Perception: Ecocritical Studies in American Art History.* Tuscaloosa: University of Alabama Press.

Buell, Lawrence. 2005. *The Future of Environmental Criticism: Environmental Crisis and Literary Imagination.* Oxford: Blackwell Publishing.

Claborn, John. 2009. "From Black Marxism to Industrial Ecosystem: Racial and Ecological Crisis in William Attaway's 'Blood on the Forge.'" *MFS Modern Fiction Studies* no. 55 (3): 566–595. doi: 10.1353/mfs.0.1626.

Cronon, W. 1996. *Uncommon Ground: Rethinking the Human Place in Nature*: New York: W. W. Norton.

DeLoughrey, Elizabeth M. 2009. *Routes and Roots* Honolulu: University of Hawaii Press.

DeLoughrey, Elizabeth M., and George B. Handley. 2011. *Postcolonial Ecologies: Literatures of the Environment.* New York; Oxford: Oxford University Press.

Dunn, R. 2011. *The Wild Life of Our Bodies: Predators, Parasites, and Partners That Shape Who We Are Today.* New York: HarperCollins.

Edelman, Lee. 2004. *No Future: Queer Theory and the Death Drive.* Series Q. Durham: Duke University Press.

Estok, Simon, and Won-Chung Kim. 2013. *East Asian Ecocriticisms: A Critical Reader.* New York: Palgrave Macmillan.

Gaard, G. 2010. "New Directions for Ecofeminism: Toward a More Feminist Ecocriticism." *Interdisciplinary Studies in Literature and Environment* no. 17 (4): 643–665. doi: 10.1093/isle/isq108.

Garrard, Greg. 2004, 2011 second edition. *Ecocriticism.* London: Routledge.

Garrard, Greg. 2010. "Ecocriticism." *The Year's Work in Critical and Cultural Theory* no. 18 (1): 1–35. doi: 10.1093/ywcct/mbq005.

Garrard, Greg. 2012a. "Ecocriticism." *The Year's Work in Critical and Cultural Theory* no. 20 (1): 200–243. doi: 10.1093/ywcct/mbs011.

Garrard, Greg. 2012b. "Worlds Without Us: Some Types of Disanthropy." *SubStance* no. 41 (1): 40–60.

Garrard, Greg. 2013. "Solar: Apocalypse Not." In *Ian McEwan: Contemporary Critical Perspectives*, edited by Sebastian Groes, 123–136. London: Continuum.

Goodbody, A., and C. E. Rigby. 2011. Ecocritical Theory: New European Approaches. London: University of Virginia Press.

Kricher, John C. 2009. *The Balance of Nature: Ecology's Enduring Myth*. Princeton, N.J.: Princeton University Press.

Latour, Bruno. 2004a. *Politics of Nature: How to Bring the Sciences into Democracy*. Cambridge, Mass.; London: Harvard University Press.

Latour, Bruno. 2004b. "Why Has Critique Run Out of Steam? From Matters of Fact to Matters of Concern." *Critical Inquiry* no. 30 (2): 225–248.

Louv, Richard. 2008. *Last Child in the Woods: Saving Our Children trom Nature-Deficit Disorder*. Updated and expanded edition. Chapel Hill, N.C.: Algonquin Books of Chapel Hill.

Luke, Timothy W. 1997. *Ecocritique: Contesting the Politics of Nature, Economy, and Culture*. Minneapolis, Minn.; London: University of Minnesota Press.

Oppermann, Serpil. 2011. *The Future of Ecocriticism: New Horizons*. Newcastle upon Tyne: Cambridge Scholars Pub.

Parini, Jay. 2013. The Greening of the Humanities 1995, accessed July 15, 2013. Available from   http://www.nytimes.com/1995/10/29/magazine/the-greening-of-the-humanities.html?pagewanted=all&src=pm.

Sagoff, Mark. 1984. "Animal Liberation and Environmental Ethics: Bad Marriage, Quick Divorce." *Osgoode Hall LJ* no. 22: 297.

Soper, Kate. 1995. *What Is Nature?: Culture, Politics, and the Non-Human*. Oxford: Blackwell.

Trexler, Adam, and Adeline Johns-Putra. 2011. "Climate Change in Literature and Literary Criticism." *Wiley Interdisciplinary Reviews: Climate Change* no. 2 (2): 185–200. doi: 10.1002/wcc.105.

Wallace, Jennifer. 1997. "Swampy's Smart Set", [Accessed July 15, 2013]. Available from http://www.timeshighereducation.co.uk/103752.article.

Weisman, A. 2008. *The World Without Us*. London: Virgin Books.

White, Lynn. Jr. 1996. "The Historic Roots of our Ecologic Crisis." In *The Ecocriticism Reader*, edited by Cheryll Glotfelty and Harold Fromm. Athens, Georgia: University of Georgia Press.

PART I

HISTORY

CHAPTER 1

BEING GREEN IN LATE MEDIEVAL ENGLISH LITERATURE

GILLIAN RUDD

WITHOUT Rachel Carson's *Silent Spring* there might be no ecology movement and thus no ecocriticism. So much is a truism; fifty years after publication, the power of her opening lyrical paragraph with its nightmare scenario of a season devoid of birdsong lives on. It taps into the same sense of place as Keats's "Belle Dame Sans Merci," whose line "And no birds sing" seals the mood of things being badly amiss in its romanticized medieval landscape. Genuine medieval texts offer similar moments when birdsong in particular is taken as an indication of how things stand in the world at large. For example, the discomfort of Gawain travelling in winter in *Sir Gawain and the Green Knight* is indicated most poignantly through a moment of fellow-feeling with the birds, a moment noticed by the narrative if not by Gawain himself, as he rides through a landscape "With mony bryddes unblythe upon bare twyges, /pitosly there piped for pine of the colde" (with many unhappy birds on the bare twigs, who peeped piteously from the pain of the cold).[1] Such moments not only confirm literature's role in reflecting deep-seated associations, but also consolidate a sense of continuity between us (whoever we may be) and people of other communities and ages, a sense which is variously challenged and asserted. Birdsong is a sign that all is right with the world, even in the case of *Sir Gawain and the Green Knight*: winter *is* cold and it is only right to be miserable when forced to travel in it.

A similar desire for, and assumption of, continuity and common experience may be found in Professor Martin Rees's 2010 Reith Lectures. President of the Royal Society and Astronomer Royal, Rees asserted in his first lecture, entitled "The Scientific Citizen":

> The dark night sky is an inheritance we've shared with all humanity, throughout history. All have gazed up in wonder at the same "vault of heaven," but interpreted in diverse ways.[2]

Rhetorically effective, correct in general, yet inaccurate in detail (the night sky gazed upon by those in the southern hemisphere is not the one seen by those in the northern), this statement is a testament to the desire for a sense of common humanity, something that perhaps tells us what it is and, crucially, always has been to be human. Rees's point is that the object of observation has been the same, that the universe is in that way eternal, but the crux of the matter for him is diversity of interpretation. In this he echoes an assertion made by Boethius in the sixth century in his *Consolation of Philosophy*, a work whose influence was felt throughout the Middle Ages: "all that is known is known not through its own nature but through the nature of those who apprehend it."[3] Taken seriously, such remarks make us aware that our understanding of the world around us and indeed our place in it are contingent upon our own attitudes and prevailing beliefs concerning issues of place and human/nature relations. This is precisely the awareness that underpins Neil Evernden's *The Social Creation of Nature* (1992) in which Evernden demonstrates "the inherent volatility of the concept of nature" (xii) and puts a good case for "nature" as a social concept which in effect rests on exactly the kind of apprehension Boethius identified. For Evernden, a noticeable shift in the understanding of "nature" occurs in the Renaissance, as humanism takes over from Christianity in defining humankind's relation to the nonhuman world. For Lynn White, that shift occurred far earlier, when Christianity itself become the dominant force. In his essay, "The Historical Roots of our Ecologic [sic] Crisis" (1967) White places the blame for our current crises firmly at the door of Judeo-Christianity, whose one Creator God made Adam his steward, setting him above creation both morally and instrumentally.

Although White makes Christianity responsible for this rift between humans and the rest of the natural world, medieval thinkers would have recognized some of his complaints as similar to those voiced by Nature in Alan of Lille's work *De Planctu Naturae* (*The Complaint of Nature*) in which Nature, as vice-regent of God, upbraids Man for disobeying her laws and thus allowing the world to fall into decay. A similar lament can be found in Langland's *Piers Plowman* where Wil, the poem's protagonist, regrets that humans do not follow the law of Kynde, whom Wil calls "Kind my creator" (B.XI.325) thus making him a figure of both Nature and God, both meanings attested by the *Middle English Dictionary*. It is this kind of reference to nature which allows Caroline Merchant (*The Death of Nature*, 1982) to offer a contrasting opinion to White's regarding the medieval period. For her it is the last era when a more holistic view of the world prevailed, in which humankind was conscious of being part of a larger system in which each element had its place in the divine plan. Her view is born out by Langland's use of the common trope of the book of nature that underpins Wil's encounter with Kynde, mentioned above, but Merchant's sense of such apprehension being lost to us is countered when that same trope is used with familiar ease by Martin Rees in the second of his Reith lectures, in which he summed up the anxiety pervading twenty-first century discussions of human/nature relations in these terms: "We're destroying the book of life before we've read it."

Rees's use of the trope indicates a sense of continuity between the Middle Ages and the present day, but for Evernden the concept of "the book of nature" not only epitomizes "the medieval mind" but also marks the greatest contrast between medieval and modern relations to nature: "It is difficult to imagine walking through a world which is actually able to inform one, and in which what is seen is never 'all there is' " (Evernden,

41–42). Yet the sense of wonder evident in Evernden's words, a sense which marks both "the medieval" view of the world and his view of that medieval mindset, is related to the wonder that Rees seeks to rekindle and that Stephen Clarke advocates as the best way of achieving a properly respectful attitude to animals in particular (Clarke, 1993; Rudd, 2003).

For a medievalist, the question of how animals appear in a text is often linked to questions about how allegory works, but by no means all animals in medieval texts are allegorical. The range of animal presence runs the gamut from realism to hybrid imaginary beasts (Rowland, 1973; Salisbury, 1994; Salter, 2001) and crucially also includes the fact that the very books in which we read such representations are made out of animals themselves; often the parchment retains the scars and marks of the animal whose skin it was (Holsinger, 2009; Ryan, 1987). Animal studies is itself a large area, too large to enter upon here, but it is worth noting Lisa Kiser's insightful remark concerning Margery Kempe's use of animal imagery to convey and empathize with the suffering of Christ: "why could we not also say that these structures allowed medieval people a chance to think about the lives of animals?" (Kiser, 2009, 314–15). This is a salutary reminder that figurative language creates a reciprocal relation between the entities being compared.

Such continuities and discontinuities make ecocritical study of early texts particularly rich. As with every period, it is perilous to posit that a single mindset typifies the era; there are marked contrasts between Aquinas and Augustine, who set great store by the belief that it is reason which distinguishes humans from other animals, and St. Francis, who advocated a sense of connection not separation between humans and the rest of creation. Unsurprisingly, recent studies which reflect our current environmental interests and anxieties, even if they are not explicitly ecocritical, advocate a return to a more Franciscan apprehension of the world (Salter, 2009; Sorrell, 1989). Likewise, much work has been done on landscape in medieval literature which is not deliberately ecocritical, yet offers insight and information that can only enhance our current ecocritical understanding of literary text and of the attitudes they both challenge and convey (Pearsall and Salter, 1973; Saunders, 1993; Sobecki, 2008). These works discuss in depth how medieval texts reflect human attitudes to the nonhuman world, but they take for granted that the nonhuman world is simply other than the human and appears in texts as something to be considered in the light of human concerns, often symbolically significant even when not part of overt allegory. Such studies do not comment upon human/nature relations with any sense of ecological urgency.

Alfred Siewers's *Strange Beauty: Ecocritical Approaches to Early Medieval Landscape* (2009) very clearly does. Drawing on the tenets of Arne Naess's Deep Ecology, on Heidegger and more deeply on the ninth-century philosophy/theology of the Irishman, John Scottus Eriugena, Siewers demonstrates how the concept of the Otherworld did not divide the actual physical landscape from a sense of the magical and nonhuman, but rather offered ways of incorporating such metaphysical responses to the natural world into explanations of the world in which we live, geographically, physically, and spiritually. Related to J. R. R. Tolkien's notion of the medieval "otherworld" as a "subcreation" and to Northrope Frye's remarks on a "green world tradition" (Siewers, p. 143), Siewers's study also demonstrates how medieval literary criticism offers fertile ground for the investigation and development of ecocritical understanding not just of texts, but of cultural attitudes. There is something deeply appealing about a mythical world in which humans are more explicitly connected to and less removed from (possibly therefore also less responsible for) the rest of life on the planet. In short, where human time frames and concepts are not even challenged, but simply set aside as all but irrelevant. Like Evernden, Siewers identifies the Renaissance as the moment of change in attitude, but his Renaissance is that of the twelfth century, not the fifteenth.

Such continuities and discontinuities mark the perceived relations between our current ecologically informed outlook and that of earlier periods, as much as they do the variety of relationships between humans and nature, however "nature" is defined. However there is one particular discontinuity that has been hitherto largely unexplored: the connotations of the word "green."[4] This simple word has an unexpectedly wide range of associations, several of which have been noted by earlier scholars either in fairly straightforward linguistic terms (Heather, 1948) or in particular literary studies which have sought to pin down word to a specific meaning for a specific poems (Brewer, 1997; Robertson, 1954), since when the matter has been largely left to rest. Now that it bears new meanings in the twenty-first century, it is surprisingly revealing to revisit this small word and explore the associations available in Middle English. Green for many now is Good. It is, for some at least, the color of ethical and political awareness, equal respect for the human and nonhuman world, animal, vegetable, and mineral, both collectively (as part of a larger and complete system, perhaps) and in its constituent parts as each animal, plant, or landscape is accorded intrinsic worth. For Chaucer and his contemporaries, by contrast, green was the color of falsehood, unreliability, and deception, as well as the color of the natural world and of vigorous new life. Looking at some of the ways green acts within medieval texts can tell us more about the associations that continue to sustain our responses to the natural world and the types of human/nature relations available to us, as well as provide some hints as to why many remain hesitant to embrace the concept of "being green."

"IN STEDE OF BLEW, THUS MAY YE WERE AL GRENE"

The line above is taken from the poem known as *Against Women Unconstant*, firmly associated with Chaucer by Stowe in 1561. Skeat endorsed this attribution in 1900, and it has survived later queries to be now largely accepted. However while the attribution attracts little question, the choice of title is, as the Riverside editors note, "unfortunate." The scribes who recorded the poem in the manuscripts were content to leave the poem titleless, or designated it simply "balade"; the title by which it is now known is Skeat's adaptation of Stowe's title which generalizes to all women a fickleness of affection that the poem itself attributes specifically to one addressed as "madame" in the first line. The poem itself is a short lyric of three rhyming stanzas with the refrain, "In stede of blew, thus may ye were al grene." A literal translation might read: "Instead of blue, therefore you should wear entirely green." 'May' here has the force of "ought to" while retaining some of the veneer of politeness still implied in modern usage in the phrase "may I." The refrain is thus a rather pointed comment: blue is the color of constancy and fidelity; green of fickleness and changeability. The woman addressed by this poem is so repeatedly fleeting in her affections of every kind, from her relations with servants to lovers, that green is the color appropriate for her, rather than the blue that the refrain implies is her habitual choice.

It may seem that beyond the happy chance of using the opposition of blue (constant, faithful) with green (changeable, fickle) and thus demonstrating the medieval association of green with undesirability, this poem has little to offer an ecocritic; to a large extent that is true. However, one should not overlook happy chances, nor, in this case, one particular comparison which reveals something about how we still habitually view the natural world and why being aware of the associations of "green" in previous eras may shed some light on the fortunes of green concerns today. The poem's second, central, stanza contains the lines:

> Ther is no feith that may your herte embrace,
> But as a wedercock, that turneth his face
> With every wind, ye fare, and that is sene;
> In stede of blew, thus may ye were al grene. (11–14)

It is safe to presume that the kind of faith the poem refers to is faith in romantic love rather than religious belief, but it is lines 12 and 13 that draw the attention here. The simile is proverbial and immediately understood—the lady's affections switch as quickly as the wind changes—but further consideration reveals some deeper prejudices. The comparison is between the woman and weathercock, but of course the weathervane itself is not being fickle when it swings round. Far from it, it is being true to its function, which is to turn readily and thus indicate the direction of the wind. We might accuse the winds of being fickle and indeed such an accusation underpins this simile, but what is really revealed is our human dislike of changeability, particularly if it seems random and wayward. There, surely, lies the rub. Change is all well and good if it is desired, known and controlled, but change that lies outside our power, and quite possibly beyond our full understanding as well, is unpredictable and so disconcerting—and that makes it undesirable, even threatening. Predictability and control are not of course synonymous, but if we can predict something we can at least decide how to respond to it and shape our lives accordingly, and that in turn gives us some sense of being in control, if not of the thing itself, at least of our actions and reactions. A prime example here might be the change in seasons. The chaos, devastation and fear that results from "unseasonable" weather, be it prolonged drought or sudden floods, is proof of how far we rely on predictable season change and our belief that we know how to live alongside it, how to exploit it indeed. Coming full circle, weathervanes are one, humble, instrument humans have used to inform themselves about the kinds of change that are known to happen. If we know which way the wind blows we can act accordingly, be the wind actual or metaphorical. One might go so far as to say that it is in the nature of winds to change; it is one of the known unknowns of life.

Upon further scrutiny, though, a paradox becomes apparent. The bias of the poem is against change and for constancy. Yet while we may desire reliable responses in our romantic relations, a weathervane that is always stuck pointing in one direction is useless. Nor do we want the wind to be forever coming from the same place. We need change, we just prefer to know when it is coming; even in our romantic relationships a little variety of response is often welcome. So that while the simile seems to support the lyric's slightly waspish refrain, it in fact also undercuts it. It is not change *per se* that is bad, but the wrong kind of changeability in the wrong place. Hence the neatness of the use of color of clothing as an indication of character.[5] What people wear may indicate their personality, but it is not expected to encompass all of it. The point here is that this particular lady is so inconstant that wearing nothing but green (al grene) would in fact be utterly appropriate. Blue, the color of fidelity, is clearly out of place. It seems unlikely that the addressee of *Woman Unconstant* took such notions to heart, although one might like to imagine that she laughingly adopts green clothing forthwith and thus having thus changed her habit, finds no need to change her habits.

As mentioned above, while this lyric is associated with Chaucer, his authorship cannot be proven beyond all doubt. If anything, the question mark over this attribution is more useful than troubling as the oppositional use of blue and green in this refrain indicates how widespread and immediate the associations of blue with constancy and green with evasion were. Whoever the author was they did not have to explain that contrast: it was there ready and waiting. We find it again in the Squire's Tale lines 644–47. This is definitely by Chaucer but the association is drawn upon by Canacee, the heroine of the Squire's rambling and incomplete romance, who is nursing a forlorn female falcon back to health. This falcon has been betrayed in love by a tercelet, who switched his devotion from her to a hawk he saw flying past one day, thus reversing the gender roles of fickle and faithful found in the *balade*. While the genders are reversed, the color associations are not. Canacee makes a pen ("mewe") for the distressed falcon and chooses to line it with blue velvet as a sign of her fidelity: "... she made a mewe/And covered it with velu-ettes blewe,/In signe of trouthe that is in women sene" (643–5). In contrast, the outside of the pen is painted green, in accordance with the "false fowles" (treacherous birds, 647) painted thereon. Trust and stability inside in blue; treachery and change outside in green. Once again the binary opposition is not explained, simply accepted as a given.

Not that green needs to be paired with blue to be a sign of duplicity. The merry yeoman encountered on the road by the (stereotypically) corrupt summoner in the Friar's Tale wears a green jacket, "a courtepy of grene" (1382). When pressed for his name, this plausible fellow happily identifies himself as a fiend (1448), something which does not seem to perturb the summoner in the least, as the two proceed amicably together along the road. Although this fiend does not dress in green entirely, as the lady of the *balade* is exhorted to do, his choice of jacket color is a clear indication of his character.

He is out to trick and in the best folk-tradition, the subject of his trickery, the summoner, has fair warning of the danger he is in, as the fiend openly tells him who he is and how he operates. It thus comes as no surprise when the summoner is damned to hell by an old woman he tries to frighten into giving him money, and is promptly swept off by his fiendish companion. The story is gratifying in its swift completion and the detail of the color of the fiend's clothing merely serves to enhance this satisfaction as the audience is expected to register the danger signals sent out by the green jacket. Green, then, is established as the color of trickery and should only be worn, it seems, by those who wish to signal their unreliability.

Let us not, however, be too simplistic in our understanding of how green should be read. The Friar's fiend combines integrity with his trickery: he does not deceive the summoner, nor does he lure him into actions he otherwise would not have taken; he takes people or things for his master, Satan, only when the curse damning them reflects true intent. When a carter curses his three horses when he is stuck the mud, then blesses them when the cart is free, the horses are safe (1540–70). As the fiend says, "The carl spak oo thing, but he thoghte another" (1570) and so neither horses nor carter are the fiend's due. The widow, in contrast, not only damns the summoner in anger, but repeats her curse when courteously asked by the fiend if she means them. Moreover, the summoner himself has uttered the fateful words: "the foule feend me fecche/If I th'excuse…" (1610–11). This summoner, now a figure of human fecklessness, not just greedy exploitation of the poor, has been warned to be attentive to how far words match actions, but carries on regardless.

But there is another reason why this fiend might be wearing green. In a move that offers some support for White's contention that Christianity seeks to silence paganism in part by denying the kinds of relation to the natural world it offered, D. W. Roberston argued in 1954 that green was so well established as the devil's color, that Chaucer's contemporaries would immediately have recognized it affirming the devilish origins of the Friar's fiend. His article "Why the Devil Wears Green" traces the link between green as the color adopted by hunters and the devil as a hunter of human souls and is rooted in the work of the fourteenth-century humanist, Pierre Bersuire. Unexpectedly perhaps, green is a hunter's color not as a form of camouflage, but because green is pleasant and appeals to animals who seek out green places (Robertson, 471). The color green is acting as a lure. This link obviates the need to see Chaucer's Tale as allowing any space to the Celtic world, whose "green otherworld" had been championed by R. M. Garrett in discussion of *Sir Gawain and the Green Knight* and by Tolkien and Gordon in their edition of that poem. However, if we follow the lead of Garrett, Tolkien and Gordon, the Friar's Tale becomes more than a moral tale or a Christian parable.[6] It becomes instead a text in which both the Christian and Pagan traditions are in play, but not necessarily addressing each other directly. The result is a kind of palimpsest. The canny widow who rumbles the summoner may also realize that the gentleman in green is the Christian devil who needs the whole-hearted curse of a morally outraged Christian to enable him to carry the summoner off to Hell. Or she may recognize that the green jacket in this case indicates a pre-Christian tradition in which fairies are dangerous creatures out to trick the unwary and carry them off. In that case the readiness with which she repeats her words damning the summoner may reveal her knowledge of the ruse being employed by this plausible fellow and her quick-wittedness in exploiting it with the added pleasurable twist of thus giving Pagan forces the power to overcome Christian church administration. The green indicates the gentleman is a Celtic fairy, while the action of the Tale shows that the Celtic underworld has been merged with Christian Hell. That merging has also repressed the green world of nature, designating it as definitely evil, devilish, where in the Celtic tradition it is Other and disconcerting, but not invariably bad.

"Under a Forest Side"

The fateful meeting of summoner and fiend occurs on the road at a point where it passes "under a forest side" (FT 1380). This is a liminal place, not in the forest but alongside it, indicating the chance of salvation open to the summoner at this point. This detail occurs also in the Wife of Bath's Tale, which precedes the Friar's. Here the knight who has been set the supposedly impossible task of discovering what women want (again the folkloric elements are obvious) comes across the hag who has the answer "under a forest side" (WBT 990). As if to emphasize the point, the hag is revealed alone "on the grene" (WBT 998), a setting which makes her the hunter and the knight the beast attracted to a green place (Robertson, 471). The action of both Tales quickly diverts our attention from the "forest side" to the words spoken there, but the significance of this place as a natural site outside human norms and acting as a touchstone for individual ethics is there, even if Chaucer chooses not to emphasize it.

The Wife's and Friar's Tales suggest that knowing how the green wood could and should be read is a useful skill. Their green, forest side locations are not the same as the forests explored by Saunders or Harrison, being closer to Dana Phillips's "niches" (Phillips 1999), but as forest *sides* they remind us of the possibility of choice. Like the summoner and the knight, humans could act differently; they could stand less upon their dignity as individuals (or species) with a particular status, insist less upon their distinction from the rest of the world, stop believing themselves above the rules that seem to apply to others. The Wife's knight learns the lesson and is rewarded, while the Friar's summoner is swept off to Hell. Each chooses his companion, and must abide by that choice, but the moment of choice is signaled by the landscape.

Once we start to read green in these terms, we see that green is not so much a symbol of trickery as of a different system of values, one which prizes changeability and an ability to adapt over inflexible and established reactions, variety over consistency; in short, one less amenable to rules set by those who like to be in control of resources. The Friar's fiend is not making the humans act in any particular way, but he is enacting the consequences of what they do, and what the summoner does reflects in turn his attitude to those he meets. Likewise, the hag in the Wife of Bath's Tale is so repellent that the knight is loth to believe she can know anything of value. He accepts her help only because he has tried everything else. Nor are these two by any means the only figures in medieval literature to be associated with greenness and to challenge the status quo. The Green Knight of *Sir Gawain and the Green Knight* famously and unapologetically dresses entirely in green and issues an outright challenge to the prevailing codes of behavior as represented by Arthur's court.

This giant knight is very green. His greenness extends beyond his garments to his skin and beard and even to his horse. As the poem puts it: "and oueral enker-grene" (150). This "enker-grene" is probably the bright green we think of as spring green, which fits well with the usual reading of this figure as some kind of representation of the natural world, who rides into Arthur's court at Camelot during the mid-winter, Christmas festivities, carrying an axe and a holly branch and challenging anyone who dares to a beheading game. Here greenness may not be specifically devilish, but it is clearly not entirely human either. Moreover, since the poem presents Arthur's court as representative of Christian ethics, it is easy to read Camelot as Christianity, while the Green Knight embodies the natural world, demanding respect through his mid-winter challenge. Such a reading is aided by the fact that the Green Knight's castle seems to be in the middle of a wood (as discussed by Saunders) that might well evoke the associations of both civilization and its opposites delineated by Harrison (1992). In the main, this figure is seen as something which Arthur's court believe must be overcome, whether that be because he is a type of wild man (Benson, 1965), a representative of the Celtic other (Ingham, 2001) or more broadly part of the pagan elements of the poem, which the narrative shows exist alongside Christianity, even if the Christian figures themselves (such as Gawain) seek to overthrow them (Tracy, 2007). The Green Knight's personal affiliation with the natural world is suggested by his entrance, when he rides into Camelot bearing a holly branch in one hand and an axe in the other (206–9). He is thus ambiguously placed between being nature anthropomorphized, a type of Green Man, and a representative of human husbandry. It is possible to read this figure as indeed being neither one nor the other, but a balance of both (Rudd 2011), reflecting the concept of nature in equilibrium which Joel Kaye explained was in fact the dominant understanding of "balance" up to the late middle ages (Kaye 2008).

Such a reading is broadly in sympathy with White's view that the "spirits *in* natural objects, which formerly had protected nature from man, evaporated" (White, p. 11). Indeed the ending of the poem could be seen as presenting the very "evaporation" he describes. Gawain has met the Green Knight's challenge, first by beheading him in Arthur's hall, then by travelling to the significantly named "green chapel" to accept a return blow the following year. The challenge was not without its perils, but Gawain has survived them all and the Green Knight acknowledges this by giving Gawain a mere nick in the neck, rather than swiping his head off entirely. After exacting this price and congratulating Gawain on his success, the Green Knight invites him back to his hall to celebrate, but when Gawain refuses, opting instead to return to Arthur's (Christian) court, the Green Knight simply disappears: "the knight in the enker-grene/Whiderwarde-so-euer he wolde" (2477–8). This last mention of the otherworldly figure simultaneously reminds us of his greenness and re-asserts the mystery of his origins as he melts back into the landscape; arguably there is no clearer example of the spirit within natural objects disappearing in the face of Christian rejection, as represented by Evernden and Merchant.

Within this poem, too, the blue/green binary exists, though it is latent and rarely remarked upon. Gawain, the hero of the piece, arrives at a castle in the midst of winter to be welcomed by its host Bertilak (later found to be the alter-ego of the Green Knight). As part of the hospitality, Gawain is provided with fresh clothes from which he chooses each day what he is to wear. The poem does not always detail Gawain's dress during his time with Bertilak, so it is surely significant that on the day when Gawain accepts the gift of a green girdle from his host's wife, we learn that he wears a blue robe (1928). The poem makes no comment beyond telling us that it reaches to the floor, but it is a nice point that by thus dressing in blue, Gawain casts himself in opposition to the Green Knight/Bertilak, his opponent-cum-host. It is also an irony that he wears the color of fidelity and truth at the very point in the poem where both have been most compromised. According to the rules of the exchange of winnings game he and Bertilak have been playing, Gawain ought to declare a girdle pressed upon him by Bertilak's wife as the spoils of his day; according to the rules of chivalry, he is honor-bound both to accept the gift and to keep it a secret, since the Lady specifically requests this. Gawain's position is thus compromised, but since he has resisted the Lady's seduction attempts, perhaps he can feel justified in dressing in blue, the color of fidelity. So here the blue/green binary may be detected, adding a further layer of meaning to the sequences of blow and counter-blow, of challenge and quest, of Christian versus Pagan or of human versus nature operating in this poem. All of which makes it easy to regard this poem as an example of the medieval Christian view in which green is linked with a fiendishly challenging if not outright hostile natural world (hostile to humans, that is) and further broadly connected to a Pagan outlook which itself challenges (or seeks to overthrow, or is overthrown by) Christian hegemony. The Norse derivation of "enker-grene" is fuel to the fire of this kind of reading and invites readings such as those established by Tolkien and Gordon, which link the Green Knight himself with pre-Christian beliefs and attitudes to the nonhuman natural world. But such easy association of Norse with non-Christian rather overlooks the fact that by the fourteenth century Christianity was well established in Scandinavia as well as the rest of Europe. Such readings more accurately reflect our latter-day desire to find different paradigms for human/nature relationships in pre- or non-Christian societies.

Moreover, greenness in *Sir Gawain* is not straightforwardly negative. The Green Knight is an ambiguous figure: jovial, not entirely human, willing to challenge Arthur's court but not seeking to destroy it. His challenge is after all a seasonal *game* and one which Gawain survives, despite all expectations. This elusive green figure epitomizes not so much the natural or pagan worlds, but the world of green itself; a world which has been revealed to be multifaceted and paradoxical. It finds a latter day parallel in our current concepts of being green. Dana Phillips attacks the popular version of ecology for its uninformed and partial adoption of scientific findings—ecosystems are many, not one; local and patch, not global (Phillips 1999, 580). True enough, but like Gawain we tend to carry our versions with us. The problem is one of accuracy of imagination, rather than fact—the concept is mightier than the science, but even so we tend to overlook the details. There is a battle between diversity and uniformity, changeability and consistency, played out in a myriad ways in our literature which feeds into our ability to imagine, or not, alternative ways to relate to and live within the planet we inhabit, the environments we create, and those we destroy. Reading earlier literature with attention might tell us a little about why we think as we do. It cannot offer solutions, but it can offer alternative patterns of thought, tools that enable us to imagine more fully some of the claims made by ecologists. Thus the encounters between Gawain and his Green Knight, the knight and the hag, the summoner and the fiend might be read as examples of Naess's defense of Deep Ecology: "Man may be the measure of all things in the sense that only a human being has a measuring *rod* but what he measures he may find to be greater than himself and his survival" (Naess, 270). For Chaucer the nonhuman world is fascinating but not to be valued in ethical terms. He is no "green" but his use of literary tropes and traditions reveals the variety of ways in which the natural world is used or abused, something from which to seek shelter, as Gawain does, but also something to contemplate, a rich source of philosophical lessons, if not exactly a refuge. *Sir Gawain and the Green Knight*, in contrast, seems to rejoice in diversity and more fluid, adaptive human/nonhuman relations. For both authors green, whether associated with a place or a person, indicates a moment of choice, or of change; a point where things are not fixed and sure, but liable to alteration. Moreover, it indicates that whatever choice we make, there will be consequences by which we must abide. We might like to consider our options carefully.

Notes

1. *Sir Gawain and the Green Knight*, ed. John Burrow (Harmondsworth, Penguin, 1972, rpt 1982) lines 746–7. This edition modernizes the letter forms and some spellings; the translation is my own, but the poem has been much translated.
2. Martin Rees, Reith Lectures 2010, "Scientific Horizons." Lecture 1, "The Scientific Citizen," transmission 1st June 2010, BBC Radio 4. Transcripts available from http://www.bbc.co.uk/programmes/b00sk5nc.
3. Boethius, *The Consolation of Philosophy*, book 5. 6.1. Translated with introduction and explanatory notes by Peter Walsh (Oxford: Clarendon Press, 1999) p. 110.
4. I am grateful to Natalie Hanna for allowing me to draw on her current work on *green* as a color term in Middle English literature. The MA dissertation (2011) arising from her research explains in greater depth the range of meanings available to a fourteenth-century author and reader; I have profited much from our conversations on the topic.
5. As opposed to indicating social position, something the sumptuary laws both tried and signally failed to police. These laws placed restrictions on the cost of materials individuals could use in their dress, but not on their color. See Keen 1990, pp. 9–11; 14–16.
6. It may seem out of touch to refer back to arguments between critics in the 1950s, but these were not just critics but highly influential editors of core texts whose views are reflected

in the notes of the standard editions still used today (the *Riverside Chaucer* (Benson et al. 1988) is based on Robertson's Oxford edition of Chaucer's *Complete Works* and Davies's revised edition of Tolkien and Gordon's *Sir Gawain and the Green Knight* remains the most commonly cited and probably widely used of the various editions of the poem). Their views thus still influence our understanding of medieval literature as their notes will have shaped our own readings of these works, initially at least.

References

Benson, Larry D. (1965), *Art and Tradition in Sir Gawain and the Green Knight* (New Brunswick, NJ: Rutgers University Press).

Benson, Larry D. et al., eds. (1988), *The Riverside Chaucer* (Oxford: Oxford University Press).

Brewer, D. S. (1997), "The Colour Green." In D. Brewer and J. Gibson (eds.), *A Companion to the Gawain-Poet* (Cambridge: Cambridge University Press).

Clarke, Stephen (1993), *How to Think About the Earth: Philosophical and Theological Models for Ecology* (London: Mowbray).

Hanna, Natalie (2011), "Colour Symbolism and Semantics in Medieval Literature: Revisiting Chaucer's 'Grene,'" unpublished MA Dissertation, Liverpool, UK.

Harrison, Robert P. (1992), *Forests: The Shadow of Civilisation* (Chicago and London: University of Chicago Press).

Heather, P. J. (1948), "Colour Symbolism: Part 1," *Folklore* 59: 4, 165–83.

Holsinger, Bruce (2009), "Of Pigs and Parchment: Medieval Studies and the Coming of the Animal," *PMLA* 124: 2, 616–23.

Ingham, Patricia (2001), "'In Contrayez Straunge': Colonial Relations, British Identity, and Sir Gawain and the Green Knight," *New Medieval Literatures IV*, 61–93.

Kaye, Joel (2008), "The (Re) Balance of Nature, ca. 1250–1350." In Barbara Hanawalt and Lisa Kiser (eds.), *Engaging with Nature: Essays on the Natural World in Medieval and Early Modern Europe* (Notre Dame, Indiana: University of Notre Dame Press, 2008), pp. 85–114.

Keen, Maurice (1990), *English Society in the Later Middle Ages 1348–1500* (Harmondsworth: Penguin Books).

Kiser, Lisa (2009), "Margery Kempe and the Animalization of Christ," *Studies in Philology* 106: 3, 299–315.

Naess, Arne (1984), "A Defence of the deep ecology movement," *Environmental Ethics* 6, 265–70.

Pearsall, Derek A. and Elizabeth Salter (1973), *Landscapes and Seasons of the Medieval World* (Toronto: University of Toronto Press).

Phillips, Dana (1999), "Ecocriticism, Literary Theory and the Truth of Ecology," *New Literary History* 30: 3, 577–602.

Rees, Martin (2010), "Scientific Horizons," The Reith Lectures, transmission June 2010, BBC Radio 4. Transcripts available at http://www.bbc.co.uk/programmes/b00sk5nc.

Robertson, D. W. Jr. (1954), "Why the Devil Wears Green," *Modern Language Notes* 69: 7, 470–72.

Rowland, Beryl (1973), *Animals with Human Faces: A Guide to Animal Symbolism* (Knoxville, TN: University of Tennessee Press).

Rudd, Gillian (2003), 'Thinking through Earth in Langland's *Piers Plowman* and the Harley lyric "Erthe toc of Erthe,"' *Ecotheology: The Journal of Religion, Nature and the Environment* 8: 2, 137–149.

Rudd, Gillian (2011), "The Green Knight's Balancing Act." In David Matthews and Anke Bernau (eds.). *In Strange Countries: a festschrift for J. J. Anderson* (Manchester: Manchester University Press), pp. 25–45.

Salisbury, Joyce E. (1994), *The Beast Within: Animals in the Middle Ages* (New York: Routledge).

Salter, David (2001), *Holy and Noble Beasts: Encounters with Animals in Medieval Literature* (Woodbridge, Suffolk: D. S. Brewer).

Saunders, Corinne (1993), *The Forests of Medieval Romance* (Woodbridge: D. S. Brewer).

Siewers, Alfred K. (2009), *Strange Beauty: Ecocritical Approaches to Early Medieval Landscape* (Basingstoke, UK: Palgrave Macmillan).

Sorrell, Roger D. (1989), *St. Francis of Assisi and Nature Tradition and Innovation in Western Christian Attitudes toward the Environment* (New York and Oxford: Oxford University Press.

Tolkien, J. R. R. and E. V. Gordon, eds. (1966), *Sir Gawain and the Green Knight*, 2nd rev. ed. N. Davis, (Oxford: Clarendon Press).

Tracy, Larissa (2007), "A Knight of God or the Goddess? Rethinking Religious Syncretism in Sir Gawain and the Green Knight," *Arthuriana 17*: 3, 31–55.

White, Lynn (1967), "The Historical Roots of our Ecological Crisis." In David Schmidtz and Elizabeth Willott (eds.), *Environmental Ethics: What Really Matters, What Really Works* (Oxford: Oxford University Press, 2002), pp. 7–14.

Further Reading

Hanawalt, Barbara A. and Lisa J. Kiser, eds. (2008), *Engaging with Nature: essays on the Natural World in Medieval and early Modern Europe* (Notre Dame, IN: University of Notre Dame Press).

Pluskowski, Aleksander, ed. (2007), *Breaking and Shaping Beastly Bodies: Animals as Material Culture in the Middle Ages.* Oxford: Oxbow.

Resl, Brigitte, ed. (2007), *A Cultural History of Animals in the Medieval Age.* Oxford: Berg.

Rudd, Gillian (2007), *Greenery; Ecocritical Readings of Late Medieval English Literature* (Manchester: Manchester University Press).

Ryan, Kathleen (1987), "Parchment as Faunal Record." *MASCA: University of Pennsylvania Journal 4.3*: 124–38.

Schmidtz, David and Elizabeth Willott, eds. (2002), *Environmental Ethics: What Really Matters, What Really Works* (Oxford: Oxford University Press).

Simmons, Ian G. (1993), *Interpreting nature: cultural constructions of the environment* (London: Routledge).

Sobecki, Sebastian (2008), *The Sea and Medieval English Literature* (Woodbridge, Suffolk: D. S. Brewer).

Yamamoto, Dorothy (2000), *The Boundaries of the Human in Medieval English Literature.* Oxford: Oxford University Press.

CHAPTER 2

··

SHADOWS OF THE RENAISSANCE

··

ROBERT N. WATSON

FIRST of all, who cares? If the environmental crisis is a present and pressing issue based in technology and economics that threatens large-scale future effects, why should green thinkers spend precious time attending to the distant cultural past?

My answer is that the main cause of and likeliest solution to the problem are both human, and that cultures are stubborn and powerful beasts that can be coaxed in new directions, but rarely yield to threats (however shocking or awesome) or direct admonishment (however valid and urgent). The attitudes toward nature underlying the current heedless conduct of so many of the world's industrial societies took shape hundreds of years ago and cannot be effectively addressed until they are understood. The assumption that our crisis is entirely recent—pollution *ex nihilo*—and addressable only by focusing on our present politics reflects a narrow, anti-ecological view. Our species will wither alone in the shadows of an ancient loss, like the forsaken knight of Keats's "La Belle Dame Sans Merci," unless we cast some light on the antecedent relations between human and nonhuman life.

Most historically informed observers now assume that modern attitudes toward nature began with the Romantics, but even this broader view overlooks a very significant rehearsal, two centuries earlier, for nature-lovers' battle against emerging industrialist and consumer-capitalist tendencies. Doubtless the story goes back even further: from the earliest instances of epic, pastoral, and georgic, literature has offered a critique as well as an expression of the nostalgia for an inviolate nature natural world that has always been not quite with us. As the argument of Pico della Mirandola's "Oration on the Dignity of Man" convinced many Renaissance intellectuals, the human species is characterized by its unique resistances to nature as well as its unique modes of self-consciousness.

The arts of the English Renaissance reflect an extensive and uneasy meditation on the shadowy boundary between ourselves and our environment. That meditation is haunted by fears of becoming either too open or too closed: either permeable to forces alien and adversarial to the self, or sealed off from the sustaining sources of life. Such concerns cannot have been unique to that era, or even this species: every living creature needs to differentiate but also connect, exclude but also absorb, wall the body with skin but eat and excrete. Regulating these apertures is the systole and diastole at the heart of identity. Amid the cultural transformations of the Renaissance, however, this balance acquired particular inflections and articulations. Humoral theory offered a particular way of construing the fact that health depends primarily on the right balance of ingestions and purgations, but the dilemma presented itself in many other forms as well. At the level of body-politic rather than body—no less essential for the human being, and with new complications under urbanization and nationalization—each self must defend its interests while still participating in the interests of a community. On a larger scale, Renaissance nation-states were struggling with unprecedented obligations to interact with foreign traders and colonial territories—and therefore with alternative belief-systems—without enduring any fatal contamination.

By the end of the sixteenth century, many Europeans began to worry that the time-honored project of controlling and distancing nature had gone too far. As the moralistic Duke of Albany warns in Shakespeare's *King Lear,*

> That nature, which contemns it[s] origin,
> Cannot be border'd certain in itself;
> She that herself will sliver and disbranch
> From her material sap, perforce must wither
> And come to deadly use. (4.6)

But Albany seems—as perhaps Rosse does also, when he warns in *Macbeth* against "Thriftless ambition, that wilt ravin up/Thine own life's means!" (2.4)—a bit naïve about the problem. As both tragedies persistently remind us on secondary levels, the fact that nature is necessary to human life does not make it friendly to human aspirations. The hundred-thousand-year war against vermin, predators, and other enemies of the proud, hungry human domain was newly complicated by skeptical, scientific, and theological challenges to established assumptions about human self-containment and self-sufficiency. The terrifying degree of passivity dictated by Calvinist soteriology emerged alongside a new recognition of the overwhelming power of nature that would find fuller expression in the Romantic sublime and, more recently, in the deep ecology movement. The Reformers' severe construals of the Fall from the Garden authorized human efforts (manifest especially in Baconian science) to suppress nature, but also emphasized our insufficiency for that project—an emphasis perhaps visible in the plain stone and wood of Protestant churches.

What the futile primitivist impulses of many sophisticated Northern Europeans in the first half of the seventeenth century evidently suggested to some remarkable artists was that one could re-connect perfectly with nature only by becoming nothing other than nature: only by the erasure of will and consciousness itself, through death, could we achieve direct uncompromised participation in the life beyond the self. This iconoclasm of the cogitating self may be the root of what Greg Garrard has rightly flagged as the "pernicious" modern idea that "nature is only authentic if we are entirely absent from it."[1] Similarly pernicious—as the fates of characters such as Coriolanus and Leontes suggest, wielding fire against their kin in hopes of purifying themselves—was the fantasy of freeing humanity from the natural taint, the original sin of vitality that entails mortality. Short of that consummation, to be human was to endure a constant tension between the mortal, biological body and the immortal soul, with its self-conscious imaginarium.

No middle ground was accessible, no matter how hard the Cartesians scrutinized the pineal gland, or the anatomists the other core mysteries of the corpse. Yet each person inhabited that no-man's-land—here Michel Montaigne is more evocative than John Donne—as neither quite an island nor entirely part of the main. Like Andrew Marvell's mower, Renaissance man could no longer find his home—the etymological sense of "eco." No wonder these homesick creatures wandered and wondered, and worried and wrote, especially about whether they could lovingly dissolve into nature or proudly define themselves against it.

The resulting artworks make visible a dangerous inherited flaw in contemporary environmentalist attitudes—a flaw that I believe William Shakespeare had already captured in the character of Jaques in *As You Like It*, whose sentimental critique of Duke Senior's deer-hunt (in Act 2, Scene 1) proves to be itself an anthropocentric imposition on nature. Jaques finally realizes that he needs to retreat from the world in order to reconsider his grasp of it. Perhaps he would end up writing some good ecocriticism.

A longstanding Christian assumption that the ultimate reality lies in God's intentions was slowly but surely being replaced by a dispiriting sense that reality ultimately consists of material objects. This was the threat lurking in the recovery of classical atomism; and when Baconian empiricism interjected some similar material into the collective cultural body, the second exposure threatened to provoke something like anaphylactic shock. The vitalist movement in seventeenth-century England—which seems, in retrospect, a fascinating mix of mysticism and biology—was one attempt to treat that reaction, offering an antidote to the mechanistic tendencies of the era.

The significance of this shift may be obscured if we view it as merely one facet of the increasing tendency of intellectuals to believe more firmly in physical sciences than in religious doctrines. It marks a massive alteration in the relationship between words and things—an alteration that made external physical reality inaccessible in a radical new way. The Protestant Reformation arose, in the sixteenth century, largely from a fear that material objects were coming between human beings and the divine Word. Scholars working either in scientific research or in literary theory will recognize that now the dominant fear is almost the opposite: a fear that language (as the epitome of our cognitive representational functions) comes between human beings and the physical universe, which we deem fundamental reality. Is the essence of things God's secret plan for them, or do we now mostly accept the view emerging in the late Renaissance that belittled postlapsarian language as a crude instrument offering no direct contact with the essences that hover tantalizingly just beyond the reach of our lexicon? Is the Word an ultimate revelation, or are words instead a mob of mediating obfuscations? The treatment of nature, then and now, depends on how those questions are answered.

Technology was swiftly advancing throughout Europe, the English language was burgeoning, and the urban life was proving irresistible both to displaced agricultural

workers seeking their way in an economy also changing rapidly, and to aristocrats pursuing interests (both financial and cultural) in that post-feudal society. At the same
time—in the amalgam of guilt and triumphalism that so often troubles refugees from
a dying culture—they began compulsively boutiquing and enshrining the green world
of natural simplicities they believed they had forfeited in pursuit of new values. The
defense of Mayday and Midsummer rituals became an effective tactic in the Stuart
monarchs' struggle against the Puritans, by enlisting the reactionary aspect of popular rural nostalgia. The sixteenth century produced a bumper-crop of pastoral literature (with its faux-naïve poses), and gardening manuals that promised—as many
still do—little backyard escape-hatches from the ills of modernity. Aristocrats began
investing, not only in country pavilions, but also in paintings of landscapes instead of
Biblical scenes. As the market for Dutch art indicates, such things were especially popular with sophisticates such as Queen Henrietta Maria, in a casual-dress rehearsal for
the association of nature with childhood, simplicity, and deep truth that most cultural
historians assume began almost two hundred years later, with English and German
Romanticism. In between, European culture had mostly swung into a Neoclassical
mode, forcing nature into geometric forms, as if, after decades of futile efforts to recap-
ture that lost world of nature as itself, the elites chose to compel nature to imitate art
instead—serving the devil abstraction, because the biophilic god had failed to provide its supposed blessings of simplification and authenticity. Pressing too hard on
that cookie-cutter eventually provoked the protests known as Romantic poetry, philosophy, and landscape architecture, but that that was by no means the first step in the
dialectic, which finally has less to do with whether we like trees or not than with how
we want to take hold of the world that our complex consciousness brings to us in such
multiple and malleable forms. The debate about whether to understand reality as a
stable external entity or instead a construction (woven by the perceiving mind on the
available cultural framework) is hardly unique to ecocriticism, but nowhere is it more
obviously crucial.[2]

The major modes of Renaissance nostalgia—for lost nature, for maternal nurture
(including that of the Virgin Mary), for Eden, and for the Classical world and its own
lost Golden Age—all suggest a culture haunted by differentiation, by humanity's alien
status in a potentially harmonious universe. Longstanding human anxieties about being
dominated by nature, or being too deeply implicated in it, gave way to anxieties about
being separated from it. In Holland, one could buy a tulip bulb, and find oneself holding an evanescent financial-derivatives marker instead; even the land there was largely
a product of technology. Forests and wilderness were shrinking rapidly across Europe
and especially Britain. The stench of London and other cities (from crowding without
ventilation, open sewers, and coal smoke[3]) would have made it difficult to construe this
change as the Christian progress from Eden to a New Jerusalem. An increasingly subju-
gated nature could become an object of uneasy sympathy, rather than a rival heroically
overcome: Mission Accomplished, but the occupation could be hellish. The only relief
would be either to take total control of nature, as the new empirical science was striving to do, or else to surrender and retreat into the symbiotic subsistence of rural feudal

agriculture; everything in-between was a quagmire—a "nine men's morris…fill'd up with mud," as in the climate-change lament of *Midsummer Night's Dream* (2.1.98).

At least four forces worked synergistically in the late Renaissance to magnify these discomforts. Nascent capitalism not only destabilized personal identity, but also allowed money to alienate work from product and ownership from object, introducing an abstract mediator into the process of valuation and alienating the field-hand from the field. The urbanization accompanying capitalism promoted not only a new kind of anonymity, but also the recognition that a past more directly linked to the land that provided life has been forfeited. Technological innovations, in providing better approximations of the world, obliged people to face the fact that approximate reproduction of the outside world was all their mortal consciousness could ever hope to achieve. Protestants strove to replace the complicated institutional mediations of Catholicism with a direct link between the Savior and the sinner through reading of the Bible, but were also forcefully reminded that their world was an allegory, and that they could no longer see their distant God except through a shadowy glass.

Many of the largest projects of late Renaissance culture seem designed either to recover the possibility of seeing things as they absolutely are, or—more often—to reconcile people to accurate accommodative representations in the place of the things themselves: cartography, historiography, philology, empirical science, Bible translation, value-regulated currencies, optics, linear perspective in painting, even representative government as an alternative to absolute monarchy. But (as audiophiles complain) there is no truly lossless form of compression, certainly not for the orchestrations of nature. Shakespeare's contemporaries heard a prophecy like the ominous one heard by Leontes in *The Winter's Tale*, who forfeited his "blossom" child in a hyper-civilized fit of egoism: their lives would be cold and empty—a silent spring, if any—"if that which is lost be not found" (3.3.46, 3.2.135–36). And what seemed lost was every-thing, which acquired the code-name of "nature."

The arts of the later Renaissance evince an often self-conscious desire to return to nature, hoping there to recover a direct experience of absolute reality in all its lovely simplicity. "In Tudor London the building of 'summer houses' or garden pavilions in the rural suburbs and adjacent villages became popular among the well-to-do.…John Stow described how on May Day Elizabethan Londoners 'would walk into the sweet meadows and green woods, there to rejoice their spirits with the beauty and savour of sweet flowers, and with the harmony of birds.' "[4] These were arguably the totemic gestures of a civilization carrying flowers, at the fringes of the city, to the grave of an ancestor it had slain.

This assumption that nature is both a savior (of body and spirit alike) to be revered, and a subject to be visited paternalistically in the progress of the human sovereign, now seems pervasive. It informs countless well-meaning children's books and green-tourism projects, as well as a range of other advertising campaigns that seek innocence by association. Simple Green is a popular cleaning fluid, supposed to wipe harmlessly away the messiness of modern life; so it was also in Renaissance pastorals. That genre shaped our notion of nature as a retreat where redemptively authentic experience awaits: an opportunity to find oneself as well as to critique the social milieu.

Encounters with nature may be better understood, however, as opportunities to lose the illusion of a bounded and self-sufficient human identity. Nature offers a rendezvous not with a prior self but with that which is prior to the self; it drowns human pride in a troubled, oceanic love of the incalculable emergent aspects of an evolving biosphere. Making nature an antidote for the complexity of our cognitive ecosystems involves a denial of the indispensable complexity of nature. Ecocritics must instead make vivid, as Shakespearean drama often does, the beautiful patterns of our interdependences. Renaissance theology offered a model of the universe as benignly collaborative. Providentialism was teleological in ways that Darwinism (rightly understood) is not, and it posited moral rather than biological causes, and the orientation was anthropo-centric: bees were systemically important because they taught orderly collective indus-try, not because they pollinated; flies similarly punished, rather than merely exploited, human uncleanliness. Still, the template of mutual reliance and life's plenitude antic-ipated (as several of us have argued, most recently and extensively Gabriel Egan) the Gaia-hypothesis of many contemporary ecological advocates.

Although I continue to find affirmations and implications of the *Back to Nature* hypothesis (some of which I will describe here),[5] I have also come to see this longing as constantly struggling against an opposing drive toward human autonomy—a fear, not of being too closed off from nature, but of being (or knowing oneself to be) saturated by it. Invite Gaia to your house, and she will bring along infestations of relatives. In the realm of architecture (with the growth of private spaces such as the closet), the habits of manners (with the emergence of what Norbert Elias calls *homo clausus*[6]), the concep-tion of physical selfhood (the Neoclassical erasure of what Bakhtin calls the Renaissance "grotesque body"[7]), even in the understanding of the skin (which was increasingly understood as a definitive boundary protecting the self rather than a permeable mem-brane integrating that self with the world[8]), interpenetration with the world was not so much sadly lost as stridently abjured. The threat was registered not only in Giuseppe Arcimboldo's portraits of human faces composed entirely from plants and animals, but also in Jacob van Ruisdael's vast landscapes that swallow up a few tiny, faceless human figures in their shadows.

What I have been describing as the yearning of human beings for integration with an external nature they could no longer authentically engage thus co-existed with a nearly opposite yearning for exactly that kind of clear and stable boundary: for differentiation from a nature from which they could never actually disengage. Perhaps this seeming contradiction reflects a frustrated (and suggestively anti-Cartesian) desire to grasp other life-forms entirely through the mind, set against a frustrated desire to exclude such life-forms completely from the body. These are symptoms of the desire for immor-tality, which often ironically proves fatal—for tragic heroes, but also perhaps for societ-ies that spurn their foundations in an organic ecology.

Shakespeare's *Midsummer Night's Dream* offers a rich example of this understand-ing that our lives are profoundly—at times, disturbingly—intertwined with other crea-tures, despite the proud claims of autonomy made by the human race and each human self. This comedy (as I have argued at length elsewhere[9]) acknowledges what Theseus proudly denies: that while human beings blunder along, a nightly world of "shadows" sorts out our mating and feeding and sleeping, patches our wounds, and fights off the demon death. Vermiculation was a common terror, but (probably about the same time Shakespeare wrote *Midsummer Night's Dream*) Thomas Muffet observed that "there are collected in us some putrefied excremental superfluous parts, which the more bounti-ful hand of Nature changeth into Worms, and so cleanseth our bodies; as we account it a good sign of health to be full of lice, after a long disease: also they consume much superfluous moisture in mans body, and unless they grow too many (for then they feed on our nutrimental juice) they are a great help to the guts."[10] Modern gastroenterol-ogy, microbiology, and endocrinology teach a similar lesson about the mostly invisible entities at work in us. In the mysteries of love and the fairyland, Shakespeare codes the world we do not know, but could not live without. In biology as in so many areas of early modern science, "magic" is the place-holder for phenomena with pending explanations.

Theseus stands at an apex of rationalist civilization, but (as Shakespeare's audience would have known) his myth embroils him in messy engagements with centaurs, mino-taurs, goat-men, demi-gods, and hunting-hounds. When Bottom translated into an ass, and the young lovers indistinguishably metamorphosed by love and flower-juice into the plants and predators of the wilderness as the wildness of passion overcomes them, the barriers by which humanity distinguishes itself from ambient nature col-lapse in merriment. This acceptance of mortal collectivity is a standard comic motif, but Shakespeare is not blind to its tragic aspects; like the happy lovers framing the Pyramus and Thisbe tragedy that might have been their own, neither scenario is a truth that can-cels the other. At the end of the play, the fairies promise fertility, but must also stand on guard against inward corruption, including misprints in the genetic alphabet that mis-shape human bodies and hence human lives:

> And the blots of Nature's hand
> Shall not in their issue stand;
> Never mole, hare-lip, nor scar,
> Nor mark prodigious, such as are
> Despised in nativity,
> Shall upon their children be. (5.1.409–414)

The specific instances of deformity cited—"mole" and "hare lip"—warn that therio-morphism, which is a source of laughter through most of the play, can be a source of sorrow as well. But the greatest sorrows in Shakespeare befall figures such as Hamlet, Macbeth, King Lear, and Coriolanus, whose revulsion from the common aspects of life locks them tragically into the prison of prideful human selfhood.

Bruno Latour also notices that we undervalue shadows. His influential *Politics of Nature* offers a broader, more abstract warning about the same error my *Back to Nature* was tracing in a specific historical moment of artistic production.[11] Latour defends the messy accretion of human needs, defined loosely as politics and carried within the social sciences, against the magisterial claims of Science with a capital S, which asserts an absolute truth established by technology that trumps any collective and/or relativistic view. This assertion has direct implications for twenty-first- century geopolitics—as Greg Garrard notes "Deploying science allowed developed countries to claim to speak for the whole world, a process called 'scientification' "[12]—but I believe it emerged from the moment when seventeenth-century empiricism promptly ran up against epistemological limits it could not afford to acknowledge.

Latour complains that Scientists have been cast as Platonic philosopher-kings because they supposedly see reality in an unmediated fashion, and therefore have the authority to report to us all on an ontologically superior world we receive only in shadow, distorted by our human interests and sympathies. Modern society is thus ruled by "a Constitution that organizes public life *into two houses*. The first is the obscure room, depicted by Plato, in which ignorant people find themselves in chains, unable to look directly at one another, communicating only via fictions projected on a sort of movie screen; the second is located outside, in a world made up not of humans but of nonhumans, indifferent to our quarrels, our ignorances, and the limitations of our representative fictions."[13] With access to an oracle called Nature, scientists declare themselves the rightful curators of Truth. *Il n'y a pas de hors*-tech. But it is, Latour implies, an incomplete and inhumane truth, wrongly dismissive of lived experience and the economy of suffering—what he terms "politics."

The late Renaissance, as I described it, was already composing and endorsing this so-called Constitution: nonhuman nature became associated with reality, with a founded and stable and unmediated and therefore superior Truth, to which access was desirable but nearly impossible, and to which obeisance was owed. This might seem to be a useful belief for environmentalist purposes, since it induces reverence toward other life-forms and a yearning to re-establish harmonious relations with them. *Back to Nature* deemed this ascendancy a pyrrhic victory, however, because the assumption that nature is primarily a source of lost simplicity and authenticity still blinds us to the often irreducible and indispensible complexity of the physical world around us and drives us to possess it in ways incompatible with that fluidity. If we demand simplicity from nature, we maim it; if we ask it to legitimate us, we enslave it to our own purposes, the more so because we believe (like a Petrarchan stalker) that we are asking only to worship, in hopes of requited love. A dedication to certainty and purity, even if motivated by a real reverence for nature rather than displaced epistemological anxieties, has direct costs for environmentalism. Industrial corporations exploit the standard of certainty to excuse people from accepting the implications of global climate change and to "brownwash" litigation for pollution-induced illnesses in mudslides of contradictory "expert testimony." The standard of purity, whereby true nature exists only in isolation from human forces, makes it difficult to adopt ameliorative measures, or even to win funding for urban parks; and millenarian fantasies of Last Days and Rapture authorize ignoring the long-term future of the Earth, imagining all our pollutants as merely a candy-wrapper tossed from a moving car that some patriarchal authority will neatly incinerate. My concern on this point resembles Latour's conclusion that the Constitution's over-valuing of Nature ontologically ends up meaning that "*under the pretext of protecting nature, the ecology movements have also retained the conception of nature that makes their political struggle hopeless.*"[14]

Latour's approach and mine provoke opposite critiques, however. He warns that his fellow-rebels against this oppressive Constitution "shall be told calmly that one must be very careful 'not to mix the sublime epistemological questions'—on the nature of things—'with the lowly political questions'—on values and the difficulty of living together. It's really so simple! If you try to loosen the trap by shaking it, it will close more tightly still, since you will be accused of seeking to 'confuse' political questions with cognitive ones! People will claim that you are politicizing Science...."[15] The response to my argument has been the converse: that I am losing the urgent eco-political questions by allowing them to sublimate into epistemological questions, confusing a political project with an enervating, attenuating cognitive inquiry, and thereby *de*-politicizing environmental science. Several reviews of *Back to Nature* complain that it is not really ecocriticism at all, because it neglects to advocate environmentalist policies or put its scholarship directly and unambiguously in their service.

As we respect the intricate and resilient character of ecosystems, formed by protracted evolution in various climates, we must respect the same qualities in human cultures. If we assume that our Green beliefs are the inevitable revelation of an absolute practical and ethical truth that had been inexplicably ignored, we will keep stumbling over the tangled historical undergrowth we refuse to see. Analyzing the forces that shaped current attitudes toward nature—which literary criticism allows us to do—offers the best chance of revealing the destructive ones as contingent and therefore dispensable. If we neglect or even disdain to do that intellectual work in depth and in good faith, we are left with nothing but the paternalism that has already bred resentment against environmental causes. If we fail to do the cultural work to make the scientific jeremiads tolerable—fail to situate them in a familiar and positive set of narratives—the rescue of distressed Gaia is likely to fail also. Have our fellow-citizens really never heard the slogans or the data behind them, or never developed the moral imagination to register the agony behind the data? Or have we eco-scholars not really understood the traditions and anxieties that keep people from accepting and applying what they hear?

Renaissance communities had to fight off crop-pests and pestilences, but present ecological problems derive from an inability to understand that we are using more pesticides and more antibiotics than are good for us. Perhaps people cannot recognize that over-achievement because of culturally entrenched assumptions about nature as an external object, and therefore about the desirability of controlling and simplifying the biosphere. If so, then opening those assumptions to question, by historicizing them, could ultimately prove valuable in ways that one more chant against polluters or one more chart about climate change may not.

In fact, without some arcane and disinterested academic research, the entire problem of anthropogenic climate change might still be unrecognized and hence entirely unaddressed. James Hansen, at Columbia University when that campus was the flashpoint of late-1960s radicalism, chose to be more hard scientist than hot activist—and thereby became the single most important figure in discovering and publicizing the vicious cycle of global warming. Research is not necessarily the adversary Latour condemns as Science; in fact, the complex practice called the humanities—especially when grounded in cultural history—is close kin to the extended subjective conversation and negotiation Latour endorses as politics. The history of ideas—often best recovered through the criticism of art—should not be dismissed by absolute Politics any more than politics should be dismissed by absolute Science. Monoculture may be no better a strategy for environmentalism than it is for the environment. There is room—there is need—for many kinds of work in the fields of Green. What follows are a few further examples, exploring the relationship between early Protestant culture and the emergence of a sympathetic valuation of nonhuman life.

As nature became the idol through which a lost ultimate reality was both worshipped and mourned in late Renaissance Europe, because a dualistic culture of representation imposed a kind of collective solipsism, so the natural world began occupying the pictorial spaces formerly occupied by a supernatural God. This was a predictable consequence of iconoclasm, and a plausible anticipation of Deism, but it had some surprising side effects. By detaching the compelling and conjoined emotions of guilt and pity from their traditional visible objects—holy martyrs, especially the crucified Christ—Reformation iconoclasm inadvertently cathected those emotions onto the creatures who die for our suppers.[16]

FIGURE 2.1 "Woman with Dead Birds," panel by Jacques de Gheyn II (1565–1629); Sweden, private collection.

Jacques De Gheyn the Younger was noted for producing many naturalistic drawings of nonhuman creatures before that became common practice; there is little direct evidence of his theology, and his wife was Catholic, but he was chiefly patronized by Prince Maurice, the leader of Dutch resistance against the rule of Catholic Spain, and apparently refused to have a Catholic priest at his deathbed. His *Woman with Dead Birds* (Figure 2.1) has baffled art historians, but—especially if one notices the white cross formed by the wound in the side of the central bird—it makes sense as a kind of quiet *Beeldenstorm*, a secularization of traditional Christian images such as Michelangelo's Collona Pietá (Figure 2.2).

The moralizing verse Michelangelo placed on this Cross—*Non vi si pensa quanto sangue costa*, from Canto 29 of Dante's *Paradiso*—could be applied to this later instance as well: people do not think about how much blood this martyrdom costs. It would doubtless have applied for Ranters such as Jacob Bauthumley who could "see God in all creatures, man and beast, fish and fowl."[17]

The gap between these pictures may seem as deep thematically as it is narrow compositionally, but in both dimensions it resembles the gap between a dozen centuries decisively insulated from any moral acknowledgment of the oppression of nonhuman animals, and the century in which (despite a desperate rear-guard action formulated by René Descartes and carried out ruthlessly by Enlightenment anatomists) that relationship was audibly and visibly registered as tyranny and martyrdom. Furthermore, that

FIGURE 2.2 Study for the Colonna Pietá by Michelangelo Buonarroti (1475–1564); black chalk on paper; early 1540s; © Isabella Stewart Gardner Museum, Boston, MA, USA/The Bridgeman Art Library.

gap may be bridged not only by various Renaissance paintings of the dead Christ with three winged angels (by Palma Il Giovane, Albrecht Durer, Antonello da Messina, and others), but even by De Gheyn's own painting of this same female model in the same costume holding the infant Christ above the winged heads of three cherubs (Figure 2.3).

This instance from the visual arts is a small and quirky piece of what I now believe is a significant correlation between Protestant resistances and cross-species sympathies. Compassion for nonhuman animals hitchhiked some distance ahead on the vehicle of iconoclasm, but other aspects of Protestantism carried it much further, and at times even allowed it to drive.

Animal-rights (or at least, anti-cruelty) sentiment in seventeenth-century England appeared predominantly on the Reformist—and especially Puritan—side of the era's culture-wars. The great Protestant martyrologist John Foxe was evidently alert to non-human martyrs as well: "Such is my disposition that I can scarce pass the shambles where beasts are slaughtered, but that my mind recoils with a feeling of pain."[18] Opposition

FIGURE 2.3 Half-length Figure of the Virgin Mary; panel, by Jacques de Gheyn II (1565–1629); MuseoBardini, Florence, Italy.

to bear-baiting, hunting, and other blood sports was led by a series of notables from the Reformation sects and campaigns: Marian martyrs, Civil War revolutionaries, and leading figures in radical Protestant groups such as the Diggers, Levellers, Adamites, Quakers, Ranters, and Familists. Many of the early English zoologists, including the Thomas Muffet who depicted worms as benign symbionts rather than parasites, and the Edward Topsell ("a cleric of distinctly puritan stripe"[19]) in whose history of beasts Muffet's work was published, were trained in intensely Puritan colleges. Although Thomas More is important earlier, Margaret Cavendish may be the only high-church Royalist likely to rank among the top twenty-five British advocates for animals in the late Renaissance. Furthermore, the earliest modern law against cruelty to domestic animals appears to be one enacted by the Puritans of the Massachusetts colony in 1641.

Animals certainly found few real advocates in the centuries preceding the Reformation. Peter Singer's landmark work *Animal Liberation* found no direct objections to cruelty toward nonhuman creatures for more than twelve centuries, between Porphyry and Montaigne. Yet the argument against human exceptionalism and consequent human privilege had long been available through classical skepticism. As Keith Thomas observes, "What is new about the early modern period is that, when Montaigne in the sixteenth century and the French libertins in the seventeenth revived the old attack...they found now for the first time there were writers in the Christian tradition prepared to agree with them."[20] Especially, I would say, within one nontraditional form of Christianity: in England, at least, Calvinism took over the ancient skeptics' project of humbling human reason, and thereby human pride, and therefore human privilege.

Commentators tend to accept as fact Thomas Macauley's claim that the Puritan opposition to cruel sports had nothing to do with sympathy toward animals, but only with antipathy toward human pleasure, especially in frivolous violations of the Sabbath. The bear-baiting allusions in the tormenting of the "Puritan" Malvolio in *Twelfth Night* may have had an ironic point. For many Reformers, however, the chief sin was causing and enjoying the suffering of beasts, and several key themes coalesce in a 1626 sermon by the Puritan minister Robert Bolton: kindness to animals is associated with vegetarianism, whereas cruelty demonstrates that we are, in significant moral and theological aspects, inferior to the beasts (equated by Bolton with human convicts) that we imagine ourselves entitled to torment.[21] Three points made by Bolton and other radical Reformers— that human reason is not so superior to the faculties of other creatures, that suffering is similarly shared, and that therefore the Golden Rule applies to human–animal interactions—prove crucial for animal advocates in subsequent centuries.

Class warfare mapped itself onto the human–animal division, and not just around the aristocratic privileges of the hunt. The Puritans' sense of themselves as theologically elect but socially preterite, always on the brink of martyrdom by the earthly powers that were, must have encouraged them to identify with the helplessness—and must have made vivid the consequent misery—of enslaved or hunted creatures (Lovelace's insect poems after the Cavaliers' fall from power show a similar imprint). In opposing the Divine Right claims of the Stuarts and the authority of Archbishop Laud, Puritans might have internalized a model for questioning the presumed reign of humanity over the animal kingdom, which had often been explained by exactly that analogy. Certainly, as outgunned outsiders, they were primed to see the tyranny of self-indulgent powers that claimed divine sanction, and to invoke against it the Golden Rule—"as ye would that men should do to you, do ye also to them likewise" (Luke 6:31; cf. Matthew 7:12)—which could then have been applied across species.

That Rule applied also to what Protestants especially had to wish God would do unto them. The absolute dominion of the Calvinist God would have resembled the unlimited dominion the human race claimed over the animal kingdom. The natural-supernatural fear that God might exercise His power with the same ruthlessness exercised by humanity made Protestants eager to remember that there were piteous virtues within Christianity, precisely where the sufferers could make no valid claim to rights. The Golden Rule leads to the Lord's Prayer—or perhaps the other way around.

This anxious application of the Golden Rule also contributed to a resurgence of vegetarianism. Although many radicals undertook this regimen more to mortify their own flesh than to protect the flesh of others, the latter motive remains visible. Protestants were obliged to articulate the protective rather than penitent aspect of vegetarianism lest they be mistaken for closet Catholics, whose Lenten fasting from meat was attacked by Reformers (including Martin Luther himself) as a superstitious refusal of food authorized by God: bad children turning up their noses at father's cooking. When Philemon Holland—whose clergyman father had fled to the Continent from the Catholic reign of Mary—translates Plutarch's arguments for vegetarianism in 1603, his synopses struggle with exactly this conflict, even while his translation slips in a characterization (nowhere in Plutarch's original) of the cooked bodies as "idols."[22] As the dynamics of Renaissance multiculturalism brought the ancient dietary arguments of Plutarch, Pythagoras, and Diogenes back into play, the economic imperatives of trade exposed Europeans to Indian notions of *ahimsa*: the obligation to avoid harming other beings. This imperative was partly based on a doctrine of reincarnation that made carnivorous eating a version of cannibalism, as it also was for Pythagoras. Feste is joking in *Twelfth Night* when he insists that Malvolio will be "still in darkness" until he accepts "th' opinion of Pythagoras, and fear to kill a woodcock, lest thou dispossess the soul of thy grandam," but it is an uneasy joke (4.2.57–60). The Protestant argument that the Catholic doctrine of Real Presence made Communion into cannibalism may also have provoked a broader revulsion from the eating of flesh and blood.

Cross-species kinship may have been just one more thing—along with unaccustomed freedoms of body and mind—that became visible through the cracks revolutionary movements tend to open in the cultural boundary. The longstanding association of vegetarianism with radical sects, including Christian heretics such as the Manichees and Cathars (as Francis Bacon was uneasily aware[23]), suggests that it may have been more the radical than the Reformed aspect of the radical Reformation that explains this pattern of association. Without traditional and institutional buffers, people might have found themselves looking face to face, in both joy and suffering, at their fellow creatures.

Protestantism was especially apt for both this general function of revolutions and the specific vision of protecting other animals because of its implicit and often explicit promise of a return toward something like Eden. The glimpse forward was also a great leap backwards, toward the antediluvian version of good husbandry, in which "God said, Behold, I have given you every herb bearing seed, which is upon the face of all the earth, and every tree, in the which is the fruit of a tree yielding seed; to you it shall be for meat" (Genesis 1:29). With the fantasy of living in that garden—vivid in the titles and raptures of gardening books in this period[24]—came efforts to behave there much as Adam and Eve supposedly did. Vegetarianism could plausibly cast itself as a return to a glorious past that had been tarnished or squandered in the interim: not just Eden, but primitive Christianity (including some early monastic deprivations), and similarly not just a progressive and affectionate engagement with the biological world, but also a return to Eastern philosophers. Reports from Asia convinced Sir Thomas Browne that vegetarianism was actually survivable, and the Puritan-affiliated Sir Isaac Newton that it was fundamentally moral: "the third major law that Newton identified—much more controversially and unexpectedly—was the commandment of 'mercy to animals.'"[25]

Plutarch's chapter against meat-eating immediately follows a misanthropic chapter arguing "That Brute Beastes Have Use of Reason"; the same points coincided in the late Renaissance. Topsell's complaint that "They which love any beast in a high measure, have so much lesse charity to man" was aimed at cat-lovers[26]—for Puritans, pets were animals made idols—but it echoes an emerging (and not unfounded) complaint against Puritans themselves. For Puritans, however, the cause and effect may have been reversed: Calvinism's deprecating assessment of humanity led to a charitable view of other creatures.

Sympathy *for* animals depended on identification *with* them—a point that may now seem obvious, but may not have been obvious at all around 1600. It depended on leveling the human–animal hierarchy, which in turn depended on challenging the valuation of human intellect over the passional experience of the body. The Parliamentary soldier George Wither's *Hallelujah: or Britain's Second Remembrancer* (1641) shows very clearly how the modeling of servile Puritan humility on that of domesticated animals leads to an impulse to protect that animal from wretchedness:

> Why should not I, O gracious God,
> More pliant be to thy command;
> When I am guided by thy word,
> And gently reined by thy hand?
>   Ashamed I may become to see
> The beast, which knows nor good nor ill,
> More faithful in obeying me
> Than I have been to do thy will.
>   From him therefore, Lord, let me learn
> To serve thee better than I do;
>   And mind how much it may concern
> My welfare to endeavor so.
>   And though I know this creature lent
> As well for pleasure as for need;
> That I the wrong thereof prevent,

> Let me still carefully take heed.
>   For he that willfully shall dare
> That creature to oppress or grieve,
> Which God to serve him doth prepare,
> Himself of mercy doth deprive.

The good behavior of these "faithful" creatures was all the more admirable for lacking knowledge of good and evil to corrupt them inwardly or guide them outwardly: it suggests a miraculously imputed righteousness. That righteousness is based—as in the Protestant revision of Catholic Christianity and as in the back-to-nature impulse I have been describing in this period—in simplicity rather than cultural grandeur and scholastic intricacy. The closing lines again reveal that Calvinists' desperate need for gratuitous kindness from their deity encouraged the modeling of such kindness in dealing with the defenseless creatures born to serve them.

Furthermore, animals were obviously good at the weirdly negative characteristic essential to so much Calvinist soteriology: the absence of disbelief. Once piety is understood, not as a ceremonial practice as it often was within Catholicism, but instead primarily as a condition of perseverance, humility, and passive obedience toward greater powers, as it often was under Calvinism, beasts will almost inevitably become exemplary rather than negligible. In *The Witch of Edmonton* (1621), the good-hearted bumpkin hero Cuddy urges the articulate devil-dog to revert to ordinary canine existence, because the lapses of a real dog are merely venial compared to those of a diabolically possessed one, whose deeds (the play suggests) are only too similar to human sins.

Martin Luther argued that, while the Fall had disastrous consequences for human beings, it left animals relatively untouched: "Among the beasts the creation or nature stayed the way it was created. They did not fall by sinning, as man did.... they do not hear the Word, and the Word does not concern itself with them; they are altogether without the Law of the First and the Second Table."[27] *Not* participating in language—even when it is God's own incised Word—now confers more sanctity (even if that sanctity cannot confer salvation) than participating. Under Protestant theology, the power of articulation, by which humanity was (and still is) commonly exalted above other species, actually limited or compromised our piety—or at least, aggravated our impiety, because it gave us Commandments to break, where Wither's "pliant" livestock simply obey "commands." Caliban learns only to curse when he learns human speech—but he seems to ascend toward Grace when he (like the animals listening to Orpheus) hears beautiful sounds and gazes up uncomprehendingly at the still-indistinct light pushing through the clouds (*The Tempest*, 1.2.364–5, 3.2.135–43).

As with language, so with reason. Alongside the recovery of classical skepticism, which hit Renaissance intellectuals with remarkable force,[28] Calvinist doctrines devastated a longstanding confidence that humanity enjoyed some mental dominion over the world that would both match and justify more material forms of domination. Since rationality was the primary distinction most commentators offered between human and other animals,[29] this loss not only unsettled the sovereignty of human over other animals, but also blurred the boundary between them. In the absence of any Right Reason capable of leading humanity reliably toward God, the saving attributes had to be found elsewhere.

With Protestant theology focused on the inward experience of each human individual as significant, and salvation no longer mass-produced by human ritual, the masses of nonhuman life-forms could be recognized as comprised of individuals capable of suffering and eager for survival, instead of seeing them only as part of a collective entity and fungible resource called nature. Vitalism and pantheism—two quite important intellectual movements emerging in mid-seventeenth-century England—may be viewed as microcosmic and macrocosmic versions of this perspective. In this vale of soul-making, each entity has, or is, a proprietary piece of the divine energy. Calvin himself described God as "diffused over all space, sustaining, invigorating, and quickening all things" from "above the rank of creatures, while his transfusing vigour into all things, breathing into them being, life, and motion, is plainly divine."[30] The distance between the Calvinist God and man renders negligible the distance between man and beast. A world everywhere fully charged with God's meanings replaced the Catholic funnel of Grace that, from an accessible locale on high, narrowed downward through cathedral and priesthood to the human soul, with the rest of the world presumed relatively contemptible.

Renaissance intellectuals toyed with upending, not just leveling, the Chain of Being hierarchy. Desiderius Erasmus asked, "What more vile than the dung-beetle? Yet the dung-beetle is clean compared to the sinner in his squalor."[31] Although Erasmus loved irony, admiring lowly creatures was not just a joke—or at least, it did not remain one. Perhaps the paradoxical encomium to animals, like Dutch paintings of those animals, was a fluke or quip that became serious in the context of other cultural forces.

As praises of animals began emerging across late Renaissance Europe (and in sixteenth-century England, the great Protestant poets Sidney and Spenser led the way), many of them alluded to the Reformation doctrine of a mysterious God for whom the lowest was the most exalted; and even misattributions showed a strong "tendency to associate animal encomia with the Reformers."[32] For a long time this renewed classical mode looked more like disputational display-behavior than like a socio-political movement. Dix Harwood overstates the case, but is not fundamentally mistaken, in claiming that, apart from a few widely scattered authors, "only Shakespeare shows tenderness toward the hare, the fly, the beetle, and other helpless things; then compassionate voices fall almost silent until the age of Anne."[33] *Venus and Adonis* certainly shows how intensely Shakespeare could register the anguish of a snail or a hare, and *Henry VI, Part II* (3.1.210–20) vividly equates a human mother's mourning with that of a dam whose calf is cruelly dragged to the slaughterhouse. Hamlet, fresh back from Wittenberg, condemns Gertrude's hasty remarriage by observing that "a beast that wants discourse of reason,/Would have mourn'd longer" (1.2.150–51). The comment places him squarely in a tradition, also rooted in Wittenberg, that lamented the human fall into an "unweeded garden" by comparing human beings unfavorably—and not just in physical abilities, but in spiritual qualities—to supposedly lesser creatures.

As early as *Titus Andronicus*, one key mark of the outsider, hovering on the boundary between madness and genius in his suffering, is an acknowledgment of the emotional anguish of supposedly negligible creatures. Now that his daughter's arms and tongue are "stumps," so she can no longer speak or write, Titus sees his grandson as a "sapling" also, and those associations allow him to imagine, reciprocally, the suffering of pruned trees:

> TITUS: Peace, tender sapling; thou art made of tears,
> And tears will quickly melt thy life away. [*Marcus strikes the dish with a knife*]
> What dost thou strike at, Marcus, with thy knife?
> MARCUS: At that that I have kill'd, my lord—a fly.
> TITUS: Out on thee, murderer! thou kill'st my heart!
> Mine eyes are cloy'd with view of tyranny.
> A deed of death done on the innocent
> Becomes not Titus' brother. Get thee gone,
> I see thou art not for my company.
> MARCUS: Alas, my lord, I have but kill'd a fly.
> TITUS: "But"? How if that fly had a father and mother?
> How would he hang his slender gilded wings
> And buzz lamenting doings in the air!
> Poor harmless fly,
> That, with his pretty buzzing melody,
> Came here to make us merry! and thou hast kill'd him.
> MARCUS: Pardon me, sir, it was a black ill-favor'd fly,
> Like to the Empress' Moor, therefore I kill'd him.
> TITUS: O, O, O,
> Then pardon me for reprehending thee,
> For thou hast done a charitable deed.
> Give me thy knife, I will insult on him;
> Flattering myself as if it were the Moor
> Come hither purposely to poison me.--
> There's for thyself, and that's for Tamora.
> Ah, sirrah!
> Yet I think we are not brought so low,
> But that between us we can kill a fly
> That comes in likeness of a coal-black Moor.
> MARCUS: Alas, poor man, grief has so wrought on him,
> He takes false shadows for true substances. (3.2:50–80)

The sane man somehow knows that insect grief is a false shadow, and human grief a true substance; but the fall into helpless misery, and into disillusionment about the supposed moral qualities of the human race, enables a piteous identification with other forms of life, and a recognition that murder, tyranny, and innocence are terms applicable outside the realm of the human. That identification is presumed a symptom of madness, but it is based around an economy of suffering, like Isabella's assertion about the crushed beetle in *Measure for Measure* (3.1.78), which anticipates the ethics of Jeremy

Bentham and (in its cross-species application) Peter Singer. Granted, there is—as in some other Deep Ecology arguments—an enabling element of racism here, making the "coal-black Moor" unworthy of even animal privileges. Granted, too, Titus is himself obviously projecting his parental anguish (like King Lear supposing that Mad Tom had bad daughters). Yet he does, thereby, come to perceive the peculiar and exquisite beauties of even this scorned and minute form of life. Calling aesthetic attention—however anthropomorphic—to the fly's "slender gilded wings" and "his pretty buzzing melody" may be an essential part of a political project.

Marcus's tactic for recovering Titus's allegiance and restoring his vengefulness also shows that human beings whose initial reflexive level of dismissiveness toward animal misery has collapsed can be led back away from empathy by converting (through an emphasis on "likeness" that Titus revealingly adopts) other creatures into allegories for human attributes. That is how they were mostly treated—and often scapegoated—in Renaissance psychology and fable, until empirical science began (though it never completely manages) to allow them to be themselves, and ecological advocacy authorized them to be for themselves.

The conversation between Titus and Marcus thus offers not only a glimpse into the future of animal-protective sentiments, but also a clue to two of their sources (the projections of persons driven into misanthropy, and the revived tradition of mock encomia), and also to the cultural mechanisms that had thus far kept real identification and admiration, and hence sympathy, safely contained for a society where survival still required direct daily combat against competing non-human creatures. The conversation also paradoxically illuminates—though it takes a breakdown approaching madness to see the light—two still-epidemic human pathologies: genocidal warfare enabled by associating another race with nonhuman animals, and the germicidal fantasy that (despite the argument I see in *Midsummer Night's Dream*) other life-forms are presumptively toxins without which the human family could be immortal. An ecocritical reading of English Renaissance literature can not only show how wrong that fantasy is, but also explain why they got it so wrong, lest we be condemned to repeat that error.

NOTES

1. Greg Garrard, *Ecocriticsm* (New York: Routledge, 2004), p. 70.
2. Laurence Buell, *The Future of Environmental Criticism* (2005) perceptively summarizes the implications of constructivism for environmentalism.
3. For a valuable summary of these early environmentalist concerns, see Ken Hiltner, *Milton and Ecology*, (Cambridge UP, 2003).
4. Keith Thomas, *Man and the Natural World, 1500–1700* (Oxford: Oxford UP, 1983), pp. 248–9.
5. Robert N. Watson, *Back to Nature: The Green and the Real in the Late Renaissance* (Philadelphia: Penn, 2006).
6. Norbert Elias, *The Civilising Process*, trans. Edmund Jephcott (Blackwell, Oxford; 1978)
7. Mikhail Bakhtin, *Rabelais and His World* (1936); trans. Hélène Iswolsky (Bloomington, 1984), pp. 23–29 and 315–67.

8. Claudia Benthien, *Skin*, trans. Thomas Dunlap (New York: Columbia UP, 2002), pp. 37–43.

9. *"Midsummer Night's* Dream and the Ecology of the Human Self," in *Ecocritical Shakespeare*, ed. Lynne Bruckner and Daniel Brayton (Palgrave, 2011), pp. 33–56.

10. Thomas Muffet, "The Theater of Insects," appended to the 1658 edition of Edward Topsell's *The history of four-footed beasts*, p. 1,111.

11. Bruno Latour, *Politics of Nature: How to Bring the Sciences into Democracy*, trans. Catherine Porter (Cambridge, MA: Harvard UP, 2004).

12. Garrard, p. 168; citing Yearley, 1996, who disagrees with Latour about the implications of this point.

13. Latour, pp. 13–14.

14. Latour, p. 19.

15. Latour, pp. 15–16.

16. Watson, pp. 166–225.

17. Preece, p. 172.

18. William Haller, *Foxe's Book of Martyrs and the Elect Nation* (London: J. Cape: 1963), p. 56. For some further instances of this correlation, see Thomas, pp. 28, 153, 158–9, 166, 174, 180–4, and 290.

19. Nicholas Tyacke, "Puritan Politicians and King James VI and I," in *Politics, Religion and Popularity*, ed. Thomas Cogswell, Richard Cust and Peter Lake (Cambridge UP, 2002), p. 24,

20. Thomas, p. 166.

21. Robert Bolton, *Some generall directions for a comfortable walking with God*, especially pp. 155–7.

22. Plutarch, *The philosophie, commonlie called, the morals*, trans. Philemon Holland, 1603; p. 572.

23. Francis Bacon, "The History of Life and Death, in *The Great Instauration*; in *Works*, 1844 ed., Vol. III, 500, 508.

24. Thomas, p. 236, lists some instances of this tendency.

25. Tristram Stuart, *Bloodless Revolution* (New York: Norton, 2007), pp. xx, 102.

26. Topsell, p. 83.

27. Luther on *Genesis* 6:58; quoted by James Fujitani, "Simple Hearts: Animals and the Religious Crisis of the Sixteenth Century," diss. UC Santa Barbara, 2008, p. 26.

28. Fujitani, p. 31.

29. This argument is made most directly and extensively in Erica Fudge, *Brutal Reasoning: Animals, Rationality and Humanity in Early Modern England* (Ithaca: Cornell University Press, 2006).

30. Calvin, *Institutes*, 13.14.

31. Erasmus, *De Immensa Dei Misericordia*, p 104; quoted by Fujitani, p. 27.

32. Fujitani, p. 71: "For example, to Philip Melancthon, the Dissertationum Ludicrarum mistakenly attributes a Laus Formicae (190–208), and the Amphitheatrum Sapientiae, a donkey eulogy. Théodore de Bèze, for his part, is attributed a parrot epitaph."

33. Dix Harwood, "Love for Animals and How it Developed in Great Britain" (Diss. Columbia Univ.; New York, 1928), p. 43.

CHAPTER 3

ROMANTICISM AND ECOCRITICISM

KATE RIGBY

THE first thing to be said about Romanticism is that it is very difficult to say what it is. Understood as a period within European cultural history, Romanticism is generally taken to span the late eighteenth to the early to mid-nineteenth centuries; but there is little agreement as to more precise dating. Many literary historians claim that the publication of William Wordsworth's and Samuel Taylor Coleridge's *Lyrical Ballads* or, in Germany, of Friedrich and August Wilhelm Schlegel's journal *Athenaeum*, both in 1798, mark the beginnings of Romantic literature. Others point to the publication of William Blake's *Songs of Innocence* in 1789, coinciding with the outbreak of the French Revolution, as an inaugural moment, while some go back further still to the publication of J. W. Goethe's sentimental best-seller, *The Sorrows of Young Werther*, in 1774, or even to Jean Jacques Rousseau's *The New Heloise* in 1761. The precise end of the Romantic period is also debated, with 1830 and 1848, years of renewed revolutionary activity, both appearing as possible cut-off dates. While the former might work for Britain and Germany, at a pinch, it is too early for such European countries as Spain and Russia (not to mention other parts of the world, such as the Americas and Australia) where a recognizably Romantic literature only emerged in latter half the nineteenth century.

To speak of a "recognizably Romantic literature" also begs a question to which there is no clear answer. The identification of a distinctive and relatively coherent Romantic "school" or "movement" occurred after the event, beginning with Heinrich Heine's "The Romantic School" (1835) and Joseph Freiherr von Eichendorff's "On the History of the Recent Romantic Poetry in Germany" (1845), both of which were critiques, albeit from opposed political perspectives (socialist and secular versus Catholic and conservative). In the English-speaking world, such characterizations followed later still, beginning with William Smith's *History of English Literature* (1864), an enlarged and revised version of Thomas B. Shaw's *Outlines of English Literature* (1846), and it was not until the 1880s that the term "romantic" began to be more widely used with reference to a discrete canon of writers from the late eighteenth and early nineteenth centuries. Subsequent literary critics and historians have expanded this canon through the inclusion of socially marginalized writers previously overlooked on grounds of class, race or gender. A range

of new definitions of literary Romanticism has also been advanced, inflected by a succession of theoretical approaches, to which a diversity of ecocritical perspectives have
now been added. So varied and even contradictory are these characterisations that, as
Aidan Day has observed, "any such attempts to summarize Romanticism inevitably end
up over-systematizing and simplifying the phenomenon. They imply a coherence [...]
which close inspection calls into question."[1]

The term "romantic" was nonetheless certainly in use around 1800.[2] According to
the OED, it first appeared in print in 1659 as an Anglicization of the French *roma[u]nt*
and referred to the enchanted world of medieval and Renaissance tales of chivalry, as
distinct from literature derived from classical models. By the mid-eighteenth century,
"romantic" was also being used to qualify landscape depictions characterised by "picturesque" wildness and frequently featuring Gothic ruins. Several of the writers who
have since come to be regarded as early Romantics turned to the romance epic and other
non-classical forms, notably Shakespearean drama and folk literature, in seeking to
break the hegemony of neoclassicist aesthetics and thereby inaugurate a new "national"
literature of and for the "common man." Blake's early songs, the *Lyrical Ballads*, and some
of Goethe's verse of the *Sturm und Drang* (Storm and Stress) period (1770s), for instance,
exemplify the revaluation ballad and folksong that had begun in the 1760s with the publication of Thomas Percy's *Reliques of Ancient English Poetry* and James McPherson's
Works of Ossian (both 1765), and while the early plays of Goethe and Schiller owe much
to the new craze for Shakespearean drama, Wordsworth's longer poems are ghosted also
by the shade of Spenserian epic and pastoral.

Coupled with this project of literary-cultural renovation was the emergence of collaborative ventures with an avant-garde edge, as evidenced in the self-consciously mod-
ernising ambition of both *Lyrical Ballads* and the *Athenaeum*, whose authors had also
chosen to live in close proximity with one another at the time. Following their move to
the Lake District, Wordsworth and Coleridge, together with Southey, were dubbed "the
Lake Poets," while the Jena group, who were committed to pioneering not only another
way of writing and thinking, but also a scandalously counter-cultural lifestyle, identified themselves as proponents of what Friedrich Schlegel famously termed "*romantische Poesie.*"[3] "Jena Romanticism" distinguished itself from the neo-classicism that had
recently been espoused by Goethe and Schiller in nearby Weimar, following their youth-
ful period of *Sturm und Drang*. In A. W. Schlegel's and G. W. F. Hegel's later lectures on
aesthetics, however, the term "romantic" was still being used more broadly to refer to
European literature from the Middle Ages on, rather than to a contemporary literary
movement. By 1801, when Schlegel gave his first lectures in Berlin, the *Athenaeum* had
folded and one of its key members, Novalis, was dead, and the "Lake poets" too were
beginning to drift apart. New groupings did nonetheless emerge, such as that of Clemens
Brentano, Achim von Arnim, and Joseph Görres in Heidelberg; Lord Byron with Percy
and Mary Shelley; and the London-based group, derisively dubbed the "Cockney
School" by hostile contemporaries, of John Keats, Leigh Hunt, and William Hazlitt.

The point that I wish to stress here, though, is that not only were there a number of significant writers who did not clearly belong to any of these groupings (such as Eichendorff

and John Clare, among the later Romantics in Germany and England, respectively), but each group also had their own distinctive agendas. For instance, while the "Heidelberg Romantics" avidly pursued the Herderian project of preserving and revivifying folk traditions, in an increasingly nationalistic and socially conservative key, the "second generation" Romantics in London launched a new form of left-leaning Hellenism. The picture becomes even more complicated when we look beyond the bounds of literature and consider other arenas of Romantic activity, such as music, painting, philosophy, landscape gardening, and natural history.

While my own ecocritical treatment of Romanticism below is necessarily highly selective, I endeavor to be attentive to the diverse and in some cases contradictory trends and tendencies that can be traced in the thought and literature of this period. Although I concentrate historically and geographically on the heyday of European Romanticism in Britain and Germany around 1800, I also consider some of the ways in which Romanticism was taken up in the "new world." If, as Isaiah Berlin has claimed, Romanticism inaugurated "the greatest single shift in the consciousness of the West,"[4] then it is clear that we are still living in its wake. From this perspective, Romanticism is not only a literary period or canon, however circumscribed, but an enduring dimension of eurowestern modernity.

NATURE AND FREEDOM

Not surprisingly, the primary foci of ecocritical interest in Romanticism have been the new ways of viewing and valuing, representing and relating to the natural world that emerged during this period.[5] Countering earlier interpretations of Romantic constructions of Nature as a mere screen for the human imagination, or an ideological phantasm masking relations of social domination, the pioneering ecocritical studies of Karl Kroeber (1974 and 1994) and Jonathan Bate (1991) emphasised the ecological dimension of Romantic understandings of the natural world and humanity's place within it, the full significance of which was only now becoming apparent in the context of an increasingly global environmental crisis: one brought about, moreover, by that process of industrial modernisation which began in the late eighteenth century and to which, in part, Romanticism responded. While a series of subsequent ecocritical publications, including the special edition of *Studies in Romanticism* edited by Bate, *Green Romanticism* (1996), and monographs by James McKusick (2000), Mark Lussier (2000), Bate (2000), Onno Oerlemans (2002), and Hutchings (2002), continued and deepened this broadly sympathetic exploration of "romantic ecology," Greg Garrard's more cautious view of the Romantic legacy as "both vital and ambiguous"[6] has been borne out in the later studies of Kate Rigby (2004), Timothy Morton (2007), and Kevin Hutchings (2009).

Like "Romanticism," "Nature" is an infamously slippery term used to refer to a range of disparate phenomena on different temporal and spatial scales. In the eighteenth century, Nature was variously dissected and mathematicized in search of its underlying "laws"; commodified as property to be exploited in the generation of wealth; aestheti-cized as "landscape"; moralized as a mode of being to which, as Rousseau influentially argued, we should "return"; revered, either as God's good creation, or, more controver-sially, as the physical aspect of the godhead; and politicised, both by conservatives, as warranting the preservation of traditional social hierarchies, and by radicals, as legiti-mating revolution in pursuit of the "rights of man." Romantic references to Nature and representations of those phenomena with which it was associated in turn engage with such prevalent constructions in diverse ways. In this opening section, I want to sug-gest how key aspects of the Romantic reconceptualization of Nature are thrown into relief when considered in relation to another core concern of this revolutionary period, namely Freedom.

By the late eighteenth century, Nature had been harnessed to the cause of human liberty in the defence of those "natural rights" most influentially promoted by Thomas Paine and enshrined in the American Declaration of Independence and the French revolutionaries' "Rights of Men and Citizens" (to which early feminists like Mary Wollstonecraft and Olympe de Gouges added the "Rights of Women"). However, there is also a sense in which Nature and Freedom were opposed to one another in the eigh-teenth century (and beyond). Within European humanist thought, Freedom was hailed as an attribute of "man" insofar as "he" alone, as made in the image of God, was pos-sessed of reason and hence capable of "free will." For Francis Bacon, the "father" of mod-ern science, the human vocation was defined as the use of reason to uncover Nature's secrets through empirical investigation in order to gain the necessary knowledge to expand the bounds of our God-given dominion over the rest of creation through tech-nology: here, the pursuit of human freedom, as noted by Theodor Adorno and Max Horkheimer in *The Dialectic of Enlightenment* (1944), is premised upon the enslave-ment of "outer," or nonhuman, nature (along with the exploitation of those subordinate humans whose labour would be appropriated in the process). This dualizing tendency, which necessarily entails also an alienation from our own "inner" nature, was reinforced by the widespread acceptance of Descartes's and Newton's view of matter as composed of inert particles functioning mechanistically in accordance with immutable laws that could be rendered mathematically. The issue here is not the validity and value of the scientific method per se, but rather the social context of its emergence, in which the discursive framing of the scientific *project*, namely as a quest for human mastery over a de-animated Nature devoid of ethical considerability, served historically to justify the treatment of the earth and its "natural resources" as freely available to be appropriated, traded and made-over by merchants and manufacturers: here, the liberty of human property owners is to be enlarged at the expense of the colonization, commodification and exploitation of those (ever expanding) portions of nature they claimed as theirs.

Several aspects of a pervasive Romantic resistance to this dualistic construction of the relationship between Nature and Freedom can be traced in Wordsworth's deceptively simple "Lines Written in Early Spring" (1798). The speaker of this "lyrical ballad" is point-edly situated, not as viewing a picturesque landscape from an external vantage-point, a position that implies an objectifying and potentially proprietorial gaze, but as reclining within a grove, immersed in an acoustic atmosphere generated by "a thousand blended notes" signalling his proximity to a vibrant collective of other-than-human beings. When in the third to fifth stanzas some of these are particularized, moreover, they are presented as interactive individuals with their own agency and ends:

> Through primrose tufts, in that green bower,
> The periwinkle trailed its wreathe;
> And 'tis my faith that every flower
> Enjoys the air it breathes.
>
> The birds around me hopped and played,
> Their thoughts I cannot measure:-
> But the least motion which they made,
> It seemed a thrill of pleasure.
>
> The budding twigs spread out their fan,
> To catch the breezy air;
> And I must think, do all I can,
> That there was pleasure there.

The verbal constructions implying an active reaching out to aspects of the environment, combined with the speaker's profession of "faith" that in doing so these birds and plants were taking pleasure in their own existence, echo Baruch Spinoza's concept of *conatus*— that is, the impulse to preserve their being and augment their capacities, to compose and recompose themselves with and through their dynamic relations with others, which he attributed to all physical entities, animate and inanimate, individual and collective. From this Spinozan perspective, the realm of Freedom is democratically expanded to incorporate the endeavors of all beings to "preserve a kinetic poise within a dynamic ensemble of relations, an ensemble that also composes them *as* individuals."[7] Far from being an exclusively human attribute, Freedom, understood as a mode of relational self-actualization, is instead jeopardized within human society: in view of the active enjoyment of life that he senses in these other-than-human beings, the speaker is moved to lament "what man has made of man." While the precise nature of this wrong is not specified, the target of the poet's repeated lament might be interpreted as those oppressive and repressive social dynamics that disallow to many humans the conative delight in their own existence apparently intended by "Nature's holy plan."

In company with the speaker himself, the birds and plants named in this surreptitiously socio-critical instance of what Raymond Williams dubs Romantic "neopastoral"[8] belong to the realm of what Spinoza termed *natura naturata*, "nature natured," the multiplicity of transient natural entities. The "Nature" to which Wordsworth here attributes a "holy plan," by contrast, alludes to the eternal generative activity of the universe, *natura naturans* or "nature naturing," which Spinoza, scandalously, equated with the physical aspect of the godhead. Echoing Spinoza's identification of God with *natura naturans*, the speaker of Wordsworth's "Lines" affirms his own kinship with other natural entities in proclaiming himself a product of Nature: "To her fair works did Nature link/The human soul that through me ran."

Wordsworth's repositioning of the human as part of Nature, coupled with the perception of all natural entities as interrelated, is often seen as exemplary of "Romantic ecology." However, similarly proto-ecological insights can already be traced within Augustan poetry, informed as it was by late seventeenth-century physico-theology.[9] Subsuming and refashioning earlier notions of the great Chain of Being, the Nature honored by Augustan poets such as James Thomson and Alexander Pope is hailed as manifesting divine providence and suffused with divine presence: as Pope avers in his "Essay on Man" (1734), "He fills, he bounds, connects and equals all" (280). Conceived as a stable and harmonious whole, Augustan Nature demands to be treated with respect by its human overlords, for, as Pope warns, "From Nature's chain whatever link you strike,/Ten or ten thousandth, breaks the chain alike" (245–46). Whereas Augustan ecology envisages Nature as a static, linear, and hierarchical "chain," however, the Romantics perceived it as something far more complex and dynamic, closer to the post-equilibrium ecology of Daniel Botkin's "discordant harmonies" than that of earlier ecological scientists such as Frederick Clements, whose concept of stable "climax" ecosystems had a distinctly Augustan ring to it. Goethe's friend, the bio-geographer Alexander von Humboldt, for example, likened the natural world in a lecture from 1827 to an all-encompassing "interlinkage, not simply in a linear direction, but in an intricate netlike interweaving":[10] no longer a chain, or even a "web," which is structured around a central point, Nature was now looking more like a decentralised "mesh," to use the metaphor favored by Morton in *The Ecological Thought*. This was a mesh, moreover, that was perpetually reweaving itself.

The possibility of perceiving the natural world not as an unchanging artefact of divine manufacture but as an autopoietic process of perpetual becoming was enabled by new research in the nascent sciences of astronomy, geology, and biology, which were uncovering the exceedingly long history of the earth and cosmos, along with that of Earth's myriad life forms. Gilbert White's *Natural History and Antiquities of Selbourne* (1789) is frequently cited as exemplary of a shift away from Linnaean taxonomy towards the proto-ecological investigation of connections between species variation and distribution and factors such as soil, climate, and topography, and a similar move can also be seen in Goethe's botanical studies from the mid 1780s.[11] What makes Romantic ecology distinctly modern, however, is the dawning recognition that such interrelationships were the product of an ongoing process of biological evolution. While each organism was seen to have an inner "formative drive," as J. F. Blumenbach put it, entire species, as Goethe and Erasmus Darwin postulated, appeared to have evolved from others (and to be evolving still), as suggested by the resemblance between the fossilized bones of now extinct creatures and those still in existence, such as the ancient megatherium and today's sloth bear.[12] Studies of rock strata, meanwhile, indicated that Earth's seemingly stable rocky mantle had been on the move for millennia, although debates raged as to whether its current contours were the outcome of violent upheaval or more gradual processes.[13] Matter itself was beginning to look more dynamic than Newton had assumed, with explorations into the fascinating phenomena of magnetism, chemical reactions and "galvanism" (electricity), even leading some, such as the German physicist

J. W. Ritter, to query the distinction between animate and inanimate objects: "the organising principle of all matter is electricity," Ritter concluded in 1800, "it unifies nature and endows everything with 'life.'"[14]

This reconceptualization of Nature as a dynamically self-transforming, thoroughly animate, and intricately interconnected "multeity-in-unity," as Coleridge put it,[15] had profound implications for human self-understanding, which were widely explored within Romantic literature and philosophy. One important manifestation of this was the reconsideration of the relationship between humans and (other) animals. In Britain especially, advocacy for the humane treatment of animals, which had been growing since the late seventeenth century, burgeoned during the Romantic period, with unloved and exploited species, such as insects, vermin and beasts of burden, featuring prominently in literary texts calling for greater respect and compassion towards non-human others.[16] The promotion of animal rights, whether by way of Jeremy Bentham's utilitarian argument against the infliction of pain on sentient beings (*Principles of Morals and Legislation*, 1789) or, more radically, the liberation of all beings from human domination advanced by John Oswald (*The Cry of Nature*, 1791), could only gain limited traction because of society's continued economic dependence on the exploitation of animals for labour, food, wool, skins and bones.[17] Opposition to live vivisection, recreational hunting and the mistreatment of domestic animals nonetheless became widespread, leading to the introduction of the first animal protection legislation in 1822 and the foundation of the Society for Prevention of Cruelty to Animals in 1824.[18] Some, including Percy Shelley, called also for the adoption of a vegetarian diet. Shelley's arguments against meat consumption in his "Vindication of Natural Diet" (1812) incorporated considerations of social justice as well as animal liberation, as he believed that a larger number of people could be fed more equitably on a vegetarian diet. Moreover, he maintained that such a diet was more "natural" and therefore healthier for humans, whose teeth and digestive system more closely resembled those of "frugivorous" animals like the "orang-outan" than of carnivorous beasts of prey.[19]

Shelley's argument from anatomy exemplifies the growing recognition of human kinship with (other) animals. This fostered a new interest in the mental and emotional life of animals, as can be traced, for example, in the animal poetry of Wordsworth and Clare, as well as in the acknowledgment (admittedly qualified and ambivalent) of human animality, whether in relation to food, as we have seen with Shelley; sex (and eating, including its corollary, elimination), in the case of Byron's raunchy *Don Juan* (1919–24)[20]; or mortality, as in Wordsworth's early poetry of death, devoid as it is of conventional metaphysical consolations.[21] Continuity, however, does not imply identity, and as Oerlemans stresses, this affirmation of "the deep-rooted commonality between humans and animals" was often coupled with an acknowledgement of the otherness and even incomprehensibility of animal consciousness.[22] While, as Greg Garrard avers, there is no necessary connection between ethics and what he calls "allomorphism,"[23] this acknowledgment of alterity did sometimes engender a type of ethical responsiveness not contingent on kinship or reciprocity. For example, whereas Coleridge's promise of liberty to the tethered young ass in the poem of that name arises from his recognition by the "pantisocratic" speaker as "brother," the unconscious blessing that the mariner extends to the slimy sea snakes in "The Rime of the Ancient Mariner" is premised on the wondrous strangeness of their unbidden appearance.[24] Animal alterity is sometimes framed considerably less favourably, however, as in the case of Coleridge's own later "Theory of Life" (1816–18), which proclaims that humans are the most highly evolved species, that is, the most fully individuated in accordance with its predetermined "ideal" (one from which the coloured races had in his view fallen away, due to adverse environmental conditions), leaving a "wide chasm between man and the noblest animals of the brute creation."[25]

The pronounced human supremacism (and implicit racism) of Coleridge's account of human-animal difference was not unique in the Romantic period. Lorenz Oken, for example, went one better than Coleridge in declaring that man was not merely the apex of the evolutionary pyramid, but "God fully manifested,"[26] while Wordsworth too affirms (only a little more cautiously) in Book 12 of *The Prelude* that, under the influence of the imagination, "the mind of man becomes/A thousand times more beautiful than the earth/On which he dwells [...] as it is itself/Of substance and of fabric more divine" (lines 446–52). Nonetheless, the recognition of what F. W. J. Schelling termed the "productivity" of Nature allowed human consciousness and creativity to be seen as an emergent property of the physical world, rather than as something added on and alien to a blindly mechanistic realm of "mere" matter. Breaking with Cartesian mind-matter dualism, Schelling maintained in his *Ideas for a Philosophy of Nature* (1797) that Nature was "visible mind, mind invisible nature," implying, as Friedrich Schlegel proclaims in his "Conversation on Poetry" (1800), that the human artistic creation arises from, and remains indebted to, the "unconscious poesy" of the earth, "the first, the original, without which there would certainly be no poesy of words."[27] In Kroeber's analysis, this Romantic insight, which he sees confirmed by contemporary neuroscience, also underpins Shelley's great verse drama, *Prometheus Unbound* (1820), whose mythic hero "embodies self-consciousness as a natural phenomenon manifesting the emergence of culture from material nature."[28]

If human freedom was grounded in Nature, including the freedom to transform the conditions of our own existence, then there was nothing inherently "unnatural" about the technological inventions that were at that time ushering in the Industrial Revolution; and as Morton (1994), observes, *Prometheus Unbound* has a distinctly technotopian edge to it. From this perspective, the key question—one that remains of vital concern to advocates of ecological modernization—becomes what kind of technological transformations should be pursued, at what cost and to whose benefit? This is a question to which I will return in my concluding discussion of Romantic utopianism. What I want to stress here, though, is how the Romantic reconceptualization of the relationship between Nature and Freedom incorporated also a valuable recognition of the inevitable limits of human self-determination.

To begin with, the Romantic discovery of "the unconscious" (*das Unbewußte*), a term later made famous by Sigmund Freud but coined by Schelling, suggested that our conscious intentions were always underpinned, and potentially undermined, by inner urgings of which we are generally unaware, disclosing the rationalistic premise of "free will" as at least partially illusory. For early Schelling and the Jena Romantics, the unconscious, which manifests itself to us, however inscrutably, in dreams and visions, inspiring our artistic creativity no less than our deepest desires, remains continuous with the entire natural world, implying that the path of reconnection with outer nature necessarily led within: a path modelled by the protagonist of Novalis's unfinished *Heinrich von Ofterdingen*, whose artistic apprenticeship entails learning how to "mine" the creative potential of the unconscious. As Ludwig Tieck and E. T. A. Hoffman indicate in their narratives of mining-induced madness, however, to take this route is also to risk solipsistic self-enclosure.[29] More generally, the Romantic discovery of the unconscious disclosed the extent to which we are strangers to ourselves, aware and in control only of a limited part of what moves and motivates us and enables us to act.

Meanwhile, the external world too was held by many Romantics to resist our efforts to render it fully knowable and entirely malleable. The most influential philosophical formulation of this point during the Romantic period was Immanuel Kant's argument in the *Critique of Pure Reason* that we can never know for certain how our knowledge of things as they give themselves to human understanding (*phenomena*) accords with the ultimate reality of things as they are in themselves (*noumena*). This does not mean that we should not endeavor to discover more about them, but that such knowledge, no matter how mathematically precise, empirically well-founded, and technically applicable, can never be pure or final, but will always be to some extent partial and provisional. This implies also that there will always be some things, including other ways of knowing, which, as Wordsworth observes of the thoughts of the birds in his "Lines Written in Early Spring," we "cannot measure."

This acknowledgment of the limits of human knowledge led to the further realization that perfectly legitimate endeavors to reshape the conditions of our existence were liable to have unforeseen consequences, as explored, for example, by Mary Shelley in her pioneering work of dystopian science fiction, *Frankenstein* (1818). Similarly, the Promethean hero of Goethe's epic drama *Faust, Part Two* (1832) dies dreaming of an emancipated society inhabiting land that he has reclaimed from the sea, even as his hastily constructed canals begin to collapse and return to swamp, ruining all that that he had achieved (at great human and environmental cost) thus far. In Heather Sullivan's systems theoretical reading of this text, *Faust* discloses "the illusion of self-directed agency [...] the illusion of those in the weave who see only their own unidirectional impetus."[30] This does not necessitate the abandonment of all human endeavours to reshape the ecosocial conditions of our existence in resigned acceptance of our subjection to uncontrollable natural forces; but it does imply a reframing of our quest for self-determination as a matter of negotiation rather than mastery, oriented not towards the mirage of autonomy from Nature, but towards the creation of more life-sustaining patterns of interrelationship among multiple more-than-human agencies and interests.

HOME AND AWAY

The first explicitly "ecological" examination of a work of British Romantic literature was Karl Kroeber's 1974 article on the fragment of Wordsworth's unfinished epic *The Recluse* known as "Home at Grasmere." In Kroeber's reading, these lines announce the project that can be traced across Wordsworth's oeuvre, namely of celebrating his natal Lake District as a "'region,' a completely interdependent, self-sufficient place," whose economically "useless" aspects he deemed intrinsic to what Kroeber terms its "ecological holiness." Several of the ecocritical studies of Romanticism that followed retained this focus on questions of place, belonging, and, to use the heavily loaded Heideggerian term adopted by Bate in *The Song of the Earth* (2000), "dwelling." Contrary to the common misperception of this preoccupation with place in "first-wave" ecocriticism as occluding a concern with social justice, Bate (1991) demonstrated how the Romantic take on place, as exemplified by Wordsworth and Clare, discloses the entwinement of destructive forms of environmental change with social structures of domination in the context of the development of more capital-intensive modes of agriculture (as Raymond Williams had argued previously in *The Country and the City*). Nor should we forget that for some leading British Romantics, such as Blake and Keats, "home" was in the rapidly industrializing city rather than in the countryside, and that the experience of, and desire to, travel was at least as compelling for many Romantic writers as was the impulse to hunker down at home.

Although neither Wordsworth nor Clare were urbanites, the former could be described as a "reinhabitant," whose writing embodies an attitude of self-conscious homecoming rather than unreflective belonging, while much of Clare's verse is riven by a sense of the imperilment of the rural homeland that he sought, increasingly desperately, to defend. While Renaissance and Augustan pastoral elided the realities of rural life from the perspective of the laboring poor, what is new and important about Romantic neopastoral, or "post-pastoral,"[31] is the stance of resistance that it offers to the growing commodification and nascent industrial exploitation of the earth. Wordsworth's "pastoral poem" "Michael," for example, breaks with earlier pastoral convention by shifting the focus from the peace and pleasure afforded the jaded city dweller by a sojourn in the country to the depredations caused by the incursion of capitalist financial relations into the subsistence economy of a more traditional rural world. Similarly, another of the "lyrical ballads," "The Female Vagrant," foregrounds the plight of the rural poor rendered homeless by the enclosure of common land. This concern also lies at the heart of much of Clare's verse, but whereas Wordsworth views those impacted by such changes from a position of relative privilege, Clare's is a voice from below. Moreover, unlike earlier poetry criticising the negative impact of modernisation on rural life, such as William Goldsmith's "The Deserted Village" (1770) or George Crabbe's "The Village" (1783), Clare's concern extends to nonhuman as well as human members of the land community, and in "The Lament of Swordy Well" and the "Lamentations of Round-Oak Waters" he even gives a voice to the wetlands and waterways that had been degraded in this process of so-called "improvement."

To construe "home" as a locus of "community," however, marks a distinction between an "inside" and an "outside" that can have unsavoury implications for those viewed as intruders. This becomes particularly apparent in the German context, where, under the impact of the Napoleonic invasion and in the absence of political structures of national unity, images of the German countryside sometimes came to stand for a *Heimat* defined less as a locality than as a the *Vaterland* of a particular *Volk*.[32] While the patriotic texts of this period, such as Clemens Brentano's *Am Rhein! Am Rhein!*, celebrating the German victory over Napoleon at the Battle of Leipzig (1813), were pitched against French imperialism, nationalistic constructions of the German land community also began to acquire an unpleasantly anti-Semitic aspect during this period, as I will discuss below.

The potential for notions of "home" to define zones of exclusion as well as inclusion points to a more general problem with Romantic "holism," where the organismic model of Nature as a unified totality, the most influential contemporary version of which is James Lovelock's Gaia theory, is used to justify the ruthless sacrifice of individuals or groups for the alleged good of "the whole": something that can really turn nasty if this model of Nature is transferred to society, as was Ernst Haeckel's Darwinian *Oekologie* during the Nazi period in Germany.[33] As Kevin Hutchings shows in his study of trans-Atlantic Romanticism (2009), the environmental determinism that emerged within some versions of Romantic holism also had adverse implications for those colonised peoples whose human agency and rights as place-makers and landholders were denied within this way of thinking. In Morton's analysis, the problematic holism that is inevitably summoned by the term "nature" impedes a genuinely ecological way of thinking about "how to share this earth with other humans, animals, plants, and inanimate things."[34] Instead, he advocates a model of "coexistence with coexistents" drawn from Jacques Derrida's and Emmanuel Levinas's ethics of "alterity," while showing that this alternative ecology is also prefigured within Romanticism, as exemplified by Coleridge's "Rime of the Ancient Mariner."[35]

In my analysis, the diverse more-than-human localized communities that are celebrated within much Romantic neopastoral could also be reinterpreted as collectives of co-existents to the extent that they are presented as places of welcome to newcomers, such as Wordsworth presents himself and his sister at Grasmere, and itinerants, like the gypsies who are said to have frequented Clare's lost commons. As Coleridge's "Rime" reminds us, moreover, Romantic literature is at least as concerned with journeying as it is with dwelling, commonly privileging wayfaring over rootedness,[36] longing over belonging. The widespread Romantic trope of travel, along with sometimes quite detailed travel descriptions, exemplify what Oerlemans terms "romantic empiricism,"[37] entailing a desire to encounter the unknown in all its material particularity—to venture, as Wordsworth puts it in Book 12 of *The Prelude*, "one bare step/Beyond the limits which my feet had trod" (145–51).

Impelled by the desire for discovery, the Romantic journeys that Oerlemans traces in the work of Dorothy and William Wordsworth, among others, involve experiences of disorientation in the face of a material reality that cannot be fully comprehended or adequately named. Yet you do not necessarily have to go abroad to encounter the incomprehensible: experiences of the "material sublime," a term Oerlemans takes from Keats and cognate with his better-known "negative capability," can also be had at home. Indeed, one of the most salient characteristics of the Romantic poetics of place is its capacity to reveal the abiding strangeness of even the most everyday and famil- iar of phenomena, "awakening the mind's attention from the lethargy of custom," as Coleridge puts it.[38] Called "forth into the light of things," as the speaker of Wordsworth's "The Tables Turned" does his book-bound friend, restored to a sense of wonderment before that which we cannot quite grasp, we might be better placed to live respectfully amongst a diversity of more-than-human others, without seeking always to subsume them to our own ends and understandings. This mode of "ecstatic dwelling," as I have argued in relation to Wordsworth's "Sonnet Composed upon Westminster Bridge" (1802) can be entered into within the cosmopolitan space of a great city no less readily than in a rural backwater, so long as the urbanised environment remains open to the more-than-human realms of Earth and Sky.[39]

The Romantic yearning to get away, however, is not always so conducive to the acceptance of a "material order (which is truly "other,") but that [...] is the ground of being":[40] in some cases, it leads right out of the physical world altogether. In much of Eichendorff's writing, for example, the Romantic trope of travel, or longing to travel, has nothing to do with an empirical or phenomenological interest in material particulars, coding instead for the mystical experience of self-transcendence associated with union with the divine: something that might be glimpsed in this life, but only fully realised in the next. The speaker of his poem "Moonlit Night" ("Mondnacht," 1812), for example, is so spiritually transported by his sense of divine presence, flowing with the wind across fields and woods, that his "soul spreads its wings and flies through the still land, as if it were flying home": home, that is, to a heavenly beyond that is ultimately not of this earth.

SACRED AND SECULAR

While Eichendorff's "Moonlit Night" is by not an isolated example of Romantic other-worldliness, M. H. Abrams's magisterial account of German and English Romanticism as entailing "the secularization of inherited theological ideas and ways of thinking" undoubtedly holds true for much Romantic thought and literature around 1800.[41] In some cases, though, the agenda was rather different: namely, in Stephen Prickett's analysis, the reconstruction of religion "in the aftermath of the divinely guar- anteed world order."[42] In my view, the Romantics' reclamation of a place for the sacred is at once a core element of their revaluation of the natural world and interlinked with the secularizing tendency traced by Abrams.

The contrapuntal movement of secularization and resacralization took a variety of forms during the Romantic period, but is formulated most explicitly in Friedrich

Schleiermacher's influential *On Religion* (1799). Addressed to the "cultured despisers" of religion among his avant-garde friends among the Jena Romantics, this extraordinary work by the young pastor who would go on to become Germany's leading nineteenth-century Protestant theologian and biblical scholar begins by looking beneath the diverse religious beliefs and practices that have arisen in different cultures in order to discern what he takes to be a universally available human experience: "The universe exists in uninterrupted activity and reveals itself to us in every moment [...] Thus to accept everything individual as a part of the whole and everything limited as a representation of the infinite is religion."[43] The "essence" of religion was thus distinct from both "metaphysics" and "morality," knowing and acting, which have become mixed up with religion in its various historically contingent cultural formations, but which are extraneous to religious experience per se. This crucial distinction signals the liberation of scientific inquiry and ethical deliberation from the strictures of religious dogma: as such, Schleiermacher's post-Kantian regrounding of religion advances the cause of secularization. Yet in relating religion to sensory perception, Schleiermacher simultaneously contributes to the Romantic rehallowing of the phenomenal world as affording the ever-present possibility of that ephemeral, ineffable (and potentially erotic) mystical experience that, he declares, is "as fleeting and transparent as the first scent with which the dew gently caresses the waking flowers, as modest and delicate as a maiden's kiss, and as holy and fruitful as a nuptial embrace; indeed, not *like* these, but *it is itself* all of these" (original emphasis).[44]

While he defends the role of the "positive religions," including Christianity, for all of its admitted "distortions and its manifold corruptions,"[45] in providing a shared context for what would otherwise remain a purely private experience, Schleiermacher looks to artists and writers for the renovation of religion against what he sees as the "new barbarism" of an era dominated by analytic and instrumental forms of rationality. This should not be interpreted as a call for a "new mythology," although this was certainly envisaged by some of Schleiermacher's contemporaries,[46] and most fully realized during the Romantic period by William Blake. Rather, Schleiermacher values works of the creative imagination in their capacity to bear witness to the phenomenology of religious experience: that "sense sublime," famously referred to by Wordsworth in his "Lines Composed a Few Miles above Tintern Abbey, on revisiting the Banks of the Wye during a Tour. July 13, 1798":

> Of something far more deeply interfused,
> Whose dwelling is the light of setting suns,
> And the round ocean and the living air,
> And the blue sky, and in the mind of man;
> A motion and a spirit, that impels
> All thinking things, all objects of all thought,
> And rolls through all things.[47]

The poetic witness to such intimations of immanent holiness functions, for Schleiermacher, as the essential counterpart and corrective to the scientific quest for knowledge and control of the physical world, for, "To want to have speculation and praxis without religion is rash arrogance. […] Man has merely stolen the feeling of his infinity and godlikeness, and as an unjust possession it cannot thrive for him if he is not also conscious of his limitedness, the contingency of his whole form, the silent disappearance of his whole existence in the immeasurable."[48]

Within the broad spectrum of Romantic reconfigurations of the sacred and the secular there are nonetheless some troubling tendencies that were discerned with great prescience by Heine. As a German Jew, he was especially perturbed by the anti-Semitic strains that had crept into the Teutonic neopaganism favored by many of his fellow students in the early 1820s, leading him to predict in his *History of Religion and Philosophy in Germany*, written in exile in Paris in the 1830s, that the German revolution would be a revolution of the Right, and it would claim to have, not God, but Nature on its side.[49] Heine correctly identifies one of the many contradictory strands in what would become the ideological arsenal of Germany's National Socialist revolution in the following century. Nonetheless, the contemporaneous example of Shelley's and Keats's fascination with classical mythology, particularly the figure of Pan as the anthropomorphic embodiment of a universal erotic impulse, suggests that the politics of neopaganism, then as now, can take a variety of directions. In Marilyn Butler's assessment, these English Romantics' paganising celebration of sexuality, shared also by Byron, represented "a challenge to arbitrary divisions between mind and body, man and his environment, man and God; and a challenge also to an institutionalised Christianity that was part of the apparatus of the State."[50]

While Heine, a sometime supporter of the Saint-Simonian socialism, would have had little problem with this libidinous and left-leaning variant, his critical analysis of Romantic Nature worship also alerts us to another problem. In his brilliant satire of ecopiety, as displayed by a group of tourists witnessing the sun set from the Brocken (a peak famous for its sublime landscape and pre-Christian sacred remains) in his *Harz Journey* (1826), Heine targets the hypocrisy of the emerging bourgeois practice of seeking a spiritual high in designated places of natural beauty when on holiday, while participating in the ruthless exploitation and commodification of natural resources during the workaday week.[51] This compensatory aestheticization and spiritualization of Nature could well be viewed as a mode of consumerism.[52] In the New World, moreover, the sacralisation of "sublime" landscapes subsequently translated into the fetish for "wilderness" experience, effectively eliding millenia of indigenous place-making.[53]

It is nonetheless important to recognise that this more recent development departs significantly from much earlier Romantic literature, which, far from idealising a putative "pure" Nature, "untouched by human hand," values most highly those hybrid places that manifest a life-enhancing collaboration—the "blended might" as Wordsworth refers to it in "Home at Grasmere"—of human and other-then-human beings and processes.[54] It is this mutuality that constitutes the "ecological holiness" of Wordsworth's Lake District; and it this that Clare saw to be endangered by those "tyrant[s]," whose "little sign[s]" of private ownership show "where man claims earth glows no more divine," as he puts it in "The Mores."[55] In this modality, the Romantic movement of resacralization serves as a mode of resistance to that strand of secularisation that has historically served the interests of power and profit in their imperious demand for the obliteration of all traces of the sacred.

Utopian and Dystopian Trajectories

By comparison with the stable and harmonious holism of Augustan physico-theology, Romantic understandings of Nature as a dynamically self-transforming and decentralised mesh opened up a more unruly prospect. For those who could no longer share Pope's faith that, so far as the divinely created natural order was concerned, " 'WHATEVER IS, IS RIGHT' " (*Essay on Man*, 294; original emphasis), the idea that natural phenomena manifested divine providence (and favored human pre-eminence) began to look like a fond illusion: one exploded, for example, in Kleist's narrative deconstruction of the contradictory meanings attributed to a natural disaster in "The Earthquake in Chile" (1807), a short story that refers back to the Santiago earthquake of 1647, but responds primarily to the philosophical and religious debates that followed the more recent Lisbon earthquake of 1755.[56] From this sceptical perspective, it became possible to imagine a global natural disaster, as Byron does in "Darkness" (1816)—a "dream, which was not all a dream," called forth by the inclement weather conditions occasioned by the eruption of the Tambora volcano[57]—in which humans could be annihilated along with the rest of the living world. Yet more disturbingly, it became conceivable that humanity alone might be wiped out, as envisaged by Mary Shelley in *The Last Man* (1826), in which the localized outbreak of a fatal and incurable disease becomes a global pandemic as a consequence of international warfare and trade, and exacerbated by the strangely (and, from a contemporary perspective, chillingly) warming climate. While Shelley here imagines the burgeoning of nonhuman life as agriculture, industry and urban civilization fall into decay, Blake, extrapolating from the environmental degradation and social injustice that he witnessed amidst the "satanic mills" of London's burgeoning manufactories, prefigured in his visionary work *Jerusalem* (1804–7) the engendering of a "desolated Earth," in which, as McKusick observes, "the skies over England are darkened with smoke, birds have fallen silent, flocks have died, harvests have failed, apples are poisoned, and the Earth's climate is marked by scorching heat and devastating storms."[58]

Blake's apocalyptic vision of the future, both in *Jerusalem* and *Milton* (1800–1804), nonetheless ultimately takes a utopian turn: one preconditioned by his religious convictions, which, while idiosyncratic, remained true to the biblical vision of ultimate redemption in the coming City of God. Significantly, though, Blake also entertains the possibility of an earthly redemption premised upon the human choice to use our powers of imagination to create a just society in which all life might thrive, as envisaged in the Great City of Golgonooza in *Milton*, in which the deployment of small-scale, non-polluting technologies enable all people to be freely engaged in creative and convivial activity, in company with diverse other creatures.[59] Here, as in the utopian vision of

Shelley's *Prometheus Unbound* and *Queen Mab*, the ideal of harmony, which is no longer assumed to pertain to Nature *per se*, is projected into the future as the desired outcome of the "active imparadising"[60] of the Earth.

The utopian trajectories traced in works such as these could well provide inspiration for ecological modernization, while Blake's vision of a "desolated Earth" foreshadows clearly what is likely to result if we fail to rise to this challenge. However, in light of the unintended consequences that inevitably beset our endeavors to remake the world in accordance with a preconceived plan, perhaps the most valuable aspect of the Romantic revisioning of humanity's potential for creative and compassionate co-existence with a diversity of more-than-human others lies in the less programmatic "utopian impulse"[61] that can be discerned across a range of Romantic texts, entailing the affirmation of the potential pleasures of earthly existence, for all its fragility and finitude. While this eudemonistic tendency is susceptible to ideological appropriation, inclining the privileged to turn a blind eye to injustice while seeking their own unlimited enjoyment, it could also provide impetus to what Kate Soper has hailed as "a new politics of consumption organised around more sensually rewarding and ecologically progressive conceptions of pleasure and fulfilment" that might just help to wean us from the "work and spend" economy that began to come into being during the Romantic period and is now, disastrously, going global.[62]

NOTES

1. Aidan Day, *Romanticism*, 5.
2. Eichner, *"Romantic" and its Cognates*.
3. Lacoue-Labarthe and Nancy refer to the Jena Romantics as the "first "avant-garde" group in history" (*The Literary Absolute*, 8). Extracts from *Athenaeum*, including the fragment on *romantische Poesie*, are included in Simpson, *The Origins of Modern Critical Thought*.
4. Berlin, *The Roots of Romanticism*, 6.
5. See Kevin Hutchings's overview of "Ecocriticism in British Romanticism Studies" (up until 2006).
6. Garrard, "The Romantics' View of Nature," 129.
7. Levinson, "A Motion and a Spirit," 377.
8. Williams, *The Country and the City*.
9. Sitter, "Eighteenth-century Ecological Poetry."
10. Humboldt, *Kosmos*, 342. The translation given here of Humboldt's expression "[e]ine allgemeine Verkettung, nicht in einfacher linearer Richtung, sondern in netzartig verschlungenem Gewebe" improves on that given in *Topographies of the Sacred* (33).
11. Rigby, *Topographies of the Sacred*, 33.
12. Richards provides a helpful account of the pre-history of Darwinian evolution in *The Romantic Conception of Life*. Nichols's *Romantic Natural Histories* is a valuable sourcebook. See also Poggi and Bossi, *Romanticism in Science* and Cunningham and Jardine, *Romanticism in the Sciences*.
13. Heringman, *Romantic Rocks*.
14. Ritter, cit. Rigby, *Topographies*, 27. Ritter is renowned for his discovery of electrochemistry and ultraviolet radiation. See also Lussier, *Romantic Dynamics*.

15. Coleridge, quoted in Abrams, *Natural Supernaturalism*, 186.
16. See, for example, Blake's "To a Fly," Robert Burns's "To a Mouse" and Coleridge, "To a Young Ass."
17. Perkins, *Romanticism and Animal Rights*, 30.
18. Ibid., 19.
19. Morton, *Shelley and the Revolution in Taste*, and Oerlemans, *Romanticism*, 98–122.
20. Bate, *Song of the Earth*, 176–99.
21. Oerlemans, *Romanticism*, 39–64.
22. *Ibid.*, 85.
23. Garrard, *Ecocriticism*, 169.
24. Morton, "Coexistence and Coexistents."
25. Coleridge, cit. Oerlemans, *Romanticism*, 135.
26. Oken, *Lehrbuch der Naturphilosophie* (1830), cit. Rigby, *Topographies*, 50.
27. Schelling, *Ideas*, 42. F. Schlegel cit. Rigby, *Topographies*, 103.
28. Kroeber, *Ecological Criticism*, 133. See also Mark Lussier on Shelley's "Mont Blanc" as an exploration of the interpenetration of mind and matter through wave dynamics in *Romantic Dynamics*, ch. 3.
29. I discuss Tieck's Runenberg" (1802) and E. T. A. Hoffmann's "Mines of Falun" (1819) in relation to Novalis's "mysticism of the mine" in *Topographies*, 140–56.
30. Sullivan, "Affinity Studies and Open Systems," 409–10.
31. On the distinction between pastoral, anti-pastoral and post-pastoral, see Gifford, *Pastoral*. On Romanticism and pastoral, see also McKusick, *Green Writing*, and Garrard, "Radical Pastoral" and *Ecocriticism*, and, with respect to North American "nature writing" in the tradition inaugurated by Thoreau, Buell, *The Environmental Imagination*.
32. Rigby, *Topographies*, 175–7 and 223–24.
33. Marshall, *Nature's Web*, 334.
34. Morton, *Ecology without Nature*, 114.
35. Morton, "Coexistence and coexistents."
36. Benis, *Romanticism on the Road*.
37. Oerlemans, *Romanticism and the Materiality of Nature*.
38. Coleridge, *Collected Works* 7, pt. 1, 80.
39. Rigby, *Topographies*, 119–27 and 248–56.
40. Oerlemans, *Romanticism*, 5.
41. Abrams, *Natural Supernaturalism*, 12.
42. Prickett, *Origins of Narrative*, 182.
43. Schleiermacher, *On Religion*, 105. For an extended ecocritical discussion of this work, see Rigby, "Another Talk on Religion to its Cultured Despisers."
44. *Ibid.*, 112–13.
45. *Ibid.*, 218.
46. The creation through art of a new, enlightened "mythology of reason" was called for, e.g., in the anonymous "Oldest System Programme of German Idealist" (1796), which is in Hegel's hand-writing but probably co-authored by Schelling and/or Hölderlin (cit. Rigby, *Topographies*, 46).
47. Wordsworth, *Lyrical Ballads*, 118.
48. Schleiermacher, *On Religion*, 102–3.
49. Rigby, *Topographies*, 170.
50. Butler, *Romantics, Rebels and Reactionaries*, 136.

51. Rigby, *Topographies*, 166–72.
52. Campbell, *The Romantic Ethic*; Morton, *Ecology Without Nature*.
53. Cronon, "The Trouble with Wilderness."
54. McKusick, *Green Writing*, 8.
55. Clare, *Selected Poems*, 91.
56. Rigby, "Discoursing on Disaster."
57. Bate, *The Song of the Earth*, 94–8.
58. McKusick, *Green Writing*, 103.
59. *Ibid.*, 104–6. On Blake's complex "environmental poetics," see also Hutchings, *Imagining Nature*.
60. Morton, *Shelley and the Revolution in Taste*, 222.
61. On the distinction between "utopian impulse" and "utopian program" see Jameson, *Archaeologies of the Future*.
62. Soper, "Passing Glories and Romantic Retrievals."

Works Cited

Abrams, M. H. *Natural Supernaturalism: Tradition and Revolution in Romantic Literature.* New York: Norton, 1973.

Bate, Jonathan (ed.). *Romantic Ecology. Wordsworth and the Environmental Tradition.* London: Routledge, 1991.

—— *The Song of the Earth.* Cambridge: Harvard University Press, 2000.

Benis, Toby R. *Romanticism on the Road: The Marginal Gains of Wordsworth's Homeless.* London: Macmillan, 2000.

Berlin, Isaiah. *The Roots of Romanticism.* London: Pimlico, 2000.

Botkin, Daniel. *Discordant Harmonies: A New Ecology for the Twenty-first Century.* Oxford: Oxford University Press, 1992.

Buell, Lawrence. *The Environmental Imagination: Thoreau, Nature Writing, and the Formation of American Culture.* London: Princeton University Press, 1995.

Butler, Marilyn. *Romantics, Rebels and Reactionaries: English Literature and its Background 1760–1830.* Oxford: Oxford University Press, 1981.

Campbell, Colin. *The Romantic Ethic and the Spirit of Consumerism.* Oxford: Basil Blackwell, 1989.

Clare, John. *Selected Poems*, ed. J. Bate, New York: Farrar, Straus and Giroux, 2003.

Cronon, William. "The Trouble with Wilderness; or Getting Back to the Wrong Nature." *Uncommon Ground: Toward Reinventing Nature*, ed. W. Cronon. New York: Norton, 1995: 69–90.

Cunningham, Andrew and Jardine, Nicholas (eds). *Romanticism and the Sciences.* Cambridge: Cambridge University Press, 1990.

Day, Aidan. *Romanticism.* London: Routledge, 1996.

Eichner, Hans. *"Romantic" and its Cognates: The European History of a Word.* Toronto: University of Toronto Press, 1972.

Garrard, Greg. "Radical Pastoral?" In *Studies in Romanticism* 35, no.3 (Fall 1996): 449–465.

—— "The Romantics' View of Nature." In *Spirit of the Environment: Religion, Value and Environmental Concern.* Ed. D. E. Cooper and J. A. Palmer. London: Routledge, 1998: 113–30.

——*Ecocriticism* (rev. ed). London: Routledge, 2011.

Gifford, Terry. *Pastoral*. London: Routledge, 1999.

Heringman, Noah. *Romantic Rocks, Aesthetic Geology*. Ithaca and London: Cornell University Press, 2004.

Humboldt, Alexander von. *Kosmische Naturbetrachtung*. Ed. Rudolph Zaunick. Stuttgart: Alfred Körner, 1958.

Hutchings, Kevin, *Imagining Nature: Blake's Environmental Poetics*. Montreal and Kingston: McGill-Queen's University Press, 2002.

——"Ecocriticism in British Romanticism Studies." *Literature Compass* 4, no. 1 (2007): 172–202.

—— *Romantic Ecologies and Colonial Cultures in the British Atlantic World 1770–1850*. Montreal and Kingston: McGill-Queen's University Press, 2009.

Jameson, Fredric. *Archaeologies of the Future: The Desire Called Utopia and Other Science Fictions*. London: Verso, 2005.

Kroeber, Karl. "'Home at Grasmere': Ecological Holiness." *PMLA* 89, no. 1 (1974): 132–41.

—— *Ecological Literary Criticism: Romantic Imagining and the Biology of Mind*. New York: Columbia University Press, 1994.

Lacoue-Labarthe, Philippe and Nancy, Jean-Luc. *The Literary Absolute. Trans. with intro. and notes, Philip Bernard and Cheryl Lester*. Albany: State University of New York Press, 1988.

Levinson, Marjorie. "A Motion and a Spirit: Romancing Spinoza." *Studies in Romanticism 46*, no. 4 (Winter 2007): 367–408.

Lussier, Mark. *Romantic Dynamics: The Poetics of Physicality*. Basingstoke: Macmillan, 2000.

Marshall, Peter. *Nature's Web: Rethinking Our Place on Earth*. New York: Paragon House, 1994.

McKusick, James. *Green Writing. Romanticism and Ecology*. New York: St. Martin's Place, 2000.

Morton, Timothy. *Shelley and the Revolution in Taste: The Body and the Natural World*. Cambridge: Cambridge University Press, 1994.

——*Ecology without Nature: Rethinking Environmental Aesthetics*. Cambridge, MA: Harvard University Press, 2007.

—— *The Ecological Thought*. Cambridge, MA: Harvard University Press, 2010.

—— "Coexistence and Coexistents: Ecology without a World." In *Ecocritical Theory: New European Approaches*. Ed. Axel Goodbody and Kate Rigby. Charlottesville: University of Virginia Press, 2011, pp. 325–50.

Nichols, Ashton. *Romantic Natural Histories: William Wordsworth, Charles Darwin, and Others*. Boston: Haughton, 2004.

Oerlemans, Onno. *Romanticism and the Materiality of Nature*. Toronto: University of Toronto Press, 2002.

Perkins, David. *Romanticism and Animal Rights*. Cambridge: Cambridge University Press, 2003.

Poggi, Stefano and Bossi, Maurizio. *Romanticism in Science. Science in Europe, 1790–1840*. Dordrecht: Kliewer Academic Publishers, 1994.

Prickett, Stephen. *The Origins of Narrative: The Romantic Appropriation of the Bible*. Cambridge: Cambridge University Press, 1996.

Richards, Robert J. *The Romantic Conception of Life: Science and Philosophy in the Age of Goethe*. Chicago: University of Chicago Press, 2002.

Rigby, Kate. *Topographies of the Sacred: The Poetics of Place in European Romanticism*. Charlottesville: University of Virginia Press, 2004.

—— "Discoursing on Disaster: The Hermeneutics of Environmental Catastrophe." *Tamkang Review 39*, no. 1 (2008): 19–40.

——— "Another Talk on Religion to its Cultured Despisers." *Green Letters 13, no.1* (2010): 55–73.

Schelling, F. W. J. *Ideas for a Philosophy of Nature* (rev. ed. 1803). Trans. E. E. Harris and P. Heath. Intro. R. Stern. Cambridge: Cambridge University Press, 1988.

Schleiermacher, Friedrich. *On Religion. Speeches to Its Cultured Despisers.* Intro., trans. and notes, Richard Crouter, Cambridge: Cambridge University Press, 1988.

Simpson, David (ed.). *The Origins of Modern Critical Thought: German Aesthetic and Literary Theory from Lessing to Hegel.* Cambridge: Cambridge University Press, 1988.

Sitter, John. "Eighteenth-Century Ecological Poetry and Ecotheology." *Religion and Literature 40,* no. 1 (2008): 11–38.

Soper, Kate. "Passing Glories and Romantic Retrievals: Avant-garde Nostalgia and Hedonist Renewal." In *Ecocritical Theory: New European Approaches.* Ed. Axel Goodbody and Kate Rigby. Charlottesville: University of Virginia Press (2011).

Sullivan, Heather. "Affinity Studies and Open Systems: A Non-Equilibrium Ecocritical Reading of Goethe's Faust." In *Ecocritical Theory: New European Approaches.* Ed. Axel Goodbody and Kate Rigby. Charlottesville: University of Virginia Press (forthcoming).

Williams, Raymond. *The Country and the City.* London: Hogarth Press, 1985.

Wordsworth, William. *Lyrical Ballads, and Other Poems, 1797–1800,* ed. J. Butler and K. Green, Ithaca: Cornell University Press, 1992.

CHAPTER 4

···

CHOLERA, KIPLING, AND TROPICAL INDIA

···

UPAMANYU PABLO MUKHERJEE

DISEASED ENVIRONMENTS

···

Introducing his influential collection of essays on medicine and nineteenth-century imperialism, David Arnold wrote over two decades ago:

> Disease was a potent factor in the European conceptualisation of indigenous society. This was especially so by the close of the nineteenth century when Europeans began to pride themselves on their scientific understanding of disease causation and mocked what they saw as the fatalism, superstition and barbarity of indigenous responses to disease.... The emergent discipline of "tropical medicine" gave scientific credence to the idea of a tropical world as a primitive and dangerous environment in contradistinction to an increasingly safe and sanitised temperate world.[1]

The complex and contested relationship between medicine, modern imperialism, and the formation of what we might call an ideology of "tropicality" have been richly analyzed by historians of medicine and imperialism following the work of Arnold and his colleagues.[2] Among the most interesting results of these investigations are the sheer material and intellectual energies invested by European imperialism and colonialism in the creation and sustenance of the paradigm of the tropical lands enveloped by an always-already diseased environment. This way of thinking about the colonized tropics (which were not always congruent with the actually existing geographical and topographical tropical locations) proved to be a key *ideologeme*, in the Jamesonian sense, of modern European imperialism as such. On the one hand, a permanently diseased environment enabled the casting of tropical (human and nonhuman) imperial "subjects" as malformed, underdeveloped, and incapable of moral, material, or intellectual progress; on the other hand, their very stuntedness invited and rationalized a palliative, civilizing presence that could only be provided by modern imperialism as the latter was understood as the vehicle of modernity itself. But, of course, as with all *ideologemes*, "diseased environment" was and continue to be a part of an immensely contested field where the legitimacy and validity of key practices and ideas of governance, economics, citizenship, "development," and identities are processed, torn apart, and re-formed. Thus, it is from the same site of the diseased environment of tropicality that we also see the normative ideas and practices of empire and capital interrogated, challenged and at least partially overcome.

The embedding of the idea of a global, tropical diseased environment through the techniques of empire in the nineteenth century should enable us to place disease and medicine as key elements in any exercise of postcolonial ecocriticism. This is not only to pay due notice to the continuing strength of the ideology of diseased tropical environments today, and what that tells us about the prevailing imperial configurations in the world-system; it is also to underline the centrality of the ideas of disease, contamination, and palliative care within what we might call the various competing ideologies of environment itself. If, as Elizabeth DeLoughrey and George B. Handley have argued recently

> We are all products of this long process of "ecological imperialism"... the "portmanteau biota" of plants, animals, and pathogens that enabled the expansion of Europe and radically transformed the globe [3]

then, it seems to me, we need to focus more on the production, circulation, and the cultural registration of pathogens and diseases than we have hitherto done in order to continue developing our understanding of the complex interactions of imperialism and environments. Excellent analytical work is being done by scholars to reveal the traffic between what DeLoughrey and Handley call "the historical process of nature's mobility, transplantation, and consumption" and the mutations and variations of aesthetic forms. But, it strikes me, looking at the crop of recent works on postcolonial ecocriticism—for example, DeLoughrey and Handley's impressively edited volume of essays (2011), Graham Huggan and Helen Tiffin's equally stimulating book (2010), Bonnie Roos and Alex Hunt's wide-ranging collection (2010), and my own much more modest and constrained effort (2010)—that we could all do more in considering how the discursive and practical detection, production, circulation, and containment of diseases contribute to specific imaginings and conceptualizations of environments—tropical or otherwise.[4] Here, I would like to make some preliminary moves towards understanding how a particular vision of a diseased tropical environment grew out of the dynamics of British imperialism in the Indian subcontinent, and how this vision was simultaneously reinforced and interrogated in the work of an writer conventionally celebrated as the "bard of empire"—Rudyard Kipling.

"THE FEVER HAS YOU BOUND"....

On a hot April's day in 1884, the nineteen-year-old Rudyard Kipling sat down to write a letter to his aunt, Edith Macdonald, on a familiar topic

As you are seven thousand miles away, I don't mind telling you that there has been a case of sporadic cholera already and, as this is the third year since we had the last epidemic, we are anticipating a festive season later on.[5]

Cholera, typhoid, plague, influenza—in short, lethal disease of all kinds are a staple theme of Kipling's nonfictional and fiction. His letters from India, for example, are liberally strewn with references to frequent fevers and accompanying depression that he claims to have suffered, and which frequently plunged him "down a gulf of dark despair."[6] In his reports and columns for the *Civil and Military Gazette,* the newspaper where he practiced his early writing skills, he published detailed and frequently gruesome accounts of these diseases and the lack of sanitary practices in India, along with extraordinarily intimate and hallucinatory accounts of his own suffering:

The fever has you bound hand and foot for the night.... the racking pains in the legs and trunks have given place to pains in the eyes and head only. The cold fits have passed away, and you have been burning steadily for the last ten minutes, preparatory to a final glissade down a rolling bank of black cloud and darkness, and out into the regions beyond. Here you are alone, utterly alone on the verge of a waste of moonlit sand, stretching away to the horizon.[7]

Kipling worked these journalistic sketches into his more famous short stories, now recognized as some of the best examples of what Patrick Brantlinger calls the "imperial gothic" genre.[8] But in addition to the production of a somatic subjectivity, sickness was also a rhetorical trope that Kipling used to construct his ideological defense of imperialism. As Thomas Pinney notes:

Fever, entailing struggle, horror and exhaustion, is the price that the Englishman pays for his position in India. In Kipling's treatment...fever unites in a single symbolic experience the strains of official work with the sense of loneliness and abandonment in a strange land.[9]

Kipling's letters frequently make this connection between personal illness and the general centrality of disease and palliative care to imperialism as such. On 27 September 1885, he wrote that "the population out here die from purely preventable causes; are starved from purely preventable causes," and attributed this to the malgovernance of the Indian rulers of the native states and uppity Bengali journalists who opposed medical reforms. He makes the characteristic move of producing the figures of Indian women as the tragic victims of their men via a rhetoric of sanitary and medical responsibility: "We might wait till doomsday till the Bengalis educate their native women; meantime they are rotting in *zenanas* [interior apartments reserved for women], for sheer want of medical attendance."[10] Two months later, he has worked this notion of a palliative imperialism into his writing:

What else are we working in the country for? For what else do the best men of the Commission die from overwork, and disease, if not keep the people alive in the first place and healthy in the second? We spend our best men on the country like water and if ever a foreign country was made better through the "blood of martyrs" India is that country.[11]

I do not intend here to rehearse the gap between the historical and material realities of epidemics and disease in imperial India, and Kipling's ideological distortions of these. The fact that epidemics in British India, and indeed, in the global imperial system of the nineteenth century, spread via the very material structures of empire itself—by its communicative network of roads, railways, and canals; its forcible and violent conversion of societies into markets dedicated to maximization of private profit; the peripatetic state of its vast armies of retribution and conquest; the emigration of (largely western European) people, livestock and plants and their settlement process in the rest of the world; and even the entrenchment of certain knowledge systems and institutions and the marginalization of others—has been firmly established by the scholarship of David Arnold, Ira Klein, Sheldon Watts, Roy Macleod, and Milton Lewis. Rather, what I would like to do here is to show how and why disease in general, and cholera in particular, were used by Kipling to echo certain key nineteenth-century medical texts by "imperial" doctors such as Edward John Tilt, James Annesley, William Twining, and James Ranald Martin. Together, these literary and medical texts created what Priscilla Wald calls "outbreak narratives" that in turn entrenched a particular vision of a "tropical" environment in general and India in particular, which continues to hold powerful sway today.[12] At the same time, the formal and discursive contradictions of this "outbreak narrative" embedded themselves deep within the fabric of Kipling's fiction and exerted decisive force over his generic and stylistic moves.

As Wald points out, the "outbreak narrative" is composed of mutually linked scientific, journalistic, and fictional incarnations. It follows a formulaic plot that begins with the identification of an emerging infection, includes discussion of the global networks throughout which it travels, and chronicles the epidemiological work that ends with its containment. As epidemiologists trace the routes of the microbes, they catalog the spaces and interactions of global modernity.[13]

This global, imperial modernity is precisely what emerges in the writings of Kipling and the British doctors of "tropical" medicine. Their use of the language of contagion and containment casts India as a (proto-) modern nation with a "population," with all the attendant connotations of communicability and material interdependence that instigates an "epidemiology of belonging."[14] But at the same time, since the rhetorical integrity of this narrative cannot be squared with its historical matter this imagining of a (proto-) "modern" nation accrues manifold contradictions:

> the obsolescence and tenacity of borders, the attraction and threat of strangers, and especially the destructive and formative power of contagion. It both acknowledges and obscures the interactions and global formations that challenge national belonging in particular.[15]

All these tensions are precisely located in Kipling's conceptualization of the relationships between the British, Indian, and global imperial dimensions. They find some of their most memorable articulations in his fictions of tropical diseases, and in particular, those that use cholera as a crucial element in their narratives.

Cholera (and its Victorian shorthand "fever") appears as crucial plot devices in a host of Kipling's shorter fiction—in the early "Thrown Away" and "By Word of Mouth," to the exceedingly sentimental and homo-social "Only a Subaltern," to the fully formed and complex imperial allegories of "The Strange Ride of Morrowbie Jukes" and "The Bridge Builders." Cholera was a crucial part of the rhetoric of disease and sickness that Kipling (and not only Kipling) used to produce India as a realm of the dead: as he wrote later in his memoir: "The dead of all times were about us... skulls and bones tumbled out of our mud garden walls, and were turned up among the flowers by the rains; and at every point were tombs of the dead."[16] This pervasive death-consciousness would remain as one of the primary interpretative lenses through which Kipling saw empire, working its way into the fabric of his fiction and travel writing. Moreover, the specific features of cholera as a disease made it a significant element in Kipling's rhetorical construction of India as death's own kingdom. In yet another characteristic passage in his memoir, Kipling wrote, "heaven knows the men died fast enough from typhoid... or from cholera, which was manifestly a breath of the Devil that could kill all on one side of a barrack-room and spare the others."[17] The seemingly inexplicable randomness of cholera, the utter impossibility of predicting its course or of preventing it, coupled with the horrifically painful nature of its progression, meant that it could be seen as an *essence* of India. It had to be defeated with the palliative tools of empire such as medicine and civic administration, but also with literary labor. Kipling would capture the disease from the point of view of the rank-and-file British soldier in stories like "The Daughter of the Regiment" that precisely enacted the drama of this imperial combat:

> You see, we was a new an' raw regiment in those days, an' we cud make neither head nor tail av the sickness; an' so was useless. The men was goin' roun' an' about like dumb sheep, waitin' for the nex' man to fall over, an' sayin' undher their spache, "fwat is ut? In the name av God, *fwhat* is ut?"[18]

Kipling's achievement in passages such as the one above is to capture the historical resonance of cholera in British India. As Arnold suggests:

> Few diseases in nineteenth-century India appeared to be as violently destructive as epidemic cholera.... cholera was important rather in terms of the dividing line it drew between European rulers and their Indian subjects and the questions it posed about the terms on which the British held India.[19]

Arnold goes on to show that cholera became widely identified, amongst both the British and the Indians, as one of the most potent symbols of the imperial experience itself:

> For British officials and Hindu villagers alike, though often in strikingly different ways, cholera stood or seemed to presage a wider political or cosmological "dis-order." In particular, either because of their severity or their historical conjuncture, the epidemics of 1817–21, 1856–7, and 1860–61 were to varying degrees identified with conquest and foreign rule.[20]

As such, cholera often became a mythic element in popular and informal circuits of Indian information and performance (often caricatured but also validated by Kipling as "bazaar gossip") that were the objects of imperial suspicion and fear. Rumors of cholera were frequently carried via the medium of frenzied religious devotees and were read as coded anti-imperial messages against foreign invasion and misrule.[21] These popular performances, with their readily interpretable messages of rebellion, made commonsensical the connection between conquest and disease, British troops and cholera, and thus had to be carefully policed and outlawed. More importantly for our purposes here, a counter-rhetoric which proposed the essential "Indianness" of the disease, of a "tropicality" that had to be combated, became one of the chief concerns of the British literature of cholera.

"Its Attack Commenced Suddenly"

The representation of cholera as an essence of the tropical Indian environment and the proper object of what I have been calling palliative imperialism, was a feature of the leading British medical texts of nineteenth century. The role of medicine in the establishment of imperial power is well documented and need not be rehearsed at any length here; it is sufficient to point out, as Andrew Cunningham and Bridie Andrews have shown, that nineteenth-century "tropical medicine" was explicitly tasked with facilitating colonial settlement.[22] In his mammoth study on the subject, Sheldon Watts has analyzed the precise connections between what he calls the "full medicalization of the West" and European imperial expansion, where "progress and development" entailed such novel disease vectors as troop trains, steamships, canals and a network of roads and highways, as well as the humans, animals, and goods that circulated via them. Cholera, in both India and Britain, became entwined with the establishment of political and economic power of a single home counties-based ruling elite.[23]

Certainly, the medical authorities of the nineteenth century carefully created a "civilizational" discourse of "tropical" diseases that was explicitly geared towards achieving imperial or colonial success and provided a template for fiction such as Rudyard Kipling's. Here, I am going to concentrate on three of the most consistent features of this discourse: the representation of India's historical and geographical environment as being "diseased"; the representation of cholera as an embodied "invasion" of the (European) body which was a problematic reversal of the historical invasion of India by the British; and finally, the recognition of cholera as being disturbingly linked to imperial or "modern" civilization itself.

The familiar trope of India's immutable history is evoked in more than a few texts of nineteenth-century tropical medicine. Edward John Tilt began his treatise on British female health in the tropics by invoking the mystique of India:

> There is a land so ancient that we neither know when, nor where its most sacred language was spoken; so ancient that the features and the dress of its present inhabitants were sculptured on Egyptian temples by Sesostris. . . . There is a land so immutable

that when, some 2200 years ago, Alexander attempted its conquest, he found them as now.[24]

In texts such as Tilt's, the alleged historical immutability of India quickly slides into a celebration of British imperialism's capacity to inhabit and decisively animate it. This thawing of frozen history is concentrated into the language of development, both physical and moral, that is seen to be the signal feature of the British enterprise. Thus, Tilt celebrates the building of canals and railways, but also talks about how a "wide-spread system of medical relief" had extracted gratitude of the millions "whom their native rulers would have inevitably let die."[25]

It quickly becomes evident that the historical immutability of India is also related to a "tropical" environment that appears disposed to material and moral entropy. James Ranald Martin wrote in his influential treatment of the relationship between "tropical climates" and endemic diseases amongst Europeans who inhabited them:

> In warm and moist climates, obesity and laxity of frame are induced.… In Bengal, as on the West Coast of Africa and other unhealthy climates, the heat and moisture combined cause a vast increase of minute vegetable and animal life, while decomposition of dead animal and vegetable matter is equally rapid, showing the aptitude of all substances to pass from the inorganic to the organic.[26]

Martin observes this environment of decay eat into the edifices of the British houses in Calcutta, which, built with the finest materials and "of such solidity that in England they would endure for centuries," soon crumble and are "fit habitations only for crows."[27] Of even greater consequence is the arrest and crumbling of the moral edifice of the inhabitants, which for Martin are linked to what he sees as India's historic underdevelopment:

> In some countries everything tends to exalt the human race, while in India everything has tended to depress it.… Improvement in Asia has been willfully arrested by the self-imposition of an arbitrary standard.… generally speaking, the agricultural and mechanical arts are in but a rude state with the Hindus, both being supposed to have remained stationary for two thousand years or more.[28]

The debilitating environment of organic and inorganic decay, a feature we might call "tropicality," in turn produces not just moral and historical disability, but also an embodied condition of disease and sickness. Cholera, one of the most dramatic expressions of this condition, can now be seen as literally infused in the atmosphere and soil of India. As James Annesley suggested, while observing that the disease prevailed in all kinds of weather and all seasons,

> It must have depended, therefore, upon the influence of some quality in the atmosphere which has been overlooked.… I have little difficulty in believing that difference to have been chiefly in its electrical state, which state may also have had an intimate relation with the exhalations proceeding from the soil of the places where the disease was predominant.[29]

One literally breathed in, and inhabited a comprehensive "disease environment" in "tropical" India:[30] In Edward Tilt's writing, the very climate of India "may be figured as a series of ague-fits, for every successive year brings its recurring stages of cold, of hot, and of sweating weather."[31]

Once imbibed, cholera demonstrated a dramatic quality that was best captured in language invoking speed and stealth. In William Twining's vivid account of the disease's progress:

> We find in Cholera, sudden and extreme prostration of strength.…. The medical man whose illness is mentioned in a subsequent part of this chapter, had no suspicion of his disease being Cholera, till about noon of the day in which he died, when he desired his servant to bring him a small looking-glass, and the instant it was brought, he said, "I see I have got Cholera, which I did not suspect before: there can be but little hope of my recovery."[32]

The image of the disease as a sudden and stealthy (Indian) assassin was amplified by each telling. Practitioners like Twining and Annesley sprinkled their accounts with anecdotes of everyday imperialists—troops as well as civilians—engaged in mundane and banal activities like an afternoon swim, or post-lunch browsing in the library, suddenly collapsing to death after a brief but intensely painful experience.[33] The language they used was of warfare, passages such as this from Twining being typical: "The invasion of Cholera most frequently appears in a violent form, between the hours of two and five a.m..… its attack commences suddenly, and without any premonitory symptoms."[34]

Perhaps the most disturbing aspect of this invasion was the horrific intimacy of the disease and the rapidity with which the human body was turned inside out via an assortment of hemorrhages and leaks. The medical texts are replete with lengthy descriptions of vomiting, diarrhea—the emptying out of the patient's insides. The very flow of blood seems to be blocked: "There is no symptom of the disease more uniform than the black, thick, and ropy condition of the blood taken from a patient in epidemic cholera."[35] In the grip of the disease, people seem to turn rapidly into specters of their former selves:

> In bad cases, the voice becomes feeble, shrill, and pectoral; respiration short, difficult, and imperfect … coldness of the whole body, but more especially of the extremities, and a shriveled state of the fingers, takes place.[36]

It is not difficult to see how this language of the spectral, with its emphasis on voiding, shriveling, shrinking, leaking, coldness, and putrefaction, directly overlapped with and contributed to the development of the nineteenth-century gothic discourse. The descriptions of sick and diseased bodies that the "imperial" medical texts yield are not so distant from the gothic bodies found in *Dracula*, *Dr. Jekyll and Mr. Hyde*, and *The Beetle*. And the conjunctural presence of cholera (and other "tropical" diseases) and the supernatural in Kipling's own "imperial gothic" tales is surely more than a coincidence. What we find in the medical texts is the materialization of nineteenth-century fantasies about the invasion of body-snatchers, a trope that was particularly useful in expressing the anxieties of an empire built on historical acts of invasion and occupation.

The combination of the rhetorical production of a diseased Indian environment and of cholera (and other diseases) as malign invading forces that must be defeated brought the imperial doctors to the consideration of just how "development" could be sustained in India. Here, the problem was frequently conceived of in racialized terms (and in unsurprisingly contradictory fashion). One the one hand, development and progress were seen as the "enlightened policy and the mechanical genius of a gifted race."[37] On the other hand, this race was seen to be ill-equipped for conquering the tropics, and must lose its imagined purity in order to do so:

> There are two ways of colonizing. The first is by "swarming," as the bees do, and as we have successfully done, to some well-chosen isothermal region, such as North America and Australia. The second is by intermarriage with aboriginals of a country, as did the Saxons, Danes, and Normans with us.… In India we have found a tropical climate, and all past experience shows that our race, if kept pure from other blood, would die out in the third or fourth generation.[38]

Thus, the problem of successful imperialism was conceived of as a problem of bio-power, of a matter of social and racial engineering. Since whenever "man migrates from the climate which contributed to generate the peculiarities of his frame… disorders of various kinds and grades may be expected," the best one could do is to mitigate this disorder by either sexual engineering ("cross-breeding") or sanitary reform. And since the first measure was likely to be politically explosive, the doctors generally plumped for designing extensive devices for the second.

The effort sometimes had interesting consequences. James Ranald Martin, for example, departed from the standard "environmentalist" paradigm to suggest that all human ecologies could be improved through sanitary reforms:

> When, again, we look back to our native country, and boast of its pure and bracing air, let us not forget the important fact, that it is man himself who has in a great measure created these salubrious climates. France, Germany, and England, not more than twenty years ago, resembled Canada and Chinese Tartary…[39]

Martin does not quite go on to debunk the "environmental" theory of "race," and as we have seen above, quickly falls back onto the stereotype of Asiatic lassitude. But he went on to spend a large part of his work recommending moderation and sobriety among European settlers, paying detailed attention to clothing, diet, exercise, sexual practices, hygiene, and even the choice of building sites, in order to better combat "tropicality."[40]

But if social engineering was seen as the key to the conquest of the tropics, the same phenomenon could facilitate invasion by diseases such as cholera. The network of modernity facilitated the conversion of diseases into epidemics:

> The engineer exults in his hundreds of miles of raised metal roads and of railway embankments through a level country, but the doctor tells him he has somehow or other so interfered with the natural drainage of alluvial plains as to develop malaria

to an extent that threatens to depopulate them. The sanitarian tells the engineer that some of his canals have been so injudiciously planned. … that they have flooded the surrounding country and greatly increased the virulence of malaria.[41]

This awareness of the terrible paradox of progress—that it could be thought of as the rationale of imperial presence as well as responsible for the very "diseased environment" of tropical India itself—frequently existed as a disquieting presence in the medical texts. Given full voice, it could potentially unleash a series of searching questions about the entire British imperial project itself, so it was disavowed as often it was raised, and remained as a residual element within the narrative of progress whose contradictory weight oddly skewed the overall rhetorical balance of "outbreak narratives":

> When we observe Cholera to have appeared progressively along great roads and navigable rivers where frequent communications by travelers, and much commercial intercourse exists, the idea of contagion is readily suggested, and it is not easy for any one to give positive proof that such idea is erroneous. … but proofs of the fact are wanting in India, while proofs adverse to the belief in contagion are numerous.[42]

The two halves of the above passage neatly mirrors the fracture in the imperial consciousness when faced with the paradox of "progress"—proof and absence of proof, avowal and disavowal, knowability and unknowability cancel each other out till we are left with an exercise in uncertainty, and this latter reveals itself as the prevailing sign of "empire writing."

"… BETWEEN DEATH AND BURIAL"

The medical ideas of the diseased tropical environment of India, of cholera in particular as an expression of a malign invasion of the human body, and of progress and development being simultaneously the mark of a palliative imperialism and a conduit for the "worlding" of diseases—all left visible marks on Rudyard Kipling's writing and thinking. They occupied crucial roles both in the narrative of his supernatural tales of imperial gothic and in realist narratives that sought to capture the practices of everyday lives. But being inherently contested and unstable ideologemes themselves they also generated structural ambiguity, narrative uncertainty, and rhetorical instability in Kipling's own writing.

Indeed, even beyond their historically symptomatic character, Kipling's writings are some of the most remarkable instances of the Victorian fictions of illness. The questions of gender (and masculinity in particular), national characterization, and civilizational development are all articulated through a narratives of contamination and disease. His early short stories, in particular, carefully crafted the trope of the stoical and heroic imperial men (and some women) working selflessly to animate Indian history with modern progress. As the narrator of "Thrown Away" says:

Now India is a place beyond all others where one must not take things too seriously.... Sickness does not matter, because it's all in the day's work, and if you die, another man takes over your place and your office in the eight hours between death and burial.[43]

But of course, the full sardonic charge of the passage can only work when the reader believes that sickness *does* matter, and it matters because it is a key element in the creation of the idea of the stoic imperial agent sticking to his or her task while fully enveloped within the lethal tropical environment. "Thrown Away" ends with the suicide of a young British man, and the necessary obfuscation of this fact by the narrator and an army official in order to preserve the general imperial morale. Between them, they concoct a story of a death by disease, of yet another life sacrificed to the imperial cause. Cholera here converts a figure of perceived moral weakness into that of stoic self-sacrifice. The interesting part of the story is that it self-consciously exhibits this latter as a fabrication, a brutally necessary lie, and this exposure inaugurates a barely suppressed suspicion about the reality of the imperial project itself (is it this that breeds incurable despair in "The Boy"?). This trope of the "necessary lie" that papers over the full horror of imperialism will receive its most famous treatment in the hands of Joseph Conrad and his *Heart of Darkness,* but is already prevalent in the early Kipling.

In other Kipling short stories like "The Daughter of the Regiment" and "Only a Subaltern," disease is used to construct a much more robust and heroic imperial figure. "The Daughter of the Regiment" is narrated in the demotic voice of one of Kipling's memorable imperial soldier figures, Mulvaney, and tells the happy story of the engagement of a fellow soldier to the eponymous "daughter," "Jhansi" McKenna. Mulvaney explains how "Jhansi" got her nickname by recalling a particularly horrific outbreak of cholera on a troop train near the central Indian city of Jhansi that killed seven soldiers in one night, including the regimental doctor, sparking mass hysteria amongst the survivors. When the commanding officer orders the women and children to evacuate the train, Bridget Mackenna, Jahnsi's mother, refuses:

"Be damned av I do!" sez Ould Pummeloe, an' little Jhansi, squattin' by her mother's side, squeaks out, "Be damned av I do, tu." ... Wid that, she turns up her sleeves an' steps out for a well behind the rest-camp—little Jhansi trottin' behind wid a *lotah* an' string.... 'twas like a battlefield wid all the glory missin'—at the hid av the regimint av women.[44]

This "regiment" of women nurses the stricken soldiers while completely disregarding their own safety, thereby gaining their own admission to the pantheon of imperial heroes. Moreover, the whole story is geared towards the regeneration and continuity of the basic imperial combat unit—the regiment—as the otherwise unattractive Jhansi is engaged to Corporal Slane at the behest of Mulvaney, whose aim is to bring back those times when "a man lived an' died wid his regiment; an' by natur', he married whin he was a *man*".[45] The heroism of the women, triggered by cholera, thus strictly serves to bolster imperial heteronormativity.

In "Only a Subaltern," imperial masculinity is again constructed through a narrative of disease and contagion. Bobby Wick, the subaltern in question, joins one of the British regiments in India where they fondly recall the civic exploits of his ex-Commissioner father ("building great works for the good of the land, and doing his best to make two blades of grass grow where there was but one before").[46] In India, he is taught by his Company Commander Revere that the "Regiment was his father and his mother and his indissolubly wedded wife," and accordingly, he forges a paternalistic bond with the soldiers under his command—especially with Dormer, a perceived malcontent and trouble-maker. This bond is emphasized when cholera hits the regiment, and Bobby returns post-haste from his vacation to nurse his men. He is warned against his frequent hospital visits: "Shouldn't go there too often if I were you. They say it's not contagious, but there's no use in running unnecessary risks."[47] But when Bobby learns that Dormer has contracted the disease and is about to die, he visits the soldier whose apparently final request is for Bobby to hold his hands. The touch and grip of the men's hands then serve to underscore the paternalist and homo-social bond that holds the regiment together:

> Bobby sat on the side of the bed, and the ice cold hand closed on his own like a vice, forcing a lady's ring which was on the little finger deep into the flesh.… An hour passed and the grasp of the hand did not relax.… Bobby with infinite craft lit himself a cheroot with the left hand, his right arm was numbed to the elbow, and resigned himself to a night of pain.[48]

The idea of contagion is here central to the charge of the passage. The suspicion that, despite medical opinion, cholera might be contagious serves to highlight the bravery and selfless love that are the key markers for imperial masculinity. Additionally, this masculinity itself is contagious, this time with positive and redemptive connotations, as Bobby's virtues flow into Dormer's body and miraculously cure him. Of course, the symmetry of the narrative requires Bobby to be infected with cholera, thereby enabling Kipling to cram the final half of the story with heightened sentimental and melodramatic language, where the news of Bobby's illness spreads like contagion through the camp ('"Wot's up?" asked twenty tents; and through twenty tents ran the answer—"Wick, 'e's down'"). The contagion of manly love and sympathy turns the previously fractious regiment into one family, and by the time Bobby dies after three days of suffering and much mass weeping, all signs of possible dissent against officers have disappeared. Thus a callous Private Conklin is beaten up by Dormer when he dares to joke about Bobby's death: "You ought to take shame for yourself, Conky! Orf'cer?- Bloomin' orf'cer?.… Hangel [angel]! *Bloomin'* Hangel! That's wot'e is!"[49] The beatification of the imperial army officer in "Only a Subaltern," then, relies on a cholera narrative and a two-pronged use of the idea of contagion. Of course, one of the central contradictions of the story that is deliberately played up by Kipling is that imperial masculinity can only be established by incorporating within it the codes of normative femininity—nursing, copious weeping and enfeeblement, physical acts of love. The narrative of disease and palliative care, here too, plays a crucial role, and serves to reveal the idea of imperial masculinity itself as being irreparably infected with femininity.

I want to end by considering how Kipling uses the full range of the contradictory possibilities of the "tropical disease" narrative to create one of his best-known "imperial gothic" stories, "The Strange Ride of Morrowbie Jukes." This is story where the traffic and the weave between Kipling's fiction and nonfiction are made deliberately evident. For example, the narrative begins by recalling that

> there is a story that if you go into the heart of Bikanir, which is in the heart of the Great Indian Desert, you shall come across...a town where the Dead who did not die, but may not live, have established their headquarters.[50]

This image of a desert haunted by living death and thus turned into an uncanny habitat clearly recalls Kipling's description of the Great Indian Desert in various sections of his travelogue "From Sea to Sea":

> If any part of a land strewn with dead men's bones have a special claim to distinction, Rajputana, as the cock-pit of India, stands first. . . .. From Delhi to Abu, and from Indus to the Chambul, each yard of ground has witnessed slaughter, pillage, and rapine.[51]

This haunted land then leads to Kipling's celebrated encounter with the uncanny in his descent into a subterranean Hindu temple in Chittor and Amber forts. These encounters are marked by a radical dissolution of the protagonist's sense of historical time and perspective, as well as by an outbreak of hysteria induced by contact:

> It seems as though the descent had led the Englishman, firstly, two thousand years away from his own century, and secondly, into a trap. . ... he had to cross the smooth, worn rocks, and he felt their sliminess through his boot soles. It was as though he were treading on the soft, oiled skin of a Hindu.[52]

This basic pattern of an encounter with the "living dead" that leads to a convulsion in the spatio-temporal coordinates of the Englishman, and his sense of being trapped in a loathsome physical contact with the Indians, provides the structure for Kipling's short story. To this, he adds an outbreak narrative in order to enhance the fictional meditation on the problematics of the imperial condition.

The story begins with a disease: Morrowbie Jukes has a "slight attack of fever," which soon gives way, however, to a semidelirious condition where he gallops on his horse aimlessly looking to shoot a dog that he imagines had been howling outside his tent. Fever and the delirium it produced were of special interest to Kipling, especially since they could be worked into the gothic and supernatural modes of registering the imperial experience.[53] Here, the affliction and the uncanny "desolate sandy stretch" of the country provide the context for a harrowing narrative of contagion that signals a crisis of imperial masculinity.

Jukes's mad ride ends in him falling down the bottom of a crater beside the river Sutlej. As a civil engineer, Jukes commands a language of science and progress that is evident in his detailed description of the angle of the crater's slope and the composition of the soil. But this is of little help to him as he quickly discovers that it is impossible to climb back up since "he had fallen into a trap exactly on the same model as that which the ant-lion sets for its prey."[54] Neither can he exit by the river, which is guarded by armed men in a boat who shoot at him at the slightest sign of approach to the waterfront. Trapped in this predicament, Jukes turns to find a gathered crowd of Indians—his fellow inhabitants of the crater.

What follows have rightly been described by many critics as a nightmare tale of imperial phobia of contact with the colonized.[55] Certainly, Jukes's first reaction to the crowd gathered about him is already marked by the classic signs of neurotically compulsive cataloging of his subjects in terms of dirt and disgust:

> They were all scantily clothed in that salmon-coloured cloth which one associates with Hindu mendicants, and, at first sight, gave me the impression of a band of loathsome *faquirs*. The filth and repulsiveness of the assembly were beyond all description, and I shuddered to think what their life in the badger-holes must be.[56]

The register of impurity is quickly used to construct a vision of mutinous Indians:

> Even in these days, when local self-government has destroyed the greater part of a native's respect for a Sahib, I have been accustomed to a certain amount of civility from my inferiors…. [Yet] The ragged crew actually laughed at me—such laughter I hope I may never hear again. They cackled, yelled, whistled, and howled as I walked into their midst.[57]

This mocking laughter inaugurates a leveling of the social and material hierarchies of empire, and Jukes is forced to live as an equal member of "a republic of wild beasts penned at the bottom of a pit, to eat and fight and sleep till we died." Leveling is also expressed in terms of embodiment, where Jukes is forced to eat what the Indians eat—crows and other unclean creatures—and drink filthy water. His body accumulates the same kind of dirt and filth that he had shuddered at initially, and he burrows in the "badger holes" just like the native inhabitants. It is not difficult to read in this Kipling's adherence to the old imperialist cliché about the barbaric anarchy that would surface in the colonies should they succeed in gaining independence, nor is it difficult to show that this also acted as a reinscription of the events of the Indian Mutiny of 1857. But for our purposes here, we should note that this "bestial republic" of the colonized is built around the notion of contagion and disease—specifically, that of cholera.

Jukes's main interlocutor in this realm of the living dead is Gunga Dass, a former employee of the colonial state. Dass's first appearance triggers a curious mixture of horror and guilt in Jukes:

> I looked at a withered skeleton, turbanless and almost naked, with long matted hair and deep-set codfish-eyes. But for a crescent-shaped scar on the left cheek—the result of an accident for which I was responsible—I should never have known him.[58]

While Dass's skeletal state speaks from the imperial gothic register, his mutilation, the only mark that makes him recognizable speaks of the empire that is responsible for his condition, despite the elision attempted via the language of "accident." It is precisely in this tone of horror and guilty admission that the story of the colonial undead is subsequently told in the story.

Dass reveals that the "reeking village" is inhabited by those who "die at home and do not die when you come to the *ghat* to be burnt." His own story reveals the central role played by the iconic imperial disease of cholera in this process of zombification. Stricken with cholera and thought to have perished from it, he was carried to the riverside cremation ground where he was found to be "too lively." Although Kipling here mobilizes the archetype of the superstitious colonized as an explanation for what happens to Dass (the ritual of the dead has already been performed and therefore he cannot be admitted back to the world of the living), it soon becomes clear that the "progressive" colonial state has an equally crucial role to play:

> They took me from my sheets when they saw that I was too lively and gave me medicines for one week, and I survived successfully. Then they sent me by rail from my place to Okara station, with a man to take care of me...[59]

Although it is of course Indians who first cure and then convey Dass to the village of the living dead, the presence of medicine and railways here speak of the palliative imperialism that was produced as one of the key rationales of British presence in the works of Kipling and many others in the nineteenth century. Modern medicine and the railway network are coupled with the so-called ancient Hindu religious rituals to produce the zombie republic that Jukes finds himself in.

The debates about cholera conducted by the imperial doctors produced a contested and contradictory idea of tropicality. The language and praxis of contagion, infection and containment were used in the ideological construction of a palliative imperialism that was needed by the stricken colonized societies; on the other hand, the same language and praxis of contagion and infection could produce a powerful interrogation of palliative and progressive imperialism itself. In Kipling's fiction and nonfiction, this contradiction produced, at the very least, a double register that turned a discomforting searchlight on, among other things, his own deeply held political belief in the empire. Cholera and disease lie behind the hallucinatory encounter with the colonial undead, but medicine, railway, the imperial civil service and all the paternalism that the latter entailed, are also decisive factors in this encounter.

The remainder of Morrowbie Jukes's story tells of the harrowing of the imperial man: "Here was a *Sahib*, a representative of the dominant race, helpless as a child and completely at the mercy of his native neighbours."[60] Dass becomes a memorable member of that species of "educated" (i.e., English-speaking petit-bourgeois) Indians who are the objects for Kipling's special vitriol. He takes pleasure in pronouncing the social death of Jukes, and reverses the colonial power-dynamic by assigning menial tasks to him. Jukes's protests are drowned out by the implacable material logic of the body: "Perhaps not tomorrow. ... but in the end, and for many years, you will catch crows and eat crows, and you will thank your European God that you have crows to catch and eat."[61] Jukes's hellish harrowing ends when the narrative register shifts from the imperial gothic to that of the imperial adventure tale: he finds out from Dass that another Briton had suffered the same fate as him, but had exercised his "racially superior" faculties by finding a way out of the trap and coding it in a map. Dass had killed him in the hope of deciphering the map and getting out, but had not been able to read it properly (his faculty of civilizational mimicry being only partially developed—he can make bad puns in English but cannot properly read it). He now proposes that Jukes should help him decode the map, then tries to kill Jukes when the two of them are escaping. But Jukes is saved by the miracle of a loyal Indian—a servant who is uncontaminated by the disease of education, and has thus simply risked his life by following the sand marks of Jukes's mad desert ride to find him in the village of the undead. Jukes escapes with this loyal servant's help, but the story ends on a disconcerting note: there is no sign of Dass. Has he managed to escape, this zombie with a diseased body and mind, ready to contaminate the colonial body politic with the idea of the "beastly republic" that, both like and unlike cholera, could overthrow the palliative empire? Kipling's writing would forever be marked by the fear and gruesome attraction of this idea.

NOTES

1. David Arnold, "Disease, Medicine and Empire," in David Arnold (ed.), *Imperial Medicine and Indigeneous Societies* (Manchester: Manchester University Press, 1988), p. 7.
2. See among others, David Arnold (ed.), *Warm Climates and Western Medicine: The Emergence of Tropical Medicine 1500–1900* (Amsterdam, Rodopi, 1996) and *Colonizing the Body: State Medicine and Epidemic Disease in Nineteenth-Century India* (Delhi: Oxford University Press, 1993); Vicento Navarro (ed.), *Imperialism, Health and Medicine* (London and New York: Pluto Press, 1981); Ira Klein, "Imperialism, ecology and disease: Cholera in India, 1850–1950," *The Indian Economic and Social History Review* 31: 4 (1994), 491–518; R. MacLeod and Milton Lewis (eds.), *Disease, Medicine and Empire, Mark Harrison, Public Health in British India: Anglo-Indian Preventative Medicine 1859–1914* (Cambridge: Cambridge University Press, 1993); Alison Bashford, *Imperial Hygiene: A Critical History of Colonialism, Nationalism and Public Health* (Basingstoke: Palgrave Macmillan, 2004); Andrew Cunningham and Bridie Andrews (eds.), *Western Medicine as Contested Knowledge* (Manchester and New York: Manchester University Press, 1997) and Sheldon Watts, *Epidemics and History: Disease, Power and Imperialism* (New Haven and London: Yale University Press, 1997).
3. Elizabeth DeLoughrey and George B. Handley, "Towards an Aesthetics of the Earth" in Elizabeth DeLoughrey and George B. Handley (eds.), *Postcolonial Ecologies: Literatures of the Environment* (Oxford and New York: Oxford University Press, 2011), p. 13.
4. Graham Huggan and Helen Tiffin, *Postcolonial Ecocriticism: Literatures, Animals, Environment* (London and New York: Routledge, 2010); Bonnie Roos and Alex Hunt (eds.), *Postcolonial Green: Environmental Politics and World Narratives* (University of Virginia Press, 2010); and Upamanyu Pablo Mukherjee, *Postcolonial Environments: Nature, Culture and the Contemporary Indian Novel in English* (Basingstoke and New York: Palgrave Macmillan, 2010).
5. Thomas Pinney (ed.), *The Letters of Rudyard Kipling*, vol.1. (Basingstoke and London: Macmillan, 1990), p. 61.

6. Ibid., p. 285.

7. Thomas Pinney (ed.), *Kipling's India: Uncollected Sketches 1884-88* (Basingstoke: Macmillan, 1986), pp. 120–121. Also see Kipling's entries for the Civil and Military Gazette for 7 May 1884 and 14 February 1885 in this volume for good examples of his sanitary ramblings through the "native quarters" of Lahore.

8. See Patrick Brantlinger, *The Rule of Darkness: British Literature and Imperialism 1830–1914* (Ithaca, NY.: Cornell University Press, 1988), p. 227.

9. Pinney (1986), p. 24.

10. Pinney (1990), pp. 91–92.

11. Ibid., p. 98.

12. See Priscilla Wald, *Contagious: Cultures, Carriers and the Outbreak Narrative* (Durham and London: Duke University Press, 2008).

13. Ibid., p. 2.

14. Ibid., p. 18.

15. Ibid., p. 33.

16. Rudyard Kipling, *Something of Myself* (London: Penguin, 1977 [1937]), p. 36.

17. Ibid., p. 46.

18. Rudyard Kipling, *Collected Short Stories*, 5 vols., ed. Andrew Lycett (London: The Folio Society, 2005), vol. 1, p. 139.

19. Arnold (1993), p. 159.

20. Ibid., p. 178.

21. Ibid., p. 173.

22. Cunningham and Andrews (1997), p. 1.

23. Watts (1997), p. 167.

24. Edward John Tilt, *Health in India for British Women and the Prevention of Disease in Tropical Climates* (London: Churchill, 1875), p. 1.

25. Ibid., p. 2.

26. James Ranald Martin, *The Influence of Tropical Climate in Producing the Acute Endemic Diseases of Europeans* (London: John Churchill, 1861), pp. 52–53.

27. Ibid., p. 57.

28. Ibid., pp. 415–416.

29. James Annesley, *Sketches of the Most Prevalent Diseases of India* (London: Thomas and George Underwood, 1829), pp. 128–129.

30. For further elaboration of this theory of "infused" theory of cholera and other diseases in the tropics, and the relationship of these to the "national character," see James Annesley, *On the More Prevalent Diseases of India* (London: Longman, 1855), p. 9.

31. Tilt (1875) p. 9.

32. William Twining, *A Practical Account of Epidemic Cholera* (London: Parbury and Allen, 1833), pp. 2–3.

33. See Annesley (1829), p. 43 and Twining (1833), p. 22.

34. Twining (1833), p. 13.

35. Annesley (1829), p. 36. Also see Twining (1833), p. 42.

36. Twining (1833), p. 4.

37. Tilt (1875), p. 2.

38. Ibid., p. 99.

39. Martin (1861), p. 4.

40. Ibid., pp. 164–193.

41. Tilt (1875), p 117.
42. Twining (1833), pp. 284–286. The idea of "contagion" was heavily debated within the impe-rial medical and administrative circles. On the one hand, it was a useful trope in the rhetor-ical creation of a "diseased" orient that must be cured or contained. James Martin declared, "The present opinion of the medical profession is, that epidemic cholera is induced by a special poison of eastern or foreign origin..." (Martin [1861], p. 516). On the other hand, the admission of contagion, as we have seen above, meant the admission of the culpability of progress and development in the creation of a disease environment. Thus, contagion remained as an irreparably fractured rhetorical site.
43. Kipling (2005), vol. 1, p. 17.
44. Ibid., pp. 138–139.
45. Ibid., p. 137.
46. Kipling (2005) vol. 2, p. 67.
47. Ibid., p. 75.
48. Ibid., p. 76.
49. Ibid., p. 79.
50. Kipling (2005), vol.2, p. 110.
51. Rudyard Kipling, *From Sea to Sea* (Leipzig: Tauchnitz, 1900), pp. 21–22.
52. Ibid., pp. 100–101.
53. Note how the feverish delirium described in a piece like "De Profoundis" published in August 1885 is echoed in the supernaturalism of one like "The House of Shadows" pub-lished a year later. See Pinney (1986), pp. 120–122 and 247–248.
54. Kipling (2005), p. 113.
55. See amongst many others, Benita Parry, "The Content and Discontent of Kipling's Imperialism," *new formations* 6 (Winter, 1988), 49–63; Zohreh T. Sulllivan, *Narratives of Empire: The Fictions of Rudyard Kipling* (Cambridge: Cambridge University Press, 1993); and D. C. R. A. Goonetilleke, "Colonial Neuroses: Kipling and Forster," *Ariel* (1974), 56–68.
56. Kipling (2005), p. 113.
57. Ibid., p. 113–114.
58. Ibid., p. 114.
59. Ibid., p. 116.
60. Ibid., pp. 118–19.
61. Ibid., p. 120.

CHAPTER 5

....

ECOCRITICISM AND MODERNISM

....

ANNE RAINE

IF British ecocriticism began with a re-greening of Wordsworth, and American ecocriticism galvanized around a reclaiming of Thoreau as nature writer, one might expect an ecocritical account of literary modernism to begin with Harriet Monroe.[1]

Best known as the founding editor of *Poetry: A Magazine of Verse*, Monroe was also an advocate for wilderness preservation; like Wordsworth, whose 1835 *Guide to the District of the Lakes* ends with a call to preserve natural beauty as "a sort of national property," and Thoreau, whose declaration that "in wildness is the preservation of the world" became a Sierra Club rallying cry, Monroe merits a mention in conservation history, and her connections with influential conservationists form an intriguing link between literary modernism and environmental activism. A few years before she founded *Poetry* in 1912, Monroe hiked the Sierras with John Muir and participated in his famous campaign to save the Hetch Hetchy Valley; a few years later she spoke in support of a proposed Indiana Sand Dunes National Park at a hearing organized by National Park Service director Stephen T. Mather, who was also an early supporter of *Poetry*.[2] And like Muir, who saw the growth of nature tourism as a "a hopeful sign of the times" (1) Monroe viewed nature parks as *modern*: she called nature preservation "the most important... spiritual and aesthetic enterprise of our time," and even declared Nature "the ultimate modern*ist*," whose untrammeled grandeur would incite American poets to knock down the "walls and roofs" of literary convention ("Back to Nature" 330, "Renewal" 322–23, emphasis added). These activities suggest that nature conservation was a significant element of popular modernity overlooked by modernist scholars and that appreciation of and concern for the natural world may be more central to literary modernism than critics have recognized.

However, it might also be said that Monroe's commitment to nature was unusual among modernists, and perhaps not unrelated to her failure to qualify as properly modern in the eyes of the "men of 1914" and later critics. Despite her view of nature as modernist, Monroe's own nature poems tend to exemplify the conventionality, sentimentality, and vague notions of "the infinite" that T. E. Hulme and Ezra Pound sought to banish from modern poetry.[3] Moreover, the very terms she used to assert poetry's value to modern readers ironically suggest that both poetry and nature are out of step with modernity. Echoing the language of wilderness preservation, she argues in *Poetry*'s inaugural issue that the modern world has "immediate and desperate need" of poetry, but also that poetry is something "rare and delicate" that threatens to be "overpowered, lost in the criss-cross of modern currents, the confusion of modern immensities" as "the world grows greater day by day, as every member of it, through something he buys or knows or loves, reaches out to the ends of the earth" ("Motive" 26). Against the global expansion of modern networks of transportation, communication, and commodity exchange, *Poetry* would serve as a kind of literary national park, "a place of refuge…where Beauty may plant her gardens, and Truth…may follow her brave quest unafraid" ("Motive" 28). This rhetorical linking of poetry with endangered nature differs dramatically from Wyndham Lewis's assertion in *Blast* two years later that modern art thrives not in the wilderness but in the machine-made second nature of the industrial age. Reversing Monroe's claim that America's wild nature would inspire modernist art, Lewis declares England an ideal site for artistic innovation because its technology has made nature obsolete (39, 41). English technology, he writes, has "reared up steel trees where the green ones were lacking[,]…exploded in useful growths, and found wilder intricacies than those of Nature" (38). England does not lack "the complication of the Jungle, dramatic tropic growths, [or] the vastness of American trees," since "in the forms of machinery, factories, new and vaster buildings, bridges and works, we have all that, naturally, around us" (39–40). And since art "must be organic with its time," modern poetry must reject rhapsodic romanticism (which worships Nature) and "pedantic Realism" (which imitates nature) and participate in the technological reinvention of the world in all its "bareness and hardness" (36, 43, 41).[4]

If Lewis's manifesto can be taken as representative, it's no wonder ecocriticism has shown relatively little interest in modernism; for Lewis, modernism defines itself in opposition both to nature itself and to the two literary genres—realist prose and romantic nature poetry—that ecocritics tend to champion.[5] Of course, not all modernists shared Lewis's technophilic antinaturalism, but most did share his sense that neither romantic naturism nor reductive realism was adequate to the goals of modern art. Take, for example, the versions of modernist aesthetics proposed by Virginia Woolf and William Carlos Williams. For Woolf in "Modern Fiction" (1925), the "essential thing" that "refuses to be contained" in outmoded literary forms is not Nature, as it is for Monroe, but a less easily definable entity that Woolf provisionally calls "life or spirit, truth or reality"; and the task of her modern novelist is not, as in realist fiction, to depict the external world (whether social or natural) but to convey the interior movements of human consciousness (149–50). And while Williams's concern for "the truth of the object" suggests a more ecocentric form of modernism than Lewis's prometheanism or Woolf's subjectivism, he shares their suspicion of romantic and realist modes of representing nature. His dismissal of poetry as "a soft second light of dreaming," with its echo of Wordsworth's "emotion recollected in tranquility," implicates romantic poetry as part of the problem—especially since for Williams the "truth of the object" for which poetry should strive is not the truth of Nature but that of the poem as a made object whose vitality "is 'like' nothing" in the natural world (247). For both Woolf and Williams, the goal of modernist innovation is not greater fidelity to nature, as ecocritics would advocate, but rather a richer apprehension of human consciousness or the construction of aesthetic objects with their own autonomous life. This lack of interest in representing nature as such is also evident in Williams's suggestion, more modest than Lewis's polemic but still likely to trouble most ecocritics, that for modernist art there is no significant difference between natural objects and technological ones: "Make it and it *is* a poem. This is modern, not the saga. There are no sagas—only trees now, animals, engines" (247–48).

It's understandable, then, that engaging with modernism has not been a first priority for ecocriticism. Among ecocritical anthologies, Laurence Coupe's *Green Studies Reader* is unusual in marking the modernist period as significant for ecocritical scholarship; and while ecocritical work has been done on some modernist writers (such as Lawrence, Stevens, and Woolf) and some ecocritical studies include analysis of modernist texts, ecocritics have tended to focus on texts that address themselves more directly to environmental concerns.[6] Meanwhile, modernist scholars have largely ignored ecocriticism. While the new modernist studies has taken a more historical and materialist view of modernism, expanding the canon and situating modernist texts within a more diverse field of discourses and practices, even such revisionist accounts rarely consider nature or ecology as part of the field in which modernist texts participated.[7] Some efforts at dialogue between ecocriticism and modernist studies have been made: as early as 1998, Carol Cantrell argued in *ISLE* that key elements of modernism, such as its critique of Cartesian dualism and interest in embodied perception, are of vital interest to ecocritics, while in modernist studies Douglas Mao described modernism as "foundationally ecological" in its concern with material objects as "something like the synecdoche of endangered nature" (10, 8). More recently, Susan Stanford Friedman has urged modernist critics to replace Eurocentric definitions of modernity and modernism with a "planetary" perspective, one that involves both "a polylogue of languages, cultures, viewpoints, and standpoints on modernism/modernity" and "a consciousness of the earth as planet, not restricted to geopolitical formations and potentially encompassing the nonhuman as well as the human" (494, 495 n.5).[8] But critics are just beginning to work out what an ecocritical or planetary account of modernism might look like, or how exactly modernist texts might speak to ecocritical concerns.

Friedman's call for a planetary modernist studies parallels developments in ecocriticism, where postcolonial and environmental justice scholars have urged ecocritics to unsettle dominant Euro-American assumptions about nature by exploring the multiple, contested versions of nature and environmentalism that emerge out of particular histories in particular places.[9] In this context, it would be misguided to attempt a singular account of modernism's relevance to ecocriticism. Not only are there obvious differences between Monroe's, Lewis's, Woolf's, and Williams's versions of modernism, but a planetary approach requires expanding the archive to include other modernisms in other parts of the world; these white middle-class British and American writers need to be read in dialogue with other writers whose experiences of modernity and its effects on particular local ecologies were quite different because of their different posi-tions within global histories of conquest, colonization, and technological change. In addition to rereading modernist ecology through the work of postcolonial writers like Édouard Glissant, Tayeb Salih, and Arundhati Roy, as Friedman proposes, we might begin with the diasporic modernism of Zora Neale Hurston, which, as Rachel Stein and Keith Cartwright have shown, challenges realist and romantic discourses of nature and race by incorporating elements of the syncretic religions of the African diaspora. At the same time, I would argue that ecocriticism still has much to gain from a more sustained engagement with canonical British and American modernisms. In what follows, I will map out some of the approaches critics have taken to reading Anglo-American mod-ernism ecocritically and make some provisional generalizations about what we might learn by doing so.

Though I will discuss a range of perspectives, I'll begin with two general claims. First, modernist texts offer rich resources for ecocriticism because modernist writers were, as Cantrell puts it, self-conscious "witnesses to the profound changes in human rela-tions with the planet that ha[d] become visible in [their] century," sharing a sense of hav-ing experienced a "revolutionary change" in "the 'given' we call nature" (25, 26). Those changes have often been understood as a process in which nature recedes into the past or into the margins of modernity, destroyed or displaced by new technoscientific practices and by the large-scale changes to the material environment those practices enable: the growth of cities, suburbs, and factories; the proliferation of mechanical devices and mass-produced consumer goods; and the expansion of national and global networks of transportation, communication, and commodity exchange. But as Donna Haraway has argued, these changes can also be understood as new *productions* of nature, new articu-lations of relationships among human and nonhuman beings and phenomena (63–68, 86–89; Heise, "Hitchhiker's" 508). As Susan Hegeman and others have noted, the land-scape of modernity included not only the industrialized urban centres with which mod-ernism is most often associated but also the rural and regional spaces that provided laborers, agricultural products, raw materials, and tourist destinations for the urban centers, and that were also transformed by modernity even as they were constructed as modernity's backward, primitive, or Edenic other (Hegeman 22).[10] And as Monroe reminds us, modernity included not only new sciences and technologies but also nature education and tourism, campaigns for nature conservation, and other manifestations of the back-to-nature movement that has functioned as a repressed and feminized other to both modern science and modernist literary culture (see Raine). This is not to deny the catastrophic effects of industrial modernity on ecosystems and life forms, but simply to suggest that analysis and critique of those effects need not rely on a simple binary oppo-sition between modernity and nature.

One way to proceed, then, is to valorize Monroe's view of modernity and modern-ism over Lewis's anti-natural one and look for evidence that modernist writers were more engaged with nature, ecology, or environmentalism than critics have assumed. This might involve exploring how nature tourism, nature education programs, or other forms of popular nature discourse influenced modernist writers' work, as critics have done for Wallace Stevens, Ernest Hemingway, and Marianne Moore; exploring affinities between modernists like William Faulkner and conservationists like Aldo Leopold, as Judith Wittenberg and Lawrence Buell have done; or reassessing the impact on modernism of what John Parham calls the Victorian ecology of John Ruskin, William Morris, and Edward Carpenter.[11] We might draw on environmental history to deepen our analysis of how modernism responded not only to industrial capitalism's transformations of particular regional ecologies but also to the work of the many environmental management organizations founded in the modernist period.[12] We might also look for affinities between canonical modernists and more overtly "ecological" writers, as John Elder does in arguing that T. S. Eliot's *The Waste Land* and Robinson Jeffers's poems both present modern culture as corrupt "because it is cut off from nature's regenerative power" (16). By 1939, when desertification in the United States and some British colonies had put the issue of soil erosion "very much before the public eye," Eliot would lament that industrial capitalist "exploitation of the earth" had depleted natural resources while doing spiritual damage to humanity, adding that Lawrence's misguided attempt to "look at the world with the eyes of a Mexican Indian" could be excused as part of a necessary "struggle to recover the sense of relation to nature and to God" (48–49).[13] How this mixture of religious, social, and ecological concerns informs Eliot's late work, and whether it is implicit in his early poetry, merits further investigation, even if his social conservatism and privileging of spiritual over material concerns limit his relevance to today's ecopolitics. A more intriguing, if similarly problematic, example is that of Ezra Pound, whose shift from Imagism to Vorticism to the encyclopedic/paratactic poetics of the *Cantos* (1925–69) represents an important link between modernist nature discourse and contemporary ecopoetics that has yet to receive much ecocritical attention.[14] While Pound shared Hulme's disdain for sentimental nature poetry, his admiration for the nature writer W. H. Hudson is another under-explored link between literary modernism and popular nature discourse. Hugh Kenner makes another kind of link in his pre-ecocritical study *The Pound Era* (1971), which reads Pound's poetics as "ecological" by arguing that his sense of "our kinship to the vital universe" and his reconception of poetry as a structure of words in dynamic interaction were informed by modern science's reconception of nature as "patterned energy" (126, 146; Pound, *Spirit* 92). More recently but in a similar spirit, Jed Rasula cites Pound as a key figure in the emergence of a field of poetic practices that are ecological in both form and theme, animated by a "composting sensibility" that attends both to our participation in material ecologies and to how poems emerge in the decaying compost of past literary models (1–2, 18–19). Yet ecocritical readings of Pound also need to consider how his critique of industrial capitalism invokes a vision of natural order informed by American nativism and Italian fascism as well as by admiration for classical and Chinese culture.[15] The question of how to read Pound's interest in Hudson and his generative influence on ecopoetics in light of the troubling politics of his vision of nature is a complex and compelling one.

My second general claim is that many of the texts most often considered modernist—those that seek self-consciously to disrupt established literary conventions—are valuable for ecocriticism precisely because their responses to modernity involve a productive questioning of conventional ideas about nature. While they may not speak very directly to the concerns of nature-endorsing ecocritics, these texts anticipate recent efforts, by scholars such as William Cronon, Donna Haraway, Bruno Latour, Tim Ingold, Jane Bennett, Stacy Alaimo, and Timothy Morton, to develop forms of ecological discourse that complicate, critique, historicize, or abandon the concept of nature while taking serious account of the agency of nonhuman beings and phenomena.[16] Read in this light, modernism's resistance to romantic and realist nature discourse does not necessarily indicate a lack of interest in or concern about the more-than-human world and the place of humans within it. Rather, it often reflects a sense that accepted forms of nature discourse relied on reductive or anthropocentric habits of thought that were inadequate to convey the world's "multifarious otherness" and often complicit with the instrumental domination of nature or the naturalization of sexist, racist, or heteronormative accounts of human nature.[17] Faced with the strange new world being produced by modern technoscience, conservationists and nature writers drew on the traditions of romantic nature poetry and domestic realism to promote a vision of nature as a transcendent source of aesthetic, spiritual, or moral value.[18] In contrast, while modernists were also interested in the nonhuman and concerned about modernity's socioecological effects, they used innovative formal strategies to disrupt, defamiliarize, distance themselves from, or imagine alternatives to conventional constructions of nature and human nature. Consequently, reading modernism ecocritically requires different strategies than reading more straightforward representations of or polemics about nature. In addition to showing how modernist texts participate in emerging discourses of nature, we also need to attend to the ways in which they resist assimilation into those discourses, since that resistance is a significant part of modernism's contribution to ecocritical inquiry.

Bart Eeckhout offers a thoughtful discussion of this issue in a recent article on Wallace Stevens that responds to Gyorgyi Voros's reading of Stevens in *Notations of the Wild*. For Voros, Stevens's poetry is ecological in the sense that it anticipates deep ecology's critique of anthropocentric humanism and reverence for "the immediacy and profound presence of earth itself" as a living whole of which humans are only a part (6, 18, 82). While others have read Stevens as concerned with material nature, Voros's innovation lies in situating his poetic meditations within the environmentalist tradition that links early wilderness advocates like Muir and Monroe with 1960s environmentalists like Gary Snyder and Arne Naess. In addition to comparing Stevens's work with that of Martin Heidegger and the deep ecologists, Voros uses biographical sources to argue that his poetry was profoundly informed by his encounter with the earth's "rough enormity" during a 1903 hunting trip in the Canadian Rockies (7, 44–45). By documenting his participation in discourses of nature tourism and wilderness appreciation more often associated with nature writers like Muir, this reading of Stevens seems to substantiate Monroe's claim that contact with wild nature would be vital to American modernism.

In Eeckhout's view, however, Voros tends to downplay the "resistance" Stevens's poems set up—the "complexities, contradictions, and multiple layers" that reflect a modernist impulse not so much to promote a particular vision of nature as to unsettle the terms in which nature is understood (174). Taking as a case study Stevens's "Earthy Anecdote" (1923), Eeckhout also begins with a biographical event—here, a 1916 business trip that included a stop in Oklahoma—and asks how it might inform this cryptic poem about "bucks...clattering/Over Oklahoma" and meeting a predatory "firecat" (179–80). But he also emphasizes how the poem prompts us to ask what exactly "earthy" means here and whether it actually conforms to the vision of Nature Voros finds in Stevens's work. For Eeckhout, even if we read the poem naturalistically, its deadpan presentation of the repetitive violence of predator–prey relationships undercuts the "essentially religious ideal of natural harmony and unity" that informs both the nature writing of Stevens's day and Voros's deep ecology-inspired ecocriticism (182). Moreover, despite Stevens's own insistence that the poem deals with "actual animals," its stylized quality, along with the odd verb "clattering" and the apparently invented term "firecat," works against a naturalistic reading. One of Eeckhout's most illuminating claims is that Stevens's use of "nonverbal sounds and symmetrically stylized movement" to portray his animal protagonists was probably inspired by the avant-garde performances of the *Ballets Russes* and thus owes as much to cosmopolitan modernism as to any encounter with Oklahoma wildlife (185–86). Yet as he also notes, the *Ballets Russes* as a formal model links the poem to a form of art that sought to transpose to a modern idiom a sense of embodied connection to the soil associated with Russian folk dance—in which case the poem's stylized patterns, which seem too self-consciously artificial to work as a realistic portrayal of animal behavior, might after all enact an oblique meditation on the bodily rhythms that link humans with the rest of nature. At the same time, the enigmatic firecat—a creature that exists only in this poem—seems to embody either the poetic imagination in its fierce resistance to quotidian reality or poetic language in its resistance to interpretive closure—including, of course, closure in the form of any particular lesson about or vision of nature (183).

As Eeckhout goes on to show, his reading of the poem's resistance to interpretive closure is compatible with Voros's claim that Stevens values Nature's resistance to human concepts, and both agree that Stevens's work challenges anthropocentric humanism and romantic notions of lyric agency. But where Voros argues that Stevens belongs in the tradition of environmentalist thought and practice that ecocritics seek to valorize,[19] Eeckhout emphasizes how the antirealist elements of his poetry unsettle some of the ecological ideas that that tradition affirms, such as the view of Nature as "unmediated, authentic, and whole" (Voros 7). What his argument shows is that reading modernism ecocritically can be richly productive, but in ways that may challenge us to reexamine or historicize some of the assumptions about nature or ecology we bring to our analysis. In addition, his discussion of the allusion to the *Ballets Russes*, and by extension the anthropological theories of rhythm, embodiment, and culture that inform modern dance,[20] suggests that while situating modernist writers in relation to the tradition of nature writing and environmentalist discourse is an important task, modernist texts also challenge us to investigate other discourses—social, aesthetic, scientific, or theoretical—that informed modernist writers' rethinking of nature, or that enable us retrospectively to recognize and understand them as such.

Responses to these challenges can be grouped into two broad categories. The first reads modernism as a continuation of the romantic reaction against Enlightenment rationality and faith in technoscientific progress, often by exploring its affinities with the work of philosophers like Heidegger, Theodor Adorno, or Maurice Merleau-Ponty. In this view, modernist writers, despite their rejection of some aspects of romanticism, shared with their romantic predecessors a desire to resist the technoscientific objectification and instrumentalization of nature. Modernist formal experimentation can thus be read as an effort to devise new artistic practices that disrupt or suspend the tendency of scientific and common-sense realism, and some forms of romanticism, to subordinate nonhuman phenomena to human concepts and values. The second approach draws more on science studies and posthumanism than phenomenology or negative aesthetics, and foregrounds the ways in which modernism was actively engaged with, rather than primarily resistant to, the sciences of its time.[21] In this view, modernist experiments in literary form aimed not so much to convey nature's irreducibility to scientific concepts as to build on the ways in which new sciences such as evolutionary biology and post-Newtonian physics—and new work in philosophy that responded to those sciences, such as Friedrich Nietzsche's and Henri Bergson's critiques of Enlightenment humanist notions of selfhood—were disrupting previous assumptions about human and nonhuman nature and offering intriguing new ways of imagining the more-than-human world. What the science-skeptical and science-inspired versions of modernist ecology share is a sense that conventional conceptions of nature were inadequate or problematic, and that a more satisfactory apprehension of things might require thinking and writing in ways that seemed unrealistic or even unnatural.

Paul Saunders offers a useful account of the science-skeptical position in his reading of Samuel Beckett's *Trilogy* (1951–53), which he sees as paradigmatic of a modernist ecology that views "the conventions of realism and the common sense view of nature it supports" as complicit with the instrumental domination of nature (54–55). Drawing on Adorno and Herbert Marcuse, Saunders argues that unlike ecocritics who view realist nature writing as the best way to foster ecological awareness, Beckett sees scientific and common-sense realism as part of the problem: by organizing the "undifferentiated substratum" of "nature-being" into intelligible and useful forms, they prevent us from apprehending nature as anything other than a reflection of human concepts and needs (55, 56). Ecological consciousness, then, requires an "enabling ignorance" embodied by the abject figure of Molloy, who has privileged access to nature-being because he is unable to share in the assumptions and habits that "distinguish forms from the formlessness that underlies them" and shape the "spray of phenomena" into both the order of nature as disclosed by science and the ordered fabric of common-sense nature (57, 58, 60). Ironically, Saunders notes, this openness puts Molloy outside the natural order; as Molloy puts it, he is "not natural enough to enter into that order," to apprehend his surroundings as the recognizable objects of realist discourse, so his narrative can only appear unrealistic and unnatural (58). In contrast, the instrumental ordering of nature is represented by Jacques Moran, a bourgeois character whose approval of botany and skill at "capturing his environment in reports" are linked to a desire for mastery (62).

Yet after getting lost in "Molloy country," Moran stops "trying to understand and dominate" and resolves to " 'let things be,' " repudiating realist description so that, rather than "imprison[ing] the birds in the language of his past reports," he can "attune himself to their language" and "find a new language with which to speak of them" (59, 61, 62). For Beckett, Saunders concludes, modernist antirealism is more ecological than realism's effort to depict nature accurately, because it seeks to avoid subordinating nature to human categories (62).

As Saunders notes, Moran's effort to "let things be" recalls the Heideggerian ecopoetics valorized by Voros and Jonathan Bate, who find in Stevens's poetry a "wise passiveness" or "openness to being," a form of *poiesis* that "permit[s] Nature to reveal itself on its own terms" (Saunders 58; Bate, *Song* 278, 268, 117–18; Voros 86). But if both Stevens and Beckett seek new literary forms that resist the technological enframing of nature, there is a difference between the Heideggerian ecopoetics of redemption that Bate and Voros find in Stevens and the Adornian/ Marcusian negative ecology Saunders finds in Beckett. As Kate Rigby puts it, an ecopoetics of redemption aims not to depict nature's outward forms but to restore a sense of wonder at the "enduring strangeness" of things and thereby "call us into a respectful relationship with an ultimately ungraspable earth" (116–18). But for Rigby Heideggerian ecopoetics, despite its emphasis on earth's unknowability, risks overestimating the capacity of poetic language to "give voice to the song of the earth" (122–3). In contrast, Saunders finds a more promising model in Moran's attempt at what Rigby calls an ecopoetics of negativity: a narrative that foregrounds its own artificiality and inability to represent the nonhuman and thereby "protects the otherness of the earth" from realism's claim to capture it in words (119). In his reading of the rest of the *Trilogy*, Saunders argues that a key aspect of Beckett's negative ecology is its acknowledgement that even if it were possible to invent a language that could "let [nature-being] itself speak," its efficacy would be limited, since it would be unrecognizable in scientific or common-sense terms and unable to "spell out manifestos or engage in environmental politics" without recourse to the realist discourse it repudiates (68, 73). Partly because of this self-critique, he concludes, modernist ecology is a valuable complement to realist ecocriticism, since it pushes us to continually "question the concepts that would guide any environmentalist project" and seek new forms in which to articulate what remains irreducible to existing concepts (72).

Douglas Mao's *Solid Objects: Modernism and the Test of Production* (1998) also defines modernist ecology in terms of its affinities with Heideggerian and Frankfurt School critiques of instrumental reason. As noted above, Mao reads modernism as "foundationally ecological" in that it seeks to preserve the radical alterity of the object *as* object, to apprehend material objects in their irreducibility to either symbols or commodities for human consumption (10–11, 22). While Mao's work does not engage with the scientific or activist conceptions of ecology that ecocritics tend to favor, his focus on objects and production rather than nature and science is useful because it helps define the historical specificity of modernist ecology as distinct from romantic ecology. Mao argues that a defining feature of modernism is its concern with objects rather than nature and reads this concern as a form of resistance not just to the enframing of nature by

Enlightenment science but specifically to the nineteenth- and twentieth-century expansion of industrial production and consumer culture.[22] For Mao, modernism's focus on objects rather than nature is also an ambivalent response not only to the subjectivism and moralism of romantic naturism but also to nineteenth-century aestheticism, which valorized consumption in such forms as Walter Pater's "sheer experience of the fleeting present" or Oscar Wilde's "self-realization through flamboyant acquisition," and was associated with homosexuality, effeminacy, neurasthenia, and degeneracy just as romantic naturism was associated with feminine sentimentality (18). Modernist writers, he argues, sought to distance themselves from these associations by defining their art in terms of production rather than consumption, the crafting of aesthetic objects rather than mere absorbing of impressions; yet production was also suspect because of its association with industrial capitalism's increasingly large-scale transformations of the planet (19). Hence modernists like Woolf, Pound, Lewis, and Stevens did not unambivalently embrace the "wise passiveness" advocated by ecocritics, but were torn "between an urgent validation of production and an admiration for an object world beyond the manipulations of consciousness" (11).[23]

Another way to read modernism as a form of romantic resistance to instrumental reason is to explore its affinities with Merleau-Ponty's phenomenology, as Carol Cantrell and Louise Westling do in their essays on Woolf's *Between the Acts* (1941). In contrast to Saunders and Mao, for whom modernist formal experimentation is ecological because it seeks to preserve the alterity of the nonhuman, Cantrell considers modernist experimentation ecological because it seeks to convey the "involvement of the perceiver within what is perceived" and thus foregrounds the interconnectedness of human and nonhuman beings and phenomena (26). In this view, the best resource for reading modernism ecocritically is not Heidegger or Adorno but Merleau-Ponty: in contrast to both the Cartesian model of scientific reason and the romantic valorization of nature's alterity, both of which posit a human subject detached from the world it perceives, Merleau-Ponty asserts that perception and language arise from the "continuity between our bodies and the world" and that knowledge involves not a predatory instrumentality but a process of "reciprocal exchange between multiple centers of perception" (Cantrell 27, 28). Similarly, for Cantrell and Westling, *Between the Acts* offers an embodied, dialogic vision of "interactions among multiple lives and life-processes" in which the social world "is not only human but collaborates within the much larger matrix of earthy life and energy" (Cantrell 33; Westling, "Virginia Woolf" 868). Rather than the romantic figure of a lone human observer confronting a monolithic Nature, Woolf uses multiple narrative voices to convey how different perceivers apprehend the phenomenal world in negotiation with others and how birds, trees, cows, wind, and rain participate in the same "weave of information in which the multiple modes of human language participate"; and by presenting human speech as an embodied, rhythmic "process in itself" as well as a "vehicle for transporting thought," she further unsettles the boundary between humans and natural phenomena, in keeping with Merleau-Ponty's view that language "belongs not only to the animal community but to the whole of the natural world" (Cantrell 35; Westling 866). Whether this participatory vision is also evident in the work of Faulkner, Gertrude Stein, or other modernists who shared Merleau-Ponty's interest in the nonconceptual aspects of perception and language is another question for further investigation—as is the question of how Merleau-Ponty's aesthetics and ethics of embodied perception might inform or complement more political approaches to socio-ecological thought and practice.

I've grouped the Merleau-Pontyan approach among the critical strategies that read modernist ecology as a form of late romantic resistance to Enlightenment technoscience because it challenges the Cartesian model of scientific reason and valorizes the aesthetic, qualitative, and organic over the rational, quantitative, and mechanistic. However, the Merleau-Pontyan approach also belongs in the second group of critical strategies: those that read modernist ecology as engaged with, rather than skeptical of, the new sciences that emerged at the turn of the twentieth century. As Westling argues, Woolf's and Merleau-Ponty's rethinking of the relations between mind and world involved a critique of Cartesian–Newtonian science, but one that was informed by the new physics of relativity and quantum mechanics, which also challenged scientific objectivity by including the observer within the field of inquiry (856). Woolf's and Merleau-Ponty's interest in embodied perception was also part of a larger rethinking of nature and human nature emerging out of Darwinian biology that included the newly material models of consciousness in the psychology and philosophy of William James and Henri Bergson. As Jeff Wallace has argued, even D. H. Lawrence's famous denunciation of science's "reduction of life to mechanism" was not so much a wholesale rejection of science as a complex engagement with new questions biological scientists were raising about the evolution of mind from matter and the human place in nature (6, 17). These examples suggest that reading modernism ecocritically calls for a more nuanced and historical account of science. Rather than viewing science as a monolithic force that always works to support technological domination (as Heideggerian and Frankfurt School accounts often do) or to naturalize dominant social ideologies (as some Foucauldian readings assume)—or, conversely, simply valorizing science's authority to reveal the facts about nature (as some ecocritics do to support ecopolitical claims) we can draw on the work of science studies scholars like Haraway and Bruno Latour to view the sciences as a heterogeneous field of competing ideas and practices that change over time, which can facilitate technological and social domination but can also foster respect for nonhuman beings and phenomena, enable critique of the ecological effects of human activities, or unsettle dominant conceptions of nature and human nature.[24] This perspective can help us to see how for some modernist writers, new scientific discourses offered intriguing alternatives to the anthropocentric humanism that often underlies both romantic and common-sense realist discourses of nature.

Another important ecocritical task, then, is to situate modernist investigations of the more-than-human world in relation to the history of the sciences as well as the history of popular nature discourse. One obvious example of a science that does not simply support technological domination is ecology, which ecologist Paul Sears and environmentalist Paul Shepard designated a "subversive science" in the 1960s because it challenged anthropocentrism and involved critical assessment of how humans affect ecosystems.

Since literary modernism coincides historically with the emergence of ecology as a science, critics like Christina Alt and Leonard Scigaj have begun to look for evidence that modernist writers like Woolf and Muriel Rukeyser took an interest in ecology as well as in other sciences more familiar to modernist critics. Here we might also recall Kenner's claim that Pound was influenced by ecology or at least by a kind of ecological zeitgeist. As Alt reminds us, however, we need to attend to the historical specificity of early twentieth-century ecology rather than assuming that it shared all the premises of later ecological science, let alone those of the postwar ecology movement that shaped the values of late twentieth-century ecocritics (8–10).[25] Ecocritics can also build on the extensive scholarship on modernist responses to Darwin and Darwinism. One important example is Robin Schulze's work on Marianne Moore, which documents Moore's engagement with contemporary debates in evolutionary biology and shows how her poetry draws on those debates to celebrate the diversity of nonhuman life, to reflect critically on "human use and misuse of the natural world," and to enact a Darwinian conception of artistic production as "endless adaptive process" ("Marianne Moore's" 5; "Textual" 288).

    I will conclude with three critical studies that show how some forms of modernist ecology drew on new scientific discourses to complicate or critique dominant conceptions of nature and human nature, and thus anticipate current efforts to move from nature-centered to posthuman, postnatural, or queer ecology. As noted above, Jeff Wallace argues in *D. H. Lawrence, Science and the Posthuman* (2005) that while Lawrence seems to be in the romantic anti-science camp, a more nuanced account enables us to view modern science as "a *source* of Lawrentian reverence and wonder for 'life' rather than an obstacle to it" and to find affinities between Lawrence's post-Darwinian materialism and contemporary posthumanism's questioning of boundaries between humans, animals, and machines (102, 6). For Wallace, Lawrence's apparent rejection of science was in fact a critical engagement with the ways in which, far from simply reducing human life to quantifiable data, modern biological science was raising profound questions about "what it meant to *be* human" and about "the position and meaning of the human intellect within the natural order" (23–24, 18). If some Darwinians, such as Herbert Spencer, found in evolutionary accounts of mind emerging from matter a progressive narrative that justified existing forms of domination by reinforcing the faith in human superiority over other animals, others, such as Bergson, found in the Darwinian view of mind as "thinking matter" a challenge to basic tenets of Enlightenment humanism (11–13).[26] As Wallace notes, it is well known that Lawrence "drew from a tradition of materialist and evolutionary thought which emphasized human kinship with 'nature,'" but less often acknowledged is the fact that this same tradition could also recognize "kinship with inorganic matter, and therefore by possible extension with mechanism and technology," as in Bergson's reconception of life as "a 'temporary articulation of the body, brain, nervous system and environment'" in which "the *integrity* of the self on traditional humanist lines is radically undermined" (6, 111). In this context, what critics have read as Lawrence's defense of the natural, organic, and "essentially human" against the "deathly mechanism" of science can be viewed as a struggle to "break free of a language of the human" that parallels the effort of later thinkers like Haraway, N. Katherine Hayles, Humberto Maturana and Francisco Varela, or Deleuze and Guattari to theorize the interrelations of human, animal, and machine without relying on "hypostatized differences of inside and outside, subject and object, organic and inorganic, nature and culture" (107, 104).

Steven Meyer offers another thought-provoking account of a science-inspired modernist ecology in *Irresistible Dictation: Gertrude Stein and the Correlations of Writing and Science* (2001). While it does not address ecocritical concerns directly, Meyer's book is valuable for ecocriticism because it shows how Stein's antirealist writing, which seems to abandon nature for an artificial world of art, can be read as an investigation of new ways of understanding entities and environments that rejects both the mechanistic and deterministic assumptions of positivist science and the Coleridgean notions of organic unity that inform humanist conceptions of nature, the self, and the work of art (4–5, 106). In a suggestive pre-ecocritical study, Harriet Chessman reads Stein's landscape writing as a form of negative ecopoetics that, by foregrounding its own status as words on a page, leaves the natural world free of human naming (133–34).[27] In contrast to this emphasis on a gap between language and material nature, Meyer reads Stein's literary experiments as a form of materialist inquiry that experiments with a new kind of organicism informed by her training in physiological psychology. In the 1890s, when Stein studied psychology with William James and brain anatomy at Johns Hopkins Medical School, neuroscientists were proposing that nerve cells are not part of a continuous network but interrelated through "contact or contiguity rather than organic connection" (80). Similarly, the words in Stein's experimental texts function as discrete entities that interact with contiguous words to form units whose form and meaning are not predetermined by any organic unity or transcendent organizing principle (111). Attending to Stein's scientific training enables Meyer to show how her writing explores language and consciousness as processes that are thoroughly material, but autopoietic rather than deterministic (72–73, 124–28). In this sense, he argues, Stein's work resonates with her friend Alfred North Whitehead's efforts to replace subject/object dualism with a new ontology of process and event, as well as with the experiments of romantic "poet-scientists" like Wordsworth and Shelley and the efforts of later thinkers like Haraway and Varela to reconceptualize relations among entities and environments as processes in which entities are neither wholly independent of their environments (as in Cartesian models of the self) nor wholly determined by them (as in some forms of Darwinism). Meyer thus shows how physiological psychology offered Stein a more open-ended alternative to established ways of thinking about mind and nature and demonstrates how a science studies approach, combined with attention to questions of form, can help reveal the ecological implications of experimental modernist texts that do not seek to represent nor advocate for nature.

My final example is Cate Mortimer-Sandilands's queer-ecological reading of Radcliffe Hall's *The Well of Loneliness* (1928), which I categorize as a science-inspired approach because it shows how Hall drew on the scientific discourse of sexology to disrupt the normative vision of nature underlying the neopastoral landscape preservation movement that was integral to British modernity (38). Like Molloy in Beckett's *Trilogy*, who has privileged access to nature-being because he is incapable of participating in the natural order of consensus reality, Stephen in *The Well of Loneliness* has special insight into the natural order because she is exiled from it—not because of an "enabling ignorance," but because of her "inverted" sexuality and identification with her father's rather than her mother's relationship to nature. As Sandilands notes, Hall's novel does not challenge conventional nature discourse through experiments with literary form; unlike Molloy, Stephen is as capable of functioning within the familiar nature of common-sense realism as she is of emulating her father's orderly and possessive relationship with his land and animals, and this is reflected in the way Hall tells her story. However, the novel is modernist in that it portrays Stephen's move to London and Paris as a passage from "home, nature[,] aristocratic ritual," and traditional heterosexuality to the "urbanity, enlightenment, ... individual creativity" and queer sexuality that are markers of a "decidedly modern subjectivity" (38). While this seems to posit a binary opposition between modernity and nature, Sandilands shows how Hall complicates that binary, presenting Stephen as an exemplary modern "nature-subject" precisely insofar as her sexual and geographical exile from nature gives her a "privileged vantage point for reflection on the moral landscape of the English countryside" (37). Moreover, while Hall's valorization of Stephen as cosmopolitan queer modernist might seem to echo nineteenth-century aestheticism's oppositional championing of the unnatural and artificial,[28] Sandilands emphasizes that Hall draws on Havelock Ellis's view of sexual inversion as a congenital—that is, biological—condition to present Stephen's "unnatural" identity as, in fact, natural—even "a facet of the same *noble* nature" that legitimates class privilege and heterosexuality and "appears to exclude the invert" (39). Sandilands thus shows how Hall finds in sexology an alternative discourse of nature with which to resist, or at least to complicate, the heteronormative nature of modern neopastoralism and wilderness appreciation.[29] As Sandilands notes, it's not entirely clear how such queer ecological critique might speak to ecocriticism's concern with our responsibility to nonhuman life forms, but her reading raises important questions about how we might put these different concerns in dialogue. It also suggests that one important area for future investigation is the connection between modernism's interest in queer sexualities and the resistance to realist and romantic nature that has made modernist texts seem unlikely subjects for ecocritical analysis.[30]

Clearly, modernist literature offers rich resources for ecocriticism, and ecocriticism's growing interest in historicizing, complicating, or moving beyond the concept of nature offers theoretical means appropriate for interpreting modernism's resistance to romantic nature anew. In conclusion, I would underscore two things: first, that reading modernism ecocritically requires careful attention to how modernism's adaptation or disruption of conventional literary forms contributes to its particular modes of ecological inquiry and critique; and second, that we need to develop a richer, more complex, and more thoroughly historicized understanding of literary modernism's relationship to romanticism, to the sciences, and to various forms of popular nature discourse. While some have called for an ecology without nature, and many of the critics I've discussed suggest that many forms of modernism are best understood using a theoretical language that does not rely on the nature/culture distinction, I would still argue, with Haraway, that nature remains a problematic but inescapable term for ecocriticism—if only because, as Harriet Monroe and many other modernists insisted, nature was integral to modernity and remained a potent, if problematic and contested, concept in modernist literature as well.

Notes

1. See Bate, *Romantic Ecology*, and Buell, *The Environmental Imagination*.
2. On Monroe's Sierra Club activities, see Schulze, "Harriet Monroe's Pioneer Modernism," and Righter 75–95. Monroe's speech on behalf of the Indiana Sand Dunes National Park is reprinted in Stephen T. Mather, *Report on the proposed Sand Dunes National Park, Indiana* (Washington: Government Printing Office, 1917), 80–81; Mather's name appears on the list of supporters of *Poetry* beginning with the September 1914 issue, the first issue that lists subscribers and donors at the back of the magazine. Both Monroe and Mather were invited to the inaugural meeting of the Illinois conservation group Friends of Our Native Landscape in 1913 (Grese 122–24).
3. A case in point is Monroe's poem "Now: Yosemite Valley," a fairly unconvincing attempt to translate into verse what Monroe called John Muir's "dithyrambic paean of praise, which flowed on as grandly as the great white waters besides us" (Monroe, "John Muir," n.p.). Modernist poet-critics were not alone in their impatience with this kind of nature writing; one journalist observed that the Hetch Hetchy hearings had "turned to 'a lot of talk about babbling brooks and crystal pools,'" and that "[n]othing much could be done until 'the New England nature lovers exhaust their vocabularies'" (Righter 78).
4. It should be noted that when Lewis uses the terms "romantic and sentimental" in this manifesto, he is referring not to romantic nature-worshipers but to the Italian Futurists' worship of machines. Clearly, however, he regarded nature-worshiping romantics with equal disdain.
5. As Kate Rigby has shown, romanticism itself involved complex and diverse attitudes toward and understandings of the more-than-human world, complexities that are compounded by the addition of American romanticism as another important influence on early twentieth-century environmental and modernist thought. Arguments about modernism's relationship to romanticism thus cannot avoid some oversimplification, and differ considerably depending on which writers and texts are taken as representative. In this essay I use "romantic" to refer not only to the work of the romantic writers themselves but also to the popular romanticism of late nineteenth- and early twentieth-century nature discourse, which was inspired by the "Lake Poets" and/or the Transcendentalists but often did not do justice to their complexity.
6. Jonathan Bate's *The Song of the Earth* includes a chapter on Stevens, and Lawrence Buell discusses Woolf, Williams, Joyce, and Faulkner in *Writing for an Endangered World*. Louise Westling focuses on American modernist fiction in *The Green Breast of the New World*.
7. There are few if any references to environmental issues in Michael North's influential *Reading 1922*, and no chapters on nature, ecology, or environment in handbooks such as *The Cambridge Companion to Modernism* (1999), *The Cambridge Companion to American*

Modernism (2005), Wiley-Blackwell's *A Companion to Modernist Literature and Culture* (2006), or the otherwise comprehensive new *Oxford Handbook of Modernisms* (2010). Two recent exceptions are Eysteinsson and Liska's *Modernism*, which includes a chapter on "Modernism and Ecological Criticism," and Stephen Ross's *Modernism and Theory*, which includes a chapter proposing "Green" theory as an important future direction for modernist studies.

8. Friedman's notion of planetarity derives from transnational studies but invokes ecocriticism in citing Ursula Heise's notion of eco-cosmopolitanism as a way to think about how various human modernities have intersected with "the earth's nonhuman species, diversities, and cosmic rhythms" (493; see Heise, *Sense of Place*).

9. See, for example, Di Chiro, Guha and Martinez-Alier, and Huggan and Tiffin.

10. Hegeman focuses on how uneven development shapes the modern landscape in the United States. On the production of rural spaces as part of the landscape of modernity in Britain, see Matless.

11. On Stevens, see Voros; on Hemingway, see Beegel; on Moore and popular nature discourse the literature is extensive, but see especially Paul and Ladino. Buell's discussion of Faulkner and Leopold appears in *Writing for an Endangered World* (170–94).

12. These include the U.S. National Park Service (1916), the Regional Planning Association of America (1923), the Civilian Conservation Corps (1933), and in Britain the National Trust (1895), the Garden Cities Association (1899), and the Council for the Preservation of Rural England (1926).

13. On the increased awareness of soil erosion in late 1930s Britain to which Eliot refers, see Hodge 161–62.

14. For a brief introduction to questions of nature and ecology in Pound, see MacPhail.

15. See Bush 76–77. For a sympathetic ecocritical reading of Pound, see Fiedorczuk. Bush reads any invocation of nature by Pound or his admirers as ideological mystification, thus foreclosing any consideration of ecological concerns; yet the political and interpretive questions he raises are important ones that future ecocritical readings need to address.

16. The terms "nature-endorsing" and "nature-skeptical" are Kate Soper's (33–34).

17. I borrow this phrase from Hugh Kenner, who uses it in a different context (*Homemade* 114).

18. On the influence of domestic fiction on late nineteenth- and early twentieth-century nature writing, see Buell, *The Environmental Imagination*, and Dunlap.

19. I have in mind here Buell's critique of the tendency of American literary history to marginalize environmental nonfiction other than Thoreau's and to situate Thoreau within a literary canon rather than a tradition of American nature writing and environmentalism (*Environmental Imagination* 8–10).

20. See Schwartz.

21. Though modernist writers' interest in science was often motivated by a desire to distance themselves from the feminized romanticism of popular nature discourse, it too can be seen as a continuation of romanticism, since as Kate Rigby and Mark Lussier have emphasized, the romantics were also engaged with the sciences of their day, and were hostile not to science per se but specifically to "the dualistic and mechanistic assumptions of Cartesian-Newtonian science" and its inability to account for "the mind's engagement with, and emergence within, material reality" (Rigby 5; Lussier 18).

22. Timothy Morton dates the rise of consumer culture to the expansion of global trade in the romantic period, and reads twentieth-century nature writing and environmentalism as a continuation of romantic consumerism (82, 92–3, 110–15). I would add that ecocriticism

also needs to attend to the historical differences between romantic consumerism in the early nineteenth-century and industrialized commodity culture at the turn of the twentieth.

23. Rigby finds a similar tension in romanticism between an "avant garde" strain that valorizes "the human mind and its powers of creation" and a "redemptive" strain that emphasizes "piety, respect, and obligation toward the world" (115).

24. On ecocriticism's invocation of science, see Love and Phillips, who both argue that ecocritics need to be more scientifically literate but disagree on what such literacy would entail. Latour and Haraway share ecocritics' view that science can play a powerful role in ecological critique, but they also emphasize the need to historicize and politicize scientific knowledge by examining the particular historical conditions and social and technological practices that enable the production and consolidation of particular scientific facts.

25. For a useful brief discussion of the distinction between ecology as a science and ecology as a popular movement, see the introduction to Keller and Golley, eds., *The Philosophy of Ecology*. Ecocritics most often get their history of ecology from Donald Worster's landmark history of ecological ideas, but see also Golley, Anker, and Bowler.

26. The idea that evolutionary science could enable a critique of anthropocentrism or a sense of kinship with other animals is not new to ecocriticism; in addition to Love's argument for the importance of evolutionary science to ecocriticism, see, for example, Nash, and the "Darwinian Landscapes" chapter of Alaimo, *Undomesticated Ground*.

27. In Chessman's view, the particular target of Stein's negative ecology is Emersonian romanticism. See also DeKoven, who suggests in a footnote to her influential feminist study of Stein that Stein's landscape writing can be read as proto-ecofeminist (169 n. 29).

28. Recent work on Wilde's engagement with Spencerian biology suggests that aestheticism's antinaturalism itself may anticipate modernist ecology in using the sciences to resist or critique conventional discourses of nature (see Gordon).

29. Not only is the wilderness important to Hall's novel (Stephen embraces urban exile so that Mary can embrace heterosexual union with Martin in the wilds of British Columbia), but Sandilands also notes that both Ellis and the socialist and gay advocate Edward Carpenter suggested a possible connection between homosexuality and appreciation for wild nature (48–50 and 57–58 n.71).

30. For a useful account of the tension between queer studies and ecocriticism, see Azzarello.

WORKS CITED

Alaimo, Stacy. *Undomesticated Ground: Recasting Nature as Feminist Space*. Ithaca: Cornell UP, 2000.

Alaimo, Stacy. *Bodily Natures: Science, Environment, and the Material Self*. Bloomington: Indiana UP, 2010.

Alt, Christina. *Virginia Woolf and the Study of Nature*. Cambridge: Cambridge UP, 2010.

Anker, Peder. *Imperial Ecology: Environmental Order in the British Empire, 1895–1945*. Cambridge, MA: Harvard UP, 2001.

Azzarello, Robert. *Queer Environmentality: Ecology, Evolution, and Sexuality in American Literature*. Farnham: Ashgate, 2012.

Bate, Jonathan. *Romantic Ecology: Wordsworth and the Environmental Tradition*. London: Routledge, 1991.

——. *The Song of the Earth*. London: Picador-Macmillan, 2000.

Beegel, Susan F. "Eye and Heart: Hemingway's Education as a Naturalist". *A Historical Guide to Ernest Hemingway*. Ed. Linda Wagner-Martin. New York: Oxford UP, 2000. 53–92.

Bennett, Jane. *Vibrant Matter: A Political Ecology of Things*. Durham: Duke UP, 2010.

Bowler, Peter J. *Science for All: The Popularization of Science in Early Twentieth-Century Britain*. Chicago: U of Chicago P, 2009.

Bryson, J. Scott. "Modernism and Ecological Criticism". *Modernism*. Ed. Astradur Eysteinsson and Vivian Liska. Amsterdam: John Benjamins, 2007. 591–604.

Buell, Lawrence. *The Environmental Imagination: Thoreau, Nature Writing, and the Formation of American Culture*. Cambridge, MA: Harvard-Belknap, 1995.

——. *Writing for an Endangered World*. Cambridge, MA: Harvard-Belknap, 2001.

Bush, Ronald. "Modernism, Fascism, and the Composition of Ezra Pound's Pisan Cantos". *Modernism/Modernity* 2.3 (1995): 75–76.

Cartwright, Keith. "'To Walk with the Storm': Oya as the Transformative 'I' of Zora Neale Hurston's Afro-Atlantic Callings". *American Literature* 78.4 (December 2006): 741–67.

Chessman, Harriet Scott. *The Public Is Invited to Dance: Representation, the Body, and Dialogue in Gertrude Stein*. Stanford: Stanford UP, 1989.

Coupe, Laurence, ed. *The Green Studies Reader: From Romanticism to Ecocriticism*. London: Routledge, 2000.

Cronon, William, ed. *Uncommon Ground: Rethinking the Human Place in Nature*. New York: Norton, 1996.

DeKoven, Marianne. *A Different Language: Gertrude Stein's Experimental Writing*. Madison: U of Wisconsin P, 1983.

Di Chiro, Giovanna. "Nature as Community: The Convergence of Environment and Social Justice". *Uncommon Ground: Rethinking the Human Place in Nature*. Ed. William Cronon. New York: Norton, 1996. 298–320.

Dunlap, Thomas. "Nature Literature and Modern Science". *Environmental History Review* 14 (1990): 33–44.

Eeckhout, Bart. "Wallace Stevens' 'Earthy Anecdote'; or, How Poetry Must Resist Ecocriticism Almost Successfully". *Comparative American Studies* 7.2 (June 2009): 173–92.

Elder, John. *Imagining the Earth: Poetry and the Vision of Nature*. 2nd ed. Athens, GA: U of Georgia P, 1996.

Eliot, T. S. *The Idea of a Christian Society*. 1939. Rpt. in Christianity and Culture. New York: Harcourt, 1960. 1–78.

Fiedorczuk, Julia. "'Pull Down Thy Vanity': Post-Pastoral Subject in Ezra Pound's Cantos". *Journal of Ecocriticism* 1.2 (2009): 55–64.

Friedman, Susan Stanford. "Planetarity: Musing Modernist Studies". *Modernism/modernity* 17.3 (2010): 471–99.

Grese, Robert E. *Jens Jensen: Maker of Natural Parks and Gardens*. Baltimore: Johns Hopkins UP, 1992.

Golley, Frank. *A History of the Ecosystem Concept in Ecology*. New Haven: Yale UP, 1993.

Gordon, Craig. "Art for Life's Sake: Oscar Wilde and Biological Individualism". Unpublished manuscript.

Guha, Ramachandra and Juan Martinez-Alier. *Varieties of Environmentalism: Essays North and South*. London: Earthscan, 1997.

Haraway, Donna. "The Promises of Monsters: A Regenerative Politics for Inappropriate/d Others". 1992. Rpt. in *The Haraway Reader*. New York: Routledge, 2004. 63–124.

Hegeman, Susan. *Patterns for America: Modernism and the Concept of Culture.* Princeton: Princeton UP, 1999.

Heise, Ursula. "The Hitchhiker's Guide to Ecocriticism". *PMLA 121.2* (2006): 503–15.

——. *Sense of Place and Sense of Planet: The Environmental Imagination of the Global.* New York: Oxford UP, 2008.

Hodge, Joseph Morgan. *Triumph of the Expert: Agrarian Doctrines of Development and the Legacies of British Colonialism.* Athens, OH: Ohio UP, 2007.

Huggan, Graham and Helen Tiffin. *Postcolonial Ecocriticism: Literature, Animals, Environment.* London and New York: Routledge, 2010.

Hulme, T. E. "Romanticism and Classicism". 1911. Rpt. in *Selected Writings.* New York: Routledge, 2003. 68–83.

Ingold, Tim. *The Perception of the Environment.* London: Routledge, 2000.

Keller, David R. and Frank B. Golley, eds. *The Philosophy of Ecology: From Science to Synthesis.* Athens, GA: U of Georgia P, 2000.

Kenner, Hugh. *A Homemade World: The American Modernist Writers.* Baltimore: Johns Hopkins UP, 1975.

——. *The Pound Era. 1971.* London: Faber & Faber, 1975.

Ladino, Jennifer. "Rewriting Nature Tourism in 'an Age of Violence': Tactical Collage in Marianne Moore's 'An Octopus.'" *Twentieth Century Literature 51.3* (2005): 285–315.

Latour, Bruno. *Politics of Nature: How to Bring the Sciences into Democracy.* Cambridge, MA: Harvard UP, 2004.

——. "Why Has Critique Run Out of Steam? From Matters of Fact to Matters of Concern". *Critical Inquiry 30.2* (2004): 225–48.

Lewis, Wyndham. "Manifesto—II". *Blast 1* (1914): 30–43.

Love, Glen. *Practical Ecocriticism: Literature, Biology, and the Environment.* Charlottesville: U of Virginia P, 2003.

Lussier, Mark. *Romantic Dynamics: The Poetics of Physicality.* New York: St. Martin's, 2000.

MacPhail, Kelly. "Ezra Pound". *The Encyclopedia of Environment in American Literature.* Ed. Geoff Hamilton and Brian Jones. Jefferson, NC: McFarland P, 2012.

Mao, Douglas. *Solid Objects: Modernism and the Test of Production.* Princeton: Princeton UP, 1998.

Matless, David. *Landscape and Englishness.* London: Reaktion, 1998.

Monroe, Harriet. "John Muir: An Appreciation". *Sierra Club Bulletin 10.1* (1916): n.p. Web.

Monroe, Harriet. "The Great Renewal". *Poetry 12.6*(1918): 320–25.

Monroe, Harriet. "Back to Nature". *Poetry 14.6* (1919): 328–30.

Mortimer-Sandilands, Catriona. "Masculinity, Modernism and the Ambivalence of Nature: Sexual Inversion as Queer Ecology in The Well of Loneliness". *Left History 13.1* (2008): 35–58.

Morton, Timothy. *Ecology Without Nature.* Cambridge, MA: Cambridge UP, 2007.

Muir, John. *Our National Parks.* Boston: Houghton Mifflin, 1901.

Nash, Roderick Frazier. "Ideological Origins of American Environmentalism". *The Rights of Nature: A History of Environmental Ethics.* Madison: U of Wisconsin P, 1989. 33–54.

North, Michael. *Reading 1922: A Return to the Scene of the Modern.* New York: Oxford UP, 1999.

Parham, John. "Was There a Victorian Ecology?" *The Environmental Tradition in English Literature.* Ed. John Parham. Farnham: Ashgate, 2002. 156–71.

Paul, Catherine. "'Discovery, Not Salvage': Marianne Moore's Curatorial Methods". *Studies in the Literary Imagination 32.1* (Spring 1999): 91–114.

Phillips, Dana. *The Truth of Ecology: Nature, Culture, and Literature in America*. Oxford: Oxford UP, 2003.

Pound, Ezra. *The Spirit of Romance*. 1910. Rev. ed. New York: New Directions, 1952.

Pound, Ezra. "A Retrospect". 1918. Rpt. in *Literary Essays of Ezra Pound*. New York: New Directions, 1968. 3–14.

Raine, Anne. "Science, Nature Work, and the Kinaesthetic Body in Cather and Stein". *American Literature 80.4* (2008): 801–3.

Rasula, Jed. *This Compost: Ecological Imperatives in American Poetry*. Athens, GA: U of Georgia P, 2002.

Rigby, Kate. *Topographies of the Sacred: The Poetics of Place in European Romanticism*. Charlottesville: U of Virginia P, 2004.

Righter, Robert W. *The Battle over Hetch Hetchy*. New York: Oxford UP, 2005.

Saunders, Paul. "Samuel Beckett's Trilogy and the Ecology of Negation". *Journal of Beckett Studies 20.1* (2011): 54–77.

Schulze, Robin G. "Marianne Moore's 'Imperious Ox, Imperial Dish' and the Poetry of the Natural World". *Twentieth Century Literature 44.1* (1998): 1–33.

Schulze, Robin G. "Textual Darwinism: Marianne Moore, the Text of Evolution, and the Evolving Text". *TEXT: An Interdisciplinary Annual of Textual Studies 11* (1998): 270–305.

Schulze, Robin G. "Harriet Monroe's Pioneer Modernism: Nature, National Identity, and Poetry: A Magazine of Verse". *Legacy 2.1* (2004): 50–67.

Schwartz, Hillel. "Torque: The New Kinaesthetic of the Twentieth Century". *Incorporations*. Ed. Jonathan Crary and Sanford Kwinter. New York: Zone, 1992. 71–126.

Scigaj, Leonard. "Ecology, Egyptology, and Dialectics in Muriel Rukeyser's The Book of the Dead". *Mosaic 38.3* (2005): 131–48.

Scott, Bonnie Kime. "*Green*." *Modernism and Theory: A Critical Debate*. Ed. Stephen Ross. New York: Routledge, 2009. 219–24.

Sears, Paul B. "Ecology—A Subversive Subject". *BioScience 14.7* (1964): 11–14.

Shepard, Paul. "Introduction: Ecology and Man—A Viewpoint". *The Subversive Science: Essays Toward an Ecology of Man*. Ed. Paul Shepard and Daniel McKinley. Boston: Houghton Mifflin, 1969. 1–10.

Soper, Kate. *What Is Nature? Culture, Politics, and the Non-Human*. Oxford: Blackwell, 1995.

Stein, Rachel. *Shifting the Ground: American Women Writers' Revisions of Nature, Gender, and Race*. Charlottesville: U of Virginia P, 1997.

Voros, Gyorgi. *Notations of the Wild: Ecology in the Poetry of Wallace Stevens*. Iowa City: U of Iowa P, 1997.

Wallace, Jeff. *D. H. Lawrence, Science and the Posthuman*. Basingstoke and New York: Palgrave Macmillan, 2005.

Westling, Louise. *The Green Breast of the New World: Landscape, Gender, and American Fiction*. Athens, GA: U of Georgia P, 1996.

——. "Virginia Woolf and the Flesh of the World". *New Literary History 30.4* (1999): 855–75.

Williams, William Carlos. *The Descent of Winter*. 1928. Rpt. in *Imaginations*. New York: New Directions, 1970. 231–65.

Wittenberg, Judith Bryant. "Go Down, Moses and the Discourse of Environmentalism". *New Essays on Go Down, Moses*. Ed. Linda Wagner-Martin. New York: Cambridge UP, 1996. 49–72.

Woolf, Virginia. "Modern Fiction". *The Common Reader*. 1925. Rpt. New York: Harcourt, 1984. 146–54.

Worster, Donald. *Nature's Economy: A History of Ecological Ideas*. Cambridge: Cambridge UP, 1977.

CHAPTER 6

....

W. E. B. DU BOIS AT THE
GRAND CANYON

Nature, History, and Race in Darkwater

....

JOHN CLABORN

INTRODUCTION

....

W.E.B. Du Bois's "Of Beauty and Death" appears as a culminating experimental effort near the end of *Darkwater: Voices from Within the Veil*, his modernist text *par excellence*: a semi-autobiographical callaloo of poems, essays, and short stories. The essay contains much of the biting social critique one would expect from the then-editor of the NAACP's *The Crisis*: depictions of black life behind the Veil, double consciousness, and the injustice of *Plessy v. Ferguson* (*Souls* 3). What come as a surprise, however, are its Thoreauvian thick descriptions of the Grand Canyon, the Rocky Mountains, and Maine's Acadia National Park. Romantic and social realist modes occupy the same page: lyrical accounts revering the "glory of physical nature" and "all the colors of the sea" are interspersed with ruminations on death and anecdotes about his journey to the national parks in a train's Jim Crow car (*DW* 174–5). Despite these themes, environmental historian Kimberly K. Smith observes that "we don't read this essay as an expression of progressive environmentalism at all; we read it as a discourse on social justice" (*AAET* 2). Why, then, does Du Bois mix environmental, racial, and existential themes in this often overlooked essay? How is it that natural beauty gives rise to this combination of strident anti-racist protest and imported German romanticism? This unusual essay can contribute to our understanding of the intersection of race, romanticism, and modernism in the ecocritical tradition.[1] From an ecocritical perspective, *Darkwater* is significant because it bridges disparate histories and aesthetic modes. It develops out of two events that seem to belong separately to environmental history and black history: the passage of the 1916 National Parks Act and the Red Summer of 1919. The 1916 Act created the National Park Service and maneuvered into place the state apparatus needed to administer the nation's designated wilderness spaces, including the Grand Canyon, which became a national park in 1919 (Merchant, *AEH* 151). The bloody riots of the Red Summer of 1919, fuelled by urban segregation and the Great Migration, ravaged the country's cities from May to September. For Du Bois, the riots were stoked in part by the unjust treatment of black soldiers during the First World War—a subject he analyzes and condemns throughout *Darkwater*. In responding to these events, Du Bois racializes romantic modes of nature writing through his notion of "double consciousness" and modernist aesthetic techniques. Double consciousness, a concept introduced in *The Souls of Black Folk*, is the "sense of always looking at one's self through the eyes of others, of measuring one's soul by the tape of a world that looks on in amused contempt and pity" (9). Later, in his 1940 autobiography *Dusk of Dawn*, he speaks of a "double environment," a concept that merges double consciousness with "environment" (understood in the broadest sense of that term):

> Not only do white men but also colored men forget the facts of the Negro's double environment. The Negro American has not only the white surrounding world, but usually, and touching him much more nearly and compellingly, is the environment furnished by his own colored group. (173)

African Americans, in other words, experience each environment doubly, as both white *and* black enfolded in one another.

Du Bois's explorations of the double environments of (black) Jim Crow and (white) national parks in *Darkwater* foreground, I argue, practices of segregation across both natural and urban spaces. Such practices involve managing and controlling space in order to include or exclude—to enforce a color line of space and aesthetic experience. When Du Bois racializes the nature discourses of the conservationist movement, he also revises their tropes in his own *Crisis*-style critique of these segregating practices. Throughout the course of "Of Beauty and Death," Du Bois reconfigures the opposition between (white) natural and (black) urban spaces, substituting a more differentiated, heterogeneous sense of modern space.

NATIONAL PARKS AND RACE: THEODORE ROOSEVELT, JOHN MUIR, AND GIFFORD PINCHOT

By the time Du Bois wrote *Darkwater*, the wilderness preservationists had been fighting for the establishment of national parks for decades. The recognition of the Grand Canyon as a national park in 1919 marks a symbolic culmination of this history of the struggle to preserve supposedly pristine natural spaces. In the dominant reading of this history, preservationists such as Sierra Club founder John Muir saw this push as a noble resistance to the expansion of eastern capital set on consuming the nation's natural resources. Against this reading of the parks' histories, Richard Grusin, borrowing a notion from Frederick Law Olmstead, argues that the formation of the parks functioned as part of a national project of "postbellum reunification"—an attempt to unify the country geographically and culturally after the North/South division of the Civil War (23). Rather than being pristine natural spaces, the parks are a "product of a complex assemblage of heterogeneous technologies and social practices," which produce a "culturally and discursively defined and formed object called 'nature'" (Grusin 3). Thus, the way people experienced wilderness and the national parks at the time depended largely on the discursive frames of writers like Theodore Roosevelt, Muir, and Gifford Pinchot. Works like Muir's *Our National Parks* and Pinchot's *The Fight for Conservation* helped shape the parks as aesthetic, political, and cultural constructions—constructions that Du Bois counters in *Darkwater*.

Besides playing a key role in the conservation movement, Roosevelt romanticized and politicized wilderness in his frontier memoir *The Wilderness Hunter*, published ten years before *The Souls of Black Folk* in 1893. Among his many accomplishments, he successfully lobbied for the Forest Reserve Act of 1891 and served as president of the Boone and Crockett Club, an influential conservation lobbying group, for six years (Cutright 182). As U.S. President, he worked closely with Pinchot to establish the national parks and federal bureaus that managed forests and game. *The Wilderness Hunter* offers an account of the future president's hunting and ranching experiences in the Dakota Badlands—a "devil's wilderness"—during the last days of the western frontier (71). Environmental justice critic Mei Mei Evans contends that there is a close relation between wilderness and American cultural identity in popular narratives such as Roosevelt's: "Nature in U.S. American popular culture is the site *par excellence* for (re)invention of the self. Locating oneself, or being located, in Nature is a thoroughly cultural activity" (182). Roosevelt's memoir, then, is an act of political self-invention; he "finds" the essence of that political identity in the Dakotas, far removed from his comfortable New York lifestyle.

In *The Wilderness Hunter* preface, Roosevelt begins by remarking that he spent much of his life "either in the wilderness or on the borders of the settled country" (xxi). He goes on to state succinctly his romanticized view of wilderness, linking it to nationalism, democracy, and masculinity: the "free, self-reliant, adventurous life, with its rugged and stalwart democracy;…it cultivates that vigorous manliness for the lack of which in a nation, as in an individual, the possession of no other qualities can possibly atone" (xxi). For Roosevelt, wilderness is both "inside" and "outside" civilization. On the one hand, removal from civilization forces him to cultivate the manly virtues of self-reliance and rugged individualism. On the other hand, this very removal "civilizes" or anthropomorphizes the wilderness as an ideal training ground for the hard-hitting political life that, in Roosevelt's eyes, someone born into the comfortable and well-connected life of New York City's elite would need (Dorman xiii–xiv).For the romantic Roosevelt, wilderness discloses the essence of great men; it helps realize a highly masculinized democracy and American nationalism.

Whilst conservationists like Pinchot advocated the "wise use" of natural resources, Muir was more romantic in his outlook, calling for large wilderness areas to be set aside (Nash 129). Beginning in the 1870s, Muir began publicizing the beauty of places like Yosemite Valley in magazines like *Harper's Monthly* and in a number of bestselling books (Gifford 29; 39). His *Our National Parks* celebrates and commodifies various national parks, emphasizing their aesthetic attraction to wealthy easterners and centering on Yosemite, Yellowstone, Sequoia, and General Grant National Parks. His passages celebrating the Grand Canyon (not yet a national park) helped sell the idea of the park to the federal government and to tourists. He repeatedly stresses the canyon's transcendence and otherworldliness: "as unearthly in the color and grandeur and quantity of its architecture, as if you had found it after death, on some other star" (35). With the "you" directed at the tourist-reader, Muir functions as a sort of guide who will lead the visitor to the romantic sublime, a construct that Du Bois would later revise. *Our National Parks* is full of descriptions like these, framing these wilderness spaces as singular, sacred, and almost entirely devoid of any sign of civilization.

Though he does champion the public good over private profit, Muir's writing also participates in a discourse that assumes a division between culture and nature—a division that Du Bois implicitly challenges as racially codified. Paul Outka convincingly chronicles Muir's latent racism, arguing that his account of the western frontier "traces the process of forgetting the explicitly racialized geography of the east and south" (156). Muir's project continues the postbellum reunification that, Outka argues, sought to repress the national trauma of slavery and the Civil War. Despite such repression, and even as they espouse the interconnectedness of all things, Muir's writings still reflect a Jim Crow discourse of segregation. Though not explicitly stated, Muir's target audience is clearly made up of white, city-dwelling bourgeois easterners: "[a]wakening from the stupefying effects of the vice of over-industry and the deadly apathy of luxury, they are trying as best they can to mix and enrich their own little ongoings with those of Nature, and to get rid of rust and disease" (*Our National* 1). This appeal is a strategic attempt to translate Muir's own values into the utilitarianism of the urban-dweller and to advertise the parks to potential tourists. But it also reflects white male fears of hyper-civilization that could lead to a national crisis of masculinity and the degeneration of the white race. The solution to the feminizing force of modernity would be a return to a primitive condition, in which the cure is, as Muir famously said, to go home to nature: "going to the mountains is going home" (*Our National* 1).

While issues of race are not explicitly addressed across Muir's oeuvre, African Americans are represented in the posthumously published *A Thousand-Mile Walk to the Gulf*. Merchant argues that Muir's views are important because he wrote at a moment when "whiteness and blackness were redefined environmentally in ways that reinforced institutional racism" ("Shades" 381). Outka describes Muir's racist rhetoric in his encounter with an African American woman and boy while hiking through the woods: "Muir's racism comes in the way he looks, in how his language and his eye collapses dark-skinned humans into the natural landscape" (160–61). As "natural" objects that Muir encounters on his wilderness journeys, African Americans are sentimentalized from within an equally sentimental view of nature as a passive landscape painting put there for the white gaze to behold. Like the naïve and cheery Captain Delano of Herman Melville's *Benito Cereno*, Muir cannot imagine black agency or culture. Stumbling across some playful black children in Florida, Muir concludes that they do not live "in harmony with Nature," for "[b]irds make nests and nearly all beasts make some kind of bed for their young; but these negroes allow their younglings to lie nestless and naked in the dirt" (*Thousand-Mile* 107). Paradoxically, African Americans are both discordant with nature and "beasts" segregated into it—they are *in* nature but not *of* it. "Harmony" with nature, it seems, is best achieved by a well-traveled, white naturalist like Muir himself. This culture/nature opposition clears the ground for a pernicious white supremacy that sees African Americans as lower than animals, wherein at least the birds know how to make shelter.[2]

Muir's much-maligned contemporary Pinchot held more controversial views about the relation between the cultural and natural worlds. Much of Pinchot's negative reputation originates in the Hetch Hetchy Valley Dam controversy, when he approved the construction of a dam in Yosemite National Park (Nash 161). But Pinchot combined his national park and wise-use advocacy with a strong, progressive stance on issues of social and economic justice—issues that merge in his nationalist rhetoric of domestication. His conservation manifesto *The Fight for Conservation* is strewn with metaphors of domesticating wilderness for the nation: the "nation that will lead the world will be a Nation of Homes. The object of the great Conservation movement is just this, to make our country a permanent and prosperous home for ourselves and for our children" (23). Pinchot saw an opposition between narrowly defined profit and the public good, seeing conservation as a way of protecting people (and nature) from the powerful interests of the captains of industry and their "great concentrations of capital" (26). Rather than repudiate the profit-motive altogether, he sought to redefine it in democratic and somewhat socialistic terms: "natural resources must be developed and preserved for the benefit of the many, and not merely for the profit of a few" (46–50). Pinchot's redefined notion of profit and attempt to synthesize conservation with cultural and economic demands offers a sort of bridge between conservation and Du Bois.

DU BOIS AT THE GRAND CANYON: "OF BEAUTY AND DEATH" AND THE SUBLIME

The Grand Canyon passage in "Of Beauty and Death" tropes the park as sublime, while at the same time invoking the racialized, complex pastoralism and double consciousness found in *The Souls of Black Folk* and other parts of *Darkwater*. That Du Bois (or any black writer for that matter) writes about the parks at all is significant in 1920, given the perceived lack of African Americans' interest in wilderness spaces. This passage also challenges Outka's white sublime/black trauma opposition, serving as an instance of African American writing on the natural sublime. By representing the Grand Canyon, Du Bois engages in the American cultural nationalism of representing the parks, but he rejects Olmsted's project of postbellum re-unification. Rather than cover over the trauma of civil war, Du Bois seeks to expose it by de-naturalizing segregation and naturalizing integration in defiance of Jim Crow and early environmentalist discourse.

The Grand Canyon passage gains much of its implied meaning through its context among the essay's fragments. The experimental form of "Of Beauty and Death" redefines and widens the scope of conventional nature writing with a modernist aesthetic of juxtaposition. It is sandwiched between a tale of segregation in the military during the First World War and a number of fragments critiquing Jim Crow. Earlier in the essay, Du Bois explicitly characterizes his overall method as "juxtaposition" in order to "compare the least of the world's beauty with the least of its ugliness—not murder, starvation, and rapine, with love and friendship and creation—but the glory of sea and sky and city, with the little hatefulnesses and thoughtlessnesses of race prejudice" (DW 174). Juxtaposition shows that the "truth" of the ugliness of Jim Crow and the beauty of the national parks (or natural beauty in general) coexist in the same world: "[t]here is not in the world a more disgraceful denial of human brotherhood than the 'Jim-Crow' car of the southern United States; but, too, just as true, there is nothing more beautiful in the universe than sunset and moonlight on Montego Bay in far Jamaica" (DW 177). Further juxtapositions of about twenty separate fragments make "Of Beauty and Death" into a sort of montage capable of producing unexpected connections and "third meanings" similar to the later dialectical montage of 1920s Soviet cinema or the French surrealism of André Breton. It can produce meanings that would usually escape the intentional control of the author, releasing a textual unconscious to run wild. Rather than writing a philosophical tract, Du Bois hopes that "out of such juxtaposition we may, perhaps, deduce some rule of beauty and life—or death?" (DW 174). The logic of juxtaposition defies syllogistic thinking, for it seeks to "deduce" underlying truths about the social totality by aesthetic accident instead of philosophical deliberation.

The Grand Canyon passage must be placed in the context of the passage immediately preceding it, where Du Bois describes a conversation with a multi-racial group of friends. A white companion suggests that they travel for recreation, but the "thought of a journey seemed to depress" the others at the table (DW 176). An unnamed black friend then gives an account of the arduous process of traveling by train. Petty Jim Crow "thoughtlessnesses" harass the black passenger before she has even boarded the train: "to buy a ticket is torture; you stand and stand and wait and wait until every white person at the 'other window' is waited on" (DW 176). After dealing with the agent's refusal to serve African Americans, the black passenger must then ride in the segregated Jim Crow car:

> Usually there is no step to help you climb on and often the car is a smoker cut in two and you must pass through the white smokers or else they pass through your part, with swagger and noise and stares.... The white train crew from the baggage car uses the "Jim-Crow" to lounge in and perform their toilet. The conductor appropriates two seats for himself and his papers and yells gruffly for your tickets before the train has scarcely started.... As for toilet rooms,—don't! (DW 176–77)

National park enthusiasts extolled the virtues of visits to wilderness spaces as a rejuvenating escape from the claustrophobia of the cities, yet the punishing ride in a Jim Crow car threatens to undermine this particular value of the parks—or specifically the *journey* to the parks—for educated blacks, the so-called Talented Tenth. Moreover, railroad companies themselves possessed a huge economic stake in establishing the parks for tourism, prospecting for new vistas as one would for gold. Such companies as Northern Pacific, for example, lobbied for the establishment of Yellowstone National Park in 1872 (Nash 111). They and others in the tourism industry sought to make the national parks, in Grusin's words, an "idealized commodity" for tourists as well as armchair tourists eager to consume verbal and visual representations like those of Muir and nineteenth-century landscape painter Thomas Moran (12). In helping to commodify and promote the parks, the railroad companies also succeeded in expanding their Jim Crow policies westward. To be sure, the reasons Du Bois gives for visiting the parks are similar to Muir's: bourgeois exhaustion with urban life and war. He affirms, too, that actually being in the national parks can offer blacks temporary respite from racism. But Du Bois asks a question about the infrequency of visitors to these places, which leads him directly to issues of race: "[w]hy do not those who are scarred in the world's battle and hurt by its hardness travel to these places of beauty and drown themselves in the utter joy of life?" (*DW* 176). Whatever their value as escape for Du Bois, getting to the parks requires navigating the Jim Crow gauntlet—petty, everyday intrusions that contrast sharply with the grandeur of the Grand Canyon.

The travel passage that follows this description of a Jim Crow car offers an unusual moment in Du Bois's prolific corpus. It begins by charting Du Bois's "great journey" that spans "over seven thousand mighty miles" across the United States (*DW* 182). Traveling through deserts, mountains, and cities, he visits, among other places, the Rocky Mountains, "the empire of Texas," and finally the Grand Canyon (*DW* 182). He also intersperses visits to cities on this trip: Seattle, Kansas City, Chicago, Los Angeles, and Manhattan. The journey, then, is diverse and sweeping both in its geographical and environmental range, for Du Bois moves from the most natural spaces to the most built and human-centered environments. In its inventorial geography marked by the essay's fragmentary, elliptical prose, the journey also invokes the close relation between natural resources and nationalism in conservationist discourse. In *The Wilderness Hunter*, for example, Roosevelt performs a similar inventory of the country's earthly gifts, naming places, regions, and animal species: the Atlantic Coast, the Mississippi Valley, "magnificent hardwood forest[s]" (1), "fertile prairies," "tepid swamps" that "teem with reptile life," Texas, the Rocky Mountains, the "strangely shaped and colored Bad Lands" (11). Unlike Du Bois, Roosevelt does not list any cities, showing the latter's sense of a distinct separation between natural and built environments. By intertwining such seemingly disparate and opposed spaces Du Bois forces us to compare them according to the logic of double consciousness.

Du Bois represents the Grand Canyon as a sublime landscape that is animated, chaotic, and even somewhat menacing, working within a tradition of nature writing about the southwestern desert region. Grusin observes that from its initial exploration in 1869 to 1919, the Grand Canyon has been troped as "cognitively inaccessible" and, he argues, the "preservation of this inaccessibility is critical to the establishment and continued attraction" of the park (103). Here, Du Bois's writing typifies both representations of the canyon and the ambivalence towards wilderness found in African American slave narratives and sorrow songs. The Grand Canyon, then, is the perfect landscape for a meeting between African American ambivalence and sublime representations of nature.

Such ambivalence towards the canyon follows the same structural logic between the human observer and nature found in Immanuel Kant's romantic theory of the sublime. According to the *Critique of Judgment*, the sense of the sublime differs from beauty: the "beautiful in nature relates to the form of the object, and this consists in limitation, whereas the sublime is to be found in an object even devoid of form" (306). For Kant, natural beauty "conveys a finality in its form" and suggests a systematic ordering even if the whole cannot be comprehended by the observer (307–8). Du Bois's visit to Acadia early in the essay exemplifies beauty in the Kantian sense. Du Bois claims, following Kant, that beauty has a certain completeness to it: "for beauty by its very being and definition has in each definition its ends and limits" (190). In contrast to beauty, the sublime provokes an "image of *limitlessness*, yet with a super-added thought of its totality" (Kant 306). The sublime is nature as excess, as a break from form and systematic ordering that produces a "negative pleasure" in the subject, who is, ambivalently, "alternately repelled" and attracted to the sublime object (307).

The ambivalence built into the experience of the sublime suggests that it has more to do with culture than with nature, with subjective feeling than the perceived thing-in-itself. In Gayatri Spivak's reading of the Kantian sublime, the subject's "feeling for nature" operates according to a metalepsis, a substitution of effect for cause (in this case, of nature for culture) (11). For Kant, sublime feeling is the result of receptivity to aesthetic experience that must be cultivated, for it is the "attitude of mind that introduces sublimity into the image of nature" (Kant 308). Spivak argues that because the sublime depends on the subject's cultivated sensibility, it is a cultural aptitude belonging, by way of implication, to the enlightened, European subject. This aesthetic capacity is important in the Kantian philosophical system because, in addition, it reveals the capacity for freedom, which for Kant is also the capacity to make ethical choices and to be fully human. Opposed to the cultured European, Spivak argues, is the "man in raw," who corresponds to the "savage," or, adjusted for the context of the Jim Crow era, African Americans. Indeed, pseudo-scientific studies like Charles Carroll's *The Mystery Solved: The Negro a Beast* (1900), novels like Thomas Dixon's *The Leopard's Spots* (1908), and D. W. Griffith's film *The Birth of a Nation* (1915) consistently portray blacks zoomorphically as animalistic, uncultured raw men (Lewis, *Biography* 276). For Kant, Spivak goes on, the raw man experiences the sublime as "*Abgrund*-affect," as terror before an abyss (Spivak 26).

In contrast to these popular portrayals, Du Bois offers a decidedly "cultured" experience of the canyon. He begins his sublime portrait with a Miltonic trope of the wounded, feminized earth: "[i]t is a sudden void in the bosom of earth, down to its entrails—a wound where the dull titanic knife has turned and twisted in the hole" (*DW* 182–83). The "sudden" appearance of the "void" mimics or attempts to recover the affective response of the first discoverers of the Canyon. Expressed as an act of phallic violence inflicted on the earth, the sublime functions as a strategy to recuperate and represent an authentic encounter with nature. At the same time, the image suggests the trauma of racial violence, specifically castration and ritual lynching. Du Bois then moves on to describe the colors of the Canyon—a tactic he uses throughout the essay to contrast the fluid mingling of colors in nature with the social rigidity of the color-line problem. The Grand Canyon "hole" leftover from the knife leaves the anthropomorphized canyon's "edges livid, scarred, jagged, and pulsing over the white, and red, and purple of its mighty flesh" (DW 183). The landscape of the canyon is likened to an inverted mountain. "It is awful," writes Du Bois, and because it appears as nature violently attacking herself (in reality, the slow violence of the Colorado River), "[t]here can be nothing like it. It is the earth and sky gone stark and raving mad. The mountains up-twirled, disbodied and inverted, stand on their peaks and throw their bowels to the sky. Their earth is air; their ether blood-red rock engreened. You stand upon their roots and fall into their pinnacles, a mighty mile" (DW 183). The canyon seems to draw its sublime power from its excesses, from a strange and paradoxical unnaturalness within nature itself.

Du Bois goes on in a mode of fervent questioning and Old Testament bombast, adopting rhetoric similar to Muir's almost twenty years before:

> Behold this mauve and purple mocking of time and space! See yonder peak! No human foot has trod it. Into that blue shadow only the eye of God has looked. Listen to the accents of that gorge which mutters: "Before Abraham was, I am." Is yonder wall a hedge of black or is it the rampart between heaven and hell? I see greens,—is it moss or giant pines? Ever the gorge lies motionless, unmoved, until I fear. It is a grim thing, unholy, terrible! It is human—some mighty drama unseen, unheard, is playing there its tragedies or mocking comedy, and the laugh of endless years is shrieking onward from peak to peak, unheard, unechoed, and unknown. (DW 183)

The repetition of "ever" and "mocking of time and space" suggests the canyon's seeming eternity, created long before humans—before "Abraham"—ever existed. The sublime here comes close to what Kant calls the "horrible," a variant on the sublime. Because, for example, a storm-wracked sea can present imminent danger to the viewer, it is "horrible," unless one has cultivated the subjective feelings capable of receiving it (Kant 308). The landscape gains some of its horror through the simultaneous absence of human presence—"No human foot has trod it"—and the canyon's uncanny anthropomorphism. This simultaneity suggests that the canyon is a human-like alien, capable of the same or even greater monstrous acts of violence similar to those perpetrated by humans overseas in war-torn Europe or the race riots at home. By the measure of traditional ecocritical litmus tests, such blatant anthropomorphism may undermine the possibility of a more ecocentric perspective in Du Bois's work, although in this case, anthropomorphism functions more as rhetorical strategy than evidence of insensitivity to the landscape's alterity. Personifying the canyon as a "mighty drama" brings it closer to the social world, as well as the natural colors—"mauve," "purple," "blue shadow," and "greens"—to the problem of the color line. The gorge becomes a symbol of integration.

A series of short meditations on the African American experience in Europe during the First World War immediately follow the Grand Canyon passage. Du Bois begins with an idyllic description of everyday race relations in Paris. Enjoying an evening out among "civilized folk," Du Bois feels thankful for the absence of the "hateful, murderous, dirty Thing which in American we call 'Nigger-hatred' " in the evening's "community of kindred souls" (*DW* 184). The intellectual's cultivated sensitivity to the natural sublime—expressed in the Grand Canyon reverie—manifests itself in a European social context as a "reverence for the Thought" that transcends the "commonplaces" of race (*DW* 184). Through juxtaposition, Du Bois suggests that the only escape from white America's racism is either into the bourgeois playground of the national parks or Europe. Set against the spirit of Roosevelt's nationalist "democracy" of American wilderness is Du Bois' exhortation to African-Americans: "[f]ellow blacks, we must join the democracy of Europe" (*DW* 165).

Parisian intellectual life, however, is no paradise: the cityscape bears the traces of the war, itself a product of European colonialism turned against itself, as Du Bois argues in "The Souls of White Folk" and *The New Negro* piece, "Worlds of Color: The Negro Mind Reaches Out." The next fragment describes a haunting image of invasion: "[t]hrough its [Paris's] streets—its narrow, winding streets, old and low and dark, carven and quaint,—poured thousands upon thousands of strange feet of khaki-clad foreigners" (*DW* 185). The sublime feelings induced by the Grand Canyon transform into the terror of the war-torn cityscape. The streets are "feverish, crowded, nervous, hurried; full of uniforms and mourning bands, with cafes closed at 9:30" (*DW* 186). In Du Bois's myth, France is saved by black American soldiers drawn from every part of the United States even as it affords them the opportunity to travel to Europe and witness its democracy. If Paris and the Grand Canyon can be seen as urban and natural democracies of color, then they are hard fought and hard won, for both mix "beauty and death." By juxtaposing this social expression of racial community in Paris with nature's mixing of colors at the Grand Canyon, Du Bois naturalizes integration and internationalizes a vision of democracy across the color line.

By intertwining the Grand Canyon and Jim Crow in these fragments, Du Bois strategically reimagines Kantian and conservationist discourse. He demonstrates not only an African American aptitude for the aesthetic experience of nature, but also its superiority to a form of nature writing that erases signs of the social world. That Du Bois, or any African American, proves capable of writing about nature so eloquently makes his nature writing an act of protest. Unexpectedly, it is the experience of racism, which would seem to (and indeed threatens to) foreclose this aptitude in the first place, that bestows the advantage of second-sight and a challenge to discourses of segregation. The black subject's second-sight saves him from the white bourgeois tourist's commodified experience of nature.

A few years later, in his Harlem Renaissance manifesto "Criteria of Negro Art" (1926), Du Bois shows his contempt for white American "excursionists," who interrupt his pastoral reverie at the Scottish lake of Walter Scott's poem "Lady of the Lake." He sets the idyllic scene: "It was quiet. You could glimpse the deer wandering in unbroken forests;

you could hear the soft ripple of romance on the waters. Around me fell the cadence of that poetry of my youth. I fell asleep full of the enchantment of the Scottish border" ("Criteria" 778). Into this scene, much like Leo Marx's "machine in the garden," intrude the vulgar Americans:

> They were mostly Americans and they were loud and strident.... They all tried to get everywhere first. They pushed other people out of the way. They made all sorts of incoherent noises and gestures.... They carried, perhaps, a sense of strength and accomplishment, but their hearts had no conception of the beauty which pervaded this holy place. ("Criteria" 778)

Here, it is the white American tourists who are the "men in the raw"; they are philistines without the capacity for aesthetic experience and they profane the "holy place." Worse yet, they drag along with them the noisy, frenzied rush of the city into the pastoral idyll, turning it into another urban space. Furthermore, Du Bois inverts white supremacy and reduces them to creatures incapable of speech or the ability to communicate at all.

In contrast, African Americans, precisely *because* of their marginalization from this vulgar version of white American culture, have an escape hatch. Du Bois states: "pushed aside as we have been in America, there has come to us not only a certain distaste for the tawdry and flamboyant but a vision of what the world could be if it were really a beautiful world" ("Criteria" 778–79). Through this reversal, Du Bois transmutes a perceived weakness into strength: African Americans become "co-worker[s] in the kingdom of culture" (*Souls* 9). The ironic gift of second-sight becomes another Kantian faculty, a unique capacity for experiencing natural beauty that not only grants African Americans access to the cultural nationalist project of the national parks but also interprets that project as integration rather than segregation. Showing the influence of his study abroad in Germany, Du Bois even grants this African American exceptionalism a flavor of German romanticism, seemingly to respond to Poundian exhortations to "make it new" with a "gift" of black folks' "new appreciation of joy, of a new desire to create, of a new will to be" ("Criteria" 779). Continuing in with more asyndeta, he claims that the "bounden duty of black America" is to step forward as custodian of the beautiful, "to begin this great work of the creation of Beauty, of the preservation of Beauty, of the realization of Beauty" ("Criteria" 782). Through participation in the cultural nationalist project of representing the sublimity of the canyon, Du Bois invokes an African American exceptionalism that previews the modernism of the Harlem Renaissance and the philosophy espoused in Alain Locke's introduction to *The New Negro* anthology.

URBAN NATURE AND MODERNISM

Though the end of "Of Beauty and Death" does not represent race riots directly, it does draw attention to spaces of urban nature that set the preconditions for the riots. Because of the dense cityscape and influx of African Americans to the cities during the Great

Migration, opportunities for outdoor recreation in urban spaces became more and more vital by 1919. African Americans' limited access to officially or unofficially segregated parks, beaches, and other spaces of urban nature became a growing source of racial tension and violence. As noted in this essay's introduction, historian Colin Fisher argues that segregated parks and beaches played a determining factor in the Chicago riots. Prior to this tragic event, Fisher claims, urban nature spaces such as Washington Park (75) or Cook County Forest Preserves (66) in Chicago were valued by African Americans as an escape from the claustrophobic South Side. In defiance of "forced exclusion from parks, playgrounds, and beaches, blacks struggled for access to open space" (Fisher 64). Without parks, many black children were left to play in marginal spaces of urban nature: open dumps, vacant lots, and rough-hewn playgrounds (67). Culminating a series of smaller skirmishes of racial violence, the riots started in July 1919 on the segregated beaches of Lake Michigan. The "black beach" was nicknamed "Hot and Cold" because it was near the industrial area of the shore (64). When fifteen-year-old South Side working-class resident Eugene Williams drifted into the "white" section of Lake Michigan beach, angry whites perceived this breach as "pollution" to their water (68). They began throwing rocks at Williams, causing him to drown. The resulting outrage from both blacks and whites made for the worst rioting in Chicago's history, lasting four days and leaving 38 dead, 537 injured, and about 1,000 homeless (64).

In the final fragments of "Of Beauty and Death," Du Bois conveys an atmosphere of racial tension as he turns his eye towards the Manhattan cityscape and its urban nature. This movement from the national parks of the west to the east suggests a frontier reversal, an importation of wilderness into urban space. After describing the broken Paris of the First World War, Du Bois sketches New York in language that echoes his portrait of the Grand Canyon: "white cliffs of Manhattan, tier on tier, with a curving pinnacle, towers square and trim, a giant inkwell daintily stoppered, an ancient pyramid enthroned" (*DW* 187). By characterizing the cityscape in these terms, Du Bois makes it a part of nature, an example of what many ecocritics have called "urban nature writing" (Bennett and Teague 31). Du Bois also invokes the seasonal cycles: "[w]e would see spring, summer, and the red riot of autumn, and then in winter, beneath the soft white snow, sleep and dream of dreams" (*DW* 190). The "red riot" conflates two events, one social and the other natural: the Red Summer, which actually continued into late September, and the changing colors of leaves in the fall.

At the same time that it represents urban nature, the end of "Of Beauty and Death" also reflects the 1919 race riots. After the riots, David Levering Lewis says that Du Bois's mood "verged on apocalyptic bitterness"—a mood clearly reflected in the sardonic humor of the apocalyptic short story "The Comet," which follows "Of Beauty and Death" (*Fight* 13). Finalized for an early 1920 publication in the midst of the riots and at the close of the First World War, *Darkwater* is usually read within the context of these violent episodes in the long history of U.S. and international race relations. Though Du Bois claimed to have finished the manuscript in February 1918, he continued revising it until September 1919—before reverberations of the riots across the county had died down (Lewis, *Fight* 11). Oswald Garrison Villard's review of the book for *The Nation* frames it in terms of the race riots, praising the artistry of "A Litany at Atlanta," a poem about the Atlanta race riots (726). But, Villard continues, such proximity to the violent events produces excessive affect, for the book "carries with it a note of bitterness, tinctured with hate, and the teaching of violence which often defeats his own purpose" (727). The riots were, in a sense, the war brought home from Europe. last fragments of the essay, then, are permeated with the tense urban atmosphere that sparked the riots.

By making nature part of the color-line problem in "Of Beauty and Death," Du Bois maps disjunctive social and natural spaces. In his second-sight, the wilderness becomes simultaneously an ideal "integrationist" space of intermingling natural colors—an objective correlative for a democratic, desegregated society—and a compromised, fraught space mediated by the problems of the color line and modernity. This counter-narrative challenges not only the dominance of white supremacy and social Darwinism, but also an emergent environmentalism. Ultimately, for Du Bois there is no "nature" without the baggage of the color line, no Grand Canyon without Jim Crow, and no wide-open landscapes without claustrophobic cityscapes.

Notes

1. In recent years, ecocritics and environmental historians have begun, at the behest of environmental justice activists and theorists, to re-imagine African American literature ecocritically and to make Du Bois a key figure. The foundational work of Smith, Vera Norwood, Jeffrey Myers, Scott Hicks, and Carolyn Merchant have paved the way for studies such as Paul Outka's *Race and Nature from Transcendentalism to the Harlem Renaissance*, which brings together African American literary studies, ecocriticism, and trauma studies. Outka argues that the sublime of conventional (white) nature writing diverges—and sometimes converges—with the traumatic experiences of African Americans. Yet Du Bois's essay, because of its celebration of national parks, complicates Outka's white sublime / black trauma narrative. Ecocritic Kimberly N. Ruffin's *Black on Earth: African American Ecoliterary Traditions* weaves together a tradition of black environmental imagination in nineteenth—and twentieth-century literature, focusing particularly on mythic and spiritual understandings of nature. While Outka and Ruffin compare and uncover black environmental texts, my approach is more historicist, contextualizing a text not just within social but also environmental history.
2. For Muir's racist views of Native Americans, see Merchant's "Shades of Darkness: Race and Environmental History."

Works Cited

Bennett, Michael and David W. Teague, eds. *The Nature of Cities: Ecocriticism and Urban Environments*. Tucson: University of Arizona Press, 1999.

Dorman, Robert L. "*Introduction*." *The Wilderness Hunter*. Theodore Roosevelt. New York: Barnes and Noble, 2004. xiii–xx.

Du Bois, W. E. B. "*Criteria of Negro Art.*" *The Norton Anthology of African American Literature.* Eds. Henry Louis Gates Jr. and Nellie Y. McKay. 2nd ed. New York: W. W. Norton & Company, 777–84.

——. *Darkwater.* 1919. New York: Washington Square Press, 2004.

——. *Dusk of Dawn.* 1940. New York: Harcourt Brace, 1975.

——. *The Souls of Black Folk.* 1903. New York: Barnes & Noble, 2003.

Fisher, Colin. "African Americans, Outdoor Recreation, and the 1919 Chicago Race Riot." In "*To Love the Wind and the Rain*": *African Americans and Environmental History.* Eds. Dianne D. Glave and Mark Stoll. Pittsburgh: University of Pittsburgh Press, 2006.

Gifford, Terry. *Reconnecting with John Muir: Essays in Post-Pastoral Practice.* Athens: University of Georgia Press, 2006.

Grusin, Richard. *Culture, Technology, and the Creation of America's National Parks.* New York: Cambridge University Press, 2004.

Kant, Immanuel. *Critique of Judgment. 1793.* Trans. James C. Meredith. In Basic Writings of Kant. Ed. Allen W. Wood. New York: Random House, 2001. 273–366.

Lewis, David Levering. *W. E. B. Du Bois: The Fight for Equality and the American Century, 1919–1963.* New York: Henry Holt and Company, 2000.

Marx, Leo. *The Machine in the Garden: Technology and the Pastoral Ideal in America.* 1964. New York: Oxford UP, 2000.

Merchant, Carolyn. "Shades of Darkness: Race and Environmental History." *Environmental History 8.3* (July 2003): 380–94.

——. *American Environmental History: An Introduction.* New York: Columbia University Press, 2007.

Muir, John. A. *Thousand-Mile Walk to the Gulf.* Ed. William Frederic Bade. New York: Houghton Mifflin Company, 1916.

——. *Our National Parks.* New York: Houghton Mifflin Company, 1901.

Nash, Roderick Frazier. *Wilderness and the American Mind.* 1967. 4th ed. New Haven: Yale University Press, 2001.

Outka, Paul. *Race and Nature: From Transcendentalism to the Harlem Renaissance.* New York: Palgrave MacMillan, 2008.

Pinchot, Gifford. *The Fight for Conservation.* 1910. Seattle: University of Washington Press, 1967.

Roosevelt, Theodore. *The Wilderness Hunter.* 1893. New York: Barnes & Noble, 2004.

Smith, Kimberly K. *African American Environmental Thought: Foundations.* Lawrence: University Press of Kansas, 2007.

Spivak, Gayatri Chakravorty. *A Critique of Postcolonial Reason: Toward a History of the Vanishing Present.* Cambridge: Harvard UP, 1999.

Villard, Oswald-Garrison. Review of Darkwater. *The Nation 110.2865:* 726–27.

CHAPTER 7

···

PATAPHYSICS AND POSTMODERN ECOCRITICISM
A Prospectus

···

ADAM DICKINSON

Read globally, write locally.
—Charles Bernstein

THE PROBLEM

···

Imagine a science that combines ecology with soap bubbles. In 1934 the Estonian ecologist Jakob von Uexküll (1864–1944) proposed that the key to understanding ecological dynamics is to study the unfamiliar sensory cues of other organisms. In "A Stroll Through the Worlds of Animals and Men," he argues that we must first "blow, in fancy, a soap bubble around each creature to represent its own world, filled with the perceptions which it alone knows."[1] This field of significance constitutes the *Umwelt*, the subjective universe of particular living things, or as Thomas A. Sebeok defines it, "those parts of the environment that each organism selects with its species-specific sense organs, each according to its biological needs."[2] Uexküll's speculative descriptions of these alternative universes range from the constrained perspectives of ticks, house flies, snails, and molluscs to the more elaborate frames of signification represented by human scientists, such as the astronomer for whom "Fleet-footed light takes millions of years to travel through his *Umwelt* space," or the oceanographer who, instead of constellations, sees "deep-sea fish wheel around his sphere with their uncanny mouths, long tentacles and radial light organs."[3] These various soap-bubble versions of reality touch and influence each other in what Uexküll describes as melodic relations. The worlds of the bat and moth, for example, are interactions of attuned difference involving certain shared themes, such as the frequency of a bat's squeak and the corresponding register of a moth's hearing.[4] Such symphonic theories and poetic descriptions did little to endear Uexküll to the scientific mainstream of his day.

Bubbles and surface tension are also essential to science of a different sort. During one of the fantastic research trips described in *Exploits & Opinions of Dr. Faustroll, Pataphysician*, an obsessive concern with point of view and its influence on constructions of reality prompts Dr. Faustroll to change the scale of his investigation of a leaf by shrinking to "a paradigm of smallness" so that he might differently apprehend a drop of water as a "deracinated eye of malleable glass."[5] Dr. Faustroll is the creation of the French writer Alfred Jarry (1873–1907) and serves as the chief exponent of Jarry's alternative science of pataphysics,[6] first published in 1911. Pataphysics is "the science of imaginary solutions"; it studies the particulars and exceptions that ultimately inhabit and subvert the generalizing assumptions of traditional scientific systems.[7] Christian Bök insists that pataphysics exposes the failure of science to be "as 'lucid' as once thought, since science must often ignore the arbitrary, if not whimsical, status of its own axioms."[8] Pataphysical texts employ methodological constraints in poetic composition (akin to the controlling of variables in a laboratory setting) in order to uncover marginalized and unique frames of signification. In other words, pataphysical writing often involves the attempt to inhabit unconventional and exceptional *Umwelten* in order to illuminate neglected perspectives and critique the effacing power of prevailing social and disciplinary attitudes. Examples include Duchampian readymades, imaginary encyclopedias such as Luigi Serafini's *Codex Seraphinianus* (an account of the botany, physics, cuisine, and architecture of an alien world composed entirely of indecipherable script and elaborate illustrations), as well as the constraint-based and procedural writing commonly associated with Oulipo, or *Ouvroir de littérature potentielle*, which emerged from the College of Pataphysics in 1948 (an originally French-based group of writers and artists inspired by Jarry's work).

It might seem tempting at first to dismiss such intersections between science and art as poetic fancy; however, both Uexküll and pataphysics have become increasingly important to contemporary theoretical biology and postmodern poetics respectively. Uexküll's *Umwelt* theory has influenced the sciences of ethology and cybernetics, and has more recently been developed by Sebeok and Jesper Hoffmeyer (among others) into the burgeoning field of biosemiotics with its emphasis on semiosis, or signs and sign processes, as the driving force of biology. Similarly, pataphysics, "despite undertones of spoofing and quackery," as Roger Shattuck observes, offers much in the way of serious social commentary.[9] Bök maintains that "Few critics have recognized that pataphysics actually informs the innovation of the postmodern."[10]

Notwithstanding the revival of both Uexküll and pataphysics at the turn of the twenty-first century, reaching back into the past as a means of inspiring future forms of inquiry is, as Wendy Wheeler identifies, part of the logic of abduction (as defined by C. S. Peirce), and it is fundamental to ecocriticism's "attempt to find a new synthesis which has science and wonder, evolution and numinosity, somehow together in the same place."[11] Abduction (as distinct from induction and deduction) is purposeless, playful exploration; it is, like pataphysics, "a sort of 'following your nose' by which the

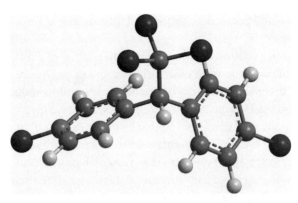

FIGURE 7.1 DDT (dichlorodiphenyltrichloroethane)

well-informed mind (that is the *Umwelt*-alert mind)" allows "itself to fall into 'the play of musement,'" and "gain access to unconscious or preconscious (or 'tacit') antecedent knowledges."[12] What might such an abductive, pataphysical postmodern ecocriticism look like?

In *Silent Spring* Rachel Carson describes how the poisonous effects of DDT (Figure 7.1) were first documented in 1945 by a small group of British investigators who deliberately exposed themselves to harm through a series of loosely controlled experiments. Carson highlights the significance of the "eloquent description of their symptoms" presented in the resulting reports.[13] In a similar performance, two Canadian environmental activists, Rick Smith and Bruce Lourie, confined themselves to an apartment in Toronto for a week in 2008 with the goal of measuring levels of pollutants in their bodies contracted from deliberate exposure to a variety of common consumer products. Both of these unconventional experiments constitute a form of performance art that evokes the methodologies of pataphysics with its intentional emphasis on subjective and local frames of signification. Smith and Lourie, for example, acknowledge that their experiment, which "began as a joke," does "not include large sample sizes, double-blind trials or other methods that constitute formal scientific research"; rather, "what matters is that they demonstrate the surprising reality that a couple of guys can manipulate the toxic substances in their bodies through the simple acts of eating and using everyday foods and products."[14] Such unusual experiments raise awareness of the indiscriminate proliferation of toxins in the environment and in so doing constitute a form of resistance to the colossal science project that the industrialized world is currently performing on the bodies of its citizens without consent.

THE OBSERVATION

Pataphysics is deeply implicated in an emerging ecocritical approach that owes more to poetics than it does to traditional analytical methodologies. In establishing a contrast between, what we might call in Deleuzian terms, the "royal science" of literary theory and the "nomad science" of poetics,[15] Charles Bernstein contends that traditional academic scholarship is characterized by consistency, explanation, and "stand-alone arguments," whereas poetics "is provisional, context-dependent, and often contentious. Theory will commonly take a scientific tone, poetics will sometimes go out of its way to seem implausible, to exaggerate, or even to be self-deprecating."[16] Bernstein laments that poetics has been displaced by literary theory as a scholarly and critical model. Pataphysics, the science of imaginary solutions, the science of exceptions, the science of particulars (Jarry employs all of these defining terms) provides a ready example of this alternative critical approach to the environment and environments. By creating imaginary research institutes and laboratories (with unconventional methodologies), by involving ambient environmental influences and procedures, and by exploring transgenic symbiosis, pataphysics succeeds in, as Bernstein says, renovating that old Poundian dictum: "The motto shouldn't be make it new but make it live."[17] As I explore further below, Bök's *The Xenotext Experiment* quite literally aims to "make it live" by inserting a poem into a bacterium. Consequently, pataphysics deserves attention not only as an object, but also as a potential *form* of ecocritical inquiry.

Dana Phillips disparages Jonathan Bate's preference for ecopoetics over ecocriticism in *The Song of the Earth* because it "allows one to write criticism as if it, too, were a form of poetry, and as if the ecocritic-cum-ecopoet were licensed to make it up as he or she goes along."[18] Notwithstanding Phillips's polemic, Bate is on to something by pursuing the exceptional critical capacities of poetics. Ecocriticism's philosophical adventure needs to be made "dirtier," Timothy Morton points out; it needs to take more risks.[19] Indeed, it could stand to be more offensive, Phillips himself admits.[20] Pataphysical texts require a criticism (which may well involve conventional techniques) that is open to the semiotic implications of its own abductive and deconstructive methodologies. However, pataphysical texts can also function *as* ecocriticism, actively morphing into a bold and innovative ecopoetics conducting research at the complex and controversial thresholds between nature and culture.

There are a number of recent examples of these sorts of pataphysical research projects with distinct ecocritical dimensions. In the 1970s and 1980s, the Toronto Research Group (TRG), founded by Steve McCaffery and bp Nichol, explored the critical potential of "rational geomancy" and its associations with environmental semiotics through a series of "reports" on the affective landscape of literary texts. Canadian poet Lisa Robertson's 2003 publication *Occasional Work and Seven Walks from the Office for Soft Architecture* presents the research of an imagined institute devoted to studying the natural history of civic surfaces in the city of Vancouver. In *Overcoming Fitness* the American writer and architect Robert Kocik provides an annotated list of speculative agencies and social services, one of which includes the Booth for Retrofection, where he proposes an audio cubicle that uses the sounds and rhythms of poetry to break the "germ barrier" in order to influence genetic inheritance.[21] While this work might be thought of as the literal embodiment of Angus Fletcher's "environment-poem," in Kocik's case the result is not simply, as Fletcher describes, to get the "reader to enter into the poem as if

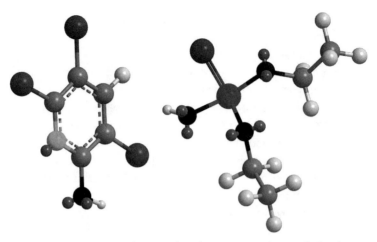

FIGURE 7.2 OPIMs (organophosphate insecticide metabolites)

it were the reader's environment of living," but to actually alter the reader's physiology in the interests of healthful attunement.[22] *The Transformation*, by American poet Juliana Spahr, which does not present its research under the auspices of an imagined institute or laboratory, is a pataphysical work of literary ethnobotany that examines the natural and social interconnections between invasive species and invasive cultures. All of these works represent explicit examples of a postmodern ecocriticism practiced as nontraditional research, as pataphysical ecopoetics.

Ecocriticism and nature writing often focus on the need to change the human self in order to deal with the ecological crisis. However, as a number of critics have argued, the nature writing "I," the self, the very question of the subject in ecocriticism requires more critical scrutiny. Phillips, for example, asserts that "Nature writers and ecocritics need to abandon their assumption that the self is a transcendental entity not to be explained in the terms of biology, common sense, and everyday life."[23] Morton emphasizes that any consideration of the self must also account for its "sitedness."[24] Stacy Alaimo calls for the recognition of a membranous "trans-corporeal" self "in which the human is always intermeshed with the more-the-human world" and its volatile chemical traffic (Figure 7.2).[25] Similarly, while critics and practitioners of innovative poetry, such as Ron Silliman, Bernstein, McCaffery, and Bök have repeatedly derided the emphasis on individual voice, and personal communication in the lyric as outdated modes of "official verse culture,"[26] such critiques of "voice, self-presence, and authenticity," Marjorie Perloff argues in *Differentials*, "must be understood as part of the larger post-structuralist critique of authorship and the humanist subject" that has emerged out of contemporary theory and the L=A=N=G=U=A=G=E poetry movement.[27] I propose in this project to redirect innovative poetics back onto the body (my body) in order to create unconventional poetry that linguistically and procedurally (through my own "body burden" testing and microbial screening) explores the writing subject and its associated flows and interchanges with the environment.

THE HYPOTHESIS

Pataphysics has much to offer a postmodern ecocriticism—both as an object of study and as a potential methodological approach given its emphasis on intersections between research and art. I will defend this claim by highlighting two characteristics of pataphysical poetics:[28] "Ambient Poetics" involves the appropriation, involvement, and reframing of found texts and other environmental influences; "Transgenic Poetics" explores symbiotic relationships in bioart that challenge conventional distinctions between text and world as well as between human and nonhuman. These are examples of what Marjorie Perloff identifies as a "new exploratory poetry"[29] emerging in contemporary poetics that has sought to recover the legacy of avant-garde projects from the early twentieth century.[30] Such research-driven, formally unconventional, sometimes unreadable poetry (requiring a "thinkership" rather than a readership, as Place and Fitterman propose in *Notes on Conceptualisms*[31]) reflects the increasing presence of new conceptual and pataphysical projects. This writing is less interested in direct expression and more concerned with constraints in compositional methodologies (such as lipograms, aleatoric techniques, digital coding, translation, bioengineering, and found texts) often under the guise of invented institutes or in the service of exceptional procedures. The work of these postmodern writers is deeply concerned with the contemporary environment not only in the context of pollution and genetic engineering, but also as a function of globalization and changes in community structures precipitated by reconfigurations of information technology.

What is the ecocritical status of texts that turn to the strict methodologies of science for imagined, unreal, or hyperreal ends? The pataphysical poetics explored below engage the environment as a complex set of semiotic and symbiotic relationships where diverse forms of signification and alternative realities and materialities interact. As Serpil Oppermann asserts, "A wholesale, discursive change in our epistemic models is necessary to create global awareness."[32] Indeed, the attempt to inhabit and expose the oppositions within normative concepts of science and nature, for example, posed by Morton (*The Ecological Thought, Ecology Without Nature*) and Bruno Latour (*Politics of Nature*) are central to pataphysical interests in "denaturing" nature, in deterritorializing (in the terms of Deleuze and Guattari) cultural *Umwelten* to other ways of thinking and framing significance (Figure 7.3).

Literary artists have a role to play in providing alternate perspectives on what it means to live and write with pollution—especially when the pollution in question is itself suspected of generating an insidious form of biochemical writing. My objective is to write a book of poetry (currently titled *Anatomic*) that will develop a semiotic map of the toxicological and symbiotic circumstances of my body. As an unusual, exceptional science project, the poetry in *Anatomic* will reflect and emerge from information and experiences gathered as a result of diverse and unconventional research methods, such as body burden testing to determine toxic chemicals in my own blood (Figure 7.3), microbial screening to reveal what other creatures share my body, as well as site-specific research into my

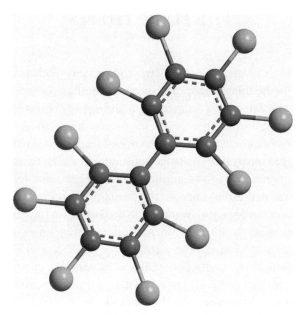

FIGURE 7.3 PCBs (polychlorinated biphenyls)

own inevitable viral infections and allergic reactions. This project combines research in theoretical and experimental scientific fields (such as biosemiotics and toxicology) with research in innovative poetics (such as constraint-based pataphysical procedures) in order to derive compositional methodologies for the creation of poems about chemical pollution as well as microbial latency and symbiosis in the human body. My aim is to complicate distinctions between nature and culture as well as between pollution and purity by reframing the body as a being overwritten by toxic chemicals yet constantly subject to the semiotic interference of other microbial life forms. Consequently, *Anatomic* asks: How can poetry respond to the predicament of a contemporary body affected by chemicals in the environment? What does it mean for the environment to write or rewrite a body in the first place?

The Experiment

Ambient Poetics

Unorthodox research methods that lead to experimental apprehensions of the physical and semiotic environment constitute a species of "ambient poetics," which is a term developed by Morton that refers to collapsed distinctions between background and foreground in artistic practice.[33] Take, for example, works that involve the environment in some way, whether as a physical process serving as a protocol for compositional

strategies, or as a textual field in which different circulating discourses (scientific, political, commercial) are translated, combined, fragmented, or reframed as an exercise in
exceptional scrutiny. Illustrations of ambient poetics include John Cage's *4'33"*, a piece of
music completely determined by its extra-musical acoustic environment, and Stephen
Collis and Jordan Scott's *DE COMP*, a re-reading of Darwin's *On the Origin of Species*
after several copies have been left to decompose in five distinct British Columbia ecosystems for a year.[34] This drive toward expanding the environment of writing by including site-specific influences and other found or appropriated texts is part of the shifting
frames of signification intrinsic to pataphysics and it is how I want to specifically understand ambient poetics. Consider, for example, Kenneth Goldsmith's conservationist
ethic: "The world is full of texts, more or less interesting; I do not wish to add any more."[35]
His conceptual projects, which he classifies as "uncreative writing," involve appropriations and transcriptions of existing texts, including a retyped edition of the *New York
Times* (*Day*), every word he spoke for a week (*Soliloquy*), and every movement he made
over the course of a day (*Fidget*). These pataphysical experiments involve controlling
for particular variables of signification; he is interested in "any method of disorientation used in order to re-imagine our normative relationship to language."[36] Goldsmith
is famous for declaring that his books do not require reading (he claims to have fallen
asleep proofreading them). Even if this were not the case, his texts demand a different
kind of reading, one that deterritorializes and displaces the conventions of literacy.

Goldsmith's works are often grounded in the placeless milieus of transportation and
information exchange. His book *Traffic*, for example, is a collection of transcribed traffic
bulletins at ten-minute intervals from the New York radio station WINS 1010 AM over
a twenty-four hour period during a holiday long-weekend. Ecocriticism has focused at
length on the importance of place, but it has had little to say so far about "non-places,"
about the placeless, transient locations associated with malls, waiting rooms, offices,
transportation, or supermarkets. The term "non-place" was developed by the anthropologist Marc Augé, who proposes that "If a place can be defined as relational, historical and concerned with identity, then a space which cannot be defined as relational, or
historical, or concerned with identity will be a non-place."[37] We might suggest that the
study of non-places represents an important frontier of emerging ecocritical concern;
after all, as Buell observes, "We may think high-mindedly that we disdain non-places
while depending on them daily."[38] These sorts of non-places are intrinsic to pataphysical projects that make use of found, ambient materials gathered from the often overlooked environments of mass communication and transportation. Both non-places and
what Jeff Derksen calls "non-sites" are environments of competing discursive forces.
Consequently, in a globalized world the proliferation of non-sites, such as toxic waste
dumps, requires varieties of experimental writing, according to Derksen, that "provide
other narrative structures—and temporal frameworks—for imagining places and histories."[39] Similarly, elaborating on Gilles Clément's idea of the Third Landscape (margins
of highways, weeds in sidewalks, and other untended spaces associated with transit and
transience), Jonathan Skinner calls for attention to the place of non-places, non-sites,
and other neglected environments by way of what he terms "biome saturation" in which

artists can dedicate themselves to locations and organisms that often fail to signify culturally or even scientifically.[40] As revealed by the results of the experiment discussed below, Harryette Mullen's focus on the supermarket in *S*PeRM**K*T* is a potential example of biome saturation, where pataphysical immersion in the ambient poetics of a non-place offers an alternate way of reading the environment.

Transgenic Poetics

In addition to ambience, postmodern ecocriticism also turns its attention to unconventional media made possible by technological innovations. Contemporary pataphysical poetics have, for example, shifted the boundaries of the text away from the codex and its metaphorical "book of life" to living organisms themselves in a manner that further blurs distinctions between art and science. In his essay "Transgenic Art," Eduardo Kac describes this emerging practice as "a new art form based on the use of genetic engineering techniques to transfer synthetic genes to an organism or to transfer natural genetic material from one species into another, to create unique living beings."[41] Kac is most famous for his transgenic creation *GFP Bunny*, which involved altering the genome of an albino rabbit to include green fluorescent protein (GFP) derived from jellyfish. The resulting bunny, named Alba, glows bright green when exposed to a specific spectrum of light. Other projects have included an enclosed ecosystem of GFP creatures (*The Eighth Day*), a genetically engineered petunia that expresses in the prominent red veins of its petals DNA from the artist's own blood (*Natural History of the Enigma*), and a sentence from the bible transposed into a genetic sequence, inserted into a bacterium that is subsequently exposed to UV light, then translated back into language to reveal the mutated text (*Genesis*).

   As might be expected, Kac's unorthodox projects have attracted controversy (Alba remains impounded in a French laboratory). N. Katherine Hayles, for example, wonders ambivalently whether Kac's meddling with genes serves to reinforce or contest human dominion over the natural world.[42] Similar concerns are expressed by Brenda Iijima about Canadian poet Christian Bök's *The Xenotext Experiment*.[43] Bök has developed a transgenic art project that uses a process of encipherment to write and translate a poem into a sequence of genetic nucleotides to be inserted into a bacterium's genome. The poem, as a set of genetic instructions, causes the organism to produce a protein, which, according to the chemical code used in the experiment, constitutes another legible poem. The formidable task for Bök involves settling on an enciphering procedure that enables mutual correlation between both the original DNA sequence of the inserted poem and the complementary RNA version of the poem produced by the organism, which is ultimately responsible for arranging amino acids into the polypeptide chains of the intended protein. Darren Wershler compares transcription, as it specifically concerns *The Xenotext Experiment*, to a newspaper cryptogram, "except that instead of one set of letters being gibberish and the other being meaningful, both sets are meaningful."[44] Bök must come up with a way to correlate letters of the alphabet so that he can write two mutually enciphering poems at the same time. The result of this experiment, according to Bök, is that "The bacterium [*Deinococcus radiodurans*] would, in effect, *be* the poem."[45] In fact, the bacterium would become a machine for writing poetry, but it would also become a potential archive more generally for human textual information: "there is probably no better way of preserving information," Bök maintains, "than in the form of living things that can evolve and survive over billions of years."[46]

The difference between Kac's *Genesis* and *The Xenotext Experiment* is that Bök's project, even though it predetermines the protein response poem, allows for the organism's active participation in utilizing the artificially inserted nucleotides as a functional element of its genetic being. The application of UV light in *Genesis*, conversely, renders the organism passively subject to external mutagenic forces. If Kac's project is about damaging the organism, Bök's is about subsisting within it like a biotrophic parasite tending toward a mutualistic symbiosis, given his project's reliance on the health and viability of the bacterium. Moreover, Bök's stated interest in exploring the possibilities of organisms as archives raises the symbiotic stakes even further. We may depend in the future on these organisms to safeguard our past. Bacteria are implicated in the deepest origins of human genetic history and they may well become storehouses for future human culture.

Anatomic will be divided into two main sections. Part One, "Symbols," will concentrate, through body burden testing, on my body as a site of environmental contamination. I will test myself under medical supervision for 68 chemicals that fall under the following groups: Phthalates (Figure 7.4); PCBs (polychlorinated biphenyls); PFCs (perfluorinated chemicals); OCPs (organochlorine pesticides); OPIMs (organophosphate insecticide metabolites); PAHs (polycyclic aromatic hydrocarbons); and

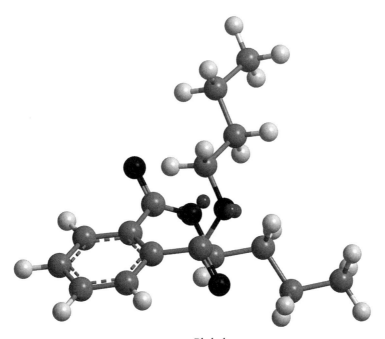

FIGURE 7.4 Phthalates

BPA (bisphenol A). All of these chemicals are widely present in the environment and believed to exist in every human to varying degrees. In addition to investigating chemical structures, industrial applications, and cultural contexts, I will research the specific adverse health effects associated with these carcinogens, hormone disruptors, neurotoxins, reproductive/developmental toxins, and respiratory toxins in order to develop poetic methodologies in which, for example, certain texts (found and created) interfere with each other. From a biosemiotic perspective, the toxicity of these chemicals stems largely from their capacity to meddle with the ways in which the body's membranous surfaces interpret chemical messages.

In Part Two, "Symbionts," I will complicate distinctions between natural and unnatural as well as questions of environmental interference by exploring ways in which the body might be said to have always been "contaminated" by the outside, by viruses, bacteria, fungi, parasites, and other organisms that have taken up residence within us over the course of a lifetime and over the course of evolutionary history. I will research specific examples relevant to my physiology. Cold sores (*herpes simplex virus*), for example, are caused by a virus that, once contracted, never leaves the body but remains latent in the central nervous system from which it reactivates occasionally according to environmental stimuli. *Varicella zoster virus* (chicken pox) is similarly dormant but prone to potential reactivation. Viruses represent explicit instances of the body being rewritten or recomposed by outside forces; moreover, they are suggestive of the parasitological theories of language proposed by Christopher Dewdney (in terms of pataphysics) and Søren Brier (in terms of biosemiotics).[47] I will also test myself for other viruses like adenovirus-36, a form of the common cold now linked to obesity, West Nile virus, and *Toxoplasma gondii*, a pervasive cat parasite that can, according to some theories, cause behavioural changes in people.[48] I also propose to screen myself to find out if I am an asymptomatic carrier of various fungi or bacteria such as *H. pylori* (ulcers) and *MRSA* (associated with drug resistance).

If toxic chemicals and viruses rewrite the body from the outside, autoimmune illnesses or allergies, such as eczema, constitute instances where the body recognizes a foreign pathogen that is neither necessarily outside the body nor necessarily harmful. The immune system must construct a biochemical "self" in order to defend the body from alien substances that it recognizes as a "non-self." It does this by producing an enormous number of receptors (called *lymphocytes*) that effectively act as a vigilant and multi-surfaced skin.[49] Consequently, this interior semiotic surface, this imaginary self, will be a focal point for various poems in "Symbionts."

THE RESULT

Ambient Poetics

The asterisks in *S*PeRM**K*T*, the title of Mullen's book-length poem, represent the letters "u are" missing from the word "supermarket." At issue here is the placelessness of identity and the legibility of space in the non-place of the grocery store. Does sperm come in a kit from the grocery store? Does food grow in packages? The identity of the consumer and the essential identities of food and health products are destabilized in the semiotic environment of the supermarket and as a consequence require a different form of personal and environmental literacy. Harryette Mullen is an African-American writer concerned in her work, as Juliana Spahr proposes, "with the relation between liberatory reading and the vectors of race, class, and gender."[50] To this I would add that Mullen is also concerned with the environment of reading and the reading of environments. The supermarket, one of the exemplary non-places described by Augé, is essentially a way station for shipping and receiving divorced from both the growing of food and the domestic sphere of consumption; it is, like the contemporary global city, an elsewhere made local through the diversity of products made available.

S*PeRM**K*T is a site-specific work that aims to "recycle and reconfigure language from a public sphere that includes mass media and political discourse as well as literature and folklore."[51] Mullen, who has professed a fascination with the dichotomy and intersection between science and spirituality, describes her compositional methodology in explicitly pataphysical terms: "Every trip to the supermarket became research and a possible excursion into language."[52] Moreover, her work intentionally builds on the experimental protocols of Gertrude Stein's Tender Buttons and its cubist or crystallographic concern with food (revealed in its multifaceted approach); Mullen's book, by extension, is about a form of household management, about the domestic duties stereotypically attributed to women. The supermarket, as an environment of language, requires of Mullen an ecopoetic approach, as evidenced by her acknowledged debt to environmental artists and collage artists who reframe and recycle detritus.[53]

The book-length poem is ultimately an experimental project in reading consumption. As Mullen notes, "You read as you stand in line."[54] The line is the governing form of the book inasmuch as each page is written with the unbroken line of prose poetry. In addition to the rows of products, whose labelling provides found-language for the poem, lines are also present in the memorized verses of commercial jingles. As Mullen points out, "twenty-five-year-old jingles are embedded in my brain... we are immersed, bombarded with language that is commercial."[55] Here are some of those jingles reread and reconfigured:

> Aren't you glad you use petroleum? Don't wait to be told you explode. You're not fully here until you're over there. Never let them see you eat. You might be taken for a zoo. Raise your hand if you're sure you're not.[56]

Augé proposes that logos and brand names become reassuring landmarks in the non-place of the supermarket.[57] However, in this case Mullen reframes these advertisements for soaps and deodorants (Dial, Zest, Dry Idea, Sure) and reads them as part of the oil economy and its capacity to infuse and displace identity. The implied connection between oil ("Aren't you glad you use petroleum?") and meat ("You might be taken for a zoo") suggests how the consumption of petrochemical products has yielded a subject dependent on packaging (socially as well as materially) and transport. The dilemma of being over there in order to be fully here is the quandary of the non-place and it is read here not simply as a geographical predicament but as social and biological one. We are oil. In the supermarket, in the world of consumerism, combustion is both an expression of individual appetite and the expansion of multinational control.

Perhaps nature is a capitalist fancy, Morton wonders in *The Ecological Thought*.[58] The supermarket, as Mullen's poem demonstrates, peddles imaginary solutions as curatives to the problem of the outside: "We dream the dream of extirpation. Wipe out a species, with God on our side. Annihilate the insects. Sterilize the filthy vermin."[59] Her pataphysical project aims to shift the *Umwelt* that frames the conventional semiotics of the supermarket in order to expose the way in which consumption has become pathology. She asserts in an interview that "We are consumers; that's how we are constructed as citizens. People consume more than they vote."[60] The final line of the book warns against failing to read the landscape of consumption: "Speed readers skim the white space of this galaxy."[61] Without careful reading of our semiotic environment we miss both the racial presuppositions of the landmarks and also fail to attend to the "white noise" of consumer culture, the din of advertising and the proliferation of non-places that assume "Homo means the same" and "Our cows are well adjusted."[62] Mullen's ambient poetics provoke, as Morton insists viable forms of this art must, "thought about fundamental metaphysical categories such as inside and outside."[63] The frame comes into focus, the semiotic field of signification expands, the *Umwelten* expand—the result is not a reified textual object, not a destination or final resting place, but a field of questions that complicate the environment of the place and the non-place.

Transgenic Poetics

Rather than germy threats to personal hygiene and household cleanliness, so omnipresent in the discourses of Mullen's supermarket, microbes have become valued hosts and colleagues in *The Xenotext Experiment*. As Margulis contends, we have microbes to thank for our lives: "humans are not the work of God but of thousands of millions of years of interaction among highly responsive microbes."[64] Life itself emerged from bacterial symbiogenesis, which is the symbiotic joining of two cells in what Margulis describes as abortive cannibalism, as a failed act of ingestion. Failed acts of this sort have resulted over time in the "truce called sex."[65] Symbiotic relationships, consequently, involve giving up a degree of autonomy in order to share the burden of overcoming certain obstacles (bacteria profit by helping termites digest wood, for example). The natural world is filled with such cases, Jesper Hoffmeyer claims, where at one level "a lack of freedom can actually pave the way to a different sort of freedom at a higher level."[66] I propose that pataphysical constraints offer a similarly counterintuitive semiotic advantage. As Bök explains in *Eunoia*, his earlier univocal Oulipian experiment, imposing immense, "crippling" compositional constraints reveals that "even under such improbable conditions of duress, language can still express an uncanny, if not sublime, thought."[67] Similarly, in *The Xenotext Experiment* authorship is constrained by the biological processes of another organism, yet the text is enriched in its capacity to be projected through time, to be expressed as part of the viability of another creature.

Just as Hayles worries about the ethical implications of Kac's work, the interference with a nonhuman organism in Bök's project potentially reinforces domineering attitudes towards nature. However, the deconstructive gesture implicit in pataphysical works like this serves to deterritorialize the conventional commercial and industrial environment of such procedures and in so doing brings to bear the invited scrutiny of artistic practice. Bök's project forces a shift in cultural *Umwelten* in order to consider the aesthetics of an activity that is normally invisible. Similarly, Cary Wolfe argues that Kac's use of the visually arresting glowing rabbit contrasts with the invisibility of genetic engineering. The appeal to the visual conspicuousness of the rabbit underscores the degree to which we cannot depend on the visible to register the effects of technology in a world of genetic engineering: "the harder you look, the less you see."[68] Bök's desire to insert what he hopes will be a "beautiful, anomalous poem, whose 'alien words' might subsist, like a harmless parasite," implies an engagement with the creature that is artistically conspicuous, nonviolent, and honest in its unavoidable anthropocentrism.[69] The experiment so far has produced "a very short poem; a very masculine assertion about the aesthetic creation of life. The organism reads the poem, and writes in response a very melancholy, feminine—almost surreal in tone—poem about the aesthetic loss of life. The two poems are in dialogue with each other,"[70] shifting in their concluding lines, by way of the chemical cipher, from "the word of life" to "any milk is rosy."[71] The discrete singularity of the word "the" becomes translated, according to the biochemically constrained act of the bacterium making a viable protein, into the inclusive and multitudinous word "any," an implicit nod, perhaps, to the organism's symbiotic predicament.[72]

We might say of *The Xenotext Experiment*, as the Canadian poet Don McKay says of thoughtfully enacted anthropocentric art more generally, that it can be seen as "an address to the other with an acknowledgement of our human-centredness built in, a salutary and humbling reminder."[73] The bacterium is a colleague in a human artistic project, a symbiont in the creation of living material (its own proteins) and non-commercial, thought-provoking information (beautiful poetry). Furthermore, the interference with bacteria need not necessarily be dismissed as ethically suspect. While I am mindful of the dangers of appearing to advocate indiscriminate invasions into the genomes of others, it must nonetheless be pointed out that, in addition to the prevalence of human experiments with microbes (ranging from bioengineering to the overuse of antibiotics), creatures have always interfered—we might say, more neutrally, intra-acted—in often subtle and fundamental ways with each other.[74] In fact, such interference has been the source of evolutionary novelty (the original pataphysical science of exceptions, we might say). As Margulis reminds us, "Viruses today spread genes among bacteria and human and other cells, as they always have. Like bacterial symbionts, viruses are sources of evolutionary variation."[75] She declares succinctly: "we are our viruses."[76] If this is the case, why not self-consciously and thoughtfully experiment with rewriting our viruses? After all, from the perspective of Bök's pataphysical proposal, it is simply a matter of viruses playing with viruses.

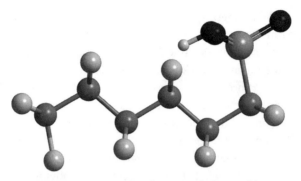

FIGURE 7.5 PFCs (perfluorinated chemicals)

COMMON POLYMER SHARED BY TWO OR MORE WORDS IN A DIFFERENT
LANGUAGE

Heart beating in Danish,
      bank, bank
Mercury monogloting in Minamata,
      ataxia
Door creaking in Arabic,
      azeeez
PCB typefacing in Monsanto,
      chloracne
Bird singing in Thai,
      jib, jib
Pharmaceuticals tap-watering in Adrenal Gland,
      fight, flight
Cannon firing in Mandarin,
      ping, pang, pa
Flame retardants keying in Keyboard and Furniture,
      dyslexia, combustion

As of this moment, my body burden tests and microbial screening are still being organized and scheduled. Consequently, in the spirit of pataphysics, this project is currently
a work of potential literature. The poem printed above is from my book *The Polymers*,[77] a
collection of poetry about plastic and plasticity that involves some of the methodological
approaches that I expect will be relevant to *Anatomic*. The poem's concerns with translation and linguistic interference enact at the textual level the endocrine disruptions believed
to be caused by exposure to volatile forms of plastic and other chemicals (Figure 7.5 and
7.6 below). As an example of ambient poetics, the poem rewrites found texts concerned
with cross-linguistic onomatopoeias, with deciphering common but uncanny cultural
practices (how are inarticulate sounds articulated in other languages?). In addition, the
poem expresses a polymeric structure through its grammatical and acoustic repetitions.

Polymer chemistry is the science of giant molecules made possible by the repetition of small units held together in long chains by chemical bonds. Culture itself is polymeric; take the proliferation of memes, the persistence of social conventions and convictions, or the insistent messages that disguise and forcefully assert industrial interests.

CONCLUSION

In *The Ecological Thought* Morton asserts that ecocritics should seek to more actively direct scientific research by proposing "experiments, based on their varied, complex, radical, and interestingly divergent ideas."[78] "Scientists should at least take a look" at these imagined experiments he insists.[79] Postmodern ecocriticism stands to gain much by both studying and practicing pataphysical modes of experimental critical inquiry. The playful poetics of pataphysics represent a serious attempt to think of art as an alternative form of science in its own right capable of expanding what matters in semiotic and material environments by interrogating distinctions between culture and nature, and between human and nonhuman. All of the pataphysical projects discussed above involve researching, sampling, or creating semiotic and biological environments and holding them up to scrutiny. To expand cultural *Umwelten* requires learning how to read in diverse ways; it means taking risks and following the abductive logic of seemingly strange, imaginary solutions. In an age when questions of biotechnology and anthropogenic environmental degradation have become vexingly pertinent, artistic/scientific work such as this that asks fundamental questions about how we write the environment and how the environment writes us is both timely and necessary.

N. Katherine Hayles suggests that to conceptualize the posthuman as the integration of human and nonhuman actors at once undermines human mastery of the

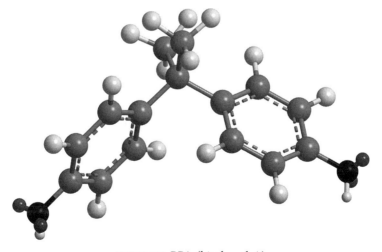

FIGURE 7.6 BPA (bisphenol A)

environment and also allows us to "fashion images of ourselves that accurately reflect the complex interplays that ultimately make the entire world one system."[80] My project is posthumanist inasmuch as it proposes that organisms are swarms of symbiotic and volatile actors (veritable non-places of being). *Anatomic* proceeds to rethink the writing subject as membranous, as a cyborg ontology,[81] as a recursive organization denaturing both the human and the nonhuman. By reframing the body as an anatomy of interfering and intra-acting messages, it is my aim to make ecopoetics and ecocriticism "dirtier" (in the spirit of Morton's "dark ecology"), to defamiliarize the subjective emphasis on the body in order to underscore both the potency of seemingly innocuous environmental toxins and the ethical potential of locating personhood in the skin, in the membranes, at the threshold of the continuous interchange between self and environment that has marked human evolutionary history.

NOTES

1. Jakob von Uexküll, "A Stroll Through the Worlds of Animals and Men: A Picture Book of Invisible Worlds," 1934, in *Instinctive Behavior: The Development of a Modern Concept*, ed. trans. Claire H. Shiller (New York: International Universities Press, 1957), 5.
2. Thomas A. Sebeok, *Signs: An Introduction to Semiotics*, 2nd ed. (Toronto: University of Toronto Press, 2001), 100.
3. Ibid., 77.
4. Jakob von Uexküll, "The Theory of Meaning," *Semiotica* 42, no.1 (1982): 77.
5. Alfred Jarry, *Exploits & Opinions of Dr. Faustroll, Pataphysician: A Neo-Scientific Novel*, trans. Simon Watson Taylor, intro. Roger Shattuck (Boston: Exact Change, 1996), 25.
6. Jarry spells pataphysics with an apostrophe ('pataphysics) in order to avoid what he sees as a "simple pun" ("*patte à physique*") (21, 119). In the pataphysical spirit of exceptions and exhaustive consistency, I have dropped the apostrophe in all references throughout this publication.
7. Ibid., 21–2.
8. Christian Bök, '*Pataphysics: The Poetics of an Imaginary Science* (Evanston, IL: Northwestern University Press, 2002), 4.
9. Roger Shattuck, introduction to *Dr. Faustroll*, xvii.
10. Bök, '*Pataphysics*, 27.
11. Wendy Wheeler, "Postscript on Biosemiotics: Reading Beyond Words—And Ecocriticism," *New Formations* 64 (2008): 139.
12. Ibid., 146.
13. Rachel Carson, *Silent Spring: Fortieth Anniversary Edition* (1962; repr., Boston and New York: Houghton Mifflin Company, [1962] 2002), 193.
14. Rick Smith and Bruce Lourie, *Slow Death by Rubber Duck: How the Toxic Chemistry of Everyday Life Affects our Health* (Toronto: Alfred A. Knopf Canada, 2009), 6, 7–8.
15. Gilles Deleuze and Félix Guattari, *A Thousand Plateaus: Capitalism and Schizophrenia*, trans. Brian Massumi (Minneapolis and London: University of Minnesota Press, 1987), 369.
16. Charles Bernstein, "The Task of Poetics, the Fate of Innovation, and the Aesthetics of Criticism," in *The Consequence of Innovation: 21st Century Poetics*, ed. Craig Dworkin (New York: Roof Books, 2008), 47.

17. Bernstein, "The Task of Poetics," 46.

18. Dana Phillips, "Ecocriticism, Ecopoetics, and a Creed Outworn," *New Formations* 64 (2008): 50.

19. Timothy Morton, *Ecology without Nature: Rethinking Environmental Aesthetics* (Cambridge, MA, and London: Harvard University Press, 2007), 188.

20. Dana Phillips, *The Truth of Ecology: Nature, Culture, and Literature in America* (Oxford and New York: Oxford University Press, 2003), 241.

21. Robert Kocik, *Overcoming Fitness* (Brooklyn, NY: Exit 18 Pamphlet Series, 2000), n.p.

22. Angus Fletcher, *A New Theory for American Poetry: Democracy, the Environment, and the Future of Imagination* (Cambridge, MA, London: Harvard University Press, 2004) 122.

23. Phillips, *The Truth of Ecology*, 196.

24. Morton, *Ecology Without Nature*, 176.

25. Stacy Alaimo, *Bodily Natures: Science, Environment, and the Material Self* (Bloomington and Indianapolis: Indiana University Press), 2.

26. Charles Bernstein, *Content's Dream: essays, 1974–1984* (Evanston, IL: Northwestern University Press, 2001).

27. Marjorie Perloff, *Differentials: Poetry, Poetics, Pedagogy* (Tuscaloosa, AL: The University of Alabama Press, 2004), 130.

28. There are other characteristics of pataphysical poetics that are relevant to ecocriticism, but space does not permit me to address them entirely. In addition to conceptual and procedural writing, Jonathan Skinner's "compass points for ecopoetics" include documentary, situationist, and sound poetics as potential modes of ecopoetic writing that I would suggest could be considered pataphysical. See: Jonathan Skinner, "Conceptualizing the Field: Some compass points for ecopoetics," *Jacket2* (September 5, 2011): https://jacket2.org/commentary/conceptualizing-field

29. Marjorie Perloff, *Poetry On & Off the Page: Essays for Emergent Occasions* (Evanston, IL: Northwestern University Press, 1998), 166.

30. Marjorie Perloff, *Twenty-First-Century Modernism: The "New" Poetics* (Malden, MA and Oxford: Blackwell Publishers, 2002), 3–5.

31. Vanessa Place and Robert Fitterman, *Notes on Conceptualisms* (Brooklyn, NY: Ugly Duckling Presse, 2009).

32. Aldo Leopold, "Seeking," *A Sand County Almanac: and Sketches Here and There* (1949; repr., New York: Oxford University Press, 1964) 244.

33. Morton, *Ecology Without Nature*, 47.

34. Oana Avasilichioaei, "Commons as folds," *Jacket2* (2011): https://jacket2.org/commentary/commons-folds

35. Kenneth Goldsmith, "A Week of Blogs for the Poetry Foundation," *The Consequence of Innovation: 21st Century Poetics*, ed. Craig Dworkin (New York: Roof Books, 2008), 144.

36. Ibid., 140.

37. Marc Augé, *Non-Places: An Introduction to Supermodernity*, 2nd ed. trans. John Howe. (London and New York: Verso, 2008), 63.

38. Laurence Buell, *The Future of Environmental Criticism: Environmental Crisis and Literary Imagination* (Oxford: Blackwell, 2005), 70.

39. Jeff Derksen, *Annihiliated Time: Poetry and Other Politics* (Vancouver: Talonbooks, 2009), 196.

40. Jonathan Skinner, "Thoughts on Things: Poetics of the Third Landscape,") ((eco(lang) (uage(reader)): the eco language reader, ed. Brenda Iijima (New York: Portable Press at Yo-Yo Labs and Nightboat Books, 2010), 46–7.

41. Eduardo Kac, "Transgenic Art," Leonardo Electronic Almanac 6, no.11 (1998): www.ekac. org/transgenic.html.

42. N. Katherine Hayles, "Who Is in Control Here? Meditating on Eduardo Kac's Transgenic Art," The Eighth Day: The Transgenic Art of Eduardo Kac, eds. Sheilah Britton and Dan Collins (Tempe AZ: Institute for Studies in the Arts, 2003), 83.

43. Brenda Iijima, "An Interview with Tyrone Williams,")((eco(lang)(uage(reader)): the eco language reader, ed. Brenda Iijima (New York: Portable Press at Yo-Yo Labs and Nightboat Books, 2010), 160.

44. Darren Wershler, "The Xenotext Experiment, So Far," Canadian Journal of Communication 37 (2012): 49.

45. Christian Bök, "Interview with Christian Bök," by Jonathan Ball, The Believer 7, no. 5 (2009): 48.

46. Ibid., 51.

47. Christopher Dewdney, Alter Sublime (Toronto: The Coach House Press, 1980) 75; Søren Brier, Cybersemiotics: Why Information is Not Enough! (Toronto, Buffalo, and London: University of Toronto Press, 2008), 330.

48. Jane Switzer, "Faster, Pussycat, Kill, Kill: A Parasite Linked to Cats Can Make People Reckless, Aggressive, Even Suicidal," Macleans, October 21, 2010, http://www2.macleans. ca/2010/10/21/faster-pussycat-kill-kill/

49. Jesper Hoffmeyer, Biosemiotics: An Examination into the Signs of Life and the Life of Signs, trans. Jesper Hoffmeyer and Donald Favareau (Scranton and London: University of Scranton Press, 2008), 241.

50. Juliana Spahr, Everybody's Autonomy: Connective Reading and Collective Identity (Tuscaloosa and London, The University of Alabama Press, 2001), 92.

51. Harryette Mullen, Recyclopedia: Trimmings, S*PeRM**K*T, and Muse & Drudge (Saint Paul, MN: Graywolf Press, 2006), x.

52. Harryette Mullen, "Interview with Harryette Mullen," by Cynthia Hogue, Postmodern Culture 9, no. 2 (1999): 17. http://muse.jhu.edu/journals/postmodern_culture/toc/ pmc9.2.html.

53. Ibid., 16; Mullen's interest in modes of reading and pataphysical methodologies is also apparent in her later work, Sleeping with the Dictionary and its self-conscious employment of Oulipian constraints.

54. Mullen, "Interview," 17.

55. Ibid., 16.

56. Mullen, Recyclopedia, 5.

57. Augé, Non-Places, 86.

58. Timothy Morton, The Ecological Thought (Cambridge, MA, and London: Harvard University Press, 2010), 125.

59. Mullen, Recyclopedia, 10.

60. Mullen, "Interview," 13.

61. Mullen, Recyclopedia, 32.

62. Ibid., 32.

63. Morton, The Ecological Thought, 142.

64. Lynn Margulis, *Symbiotic Planet: A New Look at Evolution* (New York: Basic Books, 1998), 4.
65. Ibid., 100.
66. Jesper Hoffmeyer, *Signs of Meaning in the Universe*, trans. Barbara J. Haveland (Bloomington and Indianapolis: Indiana University Press, 1996), 27.
67. Christian Bök, *Eunoia* (Toronto: Coach House Books, 2001), 103.
68. Cary Wolfe, *What is Posthumanism?* (Minneapolis and London: University of Minnesota Press, 2010), 165.
69. Christian Bök, "The Xenotext Experiment," *SCRIPTed* 5, no.2 (2008): 229.
70. Christian Bök, "Cryptic poetry written in a microbe's DNA," *New Scientist (blog)*, May 4, 2011, http://www.newscientist.com/blogs/culturelab/2011/05/christian-boks-dynamic-dna-poetry.html.
71. For an image of the full text of both poems see: Benjamin Thompson, "Event review: The Xenotext," *microbelog* (blog), August 16, 2011, http://microbelog.wordpress.com/2011/08/16/event-review-the-xenotext/
72. Bök has run into difficulties with his project despite some promising initial test results involving *E.coli*. The Xenotext protein turned out to be too small and the organism was destroying it. The preponderance of repeated letter combinations may have caused the bacterium to interpret the poem as a retrovirus, which has prompted Bök to reconfigure the way that recurrent spaces are encoded in the poem (Wershler, "The Xenotext Experiment, So Far," 54).
73. Don McKay, *Vis à Vis: Fieldnotes on Poetry & Wilderness* (Wolfville, NS: Gaspereau Press, 2001), 99.
74. Stacy Alaimo employs Karen Barad's concept of "intra-action" as way of understanding how materials do not discretely precede their relationships with each other, but emerge through combinations and interrelations. See Alaimo, *Bodily Natures*, 21, and Karen Barad, *Meeting the Universe Halfway: Quantum Physics and the Entanglement of Matter and Meaning* (Durham, NC: Duke University Press, 2007).
75. Margulis, *Symbiotic Planet*, 64.
76. Ibid., 64.
77. Adam Dickinson, *The Polymers* (Toronto: House of Anansi Press, 2013).
78. Morton, *The Ecological Thought*, 114.
79. Ibid., 114.
80. N. Katherine Hayles, *How We Became Posthuman: Virtual Bodies in Cybernetics, Literature, and Informatics* (Chicago and London: The University of Chicago Press, 1999), 290.
81. Donna Haraway, *Simians, Cyborgs, and Women: The Reinvention of Nature* (London and New York: Routledge, 1991).

PART II

THEORY

CHAPTER 8

ECOCRITICISM AND THE POLITICS OF REPRESENTATION

CHERYL LOUSLEY

> …confronting ecological problems requires making choices and deci-
> sions—about what to produce, what to consume, on what energy to rely—
> which ultimately concern the very way of life of a people; as such, they
> are not only not technical, but are eminently political in the most radical
> sense of involving fundamental social choices.
>
> —Slavoj Žižek, *First as Tragedy, Then as Farce*[1]

DOUGLAS Coupland's 2006 novel *JPod* closes with a scene where climate change
itself is made into a commodifiable spectacle. Coupland—appearing as a character in
the novel—presents game programmer Ethan with Dglobe, a prototype for a to-be-
made-in-China mass-market computer with a globe-shaped screen that simulates
planetary change on a geological scale, sped up for the electronic generation. The program—to be coded by Ethan and his jPod co-workers—not only recreates the past three
billion years of continental drift and ice ages; it uses climate-modeling algorithms to
project forward three billion years under a variety of scenarios:

> Doug said, "Gee, Ethan—I wonder what Earth would look like if Antarctica melted
>   completely? Why, let's find out! And let's do it in sixty seconds."
> Before me Earth's land masses lost their familiarity. Florida vanished, as did much of
>   Asia and all the planet's coastlines.
> "Do it again!"
> "With pleasure."
> The continents submerged once more.
> "Show me more stuff!" (512)

Ethan's demand to experience again and again the pleasure of watching the Earth transform beyond recognition and human habitation confirms Fredric Jameson's famous

quip that "it seems to be easier for us today to imagine the thoroughgoing deterioration of the earth and of nature than the breakdown of late capitalism" (xii). *JPod*—a play on Apple Inc.'s iconic consumer product "iPod"—highlights the market for imagining the destruction of the world. Ethan and his co-workers' skills in designing gore-filled video games are readily transferrable to imagining climactic apocalypse.

J. K. Gibson-Graham builds on Jameson to argue that our imaginations have been engaged more in the service of capital accumulation than directed towards creating diverse alternative economies. Coupland shows how easy the appropriation of imagination and resistance can be. Over the course of this comic novel, Ethan has experienced firsthand, in an exaggerated form of direct violence, enslavement, and noxious smell, the working and environmental conditions in China where Dglobe will be manufactured. He nevertheless detaches with ease the socio-ecological world of moral principles, political rights, and material flows from the spectacle of world destruction he codes and enjoys. Dglobe, the warming planet, appears as an autonomous object, magically brought to life by creative invention: it is the epitome of commodity fetishism. It works its magic on Ethan through the promise of work that feels like play—the promise of a new subjectivity organized around playful, voluntary networks rather than disciplinary hierarchies. The pleasures of the Dglobe performance persuade Ethan to leave his current gaming job as a nameless drone in a corporate bureaucracy and bring his creative talents to the character Coupland's entrepreneurial venture.

It is precisely the jPodders' slacker pleasures in subverting the corporation that make them the ideal workers in "Doug's world" (Coupland 514; "Doug" is what the "D" of Dglobe stands for) of "flexible accumulation" where social and employment security nets are traded for individualized risk and gain (Harvey 76). If, from a classical Marxist perspective, the jPod group is the neo-liberal version of workers failing to recognize or act in their own best interests, they are, in turn, a microcosm of North American inaction on climate change, a misrecognition of environmental conditions so smug it is, as Slavoj Žižek describes (quoting Marx), no longer tragic but farcical. "Doug's world" is as much a reprise of the 1990s American slacker comedy *Wayne's World* as a hubristic god's eye view on a malleable planet. It is time to ask: what modes of critique and action are adequate to describe and respond to this farcical cultural moment when environmental knowledge circulates *so readily* but is dissociated from any particular political project of social change?

My path to an answer involves a return to Rachel Carson's *Silent Spring*, the mass-distributed book that galvanized nature and health concerns into a recognizable social movement that politicized ecology. I suggest that we can see in *Silent Spring* the first outline of the representational challenge that ecocriticism faces: not the *representation of nature*, but the *politicization of environment*; or, in other words, how to make complex socio-ecological interactions socially visible as political concerns? I place ecocriticism within the social democratic demand—clearly and forcefully expressed by Carson in *Silent Spring*—for the creation and revitalization of political spaces and collectives for articulating demands for ecological justice. Environmental politics are not just about taking action on "environmental issues" such as climate change, but at a more basic level are the articulation of certain socio-ecological arrangements *as political con-cerns*. Despite common perception, the "environment" is not the problem or issue.[2] The problems environmentalists identify and fight include the *dismissal of the value* of cer-tain lives, communities, and affective relationships (we are subject to health risks we did not consent to, we lose treasured landscapes, the varieties life takes is diminished in the loss of entire species); the *privatization of the power* to shape common life (in corporate boardrooms, in laboratories, in credit agencies); and the *injustices and inequalities* of the distribution of ecological hazards and pleasures. Environmentalism, in other words, necessarily articulates problems at the level of the social, often, in the process, making visible new political actors and expanding the horizons of political possibility.

A Political Fable

Silent Spring tends to be evoked within the humanities for its moral statements about the value of nature, or "the web of life."[3] The achievement of *Silent Spring*, however, was its politicization of ecology: its demonstration that the study of ecological relationships had significance for public affairs. Unlike the earlier descriptive books that gave Carson her nature writing fame, *Silent Spring* presented the argument that, due to their harmful effects on people, animals, and landscapes, synthetic chemicals were a matter for politi-cal deliberation. Explicitly invoking the United States Bill of Rights, Carson repeatedly insists that pesticides are a question of the public interest: "It is the public that is being asked to assume the risks. The public must decide" (29–30). Although *Silent Spring* pres-ents a crash course in organic chemistry, Carson mobilizes science by speaking in the voice of the citizen, the "we" who have rights, including the right to know, and with that knowledge have a responsibility to make judgments based on our weighing of the evi-dence before us. Making an address to the nation, in a language of civic democracy that appealed across industrial nations, Carson closes by writing:

> The choice, after all, is ours to make. If, having endured much, we have at last asserted our "right to know," and if, knowing, we have concluded that we are being asked to take senseless and frightening risks, then we should no longer accept the counsel of those who tell us that we must fill our world with poisonous chemicals; we should look about and see what other course is open to us. (240)

Carson's ecological manifesto culminates with a vision of a reinvigorated democracy.

For Carson, this reinvigorated democracy rests on an enlightened public discourse. She places her faith in the exercise of reasoned judgment about public life. But she also makes a point about the political obscurity of technoscientific developments in empha-sizing the trope of visibility—"we should look about and see"—on which the public sphere and Enlightenment reason is founded. Accountability of the state to the citizens and reasoned discussion by citizens about their common life rest on knowledge shared in common, on what *appears* in the public domain.[4] And what is most disconcerting about the health hazards posed by DDT—like the radioactive fallout that gripped public concern at the same time—is its *invisibility*, a politically significant dimension of environmental issues that Ulrich Beck was to elaborate years later in *Risk Society*.

From her opening fable and throughout *Silent Spring*, Carson emphasizes the uncanny way in which the chemicals do their "sinister" work without being clearly or fully seen, "pass[ing] mysteriously by underground streams until they emerge and kill" (23). The pastoral America that Carson evokes in the famous fable lives with "a shadow of death" (21). The poisons are a "grim specter," a "strange blight" or "evil spell" that "has crept upon us almost unnoticed" (21–22). Given Carson's detailed reliance on empirical studies, this gothic language is not invoked to summon fear of scientific developments as harbingers of death, but rather to point to the need to shine a light on activities that happen in the shadows, and bring them into the public domain under the authority of the public's "right to know." This public enlightenment is the task Carson pursues in the body of her book. Public discussion and judgment of the acceptability of the risks and dangers can only begin, as her emphasis on clear-sightedness indicates, once the pesticides and herbicides celebrated as miracle workers can be *seen* by the broader public as the poisons or "biocides" they are (25). In the fable, the "white granular powder" is visible all along, just not as yet connected to the illnesses striking the animals and people down (22).

Carson's gothic depiction of the poisons as phantoms also points to their phantasmatic quality. The fable presents a morally significant inversion of the world of appearances: having initially implied that the invisible threat was of external origin, tapping into Cold War paranoia, Carson concludes with the famous statement that "No witchcraft, no enemy action had silenced the rebirth of new life. The people had done it themselves" (22). The blight that appears to be some foreign invasion from elsewhere in fact emerges from within. The illnesses and poisons are real, but their apparent autonomy and externality is false. The lesson Carson draws from ecology is not about safeguarding and protecting some pristine, untouchable, external nature, but about being cognizant of how porous boundaries must be, or else we could not live. DDT, Carson explains, does not just kill insects that feed on crops; it *travels*, across landscapes, through food chains, into human bodies, through bloodstreams, and across the placenta (37). And as it travels, it bio-accumulates, increasing in concentration with each step along the food chain: from insects to birds, from milk to butter, from mother to child (37). Similarly, the losses it brings as it travels have ripple effects in ecosystems. Birds vanish, while insects actually multiply. It is this eerie excess of effect over seeming intention, animating the landscape with an invisible "chain of poisoning and death" that Carson foregrounds with her gothic language (23).

Carson's juxtaposition of the seeing, knowing citizen with the phantasmatic poisons suggests a mode of environmental critique along the lines of Marx's analysis of commodity fetishism, aiming to re-embed things within their social (now socio-ecological) relations. Like the "chemical death rain" (28), commodities have real, material form. But to take them merely as things is to miss the social dimension of the commodity form, whereby anything, regardless of its particular material qualities, can be made equivalent to anything else through the medium of money. The production of a commodity as a commodity—as something to be bought and sold—is a social practice relying on social relations of labor, property, and capital. But these social relations are not visible during the commodity exchange; instead, we see the commodity as an autonomously existing entity, which seems to itself hold the power to satisfy our desires: DDT will free agriculture from the plague of pests. We have thus entered the world of fetishism, whereby "productions of the human brain appear as independent beings endowed with life" (Marx 77). As Marx writes, "a definite social relation between men assumes, in their eyes, the fantastic form of a relation between things" (77). Commodity fetishism enables relations between people to be displaced and obscured by the more lively appearance of things seemingly in direct relation with one another—the insects and DDT.

In a similar way, Carson's environmental analysis involves showing how the mysterious power of the poison, which is seemingly in a direct, merely physical relationship with our bodies or farm fields, is in fact a socio-ecological relation along water cycles and food chains and between rural inhabitants, farmers, the chemical industry, government regulators, scientific researchers, and so on. It is the presumption of discrete bodies and actors that underlies irresponsible dissemination (see also Steingraber; Alaimo, *Bodily*). Carson turns to empirical ecological studies to *make visible* the metabolic flows and social interactions within which individual organisms live. Carson's environmental politics, in turn, are oriented toward public visibility: the ecology of synthetic chemicals is placed within socio-political relations of ecological research, agricultural industries, government oversight, and public life, so that the travelling chemicals become visible on the public stage, and the responsible actors become visible in the theatre of ecological concern.

POLITICAL ECOLOGY

Undoing the phantasmatic appearance of not just commodities but the entire market economy as an autonomous sphere has been a key tenet of historical materialist thought. The artifice of market autonomy was achieved, Karl Polanyi and E. P. Thompson show, by great social disruption, with land, labor, and money being violently disembedded from the fabric of social life. "Labor," Polanyi points out, "is only another name for a human activity which goes with life itself nor can that activity be detached from the rest of life, be stored or mobilized; land is only another name for nature" (72). The fiction of their autonomy—that land and labor are merely things to be bought and sold—is what enables their degradation: "Robbed of the protective covering of cultural institutions, human beings would perish from social exposure . . . Nature would be reduced to its elements, neighbourhoods and landscapes defiled, rivers polluted" (Polanyi 73). The fields of political economy, and its offshoot, political ecology, thus begin with the refusal to treat economic and political institutions and ecological practices as if separate, unrelated spheres. The corresponding artifice of cultural autonomy—that art sits above or outside social relations—has been the focal critique developed by cultural studies.

The public exposure of social relations mystified by the appearance of objects or values as if autonomous or natural has been invaluable for environmental thought and politics. Classic ecocritical arguments in this tradition include Raymond Williams's analysis of how agricultural fields appear to flourish without the labor of workers in the English country house poem tradition, and William Cronon's historicizing account of wilderness in the United States. Wilderness, Cronon shows, was created through the claiming of territory, dispossession of Native Americans, and regulation of property, yet appears to be the physical embodiment of an original nature without people. Williams shows how literary analyses that take as self-evident the seemingly geographically based distinction between city and country miss the capital flows and property relations that join them in the service of contested regimes of political and economic power.[5] These are examples of social inequality and historical memory being repressed by the phantasmatic appearance of objects and landscapes as "autonomous nature" situated outside the social relations of property, law, labor, science, and power that produce them as such.

The historical materialist analysis is troubling because it rejects the most popular approach to environmental advocacy and ecocritical analysis: to promote the value of nature "in itself." Indeed, Steven Vogel argues that the environmentalist preoccupation with resolving Western society's apparent alienation from nature (for which the solution is reconnection to nature) contributes to the obfuscation of our environmental predicament. It sets "nature" apart as a static, unchanging entity at a time when neoliberal economics support even greater intensification and a more extensive reach in the transformation of living beings and the physical world, all the way from genomes to planetary climate. It proclaims *disconnection* while the scale, pace, and complexity of material *connections* multiplies beyond democratic accountability. Anxieties about these transformations, over which citizens seem to have such little say or control, is alleviated by the burgeoning market in "nature": nature stores, nature parks, nature-friendly products, nature television, natural food, natural burial, nature writing. "For Marx," Vogel writes, "*the appearance of nature is itself a symptom of alienation*" (196, italics in original).

Rather than attending more closely to an idealized nature, people should be paying more attention to the socio-material processes by which the world we live in is transformed. "Alienation," Vogel writes, "does not arise from our transformation of the world, but rather from our failure to recognize ourselves in the world we have transformed. We live in a society where each of us can act only as a private individual, with the result that the overall social consequences of our actions appear like 'facts of nature' about which there is nothing any individual one of us can do" (201). According to Shane Gunster, "Conceiving of our environment as natural, Vogel argues, is both symptomatic and constitutive of a profound alienation from our *social world*: it reinforces and magnifies experiences of helplessness and disempowerment that have become commonplace under capitalism" (Gunster 211, italics added). We should be suspicious of the *ease* with which a middle-class North American might "re-connect" with nature via a walk with an iPod in the woods as compared to the *difficulty* of, say, gathering knowledge about and re-organizing coltan mining and electronics manufacturing.

The appearance of *JPod's* Dglobe thus suggests a redoubled alienation, along the lines of Guy Debord's *Society of the Spectacle* (see also Ross). Ethan's infantile sense of mastery over *an Earth* reduced to a toy is compensation for his powerlessness to play any decisive role in creating his *world*. Socially impotent—unable to intervene in the social relations he morally objects to, frustrated at being a cog in the corporate wheel, and slighted by being initially left out of Coupland's business venture—Ethan substitutes, for this loss of power over his time, labor, and world, an empowered experience of visual consumption. At the same time, the simulated planet appears to Ethan—as it will to other consumers—as a mesmerizing, lively object which provides an immediate connection to a desired nature rather than to a global organization of labor and toxicity that distributes creative work to Vancouver and manufacturing to Guangzhou Economic Zone. The Earth comes to appear ever more intimate, precious, and knowable while the forces of global capitalism appear ever more distant, faceless, and uncontrollable—as if quite separate from Ethan's actual work, travel, consumption, and citizenship. The critical task is not a return to nature but a return to politics. "Alienation is overcome," Vogel insists, "by a social order where decisions about production are not left to the anarchic workings of the market but rather are made explicitly and socially, which is to say, democratically" (201).

POWER/KNOWLEDGE

For all that it points to the illusory nature of much common sense, reading objects or commodities as phantoms and fetishes is a form of ideology critique, which nevertheless insists it is possible to cut through the phantasms to reality. Carson maintained it was imperative to undertake painstaking questioning and research to trace the biocides from production through food chains to possible health effects. And yet Carson's very insistence on the public's right to know the risks we face points to how knowledge has become central to contestations of power in what Beck terms the "risk society." Beck's concept of risk points to the uncertainty associated with hazard—not every farmer applying pesticides, to take one example, will be struck ill, and some ill effects, such as cancers, do not manifest immediately but rather years down the line, when establishing a cause-effect relationship to a particular source is notoriously difficult (see Steingraber). The tobacco industry exploited minor uncertainties in the connection between smoking and lung cancer for decades, as the oil and gas industry has done with carbon dioxide emissions and climate change. Beck's point is that such uncertainties are a paradigmatic aspect of late modernity, since risks emerge as side effects of the very production of scientific knowledge and technological development—and require their apparatuses to even be identified, much less resolved, leading in turn to the production of new risks, and so on. Invisible to the senses, traveling through bodies and ecosystems over extended times and spaces, and under proprietary or state protection, hazards like nuclear radiation, synthetic pesticides—even biological ones such as *E. coli*—only become visible through "the 'sensory organs' of science—*theories, experiments, measuring instruments*" (Beck 27, italics in original). With risk, we do not just have phantasmatic forms mistakenly taken for the world itself—and which can be revealed, or made visible by historical and materialist analysis—but, closer to Foucault, sets of practices and apparatuses for knowing that materially remake the world we live in.

I bring Michel Foucault into the discussion of risk because his scholarship is most influential in showing that how we know is historically generated within an epistemic regime that authorizes the forms knowledge can take. Foucault suggests that power not only operates on a pre-formed object—on a juvenile delinquent, or crop pests, for example—but is also at work in constituting this object *as* a unit of analysis, that there is such a thing as agricultural pests amenable to chemical management: "the exercise of power itself creates and causes to emerge new objects of knowledge and accumulates new bodies of information" (51). In *Power/Knowledge*, Foucault explains that "there would be no sense in limiting oneself to discourses *about* prisons; just as important are the discourses which arise within the prison, the decisions and regulations which are among its constitutive elements, its means of functioning, along with its strategies, its covert discourses and ruses" (38, italics in original). Foucauldian environmental criticism attends to the institutions of environmental management and knowledge production by not only focusing on discourses *about* nature or ecology but attending to how such a thing as nature or ecology—or insects, or forests—becomes knowable and manageable.[6]

Shifting attention from the object of knowledge ("the environment" or the risks posed by radiation) to the rules, practices, and apparatuses that make it possible to speak of "the environment," or that govern the appearance of "radiation," has been contentious because, as a method, it places truth claims in suspension. In what has become known as social constructionism, critique operates by showing how what is taken as "natural" is always already historical and cultural, and therefore open to political contestation. But in itself, this method of criticism provides no grounds for judging between competing truth claims. Cultural theorists are adept at pulling back layer after layer of artifactuality (from gender roles to gender to sex to DNA), but the analysis tends to end with the dethroning of nature (and the appearance of a surplus element of reality still resistant to knowledge). By overemphasizing linguistic agency, and ascribing a corresponding passivity, determinism, and even stasis to nature and non-humans, social constructionist critiques risk de-materializing social struggles (see Fuss; Alaimo, *Undomesticated*). This tension created the much-discussed standoff between empiricists and postmodernists in environmental and other fields.

Postmodernists tend to critique as power moves the institutionalization of the "normal" and "natural;" ecological empiricists tend to see the "normal" as the necessary background against which a change or threat to "nature" can be identified. But such ecological naturalism ignores power relations and undermines public life and political judgment—the democratic vigor that Carson called for—by insisting that truth is located in the science, to which the public must accede (see Sandilands, "Opinionated"). On the other hand, social construction of nature critiques sometimes appear to solidify Immanuel Kant's epistemological gap between representation and the real, *concluding* rather than *beginning* with the recognition that subjects know the real through representations. "Nature" as cultural symbol and even "nature" as physical body or landscape can be understood as artifactual constructions inflected by mechanisms of power. Anthropogenic climate change is known through a discursive regime comprising representations made by measuring tools, data sets, and computer modeling—a regime which is regulated internationally by the IPCC and, in Coupland's fiction, commodified for mass consumer pleasure with Dglobe. Nevertheless, the ice core samples, pollen samples, temperature records, and glacier marks that this discursive regime mobilizes and authorizes are traces of real phenomena. Without providing grounds on which to make empirical judgments, the social construction of nature critique can be dangerously enabling of anti-naturalistic moralisms, whether Christian creationist opposition to biology, as Donna Haraway points out (*Modest_Witness*), or industry-funded climate change skepticism, as Bruno Latour notes ("Why Has Critique.")

SOCIALIZING SCIENCE

For all that the so-called science wars appeared as an entrenched dualism, "modest" methods of developing truth claims without disavowing their embeddedness in mechanisms and relations of power have emerged from the field of science studies.[7] In between truth and relativism are relative certainties, Haraway, Latour, and others suggest, certainties based not on an asocial natural world "out there" but on ever more intricate instruments and scale models enlisted in social *practices* of knowing. Modern science emerged, Steven Shapin and Simon Schaffer argue, as a technique of witnessing, which involved making an object that can be seen by others, who collectively verify its existence. The laboratory demonstration was precisely that—a *demonstration*, a making visible of a new object or property or process to gathered witnesses who agreed upon conventions of language, propriety, and technique (see also Haraway, *Modest_Witness*). Latour describes how in Louis Pasteur's laboratory (where current practices of dairy pasteurization were developed), "invisible actors—which they call microbes—show their moves and development in pictures so clear that even a child would see them. The invisible becomes visible and the 'thing' becomes a written trace they can read at will as if it were a text" ("Give" 163); "I don't know what a microbe is," Latour writes, "but counting dots with clear-cut edges on a white surface is simple" ("Give" 163). Without this translation into collective visibility, there is no science, no possibility of verification, no relative certainty.

Foucault directed attention to the "materiality of power": how it operates not just through ideas, or ideologies, but "on the very bodies of individuals" through practices of health and medicine, spatial segregation of normal from abnormal, surveillance of behavior, and so on (55). But whereas Foucault attended largely to human subjects, science studies extends the analysis of the mechanisms of power to nonhumans (see Barad; Haraway, *Simians*). Latour's work shows in detail how scientific experimentation involves the *socialization* of agential nonhumans (say microbes, or DDT, or mobile phones): the induction of active nonhumans into society through intimate acts of observation, differentiation, translation, fabrication, and mobilization that *remake* existing social relations in the process. Preferring "collective" to "society" to avoid the latter's exclusively human connotations, Latour describes how the "modern collective is the one in which the relations of humans and nonhumans are so intimate, the transactions so many, the mediations so convoluted, that there is no plausible sense in which artifact, corporate body, and subject can be distinguished" (*Pandora's* 197). Karen Barad argues instead for conceptualizing the production of scientific subjects and objects as "intra-action," which acknowledges the formation and remaking of identities and boundaries, and not only as "interaction," which tends to presume engagement between pre-existing entities. Recognizing that sciences are social—albeit involving actors and techniques not often considered social because not human—focuses analysis on the relations and actors transformed in scientific practices and claims.

If Foucault's attention to micropolitics—the multiple, dispersed, small acts and gestures of the body—illuminates one of the modes through which power circulates, science studies, too, attends to micro-level intra-actions within a laboratory or field site to illuminate how scientific practices sustain and shift social orders. Giving the example of Pasteur's invention of the anthrax vaccine, Latour argues that its historical significance lies in the double move of making the laboratory a relevant social site, and extending laboratory practices to farmers' fields. Farmers adopt routines of disinfection, inoculation, and recordkeeping; sheep and cattle are vaccinated and die at more closely regulated times; and fewer anthrax microbes can become active in the fields subject to the practices outlined by Pasteur. The laboratory generates not only new knowledge but, more crucially, "new sources of power" ("Give" 160). Microbes appear publicly for the first time, but their power is contained and regulated; laboratory scientists and statisticians gain greater legitimacy and extend their domains. The world is transformed.

These convoluted and extensive practices of mediation and intra-action that transform our world largely remain *politically invisible*, however, in what Latour often refers to as the "black box" of science and technology (see *Pandora's Hope*). For Latour, this is due to the trenchant hold of the belief in objectivity: that truth is something discovered "out there" in the world of nature. "We are prudish in matters of science," Latour suggests, "We all see laboratories but we ignore their construction, much like the Victorians who watched kids crawling all over the place, but repressed the vision of sex as the *cause* of this proliferation" ("Give" 153, italics in original). That identifiable social practices, rather than miraculous new discoveries, are what constitute scientific knowledge remains difficult to speak aloud, Latour suggests, for dropping the insistence on hard objectivity has seemed to many to be the first step to opening Pandora's box of relativism. Perhaps more crucially, however, recognizing science as a range of social spaces and practices makes them open to greater democratization.

Science studies does not, in response to the prudery of objectivity, insist upon relativism, in which all empirical judgment is to be suspended because it cannot be made absolute (nor does it naïvely suggest knowledge is solely subjective, generated from "in here"). Rather, the crucial point to take from recognizing the social production of knowledge is to see science as ever so many local sites where the world in which we live is recreated, although usually outside public visibility. Concomitantly, environmentalism might be approached not as a moral stance either against or in the name of science (or the natural), but instead, following in Carson's footsteps, as a political struggle for the public right to shape socio-ecological futures. It is a politics oriented not towards safeguarding nature from tinkering humans but to *making publically accountable* the sites and techniques where humans and nonhumans reshape the world.

ECOLOGICAL SUBJECTS

I would suggest that the call for the democratization of science falters not so much on setting aside universal knowledge-claims, but on the universality of democracy. A distrust of the capacity of the common person underlies the presumed necessity of an aristocracy of science—the sanctioned public role of experts as guardians of knowledge. *JPod* would seem to confirm this. Ethan takes Carson's straightforward alignment of the democratizing of knowledge and public action off course. Like the characters in most other Coupland novels, Ethan does not change or mature. The novel ends with a hyperbolic epilogue where Ethan declares, "Dglobe is a blast. Life is good" and everyone is "Happy, happy, happy!" (515). More disturbing than the cynically detached yet self-aware postmodernism of Coupland's landmark novel *Generation X* is the comic lack of self-reflexivity shown by Ethan and the other ex-podsters. Democratic subjectivities, however, are not merely given but are as socio-historical as the environments we simultaneously inhabit and change. Social movements as diverse as workers' emancipation and anti-colonial independence struggles have crucially involved reclaiming agency and recrafting subjectivities. Moreover, developing and broadly sharing empirical skills and knowledge has been a crucial tactic of the environmental justice movement (see Bullard; Washington, Goodall, and Rosier). Whereas Coupland's insular high-tech workers are pitted against the risk of complacency because social change is seemingly unimaginable, many contemporary environmental fictions from the postcolonial world focus on the myriad ways the global demos is excluded in conducting business as usual.

For all the urgency to empower empirically literate democratic subjects, the most prominent approach to ecological subjectivity focuses on resolving Western alienation from nature. Deep ecologists have argued for the boundary of the subject to be recognized as including its environment or habitat—a veritable "ecological self," as Freya Matthews puts it.[8] Striving toward a collapsing of the distance between subject and environment was conceptually central to Lawrence Buell's influential early ecocritical text *The Environmental Imagination*, a practice described more critically by Timothy Morton as "ecomimesis" (*Ecology* 30). The disturbing insularity of *jPod* provides an ironic example: identity for this group of high-tech workers literally is their work environment, the J-surnamed employees located together in one "pod" of cubicles in the corporate office-tower. The self-as-environment solution to alienation misses the fraught ambivalence of subjectivity as *social process*, produced through the power-inflected constitution of boundaries, identifications, and differences. Just as human beings only function as organisms through the boundary-work of skin, as Stacy Alaimo describes in *Bodily Natures*, subjectivity, too, would be undone if affectively open to all others, or if the language through which one finds a place in the social order did not also enable the reflexivity of becoming conscious of oneself and communicative with others.

In between the defensive shoring up of boundaries (imagining social liberation as the maturing achievement of an autonomous self) and their complete repudiation in an immersive blending of self and environment (the subordinate, background position that women, laborers, racialized people, and colonial subjects struggle against in the effort to become subjects of their own futures[9]) lie democratic movements that articulate new arrangements and horizons for collective life and experience. The transformation of subjects or, as it was once more narrowly conceived, "consciousness-raising"—whether feminist or working class or environmentalist—is not sufficient in itself for political or social change, but is part of the process of reforming the social institutions and practices through which unjust and debilitating social relations are sustained. Ernesto Laclau and Chantal Mouffe emphasize that social relations are contingent rather than determined, and this provides the very opening for political contestation: that collective life might be arranged differently. Recognizing such contingency also enables a democratic approach to social change, whereby politicized institutions are not known and politicized subjects not constituted in advance. Rather, as with the place of the family in Western feminism or biotechnology laboratories and test sites in environmentalism, particular social institutions become sites of antagonism through political struggle.

In a representational or mimetic model of politics, the interests of women or workers are presumed to be given by what is taken to be their common social position; or an interest in environmental sustainability might be presumed to "naturally" follow from exposure to ecological hazards or risks (or from an economic interest in avoiding the costs of climate change, or an affective attachment to pets or forests).[10] Building on the work of political theorist Antonio Gramsci, Laclau and Mouffe describe how the democratic approach, instead, "accepts the structural diversity of the relations in which social agents are immersed, and replaces the principle of representation with that of articulation. Unity between these agents is then not the expression of a common underlying essence but the result of political construction and struggle" (65). In Karen Tei Yamashita's novel *Tropic of Orange*, the mythical figure of El Gran Mojado, who embodies the people and nature of the southern hemisphere fighting back against SUPERNAFTA, both symbolizes and conjures into being subjects of economic resistance and cultural and ecological resilience (see Wallace). The tiny, spinning planet who narrates Yamashita's novel *Through the Arc of the Rainforest* and the voyeuristic Western "eyes" addressed in Indra Sinha's *Animal's People*, a novel of the ongoing environmental injustices and health effects of the 1984 Union Carbide chemical leak in Bhopal, also foreground the knowledge positions and subjectivities through which globalization processes materialize and might be contested (see Heise). Ecological subjectivities, in sum, are not some static state, achieved through enlightenment or conversion, but natural-cultural-political sites where contested futures are made and lived.

> "I prefer bleached paper to recycled paper. It looks nicer."
> "Brand new emoticons free!"
> "Hi, I'm the office ventilation system. You don't know it, but twenty-four hours a day I spew asbestos particulates into your workspace."
>
> —from *JPod* endpapers

THE HAPPY ENDING

Politics becomes farce for Marx, in Žižek's reading, when a regime "only imagines that it still believes in itself" (cited in Žižek 3). The farcical turn can have a cathartic effect: no longer frightening, the regime we work to end has become clownish and laughable; their claimed principles hollow. It becomes possible to "part *happily* with its past" (Marx, cited in Žižek 2). A diffuse, networked world such as we find in *JPod*, however, makes it more difficult to identify any singular regime against which a unified political struggle or laughter might form—a political challenge extensively outlined by Michael Hardt and Antonio Negri in *Empire*. Moreover, in Žižek's present-day reframing, it is not lack of belief but rather our belief that we have attained cynical distance from ideology that is the farce. *JPod* exemplifies this state that might be called "post-cynicism," where our practices suggest we believe in the very myth of inevitable progress and universal prosperity from which an ironic detachment is maintained. *JPod* catalogues a hollowed-out language of corporate sociality that participating employees (and readers) may hold in jest, but which, nevertheless, still mobilizes materials, people, and toxicity. The novel thus uses this hyperbolic superficiality to re-open space for critical reflection on the part of the novel's reader.

Like the "mega happy ending" version of the three possible *Wayne's World* endings, Ethan's "Happy, happy, happy!" epilogue hyperbolically satisfies the reader's genre expectations while simultaneously exposing the narrative illusion on which they rest. *JPod*, however, strives for more than the celebration of an ironic stance towards received representations. Though any hope for Ethan's possible maturation is rendered absurd, the *bildungsroman* is not replaced with the expected postmodern ironic detachment. Coupland-the-author appears as a character in the novel largely to show his disgust with Ethan's lack of change. During their brief encounters, Coupland berates Ethan for his complacency. Here is postmodern self-reflexivity turned on its head. "Doug" the character does not undo the omniscient position of the invisible narrator so much as enable the ironic exposure of the reader's complacent identification with the characters from the superior position of the know-it-better author. It is our *too easy immersion* in our socio-physical environments that the novel exposes through its redundant hyperbole, as with this series from the endpapers: "Peon. Serf. Rabble. Fodder. Filler. Driftwood. Minion. Gofer. Underling."

That climate modeling might provide the basis for a new mode of consumer pleasure is not so far-fetched given the commercial viability of television weather channels. What *JPod* more significantly points to is the ongoing representational challenge posed by commodity capitalism: how to make meaningfully visible as demands on our collective attention and action the dispersed and "slow" violence, loss, suffering, injustice, and hazardous risks produced alongside our apparent pleasures (Nixon 2)? Passé though it is, there remains an urgent political role for the cultural project of de-fetishization: for making present for democratic deliberation and accountability the destructive and unjust socio-ecological relations that produce the mesmerizing world of appearances.

Notes

1. 25.
2. See Evernden and Morton, *The Ecological Thought* for good discussions of the limits of the term and concept "environment."
3. See the collection *Rachel Carson: Legacy and Challenge* edited by Lisa Sideris and Kathleen Dean Moore for the argument to emphasize Carson's ethical thinking, although an exception is the chapter by Steve Maguire, which argues along the same lines I do here that *Silent Spring* is significant for bringing scientific debate to the public arena. See also Buell's essay "Toxic Discourse" for an emphasis on *Silent Spring*'s political significance. My account of Carson's approach to knowledge draws on Lorraine Code's *Ecological Thinking*.
4. See Sandilands, "Opinionated Natures" for discussion of the importance of appearance in environmental politics.
5. See Ryle, Head, and Lousley for elaborations of Williams's contributions to ecocriticism.
6. Excellent examples of Foucauldian environmental criticism include Agrawal, Luke, and the essays in *Discourses of the Environment* (Darier).
7. See Haraway, *Modest_Witness*, 21–39, for an extensive discussion of the conception and role of modesty in the history of science and science studies.
8. Neil Evernden's *The Natural Alien*, Chaia Heller's *Ecology of Everyday Life*, and Mick Smith's *An Ethics of Place* are approaches to ecological subjectivity that strive to expand subjectivity while aiming to avoid collapsing all boundaries between subject and environment.
9. See Plumwood for the detailed argument on environment, labor, and women as "background."
10. See Sandilands, *The Good-Natured Feminist* for an extended discussion of the limits and pitfalls of identitarian and representational approaches to politics in feminism and environmentalism.

Works Cited

Agrawal, Arun. *Environmentality: Technologies of Government and the Making of Subjects*. Durham, NC: Duke University Press, 2005. Print.

Alaimo, Stacy. *Undomesticated Ground: Recasting Nature as Feminist Space*. Ithaca: Cornell University Press, 2000. Print.

Alaimo, Stacy. *Bodily Natures: Science, Environment, and the Material Self*. Bloomington: Indiana, 2010. Print.

Barad, Karen. "Agential Realism: Feminist Interventions in Understanding Scientific Practices." *The Science Studies Reader*. 1998. Ed. Biagioli, Mario. New York: Routledge, 1999. 1–11. Print.

Beck, Ulrich. *Risk Society*. Trans. Ritter, Mark. London: Sage, 1992. Print.

Buell, Lawrence. *The Environmental Imagination: Thoreau, Nature Writing, and the Formation of American Culture*. Cambridge, MA: Belknap Press of Harvard University Press, 1995. Print.

———. "Toxic Discourse." *Critical Inquiry* 24.3 (1998): 639–65. Print.

Bullard, Robert Doyle. *The Quest for Environmental Justice: Human Rights and the Politics of Pollution*. San Francisco: Sierra Club Books, 2005. Print.

Carson, Rachel. *Silent Spring*. London: Penguin, 2000. Print.

Code, Lorraine. *Ecological Thinking: The Politics of Epistemic Location*. Toronto: Oxford University Press, 2006. Print.

Coupland, Douglas. *Generation X: Tales for an Accelerated Culture*. St. Martin's Press, 1991. Print.

———. *JPod*. Toronto: Random House, 2007. Print.

Cronon, William. "The Trouble with Wilderness; or, Getting Back to the Wrong Nature." *Uncommon Ground: Rethinking the Human Place in Nature*. Ed. William Cronon. New York: W. W. Norton, 1996. 69–90. Print.

Darier, Eric, ed. *Discourses of the Environment*. Oxford: Blackwell, 1999. Print.

Debord, Guy. *Society of the Spectacle*. Detroit: Black & Red, 1977. Print.

Evernden, Neil. *The Natural Alien: Humankind and Environment*. 1985. 2nd ed. Toronto: University of Toronto Press, 1993. Print.

Foucault, Michel. *Power/Knowledge: Selected Interviews & Other Writings, 1972–1977*. Trans. Colin Gordon, Leo Marshall, John Mepham, Kate Soper. Edited by Colin Gordon. New York: Pantheon, 1980. Print.

Fuss, Diana. *Essentially Speaking: Feminism, Nature and Difference*. New York: Routledge, 1989. Print.

Gibson-Graham, J. K. *The End of Capitalism (As We Knew It): A Feminist Critique of Political Economy*. Minneapolis: University of Minnesota Press, 2006. Print.

Gunster, Shane. "Fear and the Unknown: Nature, Culture, and the Limits of Reason." *Critical Ecologies: The Frankfurt School and Contemporary Environmental Crises*. Ed. Andrew Biro. Toronto: University of Toronto Press, 2011. 206–28. Print.

Haraway, Donna J. *Simians, Cyborgs, and Women: The Reinvention of Nature*. New York: Routledge, 1991. Print.

———. *Modest_Witness@Second_Millennium.Femaleman©_Meets_Oncomouse™: Feminism and Technoscience*. New York: Routledge, 1997. Print.

Hardt, Michael, and Antonio Negri. *Empire*. Cambridge, MA: Harvard University Press, 2000. Print.

Harvey, David. *A Brief History of Neoliberalism*. New York: Oxford University Press, 2005. Print.

Head, Dominic. "Beyond 2000: Raymond Williams and the Ecocritic's Task." *The Environmental Tradition in English literature*. Ed. John Parham and Louise H. Westling. Aldershot, UK: Ashgate, 2002. 24–36. Print.

Heise, Ursula. *Sense of Place and Sense of Planet: The Environmental Imagination of the Global*. New York: Oxford University Press, 2008. Print.

Heller, Chaia. *Ecology of Everyday Life*. Montreal: Black Rose, 1998. Print.

Jameson, Fredric. *The seeds of time*. New York: Columbia University Press, 1994. Print.

Laclau, Ernesto, and Chantal Mouffe. *Hegemony and Socialist Strategy: Towards a Radical Democratic Politics*. London: Verso, 1985. Print.

Latour, Bruno. "Give Me a Laboratory and I Will Raise the World." *Science Observed: Perspectives on the Social Study of Science*. 1983. Eds. Knorr-Cetina, Karin D. and Michael Mulkay. London: Sage, 1983. 141–69. Print.

———. *Pandora's Hope: Essays on the Reality of Science Studies*. Cambridge, MA: Harvard University Press, 1999. Print.

———. "Why Has Critique Run out of Steam? From Matters of Fact to Matters of Concern." *Critical Inquiry 30* (2004): 225–48. Print.

Lousley, Cheryl. "Knowledge, Power and Place: Environmental Politics in the Fiction of Matt Cohen and David Adams Richards." *Canadian Literature 195* (2007): 11–30. Print.

Luke, Timothy W. "On Environmentality: Geo-Power and Eco-Knowledge in the Discourses of Contemporary Environmentalism." *Cultural Critique 31* (1995): 57–81. Print.

Maguire, Steve. "Contested Icons: Rachel Carson and DDT." *Rachel Carson: Legacy and Challenge*. Ed. Lisa H. Sideris and Kathleen Dean Moore. Albany: SUNY Press, 2008. 194–214. Print.

Marx, Karl. *Capital: Volume 1: A Critique of Political Economy. 1887*. Ed. Frederick Engels. Marx/Engels Internet Archive (marxists.org), 1999. Web.

Morton, Timothy. *Ecology without Nature: Rethinking Environmental Aesthetics*. Cambridge, MA: Harvard University Press, 2007. Print.

———. *The Ecological Thought*. Cambridge, MA: Harvard University Press, 2010. Print.

Plumwood, Val. *Feminism and the Mastery of Nature*. London: Routledge, 1993. Print.

Polanyi, Karl. *The Great Transformation: The Political and Economic Origins of Our Time. 1944*. Boston: Beacon Hill, 1957. Print.

Ross, Andrew. *The Chicago Gangster Theory of Life: Nature's Debt to Society*. London: Verso, 1994. Print.

Ryle, Martin. "After 'Organic Community': Ecocriticism, Nature, and Human Nature." *The Environmental Tradition in English Literature*. Ed. John Parham & Louise H. Westling. Aldershot, UK: Ashgate, 2002. 11–23. Print.

Sandilands, Catriona. *The Good-Natured Feminist: Ecofeminism and the Quest for Democracy*. Minneapolis, MN: University of Minnesota Press, 1999. Print.

———. "Opinionated Natures: Toward a Green Public Culture." *Democracy and the Claims of Nature: Critical Perspectives for a New Century*. Eds. Ben A. Minteer and Bob Pepperman Taylor Lanham, MD: Rowman and Littlefield, 2002. 117–32. Print.

Shapin, Steven, and Simon Schaffer. *Leviathan and the Air-Pump: Hobbes, Boyle, and the Experimental Life*. Princeton: Princeton University Press, 1985. Print.

Sideris, Lisa H., and Kathleen Dean Moore. *Rachel Carson: Legacy and Challenge*. Albany: SUNY Press, 2008. Print.

Sinha, Indra. *Animal's People*. London: Simon & Schuster, 2007. Print.

Smith, Mick. *An Ethics of Place: Radical Ecology, Postmodernity, and Social Theory*. Albany: SUNY Press, 2001. Print.

Steingraber, Sandra. *Living Downstream: An Ecologist's Personal Investigation of Cancer and the Environment*. Da Capo Press, 2010. Print.

Thompson, E. P. *The Making of the English Working Class*. London: Victor Gollancz, 1963. Print.

Vogel, Steven. "On Nature and Alienation." *Critical Ecologies: The Frankfurt School and Contemporary Environmental Crises*. Ed. Andrew Biro. Toronto: University of Toronto Press, 2011. 187–205. Print.

Wallace, Molly. "Tropics of Globalization: Reading the New North America." *Symploke* 9.1–2 (2001): 145–60. Print.

Washington, Sylvia Hood, Heather Goodall, and Paul C. Rosier, ed. *Echoes from the Poisoned Well: Global Memories of Environmental Injustice*. Lanham, MD: Lexington, 2006. Print.

Wayne's World. Dir. Penelope Spheeris. Perf. Mike Myers. Paramount, 1992. Film.

Williams, Raymond. *The Country and the City*. New York: Oxford University Press, 1973. Print.

Yamashita, Karen Tei. *Through the Arc of the Rain Forest*. Minneapolis: Coffee House Press, 1990. Print.

———. *Tropic of Orange*. Minneapolis: Coffee House Press, 1997. Print.

Žižek, Slavoj. *First As Tragedy, Then As Farce*. London: Verso Books, 2009. Print.

CHAPTER 9

....

COSMOVISIONS

Environmental Justice, Transnational American Studies, and Indigenous Literature

....

JONI ADAMSON

LEADING ecocritics, often citing Shepherd Krech's *The Ecological Indian* (1999), have commented on why it is historically inaccurate and politically dubious to propagate myths about supposedly "authentic" premodern peoples who dwell in perpetual harmony with nature (e.g., Garrard 2004, 120–1, 133; Buell 2005, 23; Heise *Sense* 2008, 32; Nixon 2011, 84). Yet, references to "indigenous ecological wisdom" remain common in the oral traditions and contemporary literary works of indigenous writers, people groups, and nations. They are also emerging in the political arena, in the language of international legal instruments and constitutional and legislative reforms seeking to protect the rights of "Mother Earth." For example, in 2011, Bolivian officials implemented the Law of Mother Earth, which enshrines the right of nature to be protected and establishes a ministry to provide water, air, and all living organisms with an ombudsman to advocate for nature's rights to maintain vital cycles (Edwards 2011, n. pag.). Supported by the administration of Evo Morales, first Aymara president of Bolivia, this law mirrors and borrows from the language of the Universal Declaration on the Rights of Mother Earth (UDRME), which was drafted in 2010 at the World Peoples' Conference on Climate Change in Cochabamba, Bolivia. The UDRME attributes to indigenous peoples, nations, and organizations "a cosmic spirituality linked to nature thousands of years in the making" (UDRME 2010, Preamble n. pag.).

The language of the UDRME, UNDRIP, and Law of Mother Earth resonates strikingly with the words of indigenous movement leaders in Leslie Marmon Silko's most controversial novel, *Almanac of the Dead*. Silko's characters repeatedly express concerns for "Mother Earth" as they observe that the weather is in chaos and "the rain clouds [have] disappeared" (Silko 1991, 734, 719). While Silko's celebrated novel, *Ceremony*, helped shape the expectations that readers bring to literary works by Native American authors, *Almanac* challenged the expectations her earlier work had helped to create. Early reviewers and critics dismissed the novel as "inauthentic," even dangerous, as they expressed outrage over Silko's depiction of a Poor People's Army marching from Mexico towards the United States, where they plan to "retake the land" and join forces with a North American coalition of prison rights activists, environmentalists, Yaqui resistance fighters, homeless U.S. Army veterans, and computer hackers.

In *American Indian Literature, Environmental Justice and Ecocriticism* (2001), I focus two chapters on Silko's Army of the Poor as I explore the implications of a transnational social justice and environmental movement, made up of indigenous groups and nations, ethnic minorities and the poor, that was emerging in the 1980s to protest the increasing power and mobility of transnational corporations that—under cover of trade liberalization—were gearing up to exploit uneven economic deregulation and exacerbate the chasm between rich and poor. *American Indian Literature* (*AIL*) is the first book to link Silko's "army" specifically to the Zapatistas of Chiapas, Mexico, a mostly Mayan group of corn farmers, who formed an army in 1994 to oppose the Mexican government's entry into the tri-national North American Free Trade Agreement (NAFTA). My analysis explores why varieties of American environmentalism based on U.S. deep ecology models of conservation-oriented activism were being dismissed by indigenous groups like the Zapatistas who were, after the 1980s, consistently rejecting clichéd stereotypes of "ethnic purity" or "Indian authenticity" as they organized to oppose economic development models that were causing environmental degradation and displacement among the indigenous and the poor (Adamson 2001, 31–50, 128–79).

Book-length introductions to ecocriticism published after 2000, including Greg Garrard's *Ecocriticism* and Lawrence Buell's *The Future of Environmental Literary Criticism*, cite *AIL* for helping to move the field of ecocriticism towards a more "nuanced appreciation of the complex ecopolitical issues that permeate contemporary Native American culture and literature" and for being one of the first critical studies to help catalyze a shift towards sociocentric "eco-justice revision" (Garrard 2004, 129; Buell 2005, 119). Both field genealogies raise excellent questions about the relationship of indigenous literatures to the emergence of environmental justice approaches to ecocriticism. Garrard not only critiques the trope of the Ecological Indian but—in a sensitive and comprehensive discussion of the genocide and species extinction associated with colonization—seeks to explain why indigenous writers continue to employ images of indigenous relationship to nature that provide "some Indians with a source of pride and aspiration for themselves and their societies" (2004, 125). He cites the better-known works of Native North American fiction that I analyze in *AIL*, such as Louise Erdrich's *Tracks*, but he does not cite my analysis of *Almanac*. Instead, relying on the work of another critic who analyzes only one chapter of *Almanac*, Garrard draws conclusions about Silko's credibility to write about environmental justice based on the speech of one character, a fiery Indian lawyer named Wilson Weasel Tail. Garrard objects to this character's prediction that Euro-American society will be "vanquished" from the Americas (Garrard 2004, 129).

A close reading of Weasel Tail's speech, however, shows that he is delivering an impassioned lecture at a political rally. His subject is the role of the Ghost Dance in late nineteenth-century indigenous resistance movements (Silko 1991, 721–25). He begins by haranguing the indigenous peoples in his audience—not white people—for failing to understand that the Ghost Dance resistance movement did not end with the massacre of 150 Lakota Sioux men, women, and children at Wounded Knee, South Dakota, in 1890. His lecture is peppered with quotes from famous historical speeches by Chief Pontiac and the Paiute Prophet Wovoka who did indeed lambast "white people" and American president Ulysses Grant for breaking treaties with Indian nations and engaging in treachery that led to massive loss of life. The chapter shows audience members feeling uncomfortable about Weasel Tail's over-dramatic presentation and taking his words with a grain of salt since he is a "lawyer at heart" and thus tends to speak in the binary, yes-or-no, Socratic language of Western legal systems (Silko 1991, 725). Silko's treatment of Weasel Tail is repeated numerous times throughout the novel as she introduces other characters who are describes as "scattered crazies" who attach themselves to political movements (Silko 1991, 755), which draws the reader into deliberations with the novel's movement leaders about who can or cannot be trusted among the novel's large cast of 763 characters. Yet, based on one critic's analysis of Weasel Tail's speech, Garrard concludes that Silko attributes the ills of modern society to "white guilt" and therefore "forfeits the subtle discrimination needed to respond to environmental justice issues" (2004, 129).

I touch on Garrard's very minor comment (in the midst of his substantial and praiseworthy discussion of the Ecological Indian) only because in fields developing as rapidly as ecocriticism, the analysis, or even minor comments, of the most respected critics tend to be replicated by later ones. Similarly, in commenting on the early development of environmental justice approaches to ecocriticism, Lawrence Buell raises the question of whether or not the U.S. environmental justice movement might be too narrowly focused on environmental racism, and early environmental justice literary critics too bound to U.S. literatures, while European critics such as Joan Martinez-Alier are examining the "environmentalisms of the poor" in larger, more global contexts (2005, 116–19). This observation may have contributed to Ursula Heise's statements about the lack of transnational ecocritical approaches in the early development of ecocriticism and its "subfield" of environmental justice. Citing Buell, Heise comments that ecocriticism's foundational investment in the local takes the form of a "pronounced interest in Native American ways of life, mythologies, oratures, and literatures," which, in turn, often made it more difficult for ecocriticism to "take the step toward transnationalism" (Heise 2008, "Ecocriticism" 381, 382). Mixed borderlands identities imaged through Gloria Añzaldua's notion of *mestizaje* of the "New Mestiza," however, prepared the way for a shift in the field from localized subject to one "that reaches across national borders" (Heise 2008, "Ecocriticism" 386, 382). Then in a statement that may replicate Buell's observation about the development of environmental justice approaches, Heise observes that the subfield of environmental justice criticism hastened to focus on "environmental racism" as it occurs in local communities that function "in the particular social, racial, and ethnic structures of inequality in the US" and has tended *not* to reach "beyond the US in ways envisioned by any of the several approaches to transnational in American Studies at large"; rather, environmental justice has pushed the field in a more politicized direction comparable to "multiculturalism in American Studies" (Buell 2005, 115; Heise 2008, "Ecocriticism" 386).

More important for the analysis of environmental justice and indigenous literatures that follows, however, is Heise's important formulation, in *Sense of Place and Sense of Planet*, of "eco-cosmopolitanism," a term she coins as a kind of shorthand for ecologically inflected notions of "world citizenship" and her recognition of the ways that environmental justice case studies enrich emerging understandings of ecological citizenship in global, transnational, and cosmopolitan contexts (2008, 10, 159). I will illustrate how there has been something much more innovative than "politicized multiculturalism" going on in environmental justice criticism than leading field genealogies may have indicated and argue that Silko's *Almanac of the Dead* and Gloria Anzaldúa's *Borderlands/La Frontera* have both had more than a little to do with this. By reading these works together, I would like to examine how they have both illuminated the limitations for literary studies of theories that biologize identity formation even as they have, simultaneously, energized thinking about the organization of transnational movements coalescing around civil, human, and ecological citizenship rights, rather than ethnic, racial, or indigenous rights. Since 2007, powerful literary reconsiderations of both of these works have been catalyzed by adoption of the United Nations Declaration on the Rights of Indigenous Peoples (UNDRIP), an international legal instrument that has drawn attention to the decades-long transnational organizational work by both indigenous and non-indigenous civil and non-governmental groups that have been campaigning tirelessly since the turn of the twentieth century for recognition of indigenous cultural, legal, and environmental protections ("About UNPFII" 2009, n. pag.). Delegates to the Cochabamba Conference on Climate Change link their authority to organize in support of an indigenous "cosmovisions" to UNDRIP (UDRME Preamble, n. pag.). Together, these international documents (UNDRIP, UDRME, the Law of Mother Earth, and Ecuador's revised constitution, which now grants "Pachamama" the right to maintain and regenerate its "life cycles, structures, functions, and evolutionary processes" [*Asamblea Nacional Constituyente* 2008, Chapter 7]) are seen by many politicians and academics to indicate a significant "political reconfiguration" taking place in the Americas (De la Cadena 2010, 334). By setting Silko's and Anzaldúa's work into the context of this hemispheric reconfiguration, I will be able to examine why these two writers have been so important to indigenous literary scholars and ecocritics who are writing about environmental justice issues and seeking to understand the meaning of "cosmos," a term emerging in Latin America declarations and legislation that focuses on the issues of civil rights, human rights, ecological citizenship, and climate justice (UDRME 2010, Preamble, n. pag.).

WE ARE ALL INDIANS: NEW DIRECTIONS
IN SOCIOCENTRIC ENVIRONMENTAL
JUSTICE REVISIONISM

In a recent essay, Lawrence Buell confirms the centrality of environmental justice to future directions in ecocriticism and moves away from the notion that early environmental justice ecocritics focused too narrowly on the issue of environmental racism. He singles out *The Environmental Justice Reader* as the first critical collection to examine how literature, art, public gardens, first person "*testimonios*," and street theater were shifting environmental literary criticism towards "a fusion of cultural constructionism and social justice concerns" in support of "marginalized minority peoples and communities both at home and abroad" (2011, 96). He points to Stacy Alaimo's *Bodily Natures* and Rob Nixon's *Slow Violence* as representative of how far sociocentric environmental justice literary criticism has moved in the last decade. Alaimo's book explores how the political and activist work of minority communities (that are not always racially defined) confront biologized notions of identity and raises questions about how to understand the permeability of boundaries between the "human" and the "more-than-human." She examines communities suffering from "multiple chemical sensitivities" from the perspective of both the humanities and sciences to reveal the ways that unseen toxins transgress the boundaries of the human body to affect people in multiple racial categories. Rob Nixon's *Slow Violence* examines how the work of writer-activists such as Ogoni Ken Saro-Wiwa (whose creative work and political organization in Nigeria sought to stop the ruin of Ogoni farming and fishing lands by transnational oil corporations) exposes inattention to what Nixon calls the *attritional lethality* of environmental disasters, which exacerbate the degradation of ecosystems and increase the vulnerability of people who are poor, disempowered, and often involuntarily displaced. Nixon shows how Saro-Wiwa's writings allow his readers to "see" environmental justice threats that "remain imperceptible to the senses, either because they are geographically remote, too vast or too minute in scale, or are played out across a time span that exceeds the instance of observation or even the physiological life of the human observer" (2011, 15).

As I will show below, the concepts of a "traffic in toxins" and "slow violence" resonate strongly with the work of prominent American, Native American, indigenous, and borderlands studies scholars who have been drawn to *Borderlands/La Frontera* and *Almanac of the Dead* because they redefine the questions that shape Native American studies and its relation to American Studies and provoke debates about polarizing biologically based concepts of indigenous authenticity that can still characterize academic institutionalized forms of Native Studies and borderlands studies (Huhndorf 2009, 362; Sadowski-Smith 2008 74). Anzaldúa and Silko's depictions of bi-national indigenous communities—Yaqui, Tlaxteltaca, Nahua, O'odham, Kickapoo—contribute to long-running academic and political debates centered on the sovereign relationship of federally recognized tribes to the U.S. nation-state. By focusing on communities that fall outside the category of the "nation", both authors challenge critical paradigms based on cultural nationalism that have recently been dominant in U.S. Native Studies.

Although *Borderlands/La Frontera* and *Ceremony* have both been associated with clichéd notions of *mestiza* culture that comprises white, Mexican, and Indian elements, the later work of these two authors, including Anzaldúa's essay "now let us shift" and Silko's *Almanac*, move beyond identity-based discourses towards emphasis on civil rights and innovative new forms of coalition politics. Both Anzaldúa and Silko write about people of indigenous descent living in communities suffering from the impacts of border militarization and rising levels of toxicity connected to neocolonialism and transnational corporate agribusiness and extractive industries. As Anzaldúa's "now let us shift" reveals, her understanding of her famous *Borderlands* metaphor, "herida abierta" or "open wound," changed and expanded as a result of her own life-long struggles with diabetes and other endocrine-related illnesses (Anzaldúa 2002). Anzaldúa grew up in the 1950s working in South Texas agricultural fields and traced her illness to the chemicals encountered by indigenous workers who constantly come into contact with herbicides and pesticides and drink from a Rio Grande contaminated with arsenic from silver mines located upriver. In facing her illness, Anzaldúa proposed what she called "a new tribalism" that reimagines conventional categories of color, class, and career and moves towards a twenty-first-century politics anchored in bodily matters described in a language of "pores" and "cracks" in skin and tissue. The essay goes on to turn the reader's attention to the actual places where "worlds" and "bodies" meet: just as Alaimo's writings on multiple chemical sensitivities and Nixon's analysis of slow violence open new avenues for understanding the aims of environmental justice organizing by examining non-racialized groups of people organizing for health benefits as well as civil and human rights, Anzaldúa's later writing pushes *against* her early advocacy of biologized notions of *mestizaje* and argues for a "new tribalism." This notion of a new political "tribalism" also mirrors the coalitional connections depicted within Silko's "Army of the Poor."

Moreover, Silko's movement leaders descend from people very much like Gloria Anzaldúa's forebears who, under the pressure of colonization and the expropriation of their land under four different nation-states, Spain, Mexico, Texas, and the United States, lost the specifics of their tribal histories. For example, Lecha and Zeta, twin Yaqui sisters charged with organizing the American Southwest branch of the Army of the Poor recognize that the problem with mythical notions of "authenticity" is that they erase the historical record of indigenous or minority groups, like their Yaqui ancestors, who were harassed, killed, forced into slavery, dispossessed of their lands, and inducted into European or Mexican systems of socialization (Adamson 2001, 142). Historically, this has meant that many indigenous groups remain small and mostly unrecognized by the modern nation-states in which they live and often, because they may compete for resources or be oppressed by elite ethnic groups, may not enjoy good relations with each other. For this reason, real-life groups like the Zapatistas recognize that a politics based on ethnic identity will ultimately fail. Because Silko was in personal contact with the Zapatistas during the years she was writing her novel, she was deeply familiar with these tensions and the history of hemispheric meetings, summits and conferences convened to build leadership capacity and unity among Central and South America indigenous groups in the years before the Zapatistas uprising (Silko 1996, 153–54). She bases her fictional organizers on the leaders of indigenous and ethnic group leaders from the United States, Africa, New Zealand, and Central and South America who, from the 1960s through the 1980s, organized the summits and conferences that, eventually, would lead to international adoption of UNDRIP ("About UPFII" 2009, n. pag.).

As Maria Josephina Saldaña-Portillo explains, in Central and South America these summits and meetings often exhibited deeply historic Latin American political divisions over whether to follow an ethnic (identity-based direction) or a leftist (economic and environmental) direction. But in the decades leading up to the 1994 Zapatista rebellion, the merging of both ethnic and leftist concerns became increasingly evident, as multiple indigenous groups began forming regional and pan-continental movements that brought attention to the ways in which the neoliberal economic policies of nation-states and international lending agencies (the International Monetary Fund and the World Bank) were disregarding collective rights of indigenous, ethnic, and poor minorities and supporting national legislative reforms that would allow privatization and appropriation of indigenous lands and resources. There was growing recognition that neoliberalism would affect not only indigenous groups and the poor, but the working classes and disadvantaged minoritized groups as well. Zapatista leaders understood very well how gathering geopolitical forces would make indigenous and ethnic minorities practicing land-dependent subsistence cultures inside and outside of Mexico more vulnerable to the vagaries of the global market. They surprised the world as a guerilla movement but very quickly made it clear that their primary goal was not violence or a demand for cultural, "ethnic" or indigenous rights. Rather they were claiming a voice in Mexican governance, most immediately through electoral reform and democratic transition, and calling for a place at the table where social and environmental decisions over "economic resources for indigenous peoples" were made (Saldaña-Portillo 2003, 12, 198). However, they refused to call their movement "indigenous" or "ethnic" and repeatedly emphasized that trade liberalization would not be a problem for indigenous peoples alone, but for the entire nation. In the face of NAFTA, the Zapatistas argued, all Mexico's citizens were being treated as if they were "Indians"; obviously persuaded by this argument, Mexican workers, peasants, and popular forces took to the streets chanting "¡Todos somos indios!" (Saldaña-Portillo 2003, 255). This helps to explain why Silko's leaders actively draw together people from diverse ethnic groups and local and international backgrounds (Silko 1991, 625–26, 321, 502). It also helps to explain why The Barefoot Hopi invites all the earth's people, not just indigenous people, to work for "peace and harmony with all living things" (Silko 1991, 710). Using words that sound very much like the language of the UNDRIP and UDRME, Silko's leaders call upon all the world's people to join them as they work for civil and human rights for indigenous, ethnic, and minority groups in every nation and seek legal protections for nature as well.

ECO-ENCLAVES AND FORTRESS NATIONS

Silko's use of the name "Poor People's Army" links *Almanac* to a phrase, "environmental-ism of the poor," first circulated by Ramachandra Guha and Joan Martinez-Alier in work that documents traditions of environmental thought and activism among the world's indigenous and poor minorities and further explicated by Nixon in *Slow Violence* (Guha 2000, 98–124; and Martinez-Alier 2003). This work makes Silko's 1991 novel much more legible and helps to contradict the conclusions of literary critics who have suggested that the Army of the Poor's mission to "retake the land" implies a desire to return to premodern conditions or expel Anglo-Europeans from the Americas. Indeed, Silko's indigenous leaders are clearly seeking to build a fully modern movement that will unite diverse indigenous and ethnic minority groups fleeing unrest in El Salvador, Nicaragua, Bolivia, and Mexico with North American and African groups of all races and classes (Silko 1991, 321). However, to achieve this goal, they face problems of immense complex-ity. For example, they are dealing with an issue that Rob Nixon describes as "competitive ethnicities," or the problems that result when nation-states or transnational corpora-tions prop up certain ethnic groups in favor of others and encourage the oppression of minority groups in order to ensure the flow of wealth from extractive industries to dom-inant elites. As Nixon explain, in Nigeria, Saro-Wiwa's Ogoni people—an indigenous and ethnic minority group—were subjected to both racism by Royal Dutch Shell and discrimination by elite factions of dominant Nigerian ethnic groups profiting from oil extraction (Nixon 2011, 105).

Silko illustrates the problem of competitive ethnicities by creating a Mexican arms dealer, Menardo, who is the grandson of a Mayan shaman. Menardo is taught by Catholic school teachers to shun the "pagan" practices of his once-beloved Mayan grandfather. Later, he becomes fabulously rich selling "insurance" to protect elite Southern Mexican business owners, police chiefs, mayors, and governors who back transnational corporate development projects. Menardo's paramilitary "security forces" prevent losses that elites might suffer if indigenous guerillas planning revolution in the highlands take action (Silko 1991, 258, 260–26). Menardo also meets clandestinely with U.S. C.I.A. agents who are supplying arms for his paramilitary forces (Silko 1991, 482, 492). This shows that Silko's novel does not suggest that all indigenous people work in perpetual harmony simply because they are Indians. Indeed, scenes involving Menardo make Silko one of the first indigenous writers to link the U.S. government's Reagan-era activities in Central America to socioenvironmental degradation in the global South that was fomenting division among indigenous peoples. The novel's numerous shady characters also vividly illustrate how rifts caused by nation-states and transnational corporations would continue playing out for decades in the form of civil wars, ethnic unrest, and cartel violence.

Silko juxtaposes Menardo's paramilitary activities in support of Mexico's richest citizens with the activities of Serlo, a wealthy Columbian "scientist" who is building a steel-and-glass enclosures to house endangered plants and animals for the benefit and enjoyment of the wealthy. Serlo's "Alternative Earth Units" provide facilities where those of "superior lineage" will be able to avoid the "swarms of brown people" who threaten to pollute the world's last remaining pristine natural resources (Silko 1991, 542, 543). The Earth Units clearly parody eco-enclaves proliferating around the world from the United States to South Africa that market sustainable lifestyles and "technical fixes" such as hybrid cars and solar panels to the supremely rich who live in lightly populated, overconsuming, overmilitarized societies and who build gated communities where they practice forms of eco-apartheid. Contextualized within scenes in which Serlo is build- ing his Earth Units and Menardo is building a glass house complete with indoor water- fall, the Army of the Poor's march North to "retake the land" anticipates twenty-first century resource hoarding in what Andrew Ross has called the world's "fortress nations" (2011, 205). In *Bird on Fire*, Ross studies the same U.S.-Mexico borderlands region fic- tionalized in Silko's novel. Ross sees an interesting irony in the fact that Arizona's Governor Jan Brewer signed SB 1070, America's strictest anti-immigration policy into law in the same (Earth Day) week in April that Evo Morales convened the World People's Conference on Climate Change in Cochabamba, site of a famous popular movement in 2000 to resist privatization of the city's water supply (Ross 2011, 203). Cochabamba dele- gates expressed their solidarity with immigrants moving north because the policies and practices of "exclusionary states" are disadvantaging workers and subsistence farmers (UDRME 2010, Preamble n. pag.). The Cochabamba Conference, writes Ross, offered high-profile evidence that "environmentalism had decisively outgrown its reputation as a feel-good cause for the affluent" and become a survival toolkit for the indigenous and rural poor of the global South who were organizing to resist the effects of industrial pol- lution, economic deregulation, and large-scale extractive industries (Ross 2011, 204).

Serlo's activities call upon readers to reflect on the outcomes of policies and laws that seek to exclude the poor from the benefits of "sustainable" lifestyles. Thus, Silko anticipates future resource skirmishes between the rich and poor of the type addressed by Cochabamba delegates who demand that water be recognized as a "fundamental human right" (UDRME 2010, Art. 9 n. pag.). The novel suggests that despite the poli- cies and laws that authorize eco-enclaves, border fences and fortress nations, people from densely populated countries where significant peasant communities subsist off the land will likely continue migrating in growing numbers to more temperate zones in the Global North.

In a late 1990s interview with Ellen Arnold, Silko was asked why she ends her novel with an Army of the Poor marching toward the United States to "retake the land." She responded that this phrase should be taken to mean that the Earth will survive without humans, but if humans are to survive into the future, they will need to work together to do things "differently." Everyone will need to get "along with each other, with the earth, and the animals" (Arnold 1998, 10). Although these words were spoken a decade before the Cochabamba delegates would put the issue of climate refugees squarely on the table for discussion, they sound amazingly like the language employed in the UDRME. Delegates decry the "aggression towards Mother Earth" and declare that "violations against our soils, air, forests, rivers, lakes, biodiversity, and the cosmos are assaults against us." "Us," as noted above, is emphasized to mean all humans. To combat this violence, delegates and their allies propose an immediate shift in the world's attention from "living better" to "living well" by which they mean "supporting a society based on social and environmental justice, which sees life as its purpose" (UDRME 2010, Art. 2 n. pag.).

MAKING THE COSMOS VISIBLE

Published eight years before Shepherd Krech's *The Ecological Indian*, Silko's novel represents modern indigenous leaders fully aware of the anthropological and historical evidence disputing the supposedly peaceful and environmentally benign characteristics of their premodern Mayan and Aztecan ancestors. One of the novel's central characters, Old Yoeme, is a "keeper of the almanac," who secretly archives fragmented Mayan codices, sixteenth-century copies of the Mayan creation story, the Popol Vuh, Marx's *Das Kapital*, and nineteenth-century American farmers almanacs, as she continuously updates her collection with recent newspaper articles (Silko 1991, 570). The almanac provides the elderly Yaqui character with a clear understanding of the militaristic ruling groups who practiced human sacrifice in the years before "classic period" Mayans living in sophisticated city-states abandoned them sometime around 900 C.E. This archive documents the environmental fluctuations, overpopulation, and increasing competition for shrinking resources that led to social upheaval *before* and after the arrival of the Spanish in Mexico City (Silko 1991, 570; Adamson 2001, 140). Yoeme describes the almanac as a "living book" or "seeing instrument" for those who wish to see the present and "move beyond" (Adamson 2001, 141). She passes the "seeing instrument" down to her granddaughters, Lecha and Zeta, and to The Barefoot Hopi and Angelita and encourages them to deepen their understanding of the reasons why no one human group, indigenous or non-indigenous, should be allowed to impose a singular interpretation of "Nature" on other groups, especially if that interpretation could lead, as Yoeme articulates it, to the "end of all life on Mother Earth" (Silko 1991, 734).

The almanac allows movement leaders to see the entire "cosmos" in the sense that it illuminates pre- and post-Columbian violence and makes visible the criminality of what Rob Nixon describes as the "slow violence" of human activities that disperse unforeseen or unwanted consequences "across time and space" (Nixon 2010, 2). Silko's "seeing instrument" is based on the actual history of the Mayan codices and Books of the Chilam Balam (Jaguar Priests) that were continuously written and rewritten in the Yucatan peninsula from the sixteenth century to the nineteenth in phonetic Mayan, Latin, and classic Spanish and passed down to succeeding generations so that the astrological, ceremonial, social, and agroecological knowledges of the Maya would not be lost (Adamson 2001, 140–41). According to Marisol De la Cadena, throughout Latin America, many indigenous coalitions are forming around the notion that "ancient ancestral knowledges" can be useful in illuminating "things" in the natural world that cannot be seen by the human eye, including multi-scale relationships between species functioning in systems that heretofore have not been considered deserving of the same legal rights and protections as humans. This helps to explain why delegates to the Cochabamba Conference declared that in accordance with their ancient "cosmovisions," or knowledges that have been continuously passed down from one generation to the next, nature should be granted the "right to regenerate ... biocapacity and continue ... vital cycles" (UDRME 2010, n. pag.). Anthropologist Marisol De la Cadena draws from Isabelle Stengers's work, in which she extracts from the word "cosmopolitan" its two constituents: cosmos and politics. "Cosmos" refers to the unknown whole constituted by multiple, divergent worlds and "politics" to the articulation of which "they would eventually be capable" (Stengers 995). Stengers argues that a cosmos detached from politics is irrelevant, then dives deep into the philosophies of politics and science to explore how "our modern world," to use Bruno Latour's phrase, separated humans from nature (Latour 1993, 27). The UDRME counters this separation by urging all the world's citizens to become more aware of multiple, divergent worlds and to build a politics that would support the "recovery, revalidation, and strengthening of indigenous cosmovisions" (UDRME n. pag.).

According to Latour, the creation of the nation or "modern constitution" instituted a regime of life that created a single natural order and separated it from the social by creating ontological distinctions between things and humans that were purported to be universal. By articulating two separate spheres of science and politics, European intellectuals and scientists such as Robert Boyle and Thomas Hobbes created a modern world "in which the representation of things through the intermediary of the laboratory is forever dissociated from the representation of citizens through the intermediary of the social contract" (Latour 1993, 27). Hobbes and Boyle were thus "acting in concert to promote one and the same innovation in political theory: the representation of nonhumans belongs to science, but science is not allowed to appeal to politics; the representation of citizens belongs to politics, but politics is not allowed to have any relation to the nonhumans produced and mobilized by science and technology" (Latour 1993, 28). This separation of humanity from nature led to the "gradual extinction of other-than-human beings and the worlds in which they existed in politics. The pluriverse disappeared" (De la Cadena 2010, 345). A single anthropomorphic universe made its appearance, inhabited by diverse peoples (we now call them "cultures") who are "distanced from a single 'Nature'" (De la Cadena 2010, 345).

The Barefoot Hopi's repeated references to "Mother Earth" taps into long-held hemispheric American understandings of things unseen, or a pluriverse, often referred to "Pachamama," and understood not as a female-gendered planet but as "Source of Life" (De la Cadena 2010, 335). In Silko's novel, Lecha, Zeta, and The Barefoot Hopi use their "seeing instrument" to gaze beyond the span of a single human life to reaches of time necessary to the survival of functioning ecosystems, and to multinatural worlds that, for indigenous peoples, have never ceased to exist. The novel helps make visible some of the dynamics of contemporary indigenous "cosmopolitics" in which indigenous leaders such as Evo Morales, with his calls to all the world's people to join him to protect "Pachamama," summon a plurality into visibility that does not stop at a politicized multiculturalism, but is a project that might more properly be called "multinaturalisms."

Silko also shows how the "things" banished from politics can be "seeing instruments." For example, when an odd outcropping of sandstone emerges from underneath an erod-ing tailings pile at an inactive uranium mine near Laguna Pueblo village in New Mexico, Laguna villagers believe the formation to be the embodiment of Maahastryu, a sacred snake god who once lived in a beautiful lake near the village (Silko 1991, 761). When mining commences in the 1950s, Maahastryu disappears as the lake dries up and radio-active tailings begin piling up around the village. Forty years later, when the ancient snake god reappears in the form of a sandstone outcropping, the odd geological feature becomes a stark reminder that slow violence occurs when extractive industries displace people or interrupt their ability to provide for their own subsistence. "The old-timers," Silko writes, "had been dead set against ripping open Mother Earth" (Silko 1991, 34). However, in the words of De la Cadena, their beliefs "express an epistemic alternative to scientific paradigms (ecological and economic)" that supposedly stand in the way of "the common good (productive efficiency, economic growth, even sustainable develop-ment)" of a supposedly "homogenous humanity benefiting from an also homogenous nature" (2010, 349–50). The reappearance of Maahastryu makes visible the interruption of a socionatural world in which people were able to provide the means of their daily survival and in which other living organisms were dependent on the mountains or lakes in which they lived.

Regionally specific indigenous movements have long formed around the notion of the earth as a sentient being that takes the form of multi-scaled "lesser beings" (in the form of mountains, rivers, or lakes) considered not only material realities but also cul-ture–nature entities, or places where humans and other-than-humans coexist. De la Cadena defines "sentient beings" as geographical formations "with individual physiog-nomies more or less known by individuals involved in interactions with them" (De la Cadena 341–42). Silko illustrates how "earth-beings" become "seeing instruments" to local inhabitant populations by creating a Laguna Pueblo Indian man in his fifties who learns to "read" the odd outcropping. Sterling has just retired from his railroad job in California and returned home to New Mexico. Relatives tell him about the emergence of Maahastryu, but after an adult life spend in California, he does not value Laguna beliefs and considers the sandstone snake a joke. He prides himself, instead, on knowing the histories of America's famous criminals, including Billy the Kid, Geronimo, and Bonnie and Clyde, which he reads in *True Crime* magazine (Silko 1991, 26). After a series of mis-understandings with the tribal council, Sterling leaves the village and ends up in Tucson, Arizona, where he takes a job as Lecha and Zeta's gardener, thus becoming privy to the formation of a hemispheric movement (Silko 1991, 39). After many adventures with Lecha and Zeta, he returns to Laguna Pueblo equipped with knowledge gleaned from The Barefoot Hopi's lectures.

He immediately goes to the mine to sit at the edge and contemplate Maahastryu. Tiny black ants come out of the ground and surround him. He remembers that "the old peo-ple had believed the ants were messengers to the spirits, the way snakes were. The old people used to give the ants food and pollen" as gifts, so that they would carry "human prayers directly underground" (Silko 1991, 757). Sterling feeds the ants some of the beans he has brought with him and their success carrying them underground "lifts his spirits" (Silko 1991, 758). This interaction with the ants at the site of Maahastryu's emergence points towards understandings of "Mother Earth as living being" that can be illuminated by emerging sciences such as biosemiotics, an area of research that deals with how living things perceive and interpret their environments through chemical gradients or intensities of light. As social insects, writes biosemiotician Jesper Hoffmeyer, ant colonies have long suggested the concept of "superorganisms, with the implication that the individual insects are subunits, mobile cells, in the superorganism" (2010, 381). Citing the research of Deborah Gordon on ants responding to chemical stimuli, Hoffmeyer notes that the behavior of individual ants and colonies as a whole is not absolutely deterministic. Gordon's study suggests that large-scale patterns are established or influenced through interactions with small-scale entities. Just "as the same word can have different meanings in different situations," writes Gordon, "so the same chemical cue can elicit different responses in different social situations" (1999, 97). In a world permeated by insidious, unseen slow violence, such as imperceptible radioactivity entering an aquifer or food chain, Silko's depiction of the ants' journey with beans into the ground suggests the complexity of a "pluriverse" or a "superorganism" in which multiple biological and organic systems are constantly responding to stimuli, but not in deterministic ways. As Sterling contemplates Maahastryu and the ants, they become "seeing instruments" that make "Mother Earth's" material and biosemiotic relationships accessible, tangible, and imaginable.

Biosemiotics also suggest interesting insights into the social, political, economic, and ecological meanings of "cosmovisions" that encompass multinatural relationships. For example, as he contemplates the black ants, Sterling becomes aware that the crimes he has been reading about in *True Crime* are merely distractions that keep him from understanding the causes of large scale patterns of crime such as war or the slow violence of extractive industries that degrade socionatural worlds or threaten vital ecosystemic functions. Maahastryu allows him to consider, in the words of the UDRME, that the cosmos is a "living being with whom [humans] have an indivisible and interdependent relationship" (Art. 2 n. pag.). Silko's novel, once considered prescient because it was published in advance of the Zapatista uprising, now, twenty years later, seems even more ahead of its time as it offers readers insights into the coalitions forming around notions that multiple species, "superorganisms," and "things" might be deserving of legal rights and protections. Silko's "case study" of the fictional Maahastryu, read in the context of real-world political organization in Latin America around sentient Earth-beings, also offers affirmation of Ursula Heise's crucial insight that developing notions of "eco-comopolitanism" or world citizenship are best be understood in the context of environmental justice field work (*Sense* 2008, 10, 159).

It is important to note, writes De la Cadena, that allowing Earth-beings to count in politics does not remove all proposals for economic growth and development from the negotiating table. People, citizens—indigenous or not—can still side with a mine or dam, operate a farm or ranch, and choose jobs or money, depending on local needs. At contemporary indigenous-led gatherings all over the world today, there is often recognition of nature's multiple and heterogeneous ontologies (including its possibility as repository of mineral, hydroelectric, or timber wealth). People with differing definitions of "nature" (that may or may not include sentient beings) might weigh multiple possibilities in discussions of differing, even competing political proposals without any of these proposals being denigrated or labeled "right," "left," "ethnic," "unscientific," or "superstitious."

REASSESSING THE ECOLOGICAL INDIAN

For almost one hundred and fifty years, indigenous groups from around the world have been organizing politically both inside and outside local, regional, state, national, and international courts and institutions (About UPFII 2009, n. pag.). In an article introducing her edited edition of Penobscot writer Joseph Nicolar's *The Life and Traditions of the Red Man* (1893), Annette Kolodny calls upon ecocritics to consider this history and reassess Krech's conclusions about American Indian employment of the trope of the "Ecological Indian" as mere support for "environmental and antitechnocratic causes" (Kolodny 2007, 18; Krech 1999, 20). Kolodny writes that the Penobscots of Maine presented the first of many petitions to the governor of the state in opposition to the illegal appropriation of their lands and decimation of their natural resources in 1823. Nicolar's autobiography illustrates how Penobscot's relationship to the land is experienced as "everywhere alive with spiritual powers and kin-beings" (Kolodny 2007, 11). Thus, Nicolar's book was not written to establish some kind of authentic identity but to acknowledge that the conditions of Penobscot survival were precariously dependent on functioning ecological systems upon which they and other non-human species depended (Kolodny 2009, 92, 96). This calls attention to the fact that long before the 1970s occupation of Alcatraz Island that Shepherd Krech mentions as the date that tactical use of images of the "Ecological Indian" began, indigenous peoples had been articulating cosmovisions of worlds more multiple than those of "modern" nation-states for many decades, even for hundreds of years if we count the Books of the Chilam Balam.

At the Holistic Healers Convention convened at the end of Silko's novel, Lecha, Zeta, Angelita, The Barefoot Hopi, and Wilson Weasel Tail gather with delegates from around the world, including "affluent young whites, fearful of a poisoned earth" (Silko 1991, 734). Attendees are not united in harmony, and even display some suspicion of the motivations of other delegates. There are some "scattered crazies" in attendance (Silko 1991, 755). Their differences mirror those found among contemporary indigenous groups and organizations. Some believe in earth-beings and some do not. As De la Cadena explains, at Latin American political rallies, earth-beings do not propose what "is" or "what ought to be;" instead, they "slow down reasoning" and create "an opportunity to arouse a slightly different awareness of the problems and situations" under analysis (De la Cadena 2010, 360–61). Earth-beings do not "induce to action" but provoke the kind of thinking that would enable us to undo, or more accurately, unlearn, a single ontology of politics and thus create possibilities for new interpretations and actions (De la Cadena 360).

Silko's still-provocative novel has increasingly gained respect among scholars who study developments in transnational environmental justice organizing, indigenous literatures, and proliferating environmentalisms of the poor. Like the delegates to the Cochabamba Conference on Climate Change, Silko's organizers enlist "things" (like sentient earth-beings) into politics that are helping inaugurate an environmental movement that is more plural not because the people enacting it are bodies marked by race or ethnicity demanding rights, but because they "force into visibility the culture-nature divide that has prevented multiple worlds and species from being recognized" (De la Cadena 2010, 346).

WORKS CITED

"About UNPFII and a Brief History of Indigenous Peoples and the International System." The United Nations Permanent Forum on Indigenous Issues. http://www.un.org/esa/socdev/unpfii/en/history.html. Accessed August 17, 2009.

Adamson, Joni. *American Indian Literature, Environmental Justice, and Ecocriticism: The Middle Place*. Tucson, AZ: University of Arizona Press, 2001.

Anzaldúa, Gloria. "now let us shift." *This Bridge We Call Home: Radical Visions for Transformation*, ed. Gloria Anzaldúa and Ana Louis Keating, (New York: Routledge, 2002), 540–78.

Arnold, Ellen. "Listening to the Spirits: An Interview with Leslie Marmon Silko." *Studies in American Indian Literatures*, *10*:3 (1998): 1–34.

Asamblea Nacional Constituyente, http://www.eluniverso.com/2008/07/24/1212/1217/E8C064BD52EF420CAECDB655555BF60C.html, Accessed on April 20, 2011.

Buell, Lawrence. *The Future of Environmental Criticism: Environmental Crisis and Literary Imagination*. London and New York: Blackwell Publishing, 2005.

Buell, Lawrence. "Ecocriticism: Some Emerging Trends," *Qui Parle*. Vol. *19*. 2 (Spring/Summer 2011): 87–115.

De la Cadena, Marisol. "Indigenous Cosmopolitics in the Andes: Conceptual Reflections beyond 'Politics,'" *Cultural Anthropology 25*.2 (2010): 334–70.

Edwards, Stephen. "UN document would give 'Mother Earth' Same Rights as Humans." *Vancouver Sun*. April 13, 2011. http://www.vancouversun.com/technology/document+would+give+Mother+Earth+same+rights+humans/4597840/story.html Accessed August 28, 2011.

Garrard, Greg. *Ecocriticism*. Oxford, UK: Routledge, 2004.

Gordon, Deborah. *Ants at Work: How an Insect Society Is Organized*. New York: The Free Press, 1999.

Guha, Ramachandra. *Environmentalism: A Global History*. New York: Longman, 2000.

Heise, Ursula K. "Ecocriticism and the Transnational Turn in American Studies." *American Literary History*, *20*, No. 1–2 (Spring/Summer 2008): 381–404

Heise, Ursula. *Sense of Place and Sense of Planet: The Environmental Imagination of the Global*. New York: Oxford UP, 2008.

Hoffmeyer, Jesper. "A Biosemiotic Approach to the Question of Meaning," *Zygon* 45 no.2 (June 2010): 367–390.

Huhndorf, Shari. "Picture Revolution: Transnationalism, American Studies, and the Politics of Contemporary Native Culture," *American Quarterly 61* no.2 (June 2009): 359–81.

Kolodny, Annette. "Rethinking the 'Ecological Indian': A Penobscot Precursor." *ISLE: Interdisciplinary Studies in Literature and Environment 14.1* (Winter 2007): 1–23.

———. "Saving Maine for the Indian: The Legacy of Joseph Nicolar's *The Life and Traditions of the Red Man.*" MELUS: Multi-Ethnic Literatures of the United States. Special Issue: Ethnicity and Ecocriticism, Joni Adamson, and Scott Slovic, eds. 34.2 (Summer 2009): 81–101.

Krech, Shepherd, III. *The Ecological Indian: Myth and History*. New York: Norton, 1999.

Latour, Bruno. *We Have Never Been Modern*. Cambridge, MA: Harvard University Press. 1993.

Martinez-Alier, Joan. *The Environmentalism of the Poor: A Study of the Ecological Conflicts and Valuation*. Cheltenham, UK: Edward Elgar Publishing, 2003.

Nixon, Rob. *Slow Violence and the Environmentalism of the Poor*. Cambridge, MA, and London: 2011.

Ross, Andrew. *Bird on Fire: Lessons from the World's Least Sustainable City*. London: Oxford, 2011.

Sadowski-Smith, Claudia. *Border Fictions: Globalization, Empire, and Writing at the Boundaries of the United States. New World Series*, A. James Arnold, Editor. Charlottesville, VA: University of Virginia Press, 2008.

Saldaña-Portillo, María Josephina. *The Revolutionary Imagination in the Americas and the Age of Development*. Durham, N. C.: Duke University Press, 2003.

Silko, Leslie Marmon. *Almanac of the Dead*. New York: Simon and Schuster, 1991.

Silko Leslie Marmon, "An Expression of Profound Gratitude to the Maya Zapatistas, January 1, 1994." *Yellow Woman and a Beauty of the Spirit: Essays on Native American Life Today* by Leslie Marmon Silko. New York: Simon and Schuster, 1996: 152–154.

"United Nations Declaration on the Rights of Indigenous Peoples." The United Nations Permanent Forum on Indigenous Issues. Adopted by the United Nations General Assembly in 2007. Available online. http://www.un.org/esa/socdev/unpfii/en/declaration.html. Accessed August 11, 2009.

"Universal Declaration on the Rights of Mother Earth." World People's Conference on Climate Change and the Rights of Mother Earth. Available online. http://www.globalresearch.ca/index.php?context=va&aid=18931 Accessed September 17, 2010.

CHAPTER 10

FEMINIST SCIENCE STUDIES AND ECOCRITICISM

Aesthetics and Entanglement in the Deep Sea

STACY ALAIMO

"The question of how we should relate to that which we cannot control is still up for grabs, and as this question has become displaced ... into the ocean deeps and the depths of space, so feminists must follow"

(Bryld and Lykke 1999, 225)

A commonsensical course from the general to the specific would suggest that an essay on science studies and ecocriticism, rather than feminist science studies and ecocriticism, would be in order. Feminist theory and gender studies have demonstrated, however, that many unmarked, ostensibly ungendered fields, modes, and sites of inquiry have been shaped by the social categories of gender, race, class, and colonialism. In other words, to search for the prior or primary field of science studies as that which transcends gender is to reestablish the very hierarchies that feminist theory and cultural studies critique. Moreover, environmental criticism emerged during a period in which the most prominent science studies scholarship (at least in the United States) has been that of feminist science studies, particularly the work of Donna J. Haraway, whose work has been extremely influential for theoretically oriented humanities scholars and ecocritics alike. Thus, to invoke Bruno Latour, we have never been human, if human means something that transcends gender, race, or class. Moreover, the proper sense of moving from science studies in "general" to a supposedly more particular subset of science studies would lure us into an epistemological terrain of separate, delineated territories and fields, rather than the knots and entanglements that intertwine nature and culture, science and the humanities, the knower and the known.[1]

Haraway describes her methodology, for example, as taking "points of intense implosion or knots" such as the gene, cyborg, or ecosystem which "lead out into worlds" and exploding or disentangling them (Haraway 2008a, 38).

This may be a rather serpentine start, but it is fitting for feminist and environmentalist epistemologies to embrace our immersion within tangled banks rather than seeking to clear the ground for a more panoramic perspective. Epistemological entanglement is, I would argue, valuable for feminist science studies and for ecocriticism. Feminist science studies, interconnected as it is with feminism as a social movement, straddles the subject/object divide as it insists that the "objects" of scientific and medical inquiry are often themselves subjects. This is particularly evident in feminist critiques of medicine, allied with the women's health movements that produced their own medical information, most famously in *Our Bodies Our Selves*. Barbara Kruger's iconic postmodern artwork with the title "Your Body is a Battleground," announces a feminist sense of being that which is under siege. Exactly this sort of feminist body politics demands ways of knowing that do not fit within standard models of scientific objectivity that assume solid distinctions between the knower and the known. Granted, the situation for environmentalists and ecocritics is distinctly different from an identity politics model, as many have pointed out; it is humans that have besieged environments, ecological systems, and too many species to enumerate. No human can speak *as* "nature" of course and yet, as many have argued, it may be even more problematic to magnify the opposition between "human" and "nature," since that very opposition undergirds many of our philosophical, ethical, and environmental troubles. Wilderness models of environmentalism, in which nature is imagined as a world apart, have been complemented by those of environmental health, environmental justice, sustainability, and carbon footprint calculations—all of which link human bodies and practices to the wider material world, resulting in more entangled modes of being, doing, and knowing.

What does feminist science studies offer ecocriticism? Complicated methodologies, ontologies, epistemologies, and figurations. It undertakes incisive discursive critiques, yet it does not remain within an echo chamber of discourse. It traces the routes and interconnections between science, technology, economics, and cultural systems. It appreciates the potency of social construction and yet insists on the necessity for knowledge of the material world. Haraway, for example, insists that the figurations she unravels are "simultaneously literal and figurative" (Haraway 1997, 11). Moreover, the subject is never detached from her "object" of inquiry; instead, "we inhabit and are inhabited by such figures that map universes of knowledge, practice, and power" (Haraway 1997, 11). This sense of material-semiotic immersion parallels the theories of interaction, intra-action, and perpetual emergence in the work of Nancy Tuana and Karen Barad.[2] These models of knowing and being are especially useful for environmentally oriented thinking, which needs to account for the actions, significations, and transformations of the more-than-human world. Feminist science studies, along with the work of Andrew Pickering and Bruno Latour, provides complex ways of understanding material agency, offering scholars in the environmental humanities ways of conceptualizing how the more-than-human world acts, how scientific practices and technologies "capture" those actions, and how cultural frameworks, economic systems, and discourses are entangled with the productions of technoscience and the ever-emergent material world.

In *Bodily Natures: Science, Environment, and the Material Self*, I argue that the literature, film, photography, and activist web sites of the environmental justice and the environmental health movements manifest epistemologies that emerge from the material interconnections between the human body and the environment. By emphasizing the movement across bodies, trans-corporeality reveals the interchanges and interconnections between various bodily natures. But by underscoring that "trans" indicates movement across different sites, trans-corporeality also opens up a mobile "space" that acknowledges the often unpredictable and unwanted actions of human bodies, nonhuman creatures, ecological systems, chemical agents, and other actors. Acknowledging that material agency necessitates more capacious epistemologies allows us to forge ethical and political positions that can contend with numerous late twentieth century/early twenty-first century realities in which "human" and "environment" can by no means be considered as separate. Trans-corporeality, as a theoretical site, is where feminist theory, environmental theories, and science studies intertwine. Furthermore, the movement across human corporeality and nonhuman nature necessitates rich, complex modes of analysis that travel through the entangled territories of material and discursive, natural and cultural, biological and textual.

As the material self cannot be disentangled from networks that are simultaneously economic, political, cultural, scientific, and substantial, what was once the ostensibly bounded human subject finds herself in a swirling landscape of uncertainty where practices and actions that were once not even remotely ethical or political matters suddenly become the very stuff of the crises at hand. This is especially evident in the case of global climate change, in which an individual, household, business, university, city, or state can calculate the carbon footprint left by the avalanche of human activities that emit carbon. While carbon footprint calculations demonstrate how the actions of individuals, groups, and processes contribute to the rather abstract and complex dynamics of global climate change, people with multiple chemical sensitivities (MCS) are themselves immediately affected by the chemical-industrial world they inhabit. People with MCS exemplify trans-corporeality, as their very bodies become "scientific instruments," finely tuned registers of invisible data about the hazards of seemingly benign, ordinary places and things. Their bodies are inseparable from power/knowledge systems, through which the chemical-industrial complex seeks to delegitimize both the scientific and the subcultural knowledges of MCS. Feminist science studies is invaluable for reckoning with the economic, political, and epistemological entanglements of the material agencies that coalesce in such a way as to make certain people react to "small" amounts of "safe" substances.[3] The chemically reactive epitomize one of the most intriguing and significant aspects of the broader environmental health and environmental justice movements—the development of citizen experts, in which laypeople people participate in the production of scientific knowledge as "popular epidemiologists" (Brown 1993), "ordinary experts" (Di Chiro 1997), and "street scientists" (Coburn 2005).

While environmental health and environmental justice movements foster embodied, participatory knowledge practices, such practices may not travel well to other environmental crises, especially those involving habitats humans cannot inhabit. Movements for ocean conservation, for example, seem to float in open expanses, rather than entangled embodied places. Even though many coastal peoples have developed traditional ecological knowledges about sea creatures that they fish, hunt, or otherwise encounter, and even though there are some amateur ocean scientists, such as those operators of dive boats, whale watches, and dolphin watches, who are especially knowledgeable about and committed to marine life, for most people sea life is "encountered" in highly mediated forms—such as films, photography, websites, and aquariums. Simply put, even recreational scuba divers, exploring the top 40 meters of the ocean, are extremely limited in what they can themselves observe and experience. The ocean eludes the feminist, environmentalist, and environmental justice models of ordinary experts, embodied or situated knowers, domestic carbon footprint analysts, and trans-corporeal subjects who take science into their own hands and conceive of environmentalism as a scientifically mediated but also immediate sort of practice.

As ocean sciences gain funding, attention, and access to new technologies, and more information and images of the ocean and its creatures becomes publicized—in news stories, books, photographs, websites, and films—it will be important to consider the imbrications between scientific knowledge production, cultural narratives, and aesthetic styles, as well as the environmental and political implications of these factors. Robert D. Ballard, former Director of the Center for Marine Exploration at Woods Hole, concludes his personal history of ocean exploration, for example, with a section entitled "Leaving the Body Behind," which notes the drawbacks of human-occupied diving machines and submersibles. Tethers, for example, "remain a problem: They snap, they tangle, they restrict." Ballard argues that robotics and telecommunications technologies will allow us to

> cut the ultimate tether—the one that binds our questioning intellect to vulnerable human flesh. . . . As Jacques Cousteau used to say, the ideal means of deep-sea transport would allow us to move "like an angel." Our minds can now go it alone, leaving the body behind. What could be more angelic than that? (Ballard 2000, 311)

The desire to cut the tether, severing the umbilical-cord connection between the transcendent scientific mind and the vulnerable maternal flesh, betrays an epistemology that distances and supposedly protects the knower from the realities, complications, and risks of the material world. The predictably gendered dichotomies here, which presume the possibility of freely floating minds, erase the materiality as well as the economic and political entanglements of the very technologies that would allow scientists to, ostensibly, "cut the tether." Strangely, the figure of the angel transubstantiates the crushing waters of the deep seas to ethereal atmospheres, magically shifting from one realm to another, without tracing the scientific "cascade of mediations" that leads toward "what cannot be grasped directly" (Latour 2010: 123). Invoking angels, or, as is more commonly the case with the seas, aliens, and promoting epistemologies in which the human

remains separate from what he studies is particularly problematic for ocean conservation movements.

It is all too easy to ignore or dismiss the threats to ocean environments when they
are conceived as worlds apart from the human. Aptly, Tony Koslow opens his book *The
Silent Deep* with a *New Yorker* cartoon in which one woman at a tea party says to another,
"I don't know why I don't care about the bottom of the ocean but I don't" (Koslow 2007).
It is useful, particularly given widespread environmental devastation, to acknowledge
"the fact that we are part of the nature which we seek to understand" and to consider
that "taking account of the entangled materializations of which we are a part" may be an
ethical matter (Barad 2007, 352, 385). And yet tracing these entanglements, caring about,
feeling responsible for, or promoting the environmental health of remote reaches of the
ocean is, even for most environmentalists, an ethical-political stretch. Out of sight, out
of mind.

A sea change, however, is in sight, as the start of the twenty-first century experiences
a seemingly sudden resurgence of interest in ocean conservation and a concomitant
push for more research on ocean creatures and ecologies, especially those of the deep
seas. The TED talks, available on the web, feature a thematic cluster about marine science and ocean conservation, including Sylvia Earle's passionate plea to save the oceans.
President Obama established the Interagency Ocean Policy Task Force in 2010, creating
a National Ocean Council, and several ocean advocacy groups have gained prominence
alongside Greenpeace and the Sea Shepherds, including Oceana, Ocean Conservancy,
Blue Ocean Institute, ORCA: Ocean Research Conservation Association, Institute for
Ocean Conservation Science, BlueVoice, the United Kingdom's Marine Conservation
Society, the Chilean Centro de Conservación Cetacea, and the international Deep Sea
Conservation Coalition. This is certainly overdue, given the catastrophic overexploita-
tion of most of the world's fisheries; the wasteful and cruel use of longlines; destructive
beam-trawling for shellfish and "finning" of sharks and rays; the toxic waste (including sewage, chemicals, and radioactive waste); plastics suspended in the ocean waters as
well as in the bodies of fish and birds; and plans to increase ocean drilling and mining.
Unlike most threatened terrestrial ecosystems, however, aquatic environments remain a
mystery. Little is known, even by the scientific experts, about what creatures exist, what
their life cycles are, what they eat, and how various ecological systems work. Still less is
known about deep sea life. Biologists Michael A. Rex and Ron J. Etter muse that "Since
most of the deep sea remains unexplored we can hardly guess what other wonders exist
there" (Rex and Etter 2010, x). They explain that mainstream ecology has not incorporated the deep-sea: "One can scarcely find the term 'deep sea' in the indices of ecology
textbooks and major reference works" (Rex and Etter 2010, x).

The early twenty-firstst century is clearly a turning point for oceanic ecology and
conservation, yet marine sciences are often entangled with the commercial enterprises
that are threatening the seas. The World Ocean Council, for example, comprised of
"'the ocean business community,'" promotes "improved ocean science," in part because,
"Increased, improved, and better coordinated ocean science is important to industry
operations in the marine environment, to help ensure the business environment is as

predictable as possible" (World Ocean Council 2010). While industries and nations race to capitalize on technologies that allow for more extensive exploration and extraction from the seas, others argue that science needs to undertake fundamental projects that will allow us to have some understanding of ocean ecologies before they are disrupted by industrial fishing, dumping, and mining. John D. Gage and Paul A Tyler conclude their dense, and otherwise utterly "objective," textbook on *Deep Sea Biology* with this modest recommendation: "exploitation of [deep sea] resources should not be attempted until we fully understand the natural history and ecology of this complex ecosystem" (Gage and Tyler 1991, 406).

As the ocean and its astoundingly diverse forms of life become more publicized, more apparent, and more contested, it may be useful to analyze how sea creatures and ecologies are represented. More specifically, I would like to examine how the scientific understanding of ocean creatures becomes enlisted in more familiar models of techno-logical mastery and domination and, alternately, become highly aestheticized, perhaps even sacralized. The "cultural oscillations" that Mette Bryld and Nina Lykke analyze in *Cosmodolphins* hold sway as humans respond to the "wild other" of the ocean by taking up the "illusory positions of self-aggrandizing and self abandoning" (Bryld and Lykke 1999, 225). Bryld and Lykke argue that both these positions are "destructive and danger-ous": "While the former tries to deny that, as living beings, we cannot evade our posi-tion as objects of cosmic and biological forces beyond our control, the latter, conversely, attempts to ignore the fact that nevertheless, we do have some opportunities for sub-jective and sociotechnical intervention" (Bryld and Lykke 1999, 225). The films, texts, and photography about the ocean discussed below pose ocean life as either the vessel for heroic exploration and scientific control or a perfect specimen for aesthetic contem-plation. Such modes of understanding the material world are a far cry from models of interaction, intra-action, encounter, or companion species, as they seem to evade the recognition that humans are entangled with watery worlds. The essay will conclude, however, by suggesting that aesthetic encounters may themselves be forms of entangle-ment that may motivate concern for marine conservation.

The ocean has been portrayed as the earth's last frontier or wilderness,[4] which, in terms of American mythology, positions it as the place for narratives of domination. Unabashed masculinist narratives of exploration, discovery, and conquest grace a cover of *Wired* magazine, for example, where the guest editor James Cameron, shot from a hero-making angle, presents "The New Age of Exploration," which spotlights ocean and space exploration. The cluster leads with a full-page shot of Cameron ensconced within a very gear-heavy submersible, followed by Cameron's story, "The Drive to Discover," in which he states, "Whenever explorers go to hostile realms, whether in space or in the sea, we live or die by our machines" (Cameron 2004, 190). Cameron's film *Aliens of the Deep* documents deep ocean expeditions, in which he, along with marine biolo-gists, astrobiologists, other scientists, an astronaut, and Russian Mir space station pilots, explores the depths of the seas via submersible vehicles and rover cameras. Much of the film portrays engineering challenges and other technological dramas, highlighting the rather self-consciously enacted heroics of Cameron himself. Strangely, the viewer learns little about the ocean or about the creatures the explorers encounter and even less about ocean conservation. The scientist featured most often, Dijana Figueroa, a marine animal scientist (and an African American woman) does mention climate change, but that fleeting moment is drowned out by the rest of the film, in which exploration is promoted as an end in itself. When Cameron and planetary scientist Kevin Hand see a large gelatinous animal, Hand exclaims, "Look at that thing! That is absolutely unreal!" Cameron says, "Look at this thing. Look at this thing; It's just incredible... Beautiful." The film lingers here, letting us watch the entrancing gelatinous animal billowing like a translucent scarf. Despite their enthusiastic appreciation of the animal, one wishes a knowledgeable marine biologist, such as an expert on jellies, had been there to say something a bit more informative. Despite this arresting and entrancing scene, the film's narrative and structure makes the ocean creatures themselves subservient to space exploration or just exploration in and of itself.

Dubbing ocean creatures "aliens" is a common trope with a rather long history. Yet within this film the connection between sea creatures and (other) extra-terrestrials is not merely metaphorical. Indeed, the ocean is touted as the perfect practice arena for space explorers; marine biology is cast as a good starting point for astrobiology, and the samples from the ocean are just the "next best thing" for the planetary scientist to examine. The ethereal trumps the aqueous; the transcendent transcends the immanent. Figueroa's compelling and informative discussion of symbiosis in riftia, the giant tube worms, for example, is followed by a cut to Cameron telling Hand, "The *real* question is can you imagine a colony of these on [Jupiter's moon] Europa?" Whereas the renowned ocean scientist Sylvia Earle and other blue environmentalists use the contrast between space exploration and ocean exploration in order to argue for better funding and more interest in ocean research and conservation—the assumption being that something is wrong when we know so much more about other planets than about the depths of our own planet—a fairly linear progression appears in *Aliens of the Deep*, in which the ocean becomes subservient to the more exciting—dare we say "untethered"—expanse of space exploration. Indeed, the film concludes with an imaginary scene in which Figuero reaches out to touch an octopus-like creature that morphs into an alien.

Articulating marine depths with distant planets frames them as places to encounter pure, untouched otherness, without any of that nagging guilt, anxiety, or responsibility that may accompany the contemplation of places clearly marked by histories of colonialism, climate injustice, or environmental devastation. Casting the deep-sea animals as space aliens implies that they are from some other world. It is one thing for William Beebe, in 1932 to encounter a fish while in his bathysphere and propose that it be called, "Bathysphaera Intacta: the Untouchable Bathysphere Fish," (Matsen 2005, 157) but at this point, everything in the ocean has already been touched by human practices, if not human hands. As Tony Koslow puts it, "We may think of the deep sea as pristine, but in fact no portion of the deep sea is today unaffected by human activities" (Koslow 2007, 3). One suspects, however, that the vast expanses of the ocean and outer space exist, in the mind of Cameron, for the purpose of explorer-making. Just before the final scene in *Aliens of the Deep*, Cameron says, "Exploration is like a muscle, you have to exercise it to make it stronger." Echoing Teddy Roosevelt's belief that the United States required wilderness for patriotic manmaking, the ocean is cast as the last wilderness on earth, with one difference now, anyone, male, female, black, or white, is welcome to join the expedition, as long as they embrace the pure spirit of exploration.[5] The futuristic focus of the film fails to reckon with the racial and colonial histories lurking within narratives and discourses of "exploration" and leaves the marine animals behind.

Aliens of the Deep includes some beautiful shots of sea creatures as well as communicating the explorers' sense of awe. We see glimpses, at least, of the organisms swimming or floating in their natural environments. By contrast, organisms and species are strangely absent from Craig Venter's much publicized global expedition to genetically sample the microbial life of the seas. Microbes may not be as photogenic as jellyfish, yet the film about Venter's expedition, *Cracking the Ocean Code*, does not even bother to visually represent them, except as a ground-up crepe-like substance and then, as colorful animations of genetic code, which accurately reflects the fact that Venter is not in search of microbes per se, just their DNA. Venter, like Cameron, is a darling of *Wired* magazine. The August 2004 cover features a close-up of Craig Venter, with the long headline, "Fantastic Voyage: The Epic Quest to Collect the DNA of Everything on the Planet—and Redefine Life as We Know It. He wanted to play God, so he cracked the human genome. Now he wants to play Darwin and collect the DNA of everything on the planet." This narrative of heroic individualism, scientific progress, and the mastery of nonhuman nature reiterates the obsession with genetics, in which life—living creatures, species, and interacting ecosystems—is reduced to codes. Genes—misrepresented as discrete, mechanistic, agential entities (as Evelyn Fox Keller, Donna Haraway, and others have argued)—have become invested with the power of life itself. Sarah Franklin states that "nature becomes biology becomes genetics, through which life itself becomes reprogrammable information" (Franklin 2000, 190). The reprogrammable information is what Venter is after—that is the stuff he hopes will translate into huge profits for his private (ad)ventures. Venter's particular method of processing his samples, called "shotgunning," breaks "the long strands of DNA into millions of fragments" (Shreeve 2004, 111). (Roosevelt also haunts this story as the term "shotgunning" appears under the title "How to Hunt Microbes.") These fragments are then reassembled robotically by sequencing machines that put the bits back together (*Cracking* 2007). Despite the extreme transmogrifications of the microbes, there seems to be no worry that anything is lost, misread, or radically altered in this transformation from life to data. There is no sense of "mangling" in Pickering's terms, or of any recognition of the entanglement of technologies, procedures, economic incentives, and data. The beauty of code, supposedly, is that it floats free of messy materiality, intact and uncompromised. As the narrator in the Discovery Channel film, *Cracking the Ocean Code*, announces: "From life to disk": "What was once faint biochemical information of a living creature is now digital code ready for computer processing." The film concludes triumphantly: "And from the sea, a new epoch for all life on earth has begun." Skeptical viewers may notice, however, a rather large gulf between the actual results of this research, the collection of 1.3 million new genes, and the vaunted possibility that these microbes could, someday, maybe, address human energy and pollution challenges. Even James Shreeve, author of the *Wired* magazine article, questions the significance of what Venter has collected and reassembled: "Venter may indeed have 'collected' 100,0000 new species and tens of millions of new genes. Does he or anyone else, possess the conceptual tools needed to pull some great truth out of an ocean of information and vivify it like a bolt of lightning bringing Frankenstein's monster to life" (Shreeve 2004, 150). Shreeve's critique is well taken and yet, the "monster" here was, in fact, many different living creatures that had no need of Frankenstein's bolt of lightning. Rather than pulling a "great truth" or scattered DNA from the ocean, it may be more useful to consider marine life as always interconnected with particular environments, processes, and substances. Such considerations would, of course, still be highly mediated, but they would not culminate in the discovery of isolated genes. Instead, they would lead from "entanglement to greater entanglement" (Latour 61), as they trace interactions between forms of sea life, their environments, and the anthropogenic threats to species survival.

While the framing of Cameron and Venter as intrepid explorers overshadows the objects of their expeditions, the more taxonomical and aesthetic representations of ocean life puts each distinct species in the spotlight, framing them as distinctive and worthy of attention. Science, aesthetics, and environmentalist concern swirl together in these representations. Even as the ocean is being emptied of its life through massive industrial extractions that the quaint term "fishing" cannot begin to suggest, there is no shortage of films, television programs, coffee table books, and websites replete with stunning photos of ocean creatures. For ecocritics, it is important to point out that "Rime of the Ancient Mariner," *Moby Dick*, and *A Door into Ocean* notwithstanding, the most significant—culturally, scientifically, and politically—genre for ocean conservation may well be the highly aestheticized yet taxonomical portraits and videos of newly discovered creatures. Unlike the oceans of Cameron and Venter, which seem untainted and unthreatened by human practices, the driving force behind many of these official taxonomies and unofficial aesthetic representations is the urgent sense that time may be running out. Species must be "captured" in some way before they are lost forever. (Edward S. Curtis, rather than Roosevelt, haunts this imperative.) Against the vast backdrop of deep evolutionary time, taxonomical photographs capture a moment, framing the creature so that it can line up and be counted. The heading on the Census of Marine Life web pages, "Making Ocean Life Count," plays off the double meaning of "counting," with the hope that expanding the human knowledge of what lives in the sea will motivate ocean conservation efforts: "Better information is needed to fashion the management that will sustain fisheries, conserve diversity, reverse losses of habitat, reduce impacts of pollution, and respond to global climate change. Hence, there are biological, economic, philosophical and political reasons to push for greater exploration and understanding of the ocean and its inhabitants" (Census of Marine Life website 2010). Although the list does not mention aesthetic reasons for ocean exploration, the website, especially its image gallery, is stunningly beautiful, featuring 50 photographs of ocean creatures, most of them shots of a single organism, as well as a few shots of scientists in the field or lab. By contrast, WoRMS (World Register of Marine Species), contains a

hodge-podge mix of strikingly beautiful photographs, artistic representations of species, such as those on stamps, and rather ugly brownish and grayish photos of fish out of
water, such as jellyfish stranded on beaches or being examined in petri dishes.

The uglier photos on the WoRMS site remind us that every single thing in the ocean
is not breathtakingly beautiful, thus highlighting the fact that the striking aesthetically rendered photographs of ocean creatures has become a dominant style, a particular mode of representation and not merely a transparent window onto the world. It is
rather surprising that the Census of Marine Life, notwithstanding its serious scientific
ambitions, invites the arts to the table. The website includes a section on "Census in the
Arts": "Census discoveries have proven to be an inspiration to artists around the world.
The artwork here is a testimony to the excitement generated and the creativity it inspires
when the natural and artistic worlds come together." The page includes links to films and
documentaries, exhibits, photographs, and sculpture. The Census released three new
books in 2010 that feature photography: *Journey into the Deep: Discovering New Ocean
Creatures*, by Rebecca L. Johnson, which, as the CML points out, "features stunning photographs taken by Census scientists as well as interviews with Census researchers"; Paul
Snelgrove's *Discoveries of the Census of Marine Life: Making Ocean Life Count*, which is
a "illustrated with full-color photographs;" and *Citizens of the Sea: Wondrous Creatures
form the Census of Marine Life*. The CML website notes that this last volume "reveals the
most intriguing organisms in the ocean, captured in action by skilled underwater photographers from National Geographic and the several Census researchers" (Census of
Marine Life website 2010)

The large *World Ocean Census: A Global Survey of Marine Life* (Crist, Scowcroft,
Harding 2009) is packed with lovely photographs, graphics, maps and illustrations. The
book is divided into three sections, "What Lived in the Ocean," "What Lives in the Ocean,"
and "What Will Live in the Ocean," with chapters explaining scientific methods and technologies as well as descriptions of particular ecosystems such as hydrothermal vents and
abyssal plains. Richard Ellis' endorsement for the book begins, "If you never read a word
of this book, the photographs alone would blow you away." Famed oceanographer Sylvia
Earle's foreword to the volume promises that it is a "valuable reference" and a "place to find
white-knuckle adventure," but she emphasizes its aesthetic and ethical power:

> The images alone will cause many to re-evaluate their concepts of what astonishing
> forms are embraced within the bounds of what constitutes an eye, a heart, a body
> of living tissues. The underlying similarities shared by living things—humans very
> much included—shine through, while maintaining wonder at the infinite capacity
> for diversity: from the broad divisions of life to the individual speckles and shapes
> that distinguish each sardine, salp and starfish from every other of its kind. Above
> all, the breakthroughs in knowledge gained, and awareness of the magnitude of what
> remains to be discovered, inspire hope that the greatest era of ocean exploration—
> and ocean care—will now begin (Earle 2009, 13).

Aesthetic astonishment, sparked by the " diversity of "forms," "speckles," and "shapes,"
does not distance or exoticize the living creatures in this formulation but instead

motivates a re-evaluation of "concepts," and, significantly, swirls together with the "shin-ing" recognition of human kinship or at least "similarity" with these life forms. The aesthetic appreciation of diversity somehow becomes a sense of biological connection, which then impels the desire to both explore and care for the ocean. Aesthetics, knowl-edge, and ethics flow together in this passage. Packed with scientific information, the volume emphasizes the beauty of its subjects throughout. The microbes that *Cracking the Ocean Code* disregarded in favor of genetic animations, are granted an entire two page "Gallery" here. The statement "Microbes are intricately complicated, varied, and in many instances quite beautiful" introduces the eleven full color photos (Crist, Scowcroft, Harding 2009, 52).

Ecocritics and feminist theorists have long been critical of aesthetic captures and commodification, arguing that the glamorization of ecoporn[6] blinds people to more ordinary beauties, and, more generally participates in a culture of consumerism and instant gratification. The camera, it is claimed, follows in the path of the gun; the frame distances, contains, and controls its subject. The beautiful photographs of marine ani-mals would seem to exemplify the Enlightenment subject/object divide, where objective truth is available to all, free of perspectives, systems of power, or other entanglements. In some sense the taxonomical and enumerating aims of the Census assume this epis-temological stance, as scientists discover and present each species as a separate entity, in a clear and direct style that obscures its own technological mediations. Each species is framed as a discrete object for the human gaze—the animals themselves have no per-spective here; we do not see through their eyes—or through "Crittercams" mounted upon them.[7] These photos do not, in Bart H. Welling's terms, help us to "imagine a world that truly *looks back*" (Welling 2009, 70). Nor do the photographs reveal material entan-glements between the humans and the animals dwelling in the deep sea. Unabashed realism, indeed, a kind of luminous hyperrealism reigns. Enlightenment models of knowledge in which science brings something dwelling in the "darkness" to light play out in the high-tech representations of the heretofore undiscovered species who sud-denly appear glowing on computer screens, framed within both popular and scientific web-based journals.

None of these critiques, however, account for the potential power of these images to spark concern for ocean environments. Just as aesthetically pleasing visual images have propelled land-based environmental movements throughout the twentieth century,[8] the images of ocean life may very well be a driving force for ocean conservation movements in the twenty-first century. Moreover, given the horrific practices of industrialized "fishing," which results in up to 98 percent of the animals killed as unwanted "bycatch,"[9] it would be mistake, I think, to invoke critiques of aesthetic capture or commodification, especially when many of the animals filmed or photographed in situ need not be harmed in the process. Since most people lack the opportunity, resources, and desire to encounter sea creatures while scuba diving, and since most sea life inhabits regions that humans cannot physically visit, photographs and videos of marine life are invaluable forms of "encoun-ter." Some photographs, such as the portrait of a charming cownose ray with a goofy smile who seems to look at straight at the viewer, suggest conscious strategies of heightening a sense of encounter through the two dimensional medium (Crist, Scowcroft, Harding 2009, 213). Others, such as the full-page close up of the dappled underside of a sea star, give the illusion of physical contact (Crist, Scowcroft, Harding 2009, 173). So critique of these images must be complemented by some sort of reckoning of their potency. Perhaps aesthetic responses can entangle, as visual contemplation of the gelatinous, scaly, tentacled, or spongy creatures not only entrances but provokes an embodied sense of connection. As Simon O'Sullivan argues, the function of art is to "switch our intensive register, to reconnect us with the world." Art, he contends, "opens us up to the non-human universe that we are part of" (O'Sullivan 2001, 128).

Then again, even if the photographs open up the viewer to forms of nonhuman sea life, a momentary aesthetic and affective connection does not necessarily lead to an informed, ethical, and political trajectory that would benefit the creatures themselves. If we ask, along with J. T. Mitchell, what these pictures want from us, we could certainly surmise that they want "nothing at all" (Mitchell 2005, 48) in the sense that a sea cucumber for example (as a creature not as an image) requires nothing from humans; it is sufficient within its own watery world. And yet for us to respond with "nothing" is itself a from of (empathic?) entanglement, in the sense that an immense amount of science, political activism, policy making, and regulation would need to be enacted—all of which are entangled with each other—in the pursuit of offering these creatures the "nothing" they may well want.

The most breathtaking sea creature photographs of them all appear in Claire Nouvian's edited collection, *The Deep: Extraordinary Creatures of the Abyss*. A film director, Nouvian "worked alongside Census scientists studying the continental margins to capture some amazing photographs" (Census website). Nouvian's preface to the massive booktells how in 2001 after watching "a stunningly beautiful film" at the Monterey Bay Aquarium, her life "changed direction," as she became fascinated by creatures that she thought could not possibly be real.

> I was dazzled … speechless … astounded …
>   As crazy as it might seem, I had fallen in love at first sight.… It was as though a veil had been lifted, revealing unexpected points of view, vaster and more promising…I imagined this colossal volume of water, cloaked in permanent darkness, and I pictured the fantastic creatures that swam there, far from our gazes, the surrealist results of an ever inventive Nature. (Nouvian 2007, 12)

Interestingly, it is unclear here whether the "unexpected points of view" could be those of the animals themselves. Nouvian's enthusiasm, bordering on rapture, results in a work of equivalent intensity. *The Deep* is a stunning volume, combining substantial essays by scientists with unrivaled photographs of the creatures (many of them taken by scientists). The essays in this volume are often passionate about the creatures they describe, but it is the large and gorgeous photographs that transport their viewers to the place where Nouvian found herself "dazzled … speechless … astounded." Critic Andrew Robinson called the book, "eye-poppingly magnificent": "So much so that it provokes gasps of amazement and awe at the complexity, beauty and uniqueness of life in the abyss" (Robinson n.p.).

Notwithstanding the oversized format of the book that makes the photos even more powerful, it is the exquisite composition of each photograph that is so effective. Nouvian skillfully includes a great expanse of black space within most of the photos, suggesting both the vastness of the sea and how fortunate the viewers are to glimpse each of these creatures. Although many of these animals float in the middle of the page, some seem to be moving toward the viewer, suggesting the liveliness of the creatures and the possibility for encounters. Many of the animals are photographed in such a way that they seem to be looking back at the viewer. The eye of the octopus that inhabits just the upper edge of the page, for example, seems to curiously or coyly look at the camera. The portrait-like quality of these photos encourages us to grant these creatures—often described as strange or alien or monstrous—some sort of recognition, an ethical response perhaps, that extends across the nearly unimaginable biodiversity of the oceans. The look of these creatures calls for an expansive posthumanism that does not disavow or exclude even the "strangest" of living creatures from consideration. Somehow even the jellies and other creatures without eyes or faces call for some sort of recognition. And it is not just the fragile gelatinous creatures that evoke a sort of tenderness; somehow Nouvian manifests a sense of care in these photos. Even her captions are notable: echoing the descriptions of explorers who were unable to describe something utterly unfamiliar without the help of the familiar, they betray a whimsical, joyous fascination: "The fangtooth's menacing appearance is accentuated by the skeleton-like appearance of its strange protruding bones" (Nouvian 2007, 56); "This pair of flying buttocks is a new species of worm" (Nouvian 2007, 56); "When seen in motion, one would think it was a spider playing an invisible harp" (Nouvian 2007, 65); "It's upper jaw ... gives it the appearance of a rugby player who forgot to remove his mouthguard" (Nouvian 2007, 95); "A pram bug wields its prey's remains as a shield" (Nouvian 2007, 118). Seeking to teach and delight, her environmental motivations are clear: "Public opinion cannot possibly develop until people are enlightened about the exceptional natural heritage existing at the bottom of the seas" (Nouvian 2007, 26). Despite the term "enlightened," Nouvian's playful analogies, her enthusiasm for her subjects, the composition and arresting aesthetics of the photographs, intertwine knower and known in highly mediated ways that may still manage to provoke an encounter of sorts.

Sylvia Earle claims that the Census of Marine Life is "one of the most ambitious undertakings in the history of humankind" (Earle 2009, 12). Despite the staggering magnitude of the project and its necessarily taxonomical and enumerative aims, *World Ocean Census* betrays little sense of mastery or domination. One would assume that a group undertaking nothing less than the project of counting and categorizing all the creatures in the sea—in the past, present, and future—would epitomize the "god-trick" of "infinite vision" (Haraway 1991, 189). The first chapter, however, is entitled, "The Known, the Unknown, and the Unknowable," and many of the essays point out the extraordinary challenges—in terms of scale, sampling techniques, geographic and aquatic hardships, international cooperation of scientists, and the great void of baseline knowledge, to name a few—of determining what lives in the ocean. One chapter, "Unravelling the Mystery of New Life-Forms," begins with an epigraph by Steven Haddock, "New species aren't really new, they are just new to us. These creatures have been out there for millions of years and we are just now fortunate enough to find them and have the technology to examine them" (Crist, Scowcroft, Harding 2009, 175). Haddock displaces the anthropocentrism of the figuration of the "new species," positioning himself, far more humbly than Cameron and Venter, as the fortunate heir to both millions of years of evolution and more recent technological innovations. This chapter includes a one-page inset written by Haddock, "On Being the First to Find New Life Forms," in which he outlines his reactions to "discovering a species": "amazement," at biological variation; "skepticism" that the species must have already been seen by someone else; and "puzzlement" about how to categorize the species. Despite the "natural human instinct to categorize," Haddock states that his "favorites" are "the critters that we have no clue what to temporarily call them. Such animals are given descriptive pet names like 'Mystery Beast,' 'Weird Ctenophore,'. . . 'Blue Bomber' and so on" (Crist, Scowcroft, Harding 2009, 194).

Finding a new species is, of course, a paradigmatic moment within narratives of discovery, yet the "Mystery Beast" with its "pet name," provokes epistemological humility, rather than triumph. Compared with Venter's shotgunning method of processing microbes into paste and then code, Haddock's stance respects the organisms as distinctive creatures. Unlike twenty-first century biotechnologies, contemporary ocean science seems quaintly anachronistic—discovering new species? venturing where no human has ever gone? And it is true that explorers such as Venter and Cameron capitalize on older narratives of discovery and conquest, which are not yet dampened by gloomier late twentieth-century narratives of climate change, ocean acidification, and the massive extinction of species. Yet the *World Ocean Census* and *The Deep* intertwine science, aesthetics, and environmentalism, attempting to entangle all of us in networks of (aesthetic) pleasure, responsibility, and concern. While it may be more fitting to conclude with organizations that publicize more literal examples of oceanic entanglement, such as Blue Voice, which demonstrates how chemicals in the ocean harm dolphins and humans alike, or Captain Charles Moore's Algalita Marine Research Foundation, which vividly demonstrates how the plastic refuse of human civilization floats in the Pacific Garbage Patch as well as in the bodies of fish and birds, the threats to the ocean are so dire that it may, paradoxically, be necessary to call on something as seemingly flimsy as aesthetic pleasure to help enlist new generations of blue-green environmentalists.

My thanks to Greg Garrard for his incisive comments, which challenge me to rethink many of the arguments in this piece.

NOTES

1. For three different histories and genealogies of feminist science studies, see *Bits of Life: Feminism at the Intersections of Media, Bioscience, and Technology*, edited by Anneke Smelik and Nina Lykke.
2. See Nancy Tuana's "Material Locations: An Interactionist Alternative to Realism/Social Constructivism" and "Viscous Porosity," and Karen Barad's *Meeting the Universe Halfway*.

I don't have the space here to disentangle the commonalities and differences between the work of Haraway, Tuana, and Barad. I should note, however, that Barad's notion of entanglement is much more specific than the multiple meanings of entanglement that I am trying to invoke within this essay.

3. See Michelle Murphy, "The 'Elsewhere within Here' and Environmental Illness; or How to Build a Yourself a Body in a Safe Space" and my chapter "Deviant Agents: The Science, Culture, and Politics of Multiple Chemical Sensitivity" in *Bodily Natures*.

4. See Gary Kroll, *America's Ocean Wilderness: A Cultural History of Twentieth-Century Exploration*.

5. The background to this comment is Bonnie Mann's brilliant essay(2006), "How America Justifies Its War: A Modern/Postmodern Aesthetics of War and Sovereignty," in which she argues that American women have been "invited" to take up a militarized, masculine aesthetic.

6. See Bart H. Welling, "Ecoporn," for a theory of "ecoporn."

7. See Haraway's discussion of *Crittercam* in *When Species Meet* (Haraway 2008b).

8. See Finis Dunaway, *Natural Visions: The Power of Images in American Environmental Reform*.

9. The rates of "bycatch" vary by region and by types of fishing. Shrimp trawling, for example, has bycatch rates varying between 40 percent and 98 percent, averaging 85 percent (Fisheries and Aquaculture Department n.p.). Recent studies of bycatch focus on specific types of animals killed, such as sea turtles, pelagic birds, whales or dolphins; it is doubtful that enough data exists to support an estimated percentage of all animals killed, "incidentally," by all industrialized fishing.

WORKS CITED

Alaimo, Stacy. 2010. *Bodily Natures: Science, Environment, and the Material Self* Bloomington: Indiana University Press.

Aliens of the Deep. 2005. Dir. James Cameron and Steven Quale.

Ballard, Robert D. with Will Hively. 2000. *The Eternal Darkness: A Personal History of Deep-Sea Exploration*. Princeton: Princeton University Press.

Barad, Karen. 2007. *Meeting the Universe Halfway: Quantum Physics and the Entanglement of Matter and Meaning*. Durham: Duke University Press.

Brown, Phil. 1993. "When the Public Knows Better: Popular Epidemiology Challenges the System." *Environment* 35.8 (Oct. 1993): 17–41.

Bryld, Mette and Nina Lykke. 1999. *Cosmodolphins: Feminist Cultural Studies of Technology, Animals, and the Sacred*. London: Zed Books.

Cameron, James. 2004. The Drive to Discover. *Wired* 12.12 (December):189–191.

Census of Marine Life website. http://www.coml.org, accessed August 17, 2010.

Coburn, Jason. 2005. *Street Science: Community Knowledge and Environmental Health Science*. Cambridge, MIT Press.

Cracking the Ocean Code. 2007. Discovery Channel.

Crist, Darlene Trew, Gail Scowcroft, and James M. Harding Jr. 2009. *World Ocean Census: A Global Survey of Marine Life*. Buffalo: Firefly Books.

Di Chiro, Giovanna. 1997. "Local Actions, Global Visions: Remaking Environmental Expertise." *Frontiers* 18.2: 203–231.

Dunaway, Finis. 2008. *Natural Visions: The Power of Images in American Environmental Reform.* Chicago: University of Chicago Press.

Earle, Sylvia. 2009. "Foreword." In Darlene Trew Crist, Gail Scowcroft, and James M. Harding Jr., *World Ocean Census: A Global Survey of Marine Life.* Buffalo: Firefly Books.

Fisheries and Aquaculture Department, A Global Assessment of Fisheries Bycatch and Discards. FAO Corporate Document Repository, 1994. http://www.fao.org/DOCREP/003/T4890E/T4890E02.htm

Franklin, Sarah. 2000. "Life Itself: Global Nature and the Genetic Imaginary." In Sarah Franklin, Celia Lury and Jackie Stacey, *Global Nature, Global Culture.* London: Sage.

Gage, John D. and Paul A. Tyler. 1991. *Deep Sea Biology: A Natural History of Organisms at the Deep-Sea Floor.* Cambridge: Cambridge University Press.

Haraway, Donna J. 1991. *Simians, Cyborgs, and Women: The Reinvention of Nature.* New York: Routledge.

——. 1997. *Modest Witness @ Second Millenium. Female Man Meets Oncomouse.* New York: Routledge.

——. 2008a. "There Are Always More Things Going on Than You Thought! Interview with Nina Lykke, Randi Markussen, and Finn Olesen." In *Bits of Life: Feminism at the Intersections of Media, Bioscience, and Technology,* ed. Anneke Smelik and Nina Lykke Seattle: University of Washington Press.

——. 2008b. *When Species Meet.* Minneapolis: University of Minnesota Press.

Koslow, Tony. 2007. *The Silent Deep: The Discovery, Ecology, and Conservation of the Deep Sea.* Chicago: University of Chicago Press.

Kroll, Gary. 2008. *America's Ocean Wilderness: A Cultural History of Twentieth-Century Exploration.* Lawrence: University Press of Kansas.

Latour, Bruno. *On the Modern Cult of the Factish Gods.* Durham: Duke University Press, 2010.

Mann, Bonnie. 2006. "How America Justifies Its War: A Modern/Postmodern Aesthetics of War and Sovereignty." *Hypatia 21.* 4(Fall 2006): 147–163.

Matsen, Brad. 2005. *Descent: The Heroic Discovery of the Abyss.* New York: Vintage.

Mitchell, W. J. T. 2005. *What Do Pictures Want? The Lives and Loves of Images.* Chicago: University of Chicago Press.

Murphy, Michelle. 2000. "The 'Elsewhere within Here' and Environmental Illness; or How to Build a Yourself a Body in a Safe Space." *Configurations 8:* 87–120.

Nouvian, Claire. 2007. *The Deep: The Extraordinary Creatures of the Abyss.* Chicago: University of Chicago Press.

O'Sullivan. Simon. 2001. "The Aesthetics of Affect: Thinking Art Beyond Representation." *Angelika: Journal of the Environmental Humanities* 6.3(December): 125–135.

Rex, Michael A. and Ron J. Etter. 2010. *Deep-Sea Biodiversity: Pattern and Scale.* Cambridge: Harvard University Press.

Robinson, Andrew. "Yeti Crabs & Vampire Squids. Review of *The Deep: The Extraordinary Creatures of the Abyss.*" *Literary Review* http://www.literaryreview.co.uk/robinson_05_07.html accessed August 24, 2010: (n.p.)

Shreeve, James. 2004. "Craig Venter's Epic Voyage to Redefine the Origin of Species." *Wired* 12.08 (August): 106–113, 146.

Smelik, Anneke and Nina Lykke, ed., 2008. *Bits of Life: Feminism at the Intersections of Media, Bioscience, and Technology.* Seattle: University of Washington Press.

Tuana, Nancy. 2001. "Material Locations: an Interactionist Alternative to Realism/Social Constructivism" in Nancy Tuana and Sandra Morgen, eds., *Engendering Rationalities.* Albany: SUNY Press: 221–243.

——. 2008. "Viscous Porosity." In Alaimo and Hekman, *Material Feminisms*: 188–213.

Welling, Bart. 2009. "Ecoporn: On the Limits of Visualizing the Human." *Ecosee: Image, Rhetoric, Nature.* Ed. Sidney I. Dobrin and Sean Morey. Albany: SUNY Press: 53–77.

World Ocean Council website, accessed August 18, 2010, http://www.oceancouncil.org/site/science.php.

WoRMS: World Register of Marine Species website. http://www.marinespecies.org/, accessed August 24, 2010.

CHAPTER 11

··

MEDIATING CLIMATE CHANGE

Ecocriticism, Science Studies, and The Hungry Tide

··

ADAM TREXLER

IMAGINING climate change is an enormously difficult task. Deliberate politicized spin campaigns have contributed to public uncertainty, but setting this aside, perhaps the single greatest difficulty is that it is impossible to have a direct experience of climate. Human technologies are thoroughly invested in *weather*, from wearing animal skins to turning on the air conditioning unit, from looking at clouds to tuning in for the five-day forecast. Climate is a pattern of weather demonstrated over time, so no single storm or heat wave can be ascribed to climate change. Other difficulties abound. Direct cause and effect make a satisfying narrative, but anthropogenic global warming is expansive: tail-pipe and smokestack emissions can lead ultimately to storm surges or rising sea levels on the other side of the globe. Similarly, the effects of species loss can be difficult to see, even when they participate in ecosystems worth billions of dollars. There are no clear villains, either. Billions of people, including you and me, are implicated: buying food grown with petrochemicals; working in offices or shops or factories powered by coal plants; driving in cars or riding in buses or flying in planes that burn fossil fuels; or using the furnace or air conditioner that came with our home. The timescales of climate change are difficult as well: failing to alter the power plants built in the next five years will affect global climate through the twenty-second century, even though many of the worst changes may not be realized for fifty years.[1] Fiction can help us think about these difficulties, but the form of the novel and the state of literary criticism make the task more difficult. In order to approach climate change in fiction, it is necessary to re-examine some of our basic assumptions about what things do the work in novels.

The novel would seem to be an enormous resource: over two hundred works of fiction about anthropogenic global warming have been published in the last thirty years. Nearly all of these novels shift the fictional climate for the sake of drama. Often, the novel is set in a distant future, when the catastrophic effects of climate change have already taken place, flooding Britain or turning continents to ash. Otherwise, novelists rely on the plausible but unpredictable idea of sudden climatic change to plunge familiar characters into an unprecedented blizzard or drought. If the novel is set in the present, villains must be found, whether these are fraudulent energy corporations, corrupt governments, or individual consumers made grotesque. The majority of these novels are set in familiar cities (Washington, D.C.; New York; or London), but these locations make it all but impossible to show its effects on inhabitants of developing countries and species around the world. These shifts are not inconsequential: by making climate change spectacular, dramatic, and containable in a single setting and a cast of characters, they almost universally avoid the political problems we face in the uncertain present, trying to act on climate change before it reaches the dystopian phase that is threatened.

Climate change has proved to be even more troublesome for academic criticism. Almost invariably, writing about contemporary literature involves making claims about which authors should be included in the congealing climate canon (Brauner 206). Not only is such judgment precarious, but it also leads to a set of assumptions about literary production disowned by nearly all historicist and theoretical accounts. Harold Bloom sets out the view:

> Aesthetic criticism returns us to the autonomy of imaginative literature and the sovereignty of the solitary soul, the reader not as a person in society but as the deep self, our ultimate inwardness. That depth of inwardness in a strong writer constitutes the strength that wards off the massive weight of past achievement, lest every originality be crushed before it becomes manifest. (Bloom 10–11)

At every turn, canonical criticism privileges the human. Authorship depends on the deep, private, inward soul, rather than the material activities of research and composition, not to mention editing and printing. In practice, this also leads to characters that are not, in principle, contextualized within a society, let alone engaged significantly with nature, the pathetic fallacy notwithstanding. The "ultimate inwardness" of canonical criticism deliberately eschews analysis of both politics and *things* more generally, and rules out a sublime or sensuous experience of global warming, because a wider scientific and social infrastructure is needed to make it appear. Climate change, having everything to do with places, politics, and things—car engines and coal mines and tropical fruit—is anathema.

Many of the authors in the contemporary canon have, in fact, written climate change novels, but the evasions and transformations they find it necessary to perform are so bizarre that they are among the worst. Margaret Atwood's *Oryx and Crake* and *Year of the Flood* raises climate change as a fundamental threat to biodiversity, only to refocus completely on human exploitation and genetic modification in order to get purchase on ultimate inwardness. Cormac McCarthy's *The Road* suppresses the causes of catastrophe, turning climate change into a biblical melodrama. Ian McEwan's *Solar* ensures the problem seems all but insoluble by choosing an obese, sex-crazed physicist as an allegorical everyman. Doris Lessing's *Mara and Dann* elides any question of human causes or responses by replacing global warming with a natural ice age. Products of the authors of the contemporary Western canon, all of these novels return the focus to the internal, human soul, while evading questions of environmental justice for those not of European ancestry.[2] Also supposed irrelevant or insufficiently dramatic are the things we use to know climate change, like ice cores, temperature surveys, and computer models. Still less do they concern themselves with the political processes that might avert catastrophic anthropogenic climate change in the first place.

Environmental criticism has also elided the climate change novel, though for very different reasons. Having productively criticized the canon's anthropocentric assumptions, it has gone on to create a canon of its own, largely composed of texts that give a sensuous, immediate sense of place and describe its effects on human beings. Climate change fiction, set in the future, dispersed over the globe, when "pure" nature has all but vanished, doesn't sit easily with the ecocritical canon, but this is not the fundamental problem. In the last decade, important monographs by Jonathan Bate, Lawrence Buell, Dana Phillips, Greg Garrard, and Timothy Morton have invoked climate change as part of the "environmental crisis," without having much to say about its specific causes, possible remedies, or how literature might be involved.[3] There have been a handful of articles examining the most prominent authors of climate change novels, and a few attempts to consider literary theory and historicism in light of global warming, but there is relatively little research that takes a systematic approach to climate change literature.[4]

When a novel successfully mediates climate change, making the scientific phenomenon appear in the narrative, the possibilities of the novel are also altered. Stories about floods are as old as writing, appearing in *Genesis* and *Gilgamesh*, but when a deluge sweeps through the capital in Maggie Gee's *The Flood* or Kim Stanley Robinson's *Forty Signs of Rain*, we are encouraged to judge characters' agency and ethics in a very different way. (Mediation can also fail: when James Herbert's *Portent* tries to pin the responsibility on an evil, fat, black sorceress from New Orleans, no less than when George Bush tried to recast climate change as an invention of the Left, the internal contradictions render anthropogenic climate change absurdly unrecognizable.) If one of ecocriticism's most important insights has been the recognition that *places* in literature are far more constructive than was assumed by humanist critics obsessed by character, *things* achieve a new sort of prominence in the climate change novel. Landscapes, animals, devices, vehicles, buildings, and other people have always been formally constructive entities in fiction: in eighteenth-century society novels, the English country house contains and elevates a cast of characters, and implies a moral context judging them, while narration of the city enables anonymous, acquisitive, amorous, and amoral encounters. But the invention of the motor car in the early 1900s made very different kinds of narrative gestures possible: the hero who races from city to country house to correct a misunderstanding with his intended demonstrates a new agency over his destiny, while the narrator gains a new play with distance and immediacy not lent by stagecoaches or trains.[5] Another century on, the aristocratic Land Rover has another set of meanings. Melting ice caps, global climate models, solar technologies, and tipping points are actively altering the formal possibilities of the novel, but to understand how involves a close reading of things.

The critical difficulty here is not ignorance of climate change, but a general misunderstanding of how fiction *mediates*. Following an important argument between Buell and Phillips, environmental critics too often chose between the assertion that real, natural things (trees, to be specific) can enter a text referentially, and the argument that literary texts operate according to their own rules, with no essential relationship between a described tree and one found in the author's backyard. In practice, this amounted to cheerleading for realism and postmodern formalism, both of which have become all but exhausted as literary modes.[6] The difficulties were multiplied as ecocriticism tried to articulate a theory of interdisciplinarity: from the 1970s through the 1990s, one side claimed ecology could provide a material, nonhuman foundation for criticism by allowing it to trace a transhistorical, natural subject, like ecosystems, wetlands, or birds.[7] The other side paid lip service to the "scientific method," but claimed its findings were irreducibly socially embedded (Levin 6–7) and that criticism offered a superior approach to immaterial emanations of the mind or the "hyperreal."[8] Unfortunately, both positions attacked straw men on the other side. Literary texts are able to mediate things precisely because they are wholly unlike the thing itself. A literary description of a tree carries specific, chosen aspects of a real tree into the narrative, while suppressing other, undesirable aspects: a novel will sit comfortably in a reader's lap. The result was literary criticism that was either blinded to the interplay of things, forms, and ideologies across historical periods, or that dematerialized science's truth claims into mere historical ideas. Both are disastrous for ecocriticism, which must be able to describe the historical conditions that led to the proliferation of emissions and the truth of the greenhouse effect across history and culture.

Since the late 1990s, a number of ecocritics have turned to science studies to resolve the ontological difficulties that result from combining environmental sciences and literary criticism. In an important article, Bruce Clarke argues ecocriticism must avoid scientism, "the appropriation of science within a non-scientific context," while also avoiding the strong social constructivism that tended to dematerialize the sciences (Clarke 150). For a third direction, Clarke turned to Bruno Latour's *We Have Never Been Modern*, which argues that modernity is not a particular invention or historical moment, but rather a style of thinking and writing, often confused with science, that insists upon an untenable ontological separate between Nature and Society, objects and subjects. This modernist purification continues to operate in postmodern theory, primitivist nature appreciation, and the critique of nature as a social construction (Clarke 155–56). Science, for Latour, is not modern at all, nor is it a single, stable "method" of creating representations of things; instead, it is the practice of creating new situations for things to express their agency. (Latour's description privileges "research," leaving the door open to practices such as literary criticism, or novel-writing.) The things that emerge from this process are neither merely material, real, independent of human beings; nor are they pure intellection, constructed by the will of scientists, ideology, or discourse. Categorically, they are "hybrids," "half object and half subject," resisting human agency and producing human knowledge at the same time.

To speak of the agency of things—red dwarves or mud or dolphins—is not to ascribe interiority, intentionality, or choice to them. Interiority and intentionality are specifically human categories of agency: we express our agency and intentionality by studying red dwarves, walking around muddy puddles, and trying to conserve dolphins or teach them tricks. However, things have an agency of their own, though this is inextricable from *how* we know them: red dwarves will not radiate light beyond a certain spectrum; mud will splash despite our best wishes; dolphins will learn tricks in a way that a duck simply will not. Their "behavior" is not a choice, but it distinguishes them from otherwise similar things. Agency is a useful concept because it acknowledges things' real existence without necessitating the transcendentalist argument that we can know about them without interacting with them, as well as trouncing the common environmental canard that things are only natural if they are purely beyond human influence. Thus, Latour's model suggested a means to escape the binary opposition between naive scientific realism and anti-scientific reaction (Phillips 2003). Subsequently, environmental critics have used Latour's model of hybridity to describe human modification of animals' genes and the atmosphere (Wallace), to construct a sustainable vision of place (Ball), and to trace the dynamic historical interactions between culture and climate (Markley). Gert Goeminne and Karen François, following Emily Potter, have shown anthropogenic climate change is inextricably hybrid: it is naturally produced, operating beyond human understanding or control, but it is also socially produced and the consequence of human actions (Goeminne and François 2010). Unfortunately, there has been much less work exploring how Latour's actor-network theory might inform our interpretation of fictional texts.

Existing criticism has also tended to neglect an important feature of actor-network theory: many things are needed to produce scientific "facts." Data is not a representation of a hybrid, but rather another hybrid thing itself. To take a simplified example: from 1850 local weather has been translated into temperature by standardized thermometers; handwritten logs charted daily temperature; these records are nowadays transcribed into computer files; the files are collected into much larger data sets; models are used to describe temperature around the globe; the temperature records ultimately inform and test predictive climate models; these findings are published in academic papers, and are themselves tested by other scientific processes. In each of these steps, the thermometer, handwritten record, computer file, database, climate model, and scientific article reproduce aspects of the original weather, while also taking a new form that can be used in a different way. Also, each step is tested for whether the new thing carries along, or *mediates*, the agency of the original thing: testing these steps is much of the process of doing science. Latour uses the term "immutable mobiles" to describe hybrid things like samples, records, and databases that are both stable and moveable, material and bearing ideas.[9] Literary things are similar hybrids: the fictional Land Rover is both similar to and different from the one that nearly ran me over last week, though we could only determine precisely how by reading contextually. Moreover, the literary process of mediation can also fail to obtain. To take a previous example, climate change rendered as the fault of a fat black sorceress is radically *insufficient*: it carries none of the important features of climate change, and introduces a racism and misogyny that interrupts any consideration of the phenomena. By tracing mediation in literary texts, ecocriticism can begin to describe their innovations in the world of things.

In order to see this process of mediation at work, it is helpful to follow it through a text. Although the obvious choice would be to read one of the "better" climate change novels, a novel that actively *resists* global warming better shows the literary processes of mediation. Amitav Ghosh's *The Hungry Tide* is particularly useful in this case. With considerable formal refinement, an interest in folk tale, historical narrative, realism and translation, the novel's self-awareness marks it as worthy of formal critique.[10] Ghosh's novel has also been celebrated by postcolonial critics, who value his nuanced depiction of the interactions between Piya, an American scientist alienated from her Indian ancestry, Kanai, a Delhi businessman and translator, Fokir, an impoverished Sundarban fisherman, and Nilima, an NGO administrator.[11] The novel's preoccupations with differential power dynamics, discrete ways of knowing, and the contemporary world, make an amenable setting for poststructuralist approaches, while a back story involving repression by a Marxist regional government and the dispossession of peasantry invites a reconsideration of Marxist theory.[12] Moreover, *The Hungry Tide* pays close attention to Piya's field work, the colonial background to ecological research, the interplay between local myth and scientific knowledge, and tensions between human place and climatology, all of which makes an interesting field to explore the interconnections between science and literature.[13]

The Hungry Tide has rapidly become something of a canonical text for environmental critics.[14] Set in the Indian Sundarbans, it is preoccupied with the conservation challenges to megafauna, specifically Royal Bengal tigers and Irrawaddy river dolphins. Ecocritics have appreciated the precise, evocative descriptions of the tide country, where storms wipe away villages and islands in hours, mangrove trees and tidal currents create unique habitats, floods threaten any human settlement, and humans are always only precariously able to maintain food, shelter, and safety. These features make *The Hungry Tide* a hospitable climate for a full range of critical models to encounter an ecocritical theory of mediation, particularly because science plays a central role in the novel. At the same time, the novel pointedly avoids anthropogenic climate change, even though, driven by concerns of melting ice-caps and rising sea levels, the shallow tide country of India and Bangladesh has been at the center of cultural and political accounts of global warming. Prominent climate change novels like Kim Stanley Robinson's *Science in the Capital* trilogy and Michael Crichton's *State of Fear* are deeply concerned with the region, while other novels like T. C. Boyle's *A Friend of the Earth*, Maggie Gee's *The Flood*, and J. G. Ballard's *The Drowned World* envision climate-changed worlds that bear a marked similarity to the tide country. The combination of *The Hungry Tide's* unimpeachable literary credentials and curious omission of climate change make it an ideal text to examine literary mediation's relationship to anthropogenic global warming.

It is the *practice* of science that is central to the novel. It would be easy enough to argue that science provides a "real" context for the fiction: that hydrology provides a formal model for literary innovation; or conservation operates as an ideological structure for colonial demarcation; or scientific discourse stages a conflict between different social organizations; or ecology is disseminated differently in American and Indian culture;

or even that Piya's ecology suggests a new theory of environmental writing. Instead of science being only a ground for literary invention, though, Ghosh's fiction follows an anthropological model that reports human truth practices, based on participant observation. Ghosh trained as an anthropologist at Oxford and spent two decades as a professional ethnologist. In interviews, he has emphasized how this shaped his own methods of composition, leading his imagination to "[engage] with real life, with the lives people lead," instead of supplying the material for his novels "almost entirely out of his own head" (Aldama). *The Hungry Tide* was written after extensive research in the region, including accompanying a cetologist on a survey expedition, being introduced "to the ways of the Irrawaddy dolphin and to those of the cetologist" (Ghosh 2004 401). Ghosh's methodology, then, shares a methodological lineage with Latour's branch of science studies, which distinguished itself from the sociology of science when researchers began to perform ethnographic studies of scientific practice, following scientists into laboratories and the field.[15] Put simply, both Ghosh and Latour describe the inextricably material and social practices that allow knowledge to emerge.

Such an ethnographic model challenges basic modes of literary explanation and contextualization. Before ethnographic models influenced science studies, the results of an experiment would be described in terms of nature's truth, progress, or social forces like ideology, discourse, or capital. Similarly, critical interpretations of texts continue to use material reality, narrative, and social power as privileged means of explanation. Ethnographic approaches distinguish themselves from social scientific explanations of science by arguing that nature, society, and history are not *sources* of truth, but rather what is *produced* by scientific practice. A practice-based model of explanation also challenges the basic categories of human character and material things, as Andrew Pickering explains:

> Scientists are human agents in a field of material agency which they struggle to capture in machines. Further, human and material agency are reciprocally and emergently intertwined in this struggle. Their contours emerge in the temporality of practice and are definitional of and sustain one another. Existing culture constitutes the surface of emergence for the intentional structure of scientific practice, and such practice consists in the reciprocal tuning of human and material agency, tuning that can itself reconfigure human intentions. (Pickering 21)

Pickering's model suggests that both social constructionist and material (or naturalistic) explanations of things are incomplete, because the humans and things on which they depend emerge *from* such interaction.[16] Moreover, neither social constructionist nor naturalistic theories can provide an incontestable basis for explanations of science, because both humans and things are "mangled" together from scientific practice. In scientific practice, therefore, human and material agencies are understood in terms of each other, through the unfolding of narrative.[17] In relation to literature, this makes good sense, because literary character and literary things don't precede the narrative, but rather take their meaning from a network of other characters and things.[18] Pickering's account is also suggestive in its description of culture as the surface where human and nonhuman agency becomes further intertwined. Pickering means culture in an anthropological sense, but cultural studies' productive slippage between culture as collective ideology and culture as art is helpful here, suggesting that works of art are also things that entangle human and material agency.

One of the most important achievements of *The Hungry Tide* is the way it shows the agency of humans and nonhumans in the same framework. Too often, critics turn a novel's things into a foil for human character or social forces, or treat animals as an extra-literary phenomenon.[19] *The Hungry Tide* forestalls this mode of interpretation, giving a palpable sense of things beyond human control. After Piya falls from a boat and narrowly escapes a crocodile, she is all too aware of the reptile's will: "She imagined the tug that would have pulled her below the surface and the momentary release before the jaws closed again, around her midsection" (194). Faced with a crocodile, few critics would describe its malign agency as a social construction. Tigers too exert agency: while Kanai assumes the hundreds of tiger attacks per year are caused by humans—"overpopulation, or encroachment on the habitat, or something like that"— Nilima, the head of a local NGO, has better information, and demonstrates tigers had been killing humans at the same rate since the 1860s. For the last 25 years, scientists, government, and local people had tried countless schemes to deter the animals from their prey, but the tigers' agency proved frustratingly resistant to human intervention (240–2). Also unforgettable are the descriptions of storms that fling characters up to fifty kilometres away, hurl boats into trees, wipe whole islands into the sea, and kill as many people as the nuclear attack on Hiroshima in a single day. Things like crocodiles, tigers, and weather exert an agency that is irreducible to humans' wishes; they need to be read in their own right.

The Hungry Tide also demonstrates that humans' artefactual relationship to the world cannot be understood through established notions of character.[20] A canonical critic would be tempted to interpret Piya's scientific instruments, her range-finder, depth-sounder, data sheets on a clipboard, and GPS monitor, as props for characterization. As a graduate student, Piya buys a pair of expensive binoculars after going through dozens of catalogues, and then worries she might not have the physical strength to be a scientist after struggling to hold the heavy instrument for a few minutes, let alone the hours needed for scientific observation (73). All this could be read as an indication of Piya's care, precision, frugality, and tenacity. Even politically engaged critics build on this human-centred approach: Mukherjee is dismissive toward "Piya's gadgets" (156), arguing Piya "literally embodies the panoptical knowledge-machine of colonialism" (152), while Marzec reads her tools as showing the limits of "instrumentally-governed subjectivity" (431), preparing for Piya's humanistic transcendence of technology. However, conservative characterization, Foucauldian knowledge-power, and transcendental humanism all struggle to account for the stubborn recalcitrance of nonhuman things, as well as the ways humans and nonhumans mutually transform each other in an experimental system. In fact, Ghosh describes Piya's instruments as an ethnographer of science, emphasizing their irreducibility to human agency. The description of Piya's binoculars accentuate their material existence:

The glasses' outer casing had been bleached by the sun and dulled by the gnawing of sand and salt, yet the waterproofing had done its job in protecting the instrument's essential functions. After six years of constant use the lens still delivered an image of undiminished sharpness. (73)

The details of the binoculars, the bleached and gnawed casing, the precision of the lens, emphasizes their material importance. At the same time, both binoculars and Piya are entangled in their use. The precise, scientific observations that are delivered through the binoculars are irreducible to Piya's unaided gaze. During her first expedition, Piya's physicality is altered as well, as she develops "huge ropy muscles in [her] arms" (75), her body inserted into a "cyborg" assemblage. Just as importantly, the binoculars' patina distinguishes them from the shiny, expensive accessory of an amateur enthusiast.

To be clear, Piya and the binoculars don't represent yet another binary opposition, a symptom of mind and materiality or culture and nature. Understanding them requires an interdependent system of things. In her first expedition, Piya's agency is reconstructed as she is joined to a network of scientific things, with the binoculars, a boat, the river, and wildlife. When a herd "of possibly as many as seven thousand" spinner dolphins appears to the expedition, "at a certain point the binoculars' weight ceased to matter...the glasses fetched you the water with such vividness and particularity that you could not think of anything else' (74–75). In this moment, the dolphins are remade as scientific facts, the expensive, leaden binoculars are remade into an ecological prosthesis, and the young student is reformed as a scientific observer. Their impure, assembled agencies allow the results to be translated from field observations to data sheets, databases at the Scripps Institution of Oceanography in California, academic journals, and scientists around the world.[21] At the same time, the instrumental act of scientific observation effaces the things that make Piya a character—her pain, her aesthetic enjoyment, her inner monologue, even "intimate involvements" with other humans (112). Even the convention of third person narration shifts to the impersonal "you." Humanist critics view these transformations as a dangerous threat to human sovereignty, but this is merely an indication that our critical commonplaces can't encapsulate one of the most important and common aspects of human experience. Piya is neither "instrumentally governed," because her agency is necessary to the experimental system, nor is she an agent of colonialism, because the findings of the system are far beyond her control.[22] Piya's will is an important precondition for finding out about real dolphins, and therefore being able to conceive of conservation. By entangling ourselves with technology, we sometimes preserve things beyond us.

Critics' complaint against Piya's instrumental logic actually has more to do with the discourse of modernity than her relationships with things. For Latour and Ghosh, modernity rigorously separates nature and society: "Nature is defined by its exemption from contamination by people: it is as it were, the other of society, a province defined by its exclusion of human sociability" (Ghosh, "Wild Fictions"). Humans are correspondingly ranked on a scale from primitive to modern, based on their apparent "distance" from nature. Certainly Mukherjee and Marzec are right to object to Piya's snobbish amazement at the compatibility of her work, depending on geostationary satellites, and Fokir's, involving "bits of shark bone and broken tile" (118). Modernity's exclusions are even uglier when Piya rejects the thought of making Fokir a scientific partner, because she can't imagine him boarding a plane dressed in lungi and t-shirt (320). Curiously, both Piya and Fokir understand nature as a rigorous separation from human sociality, when Piya invokes "what was *intended*...by nature, by the earth" (301), and when Fokir argues that "when a tiger comes into a human settlement, it's because it wants to die" (295). These discursive separations between moderns and primitives, society and nature, are policed with considerable violence: at the political level, the Forest Department beats and kills humans who try to live in the purified area of the nature reserve, and Piya and Kanai find themselves unwillingly implicated in this discourse, involuntarily describing villagers through Conrad's "the horror," "something from some other time—before recorded history" (300, 326). Paradoxically, their horror is precisely at the violence Sundarban locals use to protect themselves from the (natural) tigers, suggesting that neither cosmopolitan intellectuals nor villagers in the developing world are exempt from the relentless purification of human and nature. The reader's ability to sympathize with either side is indicative of the ubiquity of modernity.

One of Latour's insights is that the purifications of modernity cannot be overcome by transcendent consciousness or postmodernism, because neither of these forms describe how things and humans actually cooperate. Piya and Fokir are not connected by a desire to commune spiritually with nature, but rather by practices of technological entanglement with natural things that they increasingly come to share.[23] As Latour has argued, "I may use an electric drill, but I also use a hammer. The former is thirty-five years old, the latter hundreds of thousands" (Latour, *Modern* 75). Piya learns it's better to "hunt" river dolphins in Fokir's canoe than a motorboat, while Fokir learns to supplement his fishing income by hunting waypoints on Piya's GPS (250). The discourse of modernity leads us to expect a successive model of history—Piya is shocked at the compatibility of their labour—but Piya and Fokir actually interact with a network of things that spans humans' earliest and most recent inventions. By looking past the discourse of modernity to humans' inescapably instrumental relationship to the world, we can begin to trace the effects of our complex entanglements with the material world.

For both scientists and literary critics, the central issue is how the agency of nonhumans can be preserved as it is circulated. Of course social power can shape knowledge—as British naturalists like "the great Gray of London" handed down erroneous judgements from the imperial centre (Ghosh 2004, 231)—but things also emerge through scientific discourse, cultures, publics, and individual experience, their agency intact. Often things move from scientists to the public: Ghosh singles out natural history as an "indispensible science of interpretation that allows the environment to speak back to us," creating knowledge that is "capable of universal application" ("Wild Fictions"). Thus, Piya's research is designed to shape public behavior, and when she loses her data sheets in the storm, the story leads friends and colleagues to fund further research. Even more tangibly, orcaella fetch up to one hundred thousand U.S. dollars on the black market, to be shown in aquariums in eastern Asia (Ghosh 2004, 306). In such cases,

environmental science mediates between the environment and the public, letting natural things "speak."

Just as often, though, cultural mediations of things are transferred to science. As a
child, Fokir learns to follow the orcaella from the legend of Bon Bibi (307), which later
allows him to show Piya the dolphin's favored haunts. European literary traditions also
allow the things to be seen, as when Nirmal recognizes a the independence of a dolphin's gaze through Rilke's mediating language: "some mute animal/raising its calm eyes
and seeing through us,/and through us. This is destiny…" (235). Things can also teach
scientists and publics: the dolphins' sensitivity to atmospheric pressure warns Piya of
an approaching cyclone, and Fokir finds fish by following the river dolphins (366–67).
The animals, mediated through scientific discourse, folk legend, and European literary
forms, exert their agency as they circulate through scientific instruments, cultures, and
natures, giving and receiving influences along the way. Instead of viewing mediation as a
substitution of the sign for the real, *The Hungry Tide* suggests that the mediated circulation of things is what makes them real.[24]

In an important sense, the form of mediation shapes the content of what is known.
One of the central problems for cultural theory is why one group's knowledge is
apparently incompatible with another's: a problem that appears between laboratories, political groups, and nations. Social accounts of incommensurability (e.g.,
Kuhn) argue that a shared paradigm, ideology or episteme differentiates one group
from another. However, Latourian accounts suggest incommensurability is rooted in
different technological assemblages of people and things, a crisis illustrated in *The
Hungry Tide* when a tiger becomes trapped in a livestock pen, having previously
killed two villagers and many of their animals. Ghosh paints a lurid, torchlit scene,
with the village's men plunging sharpened staves into the tiger, "their faces…in the
grip of both extreme fear and uncontrollable rage." The village's women and children
look on, "screaming in a maddened bloodlust 'Kill! Kill!' " (292–33), while Fokir helps
sharpen spears. Ever the conservationist, Piya is appalled, wades into the crowd to
stop it, but is dragged away by Fokir as the crowd sets the tiger on fire. The scene
frames a moment of incommensurability, and the dramatic stakes are raised by the
literary echoes of villagers torching modern civilization and burning science's monsters with it. In the controversy, the technological framework of subsistence livestock
farming co-produces the tigers' agency as malignantly pitched against humans' food
source, while the technological framework of conservation zoology (in a highly specialized labour economy) co-produces tigers' individual agency as independent of
human goals. Both technological frameworks produce an incommensurable opposition, although participants, readers and policymakers are not, in reality, completely
constrained by either framework. What none of these humans can do is distinguish
the "truth" of an unmediated tiger.[25]

Some ecocritics have suggested that the problems of mediation can be overcome
through a primary experience of things themselves, but *The Hungry Tide* shows the limitations of this strategy.[26] After Kanai falls in a mud pool and abuses Fokir, he finds himself alone on an island known for its tigers. The urbane translator becomes terrified and

crashes through tangled vegetation into a grassy clearing, where he has an unmediated experience of nature:

> He could not bring himself to look around the clearing. This was where it would be, if it was here on the island—but what was he thinking of?...The words he had been searching for, the euphemisms that were the source of his panic, had been replaced by the thing itself, except that without words it could not be apprehended or understood. It was an artefact of pure intuition, so real that the thing itself could not have dreamed of existing so intensely. He opened his eyes and there it was, directly ahead, less than a hundred metres away. It was sitting on its haunches with its head up, watching him with its tawny, flickering eyes. The upper parts of its coat were of a colour that shone like gold in the sunlight, but its belly was dark and caked with mud. It was immense, of a size greater than he could have imagined, and the only parts of its body that were moving were its eyes and the tip of its tail. (329)

In terror, Kanai pushes aside the mediating word, "tiger," and discovers a state of "pure sensation," a romantic experience where mediated nature is replaced with immediate contact. He feels tigerness with his eyes closed, and sees it when he opens them. The language here poses an unanswerable dilemma, as the "artefact of pure intuition" is uncertainly invented or real. In the moment Kanai "sees" the tiger, "its head up, watching him," "greater than he could have imagined," the description's specificity—"tawny, flickering eyes," "belly . . . caked with mud"—draws on the realist novel's conventions, exerting its own gaze and seeming more real "than he could have imagined." At the same time, Kanai is having a mythic confrontation: the island is said to be a testing ground where only those pure of heart will survive. His survival in the mythic conflict self-servingly designates him "pure," although later, Kanai's tiger story runs into trouble after Fokir and Piya are unable to find any tiger prints (another mediating inscription) and pointedly doubt his success in any such mythic trial. In this way, the passage stages a formal conflict by raising incommensurable romantic, realist, and mythic frameworks of interpretation. With no clear way to adjudicate between them, there is no means of establishing what has taken place.[27] What hangs in the balance is precisely the tiger's agency: without mediation, it becomes impossible to say whether Kanai has seen a tiger. In short, mediation enables things to emerge in narrative.

Understanding fiction as a collection of mediated things helps resolve some of criticism's main theoretical difficulties. Too often, fiction is understood as "imaginary," essentially separated from the real, in opposition to the mediating language of commerce and day to day existence. Kanai raises this model when he retells his own youth, as he abandoned poetry's "riches beyond accounting" in favor of profitable commercial translation (Ghosh 2004, 198–99). Here, most language enumerates, makes happen, and makes money, but literature is language that doesn't mediate. (This sense of literature bears a striking resemblance to "nature," defined as whatever remains uncontaminated by society.) Such a model struggles to understand literature's relationship to power, politics, knowledge, and things. But when fiction is understood as a collection of mediations of things, both its artifice and its truthfulness come into focus. Novels artfully invoke—mediate—our technologies for mediating things. By integrating technical ways of knowing the world—fishing, ecological surveys, local myth, and so on—into narrative, fiction allows us to explore the making of the real. Ghosh has made a similar point, noting novels provide "a canvas broad enough to address [the relationship between human beings and their surroundings] in all its dimensions" ("Wild Fictions"). Interpretation tests how successfully a novel mediates these technologies, by assessing the things that shape characters.

How, then, are such fictions of place to be historicized? Pickering suggests that new things constantly emerge in the world, and that new societies of humans emerge with these things. This is probably the most important achievement of *The Hungry Tide*, articulating the emergence of a new social configuration resulting from the endangered river dolphins. In the epilogue of the novel, Piya proposes a new conservation organization named after Fokir and under the sponsorship of a local NGO, creating a partnership between formerly disparate agents: ecological scientists and American environmentalists, academic funding bodies and web-based environmental contributors, a grassroots organization for women and underemployed men, local fishermen and endangered marine mammals (397). The novel also describes a contemporary transition from apparently pure science to research that is visibly implicated in capital, development, and social justice. Notably, this emergence is unthinkable outside the specific agency of *orcaella brevirostris:* its habitat ties it to the people of the tide country; its complex migration patterns and deep tidal pools demand seasoned fishermen's knowledge of local environment; its struggles to survive interest the Indian Forest Service; its unique behavior draws first world ecologists. The emergence of this organization is not subject to a logic of "dominance" by one of the actors, because their interests in *orcaella brevirostris* and each other only emerge through the project-narrative. The novel is also at pains to show that "ideological influence" alone is powerless to make new societies emerge: David Hamilton's utopian community founders on the unruly climate; a Marxist government violently exiles Sundarban settlers; Kolkata's capital never reaches the tide country; Science "with a capital S" doesn't know enough to save river dolphins or protect humans from tiger attacks; Project Tiger funds a repressive military force while failing to protect the animals. Utopian organization, leftist politics, globalized markets, scientism, and mandated environmentalism alike catastrophically fail to engage with the emergences of heterogeneous systems like the Sundarban environment. When "Fokir's" new organization emerges, the ideological structures are made the cause of a thing they could not have anticipated. As a result, the emergent organization is historically significant in its own right.

When new connections are made between epistemological things like characters, settings, animals, and objects, the past is retrofitted to cause their emergence. In *The Hungry Tide*, the same operation occurs at the level of history, romance, and description. Regarding history, a journal provides Kanai with a history of refugees who founded a Utopian community on the island of Morichjhapi, only to be exiled by a Marxist government in the name of environmental protection. It would be easy to misread this "history" as a "context" for the novel, but it is more accurate to say that the novel reconstructs history to allow itself to exist in the present. Thus, the "past" of the journal allows "Fokir's" contemporary conservation group to emerge, tying together social and environmental justice.[28] The novel's romantic arc operates similarly: a love triangle between Kanai, Piya, and Fokir should result in one of the men becoming a hero and Piya falling in love. Instead, Kanai is humiliated when he falls in the mud and claims to see a tiger; Fokir dies while shielding Piya while whispering the names of his wife and son; and Piya declines any sexual encounter in the field. Piya also denies she is motivated by intellectual ambition or political efficacy, seeking "an alibi for life" instead of a deep sense of self (126–27). This rejection of romance and heroism enables a new kind of relationship to form between Piya and the *orcaella brevirostris*, leading Ghosh to imagine a new kind of conservation organization. At key moments in the novel, moreover, description is remade as something new: as the climactic storm picks up strength, language is remade to describe it: "[The gale's noise] sounded no longer like the wind but like some other element—the usual blowing, sighing and rustling had turned into a deep, ear-splitting rumble, as if the earth itself had begun to move" (378–79). Normally passive air becomes like an earthquake, even as it tears the earth. A bit later, the transparency of sky and mysterious danger of water are inverted: "It was as though the sky had become a dark-tinted mirror for the waters of the tide country" (379). In these passages, the agency of the storm reworks standard tropes of nature, which apparently cause the phenomenon even as they are superseded.[29] This model of literary practice locates formal innovation not in authorial genius or the working out of historical forces, but rather in the mediations between new collections of things that, put together, produce unprecedented literary events.

Despite these limited innovations, *The Hungry Tide* proves to be quite a traditional novel, founded on the purifications of modernity. By his own account, Ghosh's fiction depends on an atmospheric sense of place and naturalistic dialogue, making it difficult to describe "a world that is intrinsically displaced, heterogeneous, and international" (Ghosh, "Petrofiction" 142). The novel is intensely local: save a few flashbacks, it is entirely set in the Sundarbans. As with the country house, the setting provides a framework for interrelating characters, and local myths provide a romantic interpretation of the novel's events, but this localism depends on the violent exclusion of other kinds of relationships. In effect, the tide country polices its boundaries, suppressing rival interpretations. The novel opens with Kanai's business documents being destroyed as he enters the Sundarbans and closes with Piya's scientific records being destroyed by the storm, ensuring only narrative circulates between the Sundarbans and the rest of the world. In a slightly more subtle way, characters are cut off from the world outside. Despite leading a powerful nongovernmental organization (NGO), Nalima never seems to travel out of the area. Even more implausibly, Kanai seems perfectly content to leave the BlackBerry and satellite phone at home, letting his business take care of itself. This narrative localism is presented as an ethical force: Piya's new conservation model looks after indigenous people and animals, reifying localism as a criterion of justice and excluding national and international political bodies from assessment. Global

citizenship and responsibility are also excluded. Not only are conservation efforts emanating from international scientists and national bureaucrats condemned as a violent
imposition, but the new conservation work is to depend on charity (and stories' ability to pull at the heart strings) rather than governmental taxation and the collective
obligation that implies. Similarly, the naturalistic frame is assiduously maintained: no
reference to the reader spoils the illusion with an uncomfortable feeling of responsibility. Actually, political mediation is excluded full stop: Weik has observed that the novel
omits "the disconnected political forces that cannot relate to persons and localities, but
are driven only by well-meaning concepts (at best) and global flows of capital" (136–37).
No surprise, then, that newspaper reports, scientific papers, conservation officials, and
non-local NGO workers never arrive on the scene to warn about climate change. This
absence of global modes of mediation may hold the novel together, but the cost is a sup-
pression of global warming.

    What if the *The Hungry Tide* had merely hinted at climate change, perhaps in Piya's
internal monologue? Even its mention would tear the novel's frame apart. Instead of
gathering a community of characters, global warming is documented by scientists, set in
the future, and marked by contention. It seems impossible that Piya would not recognize
that the Irawaddy dolphin is particularly vulnerable to climate change, and that conservation efforts depend on "incorporating information about cetacean populations into
national, regional and international climate adaptation decisions" (Alter 943). Climate
change also contributes to stress on the mangrove forests, which act as a natural buffer
to tropical cyclones and underpin the ecosystems for many marine invertebrate species
and fish; by 2100 sea-level rises could lead to the destruction of 75 percent of Sundarbans
mangroves. Similarly, Nalima would not really be unaware of pronouncements by the
Intergovernmental Panel on Climate Change (IPCC) that the greatest threat to the sustainable adaptation of the Sundarban population is sea-level rise, leading to flooding,
retreat of shorelines, salinization and acidification of soils, and changes in the water
table (Colette 36). If international action is not taken, wells will be fouled, crops will fail,
and eventually main islands will be wiped away, creating a refugee crisis far exceeding
Morichjhapi. On the other hand, Kanai is at the forefront of Indian development, his
translation company providing the mediations needed to convey a vast influx of global
capital into the country. It is almost certain that he would be wary of emissions reduc-
tions that might hurt economic growth, and that he would favor India's "largely negative
position" in climate negotiations, refusing to join a treaty and take on internationally
agreed binding targets, even though "India is more vulnerable to climate change than
the USA, China, Russia, and, indeed, most other parts of the world."[30] And Fokir would
seem just as likely to support Indian development as to defend his traditional method
of fishing. These differences would make the love triangle linking Piya, Kanai, and
Fokir impossible, pit the generations of Kanai and Nalima against each other, undermine the limited resolution provided by Piya's local conservation group, and destroy the
ethic of local environmental justice the novel proposes. At all costs, the future must be
avoided, as it threatens to coopt a present that has already become impossible. The heterogeneous things that produce climate change—international consumption, climate

models, carbon dioxide, international emissions accords—exceed local place, time, and character by their very nature. Global warming would simply dissolve the sensuous, local scene.

Despite, or perhaps because of these difficulties, environmental criticism has a significant role to play in the articulation of climate change. Individuals, communities, nations, and international bodies have struggled to account for climate change in their practices, even as they have expressed passionate concern. In the past thirty years, environmentalisms based on leftist politics, Utopian communities, globalized markets, scientism, and bureaucratic mandate have proved themselves all too human. Carbon credits, offsets, energy-saving light bulbs, hybrid cars, and wind farms entangle human agency with the climate's, while what passes for literary fiction tries to create authentic characters by ignoring global dynamics. If climate disaster is to be averted, far more entanglement is needed. Ecocritics have often fretted that literature is too cultural, without acknowledging culture's central role in entangling those supposedly distinct entities, nature and society. By sharing in the strategies of mediation that make up the world, fiction can articulate new connections, inventing individuals, social organizations, and things. Novels that do this are inherently impure, blending sensuous description with abstract ideas, moving between place and scientific terminology, extending beyond recognizable characters to the world of things. They cannot be chosen according to a pre-existing canon of taste because they are remaking the traditions on which literary studies depends. Such novels are part of a larger cultural project to imagine our future with climate change, using all the strategies of mediation at our disposal and inventing new ones along the way. This work is far more complex than any single novel could encapsulate, and so environmental criticism has a role as well, building connections that are simultaneously material and political.

NOTES

1. For recent data on this issue, see International Energy Agency, *World Energy Outlook 2011*, Paris: OECD/IEA, 2011.
2. Lessing's *Mara and Dann* is the most egregious in this sense, describing two white siblings passing through Africa as supreme, chosen leaders.
3. Heise indicates the problem in her monograph, but finds few literary or critical approaches to it. Garrard and Kerridge have played an important part in remedying this situation, writing articles on the topic and convening a symposium on ecocriticism and climate change in 2010.
4. For an overview of scholarship engaging with climate change and literature, see Trexler and Johns-Putra.
5. Of course, the author can just as easily invent a new kind of vehicle—a time-traveling police box, let us say—but the meaning of this invention is worked out by showing its role in the form of the novel.
6. For a sustained argument about these issues, see Phillips 2003, Chapter 1; Buell 2005, Chapter 2.

7. Joseph Carroll's *Evolution and Literary Theory* is an oft-cited precursor to this work, arguing that evolutionary biology provides a "theory" for both literary criticism and ecology and exploring literary form's role in evolutionary survival. Love is probably the most important advocate of the position that the scientific method can provide a rationale for ecocriticism.

8. For an example of the former, see Bate, 2000. For the latter, see Phillips, 1999.

9. Latour introduced the model of immutable mobiles in *Science in Action* (1987). For a succinct and recent articulation of its application to field work, see 'Circulating Reference: Sampling the Soil in the Amazon Forest' in *Pandora's Hope* (1999). Mediation, as it is used here, is entirely different from the Marxist sense of translating between base and superstructure. In Latour's formulation of hybrids, real and ideal are wholly mixed up in each thing, and the expression of these features comes through a network of other things.

10. Rollason reads the novel through ideas of translation, while Agarwal interprets it through various critical notions of language.

11. Mukherjee and Weik have analyzed *The Hungry Tide* as a novel that bridges postcolonial and environmental discourses, particularly its movement between global and local conceptions of place.

12. Marzec reads *The Hungry Tide* in the long history of enclosure laws, and invokes Deleuze and Guattari, Edward Said, and Lacan.

13. There is a much larger body of science-themed work on Ghosh's *The Calcutta Chromosome*, which spins intricate fictions around malaria and genetic research. Both Diane Nelson and Christopher Shinn have read *The Calcutta Chromosome* through Latour and Haraway.

14. Rajender Kaur has proposed the novel as a new paradigm for contemporary, transcultural environmentalism. The novel has become something of a favorite for conference papers and is also frequently used for teaching (see Garrard).

15. See especially Latour's *Laboratory Life* (with Steve Woolgar, 1979) and *Science in Action* (1987). Diane M. Nelson has also read Ghosh's work through his social science training and Latour, but sees science fiction and social science as "mixing … categories," a very different model from the one I am proposing here (248).

16. Similarly, Latour argues that modernity isn't characterized by an increasing distance between society and nature, but rather a deepened intimacy, a more intricate mesh, between the two (Latour, *Pandora* 196).

17. Latour and Haraway controversially used Greimas, the literary theorist, to delineate a limited number of ways that agency unfolded in time. By using "narrative" here, I only mean that agency is temporally emergent: its alliances seem endlessly open to me.

18. The question of pre-existence is knotty, but the simple version is this: neither microbes nor David Copperfield existed, as such, before Pasteur and Dickens, but there were historical phenomena that the terms successfully captured: disease and orphans made good.

19. Mukherjee, for one, veers away from considering animals, focusing on human oppression under a postcolonial framework. Other ecocritics have discussed animals but struggle to integrate their accounts with the humans of a novel.

20. Indeed, at least one reviewer slated the novel because "none of the many characters [come] properly alive" (Robinson).

21. Latour refers to the things that are translated thus as "immutable mobiles."

22. Although authorial intent is peripheral to the interpretive issue at stake, it is also interesting to note that Ghosh has repeatedly valorized contemporary ecological scientists like

Piya and distinguished them from colonial naturalists of the 19th century. See Ghosh 2004, 401; "Wild Fictions," 20.

23. Weik makes a similar point about Piya, Fokir, and modernity, but attributes "harmony with nature" to Fokir (127–8).

24. Nelson has used Latour to read *The Calcutta Chromosome*, finding labs make strong, "real" science "if they can mobilize the highest number of associations, linkages, resources and allies" (253).

25. Of course, most ecocritics would side with Piya, while Mukherjee's postcolonial allegiances lead him to call Piya's outrage "nauseous" and to claim she lacks "a properly ecological ethos" (152).

26. For example, Love has approvingly cited Richard Dawkins' thinly veiled threat to throw cultural relativists from planes "at 30,000 feet" (45), as well as Edward Abbey's prescription: "To refute the solipsist or the metaphysical idealist all that you have to do is take him out and throw a rock at his head: if he ducks, he's a liar" (26). Love redeploys Dawkins and Abbey to attack literary theory, and with it, critical scrutiny of mediation.

27. This hasn't stopped critics from trying to adjudicate between the alternatives. Marzec assumes Kanai has seen the tiger (434); in my reading, Kanai's experience is purposely indeterminate.

28. Nirmal is similarly retrofitted in the novel's present, changing from a failed Marxist to the heroic designer of a storm shelter (388).

29. Kaur has read the novel through more traditional tropes: pastoral, idyll, and Tennysonian nature that is "red in tooth and claw" (136), but this formal conservatism does a disservice to the "new paradigm" he also recognizes in the novel.

30. Joshi 169. There are legitimate ethical issues surrounding India's (as well as China's) right to pollute on the path to development, since their per capita emissions are and will remain lower than those in developed countries. However, the increases currently projected in India and China will nullify efforts to reduce emissions elsewhere.

Works Cited

Agarwal, Nilanshu Kumar. "A Web of 'Langue' and 'Parole' in Amitav Ghosh's *The Hungry Tide*." *The Fiction of Amitav Ghosh: An Assessment*. Ed. O. P. Dwivedi. Jaipur, India: Book Enclave, 2010. 183–93.

Aldama, Frederick Luis and Amitav Ghosh. "An Interview with Amitav Ghosh." *World Literature Today 76*.2 (Spring 2002): 84–90.

Alter, S. E., M. P. Simmonds, and J. R. Brandon. "Forecasting the consequences of climate-driven shifts in human behaviour on cetaceans." *Marine Policy 34*. 5 (September 2010): 943–54.

Ball, Eric L. "Literary Criticism for Places." *symplokē 14*. 1–2 (2006): 232–51.

Bloom, Harold *The Western Canon*. London: Macmillan, 1995.

Brauner, David. *Contemporary American Fiction*. Edinburgh: Edinburgh UP, 2010.

Bate, Jonathan. *The Song of the Earth*. Cambridge, MA: Harvard UP, 2000.

Buell, Lawrence. *The Future of Environmental Criticism: Environmental Crisis and Literary Imagination*. Oxford: Blackwell, 2005.

Clarke, Bruce. "Science, Theory, and Systems: A Reply to Glen A. Love and Jonathan Levin." *Interdisciplinary Studies in Literature and Environment 8.1* (Winter 2001): 149–65.

Colette, Augustin. *Case Studies on Climate and World Heritage*. Paris: UNESCO World Heritage Centre, 2007.

Garrard, Greg. "Ecocriticism and Education for Sustainability." *Pedagogy 7.3*: 359–83.

Ghosh, Amitav. *The Hungry Tide*. London: Harper Collins, 2004.

Ghosh, Amitav. "Petrofiction: The Oil Encounter and the Novel." *Incendiary Circumstances: A Chronicle of the Turmoil of Our Times*. Boston and New York: Houghton Mifflin Company, 2005. 138–151.

Ghosh, Amitav. "Wild Fictions." *Outlook India.com*. 22 December 2008. http://www.outlookindia.com/article.aspx?239276. Accessed August 10 2013.

Goeminne, Gert and Karen François. "The Thing Called Environment: What It Is and How to Be Concerned With It." *Oxford Literary Review 32. 1*: 109–130.

Heise, U. K. *Sense of Place and Sense of Planet: The Environmental Imagination of the Global*. New York: Oxford UP; 2008.

Herbert, James. *Portent*. London: Eos, 1997.

Kaur, Rajender. "'Home is Where the Oracella Are': Toward a New Paradigm of Transcultural Ecocritical Engagement in Amitav Ghosh's The Hungry Tide." *Interdisciplinary Studies in Literature and Environment 14.1* (Summer 2007): 125–41.

Latour, Bruno. *We Have Never Been Modern*. Trans. Catherine Porter. Boston: Harvard UP, 1993.

Latour, Bruno. *Pandora's Hope: Essays on the Reality of Science Studies*. London: Harvard UP, 1999.

Levin, Jonathan. "Between Science and Anti-Science: A Response to Glen A. Love." *Interdisciplinary Studies in Literature and Environment 7. 1* (2001): 1–7.

Love, Glen A. "Ecocriticism and Science: Towards Consilience?" *New Literary History 30* (1999): 561–76.

Markley, R. "Monsoon cultures: Climate and acculturation in Alexander Hamilton's A New Account of the East Indies." *New Literary History 38* (2007): 527–50.

Marzec, Robert P. "Speaking Before the Environment: Modern Fiction and the Ecological." *MFS 55*:3 (Fall 2009): 419–42.

Mukherjee, Pablo. "Surfing the Second Waves: Amitav Ghosh's Tide Country" *New Formations 59* (2006): 144–57.

Nelson, Diane M. "A Social Science Fiction of Fevers, Delirium and Discovery: 'The Calcutta Chromosome', the Colonial Laboratory, and the Postcolonial New Human." *Science Fiction Studies 30*:2 (Jul 2003): 246–66.

Phillips, Dana. "Ecocriticism, Literary Theory, and the Truth of Ecology." *New Literary History 30. 3* (Summer 1999): 577–602.

Phillips, Dana. *The Truth of Ecology: Nature, Culture, and Literature in America*. Oxford: Oxford UP, 2003.

Pickering, Andrew. *The Mangle of Practice*. Chicago: U of Chicago P, 1995.

Potter, Emily. "Climate change and the problem of representation." *Australian Humanities Review 46*:1 (2009). <http://www.australianhumanitiesreview.org/archive/Issue-May-2009/potter.htm> Accessed 4 November 2010.

Robinson, Andrew. "Delta of Venus" *The Times* December 6, 2004. N.p.

Rollason, Christopher. "'In Our Translated World': Transcultural Communication in Amitav Ghosh's The Hungry Tide." In *The Fiction of Amitav Ghosh: An Assessment*. Ed. O. P. Dwivedi. Jaipur, India: Book Enclave, 2010. 159–82.

Shinn, Christopher A. "On Machines and Mosquitoes: Neuroscience, Bodies, and Cyborgs in Amitav Ghosh's 'The Calcutta Chromosome'". *MELUS* 33:4 (Winter 2008): 145–66.

Trexler, Adam and Adeline Johns-Putra. "Climate change in literature and literary criticism." *WIREs Climate Change* 2:2 (March/April 2011): 185–200.

Wallace, Molly. "'A Bizarre Ecology': The Nature of Denatured Nature." *Interdisciplinary Studies in Literature and Environment* 7.2 (2000): 137–53.

Weik, Alexa. "The Home, the Tide, and the World: Ecocosmopolitan Encounters in Amitav Ghosh's The Hungry Tide." *Journal of Commonwealth and Postcolonial Studies* 13.2–14.1 (2006–2007): 120–41.

CHAPTER 12

....

ECOCRITICISM, POSTHUMANISM, AND THE BIOLOGICAL IDEA OF CULTURE

....

HELENA FEDER

IN May of 2010, the United Nations International Year of Biodiversity, geneticist Craig Venter and his research team created what he calls "the world's first synthetic life form"—a bacterium described as "a defining moment in biology;" Venter claims this single-celled organism with its made-from-scratch genome "heralds the dawn of a new era in which new life is made to benefit humanity, starting with bacteria that churn out biofuels, soak up carbon dioxide from the atmosphere and even manufacture vaccines" (Sample, "Craig Venter").[1] This new life form, invention and intervention, is a source of tremendous interest and anxiety—not unlike Alan Weisman's *The World Without Us*, "a penetrating, page-turning tour of a post-human Earth," twenty-six weeks on *The New York Times* bestseller list, *Time Magazine*'s number one nonfiction book of 2007, and likely inspiration for the 2010 television series (and iPhone App), *Life After People*.[2] This novel organism's place in material reality and, conversely, the resonance of a world after humanity in the human imagination seem to confirm what some theorists have argued, in various terms, for decades: that at some point we or the world became posthuman.

We or the world or we *as* the world? We imagine life after people because human sovereignty over the rest of life on earth intensifies exponentially, because we tell ourselves we are the world, the pinnacle of nature or "natura naturans,"[3] even as we render it less and less inhabitable for ourselves and many other creatures. Such conflation of humanity and world makes posthumanism at once terrifying and potentially appealing for ecocriticism (depending, as we will see, on which version of posthumanism is in play, whether it elides or foregrounds power relations). If evolutionary thought and the ecological sciences have taught nothing else, surely we have learned that "we" are not the world. And yet we are the world too—our bodies are themselves ecosystems, our atoms the very fibers of it. But, as D. H. Lawrence wrote of Whitman's pantheism, "All Walt is

Pan, but all Pan is not Walt."[4] While we are still here—the world is not yet without us even if it is too much with us—the apocalyptic *post* of posthumanism suggests that the Age of "Man" may lead to an age without human beings and a great many others. As Rob Nixon recently wrote, we are faced with "amorphous calamities," not only in the form of the Anthropocene but also in the age of the new "man"—the Great Acceleration in which "high speed planetary modification has been accompanied (at least for those increasing billions who have access to the Internet) by rapid modifications to the human cortex"; these increasing connections, and "the paradoxical disconnects that can accompany it," seem to redefine time itself (12).[5]

This chapter will argue that ecocriticism and posthumanism, as parallel and potentially overlapping fields concerned with biological change, must consider the implications of the growing work in biology on other animal cultures. Of course, just as this volume represents the diversity and complexity of new ecocritical enquiry (under the banners of ecocriticism, green cultural studies, ecocritique, etc.), posthumanism also comprises differing and, to a greater degree, conflicting ideas and practices.

While the term *posthumanism* seems to suggest life beyond biology, and sometimes more specifically human life beyond the current bounds of humanity, it also signals a renewed interest in the biological world, ideas of human animality and our kinship with other creatures (as we see in the field of animal studies), as well as new integrations and manipulations of information and biological technologies. Posthumanism may challenge the primacy of humanity, the idea of the Human as the all-pervasive legacy of Enlightenment essentialism, or it may champion a new teleology, a race for infinite technological power over material life. It may function as a spatial category, as a landscape of virtuality or the possibility of new connections between material agencies, a reimagining of what Darwin described in *Origin of the Species* as "a web of complex relations." Posthumanism may mean many things, some of which are mutually-exclusive: a revaluing of human animality or the desire to transcend animality; a radical, ecological sensibility or a teleological essentialism.

In *How We Became Posthuman*, N. Katherine Hayles asserts the duality of what is called posthumanism: the rejection or erasure of the body or materiality for a fantasy of disembodiment (cue the robotic and virtualized selves of the imagination) *and* the realization of that fantasy's root in the familiar subject of liberal humanism, with its disavowal of embodiment and embeddedness in pursuit of individuality and freedom. This realization makes possible the second posthumanism, the critique which reveals that the human of humanism, the free-floating Cartesian mind or the atomized subject of "free" political-economy, is itself a fantasy. This posthumanism suggests that, far from finding ourselves on the far side of an historic rupture, we may have always been posthuman, even as it offers new modes of subjectivity (Hayles 2). Building on Hayles' work, Bart Simon characterizes these models of posthumanism as "popular" versus "critical:" popular posthuman, or *transhumanist*, discourse "structures the agendas of much of corporate biotechnology and informatics as well as serving as a legitimizing narrative for new social entities (cyborgs, artificial intelligence, and virtual societies)... For popular posthumanism, the future is a space for the realization of individuality, the transcendence of biological limits, and the creation of a new social order" (2). On the other hand, critical posthumanism questions the humanism, liberal and philosophical, that still animates popular posthumanism (3). Its target is nothing short of the Enlightenment narratives of human nature which undergird much of Western philosophy and political-economy.[6]

While humanism is certainly more complex than any caricature of the Enlightenment,[7] there is no mistaking its essentialist legacy, a legacy that even critical posthumanism and ecocriticism carry forward in the idea of culture. While the binary of nature and culture has long been the subject of ecocritical analysis, critical focus has centered on the idea of nature and its role in ecological crisis (just as critical posthumanism has often focused on ideas of human nature). The idea of culture as defined by this binary has not been adequately considered. This is the most pressing problem for ecocriticism, posthumanism, and cultural studies generally.

In *What is Posthumanism?* Cary Wolfe also differentiates between transhumanist and critical posthumanisms, but argues that even critical posthumanism must change the form of its thought if it is to be truly posthuman:

> What this means is that when we talk about posthumanism, we are not just talking about a thematics of the decentering of the human in relation to either evolutionary, ecological, or technological coordinates (though that is where the conversation usually begins and, all too often, ends,); rather, I will insist that we are also talking about how thinking confronts that thematics, what thought has to become in the face of those challenges... the point is not to reject humanism *tout court*... but rather to show how those aspirations are undercut by the philosophical and ethical frameworks used to conceptualize them. (xvi)

Through connections between Derrida's work and the systems theory of Nicklas Luhmann, Wolfe considers how this posthumanism should function in the field of animal studies. He writes that the radical impact of animal studies ("what makes it not just another flavor of 'fill in the blank' studies") "is that it fundamentally unsettles and reconfigures the question of the knowing subject and the disciplinary paradigms and procedures that take for granted its form and reproduce it." Wolfe argues that the posthuman challenge of this field is lost when "the animal" becomes simply another "object" of study (xxix).

Like animal studies, ecocriticism is in the process of contesting paradigms and considering conditions of knowledge as well as the purposes of such knowledge. While I am not proposing that ecocriticism necessarily adopt, or adopt *tout court*, the exhaustive systems theory overhaul of ontology that Wolfe advocates, I do want to argue that we too must focus on our philosophical, disciplinary challenge to the anthropocentric orthodoxies of the humanities. Ecocriticism's radical challenge lies not only in recognizing other forms of subjectivity and the ecological interconnectedness of these biologically diverse subjects, but in recognizing that the relations between them are *political*—they are life and death relations. We are one animal among many in this shared world, living in interwoven interspecies communities, a series of polities themselves comprised of differing societies. This is not to say that this politics must take the form of human political relations, or that political or ethical consideration of other animals[8] depends on how "intelligent" or *like us* we think they are, but that we must begin to recognize the implications of our real similarities with and differences from other creatures.

The discussion of politics is, of course, always itself political. As Jacques Rancière suggests, what is at stake is the definition of politics:

> "Disagreement" and "dissensus" do not imply that politics is a struggle between camps; they imply that it is a struggle about what politics is, a struggle that is waged about such original issues as: "where are we?," "who are we?," "What makes us a we," "what do we see and what can we say about it that makes us a we, having a world in common?" Those paradoxical, unthinkable objects of thinking mark...the places where the question "How is this thinkable at all?" points to the question: "who is qualified for thinking at all?" (116)

Again, we are part of a common world, but a changed one, and one that is still changing rapidly for the immediate benefit of some at the expense of a great many others. In this context, to ask who is qualified for politics, what counts as political, is to ask who *counts* full stop. In Western cultures the questions of who counts is intimately bound up with the question of what counts as culture. To think politically, to think about politics, we must contest the humanist ideology of culture, the essentialist idea at the core of the humanities and Western culture in general. A radically expansive idea of culture, a non-speciesist multiculturalism, may intervene in forms of subjugation that function precisely by excluding some from the realm of culture.

Turning to biology, we find the broader and more nuanced notion of culture, what we might call a posthumanist view of culture, necessary for a more materialist ecocritical practice.[9] While the experience of nature is culturally mediated, biology reminds us that culture is itself a natural medium, created by and subject to evolutionary and other ecological processes. While some scientists continue to disagree over this use of the term *culture*,[10] *Nature* and other prominent journals have published the findings of dozens of studies demonstrating that many species learn socially and pass on traditions or skills. For example, a comprehensive synthesis of several long-term studies of chimpanzees in Africa (151 years cumulatively) documents thirty-nine group-specific, learned behavioral patterns (including tool usage): "[T]he combined repertoire of these behavioral patterns in each chimpanzee community is itself highly distinctive, a phenomenon characteristic of human cultures but previously unrecognized in non-human species" (Whiten et al. 682). A particularly resonant example of learned tool use was reported in 2007 by researchers in Senegal, who recorded twenty-two examples of chimps creating spears to hunt smaller primates ("Chimpanzees 'hunt using spears'").[11] Primates, though, are not the only culture-makers in nature; evidence of animal cultures abounds—from Hal Whitehead's work on orcas and sperm whales to Kevin Laland's studies of birds and fish.[12] Writing on animal cultures, primatologist Frans de Waal exclaimed, "one cannot escape the impression that it is an idea whose time has come" (13–14).[13] It is also an idea that has been kicking around, even if only to be dismissed, for a while now.

In *Civilization and its Discontents*, Sigmund Freud considers, albeit briefly, the existence of nonhuman cultures:

> Why do our relatives, the animals, not exhibit any such cultural struggle? We do not know. Very probably some of them—the bees, the ants, the termites—strove for thousands of years before they arrived at the State institutions, the distribution of functions and the restrictions on the individual, for which we admire them today … In the case of other animal species it may be that a temporary balance has been reached between the influences of their environment and the mutually contending instincts within them, and that thus a cessation of development has come about. (83)

Freud's question about animal culture was turned on its head (or, more accurately, stood on its feet) in 1953 when Kinji Imanishi, founder of Japanese primatology, applied ethnographic study to an animal society on the island of Koshima, creating animal cultural studies. In September of that year, Satsue Mito noticed Imo, an eighteen-month-old macaque, carry a sweet potato to a freshwater stream to clean it before eating, minimizing wear on her teeth.[14]

> She playfully repeated this behavior on the first day. Later, she improved her technique by going deeper in the water, holding the potato in one hand and rubbing off the mud with the other, occasionally dipping it in the water … Within three months, two of [Imo's] peers as well as her mother were showing the same behavior. From these potato pioneers the habit spread to other juveniles, their older siblings, and their mothers. Within five years, more than three quarters of the juveniles and young adults engaged in regular potato washing. (de Waal 200–201)

This has become a rather famous example[15] of the "struggle" Freud did not see in the animal world: cultural change through socially transmitted and learned problem solving.[16]

Building on the work of William McGrew's *Chimpanzee Material Culture* in 1992, primatologist Frans de Waal's *The Ape and the Sushi Master*, published in 2001, surveys and theorizes the methodological and conceptual issues of the growing field of animal cultural research, termed "cultural biology" (267).[17] He argues,

> The standard notion of humanity as the only form of life to have made the step from the natural to the cultural realm—as if one day we opened a door to a brand-new life—is in urgent need of correction… The idea that we are the only species whose survival depends on culture is false, and the entire juxtaposing of nature and culture rests on a giant misunderstanding. (28)

De Waal goes on to state that even aesthetics may be found in nonhuman cultures: "Given that our aesthetic sense has been shaped by the environment in which we evolved, it is logical to expect preferences for shapes, contrasts, and colors to transcend species" (36). Of course, the question of aesthetics, and its associations with "high" culture,[18] need not come into play here; as Raymond Williams observes in *Keywords*, culture is "one of the two or three most complicated words in the English language... [The Latin root] *Colere* has a range of meanings: inhabit, cultivate, protect, honor with worship" (87). While all animal species inhabit, many live and learn socially, and some cultivate or transform food (leaf cutter ants are a favorite example). Even abstractions such as honor and worship form a part of the lives of some animals. The elephant practice of ritual mourning is one such example.[19]

In fact, the social fabric of elephant life is sufficiently complex to suffer catastrophic degeneration. In 2005, Gay Bradshaw and her colleagues argued in *Nature* that human interference (poaching, culling, and habitat loss) has led to a "collapse of elephant culture." Wild elephants are demonstrating unprecedented aggression toward humans and occasionally other animals, attacking villages and crops, killing hundreds of people each year. In an interview with Charles Siebert, Bradshaw describes this wide-scale phenomenon as psychological and cultural breakdown: "Everybody pretty much agrees that the relationship between elephants and people has dramatically changed... What we are seeing today is extraordinary. Where for centuries humans and elephants lived in relatively peaceful coexistence, there is now hostility and violence. Now, I use the term 'violence' because of the intentionality associated with it..." She asks, "How do we respond to the fact that we are causing other species like elephants to... break down? In a way, it's not so much a cognitive or imaginative leap anymore as it is a political one" (Siebert). In *Elephants on the Edge*, Bradshaw contextualizes the implications of her research, interpreting elephant violence as another form of resistance to colonial oppression and global power.

> Much like other cultures that have refused to be absorbed by colonialism, elephants are struggling to survive as an intact society, to retain their elephant-ness, and to resist becoming what modern humanity has tried to make them—passive objects in zoos, circuses, and safari rides, romantic decorations dotting the landscape for eager eyes peering from Land Rovers, or data to tantalize our minds and stock in the bank of knowledge. Elephants are, as Archbishop Desmond Tutu wrote about black South Africans living under apartheid, simply asking to live in the land of their birth, where their dignity is acknowledged and respected. (71–72)

Bradshaw's work not only requires the recognition of our relations with elephants (and many other life forms) as political, it also suggests that the resistance to the idea of nonhuman animal cultures is not (or not only) intellectual but ideological. With many animals, including most mammals, and their habitats still treated as raw materials for production (much in the way other colonial subjects have been subject to horrific exploitation, physical and cultural genocide), the existence of other animal cultures, their numbers and scope, and the new political terrain they imply, present a profound challenge to power and the status quo, including scientific humanism.

Carel van Schaik's *Among Orangutans: Red Apes and the Rise of Human Culture*, which documents twenty-four cultural variants among the orangutans he observed in Sumatra (including sophisticated tool making and a variety of other socially learned behaviors), lays out the philosophical and scientific problem with traditional definitions of culture and the new biocentric corrective:

> The anthropological definitions emphasize the underlying beliefs and values of cul-
> ture bearers…The Japanese primatologist Kinji Imanishi was perhaps the first, in
> 1952, to point out that at its core, culture is socially transmitted innovation: culture
> is simply innovation followed by diffusion. This biological (as opposed to anthro-
> pological) definition leads to an operational emphasis on observable behaviors or
> artifacts, things we can actually see in animals, rather than beliefs or values, which
> we cannot. It also explains the key property of culture in humans: geographic varia-
> tion. Useful or popular innovations spread until they hit some barrier, producing
> geographic differentiation. So, if we see geographic variation in behaviors that we
> know reflect innovation and are transmitted through some socially mediated learn-
> ing process, then we have animal culture (and we can worry about how symbolic any
> of it is later on). (139)

However, in *Sense and Nonsense*, Kevin N. Laland and Gillian R. Brown agree that scientists are a long way from a consensus definition: "most social scientists would agree on
two points, that culture is composed of symbolically encoded acquired information and
that it is socially transmitted within and between populations, largely free of biological constraints. Is that the way evolutionists regard culture? For the most part it would
seem not" (310).[20] Put most simply, our notion of culture is culturally (and, more narrowly, disciplinarily) constructed; the emphasis on a narrow notion of symbol, along
with symbolic learning and syntactic communication, is only one of the anthropological
biases underlying some definitions of culture.

The definition of culture de Waal uses is as follows:

> Culture is a way of life shared by the members of one group but not necessarily with
> the member of other groups of the same species [local variations]. It covers knowl-
> edge, habits, and skills, including underlying tendencies and preferences, derived
> from exposure to and learning from others. Whenever systematic variation in
> knowledge, habits, and skills between groups cannot be attributed to genetic or eco-
> logical factors, it is probably cultural. The way individuals learn from each other is
> secondary, but that they learn from each other is a requirement. (31)

Within the parameters of this definition, de Waal and other biologists have documented
a number of examples of culture in a range of species: socially learned practices such
as complex nut-cracking by chimps in the Guinea forest; the tool-use of Sumatran
orangutans; and self-medication in a variety of primates. Again, cultural practices
are not limited to primates: Dorothy M. Fragaszy and Susan Perry's *The Biology of
Traditions: Models and Evidence* published the findings of nearly a dozen separate studies of social learning and traditions among nonhuman creatures, from fish and dolphins
to birds and rats.

As the title of Fragaszy and Perry's book suggests, not all biologists are comfortable
with the use of the term "culture," despite the fact that the idea of nonhuman cultures

has a great deal of support (primatologist William McGrew, a "pro-culturalist," has characterized this state of affairs as "the controversial, value-laden use of the 'c' word" [127]). In fact, in their Introduction to *The Question of Animal Culture*, editors Laland and Bennett G. Galef refer to "the recent spate of articles in prominent scientific journals, newspapers, and news magazines that argue that differences in the behavioral repertoires of animals living in different locales provide evidence that they, like humans, are cultural beings." (1) While several researchers in the collection advocate the idea or actuality of nonhuman cultures without any or many qualifications, others do not, in part because of the interdisciplinary nature of this research:[21] there are varied methodologies, differing ideas of evidence, and basic definitional disagreements. One author's nonhuman "culture" is another's animal "tradition," "pre-cultural" practice, or social learning. Nevertheless, "There is nothing more circular than saying that we, humans, are the product of culture if culture is at the same time the product of us," de Waal and Kristin E. Bonnie argue in their chapter. "Natural selection has produced our species, including our cultural abilities, and hence these abilities fall squarely under biology. This inevitably raises the question whether natural selection may have produced similar abilities in more than one species." (19)

In the decades since Mito and Imanishi first discovered the cultural innovation of potato washing on Koshima island, the macaques have shifted their practices by dipping their potatoes in the ocean, rather than freshwater. On a recent trip to the island, de Waal observed this first hand:

> Walking in shallow water, they would alternate dipping a potato in and chewing off a piece. They did not do much rubbing in the water, probably because these potatoes were prewashed: there was hardly any dirt to be removed.... For this reason, Japanese scientists have changed their terminology... Assuming that it is the salty taste of the water that the monkeys are after, they now speak of "seasoning." (204)

Not only have cultural practices now been documented, but even the evolution of such practices.

The study of nonhuman cultures overlaps with the biological study of human cultures. The charge leveled at the former, anthropomorphism, is related to the charge of determinism leveled at sociobiology and its descendants.[22] In the first case, critics mischaracterize anthropomorphism as anthropocentrism, whereas de Waal distinguishes between "animalcentric anthropomorphism" and "anthropocentric anthropomorphism:" "The first [makes every effort to take] the animal's perspective, the second takes ours. It is a bit like people we all know, who buy us presents that they think *we* like versus people who buy us presents that *they* like. The latter have not yet reached a mature form of empathy, and perhaps never will" (77). He argues that if anthropomorphism is risky, "its opposite carries a risk too. To give it a name, I propose *anthropodenial* for the a priori rejection of shared characteristics between humans and animals when in fact they may exist" (de Waal 68–69).[23]

The second case is a variation on a theme if not a mirror image. If nonhuman cultural studies, or cultural biology, is allegedly mired in false, sentimental identifications, then the biological study of human behavior coldly denies the unique significance of human thought, feeling, and freedom by claiming a biological basis of culture—treating *us* like "mere" animals! In his 1996 retrospective *In Search of Nature*, E. O. Wilson defends the evolutionary study of human and other animal behavior from charges of determinism:

> Concern over the implications of sociobiology usually proves to be a simple mis-understanding about the nature of heredity. Let me try to set the matter straight as briefly but fairly as possible. *What the genes prescribe is not necessarily a particular behavior but the capacity to develop certain behaviors and, more than that, the tendency to develop then in various specified environments*... It is this *pattern* of possibilities and probabilities that is inherited. (89–90, italics in original)

Laland and Brown concur: "When researchers talk about genetic influences on human behavior, they do not mean that the behavior is completely determined by genetic effects, that no other factors play a role in our development, or that a single gene is responsible for each behavior" (17). In fact, "developmental biologists are agreed that the very idea that an individual's behavior can be partitioned into nature and nurture components is nonsensical, as a multitude of interacting processes play a role in behavioral development." (18)

The notion of human freedom latent in this charge of determinism is, at root, a notion of human supremacy only conceptually possible if the rest of the living world is determined. Both logic and daily experience suggest, however, that nothing is determined and, equally, nothing is "free." We fear biological determinism not only because of the use made of the idea in the past, but also because Western culture at large continues to attribute every action and desire of other animals to a reductive notion of their biology, summed up in the derogatory (and tautological) use of the term "instinct." It is a short-hand way of saying that *they* are machines, organic machines acting under the rubric of their design.[24] This, of course, is no truer of "them" than of us. De Waal reminds us that if biology restricts our freedom, culture does so to the same extent. "And where do our cultural capacities come from?" he asks. "Don't they spring from the same source as the so-called instincts?... Whereas we can fully expect that definitions of culture will keep changing to keep the apes [and other animals] out, the proposals heard thus far seem insufficient to do so" (236). Just how far some scientists will go to keep changing definitions of culture to keep the "riffraff" out is itself a question of culture.[25]

Perhaps those who expressed horror at Wilson's *Sociobiology*, scientists and scholars in the humanities alike,[26] did so not because, or simply because, they misunderstood the text (or, as Wilson has it, took the notion of heredity to be deterministic) but because of the most pervasive form of liberal humanism: anthropocentric rationalism. "To be anthropocentric," Wilson writes, "is to remain unaware of the limits of human nature, the significance of biological processes underlying human behavior, and the deeper meaning of long-term genetic evolution" (100).[27] Val Plumwood characterizes anthropocentric rationalism, this dominant form of reason, as "a doctrine about reason, its place at the apex of human life, and the practice of oppositional construction in relation to its 'others,' especially the body and nature, which are simultaneously relied upon but disavowed or taken for granted" (18). It is doctrine of reason as power, which erases the subjectivity of other beings, creating living "resources" available for consumption. While this functional "misunderstanding" of the world enables its domination, it also misunderstands the enabling conditions of human life, of embodiment and embeddedness, at our peril.

"The question of the purpose of human life has been raised countless times; it has never yet received a satisfactory answer and perhaps does not admit of one...," argues Freud. And yet,

> Nobody talks of the purpose of the lives of animals, unless, perhaps, it may be supposed to lie in being of service to man. But this view is not tenable either, for there are many animals of which man can make nothing, except to describe, classify, and study them; and innumerable species of animals have escaped even this use, since they existed and became extinct before man set eyes on them. (24)

Here Freud presents us with the story of the first human question (what is the purpose of human life?) as the very origin of culture. It only makes sense, then, that nobody talks of the purpose of lives of animals. Our purpose, as our story goes—the story that seems the very foundation of Western culture—relies on their distinct lack of purpose. Whether the story is religious (God has made using his image and our purpose is to please him) or teleological (we are the unique pinnacle of life on earth) or both doesn't make a substantive difference. In either case, this story is a defense-narrative, what Freud calls a *détour* en route to a mature, frank acceptance of human powerlessness and finitude: "If the believer finally sees himself obliged to speak of God's 'inscrutable decrees,' he is admitting that all that is left to him... is an unconditional submission. And if he is prepared for that, he probably could have spared himself the *détour* he has made." (36) What Freud called the reality principle we might call the biological conditions of life: the fact that human beings are not deities, cannot master nature or control their fate, but are, in fact, animals that evolved and continue to evolve with other life forms. "This recognition," writes Freud, "does not [need to] have a paralyzing effect. On the contrary, it points the direction for our activity." (37)

The implications of this new work in cultural biology are far-reaching and radical: we do not have to look to the sky to see that we are not alone in the universe. In her field-making introduction to *The Ecocriticism Reader*, Cheryll Glotfelty writes, "In most literary theory 'the world' is synonymous with society—the social sphere. Ecocriticism expands the notion of 'the world' to include the entire ecosphere." (xix) We must take this formulation a step further: ecocriticism must not only expand our notion of "the world" but also of "the social." Although we are not the only species that use culture to alter our environment, we are at the moment the only ones endangering the existence of a *great many others*. Despite Venter's pronouncement that his new bacterium "heralds the dawn of a new era in which new life is made to benefit humanity," the new era doesn't sound *so* very new; other life forms have long been *made* to benefit humanity. That is, made to benefit some of us, in the short term, with widespread suffering and the risk of more.

For political intervention in this historical, ecological crisis, in which a great many real beings suffer, we must change our conception of the human and the nonhuman, of animality itself. The post-anthropological concepts and findings of cultural biology topple the humanist idea of culture perpetuated by various ecocriticisms and posthumanisms, and the humanities generally. The realization that the human animal is one of many life forms engaged in the interwoven (indeed, co-creating) processes of nature and culture (or naturecultures) is the first step toward a posthumanist multiculturalism, an ecocultural materialist practice—toward concepts of subjectivity and knowledge, and knowledge itself, transformed by interconnected social and ecological worlds. It is a step toward a political sensibility in cultural theory and analysis attuned to anthropodenial as well as anthropomorphism, one willing to explore the messiness of needs and our responsibilities to similarity and to difference.

NOTES

1. "To mark the genome as synthetic, they spliced in fresh strands of DNA, each a biological "watermark" that would do nothing in the final organism except carry coded messages, including a line from James Joyce: "To live, to err, to fall, to triumph, to recreate life out of life."" (Sample, "Synthentic.")

2. See http://www.worldwithoutus.com/about_book.html. *Life After People* is a series on the History Channel: "In every episode, viewers will witness the epic destruction of iconic structures and buildings, from the Sears Tower, Astrodome, and Chrysler Building to the Sistine Chapel–allowing viewers to learn how they were built and why they were so significant....The series will also explore the creatures that might take our place. With humans gone, animals will inherit the places where we once lived. Elephants that escape from the LA zoo will thrive in a region once dominated by their ancestors, the wooly mammoth. Alligators will move into sub-tropical cities like Houston—feeding off household pets. Tens of thousands of hogs, domesticated for food, will flourish. In a world without people, new stories of predators, survival and evolution will emerge. Humans won't be around forever, and now we can see in detail, for the very first time, the world that will be left behind in *Life After People: The Series.*"See http://www.history.com/shows/life-after-people/articles/about-life-after-people

3. See Frederick W. Turner's "Cultivating the American Garden" in *The Ecocriticism Reader*.

4. In "Pan in America" Lawrence writes, "Lucy Gray, alas, was the form that William Wordsworth thought fit to give the Great God Pan. And then he crossed over to the young United States.... To this new Lucifer Gray of a Pan Whitman sings the famous *Song of Myself*: "I am All, and All is me." That is: "I am Pan, and Pan is me." The old goat-legged gentleman from Greece thoughtfully strokes his beard, and answers, "All A is B, but all B is not A." Aristotle did not live for nothing. All Walt is Pan, but all Pan is not Walt" (*Phoenix* 23–24).

5. See *Slow Violence and the Environmentalism of the Poor*.

6. Of course, there are less critical "critiques" of popular posthumanism. As Simon notes, Francis Fukuyama's *Our Posthuman Future: Consequences of the Biotechnology Revolution* resurrects an idea of human nature to battle popular posthumanism, a move "emblematic of the contradictions that arise when a historically humanist public culture confronts contemporary corporate technoscientific fantasies of infinitely malleable life" (1–2).

7. A point Neil Badmington makes in "Theorizing Posthumanism."

8. As Derrida argues in *The Animal That Therefore I Am*, there is no simple, wholly positive way to refer nonhuman animals. Derrida's "animot" (41) seems a better option but
it too falls short of the mark. I will use terms interchangeably, favoring other animals,
animals, and animal-others as they remind us of our animality and the reality of our political relations with the larger animal world—that is, their current position as Other in our
(and their) world. The meat industry is one obvious example. As Achille Mbembe asks in
"Necropolitics": "Is the notion of biopower sufficient to account for the contemporary ways
in which the political, under the guise of war, of resistance, or of the fight against terror,
makes the murder of the enemy its primary and absolute objective?" (12). Though Mbembe
here writes about human bodies, he might just as well be writing about other animal bodies
too—as Derrida argues in *The Animal*, we have been waging war on "animot" for generations, a "violence, which some would compare to the worst cases of [human] genocide. In
fact, Mbembe's rationale for the idea of necropolitics seems a perfect description of the
meat industry: because "biopower" does not adequately explain "contemporary forms of
subjugation of life to the power of death…I have put forward the notion of necropolitics
and necropower to account for…the creation of *death-worlds*, new and unique forms of
social existence in which vast populations are subjected to conditions of life conferring
upon them the status of *living dead*" (39–40).

9. Animal studies does not yet seem to have processed the idea of nonhuman cultures, nor
has ecocriticism, though an interest in biological research is rapidly growing. Glen Love's
Practical Ecocriticism, published in 2003, sought "to help initiate, on the ground level, a more
biologically informed ecocritical dialogue about literature and its relationship to nature and
to environmental concerns" (11). Love goes to stress that "Biological evolution and cultural
evolution are not independent but interrelated; hence such scientists' descriptions of the
process as "coevolutionary" or "biocultural" " (19). Though Love doesn't discuss nonhuman
cultures he does note that the "traditional reluctance of many scientists and philosophers
to attribute consciousness to animals must be questioned in the face of new evidence" (33).
More recently, in "Eluding Capture: The Science, Culture, and Pleasure of 'Queer' Animals,"
Stacy Alaimo wrote, "Nonhuman animals are also cultural creatures, with their own sometimes complex systems of (often nonreproductive) sex…. Rather than continuing to pose
nature/culture dualisms that closet queer animals as well as animal cultures…we can think
of queer desire as part of an emergent universe of a multitude of naturecultures" (57–60).

10. There are skeptics, chief among them psychologist Bennett G. Galef, co-editor with Kevin
N. Laland of the recent volume, *The Question of Animal Culture* (discussed later in this
chapter).

11. "Researchers documented 22 cases of chimps fashioning tools to jab at smaller primates
sheltering in cavities of hollow branches or tree trunks. The report's authors, Jill Pruetz and
Paco Bertolani, said the finding could have implications for human evolution. Chimps had
not been previously observed hunting other animals with tools" (BBC).

12. For example, see "Culture in whales and dolphins," by Luke Rendell and Hal Whitehead
in *Behavioral and Brain Sciences*, and Whitehead's *Sperm Whales: Social Evolution in the
Ocean*. On fish and birds, see Kevin N. Laland and William Hoppitt's "Do Animals Have
Culture?" in *Evolutionary Anthropology*. While they take issue with the famous example
of the potato-washing macaques, they do claim that some birds, whales, and fish have
culture: "Cultures are those group-typical behavior patterns shared by members of a community that rely on socially learned and transmitted information…. According to the

preceding definition, which animals have culture? There are two kinds of answers to this question. The first kind is based exclusively on hard experimental evidence. That is, for which species do we have reliable scientific evidence of natural communities that share group-typical behavior patterns that are dependent on socially learned and transmitted information? The answer, which will surprise many, is humans plus a handful of species of birds, one or two whales, and two species of fish" (150–151). Also, see the recent issue *Culture Evolves* (edited by Andrew Whiten, Robert A. Hinde, Christopher B. Stringer, and Kevin N. Laland.), and John M. Marzluff and Tony Angell's *In the Company of Crows and Ravens*, which includes "a detailed look at the cultural life of crows, exploring their behavior and traditions and our influences on them." Excerpt available online at http://yalepress. yale.edu/yupbooks/excerpts/crows_and_ravens.asp.

13. Even Animal Planet network has a webpage on animal culture. Here is a sample from their five-page overview, available online at http://animals.howstuffworks.com/animal-facts/ animal-culture-info.htm: "Primates are not the only animals in which scientists have discovered evidence of cultural transmission of behavior. Researchers believe the best nonprimate evidence for culture is found in songbirds, which include thrushes, jays, wrens, warblers, finches, and other common backyard birds. Many studies have indicated that songbirds learn their melodies from parents and neighbors of the same species. Songs within a particular species show regional variations similar to the regional dialects (variant forms of speech) common in human populations.... [B]iologists think of the songs as culture because they represent behaviors that are transmitted through learning and imitation rather than being genetically determined."

14. Imanishi concluded that the advantage to washing potatoes is the wear it saves on teeth. While Satsue Mito first observed and reported this behavior, Imanishi interpreted the behavior and his team conducted the formal research confirming social transmission.

15. See Sara Shettleworth's *Cognition, Evolution, and Behavior* for a skeptical reading of this famous evidence. Also, see Galef's well-known 1990 article, "The Question of Animal Culture" in *Human Nature*. De Waal discusses Galef's argument in *The Ape and the Sushi Master*: "Galef questioned whether the spreading of potato washing had anything to do with imitation. The Canadian psychologist was right to take a close look at the evidence and to insist that scientists carefully weigh the options when they see a behavior spreading in a population.... But given Galef's valid warning, it was all the more disturbing that he himself made so little effort to verify his own assumptions, for example, by actually visiting the island in person" (207).

16. Potato washing, however, is not the only example of socially learned behavior on Koshima Island. "In 1956, she [Imo] introduced a solution to the problem that wheat thrown on to the beach mingles with sand. Imo learned to separate the two by carrying handfuls of the mixture to nearby water, and throwing it into it. Sand sinks faster than wheat, making for easy picking. This sluicing technique, too, was eventually adopted by most monkeys on the island" (de Waal 202).

17. De Waal notes that this term was first proposed by Imanishi in 1950 (381).

18. However historically, of course, it was just this view of culture often used to deny the existence of culture in various human groups.

19. For example, see work by Cynthia Moss, including "African Elephants Show High Levels of Interest in the Skulls and Ivory of Their Own Species" in *Biology Letters* and *Elephant Memories*. Also, see Marc Bekoff's *The Emotional Lives of Animals*. Finally, see Derrida's comment on this phenomenon in *The Animal That Therefore I Am*.

20. Even among social scientists definitions vary significantly; in 1952, A. L. Kroeber and C. Kluckholm published an article citing 164 different definitions of culture held by social scientists.

21. The emergent field of nonhuman social studies includes primatology, behavioral ecology, evolutionary biology, ethology, comparative psychology, and (to a lesser extent) anthropology.

22. In 1975, E. O. Wilson's *Sociobiology: the New Synthesis* applied Darwinian principles to human behavior. Wilson coined the term sociobiology, and from this discipline grew other evolutionary approaches to behavior: behavioral ecology, evolutionary psychology, and gene-culture co-evolution. For an explanation of the differences between these fields, see Laland and Brown's *Sense and Nonsense*.

23. As Marc Bekoff writes, "I know no practicing researcher who doesn't attribute emotions to their companion animals—who doesn't freely anthropomorphize—at home or at cocktail parties, regardless of what they do at work. (This anthropomorphizing is nothing to be ashamed of, by the way;…these scientists are simply doing what comes naturally. Anthropomorphizing is an evolved perceptual strategy; we've been shaped by natural selection to view animals in this way.)" (10). Just as our survival depends on the survival of a great many other creatures, it seems reasonable to assume this evolved capacity of anthropomorphism, and the biophilia it engenders, is necessary for human (and other animal) survival. Bekoff argues, "If we don't anthropomorphize, we lose important information…. it is a necessity, but it also must be done carefully, consciously, empathetically, and biocentrically. We must make every attempt to maintain the animal's point of view" (124–125).

24. Eileen Crist refers to this as "mechanomorphism." See *Images of Animals: Anthropomorphism and the Animal Mind*.

25. In "An Ape Among Many: Animal Co-Authorship and Trans-species Epistemic Authority," Bradshaw writes that science has traditionally excluded nonhuman animals from the creation of knowledge and its application to their lives, even in environmental policy. There is new science, however, which includes other species in the project of human knowledge, challenging old epistemological assumptions about other animals. Bradshaw discusses languaged ape and human participatory action research (PAR) at the Great Ape Trust as one example of trans-species science, work which contradicts the idea that language and knowledge are properties unique to humans.

26. For just one example, see Richard Levins and Richard Lewontin's otherwise intelligent *The Dialectical Biologist*, in which they dismiss Wilson as wholly reductive: "A recent avatar [of vulgar reductionism] is Wilson's (1978) claim that a scientific materialist explanation of human society and culture must be in terms of human genetic evolution and the Darwinian fitness of individuals" (134).

27. Or, "culture is created and shaped by biological processes while the biological processes are simultaneously altered in response to cultural change" (Wilson 111).

Works Cited

Badmington, Neil. "Theorizing Posthumanism." *Cultural Critique* 53 (2003): 10–27.
Bekoff, Marc. *The Emotional Lives of Animals*. Novato, CA: New World Library, 2007.

Bradshaw, Gay, A. N. Schore, J. L. Brown, J. H. Poole, and C. J. Moss. "Elephant breakdown." *Nature* 433 (2005): 807.

Bradshaw, Gay. *Elephants on the Edge: What Animals Teach Us about Humanity*. New Haven and London: Yale UP, 2009.

Bradshaw, Gay. "An Ape Among Many: Animal Co-Authorship and Trans-species Epistemic Authority." *Configurations* 18.1–2 (Winter 2010): 15–30.

Bradshaw, Gay. Email to Helena Feder. 20 July 2011.

"Chimpanzees 'hunt using spears.' " *BBC/Science/Nature*. 22 February 2007. <http://news.bbc.co.uk/2/hi/science/nature/6387611.stm>

Crist, Eileen. *Images of Animals: Anthropomorphism and the Animal Mind*. Philadelphia: Temple, 1999.

de Waal, Frans. *The Ape and the Sushi Master: Cultural Reflections by a Primatologist*. New York: Basic Books, 2001.

———. and Kristin E. Bonnie. "In Tune with Others: The Social Side of Primate Culture." *The Question of Animal Culture*. Ed. Laland, Kevin N. and Bennett G. Galef. Cambridge and London: Harvard UP, 2009. 19–40.

Fragaszy, Dorothy M. and Susan Perry. *The Biology of Traditions: Models and Evidence*. Cambridge: Cambridge UP, 2003.

Freud, Sigmund. *Civilization and its Discontents*. Trans. James Strachey. New York and London: Norton, 1930, 1961.

Fukuyama, Francis. *Our Posthuman Future: Consequences of the Biotechnology Revolution*. New York: Farrar, Straus, Giroux, 2002.

Galef, Bennett. "The question of animal culture." *Human Nature* 3.2 (1992): 157–178.

Glotfelty, Cheryll. Introduction. *The Ecocriticism Reader*. Athens: Georgia UP, 1996.

Hayles, N. Katherine. *How We Became Posthuman: Virtual Bodies in Cybernetics, Literature, and Informatics*. Chicago and London: U of Chicago P, 1999.

Laland, Kevin N. and Bennett G. Galef, ed. *The Question of Animal Culture*. Cambridge, MA, and London: Harvard UP, 2009.

———and Gillian R. Brown. *Sense and Nonsense: Evolutionary Perspectives on Human Behavior*. Oxford: Oxford UP, 2002.

———. and William Hoppitt's "Do Animals Have Culture?" *Evolutionary Anthropology*. 12.3 (2003): 150–159.

Lawrence, D. H. *Phoenix*. Harmondsworth: Penguin, 1985.

Levins, Richard and Richard Lewontin. *The Dialectical Biologist*. Cambridge, MA, and London: Harvard UP, 1985.

Love, Glen A. *Practical Ecocriticism: Literature, Biology, and the Environment*. Richmond: U of Virginia P, 2003.

Marzluff, John M. and Tony Angell. *In the Company of Crows and Ravens*. New Haven and London: Yale UP, 2005.

Mbembe, Achille. "Necropolitics." *Public Culture* 15.1 (2003): 11–40.

McGrew, W. C. "Ten Dispatches from the Chimpanzee Culture Wars, plus Postscript (Revisiting the Battlefronts)." *The Question of Animal Culture*. Ed. Laland, Kevin N. and Bennett G. Galef. Cambridge and London: Harvard UP, 2009. 41–69.

Moss, Cynthia. *Elephant Memories: Thirteen Years in the Life of an Elephant Family*. Chicago and London: Chicago UP, 2000.

Nixon, Rob. *Slow Violence and the Environmentalism of the Poor*. Cambridge, MA, and London: Harvard UP, 2011.

Plumwood, Val. *Environmental Culture*. London and New York: Routledge, 2002.

Rancière, Jacques. "A few remarks on the method of Jacques Rancière." *Parallax* 15.3 (2009): 114–123.

Rendell, Luke and Hal Whitehead. "Culture in whales and dolphins." *Behavioral and Brain Sciences* 24 (2001): 309–382.

Sample, Ian. "Craig Venter creates synthetic life form." *Guardian* 20 May 2010. <http://www.guardian.co.uk/science/2010/may/20/craig-venter-synthetic-life-form>

———. "Synthetic life breakthrough could be worth over a trillion dollars" *Guardian* 20 May 2010. <http://www.guardian.co.uk/science/2010/may/20/craig-venter-synthetic-life-genome>

Siebert, Charles. "An Elephant Crackup?" *New York Times Magazine*. 8 October 2006. http://www.nytimes.com/2006/10/08/magazine/08elephant.html?pagewanted=all&_r=0. Accessed August 10 2013.

Simon, Bart. "Introduction: Toward a Critique of Posthuman Futures." *Cultural Critique* 53 (2003): 1–9.

van Schaik, Carel. *Among Orangutans: Red Apes and the Rise of Human Culture*. Cambridge and London: Belknap, 2006

Whitehead, Hal. *Sperm Whales:Social Evolution in the Ocean*. Chicago and London: Chicago UP, 2003.

Whiten, Andrew, Jane Goodall, William C. McGrew, Toshisada Nishida, Vernon Reynolds, Yukimaru Sugiyama, Caroline E. G. Tutin, Richard W. Wrangham and Cristophe Boesch "Cultures in Chimpanzees." *Nature* 399 (1999): 682–685.

Williams, Raymond. *Keywords*. Oxford: Oxford UP, 1976, 1985.

Wilson, Edward O. *In Search of Nature*. Washington D. C.: Island, 1996.

———. *Sociobiology: the New Synthesis. 25th Anniversary Ed*. Cambridge and London: Harvard UP, 2000.

Wolfe, Cary. *What Is Posthumanism?* Minneapolis and London: U of Minnesota P, 2010.

CHAPTER 13

···

FERALITY TALES

···

GREG GARRARD

ONE of the most exciting things that occurred in my thirteenth year was that I acquired a Sinclair ZX Spectrum computer. To a young geek, its powers were awesome: eight colors, a keyboard with rubbery little keys, and, in the deluxe version, 48 kilobytes of memory. Programs had to be loaded from cassette tapes, which could take up to half an hour. The computer I'm using right now has 43,690 times as much memory, stores much of its information on an Internet server somewhere else for instant access and can display more colours than humans can discriminate. Similar, if less dramatic, stories could be told of medicine, astronomical observation, materials engineering, and a plethora of other fields of enquiry. The advancement of technological and scientific learning is real and cumulative, and is—apocalypse aside—impossible to reverse. Ecological modernization is an increasingly important objective of scientific progress, as well as arguably the only viable way forward for environmentalism.

Moral and political progress is also real. Gender, racial, and sexual equality; disability rights; and increased attention to animal welfare are all important forms of liberal moral improvement, but unless they are entrenched in political constitutions, they are not cumulative and seem far more easily undone by ideological changes. The reason is that the human animals supposedly running the show are as fallible and contradictory as they have always been, which imposes important limits on our moral responses, as psychologist Daniel Gilbert has argued in an article memorably titled "If Only Gay Sex Caused Global Warming":

> Although all human societies have moral rules about food and sex, none has a moral rule about atmospheric chemistry. And so we are outraged about every breach of protocol except Kyoto. Yes, global warming is bad, but it doesn't make us feel nauseated or angry or disgraced, and thus we don't feel compelled to rail against it as we do against other momentous threats to our species, such as flag burning. The fact is that if climate change were caused by gay sex, or by the practice of eating kittens, millions of protesters would be massing in the streets. (Gilbert)

Whereas scientific knowledge begets more knowledge so long as the global research base exists and continues to communicate, moral wisdom has to be learned, painfully and unreliably, by every generation afresh.[1]

Does art belong with science, or with morality? Politicised forms of literary criticism—Marxism, feminism, ecocriticism—have seen themselves as progressive, but they seem not to have been accompanied by sustained and cumulative literary movements. Art changes, perhaps even develops, but does not progress. If Ian McEwan's *Atonement* is a better novel than *Crime and Punishment* or *Nineteen Eighty-Four*, it is not because it is more recent. Partly this is because the occurrence of novels and poems is *singular*, in the sense articulated by Derek Attridge. Literary works are non-commensurable, their authority and inventiveness attributed, unlike a valid scientific experiment, to a specific individual or group. Indeed, the word "experimental" has precisely opposed meanings in the arts and the sciences: as Attridge points out, "The very term 'experiment' paradoxically combines the notions of a controlled, repeatable physical process and the unrepeatable trying-out of new procedures" (Attridge loc. 547). Partly it is because literature responds far more avidly to the relative stability of humans' natures (the term I prefer to "human nature") than to technological and even broader historical changes. Even so, I want to argue that literature and literary criticism can contribute to scientific progress, provided we conceive of it more generously than we have heretofore. The potential for such interdisciplinary progress is most obvious in the two fields of the humanities most closely allied to the natural sciences: ecocriticism and animal studies.

According to biologist E. O. Wilson, "The greatest enterprise of the mind has always been and always will be the attempted linkage of the sciences and humanities" (6), a project he calls "consilience." It is an immense and progressive ambition for research across the academic disciplines, yet his version of it insists on locating physics at the head of a rigid hierarchy of coordinated scientific explanation. Only if they submit to the authority of the natural sciences will the humanities be permitted to contribute to human and biospheric welfare and the advancement of knowledge. "Ferality Tales" is inspired by Wilson's hopes, but seeks to show that the various epistemic frameworks of the disciplines can and should collaborate successfully on more or less equal terms. As Stephen Rose says, "Our world may be—is, I would claim—an ontological unity, but to understand it we need the epistemological diversity that ... different levels of explanation offer" (95).

Ferality, the condition of existing in between domestication and wildness, is an ideal test case for three reasons: it is a key point of dispute between environmental ethics and animal rights; it is a subject on which scientific perspectives have changed dramatically in recent years; and it has inspired some superb fictions over the course of the twentieth and early twenty-first centuries. We will therefore be locating ferality by *triangulating* from animal studies and ecocriticism, ethology and evolutionary ecology, and literary fiction, using the insights (and perhaps lacunae) of each to produce a multifaceted, interdisciplinary projection of this concept.[2]

FERALITY: BETWEEN ANIMAL STUDIES
AND ECOCRITICISM

Linnaeus's epochal taxonomy *Systema Naturae* (1735 first edition) boldly classified humans among the human-like apes, causing both theological and scientific dismay. Writing to a colleague, Linnaeus responded: "It is unacceptable because man has been categorised among the *Anthropomorpha*, but man knows himself" (148). It seems, indeed, that self-knowledge is what defines this species—if anything does. Pursuing this strange basis for categorization, Giorgio Agamben comments that Linnaeus

> does not record—as he does with the other species—any specific identifying characteristic next to the generic name *Homo*, only the old philosophical adage: *nosce te ipsum* [know yourself]. Even in the tenth edition, when the complete denomination becomes *Homo sapiens*, all evidence suggests that the new epithet does not represent a description, but that it is only a simplification of that adage, which, moreover, maintains its position next to the term *Homo*. It is worth reflecting on this taxonomic anomaly, which assigns not a given, but rather an imperative as a specific difference. (loc. 255)

But if *Sapiens* alludes not descriptively to the wisdom of our kind (how could it, indeed), but to the faculty required to recognise ourselves at all, "*Homo sapiens*," argues Agamben, "is neither a clearly defined species nor a substance; it is, rather, a machine or device for producing the recognition of the human" (loc. 268–69). To shape ourselves *to* ourselves we need animals, because man is "a constitutively 'anthropomorphous' animal (that is, 'resembling man,' according to the term that Linnaeus constantly uses until the tenth edition of the Systema), who must recognize himself in a non-man in order to be human" (loc. 272).

Located at—or even *as*—the species boundary is, Agamben says, the feral man, which Linnaeus categorizes as a biological variant of our species, *Homo ferus*. To Agamben, "the *enfants sauvages*, who appear more and more often on the edges of the villages of Europe, are the messengers of man's inhumanity, the witnesses to his fragile identity and his lack of a face of his own" (loc. 295). Although the feral man is *recognized as human*, he or it "seems to belie the characteristics of the most noble of the primates point for point: it is *tetrapus* (walks on all fours), *mutus* (without language), and *hirsutus* (covered with hair)" (loc. 292). Just on the other side of that imaginary boundary is the animal, through whose difference and inferiority *Homo sapiens* habitually defines himself, as if gazing into a kind of weird anti-mirror. And if the domestic animal is the one who affirms our power and sovereignty most unambiguously, perhaps the feral animal is the one who, like the feral man, refuses to face us, and in doing so, frustrates our preening self-identification.

Such seems to be the view of animal studies critic Philip Armstrong, for whom "ferity" (as he calls it) is a subversive energy of quite stunning breadth and force. The autonomous agency of animals it embodies "provided a means to disrupt the instrumentalist paradigm that united Cartesian philosophy, new scientific practice, capitalist economics, and colonial domination over populations and terrains" (38). The enduring Freudian commitments of cultural studies, from which animal studies largely derives, are evident in his assertion that, "As the history of modernity shows ... the attempt to eradicate, regulate, commodify or otherwise manipulate wildness tends to result in ferity—the return of wildness, or an escape back to it, or its redirection into unexpected modes" (189). In truth, though, if the return of the repressed is bad psychology, the return of the wild is even worse ecology; much of the time when industrial modernity seeks to eradicate wildness, it simply succeeds. The key point, though, is that an animal studies perspective that has inherited a preoccupation with transgression will no doubt be inclined to *celebrate* the feral animal along with Armstrong. Domestication will be read as perhaps the earliest form of oppressive "bio-power," which seeks to minimize or eliminate animal agency altogether.

Armstrong is not the only advocate of ferality as a subversive force. Another writer from the Southern hemisphere, Adrian Franklin, indicts environmentalist concern about feral animals as a form of nationalism, insisting that

> ...the species-cleansing of outsider categories of animal based on the logic and demands of ecology reinforces the solidarity of human nationalism. Nationalism has always thrived on the rhetorical advantages of ecology. Ecology not only deals with communities that are tied to specific territories but gives them an unswerving sense of order ordained by nature itself. (17)

In truth, many forms of nationalism (most notably American Republicanism since the 1980s) are hostile to environmentalism, and the few opportunistic alliances that have existed, as between the German Nazis and conservationists, have proven both superficial and transient.[3] Franklin's characterization of "ecology" as a rigidly territorializing discourse also seems unencumbered by any detailed knowledge of it as a science: he supports his argument with highly selective, tendentiously interpreted examples of popular environmentalism rather than references to scientific papers. While Franklin is right to suggest that, practically and perhaps morally, feral animals cannot be exterminated from Australia, he provides inadequate evidence for the claim that "Feral animal control does not follow from the science of land and nature but from moral, cultural, ethical and political discourses" (177). In Franklin's account, the acceptance of feral animals by Aboriginals legitimizes their presence as part of a jolly "hybrid" mix, and biodiversity (which he claims is enhanced, not destroyed, by feral animals) is celebrated by means of a lazy and unexamined analogy with cultural diversity.

The question is particularly pointed in Australia, which is plagued by feral and invasive exotic species, but which was also the birthplace of modern animal rights. As Peter Singer observes of the ethics and language of "pest control":

> The farmer will seek to kill off the "pests" by the cheapest method available. This is likely to be poison. The animals will eat poisoned baits, and die a slow, painful death.

No consideration at all is given to the interests of the "pests"—the very word "pest" seems to exclude any concern for the animals themselves. But the classification "pest" is our own, and a rabbit that is a pest is as capable of suffering, and as deserving of consideration, as a white rabbit who is a beloved companion animal. (233)

In practice, animal advocates have campaigned vociferously, and sometimes successfully, against extirpation campaigns directed against feral and invasive animals. For instance, when Italian wildlife authorities sought to assess the impact of introduced grey squirrels in 1997 as a prelude to the introduction of control measures, animal rights advocates took them to court. By the time the legal process found in favour of the conservationists three years later, the squirrel population was too big to eliminate. Thus Dan and Gad Perry's assessment laments that "The responses of [wildlife] managers and animal rights proponents to environmental issues remain mostly diametrically opposite, leading to ongoing friction" (Perry and Perry 31). Having said that, Perry and Perry also give an example of successful compromise over lethal control of feral pigs in Texas, and major organizations such as PETA in the United States and the RSPCA in the United Kingdom and Australia support humane population control.[4]

On the other side of the argument, passions also run high. In the early work of "land ethic" proponent J. Baird Callicott, domestication seems to have an almost mystical power to denature animals:

Domestic animals are creations of man. They are living artefacts, but artefacts nevertheless.... There is thus something profoundly incoherent ... in the complaint of some animal liberationists that the "natural behaviour" of chickens and male calves is cruelly frustrated on factory farms. It would make almost as much sense to speak of the natural behaviour of tables and chairs. (50)

Because domestic animals have been "bred to docility, tractability, stupidity, and dependency," he claims, "It is literally meaningless to suggest that they be liberated" (51). It is significant that he does not include dogs in his list of denatured animals, as his demeaning list of traits would not comfortably encompass Rottweilers (docile?), Jack Russell terriers (tractable?) and Border Collies (stupid?). Released feral animals, claims Callicott, reveal the truth of the situation: they either die, confirming their enfeebled vulnerability, or—like feral mustangs—they survive, "begin to recover some of their remote wild ancestral genetic traits and become smaller, leaner, heartier, and smarter versions of their former selves" (51).

It is not hard to see why Callicott's uncompromising land ethic, which subordinates all individual rights—human and animal—to the supraorganismic interests he vests in the ecosystem, was chastized by Tom Regan as "environmental fascism" (Regan 362). On the other hand, Callicott's ire is understandable given the immense destructive capability of feral animals, which is well known to environmentalists and conservation biologists. Perhaps the worst example is the rabbit, introduced to Australia as a game animal by a farmer in 1859. So rapid was their spread across the country that, as Clive Ponting reports, "in the mid-1880s 1.8 million rabbits were killed in Victoria and nearly 7 million in New South Wales without perceptibly slowing up their relentless spread" (171). Before the introduction of myxomatosis the rabbit population was as high as ten billion, leading to profound ecological changes in the Australian Outback. Feral cats have been held responsible for the extinction of several insular species of bird (including the famous Stephens Island wren, supposedly killed off by the lighthouse keeper's cat) and are considered another imported scourge of Australia's native wildlife, along with feral camels and horses (or "brumbies"). Dogs have not had such bad press, although Robert Whittaker notes that "Domestic dogs can also be devastating, and feral populations have been responsible for the local extinction of land iguanas in the Galápagos" (231).

In this, as in so many matters ecological, generalizations are risky: the impact of ferality depends on the particular species and the habitat into which it escapes. The singularity of literary landscapes is such that I cannot "control" for (fictional) habitat—although it is worth noting all three of my texts are situated in cold northern climes—and so I propose to limit the variables by focusing on a single species: *Canis familiaris*, or the domesticated dog.

FERALITY: BETWEEN ETHOLOGY AND EVOLUTIONARY ECOLOGY

Just as "human" depends, as we have seen, on "animal" for its meaning, "feral" depends on "domestic" and "wild." Until the 1980s, a view prevailed, in both popular and scientific accounts of domestication, that S. K. Robisch has dubbed "the campfire myth," in which the ancestors of modern dogs were irresistibly attracted to the warmth and smell of roasting meat of cavemen's campfires and were tamed first by familiarity and later by deliberate selection. How flattering a story it is to us is evident from Jack London's *White Fang*, which tells the story of a wolf cub that accepts domestication, effectively recapitulating speculative phylogeny as fictional ontogeny.[5] White Fang's mother, Kiche, is half dog and half wolf, an ancestry that presumably accounts for her reaction to the proximity of an Indian encampment:

> A new wistfulness was in her face, but it was not the wistfulness of hunger. She was thrilling to a desire that urged her to go forward, to be in closer to that fire, to be squabbling with the dogs, and to be avoiding and dodging the stumbling feet of men. (loc. 1671)

To the wolf-dog—even so powerful a one as White Fang—acceptance of the domination of man is akin to spiritual revelation, but more firmly grounded in the facts of life:

> No effort of faith is necessary to believe in such a god; no effort of will can possibly induce disbelief in such a god. There is no getting away from it. There it stands, on its two hind-legs, club in hand, immensely potential, passionate and wrathful and

loving, god and mystery and power wrapped up and around by flesh that bleeds when it is torn and that is good to eat like any flesh. (loc. 2261)

London promotes us to a peculiar sort of divine condition: weak, edible creatures made by evolution to transcend, and ultimately to direct, evolution. He certainly intended the privileged rank of the dog as man's lieutenant to remain undemeaned, but given the tool-centred construction of prehistory that dominated twentieth-century culture—with its ages of Stone and Bronze and Iron—it was only a couple of short hops from good soldier to fine instrument, and thence to Callicott's stupid artefact. Donna Haraway passes scathing judgment on such narratives:

> Dogs are said to be the first domestic animals, displacing pigs for primal honours. Humanist technophiliacs depict domestication as the paradigmatic act of masculine, single-parent, self-birthing, whereby man makes himself repetitively as he invents (creates) his tools. The domestic animal is the epoch-making tool, realizing human intention in the flesh, in a dogsbody version of onanism. Man took the (free) wolf and made the (servant) dog and so made civilization possible. Mongrelized Hegel and Freud in the kennel? Let the dog stand for all domestic plant and animal species, subjected to human intent in stories of escalating progress or destruction, according to taste. (28)

The campfire myth is anthropocentric twice over: once because it assumes that domestication is something (good or bad) *we did to wolves*, and again because it neglects the examples of domestication that do not involve humans at all.

Ants of several different species, for example, have domesticated fungi that provide the nest with food by digesting plant material. Their careful maintenance of the right temperature and humidity for the fungi leads evolutionary biologist Darcy Morey to describe the ants' work as "complex agriculture" (61). Regarding human's domestication of plants, Michael Pollan counter-intuitively sets out in *The Botany of Desire* to understand the qualities in plants that attracted—even seduced—humans, more or less unconsciously, to domesticate them. "We automatically think of domestication as something we do to other species," he says, "but it makes just as much sense to think of it as something certain plants and animals have done to us, a clever evolutionary strategy for advancing their own interests" (xvi). Given that there are roughly 100–200000 wolves in the world, and as many as half a billion dogs, the evolutionary gamble of domestication seems to have paid off for the ancestors of dogs.

The new scientific consensus is, according to Ádám Miklósi, that "the natural environment of the dog is that ecological niche which has been created by humans" (10), and that it was the palaeolithic midden, not the fireside, that was most likely to have been the primal scene of domestication. More remarkably, the scientific evidence suggests that "not only have convergent processes made dogs fit for the anthropogenic environment, but also that dog and human behaviour actually share some important features" (237). Even though the underlying causal pathways are probably different due to our lack of close evolutionary ancestry, dogs have, for example, converged with human children to some degree in terms of their attachment behaviors. Like children, but unlike chimpanzees and socialised wolves, dogs pay careful attention to the gaze and gestures of adult humans, and respond to their referential aspects. Perhaps most endearingly, Miklósi found that, whereas socialised wolves carried on worrying indefinitely at a frustrating puzzle task, "after a few attempts most dogs stopped trying and looked at their owner who was standing behind them" (179).[6] David Paxton purports to show that, so intimate has dog–human co-evolution been, that *our* brains have changed so as to enhance our complementary capacities. In short, we do some of their thinking for them, while they do most of our smelling for us, while together "we and dogs make up a composite animal that has the ability to speak" (loc. 179). Although sceptical of Paxton's claims, Donna Haraway prefers such "remodeled versions [of evolution] that give dogs (and other species) the first moves in domestication and then choreograph an unending dance of distributed and heterogenous agencies." (28) In evolutionary terms, domestication is not subjugation, but rather a specialized form of symbiosis. Like all intimate relationships (and in contrast to the fuzzy, feel-good notion of symbiosis prevalent in popular ecological discourse), domestication includes the potential for anguish, cruelty, and incomprehension on both sides, as well as joy, love, and mutual benefits. We have eaten dogs, at times, and they have eaten us. But, as the Australian Aboriginal saying has it, it *is* dogs that make us human.

The situation of feral dogs is therefore, in reality, mainly sad, rather than excitingly liberated or subversive as Armstrong's analysis would lead us to expect. Luigi Boitani, a leading expert on "free-living" dogs of all kinds, estimated in 1995 that there were around 800,000 feral dogs in Italy, a number that could only be sustained by a regular influx of abandoned animals given the extremely high mortality rate of their litters. The low chances of survival of feral puppies seem to be made worse by the minimal or non-existent paternal care dogs exhibit, as contrasted with wolves,[7] and their seeming lack of the pack organization typical of other canids. Although it may be unwise to generalize since all observers note the genetic diversity of feral dogs and the wide variety of ecological factors they encounter (Boitani et al.), it would seem that feral dogs literally cannot live without us.

Crucially, for our purposes, Miklósi insists that "Adult socialized offspring from feral dogs should be indistinguishable from other dogs living in human families. Note that in this sense feralization is the opposite process to socialization and not to domestication, which was often implied in earlier writings" (86). Given this shift in the understanding of dogs' natures, we might expect to encounter two typical manifestations of ferality in fiction: as an *existential condition* midway between more-or-less reified notions of domesticity and wildness, reflecting the old anthropocentric consensus; and the representation of ferality as a *developmental vicissitude* befalling our most intimate symbiont. Anthropomorphism is less of a problem than lupomorphism in these ferality tales: the dog seems inherently (and surprisingly) resistant to disnification, but is at considerable risk of departing domesticity only to arrive at ferality as, effectively, a wolf. As we have seen, anthropomorphic representations are better supported on scientific grounds than lupomorphic ones.

THE CALL OF THE WILD

Our first ferality tale is also by far the most famous. The author of *The Call of the Wild* (1903), Jack London, was flattered by dozens of imitators, although as S. K. Robisch points out, he "may have been easy to copy, but he was hard to match" because "no matter how many writers revived [his] characters, they would always belong to London, who before he invented them met their real counterparts in the world" (294). London was sensitive both to contemporary scientific thinking about wolves and dogs, and astutely observant of the human–canid moral and material economy of the Klondike Gold Rush. For example, say Raymond Coppinger and Richard Schneider, "London was right in making 'Buck' a cross between a Saint Bernard and Scottish sheepdog, stolen in one of the lower 48 states. Buck and his fellow captives were dog derivatives, not wolf derivatives" (Coppinger and Schneider 26). Contemporary photographs show a mishmash of mongrels in the traces, by contrast with the uniformity of present day Alaskan huskies.[8] At the same time, though, *The Call of the Wild* is also shaped by London's seriously complex ideological commitments, which led him, as Robisch observes, to attempt "to synthesize no less than Darwinism, atavism, early Marxist socialism, the Nietzschean concept of the over-man, and the tricky relationship between deterministic naturalism and survivalist self-reliance" (290). As a result, he over-emphasizes the importance of dominance hierarchies among sledding dogs, thrilling bloodthirsty readers with Buck's campaign to oust the lead dog Spitz. As the old leader disappears beneath a mass of murderous dogs, Buck looks on, "the successful champion, the dominant primordial beast who had made his kill and found it good" (loc. 474). The victory is the logical conclusion of Buck's brutal re-education from the effete "morality" of his comfortable California upbringing to the "primitive law" that prevails in the howling North, via a man in a red sweater in Seattle who sets him on the path from "dog" back to "wolf" by bludgeoning him with a hatchet.

According to London's half-mournful, half-thrilled Spencerian Darwinism, "wild" and "civilized"—and their canid symbols, "wolf" and "dog" too—are existential conditions at least as much as they are biological ones. So when Buck experiences "species memory" erupting from his unconscious being, we are to perceive ancient necessities awoken by strange, modern contingencies like the Gold Rush: "The domesticated generations fell from him. In vague ways he remembered back to the youth of the breed, to the time the wild dogs ranged in packs through the primeval forest and killed their meat as they ran it down." (loc. 275). Dim memories of the Californian "Sunland" are brushed aside by inherited recollections of lying by campfires beside his prognathous and brachiating caveman master. Even then, the atavistic inner wolf struggles to dominate the loyal dog Buck who takes pride in his strength and skill in the traces, much like the faithful "Dave" who demands to die in them.

The inner conflict reaches its climax when John Thornton rescues Buck from the cruel, "callow" greenhorns Hal and Charles. Their deserved demise begets a contest of civilising "love" and "wild," wolfish wiles in the dog, a contest sharpened by the "blood longing" aroused in him by hearing a chorus of wolves: "in spite of this great love he bore John Thornton, which seemed to bespeak the soft civilizing influence, the strain of the primitive, which the Northland had aroused in him, remained alive and active" (loc. 832). Ultimately, though, long days convalescing at his master's feet are outweighed by the thrill of a *four day* lone pursuit of a bull moose—perhaps the most extreme "tall tale of the Klondike" in the novel. Ferality makes Buck the perfect predator, supposedly combining the ancient instincts of the wolf with the enhanced intelligence bred by man. Having taken bloody revenge on the Yeehat Indians for their murder of Thornton, he haunts the remote woods of the Northland, prompting Robisch's comment that "If Buck is an Evil Spirit, then turning feral means going bad.... In the climax of *The Call of the Wild* Buck's conversion to 'evil' reaches beyond the bestial state even while the bestial state is valorized as pure" (317). London's ambivalence may extend still further, however, as Buck is "evil" specifically towards humans who are represented as savage themselves. Evil cancels out evil, but does not make him good; rather, Buck's feral power makes him an *Uberhund*, beyond good and evil, a potent denizen of London's intensely moralized domain of "wild" amorality. As the novel ends, the transformation from anthropomorphized focalizer to lupomorphic enigma remains uncompleted: the unnamed "Ghost Dog" who rips the throats of the Yeehats also returns annually to mourn John Thornton, and his forsaken domesticity.

"As Birds Bring Forth the Sun"

Our second case is the eponymous story from Canadian writer Alistair Macleod's collection *As Birds Bring Forth the Sunand Other Stories* (1986). As with so many of Macleod's flinty stories, it is set in the rugged and unforgiving environment of Cape Breton, Nova Scotia, where men struggle daily to make a living. The legendary quality of "As Birds Bring Forth the Sun" is enhanced by the careful balance of scepticism and respect maintained by the narrator, the contemporary great-great-great-grandson of a man who rescues an injured puppy from under the wheels of a cart and nurses it by hand back to health. The immense dog she grows into is devoted to her savior. Even so, "She was never given a name but was referred to in Gaelic as *cù mòr glas*, the big grey dog" (loc. 1809). When she is in heat, the man finds a dog nearly big enough to mount her, then takes them both to the seashore where there is a hollow she can stand in to mate. The sturdy roughness of the man only emphasizes the intimacy of the scene: "He was a man used to working with the breeding of animals, with the guiding of rams and bulls and stallions and often with the funky smell of animal semen on his large and gentle hands" (loc. 1817). Taking herself off to whelp, the *cù mòr glas* disappears from the man's home.

The dramatic climax of the story is a mirror image of another tale of misrecognition and tragic irony, best known in the British Isles as the story of a wolfhound named Gelert, but apparently folkloric around the world: returning from a hunt, King Llewellyn finds his faithful dog in his child's bedchamber covered in blood, and the child gone. But after he has killed the dog in anger, he discovers the child unhurt—and a dead wolf that Gelert has fended off to boot. In Macleod's story, it is the dog that goes away, and when the man succeeds in finding her a year later, she bounds up to him on the shoreline joyfully, knocking him over in the surf. Her six pups, now full grown, "misunderstood, like so many armies, the intention of their leader" (loc. 1834). They rip away his jaw and throat in front of his horrified sons, mortally injuring him.

The terrible story is recounted around the region: "All of his caring for her was recounted over and over again and nobody missed any of the ironies" (loc. 1869). The dog, now known as the *cù mòr glas a' bhàis* or big grey dog of death, goes on to haunt the family, a curse transcending the generations:

> This is how the *cù mòr glas a' bhàis* came into our lives, and it is obvious that all of this happened a long, long time ago. Yet with succeeding generations it seemed the spectre had somehow come to stay and that it had become ours—not in the manner of an unwanted skeleton in the closet from a family's ancient past but more in the manner of something close to a genetic possibility. In the deaths of each generation, the grey dog was seen by some—by women who were to die in childbirth; by soldiers who went forth to the many wars but did not return; by those who went forth to feuds or dangerous love affairs; by those who answered mysterious midnight messages; by those who swerved on the highway to avoid the real or imagined grey dog and ended in masses of crumpled steel. (loc. 1889)

In fact, as soon as the pregnant bitch lopes off across the ice, she tilts from tangible reality into an allegory of what lies beyond the embattled refuge of the man's hearth and threshold: a beckoning wildness, meaning death. A curse modernized and naturalized as a "genetic possibility" is a curse nonetheless.

The *cù mòr glas a' bhàis* is woven into family legend, itself a synecdoche of traditional Cape Breton Gaelic culture, but her immortality costs her animality. The dog's ferality comes to embody a lethal, fascinating chthonic energy that asserts itself even as it is dismissed as superstition. Thus, at the close of the story, the narrator and his five grey-haired brothers gather round the deathbed of their own father, fearing that, against their will, they will seem to have fulfilled the curse:

> Sitting here, taking turns holding the hands of the man who gave us life, we are afraid for him and for ourselves. We are afraid of what he may see and we are afraid to hear the phrase born of the vision. We are aware that it may become confused with what the doctors call "the will to live" and we are aware that some beliefs are what others would dismiss as "garbage." We are aware that there are men who believe the earth is flat and that the birds bring forth the sun. (loc. 1916)

The phrase "we are aware" seems an agnostic disavowal of visions and delusions, but because the beauty and mystery of the story's title broods over it throughout while the grey-haired sons gather around the deathbed at its conclusion, the undertow of mythicized ferality prevails over the narrator's superficial urbane scepticism.

The dog's presence is richly realized at the beginning the story—especially when she is an injured puppy with 'bulging eyes and...scrabbling front paws and ... desperately licking tongue'—only for her to become, as the Afterword points out, "a sort of canine banshee," recalling too "Finn McCool's great dog Bran loping across the Giant's Causeway from Ireland to Scotland and Charon's dog Cerebus guarding the gates to the underworld and keeping watch over the River Styx" (loc. 2645). Is being legendary an elevation or a demotion? Either way, it might seem either perverse or puritanical to object to such allegorization: it is the fate of most fictional animals, and figurality is in any case impossible to police. Allegorical animals sometimes bite or whimper, while even the realistically drawn canines of our next tale find symbolic resonances clustering round them whether Hornung wills it or not. Still, one would like to see more curiosity about dogs themselves. They always reward it.

DOG BOY

Eva Hornung's brilliant novel *Dog Boy* (2010) betrays immense curiosity about dogs on the part of the author, as well as her determination to resist both allegorising and crudely anthropomorphizing them.[9] To the child protagonist Romochka, abandoned or orphaned in anarchic post-Soviet Moscow, a family of feral dogs represents not an existential threat or lure but a haven from hunger and cold.[10] By following them home, he has unwittingly "crossed a border that is, usually, impassable—not even imaginable" (15); unlike the earlier ferality tales, though, this border runs erratically *through* the modern cityscape, not simply between it and a putative "wilderness." On its far side, Romochka's nature as a feral child is shaped in complex intra-action with his canine companions, as he moves through phases of vulnerability, affection, fear, and power.

First to be tried and abandoned is the conventional relationship of boy to puppies: he names them, then forgets their names, then names and forgets again. Soon the desperate child admits his need and suckles from the dominant female, Mamochka, catching faint hints of the scent-world the dogs inhabit:

> His suckle siblings were all milk-spiced, but the three older dogs had strong saliva and rank muzzles, each different, unequal in experience. They carried their own body odour on their tongues, their own signature in faint urine, paw, skin and anus—and their authority in their teeth, clean and sharp. They carried their health and their abilities in their kiss. He tumbled over the puppies too, kissing each dog on their return to the lair, then smelling their necks and shoulders to see what they might have done, might have found today. He, like the puppies, found the smell on their mouths and bodies tantalising, but he couldn't read the stories. (19–20)

As he grows together with the dogs, he becomes still more "animalistic," but rather than connoting only chaos or lethal violence,[11] ferality represents a viable alternate social order: filthy, stinking, impoverished, but also alive with affection and pervaded by a kind of morality. "Everything [is] ritual" in the lair (27), much like the finely calibrated world of canine play revealed by Marc Bekoff's studies (Kalof and Fitzgerald).

Hornung vividly conveys how Romochka's perceptions become attuned to the canine "environment," in the sense of the word articulated by Richard Lewontin in *The Triple Helix*:

> …it is the biology, indeed the genes, of an organism that determines its effective environment, by establishing the way in which external physical signals become incorporated into its reactions. The common external phenomena of the physical and biotic world pass through a transforming filter created by the peculiar biology of each species, and it is the output of this transformation that reaches the organism and is relevant to it. (64)

Romochka is able to access this phenomenological environment—known to biosemiotics as the organism's *Umwelt*—both because of the convergent evolution of humans and dogs, and because of his developmental intimacy with them. It may not be possible to know what it is like to be a bat, but a dog might not pose nearly as many problems (see Uexküll loc. 159–80, 957, 1009, and passim).[12]

Romochka's life with the dogs allows his co-evolutionary potential to be realized, but the ancient compact still requires he do his part *as human*. His physical limitations—useless nose, small teeth—frustrate him so long as he hopes to become more canine, but when he works with Black Sister to flush out a rat she shows him what interdependence requires of him:

> Black Sister crouched down, tail wagging, eyes shining in the gloom, snuffing away at the gap under the wood pile. She turned to him with a look of such hope and expectation that he was stirred. She trusted him to help her get that rat, she really did! An urgent pride flooded him. He would help, no matter what. (50)

The scene recalls Miklósi's experiments with dogs and socialized wolves described above: the contingent developmental ferality of Black Sister has not altered her evolutionary propensity to look to a human companion to solve problems. Her mute appeal comes in the context of a powerfully anti-anthropocentric narrative in which the dogs enable Romochka to survive and, as Agamben suggests, recognize himself ultimately as *Homo sapiens*. By contrast, the animal studies perspective, in which domestication is represented as a form of repressive bio-power, is inconsistent with the way it is the dog's gaze that elicits Romochka's human subjectivity, not the other way round.

Until Part IV, when attention shifts to the attempts of scientists at the Children's Centre to comprehend Romochka and the younger adoptee Puppy, the novel develops a powerful and sustained critical analogy between the feral dogs and the *bomzhi*, or homeless people. To the regular citizens of Moscow, both are alike repulsive and degraded: when Romochka and his canine siblings assault and rob a woman of her shopping bags, she screams ' "Filth! Bomzh! Animal!" ' (89). Like the *militzia* officer who comments that "Feral kids are worse than rabid dogs" (135), the woman's crudely zoomorphic rhetoric abjects dogs and "feral" people as subhuman, taking for granted an anthropocentric vertical hierarchy of value. But Romochka, while he is upset by her insult, inhabits a far more complex moral and perceptual landscape, in which "enmity between feral dogs and bomzhi is seasonal, and winter is its peak" (82). His fear of feral people stems from the contrast between the chaos of their lives and the love and discipline among the dogs:

> Sometimes [the bomzhi] seemed to him just like sick dogs or lone strays. You couldn't predict when they would be dangerous. Some of them didn't know how to behave, either with him or with each other. They fought and yowled, ripped and tore each other over food and scraps of metal. They stole from each other, beat each other senseless, even killed. They mated even when one of them didn't want to. At other times they touched each other with a tenderness that filled him with confusion and longing. (85)

Romochka's zoomorphism is critical and sophisticated, based not on a fantastical "beast within" but on a precise, observant analogy between the most desperately disordered humans and the clanless dogs.

The civilized Muscovites Romochka encounters when he ventures into the subway are likewise represented zoomorphically, but not denigratingly:

> Crowds of people stood near the edge of the platform, each person almost touching the next, yet just distant enough to be alone. They were clearly not a pack. It was as if all these strangers had somehow agreed that their personal territory could be shrunk for the purpose of waiting for trains. People stared blankly up the tracks or straight ahead, none meeting another's eyes. (117)

Much as London used focalization through Buck to expose the cruelty he saw as latent in human nature, Romochka's alienated feral viewpoint reveals our complex unconscious negotiation of social estrangement and physical intimacy.

The last two parts of the book shift attention to the questions of developmental psychology that make historic cases of "feral children" so painfully fascinating: what aspects of normal human behaviour can develop in a child raised by dogs? How might one distinguish between that presumably deprived upbringing and the mental "retardation" that might lead such a child to be abandoned in the first place? But Dr. Dimitry Pastushenko's epiphany about Romochka comes when he acknowledges for the first time that, far from being rendered *subnormal* by nature or nurture, the boy is, so to speak, bilingual across species. Ferality has made the boy a "master of *passing*" between worlds:

> He'd done so for three months now in the centre—among *experts*, no less. Among dogs ... well, Dimitry could only begin to guess [...] Romochka could cross ... over. (229)

Such bicultural fluency is similar to what dogs learn when properly socialized in both canine and human codes of behavior.

Immediately after this realization, Dimitry is forced to acknowledge the independent agency of animals when he sees a feral dog take the subway two stops on its own: "Why had dogs always seemed thing-like, symbolic," he asks himself, "when they were in fact person-like and about as symbolic as he was" (234). The truth about Romochka's nature turns out to be radically incomplete without taking into account his feral family, just as human nature is incomprehensible in isolation from our evolutionary companions, pre-eminently the "domestic" dog. As Donna Haraway puts it, dogs are "Partners in the crime of human evolution, they are in the garden from the get-go, wily as Coyote" (5).

Eva Hornung's *Dog Boy* therefore unites in a single novel the two opposed meanings of "experimental" discussed above. It incorporates evidence, derived from repeatable scientific studies such as Miklósi's comparative ethology of wolves and dogs, of human–canine co-evolution, and portrays ferality as a developmental phenomenon rather than the outcome of an existential struggle. At the same time, the biological specificity of the dogs—the fact that they do *not* stand for all animality everywhere and always—endows them with the transformative otherness that, according to Attridge, "enters, and changes, a cultural sphere" (loc. 524) when singularity manifests in a particular act of reading. First, Attridge implicitly denies that animals are extrinsic to the "cultural" sphere: "I take the relation between the human and the non-human in all its forms to be a significant part of what I am calling 'culture'" (loc. 569). Later this relation is acknowledged as a crucial example of alterity as defined in *The Singularity of Literature*:

> We can specify the relation between the same and the other a little more fully by thinking of it in terms of that which the existing cultural order has to occlude in order to maintain its capacities and configurations, its value-systems and hierarchies of importance; that which it cannot afford to acknowledge if it is to continue without change. (loc. 746)

The tremendous ethical import of a novel like *Dog Boy* lies, according to Attridge's persuasive argument, in the unprecedented and unpredictable cultural dynamic it sets in motion: "[Singularity] is produced, not given in advance; and its emergence is also the beginning of its erosion, as it brings about the cultural changes necessary to accommodate it" (loc. 1338). A culture altered by the alterity of Hornung's dogs—call it biocentric, call it posthumanist, call it the advent of Timothy Morton's "Ecological Thought"— would *interdifferentiate* within and between species, rather than constructing a simplistic binary of human and animal that must thereafter be either defended or undermined. As Morton puts it, "Humans may be 'animals,' but 'animals' aren't 'animals'" (Morton 62). Dogs, in particular, are not animals.

Conclusion

Canis familiaris is a designation almost as odd as *Homo sapiens*. According to the biological species concept, which is based on the ability to interbreed, *Canis familiaris* is a subspecies of *Canis lupus*, somewhat as some scientists claim that we are really the "third chimpanzee" (genus *Pongo*) (Diamond). Presiding alone over the genus *Homo* is, on this view, justifiable only on theological, not taxonomic, grounds. As part of our family, our evolutionary familiar and first domesticate,[13] the dog has been promoted by *Pongo sapiens* from *Canis lupus* ssp. *familiaris*, perhaps in recognition of their role in our self-recognition. As James Serpell points out, though, our good lieutenant remains liminal:

> To be loved by a paragon is one thing, to be adored by a creature that eats shit, sniffs genitals and bites people is quite another.... In symbolic terms, the domestic dog exists precariously in the no-man's-land between the human and non-human worlds. It is an interstitial creature, neither person nor beast, forever oscillating uncomfortably between the roles of high-status animal and low-status person.... it has become a creature of metaphor, simultaneously embodying or representing a strange mixture of admirable and despicable traits. (Serpell 254)

If the dog lies on the boundary between human and animal, at once imaginary and effective as it is, feral dogs inhabit the border's border. They possess the agential energy idealized by Armstrong as a generalized "ferity," but are as likely to direct it back towards enhanced intimacy as subversion. Conversely, while some feral species are undoubtedly destructive, environmentalist generalizations about ferality as a kind of biological pollution (worse even than chemicals or radiation because self-sustaining) are belied by studies of dog populations that show they would vanish without human waste to feed on and abandoned dogs to replenish their numbers.

Despite the contempt of some environmentalists, the dog's domesticity is not denaturing, and its seeming wildness provisional, not existential: feral dogs are only ever one socialized generation away from return to the human fold. If there is progress in fictional ferality tales as much as in the science of ferality, we might expect it to manifest as a *resistance to allegorization*, so that fictional dogs can *be dogs*, rather than (or as well as), having to mean something. At the same time, though, in the most sophisticated of these tales, the hardship and scandal of ferality for both its human and canine victims recasts the symbiosis of people and dogs not as biopolitical oppression, but as the most ancient and demanding of moral responsibilities for *both* parties.

ACKNOWLEDGMENTS

I am grateful to the contributors to the ASLE discussion list for their suggestions of texts for this essay. It is a consistently valuable and encouraging resource. The idea of "resistance to allegorization" as an indication of progress in the representation of animals emerged in the context of my supervision of Jude Allen's dissertation on metamorphic narratives in twentieth-century literature. As so often in the agonistic intimacy of the symbiosis of student and supervisor, it is hard to say exactly whose idea it was.

Notes

1. This distinction, which is probably obvious to everyone else, was first pointed out to me in a lecture by philosopher John Gray.

2. The terms "triangulation" and "projection" are borrowed from cartography. The former uses trigonometry to establish the position of an unknown point by making it a vertex of a triangle formed with two known points. A projection converts the coordinating lines of latitude and longitude on a mapped globe into a flat plane. In metaphorical terms, triangulation attempts to situate a term—"ferality," in this case—by estimating its position from several disciplinary perspectives. Like a cartographic projection, a conceptual projection aims at once to be precise and to fulfill, by means of necessary distortion (a certain flattening, let us say), a particular purpose.

3. At one time I would have agreed with Franklin: "An Absence of Azaleas: Imperialism, Nativity and Exoticism in Romantic Biogeographical Ideology," *Wordsworth Circle*, 28:3 (Fall 1997):148–55. But the evidence has made me change my mind: "Heidegger Nazism Ecocriticism," *Interdisciplinary Studies in Literature and the Environment*, 17:2 (Spring 2010): 251–71.

4. See, for example, Adam Gabbatt, 'Australian camel cull plan angers animal welfare groups.' *The Guardian*, November 26, 2009. Available at http://www.guardian.co.uk/world/2009/nov/26/australia-thirsty-camels-animal-welfare. Also this impeccably balanced article from the Daily Mail: Richard Shears, 'Massacre at murder spring: The shocking cull of wild horses in the Aussie outback.' *Mail Online*, November 17, 2007. Available at http://www.dailymail.co.uk/news/article-494610/Massacre-murder-spring-The-shocking-cull-wild-horses-Aussie-outback.html.

5. Ernst Von Haeckel, coiner of the term *oecology* and translator of Darwin into German, came up with the fascinating—though incorrect—notion that the embryonic development of individual organisms (ontogeny) "recapitulated" the evolutionary development of the species (phylogeny). Gestation, on this view, compresses into a few weeks and months the aeons of deep time.

6. Another amazing example of convergence is the collie, Rico, who could recognize the labels for 200 different objects, and when prompted with a name he did not know, preferentially chose the unknown object from amongst three known ones (J. Kaminski, J. Call, and J. Fischer, "Word Learning in a Domestic Dog: Evidence for 'Fast Mapping,'" *Science*, 304:5677 (2004): 1682–1683. Fast mapping has only previously been observed in human children. There is, moreover, some evidence of social learning in dogs, involving both canine and human teachers.

7. We might well conclude, on Boitani's evidence, that depictions of free-living or feral dogs as "pack animals" are in fact *lupomorphic*.

8. The Alaskan husky is, despite its wolfish appearance, a recent phenomenon, bred out of the Gold Rush mongrels and Siberian huskies, and refined since then. As Coppinger and Schneider point out, Native Arctic dogs and Alaskan malamutes are too big for sledding.

9. For an extended discussion of the distinction between crude and critical anthropomorphism and zoomorphism, see my *Ecocriticism* (Routledge 2011), pp. 152–170.

10. A *Financial Times* article shows how much a part of Moscow life the feral dogs are, and explains that the extermination sweeps are now a thing of the past: 'Moscow's Stray Dogs', Susanne Sternthal, 16 January 2010, http://tinyurl.com/c9rd9ce, [accessed 20 August 2013]

11. "Animalistic" and "bestial" are key examples of crudely zoomorphic language, which typically demeans humans by representing them as (completely imaginary) animals. See note 5.
12. Thomas Nagel's famous essay admits as much, asking "What is it like to be a bat?" specifically because its *Umwelt* is so obviously inaccessible. The main point of his essay, though, is to challenge "psycho-physical reductionism," or the attempt to reduce the mind/body problem to a merely scientific issue. Knowing in precise detail how bats perceive the world does not, he argues, give us any access whatever to its subjective experience. If the same is true of humans, neuroscience cannot shed any light on what it is like to be human.
13. The *OED* includes among the meanings of "familiar": "1.a. Of ... one's family or household ...; 2.a. extremely friendly, ... intimate; 3. Of animals: ... domestic, tame."

Works Cited

Agamben, Giorgio. *The Open: Man and Animal.* Stanford, Calif.: Stanford University Press; London: Eurospan. Kindle. Stanford University Press, 2004. Print.

Armstrong, Philip. *What Animals Mean in the Fiction of Modernity.* London: Routledge, 2008. Print.

Attridge, Derek. *The Singularity of Literature.* London: Routledge, 2004. Kindle.

Boitani, Luigi, Francesco Francisci, Paolo Ciucci, and Giorgio Andreoli. "Population Ecology and Biology of Feral Dogs in Central Italy." *The Domestic Dog: Its Evolution, Behaviour, and Interactions with People.* Ed. Serpell, James. Cambridge: Cambridge University Press, 1995. Print.

Callicott, J. Baird. "Animal Liberation: A Triangular Affair." *Environmental Ethics.* Ed. Elliot, Robert. Oxford: Oxford University Press, 1995. 29–59. Print.

Coppinger, Raymond, and Richard Schneider. "Evolution of Working Dogs." *The Domestic Dog: Its Evolution, Behaviour and Interactions with People.* Ed. Serpell, James. Cambridge: Cambridge University Press, 1995. 268p. Print.

Diamond, Jared M. *The Rise and Fall of the Third Chimpanzee.* London: Vintage, 1992, 1991. Print.

Franklin, Adrian. *Animal Nation: The True Story of Animals and Australia.* Sydney: UNSW Press, 2006. Print.

Garrard, Greg. *Ecocriticism.* New Critical Idiom. Abingdon, UK: Routledge, 2011. Print.

Gilbert, Daniel. "If Only Gay Sex Caused Global Warming." *Los Angeles Times* July 2, 2006. Print.

Haraway, Donna Jeanne. *The Companion Species Manifesto: Dogs, People, and Significant Otherness.* Chicago, Ill.: Prickly Paradigm, 2003. Print.

Hornung, Eva. *Dog Boy.* London: Bloomsbury, 2010. Print.

Kalof, Linda, and Amy J. Fitzgerald. *The Animals Reader: The Essential Classic and Contemporary Writings.* Oxford: Berg, 2007. Print.

Kaminski, J., J. Call, and J. Fischer. "Word Learning in a Domestic Dog: Evidence for 'Fast Mapping.'" *Science* 304:5677 (2004): 1682–83. Print.

Lewontin, Richard C. *The Triple Helix: Gene, Organism, and Environment.* Cambridge, Mass.; London: Harvard University Press, 2000. Print.

London, Jack. *"The Call of the Wild" and "White Fang."* Ed. M. Mataev. 2010. Kindle.

Miklósi, Adam. *Dog Behaviour, Evolution, and Cognition.* Oxford: Oxford University Press, 2007. Print.

Morey, Darcy. *Dogs: Domestication and the Development of a Social Bond*. Cambridge: Cambridge University Press, 2010. Print.

Morton, Timothy. *The Ecological Thought*. Cambridge, Mass.; London: Harvard University Press, 2010. Print.

Nagel, Thomas. "What Is Like to Be a Bat?" *The Philosophical Review* LXXXIII:4 (1974): 435–50. Print.

Paxton, David. *Why It's Ok to Talk to Your Dog: Co-Evolution of Humans and Dogs*. 2011. Kindle.

Perry, Dan, and Gad Perry. "Improving Interactions between Animal Rights Groups and Conservation Biologists." *Conservation Biology* 22:1: 27–35. Print.

Pollan, Michael. *The Botany of Desire: A Plant's Eye View of the World*. 1st ed. ed. New York: Random House, 2001. Print.

Ponting, Clive. *A Green History of the World*. London: Penguin, 1992, 1991. Print.

Regan, Tom. *The Case for Animal Rights*. London: Routledge & Kegan Paul, 1983. Print.

Robisch, S. K. *Wolves and the Wolf Myth in American Literature*. Reno, Nev.: University of Nevada Press, 2009. Print.

Rose, Steven P. R. *Lifelines: Life Beyond the Gene*. Fully rev. ed ed. London: Vintage, 2005. Print.

Serpell, James. "From Paragon to Pariah: Some Reflections on Human Attitudes to Dogs." *The Domestic Dog: Its Evolution, Behaviour and Interactions with People*. Ed. James Serpell. Cambridge: Cambridge University Press, 1995. Print.

Singer, Peter. *Animal Liberation*. 2nd ed., with a new preface by the author. ed. London: Pimlico, 1995. Print.

Uexküll, Jakob von. *A Foray into the Worlds of Animals and Humans: With a Theory of Meaning*. Trans. Joseph D. O'Neil. Minneapolis, Minn.: University of Minnesota Press, 2010. Kindle.

Whittaker, Robert J. *Island Biogeography: Ecology, Evolution, and Conservation*. Oxford: Oxford University Press, 1998. Print.

Wilson, Edward O. *Consilience: The Unity of Knowledge*. 1st ed. New York: Knopf, 1998. Print.

CHAPTER 14

···

BIOSEMIOTIC CRITICISM

···

TIMO MARAN

BIOSEMIOTICS, described in the most general way, is a discipline that examines sign processes, meanings, and communication in and between living organisms. Biosemiotic criticism could be defined as the study of literature and other manifestations of human culture with an emphasis on the biosemiotic understanding that life is, down to its most fundamental levels, organised by sign processes. A rather similar term—*literary biosemiotics*—was proposed by W. John Coletta in 1999,[1] but I prefer *biosemiotic criticism* for the same reason that I believe *ecocriticism* should be favored over *literary ecology*: both paradigms strive to account for the environmental aspect of various cultural phenomena, not only literary works. The present essay gives a brief overview of biosemiotics as a synthetic biological discipline, draws up a list of possibilities for describing humans' semiotic relations with their environment, and discusses some synthetic applications and models. It must be noted, however, that biosemiotics is a recent and quickly developing discipline that is still negotiating its theoretical base and conceptual framework. The present essay develops a perspective of what biosemiotic criticism might be, but the reader should be aware that alternative possibilities exist.

INTRODUCTION TO BIOSEMIOTICS

···

For most people in the humanities, at least in Europe, the word *semiotics* is associated, first of all, with the structuralist tradition, the semiology of Ferdinand de Saussure, the Prague linguistic circle, Louis Hjemslev, Claude Lévi-Strauss, Roland Barthes, and other representatives of the same tradition of thought. On the other hand, biosemiotics relates to another tradition of thought that, inside of semiotics, has become more and more eminent in the recent decades. This tradition proceeds from the semiotics of the American philosopher Charles Sanders Peirce and has been elaborated by his students or followers Charles W. Morris, Thomas A. Sebeok, Jesper Hoffmeyer, John Deely, and many others. The central concept for this tradition (or semiotics proper as opposed to semiology) is the concept of sign, or its dynamical aspect—semiosis, that in the most general way can be described as a mediated relation or mediated change. To pick one among the many definitions of sign by Peirce, a sign is "something which stands to somebody for something in some respect or capacity."[2] As to semiosis, Peirce has described it as "an action, or influence, which is, or involves, a cooperation of *three* subjects, such as a sign, its object, and its interpretant, this tri-relative influence not being in any way resolvable into actions between pairs."[3] Peirce's complex terminology remains outside the scope of the present article; let it simply be noted that Peirce's semiotics deals with the mediated or triadic relations (as being opposed to dyadic or physical relations between objects). Unlike European semiology, which focuses on sign structures or systems, Peircean semiotics is also capable of dealing with various local sign relations in nature. There are various examples of such relations in nature that have sign property: for instance, courtship feeding where a female passerine displays a begging behaviour with flapping wings, head, and neck bended down and beak opened that may be a sign of dependency relationship and relates to the feeding behavior of chicks; or replacement behavior in which a kitten who plays with a ball of yarn and bites it as if it were a prey animal is at the same time also aware of the difference and does not try to eat the yarn.

Another important source for biosemiotic paradigms has been the meaning-centred *Umwelt theory* of the Baltic-German biologist Jakob von Uexküll (1982, 1992).[4] He has described an animal and that part of the environment it lives in as mutually coupled through meaning relations containing perception and action and through correspondence between animal body forms and environmental objects. Uexküll argued that those and only those parts of the environment meaningfully linked with an animal are present for it and are contained in its subjective universe or *Umwelt*. Nature, in Uexküll's view, is construed by meaningfully connected perception and action points of different animal species, or points and counterpoints, as he borrows musical terms for expressing this holistic understanding. While Peircean semiotics provides biosemiotics with a view of relational signs capable of connecting organisms and objects in the environment, Uexküll's theory of meaning allows sign processes to be grounded in bodily and biological organization but to be also seen in the framework of ecological relations that connect animal species and bind together ecosystems.

The meeting of Peircean semiotics and Uexküllian biology has probably been a prerequisite for the biosemiotic maxim, according to which semiosis is intrinsically connected with life. Thomas A. Sebeok, a Hungarian-born founder of biosemiotics, linguist, and semiotician has expressed this thought as follows: "the process of message exchanges, or *semiosis*, is an indispensable characteristic of all terrestrial life forms,"[5] and also: "semiosis, independent of form or substance, is thus seen as a universal, criterial property of animate existence."[6] This idea has later been repeated in different wordings by Jesper Hoffmeyer, Kalevi Kull, Marcello Barbieri, and other leading biosemioticians. Biosemiotics has examined various processes in living systems as semiotic, from the transmission of genetic and molecular information on the cellular level up to intra- and interspecific communication in animals.[7] Central principles of biosemiotics include self-organization and self-regulation of living systems; code-duality, such as the parallelism of digital and analogic information in the development of life; embodiment of communicative and interpretive processes; the organism's inside–outside boundary as a semiotic filter or translation mechanism;[8] sign processes as regulators of ecological relations and ecological communities; organisms as active shapers of their semiotic niches or *Umwelten*; and the growth of complexity of semiotic processes in biological evolution.[9] Additionally, the history of biosemiotics can be interpreted in different ways as well as ramified by influences from phenomenology, hermeneutics, cybernetics, system theory, genetics, molecular biology, system biology, evolutionary developmental biology, and other fields.[10] In general, the present essay focuses on two of several subfields of biosemiotics: zoosemiotics, the study of semiosis, communication and representation of animals;[11] and ecosemiotics, semiotic relations between culture or organisms carrying it and the natural environment.[12] These two subfields seem the most relevant for considering the connections between semiotic processes in nature and in human culture.

For the humanities, the emergence of biosemiotics widens the sphere of semiotic processes to embrace all living organisms on Earth, thereby ensuring that human cultural and semiotic activities cannot be treated as a semiotic island in the vast ocean of unsemiotic void. Rather, human culture should be considered as being surrounded by a multitude of other semiotic systems, some partly accessible, some rather different from ours. The issues that biosemiotics can bring to the attention of the humanities would include: (1) communicative and sign relations between human cultural activities and other semiotic subjects and their representations in literature and other cultural texts; (2) interrelations between environmental information and literary texts or other human cultural representations and the question of whether the latter may be motivated by the former; (3) the presence and traces of human bodily perception, sensations, and biological organization in literary texts and other human cultural representations; and (4) resemblances and analogies between literary texts or other cultural representations and elements of nature as such and the use of biosemiotic research models in the study of human culture in this aspect. These different possibilities and their practical applicability will be discussed more systematically in the following pages. In general, biosemiotic criticism emphasizes contextual and ecological reading and interpretation of the manifestations of the human culture and their natural surroundings.

SEMIOTICS OF HUMAN–NATURE RELATIONS

One central question for discussion between biosemiotics and ecocritical studies on both the object and the paradigmatic levels is the relatedness of human cultural activities and nonhuman nature through semiotic means. The success in answering this question will settle whether biosemiotics as a paradigm of natural science has anything to offer to ecocriticism and whether the project of biosemiotic criticism is viable at all.

Monist–dualist debates run deep in Western philosophy, the humanities and biological science[13], but it seems that biosemiotics—by considering the capacity to interpret as an intrinsic property of the living matter—can add some fresh arguments to this discussion. I propose that the existing biosemiotic landscape can be organized around five types of relations bridging the human–nature divide: evolutionary, communicative, hierarchical, significational, and analogical. This typology should be taken as a tentative attempt to conceptualize the field of biosemiotic criticism.

1. Among these five possibilities, the *evolutionary* approach of relating humans with nonhuman nature is indeed most common in the humanities. It is based on the understanding of humans being descendants of the animal world, and it is applied by many Darwinian schools of humanities, such as literary Darwinism and evolutionary psychology, that seek to explain human culture through its evolutionary origin.[14] Such approaches have often been accused of inclining towards biological determinism and reductionist descriptions as they may, for instance, try to explain human cultural texts by animal instincts and motivations. Although interest in the biological origins of human language and other semiotic systems is definitely present also in biosemiotics,[15] the Darwinist way of relating humans with nonhuman nature is generally not characteristic of biosemiotics. What could be, however, a fruitful approach for biosemiotic criticism, would be to search for and identify such bases of similarities, provided by biological evolution, that function as points of departure both for zoosemiotic and linguistic modelling (on these concepts see below). Examples of such basic similarities include orientation on the vertical bottom-up axis that is a connecting feature for most animal and plants;[16] the baby-schema ("Kindchen-schema,"[17] or in English, "neotenic features"), a complex of face proportions characteristic of juvenile animals that is feature common to most vertebrates; or group relations and group hierarchies that is a connecting feature for most mammals. A resemblance on a certain level of biological organization provides the common ground on which interspecific communication and interpretation can be built (e.g., anthropomorphic depiction often uses and exaggerates the baby-schema features). The evolutionary connectedness of humans and animals can also be used as an argument in the humanities in a new way: instead of considering literary expression a means to maximize authors' reproductive success, it is possible to study, for instance, the aesthetical and artistic behavior of other animal species.[18]

2. The *communicative* approach makes an attempt to widen the sphere of subjects that have culture or communication ability, in other words, to extend this sphere over the borders of our species, including at least some higher social mammals and birds. Such approach is characteristic of, for instance, cognitive ethology, cultural biology and some schools of environmental philosophy dealing with animal rights issues. In biosemiotics (or in zoosemiotics, to be exact), the communicative approach is present in debates as to whether any other animal species besides humans have language-like communication or to what extent humans can decode the communication systems of other species. These questions relate to the topic of the fundamental features of human language itself. In this discussion, Charles F. Hockett's list of design features of human language and its

applications in other communication systems remains a classical and still actively used source.[19] There are also many ethological research studies, such as descriptions of ethograms or vocabularies of different species (a list of vocalizations of chaffinch by William H. Thorpe being an elegant example[20]). In essence, the communicative approach argues that instead of talking about the opposition between the humans and the environment, the environment itself can be seen as twofold, including the physical environment as well as semiotically competent animals who are much more similar to humans than we are to rocks or rivers. Animals' actions have at least local intentionality, and this may turn them into an active party in the communicative relations with humans. At the same time, attributing language to other species besides humans is rarely done in biosemiotics, as the structural complexity of human language (especially because of lexical syntax) appears to far surpass any other communication system on Earth.

An interesting compromise and concept in this respect is that of "primary modelling system" or "zoosemiotic modelling system," introduced by Sebeok, who argued that human capacity for linguistic communication is both ontogenetically and phylogenetically preceded by yet another modeling system—the-world-as-perceived—, where signs are distinguished by the organism's species-specific sensory apparatus and nervous system and aligned with its behavioural resources and motor events.[21] According to Sebeok, we possess at least two mutually sustaining modeling systems: the anthroposemiotic verbal, which is unique to the human species, and the zoosemiotic nonverbal, which unites us with the world of other animals. Verbal modeling may link further to higher ideological, poetic, artistic, or religious forms of modeling.[22] Direct and spatial perceptions, tactile and smelling sensations, as well as many occurrences of nonverbal communication[23] belong to the sphere of nonverbal modeling. Language does not have good resources for describing these kinds of phenomena, although it is certainly possible to express them. A particular target for biosemiotic criticism would be the manifestations of zoosemiotic modeling in a range of cultural artefacts.

3. The approach that I describe as *hierarchical* questions how we humans understand ourselves. The hierarchical approach argues that we are not uniform subjects, but rather hierarchical structures that contain many interacting layers of organization, all of which have their own subjectivity, memory, and semiotic competence. These claims are often supported by studies from neurology and molecular biology. For instance, Jesper Hoffmeyer has described the human immune system as a semi-autonomic agency with its own memory and activity and argued that the structure and functioning of the human nervous system is closer to swarm intelligence than a singular subject.[24] Similarly, Sebeok has introduced the concept of a semiotic self: it is a multilayered structure, based on all the memory-capable codes in the body,[25] including at least immunological, neurological, cognitive, and, in the case of human animals, also verbal and narrative layers. In her book *The Whole Creature: Complexity, Biosemiotics and the Evolution of Culture*,[26] Wendy Wheeler argues for the interrelations between social, psychological, neurological and immunological systems in humans, referring to psychoneuroimmunological

(PNI) studies of Paul Martin, Candace Pert, and others. Emphasizing the interactional nature of the human subject on different levels may also open biosemiotics up to issues of social criticism and theories of education and development in this context.[27]

4. The next way for human cultural activities to be related with nonhuman nature could be called *significational*, and this proceeds from the very heart of the logic of semiotics. The concept of significationality refers here to the works of the German semiotician Winfried Nöth,[28] who has used this term to denote semiotic processes involving natural signs. For St. Augustine, from whom the concept of natural signs derives, natural signs lead to the knowledge of something else, but they are not used intentionally for communication (the footprints indicating the presence of an animal being a classical example). Natural signs can function because there are some correspondences or structural relations present in the natural world; for example, there can hardly be any animal footprints present in the landscape if no actual animal has visited this spot.

In arguing for the accessibility of natural environment for the living organism, biosemiotics may rely on some psychological or philosophic theory, such as James J. Gibson's concept of environmental affordance[29] or Michel Polanji's philosophy of tacit knowledge.[30] In its philosophical grounding, biosemiotics more often relates to pragmatism or scholastic realism (*sensu* John Deely[31]). For natural signs to function, the natural environment and the realm of representations need to be bridged, which presumes developed structurality in both. On the level of practical analysis, this may also mean juxtaposing literary representations of nature with collateral sources of knowledge such as scientific, folkloristic, or common-sense understandings of nature, as undertaken, for instance, by Kadri Tüür in her analysis of bird sounds in nature writing.[32]

To understand the functioning of natural signs, Peircean semiotic theory, which underlies much of contemporary biosemiotics, can also be helpful. As I mentioned before, a Peircean sign is essentially tripartite, consisting, first, of something that enters the attention of an individual—this would be a sign in the narrow sense or a *representamen*; second, of some object that this sign refers to; and third, of an interpretant that is some further thought, reaction or application related to this object. In such a tripartite structure, every sign is temporally organized, as it relates what is perceived to some object that has been before and leads to some future activity. Related to this, tripartite signs may induce motivatedness and intentionality into semiosis, as objects generate interpretants, whereas their properties remain constraints for possible interpretation.[33] Peirce explains, "I define a Sign as anything which is so determined by something else, called its Object, and so determines an effect upon a person, which effect I call its Interpretant, that the latter is thereby mediately determined by the former."[34] At the same time, Peirce's view is not deterministic, as an interpreter also needs to be capable of regarding a sign as a representamen of something else, and different individuals may interpret the same physical aspect of the sign (or the so-called sign vehicle) differently.

In principle, Peirce distinguishes three possibilities for how a representamen or sign in the narrow sense can be related to the object. In symbols, the signs characteristic of human linguistic communication, the relation is based on habit or convention. In addition to symbolic signs, Peirce speaks about icons, in which the relation between the representamen and the object is based on resemblance, and about indexes, where the relation is physical or spatial. We can see that in icons and indexes the motivatedness of the sign arises from the things present in the environment, whereas in the case of symbols it is induced because of human conventions. This rather complex semiotic vocabulary is introduced in order to show that for Peircean semiotics, human cultural artefacts can be *immediately* related to the environment if they include iconical or indexical aspects. Examples of iconical sign relations on the lexemic level of human language are metaphors and onomatopoeia;[35] examples of indexical signs are deictic words. There are probably more possibilities for iconic and indexical relations in sentence structure and on the narrative level. We can also think of the natural environment inspiring us to create a piece of nature writing as a certain type of motivated sign activity.

Biosemiotics, stemming from the Peircean tradition, when applied to nature–culture relations, appears to establish an ecological perspective by emphasizing relations between nature writings, films, art, and so on, and the natural environment. This is especially so if one considers that also ecological relations between species have an essentially semiotic nature (forming what might be called *semethic interactions*[36]) by being shaped by processes of recognition and communication. A significational approach may lead to describing literature or other human cultural representations, human experience and the nonhuman environment as a nonhierarchical complex bounded together by sign relations, which is a local memory tradition or a local semiosphere. It may, for instance, deserve attention and reconsideration from this specific semiotic perspective that some particular landscapes and geographic areas have inspired their peculiar traditions of nature writing, with common motives and implicit references between the works of different authors.

5. The fifth possibility argues for the existence of deep structural parallels between the communication within and amongst living systems and those of human cultural manifestations, and suggests the possibility of using biosemiotic methods for describing literature or other representations in human culture on this basis. Such a possibility is historically influenced by studies of the genetic code and its possible analogy to human language, noted by linguists in the 1960s.[37] Recent developments of this line of thinking include the Prague school of biohermeneutics[38] that argues for the hermeneutic nature of the living world, life's own role in creating the world in the evolutionary process and the possibility of using narrative strategies in understanding it. Similar ideas may depart from Peircean semiotics. For instance, W. John Coletta has studied the necessary conditions in nature for sign relations to emerge and underlined several parallels between the functioning of language and nature.[39] Following the Peircean tradition, he has written about what he calls the "literary dimensions of nature": nature's embeddedness in language, its ironic and agentive features, its self-organizing and self-maintaining properties, its emergent properties, and its semiosis or signing action.[40] His topics include resemblances between the functioning of language in predication and ecological

relations, such as predation; he has also discussed human metaphors with reference to biological adaptations or natural metaphorics already present in the environment. For instance, Coletta argues that the specific resemblance between the coloration of a prey species and its natural background may produce a relationship similar to predication in human language. In the case of the fish Rock Beauty or *Holocantus tricolor*, with a yellow head and dark rock-like body, "the relationship between the indexical, specifying head of the fish and the iconic, complementary rock-like body of the same fish [...] produces at least the effect of the phrase 'this yellow fish behind the rock' in the mind of interpretant or predator..."[41]

A practical research method inspired by a possible analogy in the functioning of nature and cultural representations would be to use Uexküll's *Umwelt* analysis in the study of literary texts. Uexküll used this analysis to describing different animal *Umwelten* in comparison and in relation to each other. The research method allows for the formation of hypotheses about how the *Umwelten* of two species interact, as well as what the meaning of the characteristic behaviors of one animal might be for another, and vice versa. The groundwork for the *Umwelt* analysis is laid by von Uexküll in the book *The Theory of Meaning*,[42] in which he analyses the *Umwelt* of a tick and the mammals' place in it. The analysis consists of three parts. At first Uexküll determines the carrier and the receiver of meaning, thus establishing the position of the subject for the analysis. Then he describes the links between one animal's sensory organs and the activities or features of another as corresponding points and counterpoints. Both parties are enclosed in their species-specific *Umwelten* and have their species-specific bodies and functionalities to use. As the third step of the analysis, on the basis of correspondence between different meaning points, Uexküll infers a common meaning rule connecting both organisms. For example, in the relation between the tick and an unspecified mammal, the meaning relation for the tick could be expressed as: "recognition and attack of the prey and extraction of blood."[43] We can assume that such method could also be used in the analysis of some literary novels, in which the different position and relations of the protagonists are the central theme. The Uexküllian approach would emphasize the subjective worlds of the protagonists, invite the discovery of correspondences in their characters, dialogues, and deeds (that could be either affirming or destructive), and examine the meaning of such relations on a higher level, either for the rest of the community in the narrative or for the structure of the book.

TOWARDS HYBRID RESEARCH MODELS

When we look at the works of contemporary authors who are trying to bridge biosemiotics (or semiotic thinking more generally) and cultural or literary criticism, there appears to be a common endeavor to undermine the dualistic pairs of culture–nature, text–world and to develop a new framework that would connect semiotic processes in human culture with those outside it. Often, writings in biosemiotic criticism arrive at an understanding that this work cannot be completed only on the level of applied research but that a more general epistemological or paradigmatic shift is needed.[44] This positional change would include a new understanding of the relations between the text and the world, the text and its reader, and the text and the researcher as semiosis-based. The natural environment, both in its animate and its physical existence, needs to be reinterpreted as holding semiotic potential. And as is accepted in the semiotics of culture, eventually the activity of the researcher can be interpreted as a continuation of the sign process that led to the writer's inspiration, the creation of a text, and its interpretation by the reader; and the resulting review or analysis can be regarded as yet another layer of signs or texts in the same semiotic series.

For literary analysis, especially regarding nature writing as a research object, developing synthetic research models that could account for a written text and the natural environment in the same framework is an essential task. There exist several models, attempting to relate culture to the environment that it represents or is otherwise connected to, that are focused either on the natural or cultural component and that are either more or less explicitly semiotic than others. For instance, the British education theorist and semiotician Andrew Stables has introduced the notion of "landscape as text" and argued that the blurring of the concept of author in modern literary theory makes it possible to open the concept of text to natural phenomena. Stables notes that in landscapes the network of shared meanings extends beyond the human sphere and that it is difficult to draw a dividing line between the creative activities of humans, other life-forms, and natural forces.[45] This parallel allows us to introduce as well the concept of environmental literacy as a natural equivalent to the competence of orienting in literary realms. A rather similar approach is introduced by an American cultural geographer Anne W. Spirn who has described the physical environment using language-related terminology. In her view, landscape contains "patterns of shape, structure, material, formation, and function"; it is "pragmatic, poetic, rhetorical, polemical" and can be "spoken, written, read or imagined."[46]

In addition to arguing that nature or some of its elements have text-like characteristics, it is also possible to describe human cultural texts and nature-as-text as mutually intertwined. David Abram, in his investigation into the phenomenology of the more-than-human world,[47] has described the mutual coupledness of texts and landscapes in many Native American (Amahuaca, Apache, Koyukon) and Australian traditional cultures. In these cultures, songs and tales help members of that culture to remember the properties, resources, and dynamics of the landscape as well as the proper behavior toward it, whereas the variability of landscape acts as a visual mnemonic pointing to the stories, teachings, and traditions of the culture. The same would seem to apply at least to some extent also to modern nature writing, in which the written texts and the natural environment connect and intertwine in complicated ways. Relying on the use of the concept of text in the Tartu-Moscow semiotic school, I have proposed the concept of "nature-text" as one way to integrate in a single research model representations of nature in culture and nature in its own semiotic activity.[48] "Nature-text" refers to the unit that is formed through meaning relations between the written text that speaks about nature and points to nature and the depicted part of the natural environment itself. Such interaction can significantly shape possible interpretations of the text, especially in cases when sign relations with the local environment are more intense than cultural meanings. It is remarkable that in the case of "nature-text," the written text does not need to convey all meanings, as they are present in the environment and familiar to the reader. Think for instance about geographies or climate conditions of a particular place: quite often nature essays leave these unspecified, assuming that reader has some experience of the place. Pointing to them is often enough, and the gaps in the fabric of the text may be as important as the explicitly expressed meanings.[49] Such claims could also be supported by Gregory Bateson's observations on the redundancy present on different levels between a unit of meaning (text) and its surroundings that together constitute a cybernetic system regulated by redundancy restraints and feedback loops.[50] In such a case, the reading of a cultural text becomes a doubly interpretative activity, where the written text is read in relation to personal experience of the environment.

An understanding of the interwovenness of the natural environment and symbolic or literary expressions may also rise at a higher level of complexity of culture. For instance, Alfred K. Siewers, a medievalist at Bucknell University, has found use for the semiotic approach in his studies of Celtic literature.[51] He has introduced the concept of eco-semiosphere to describe a fantasy world (for instance Celtic Otherworld) or culture that is closely and reciprocally related to an eco-region of the Earth, each forming the other in a locality. In eco-semiosphere, there is a rich engagement of cultural narrative in an overlap between regional semiosphere and biosphere. The concept itself is adapted from Juri Lotman's "semiosphere," but with an emphasis on the role of physical landscape and geography. It is remarkable that Lotman, in his turn, derived the concept of semiosphere from a biological source—from Vladimir Vernadsky's "biosphere," and the original meaning of both concepts emphasizes the *place for* life or semiosis that is inhabited but at the same time influenced by the living or semiotic activities. In other words, a semiosphere is wider than just a collection of written texts, and it extends as far as any possible influences of semiotic processes reach in the world and perhaps also as far as any possible influences of the world reach in the texts.

These different attempts to propose new research models appear to have some common traits: the role of the nonhuman environment is emphasized, the environment is considered in most cases to be an active and dynamical player, and human cultural phenomena are regarded as open to the environment or as intertwined with the environment. Such approach does not attempt to hierarchize the nonhuman environment, human experience, and representations, but rather regards these as a complex bounded together by sign relations. Accordingly, biosemiotic criticism can also be understood as a truly ecological approach towards literary texts, in the sense that it tries to consider the texts themselves in their creation and interpretation in the context of a wider environment that is not only textual or cultural but includes also animate subjects and the physical realm as well as interpreters and protagonists as embodied biological creatures with their own environmental relations and being.

ACKNOWLEDGMENTS

The research has been supported by the European Union through the European Regional Development Fund (Centre of Excellence CECT, Estonia), by Estonian Science Foundation Grant No. 7790.

NOTES

1. W. John Coletta, "Literary Biosemiotics and the Postmodern Ecology of John Clare," *Semiotica* 127, no. 1–4 (1999).
2. Charles Sanders Peirce, *The Collected Papers of Charles Sanders Peirce* (Cambridge: Harvard University Press, 1994), CP 2.228.
3. Charles Sanders Peirce, *The Essential Peirce. Selected Philosophical Writings II*, ed. Nathan Houser, et al. (Bloomington, IN: Indiana University Press, 1998), EP 2.411.
4. Jakob von Uexküll, "The Theory of Meaning," *Semiotica* 42, no. 1 (1982); Jakob von Uexküll, "A Stroll through the Worlds of Animals and Men: A Picture Book of Invisible Worlds," *Semiotica* 89, no. 4 (1992).
5. Thomas A. Sebeok, "Communication" in *Thomas A. Sebeok. A Sign is Just a Sign* (Bloomington, IN: Indiana University Press, 1991), 22.
6. Thomas A. Sebeok, "Zoosemiotics: At the Intersection of Nature and Culture," in *Thomas A. Sebeok.Essays in Zoosemiotics* (= *Monograph Series of the TSC* 5) (Toronto: Toronto Semiotic Circle; Victoria College in the University of Toronto, 1990), 47.
7. In the case of interest for more specific topics, see Springer's book series and journal both under the title "Biosemiotics", such as Donald Favareau, ed., *Essential Readings in Biosemiotics. Anthology and Commentary* (Dordrecht: Springer, 2009).
8. For an introduction to these principles, see Jesper Hoffmeyer. *Biosemiotics: An Examination into the Signs of Life and the Life of Signs*, Donald Favareau, ed. (Scranton, PA: University of Scranton Press, 2008), esp. ch. 2, 4, 7.
9. For various interpretations in biosemiotics, see Myrdene Anderson, "Biology and Semiotics," in *Semiotics in the Individual Sciences*, ed. W. A. Koch (Bochum: Brockmeyer, 1990); Claus Emmeche, Kalevi Kull, and Frederik Stjernfelt, *Reading Hoffmeyer, Rethinking Biology* (=Tartu Semiotics Library 3) (Tartu: Tartu University Press, 2002); Frederik Stjernfelt, "Tractatus Hoffmeyerensis: Biosemiotics as Expressed in 22 Basic Hypotheses," *Sign Systems Studies* 30, no. 1 (2002); Kalevi Kull, Claus Emmeche, and Donald Favareau, "Biosemiotic Questions," *Biosemiotics* 1, no. 1 (2008); Kalevi Kull et al., "Theses on Biosemiotics: Prolegomena to a Theoretical Biology." *Biological Theory: Integrating Development, Evolution, and Cognition* 4, no. 2 (2009); and Kaveli Kull and Claus Emmeche, eds, *Towards a Semiotic Biology. Life Is the Action of Signs.* (Singapore: World Scientific, 2011).
10. See Donald Favareau, "The Evolutionary History of Biosemiotics," in *Introduction to Biosemiotics: The New Biological Synthesis*, ed. Marcello Barbieri (Berlin: Springer, 2006); Timo Maran, "Why Was Thomas A. Sebeok Not a Cognitive Ethologist? From 'Animal Mind' to 'Semiotic Self,'" *Biosemiotics* 3 no. 3, 315–29 (2010); Kalevi Kull, "Biosemiotics in the Twentieth Century: A View from Biology," *Semiotica* 127, no. 1/4 (1999); and Marcello Barbieri, "A Short History of Biosemiotics," *Biosemiotics* 2, no.2 (2009).

11. Timo Maran, Dario Martinelli, and Aleksei Turovski, "Introduction," in *Readings in Zoosemiotics*, ed. Timo Maran, Dario Martinelli and Aleksei Turovski (Berlin: Mouton de Gruyter, 2011. In press).

12. Winfred Nöth, "Ökosemiotik," *Zeitschrift für Semiotik* 18, no. 1 (1996); and Kalevi Kull, "Semiotic Ecology: Different Natures in the Semiosphere," *Sign Systems Studies* 26 (1998).

13. I refer here mostly to questions of continuity or discontinuity of mind and matter, humans and other animals, and culture and nature.

14. See, for example, Robert Storey, *Mimesis and the Human Animal: On the Biogenetic Foundations of Literary Representation* (Evanston, IL: Northwestern University Press, 1996); and Joseph Carroll, *Literary Darwinism: Evolution, Human Nature, and Literature* (New York: Routledge, 2004).

15. See, for example, Wendy Wheeler. *The Whole Creature: Complexity, Biosemiotics and the Evolution of Culture* (London: Lawrence and Wishart, 2006); and Terrence W. Deacon, *The Symbolic Species. The Co-Evolution of Language and the Brain* (New York: W. W. Norton, 1997).

16. The essential connection between the biological organization and language in humans has been argued by cognitive linguistics to be embedded in conceptual metaphors (for up–down organization of so-called orientational metaphors: good–bad, life–death, more-less, and so on. See George Lakoff and Mark Johnson, *Metaphors We Live By* (London: The University of Chicago Press, 1980), 1522.

17. Konrad Lorenz, "Die angeborenen Formen möglicher Erfahrung," *Zeitschrift für Tierpsychologie* 5, no. 2 (1943), 278.

18. Thomas A. Sebeok, "Prefigurements of Art," *Semiotica* 27, no. 1–3 (1979); Dario Martinelli, *Zoosemiotics.Proposals for a Handbook (= Acta Semiotica Fennica 26)* (Imatra: Finnish Network University of Semiotics; Imatra: International Semiotics Institute; Helsinki: Semiotic Society of Finland, 2007).

19. Charles F. Hockett, "Logical Considerations in the Study of Animal Communication," in *Animal Sounds and Communication*, ed. Wesley E. Lanyon and William N. Tavolga (Washington: American Institute of Biological Sciences, 1960).

20. William H. Thorpe, "The Learning of Song Patterns by Birds, with Especial Reference to the Song of the Chaffinch Fringilla Coelebs," *Ibis* 100, no. 4 (1958).

21. Thomas A. Sebeok, "In What Sense Is Language a 'Primary Modeling System'?" in Thomas A. Sebeok, *A Sign Is Just a Sign*, 49–58. Bloomington, IN: Indiana University Press, 1991.

22. See Thomas A. Sebeok and Marcel Danesi, *The Forms of Meaning: Modeling Systems Theory and Semiotic Analysis* (Berlin: Mouton de Gruyter, 2000), but also Juri M. Lotman, "Primary and Secondary Communication-Modeling Systems," in *Soviet Semiotics: An Anthology*, transl. and ed., D. P. Lucid (Baltimore: The Johns Hopkins University Press, 1977) for possible elaborations of modeling systems theory.

23. Alf Hornborg, "Vital Signs: An Ecosemiotic Perspective on the Human ecology of Amazonia," *Sign Systems Studies* 29, no. 1 (2001): 128.

24. Jesper Hoffmeyer, *Signs of Meaning in the Universe.* Transl. B. J. Haveland (Bloomington, IN: Indiana University Press, 1996): 83–88, 113–120.

25. Thomas A. Sebeok, "Tell Me, Where is Fancy Bred?" The Biosemiotic Self," In Thomas A. Sebeok, *Global Semiotics* (Bloomington: Indiana University Press, 2001), 124.

26. Wendy Wheeler, *The Whole Creature.*

27. See Andrew Stables, *Living and Learning as Semiotic Engagement. A New Theory of Education* (Lewiston: The Edwin Mellen Press, 2005); and Wendy Wheeler, *The Whole Creature.*

28. Winfred Nöth, "Ecosemiotics and the Semiotics of Nature," *Sign Systems Studies* 29, no. 1 (2001): 72.

29. James J. Gibson, *The Ecological Approach to Visual Perception* (Hillsdale, NJ: Lawrence Erlbaum, 1986).

30. Michael Polanyi, *Personal Knowledge. Towards a Post-Critical Philosophy* (London: Routledge, 1962).

31. John Deely, *Four Ages of Understanding: The First Postmodern Survey of Philosophy from Ancient Times to the Turn of the Twenty-First Century* (Toronto: University of Toronto Press, 2001).

32. Kadri Tüür, "Bird Sounds in Nature Writing: Human Perspective on Animal Communication," *Sign Systems Studies* 37 no. 3/4 (2009).

33. Here, motivatedness should be understood as limited (because of constrained relations of object-sign-interpretant) possibilities for interpretation, and intentionality as directedness of semiosis because of these limitations.

34. Charles Sanders Peirce, *Semiotic and Significs: The Correspondence between Charles S. Peirce and Victoria Lady Welby*, ed. Charles S. Hardwick and J. Cook (Bloomington, IN: Indiana University Press, 1977), 80–81.

35. Metaphors and onomatopoetic words can be considered iconic to the extent that the perception of the relation to their referent is based on similarity.

36. Jesper Hoffmeyer, *Biosemiotics: An Examination into the Signs of Life and the Life of Signs*, ed. Donald Favareau (Scranton, PA: University of Scranton Press, 2008), 189.

37. Roman Jakobson, "Linguistics in Relation to Other Sciences," in *Roman Jakobson. Selected Writings II. Word and Language* (The Hague: Mouton, 1971), 677–81.

38. Anton Markoš, *Readers of the Book of Life: Conceptualizing Developmental Evolutionary Biology* (Oxford: Oxford University Press, 2002); and Anton Markoš, Filip Grygar, László Hajnal, Karel Kleisner, Zdenek Kratochvíl, and Zdenek Neubauer, *Life as Its Own Designer: Darwin's Origin and Western Thought* (Dordrecht: Springer, 2009).

39. Coletta, "Literary Biosemiotics"; W. John Coletta, "Predation as Predication: Toward an Ecology of Semiosis and Syntax," *Semiotica* 109, no. 3–4 (1996); W. John. Coletta, "The Semiosis of Nature: Towards an Ecology of Metaphor and a Biology of Mathematics," *The American Journal of Semiotics* 10, no. 3–4 (1993).

40. Coletta, "Literary Biosemiotics," 251.

41. Coletta, "Predation as Predication," 230.

42. Uexküll, "The Theory of Meaning," 52–57.

43. Uexküll, "The Theory of Meaning," 57.

44. See, for example, Wendy Wheeler, "Postscript on Biosemiotics: Reading beyond Words— and Ecocriticism," *New Formations* 64 (2008): 137–54; Coletta, "Literary Biosemiotics."

45. Andrew Stables, "The Landscape and the 'Death of the Author,'" *Canadian Journal of Environmental Education* 2, no. 1 (1997).

46. Anne W. Spirn, *The Language of Landscape* (New Haven: Yale University Press, 1998), 15.

47. David Abram, *The Spell of the Sensuous. Perception and Language in a More-than-Human World* (New York: Vintage Book, 1996).

48. Timo Maran, "Towards an Integrated Methodology of Ecosemiotics: The Concept of Nature-Text," *Sign Systems Studies* 35, no. 1/2 (2007).

49. Maran, "Towards an Integrated Methodology of Ecosemiotics," 280.

50. Gregory Bateson, *Steps to an Ecology of Mind* (Chicago: The University of Chicago Press, 1973), 405–31.

51. Alfred K. Siewers, *Strange Beauty. Ecocritical Approaches to Early Medieval Landscape*, (New York: Palgrave Macmillan, 2009).

REFERENCES

Abram, David. *The Spell of the Sensuous*. Perception and Language in a More-than-Human World. New York: Vintage Book, 1996.

Anderson, Myrdene. "Biology and Semiotics." In *Semiotics in the Individual Sciences*. Edited by W. A. Koch, 254–81. Bochum: Brockmeyer, 1990.

Barbieri, Marcello. "A Short History of Biosemiotics." *Biosemiotics 2*, no. 2 (2009): 221–45.

Bateson, Gregory. *Steps to an Ecology of Mind*. Chicago: The University of Chicago Press, 1973.

Carroll, Joseph. *Literary Darwinism: Evolution, Human Nature, and Literature*. New York: Routledge, 2004.

Coletta, W. John. "The Semiosis of Nature: Towards an Ecology of Metaphor and a Biology of Mathematics." *The American Journal of Semiotics 10*, no. 3–4 (1993): 223–44.

Coletta, W. John. "Predation as Predication: Toward an Ecology of Semiosis and Syntax." *Semiotica 109*, no. 3–4 (1996): 221–35.

Coletta, W. John. "Literary Biosemiotics and the Postmodern Ecology of John Clare." *Semiotica 127*, no. 1–4 (1999): 239–72.

Deacon, Terrence W. *The Symbolic Species*. The Co-Evolution of Language and the Brain. New York: W. W. Norton, 1997.

Deely, John. *Four Ages of Understanding: The First Postmodern Survey of Philosophy from Ancient Times to the Turn of the Twenty-First Century*. Toronto: University of Toronto Press, 2001.

Emmeche, Claus, Kalevi Kull, and Frederik Stjernfelt. *Reading Hoffmeyer, Rethinking Biology (Tartu Semiotics Library 3)*. Tartu: Tartu University Press, 2002.

Favareau, Donald. "The Evolutionary History of Biosemiotics." In *Introduction to Biosemiotics: The New Biological Synthesis*. Edited by Marcello Barbieri, 1–67. Berlin: Springer, 2006.

Favareau, Donald, ed. *Essential Readings in Biosemiotics*. Anthology and Commentary. Dordrecht: Springer, 2009.

Gibson, James J. *The Ecological Approach to Visual Perception*. Hillsdale, NJ: Lawrence Erlbaum, 1986.

Hockett, Charles F. "Logical Considerations in the Study of Animal Communication." In *Animal Sounds and Communication*. Edited by Wesley E. Lanyon and William N. Tavolga, 392–430. Washington: American Institute of Biological Sciences, 1960.

Hoffmeyer, Jesper. *Signs of Meaning in the Universe*. Translated by B. J. Haveland. Bloomington, IN: Indiana University Press, 1996.

Hoffmeyer, Jesper. *Biosemiotics: An Examination into the Signs of Life and the Life of Signs*. Edited by Donald Favareau. Scranton, PA: University of Scranton Press, 2008.

Hornborg, Alf. "Vital Signs: An Ecosemiotic Perspective on the Human Ecology of Amazonia." *Sign Systems Studies 29*, no. 1 (2001): 121–52.

Jakobson, Roman. "Linguistics in Relation to Other Sciences." In *Roman Jakobson. Selected Writings II. Word and Language*, 655–96. The Hague: Mouton, 1971.

Kull, Kalevi. "Semiotic Ecology: Different Natures in the Semiosphere." *Sign Systems Studies 26* (1998): 344–71.

Kull, Kalevi. "Biosemiotics in the Twentieth Century: A View from Biology." *Semiotica* 127, no. 1/4 (1999): 385–414.

Kull, Kalevi, Claus Emmeche, and Donald Favareau. "Biosemiotic Questions." *Biosemiotics* 1, no. 1 (2008): 41–55.

Kull, Kalevi, Terrence Deacon, Claus Emmeche, Jesper Hoffmeyer, and Frederik Stjernfelt. "Theses on Biosemiotics: Prolegomena to a Theoretical Biology." *Biological Theory: Integrating Development, Evolution, and Cognition* 4, no. 2 (2009): 167–73.

Kull, Kalevi and Claus Emmeche, eds. *Towards a Semiotic Biology: Life Is the Action of Signs*. Singapore: World Scientific, 2011.

Lakoff, George and Mark Johnson, *Metaphors We Live By*. London: The University of Chicago Press. 2003[1980].

Lorenz, Konrad. "Die angeborenen Formen möglicher Erfahrung." *Zeitschrift für Tierpsychologie* 5, no. 2 (1943), 235–409.

Lotman, Juri M. "Primary and Secondary Communication-Modeling Systems." In *Soviet Semiotics: An Anthology*. Translated and edited by D. P. Lucid, 95–8. Baltimore: The Johns Hopkins University Press, 1977.

Maran, Timo. "Towards an Integrated Methodology of Ecosemiotics: The Concept of Nature-Text." *Sign Systems Studies* 35, no. 1/2 (2007): 269–94.

Maran, Timo. "Why Was Thomas A. Sebeok Not a Cognitive Ethologist? From 'Animal Mind' to 'Semiotic Self'." *Biosemiotics* 3, no. 3 (2010), 315–29.

Maran, Timo, Dario Martinelli, and Aleksei Turovski. "Introduction." In *Readings in Zoosemiotics*. Edited by Timo Maran, Dario Martinelli and Aleksei Turovski. Berlin: Mouton de Gruyter, 2011. *In press*.

Markoš, Anton. *Readers of the Book of Life: Conceptualizing Developmental Evolutionary Biology*. Oxford: Oxford University Press, 2002.

Markoš, Anton, Filip Grygar, László Hajnal, Karel Kleisner, Zdenek Kratochvíl, and Zdenek Neubauer. *Life as Its Own Designer: Darwin's Origin and Western Thought*. Dordrecht: Springer, 2009.

Martinelli, Dario. *Zoosemiotics. Proposals for a Handbook* (= *Acta Semiotica Fennica* 26). Imatra: Finnish Network University of Semiotics; Imatra: International Semiotics Institute; Helsinki: Semiotic Society of Finland, 2007.

Nöth, Winfred. "Ecosemiotics and the Semiotics of Nature." *Sign Systems Studies* 29, no. 1 (2001): 71–81.

Nöth, Winfred. "Ökosemiotik." *Zeitschrift für Semiotik* 18, no. 1 (1996): 7–18.

Peirce, Charles Sanders. *Semiotic and Significs: The Correspondence between Charles S. Peirce and Victoria Lady Welby*. Edited by Charles S. Hardwick and J. Cook. Bloomington, IN: Indiana University Press, 1977.

Peirce, Charles Sanders. *The Collected Papers of Charles Sanders Peirce*. [Electronic version (Folio Bound Views); volumes 1–6 edited by C. Hartshorne and P. Weiss, 1931–5; volumes 7–8 edited by A. W. Burks, 1958] Cambridge: Harvard University Press, 1994.

Peirce, Charles Sanders. *The Essential Peirce. Selected Philosophical Writings II*. Edited by Nathan Houser, et al. Bloomington, IN: Indiana University Press, 1998.

Polanyi, Michael. *Personal Knowledge*. Towards a Post-Critical Philosophy. London: Routledge, 1962.

Sebeok, Thomas A. "Prefigurations of Art." *Semiotica* 27, no. 1–3 (1979), 3–74.

Sebeok, Thomas A. "Zoosemiotics: At the Intersection of Nature and Culture." In *Thomas A. Sebeok. Essays in Zoosemiotics (= Monograph Series of the TSC 5)*, 37–47. Toronto: Toronto Semiotic Circle; Victoria College in the University of Toronto, 1990.

Sebeok, Thomas A. "Communication." In *Thomas A. Sebeok. A Sign Is Just a Sign*, 22–35. Bloomington, IN: Indiana University Press, 1991.

Sebeok, Thomas A. "In What Sense Is Language a 'Primary Modeling System'?" In Thomas A. Sebeok. *A Sign Is Just a Sign*, 49–58. Bloomington, IN: Indiana University Press, 1991.

Sebeok, Thomas A. "Tell Me, Where Is Fancy Bred?" The Biosemiotic Self." In *Thomas A. Sebeok. Global Semiotics*, 120–7. Bloomington: Indiana University Press, 2001.

Sebeok, Thomas A. and Marcel Danesi. *The Forms of Meaning: Modeling Systems Theory and Semiotic Analysis*. Berlin: Mouton de Gruyter, 2000.

Siewers, Alfred K. *Strange Beauty. Ecocritical Approaches to Early Medieval Landscape*. New York: Palgrave Macmillan, 2009.

Spirn, Anne W. *The Language of Landscape*. New Haven: Yale University Press, 1998.

Stables, Andrew. "The Landscape and the 'Death of the Author.'" *Canadian Journal of Environmental Education 2*, no. 1 (1997): 104–13.

Stables, Andrew. *Living and Learning as Semiotic Engagement*. A New Theory of Education. Lewiston: The Edwin Mellen Press, 2005.

Stjernfelt, Frederik. "Tractatus Hoffmeyerensis: Biosemiotics as Expressed in 22 Basic Hypotheses." *Sign Systems Studies 30*, no. 1 (2002): 337–45.

Storey, Robert. *Mimesis and the Human Animal: On the Biogenetic Foundations of Literary Representation*. Evanston, IL: Northwestern University Press, 1996.

Thorpe, William H. "The Learning of Song Patterns by Birds, with Especial Reference to the Song of the Chaffinch Fringilla Coelebs." *Ibis 100*, no. 4 (1958): 535–70.

Tüür, Kadri. "Bird Sounds in Nature Writing: Human Perspective on Animal Communication." *Sign Systems Studies 37* no. 3/4 (2009): 580–613.

Uexküll, Jakob von. "The Theory of Meaning." *Semiotica 42*, no. 1 (1982): 25–82.

Uexküll, Jakob, von. "A Stroll through the Worlds of Animals and Men: A Picture Book of Invisible Worlds." *Semiotica 89*, no. 4 (1992): 319–91.

Wheeler, Wendy. *The Whole Creature: Complexity, Biosemiotics and the Evolution of Culture*. London: Lawrence and Wishart, 2006.

Wheeler, Wendy. "Postscript on Biosemiotics: Reading beyond Words—and Ecocriticism." *New Formations 64* (2008): 137–54.

CHAPTER 15

···

PHENOMENOLOGY

···

TIMOTHY CLARK

INTRODUCTION

···

IT may seem odd at first to have an essay entitled "Phenomenology" in a book on eco-criticism. The forbidding term seems hardly prominent in critical essays and contro-versies. Nevertheless, forms of "phenomenological" thinking have been a resource for many critics, and work informed by phenomenology is widespread. At the same time, as a final section argues, the emerging intellectual demands of thinking about climate change and such concepts as the Anthropocene are beginning to give ecocritical work heavily indebted to phenomenology a slightly dated, twentieth-century feel.

"Phenomenology" means several disparate things. Its famous slogan, "to the things themselves," is usually associated with the so-called "founder" of phenomenology, the philosopher Edmund Husserl (1859–1938), though it is the later "existential phenom-enology" associated with Martin Heidegger (1889–1976) and developed by figures such as Maurice Merleau-Ponty (1908–61) and Simone de Beauvoir (1908–84) that is mostly of concern here.[1]

Phenomenology presented itself as a challenge to deep assumptions in Western soci-ety about the nature of thought and theorizing, especially the assumption that any intel-lectually defensible account of things and of ourselves should necessarily form a part of the dominant natural-scientific conception of nature. Arguing that the authority of science had overreached itself, phenomenologists saw themselves as offering a new dis-cipline of thinking on bases other than scientism.

A sense of why phenomenology has been so important, and what it claims are, can be traced in an argument about that vague but crucial term "the environment." In "The idea of environment," David E. Cooper argues against the current dominant understanding of this tired word, calling instead for an understanding of "environment" informed by phenomenology (reworking some arguments from Martin Heidegger's *Being and Time* (1927)).[2] A distinguishing feature of the phenomenological mode of thought is that, first; it discounts any intellectual presuppositions about its object of concern, presuppositions as to what is more "real" or "factual" or "merely subjective" in what appears to us (the "environment" in this instance). One simply begins with what presents itself as evident to a consciousness that has tried to purge itself of all presuppositions. Taking "environment" in the basic etymological sense of that-which-surrounds, a milieu, an ambience, Cooper thus sets out to describe without presupposition the essential features of the way one's surroundings impinge upon awareness. In this sense, "An environment is something for a creature, a field of meanings or significance" (169):

> The beech at the end of my garden belongs to my environment, despite being further away than the rubble beneath the floor where I stand, which does not. A badger in a set by a motorway has the trees on his side in his environment, even though some of these trees are further away than the ones just over the road. City dwellers from different sides of the tracks may share an environment less than hill farmers living miles apart. (168)

Although Cooper uses here his own environment as an example, the issue is to highlight the invariant, general features that would emerge for anyone giving this kind of attention to their "environment," to describe, that is, a basic "environmentality." This is what the later Husserl called a "life-world." The world uncovered through phenomenological attention is one giving itself as already full of incipient implication, a network of meaning in which one knows one's way:

> In calling an environment a field of significance I mean . . . that the items within it signify or point to one another, thereby forming a network of meanings. It is this which confers cohesion, a certain "wholeness," on an environment, rather as episodes in a novel belong to a coherent narrative through pointing back and forth. The German philosopher Martin Heidegger describes a person's world—for example, a farm with its equipment, inhabitants, and surrounds—as constituting a "referential totality." For the various items which belong there—a cow's udder and a milk pail, say,—point towards one another and take on significance only as parts of a whole (p. 170).

To use one of phenomenology's technical terms, our relation to things is essentially an "intentional" one, meaning not that that they are the object of will or choice but that all living consciousness is "intentional" in the sense of necessarily relating to something outside itself. For any such intentionality the world is a totality of such relations, a network of significances that our daily practices foreground (e.g., the need for shelter, food etc.). Reality is first of all, something "meaning-ful" in that sense. It is this stress on the primacy of meaning that has made phenomenology a resource for environmental politics.

For Cooper, another import of the phenomenological attention to things is that the self and its world are inseparable. Any dualism which describes reality in terms of there being an isolated consciousness, a me, on one side and a realm of objects on the other (and then puzzles over how to relate the two) has only confused itself by falsely dividing an existence which was already, fundamentally and originarily, a "being-in-the-world" (Heidegger).

Phenomenology seemed to offer a powerful answer to a major dilemma of post-enlightenment life: that the more natural science succeeds in modeling and understanding the world in terms of material processes governed by natural laws, the more that world seems deprived of any meaning or significant mystery. At issue is the social and political privilege that is often given to scientific conceptions of objectivity as a realm of value-free fact established through a rigorous procedure of abstraction, generalization and formal modeling. Phenomenologists argue that to over-privilege a method which strips nature of all its experienced qualities may leave us with a misleading abstraction, for even scientists and scientific work exist in and begin from that immediate life-world which it is the task of phenomenology to articulate. It is one thing to use the scientific method to isolate a reliable model of things for specific purposes (e.g., ascertaining the geology of the local area with a view to recommendations about the foundations of a house), but quite another to say that the realm of neutral facts made available by this method is the one *true reality* to which all others are subordinate, or in terms of which they must be explained. Phenomenology is a critique of this ontological prejudice.

It is this latent scientism that Cooper rejects in that notion of "the Environment" ironically dominant in much green talk. That tired phrase must be acknowledged as too often an awkward blend of secondhand ecological science and moralism. It is frequently associated with a vocabulary stressing the interdependence and interconnections of ecosystems, assertions based in ecological science but often remote from the immediate experience of those making them. Cooper writes, "Ecological accounts of environments, even when their novelty is exaggerated, are very much in the main scientific tradition. They purport, that is, to be "objective" in the sense of describing the world in terms which are as free as possible from those which render "subjective" attitudes and feelings" (171). As a realm of energy exchanges, food chains and population dynamics, the "environment" in the ecological sense is a long way from the environment in the phenomenological sense: "Every thing that makes an environment special *for* a creature—from the inside, so to speak—is outside the scientific domain" (171). So, ironically, the familiar notion of "the Environment" is "symptomatic of just that 'scientism' of which "new" environmentalists complain" (171). Instead, it is the defense of environments as habitable life-worlds that ought, more fruitfully, to be the issue of a green politics.

This may be a good place to sum up. The aspects of phenomenology of most relevance to environmental thinking have been; (1) the rejection of scientism and a return to "things themselves," that is, the affirmation of the primacy of experience over those approaches that strip it of all lived qualities and leave a partial or questionable abstraction in its place; (2) second is the argument that the realm of value, meaning and so on(the axiological) is not excluded from reality as a matter of method, but uncovered as a pre-given element of experience. This, according to Charles S. Brown and Ted Toadvine, phenomenology becomes, necessarily, *eco-phenomenology*, "that is, a study of the interrelationship between organism and world in its metaphysical and axiological dimensions."[3]

A third point also follows, of particular import to literary criticism. (3) Because a phenomenologist does not claim to be building up some system of philosophical "arguments" or "theses," but to be practicing a patient discipline of describing the fundamental modes in which things present themselves to us, the practice of phenomenological writing is closer to the arts of language than is usual among philosophers. To use Simon Glendinning's wry term, phenomenology is not "argumentocentric."[4] The claim of a phenomenological text may be mediated through language that appeals to our imaginative capacities as much as to our ratiocinative ones. When Martin Heidegger devotes several hundred pages to the minutest and subtlest accounts of forms of boredom, or when Alphonso Lingis evokes our pregiven participation in animality, the distinction between a philosophical and literary text becomes relatively otiose.[5] Phenomenology easily becomes an affirmation of the cognitive value of literature and literary language, seen as a genuine mode of engaged, embodied non-formalized knowledge and perception. Charles S. Brown, for instance, draws on phenomenology to defend environmental nonfiction as a source of genuine cognitive insight into the natural world. Such writing, often engaged with the way non human entities and creatures give themselves to unbiased attention as having intrinsic value, is already a philosophical refutation of anthropocentrism.[6]

Phenomenology in Ecocritical Practice

Let us turn then to two thinkers who can be said to practice a kind of green phenomenology, Gernot Böhme and David Abram.

(1) *An aesthetic of natural forms.* For Böhme one promise of phenomenology is that of a new, environmentally sensitive aesthetics of the natural world. In his *Für eine öklogische Naturästhetik* (Towards an Ecological Nature Aesthetic) (1989), *Atmosphäre* (Atmospheres) (1995), and *Die Nature vor uns: Naturphilosophie in pragmatischer Hinsicht* (The Nature before Us: Nature Philosophy from a Pragmatic Point of View) (2002) he sketched an "ecological nature aesthetic" indebted to phenomenological thinking.[7]

What is the aesthetic allure of many natural forms? For the past several hundred years the discipline of aesthetics has developed with an almost excusive reference to the qualities of artifacts, so that attention to the natural world has usually been secondary. Characteristics derived from reflection upon art are sometimes transferred to natural forms, as in the eighteenth-century cult of the "picturesque," of landscapes which seem to reproduce the qualities and composition of a painting. So, for Böhme, an aesthetic of natural forms would need to eschew the intellectualism of traditional aesthetics with its narrow focus on the artwork and on the phenomena of communication, that is, the assumptions that an artwork has a cultural meaning, that it is saying something other than itself, a mode of thinking not evidently applicable to natural forms. He develops a classic phenomenological argument: the aesthetic is not some sort of subjective or value-laden add-on projected upon reality conceived as more truly a realm of "objective" and value-neutral "fact," it is rather revealed as an integral feature of the way things present themselves and are experienced. Natural beauty is not a projection of art-derived modes of seeing but a matter of real presences registered by the human body as itself part of nature. Böhme endorses efforts by J. W. von Goethe and Wilhelm von Humboldt to articulate the expressive qualities of various natural forms, qualities understood as inherent to their perception, not as anthropomorphic projections (*Atmosphäre*, 142–52). Böhme also refers to the art of English landscape gardening, its consistent, reproducible methods of producing moods or atmospheres which are universally recognized (*Für eine öklogische Naturästhetik*, 79–84). As this example also shows, the aesthetic natural atmospheres which phenomenological attention uncovers are both objective (landscape gardening is not arbitrary) and also, within strict physical constraints, things which human beings can sometimes make for themselves.

Aesthetic atmospheres for Böhme are inseparable from the fact that the body, as a part of nature, participates in the showing and letting-be-felt of things in their multiplicity and varied tonalities. To cultivate an ecological aesthetic necessarily entails acceptance of oneself as a finite body, one that exists in reciprocity with natural forms and processes. It urges human beings, especially in the West, towards a less deceptive and destructive understanding of their own nature:

> Humanity in the age of enlightenment understands itself as a rational entity—and we thus exclude the body from our self-definition. The body becomes for us not that nature that is already ourselves, but rather nature next to us, something external. (*Für eine öklogische Naturästhetik*, 32; my translation)

(2) *A defense of animism (David Abram).* A feature of Cooper's phenomenological exercise is that, unlike Heidegger, he refuses to identify "intentionality" with human beings alone: "Animals too, dwell in fields of significance; the droppings at the entrance to the tunnel indicate a fox, which signifies a threat to the badger's young, whose squealing expresses hunger, which refers the badger to the berries behind that tree, the scent on which means the recent presence of a fox, which indicates etc." (170). The "environment" in this sense is part of an identity. "A badger is not in its set in the way a clod of earth is; the roof of its tunnel is the roof of its home" (168). To damage the "environment" of the badger is tantamount to an assault upon the badger itself.

The focus on the nonhuman as much as the human also characterizes David Abram's *The Spell of the Sensuous*,[8] perhaps the best-known and most influential application of phenomenological thinking to environmental criticism. Abram effectively works through the fuller implications of the argument already described in Cooper that "the creature is … part of its environment, though one could as truly say that the environment is part of it" (178). The phenomenology that Abram follows is that of Merleau-Ponty with its focus on the place of the body as the locus of intentionality, of bodily perception as a condition of thought and language. In this counter-stress on embodiment as the crux of "intentionality," the body is not understood as that entity studied of medical and scientific research, as if it were one object that I happen to encounter among other objects, but phenomenologically, as the primary mode in which humans find themselves in a world, as the ground of self-consciousness in self-perception. Human experience of the world is necessarily a bodily, an incarnate one, and this always gives us a basic sense of orientation among things. Bodily sentience already structures the "life world" around any living thing, in terms of possibilities of warmth or cold, nourishment or threat. It is through the body that we live in a world already full of incipient "meaning" and implication:

> Easily overlooked, this primordial world is always already there when we begin to reflect or philosophize. It is not a private, but a collective, dimension—the common field of our lives and the other lives with which ours are entwined—...the world as we organically experience it in its enigmatic multiplicity and open-endedness, prior to conceptually freezing it into a static space of "facts." (40)

Since possession of bodily sentience is a shared feature of all living things, a certain basic common intelligibility exists between creatures. Possibilities of shelter, danger, nourishment, of reproductive chances all structure the life-world of nonhuman creatures in ways analogous to the kinds of "environment" uncovered in Cooper's essay. Perception *signifies*, in multiplicitous but not incoherent ways. What looks to a squirrel like a safe route through the trees will look to a heron as difficult barrier to be avoided. Phenomenology uncovers the various significances of a lived environment, even as a kind of "originary language common to both people and animals" (87). Abram pushes hard such phenomenological description, reading it as a distinct, ontological claim. He affirms the later, more metaphysical Merleau-Ponty who writes "less about 'the body'" (which in his earlier work had signified primarily the *human* body) and begins to write instead of the collective "Flesh," which signifies both *our* flesh and "the flesh of the world." (66).

Abram's investment in an understanding of bodily perception goes beyond Merleau-Ponty. First, he affirms what he sees as a "startling consonance" between Merleau-Ponty's work and "the worldviews of many indigenous, oral cultures" (69). He reads these as living a fulfilled reciprocity with the natural world, a respectful participation of the human in a realm of multiple natural agencies, as opposed to the anthropocentrism of literate Western cultures that take the sphere of human culture as solely of significance. Second, for Abram phenomenology becomes part of a philosophical and ethical defense of *animism*, which is no longer to be dismissed as an obsolete belief system. Often falsely caricatured as projecting some mysterious spirit or awareness into inanimate things, animism is more truly described in terms of a general sensitivity to real, nonhuman agency:

> When we attend to our experience not as intangible minds but as sounding, speaking, bodies, we begin to sense that we are heard, even listened to, by the numerous other bodies that surround us. Our sensing bodies respond to the eloquence of

certain buildings and boulders, to the articulate motions of dragonflies. We find ourselves in a listening, speaking world. (86)

Abram argues that an originary reciprocity with the world known to oral culture
was lost through the technologies of print and writing, as the psychic effects of these
divorced the human from its immediate surroundings, projecting a world of inherited law, cultural narratives, and administrative systems, all made possible and sedi-
mented by the written record. So whereas people in an "indigenous and oral" context,
experienced "their own consciousness as simply one form of awareness among others" (9), writing made possible the dangerous illusion that human culture is the sole
environment, or at least the only one that signifies. The phenomenological discipline
of being minutely attentive to the ways in which we are actually conscious of things
can help us escape from the numbed condition of a merely lettered consciousness.
Phenomenology becomes a redemptive force, revealing that, underneath, "we are *all*
animists" (57).

Although both focus on embodiment as the primary mode of human intentionality,
there are striking differences between the arguments of Böhme and Abram. For Abram,
phenomenology is at the service of a project of retrieval, that of an original human
nature, supposedly long suppressed in modern, urban people. Phenomenological
attention may uncover a deeper nature within us. Abram's argument becomes another
version of the story of a human fall from a condition of supposed plentitude. For
Böhme, however, phenomenology is not an implicit primitivism. It engages with atmospheres which are at once objective and a matter of human enhancement or making.
Furthermore, acknowledgment that pristine nature no *longer* strictly exists, either in
the natural world beyond us or in nature as our own bodies, means that we need to
develop an explicit "Nature politics," one whose topic would be what kind of "nature"
we wish to inhabit, just as ordinary politics concerns what kind of society we which to
live in. It is not then a matter of uncovering some lost or original human relationship
with nature but of helping us discover, enhance, or even create the kinds of environments we find valuable.

The popularity of Abram's book among ecocritics, especially in North America,
was in spite of the fact that it contains almost no models of literary reading or analysis. Abram acknowledges that his program would not be one of somehow reviving oral
cultures in modern society, and speaks very briefly elsewhere of writers who achieve
similar effects in the written medium.[9] The comparison with Böhme is again instructive.
His concern with atmospheres as modes of engagements that can yet also be created
by human beings enables a far more resourceful reading of art, its history and current
situation. To give one simple example, Böhme describes an installation of Franz Xaver
Baier at the Hessischen Landesmuseum Darmstadt. Baier placed, singly or in groups,
zinc buckets full of ripe fragrant apples at selected positions in the museum, often right
next to various esteemed paintings. Böhme is fascinated by the effect this simple action
has in defamiliarizing and questioning the modes of attention toward art that dominate
in a museum or exhibition space ("The peculiar aura of sanctity, that mix of the cultish

and an exhibition atmosphere is suspended and made perceptible as such by the banal and frugal objects" [*Die Nature vor uns,* 243]). Such installation art disturbs modes of conventional comportment, simply by affirming a realization that "we ourselves, qua bodily, are nature" (244):

> Should art make of the body its theme as that nature which we ourselves are, then it would have a vastly unknown realm for investigation and would mediate to modern people an experience of themselves which they have long repressed. (*Die Natur vor uns,* 228)

In a study of 1996, Böhme and his brother Hartmut survey the long history of the ancient doctrine of the four elements (fire, earth, air, and water) as principles of both physics and psychology, notions long since superseded by the work of the scientific enlightenment.[10]Attentive to a deeper cultural history, however, the Böhmes discuss how an unformalized version of the ancient symbolic framework of the elements still survives in modern lyrics reacting to environmental crisis, with their images of a disturbances of the air, earth, fire, or water as primary conditions of health (301) (one might think too of the place of the elements in texts such as T.S. Eliot's *The Waste Land* (1922) or in Gary Snyder's *Mountains and Rivers without End* (1996), images suggesting a disturbance to the basic environmentality of life). Modern painting likewise shows this too:

> In contemporary art the elements are no longer what they are according to the scientific-technical approach, and yet they appear far removed from being gods and emotional powers. They appear as partners of the human in its bodily-sensory existence. (*Feuer Wasser Erde Luft,* 302)

Other questions arise at this point. Abram laments a lost "harmony" or "fusion" with nature, calling for a re-connection to one's supposedly truer self, and Böhme likewise sees art as the retrieval of the fact that "we ourselves, qua bodily, are nature" (244). Is the phenomenological method here in danger of dwindling to the instrument of the crude romantic meta-narrative that perpetually threatens thinking in environmental criticism? This is to posit a fall from some lost state of harmonious interrelation or "unity" of human and nonhuman, something supposedly severed at some point—by the rise of writing in Abram's case—an alienation held to be answered by some rather implausibly redemptive change of consciousness. Is not the body, in these late romantic programs, idealized as a possible agent of transformation?

Abram also exemplifies what is arguably a common weakness in ecocritical engagements with philosophy. This is the distinctly unphilosophical practice of picking up an isolated or piecemeal arguments from a philosopher in order to serve an agenda assumed in advance to be valid, one usually couched in terms of "reuniting" the human with nature, or as reinforcing that romantic anti-intellectualism that pits immediate experience against the supposedly mentalistic or abstract. For instance, there is nothing in either Abram or Böhme on the now substantial body of thought criticizing the bases of phenomenology itself, the work of Jacques Derrida for instance.[11]

Ted Toadvine argues against "phenomenologically oriented approaches to environmental philosophy" that use Merleau-Ponty to affirm an original oneness or kinship between the human and nature.[12] Such "humans as part of nature" arguments, he claims, can become reductive, denying the challenging otherness of natural forms and other creatures by too appropriative a conception of their kinship to us—a kind of intellectual anthropomorphism, one might say. Instead, Toadvine postulates a kind of post-phenomenology that is sensitive to the opacity and otherness of things and that does not excessively posit nature as continuous, homogenous, predictable and assimilable. Toadvine is concerned with that wild or brute element of being that is not necessarily a part of the horizon of possible experience, nor "a modality of consciousness, nor even a perceiving corporeality" (148). Phenomenology of the older kind is in danger of overlooking the degree to which the world is more and other than the meanings given to an intentionality:

> What is called for is not a new "philosophy" of nature, but an ethics of the impossibility of any "philosophy" of nature. The basis for such "impossibility" is phenomenological, but in a way that stretches this method, perhaps to the breaking point. (140)

For instance, "there is an opacity of my body as a desiring being which subjectivity cannot penetrate, just as there is an ecceity [thisness] and resistance of matter which cannot in principle be comprehended or brought into the circuit of language." (149)

ECOPHENOMENOLOGY AND BEYOND PHENOMENOLOGY?

What of phenomenology and ecocriticism in the future? The issue can perhaps be expressed in the following postulate: all that is most challenging in the twenty-first century about the environmental crisis—politically, socially, psychologically, and philosophically—can be gauged to the degree to which it challenges or even eludes altogether a phenomenological approach.

Three issues stand out. The first presents phenomenology with the question of our access to the lived environments of nonhuman animals.

How far can elements of our own animality and embeddedness enable a sense of the intentionality of a nonhuman creature?[13] To develop phenomenology in relation to inhuman modes of intentionality is an immense and exciting challenge. It is a question that may open new ways of reading and valuing those literary texts on animals which try to transcend the weakly anthropomorphic. It also throws a new defamiliarizing light on many assumptions about the peculiarity of being human. Essays collected in *Phenomenology and the Non-Human Animal* (2007)[14] discredit many features of inherited dogmatic distinction of human and animal, especially notions of human exceptionalism that rest on some idealization of human reason or reflection as transcending the natural world in order to view it from some supposed outside.

Toadvine asks of phenomenology itself the difficult question: "despite its value for describing the nonhuman animal lifeworld and its overlap with our own, does phenomenology actually avoid the problem of human exceptionalism, or does it simply reinscribe it on another register?"[15] If the phenomenological method serves only to identify human intentionality with an ability to reflect which also severs it from its natural environment, does it not risk serving the terms of a familiar human/animal distinction? When Heidegger describes animal intentionality as a condition of being totally captivated or captured by its surroundings, as opposed to human power of reflection, does he not make the human the site of a dogmatic rupture from other life?[16] Toadvine avoids re-erecting a discredited human exceptionalism through another reading of Merleau-Ponty's late work, tracing as it does the human reflective capacity to the nature of sentient life more generally, to the fact that touching is also, reciprocally, the capacity of being touched: "Animal being is, on this view, just as much as human being, an interrogative fold within the world's flesh" ("How Not to Be a Jellyfish," 52). In relation to phenomenology:

> A double movement is required, which, on the one hand, opens a space for the positive description of the meaning of the animal's world as other than merely a modification of the world of the human subject, while, on the other hand—and this is perhaps the more complicated task—the human as such much be reconceived as neither opposed to nor reducible to the animal. (41)

A second huge issue is that of the possible gender assumptions being made in assertions about human intentionality.Neither Böhme and Abram take up another controversy in existential phenomenology, that of the degree to which their accounts of constitutive bodily experience are tacitly gendered, based on the male body alone. For instance, for De Beauvoir and thinkers influenced by her, the experience of pregnancy suggests modes of intentionality and self-other relations that escape the privilege of the visible in Merleau-Ponty's thinking. Sara Heinämaa writes:

> The body is not a solid closed volume but has an internal space capable of opening to another... For the woman, her body is not constituted as a solid object but rather as a fold which is capable of opening up to form an inner space that can house another sensing being. This opening is experienced in erotic encounters but more vigorously in pregnancy.[17]

A third challenge for phenomenological approaches lies in the global scale of some environmental issues. It is increasingly accepted that the planet has now entered a new geological epoch, the Anthropocene. The term, first coined by the chemist Paul Crutzen, names that epoch, arguably even long underway, in which human activities have become a geological force on a global scale.[18] To live in the Anthropocene seems to present a host of new and largely unprecedented questions and dilemmas for human self-conception, for ethics, philosophy, economics and politics.

Take the notion of a "carbon footprint." What kind of metaphor/concept is it? The image translates the quantity of carbon emissions for which I am directly responsible, into a sensory image, a footprint. In reality my "footprint" is an impact that escapes immediate apprehension, including that of phenomenology. It only in fact makes sense through a process of complex mediation, involving physics, meteorology, and so on. In other words, though crucial, it comes to our attention only through a great deal of scientific mediation. It requires that very notion of "environment" of which Cooper is suspicious. The metaphor—or catachresis—of the "footprint," translates the scientific data into something intelligible in terms of the individual human body and its immediate surroundings.

A second way in which the very notion of a carbon footprint eludes phenomenology relates to scale effects. If it were just a matter of my own emissions there would be no controversy. The size of my carbon footprint is of no interest or significance in itself except in relation to the incalculable effect of there being so many millions of other footprints over an uncertain timescale, which is something beyond my individual phenomenological horizon entirely. Third, the significance of "carbon footprint" is one in which the finitude of the planet is inherent—crudely, if the planet were larger, my personal footprint would be smaller. "Carbon footprint" becomes a very peculiar catachresis, collapsing huge and tiny scales upon each other, eluding the phenomenological approach.

Consideration of scale effects and the foregrounding of vast but not immediately perceptible planetary impacts seem set to be definitive features of environmental thinking in the Anthropocene, but both are outside the scope of phenomenological attention, which seem bound to older, insufficient conceptions of localism and with overcoming individual alienation. How could phenomenological attention, presented with a modern Western breakfast, intuit that the food miles that went into it may circle the globe?

How this shift will affect individual ecocritical readings, mostly trapped in the old paradigms, is still hard to say. To close this essay, here is one example, admittedly a fairly easy one, of this kind of post-phenomenological quandary. It concerns a poem by Gary Snyder, the first poem of his first collection *Riprap* (1959):

> Mid-August at Sourdough Mountain Lookout
> Down valley a smoke haze
> Three days heat, after five days rain
> Pitch glows on the fir-cones
> Across rocks and meadows
> Swarms of new flies.
> I cannot remember things I once read
> A few friends, but they are in cities
> Drinking cold snow-water from a tin cup
> Looking down for miles
> Through high still air.[19]

This seems a poem of bucolic meditation, a celebration of solitude in a nonhuman environment that liberates the speaker from the pressures of a social identity. This is how most readings take it, reading on the individual scale as affirming a process of natural therapy and self-discovery. For Timothy Gray, it is about a process of "de-education"

("I cannot remember things I once read") of "the poet hoping to commune with his natural surroundings."[20] In Tim Dean's loosely phenomenological reading, the poem becomes a celebration of being free "from the ties of the civilized."[21] Here the 'I'"does not order or dominate the landscape in any way"[22] but is situated in the natural realm, as a part of that realm, rather as in Cooper's preferred sense of environment. The looking is seen as nonpurposive, "not subsumed here to any other measure and this function."[23]

Nick Selby, however, argues that this is a poem about work, to be situated in relation to American conceptions of work and constructions of landscape.[24] The speaker's seeing is deeply purposive, for it is part of the task of being employed as a fire-watcher, as the young Snyder was. The specific details of the landscape are focused on appearance that, after three days of heat, may indicate fire or look like fire or smoke ("Pitch glows on the fir cones/Across rocks and meadows/Swarms of new flies"). Contrary to the familiar association of such reveries with leisure, or as the space for values to be opposed to the realm of productive work, the mountain is a place of work and the trees a potential crop. Selby explores Snyder's poetics as one in which a poem is itself a workplace for examination of the crucial part played in American conceptions of cultural identity by varying appropriations of the land as a cultural text.

All three ecocritical readings see what Snyder is engaging as valuable in loosely green terms, whether this is a familiar exposure to the natural world as a kind of personal therapy, an affirmation and chastening acceptance of the finitude of the human measure, or a staging of poetic writing as itself a mode of work critical of various ways in which American culture has appropriated the landscape.

In fact, however, at the global scale now demanded by the thought of climate change, *all* these positive evaluations seem questionable or inadequate. It turns out that the fire-watcher depicted in the poem is actually engaged in an environmentally destructive practice. Wryly acknowledging in retrospect the joke on himself, Snyder observed in 2007 that to suppress small fires, now understood as ecologically benign, is only to encourage conditions for a massive and genuinely destructive fire at a later date, as debris builds up.[25] Counterintuitively, what looks like environmental protection on the small scale is actually environmental destruction on the regional and even on global one, for, in the Anthropocene, deforestation is a planetary issue.

Clearly the later understanding of fires in the forest ecosystem, casts an ironic light over the reading of Snyder's poem in terms of what comes to seem, retrospectively, a premature green moralism in the readings by Dean and Gray, yet the methodological nationalism of Selby's reading also becomes untenable. Modes of thinking tied to phenomenology, or indeed to any thinking inherently tied to the scale of the individual life, are likely to be circumscribed or incomplete.

The Anthropocene also questions the adequacy of the kinds of ethical programme that follow from a green phenomenology. Both Cooper and Abram advocate environmental activism as a form of phenomenologically informed and conception of localized care. Cooper looks to "emerging, mutually supporting league of little, local pockets of resistance" rather than "exhortations to 'global awareness' ..." (Cooper, 179; compare Abram, 268). Such an ethic of local care needs to be supplemented by Timothy Morton's alternative and counter-intuitive definition: "the environment is that which cannot be indicated directly." (175)

David Wood writes:

> If my tree is dying, I notice. But the earth slowly dying is not obvious, not something I can see at a glance out of my window.... there is a gap between what I can see and what may really be happening. The glance is ripe for education.[26]

Where, especially in the Anthropocene, does "my environment" end? Someone living a high-carbon lifestyle in New York or the Scottish Highlands is already lurking as a destructive interloper on the floodplains of Bangladesh.

Where then to take an environmentally engaged phenomenology? Wood proposes an *ecophenomenology* "in the double sense of a phenomenological ecology, and an ecological phenomenology" (229). This would rethink and revise what is arguably too dismissive an account of the scientific attitude in traditional phenomenology. Its opposition between approaching reality as either a realm of natural causality or as a life-world full of meaning may now seem far too crude. For example, to stress the body as the locus of intentionality is also to acknowledge the degree to which bodily existence is lodged in the natural world, in ecological streams of energy exchange, and structured through the long-term biological engineering of evolutionary processes. Intentionality is not reducible to but neither is it independent of such physiological facts as those that structure the sensorium in certain ways, or render particular foods attractive or impossible. Wood writes: "these sorts of connections illustrate how much a certain naturalization of consciousness would require, at the same time, an expansion of our sense of the natural" (224).[27] A kind of scientific or ecological literacy is called for, to highlight deeper structuring forces, elements of an impersonal purposiveness, within my own sense of the meanings of things.

A new ecophenonomology, then, would do two things. First, an enhanced scientific literacy would address the limits of inherited phenomenology—helping bridge the gap between seeing that a tree is dying and understanding that the planet is dying, something foreclosed in Cooper's sense of the "environment." Ecophenomenology would involve "an enhanced attentiveness to the complexity of natural phenomena, and the ease with which that is hidden from view by our ordinary experience" (155). Second, however, it would still continue the older task of resisting the tyranny of the scientific as the solely accepted model of the real. Wood's example of such tyranny is the use of ecological science by some deep ecologists to offer a stance in which any singular life only has significance as part of a chain of relations—a view that is arguably slides towards the ecofascist. Ecophenomenology, by reaffirming the individual life-world in its idiosyncrasy, would remind us that the "whole" "is dependent on the continuing coordination of parts that have, albeit residual, individual interests" (226–27). Ecophenomenology would become a kind of boundary discourse, more deconstructive than otherwise, refusing the premature closure of given areas of questioning, modes of disciplinary competence, procedures of reading and assumptions of scale.

NOTES

1. For useful introductory material see the essays in Hubert L. Dreyfus and Mark A. Wrathall eds., *A Companion to Phenomenology and Existentialism* (Oxford: Wiley-Blackwell, 2009); Dermot Moran, *An Introduction to Phenomenology* (London: Routledge, 2000); Simon Glendinning ed., *The Edinburgh Encyclopedia of Continental Philosophy* (Edinburgh: Edinburgh University Press, 1999).
2. "The idea of environment," in David E. Cooper and Joy A. Palmer eds., *The Environment in Question: Ethics and Global Issues* (London: Routledge, 1992), 165–80. Compare Heidegger, *Being and Time,* trans. John Macquarrie and Edward Robinson (Oxford: Basil Blackwell, 1980), 91ff.
3. "Eco-phenomenology: An Introduction," in Charles S. Brown and Ted Toadvine eds., *Eco-Phenomenology: Back to the Earth Itself* (Albany: SUNY Press, 2003), xi–xxi, xiii.
4. Simon Glendinning, *In the Name of Phenomenology* (London: Routledge, 2007), 23.
5. Heidegger, *the Fundamental Concepts of Metaphysics: World, Finitude, Solitude,* trans. William McNeill and Nicholas Walker (Bloomington: Indiana University Press, 1995); "Bestiality," in *Animal Others: On Ethics, Ontology, and Animal Life*, 37–54.
6. "Respect for Experience as a Way into the Problem, of Moral Boundaries," in *Nature's Edge: Boundary Explorations in Ecological Theory and Practice*, ed. Charles S. Brown and Ted Toadvine (Albany: SUNY, 2007), 83–91, 90.
7. *Für eine öklogische Naturästhetik* (Frankfurt am M. Suhrkamp, 1989); *Atmosphäre* (Frankfurt am M. Suhrkamp, 1995); *Die Nature vor uns: Naturphilosophie in pragmatischer Hinsicht* (Kusterdingen: Die Graue Edition (2002). Surprisingly, little of Böhme 's work is available is English, but see "An Aesthetic Theory of Nature: An Interim Report," in *Thesis Eleven* 32 (1992:90–102; and "Aesthetic Knowledge of Nature," in *Issues in Contemporary Culture and Aesthetics* 5 (1970): 27–37. All translations in this essay are my own.
8. David Abram, *The Spell of the Sensuous* (New York: Vintage Books, 1996).
9. "Between the Body and the Breathing Earth: A Reply to Ted Toadvine," *Environmental Ethics* 27 (2005): 171–90, 179.
10. *Feuer Wasser Erde Luft: Eine Kulturgeshchichte der Elemente* [Fire Water Earth Air: A Cultural History of the Elements], (Munich: C.H. Beck, 1996).
11. See W. McKenna and J. Clarke Evans eds., *Derrida and Phenomenology* (Boston: Kluwer Academic Publishers, 1995).
12. "The Primacy of Desire and its Phenomenological Consequences," in *Eco-Phenomenology*, 139–53, 139.
13. I develop this issue in more detail in Chapter 20, "Anthropomorphism," in *The Cambridge Introduction to Literature and the Environment* (Cambridge: Cambridge University Press, 2010).
14. Corinne Painter and Christian Lotz, eds., *Phenomenology and the Non-Human Animal: At the Limits of Experience* (Dordrecht: Springer, 2007).
15. "How Not to Be a Jellyfish: Human Exceptionalism and the Ontology of Reflection," in *Phenomenology and the Non-Human Animal,"* 39–55, 42.
16. For Heidegger and Derrida on animality, see Matthew Calarco, *Zoographies: The Question of the Animal from Heidegger to Derrida.* (New York: Columbia University Press 2008).
17. "Feminism," in *A Companion to Phenomenology and Existentialism* (2009), 502–15, 510.
18. See Crutzen's chapter in Eckart Ehlers and Thomas Krafft, eds, *Earth System Science in the Anthropocene* (Berlin; Springer, 2006).

19. In *The Gary Snyder Reader: Prose, Poetry, and Translations* (Washington DC: Counterpoint, 1999), 399.
20. Timothy Gray, *Gary Snyder and the Pacific Rim. Creating Countercultural Community* (Iowa City: University of Iowa, 2006), 107.
21. Tim Dean, *Gary Snyder and the American Unconscious: Inhabiting the Ground* (New York: St. Martin's Press, 1991), 21.
22. Ibid.
23. Ibid, 92.
24. Nick Selby, " 'Coming back to oneself / coming back to the land.' Gary Snyder's Poetics," in *Reading under the Sign of Nature: New Essays in Ecocriticism*, ed. John Tallmadge and Henry Harrington (Salt Lake City: University of Utah Press, 2000), 179–97.
25. *Back on the Fire: Essays* (Emeryville CA: Avalon, 2007), 83.
26. "What is Eco-Phenomenology?, in Brown and Toadvine eds. *Ecophenomenology: Back to the Earth Itself* (Albany: SUNY Press, 2003), 211–32, 230.
27. For Ray Brassier, Daniel Dennett, and Thomas Metzinger, the insights of modern neuroscience undermine the authority of the basic phenomenological principle of unbiased attention to things as they present themselves. The seemingly primary immediacy of consciousness, the first person point of view, "can and should be understood as a phenomenon generated by sub-personal but perfectly objectifiable neurobiological processes" (Ray Brassier, *Nihil Unbound: Enlightenment and Extinction* (New York: Palgrave Macmillan, 2007), 31.

CHAPTER 16

··

DECONSTRUCTION AND/AS ECOLOGY

··

TIMOTHY MORTON

THE DARK SIDE OF THE THING

··

WHEN my son Simon was about nine months old, he started turning objects—baskets, toy trucks, stuffed animals—over and over.. He was trying to see their other sides. Of course, when Simon arrived at the other side, the original side became the other side. So he would turn the object over again to see the new other side. The game occupied him for long stretches of time. This hidden dimension was *irreducible*: no matter how many times Simon turned an object over, it would never reveal its obscure reverse. This didn't dampen his enthusiasm.

At the same time, Simon began to take an interest in books and writing. This curiosity was exactly the same as his newfound awareness of the hidden sides of things. He tried to turn pages, though his baby fingers only succeeded in overturning entire books. Still, it was evident that page turning was congruent with the turning of other objects. In effect, Simon was turning over the "pages" of objects, just as we turn the pages of a text "to see what happens next."

We think of writing and reading, unlike talking and walking (let alone handling objects) as a little unnatural—perhaps especially if we are nature writers. The phrase "nature writing" seems almost oxymoronic given ecocritical assumptions that writing is rather unnatural. Yet writing and reading are part of whatever "nature" is. What is DNA if not a text inside cells, a set of recipe-like instructions (algorithms) for producing life forms? Just like reading, our awareness of the environment contains difference—hidden dark sides that structure our experience of the side exposed to view. Think of walking through a forest—an especially vivid example because each tree is like a letter in a vast multidimensional script (trees don't conveniently go from left to right, except in an orchard), and you can easily lose your way. The irreducibly hidden dimension of things has been well explored by phenomenological philosophers who examine experience: Edmund Husserl, Maurice Merleau-Ponty, and Martin Heidegger. It's marvelously described in David Abram's *The Spell of the Sensuous*.[1] Each writer engages with reading in order to articulate the shadowy hidden qualities of the thing.[2] The emerging school of object oriented ontology takes Heidegger's argument one step further, applying the dark side of things not only to human–thing relationships, but also to the way things encounter one another. Object-oriented ontology calls these encounters "translations."[3]

Texts are environmental, not simply because they are made of paper and ink that comes from trees and plants (or other terrestrial sources), or because they are sometimes about ecological matters. Reading is *formally* ecological, since in order to read we must take account of the dark sides of things, as intimately connected to the "lighter" sides as the recto and verso of a piece of writing paper. Reading discovers a constantly flowing, shifting play of temporality, and a constant process of differentiation—like evolution. All texts are environmental: they organize the space around and within them into plays of meaning and non-meaning.

Some writers in the lineage of deconstruction such as Heidegger and Paul de Man argue that the dark side of things is what poetry is about.[4] The turning of pages brings to mind what Denise Levertov says of ocean waves, in lines whose repetition establishes a wave-like ebb and flow:

> and as you read
> the sea is turning its dark pages,
> turning
> its dark pages.
>
> ("To the Reader," 8–10)[5]

Levertov's repetition wonderfully suggests turning a page, then turning it back to redo the sequence, the second time with a little hesitation; or turning another page, this time more slowly. Repetition disorients our sense of direction. The repeated phrase introduces a gap between "turning" and "its"; or it illuminates a gap that was already there. Shadowy reverse sides appear everywhere: between the first "turning" and the second, between words, forward onto the next line, then backward ("Did I really read that?") onto the previous one. Hesitantly luxuriant reading is precisely what the poem is talking about on another level. It is as if, while we are reading the poem, the sea is reading itself, in a mysterious self-pleasuring narcissism (repetition is always strange and erotic).

An automated process occurring without conscious input, like a book reading itself, is not a bad image for a computer program, or for DNA–RNA transcription and translation. Nor is it a bad image for Nature (I shall capitalize the term from now on to make it seem slightly strange), often imagined to be "just happening" (and as a book—the question is, what kind of book?). There is something uncanny about this "just happening": on the one hand it makes us anxious about being automated puppets; on the other it suggests that puppets have powers of thought and reflection. The book that reads itself doubles the book into reader and text: the sea as reader, and the sea as something that is read (the ocean and its waves). Is this one thing, or two? All statements function a little like the Cretan liar paradox: "I am lying" means that the *I* telling you "I am lying" is different from the *I* about whom it is said, "He is a liar." A weird doubling is hardwired into language like a vanishing point, the place in perspective paintings that organizes how we see them.

The hidden dimension definitely exists. Yet as soon as you go round the back of a tree, or fly around the moon, the dark side is no longer there: it has been displaced. You can't get rid of the dark side, but it keeps disappearing, just ahead and just behind. This dark side manifests between pages, sentences, and words. You never know what the end of a sentence is going to be until after you have read it. So you project ahead—what Wolfgang Iser calls "protension"—and retrospectively—("retention").[6] The "present" of the text is a moving blank that travels as we read.

Writing is drawing lines that differ from each other enough to be recognizable as letters. There are all kinds of ways of drawing a letter /t/ for example.[7] As long as a /t/ differs enough from other letters, it will function as a /t/. This good-enough criterion is like evolutionary "satisficing": evolution is fine with physical traits that don't kill you before you pass on your DNA. One only needs to look and quack enough like a duck to actually be a duck.[8] Structural linguistics holds that letters, words, and sentences manifest through negative difference: /t/ is /t/ insofar as it is not /p/, "tree" is not "treat," and so on. (DNA expression is a matter of which genes are turned off.) There must therefore be some minimal difference that distinguishes a /t/ from a non-/t/. A piece of /t/ must therefore be legible as /t/: humans are capable of discerning letters by their tips alone, when the shape of those letters is all but covered.

There should be some minimal difference that distinguishes a significant piece of a letter from an insignificant squiggle (Figure 16.1). How, for example, can you tell that the bird Woodstock in the Peanuts cartoons is talking, even though his language is illegible little grass-like lines?

FIGURE **16.1.** Copyright Charles M. Schultz.

When we reach this level, however, something strange happens. We can't rigorously distinguish between a mark and a squiggle, unless we have decided beforehand what counts as significant and as insignificant. Consider a pattern of squiggles. Does the patterned quality—the repetition of a certain sequence of squiggles or a certain shape of squiggling—fall on the "hither" or the "yonder" side of meaning? Crystals are patterned; DNA is patterned; viruses are giant crystals of RNA, some with very regular surfaces—the common cold is an icosahedron. Which of these patterns is meaningful? On which ontological level does the meaning manifest? What about other levels? Are they totally devoid of meaning?

Any given system of signs entails another system that distinguishes meaning from non-meaning, for instance to establish differences between marks and squiggles (grammar). Grammar as such—what makes signs meaningful—is already a kind of philosophy. In inventing Tibetan, Buddhism had a unique opportunity to encode its non-dualism directly into grammar.[9] There is no exit from metaphysics into some special non-metaphysical realm; yet every metaphysical realm we can conceive of is shifting and unsteady at its core. We are in an infinite regress, since the system that differentiates between mark and non-mark is also made of language, which is made of marks, and so forth. No matter how we endeavor to maintain the consistency of the system, what differentiates between mark and squiggle—the difference of difference, as it were—remains ambiguous. At the "bottom" of any system there lies some fundamental inconsistency that ironically guarantees that everything above that level will be coherent—the ambiguity may affect every other level. You are reading this sentence because at some level it's made of meaningless squiggles. A similar problem is intrinsic to life forms too, because DNA and RNA are molecules that read and translate and encode: squiggles and marks, at the same time. One distinguishing feature of letters is that they can be replicated, but as any medieval scribe will tell you, this involves error. Evolution is repetition with differences—as in poetry, these "errors" are functional, producing novelty and significance. (I deliberately omit, for now, any rigid assertion of a thin and precise boundary between "deliberate" and "accidental" error.) And on levels up from the genome, life forms are ambiguous and incoherent. The ironically titled *The Origin of Species* proves that there are no species as such: a deconstructive view of Darwinism holds that it's radically impossible to distinguish decisively between a species, a variant, and a monstrosity.[10]

According to what Jacques Derrida called deconstruction, texts (including life forms) talk about their fundamental undecidability—an irreducible dark side. In mathematical terms, we are talking about entropy. If you think of entropy as an amount of information that you can't be sure about (Shannon entropy), then a coin has an entropy of 1 bit since it has two sides (it can be tossed to read heads or tails). Printed English text has an entropy of between 0.6 and 1.5 bits per letter.[11] That means that recognizing the predictable meaningfulness of a string of letters in printed English can be as unlikely a predicting coin toss, even slightly more. Shannon entropy is a way for mathematics to say that things have hidden dark sides. For every head there's a tail, for every recto there's a verso, for every letter there's a squiggle.

Life forms contain codes. These codes operate like human languages, through differ-ences. From a simple menu of four amino acids, combined in different ways, you can obtain all life forms, just as you can construct Shakespeare and *Reader's Digest* from the same alphabet. Since life forms are texts—cladistics calls them *phenotypes*, forms based on a certain *genotype*—they manifest hidden dark sides. This manifestation goes all the way down to the life–non-life boundary, just as language goes all the way down to the mark–squiggle boundary. In order to have DNA there must be ribosomes (factories that make enzymes); and in order to have ribosomes, there must be DNA—an infinite regress. The regress necessitates something like what Sol Spiegelman calls RNA World, a paradoxical "pre-living life" in which RNA is attached to a non-organic replicator such as a certain kind of silicate crystal.[12] A replication system was already in place before "life" began: Stuart Kauffman's theory of autocatalysis, for instance, in which some structures can become their own catalysts, applies to RNA, which existed before DNA. It becomes meaningless to talk about a single evolutionary origin. Like deconstruction, evolutionary biology rejects teleology: the claim that beings tend towards an end or emerge from an origin. At any given moment, boundaries between and within life forms are disturbingly arbitrary, at least from their genomes' point of view: "Organisms and genomes may . . . be regarded as compartments of the biosphere through which genes in general circulate" such that "the whole of the gene pool of the biosphere is available to all organisms."[13]

Deconstruction holds that meaning and unmeaning secretly depend upon one another. Before we interpret marks as marks, a grammar is already in place; all texts are made of squiggles that encode how we are to read them. The endless play of the dark side of things is what deconstruction calls *différance,* whose different spelling you can read but not hear (the word itself has its own dark side). The trouble with *différance* is that you can't get rid of it: when you try, it appears somewhere else, a shadow forever haunting your conceptual illumination. *Différance* is a humiliating fact akin to Copernicus' dis-covery that the Earth goes around the Sun, or Freud's discovery of the unconscious, or Darwin's discovery of evolution.[14] Each discovery is decentering, since each one ascer-tains that we are not directly, totally in charge of meaning and existence. (By "we" I mean conscious beings; bonobos might find Copernicus humiliating too.) Since "humilia-tion" literally means "being brought close to earth," it is a good sign when ecocriticism ponders these modes of thinking.

Deconstruction is not nominalism: it tells us something profound about our actual universe. It would be a big mistake to see deconstruction as saying that things only exist insofar as we have names for them. Nominalism preserves a boundary between things and signs for things. Deconstruction disturbingly suggests that this boundary cannot be accounted for within nominalism as such: nominalism too has a hidden shadow. Another way to fend off deconstruction is to say that it is "just" about texts; but since many phenomena in our universe can be described as texts, deconstruction must apply to them. There is nothing to stop scholars from combining deconstruction with science; this includes writers like Heidegger, from whom Derrida derives the term deconstruction and from whom he inherits the idea of the irreducible human displacement from any center of meaning. As Derrida himself and others have asserted, there is no contradiction between deconstruction and Darwinism.[15]

Deconstruction is the secret best friend of ecocriticism, despite how some versions of ecocriticism want to rough it up. We can't unthink the last thousand years of philosophy and science, and in particular, the humanities can't unthink deconstruction. Far from totally demystifying things, deconstruction, like evolution, reveals a situation even more mysterious, uncanny, and intimate than other forms of environmental criticism. Yet deconstruction must investigate the sacred cows of ecological criticism, for instance the "world" that ecocriticism wants to re-enchant. The notion of "world" is a potent force in imagining Nature. What exactly is this world? Let's begin with some bad news: there isn't one.

WE AREN'T THE WORLD

The dark side of things is well known to phenomenology, the philosophical study of experience. But only up to a certain limit. Phenomenology is in danger of reifying the difference between the hidden side and the unhidden side, turning it into a thing-like, solid, independent, and "real" fact. Phenomenological criticism of the environment (ecophenomenology) often opposes a more rigorous application of its insights into how hidden dimensions structure meaning. Ecophenomenology urgently wants to assert that walking, for instance, is a stronger, more virile form of reading; and to disavow the illusory, passive, feminine aspects of phenomena. Perhaps this is why Abram turned from conjuring tricks to ecophenomenology, seeming to offer salvation from empty, formal trickery. Yet Nature is precisely a find-the-Lady trick: now you see it, now you don't. Many cultures characterize Nature as the Trickster. As the psychoanalyst Jacques Lacan proclaimed, "What constitutes pretense is that, in the end, you don't know whether it's pretense or not."[16] Derrida attended Lacan's lectures in the 1960s.

"Worlds" fascinate phenomenology. They possess a coherent hither and a yonder, height and depth: they bestow a sense of meaningful dimensionality. Like a powerful movie, "world" suggests feeling surrounded by or embedded in a field rich with significance. Relying on touchy feely ideologies of "embeddedness," ecophenomenology resists the humiliating darkness of things: the way things elude our grasp (conceptual and physical), the way the darkness might not conceal depths, but a depthless opaque surface. Coherent dimensionality conceals what Derrida would call "the rules of its game," the flickering between categories on at least one level of its generative structure.[17]

The Lord of the Rings is a marvelously constructed "world": J. R. R. Tolkien developed the languages and histories of Middle Earth long before he sat down to write the story. Middle Earth is perfect for thinking about how deconstruction might consider ecology and environmentalism. Inevitably, this line of thinking seemingly runs counter to conventional ways of understanding Tolkien, though Patrick Curry has recently argued that Tolkien's work is surprisingly postmodern.[18] Middle Earth deals in all kinds of figurative patterns dear to environmentalism's heart: a certain Romanticism (as opposed to modernism or postmodernism); the Scandinavian and Germanic (as opposed to the Persian or Chinese); depth (as opposed to surface); life (as opposed to artifice); agriculture (as opposed to industry—just think of Saruman's production of fighters who are weirdly cloned); magic (as opposed to technology—Gandalf's fireworks versus Saruman's high explosives); sincerity (as opposed to irony); being straightforward (as opposed to being "queer," frequently used to describe the foreign, the unnatural and the evil).[19] One could easily imagine texts in which, say, irony and sincerity were not opposed—just read Wordsworth (which is itself ironic, since some ecocriticism seems to have a tin ear for this quintessentially Wordsworthian blend). Ecocritical Romanticism is precisely a hear-no-deconstruction, speak-no-deconstruction approach to Wordsworth and his ilk, strategically deaf to the works of Geoffrey Hartman, De Man, and Derrida himself, to name but three.

What is this strange hybrid fantasyland, made of pieces of other text (myth, legend, fairy tale), yet appearing ever so seriously not to be mere fantasy or mere collage? A land designed to fill a gap Tolkien perceived in the English imagination, a sort of supplementary national myth, like the sagas of Scandinavia. That's the trouble with supplements: Do they enhance what's already there? Or do they add something that is lacking? More drastically, do they reveal or disguise?[20] Some say spices (a common culinary supplement) bring out the taste of meat; others say they hide it. Deconstruction argues that in any system of meaning, there is at least one sign functioning in such an ambiguous manner, like a kind of skin between what the system includes and what it excludes. Many texts endeavor to erase any trace of this ambiguous functioning—and then to erase any trace of erasure, just to be safe. Only consider a fundamentalist interpretation of the Bible as the literal word of a single, male God. If published as an essay or a book, such an interpretation is forced to edit out all kinds of inconsistencies in the source text—and then erase the trace of this tampering.

Tolkien imbues the dark side of things with the mystery of traveling down a road, in a suggestive song of the hobbit Bilbo Baggins, recalled by his nephew Frodo as he begins his own journey. It's as if Frodo is trying to "read" Bilbo in his recitation (repetition) of this song, which is itself about walking as a kind of reading, and the road as a text that goes "ever on and on":

> The Road goes ever on and on
>> Down from the door where it began.
> Now far ahead the Road has gone,
>> And I must follow, if I can,
> Pursuing it with eager feet,
>> Until it joins some larger way
> Where many paths and errands meet.
>> And whither then? I cannot say.
>
> ("The Road Goes Ever On and On," 1–8)[21]

Bilbo admonishes Frodo: "He used often to say there was only one Road; that it was like a great river: its springs were at every doorstep, and every path was its tributary. "It's a dangerous business, Frodo, going out of your door," he used to say. "You step onto the Road, and if you don't keep your feet, there is no knowing where you might be swept off to."[22] Some philosophers want to disambiguate walking along a path from reading a text, which they would treat like the old ad for Yellow Pages: "Let your fingers do the walking." Bilbo's Road is congruent with deconstruction's view of "textuality," which doesn't stop at the covers of a book: the Road does not stop at the end of a particular street.[23] The "on and on" quality of textuality is *différance*—the play of differentiation. Yet Tolkien's world has coordinates: a beyond and a close-at-hand, a past and a present, good and evil, inside and outside. Bilbo's Road goes "on and on" within a certain dimensionality. The "Black Speech" of Mordor contains traces of Arabic: in Tolkien, orientalism functions as a sign of threatening otherness.[24] Elves speak a mixture of Welsh and Hebrew, combining two mythical worlds in a single unit, magical yet sealed from the (evil) orient (Mordor is in the far east of Middle Earth).

"World" depends upon a decision to limit the ambiguous Road, the hide-and-seek game of difference and dispersal (*différance*). Draw a boundary around any set of things—say we decide that "Middle Earth" means those qualities listed above—then *this* thing, the bounded set of things, also has a dark side: the "opposite" qualities, and those ambiguous qualities that fall between the cracks. This dark side secretly allows the light side to exist. Once I have decided (in speech, thought or action) that my world consists of my house, my family, and part of the street on which I live, this world has a dark side consisting of other worlds and non-worlds existing beyond its boundary. Using more rigorous concepts, a certain ecosystem consists of certain interacting species; but this interaction depends upon bordering systems. We could travel around Earth filling in the dark spots. Why stop there? The biosphere depends on Earth's magnetic field, which prevents life forms from being scorched by solar winds. Organic compounds may have arrived on Earth from material in comets. Think about how carbon travels around between plants, animals, the atmosphere, out into space, and so forth. Thinking of ecosystems involves thinking without thin, rigid boundaries between inside and outside, because in order to exist at all, the ecosystem must exchange with circumambient phenomena. Indeed, thinking in systems theory seems remarkably close to thinking in deconstruction.[25] In the same way the meaning of one word is another word, and so on round the mulberry bush of the dictionary—but what results is not a nice circle, but a confused tangle.

Some defend "worlds" by claiming that since they work for some people, we shouldn't deprive them,[26] an empty pragmatism that is often disguised as primitivist respect for the other. Such respect can go to absurd levels, for instance the claim that non-Westerners don't or can't care about global warming, since they don't live in a world created by the technologies that generate and map global warming—as if no Pacific islander had given a thought to rising sea levels, or used a cell phone. This claim borrows the idea of "life-world" form phenomenology and draws a rigid line around it, but it's not rational to argue that worlds should be preserved because they "work" for people, the way a good story "works." Witch-ducking stools "worked" for persecutors of witches in the early Renaissance. If they existed today should we leave such instruments of torture intact because they helped construct a meaningful "world"? Imagine the notion of "world" taken to the horrifying absurdity: a defense of concentration camps.

There is indeed something rather fascist about "worlding"—the notion that certain technologies create certain worlds (to a hammer, everything looks like a nail).[27] This idea, derived from Heidegger, provides a way of thinking of other cultures as different "worlds" with a different hither, different yonder, and so on. This is indeed the case: concepts vary drastically and so does the language in which people have them. But worlding easily devolves into something like team sports. In *The Lord of the Rings* and Peter Jackson's film adaptations, each "race" has its own weapons, language, and codes of conduct.[28] Their worlds are rigidly insulated from one another, despite how the races keep interacting. This rigid insulation and competition is also a fascist fantasy: a worldwide Olympics of death, unto eternity, may the best elf win. (Tolkien's rather English version stages the rise of an enlightened ruler over the factions, a good imperialist fortified and chastened in the wilderness.)

The temptation arises to over-design everything down to the last syllable—in the films the sword pommels of the Kingdom of Rohan differ from those of the adjacent kingdom of Gondor. Wagnerian *Gesamtkunstwerk*, the prototype of aesthetic "worlding," is only possible through modern technological devices such as conductor-led orchestras and special lighting effects, creating snow-globe-like distances between the audience and the spectacle, distances that only enhances the spectacle's immersive and seductive effects. "World" is a modern product, made to look ancient and non-Western. Yet as we have discovered, things must fuzz out and on at least one level there must be some inconsistency. It would be better to invert the 1980s charity song: "We Aren't the World."[29]

Science and technology have placed human beings in a position of bad faith with respect to "world." We don't really believe in *world* but we cleave to it nevertheless, cynically. The "end of the world" does not make things easier—it imposes all kinds of disturbances and judgments. Leaving no stone unturned has resulted in an all too clear awareness of the irreducibility of the dark side of things. Consider global warming denial. Sarah Palin's late 2009 editorial in the *Washington Post* condemned "scare tactics pushed by an environmental priesthood that capitalizes on the public's worry and makes them feel that owning an SUV is a 'sin' against the planet."[30] Palin's text reveals a paradox of right wing ideology: it enjoins us to obey authority without question, submit to "traditional values" and so on. Yet it contains an equally necessary implicit message to enjoy, to commit crimes without guilt: hence the message about enjoying SUVs.

Global warming science deprives the anti-environmentalist right of its world: the minimal apparatus that enables the functioning of their two levels: the explicit, condemning sin, and the implicit, encouraging violations—a split form familiar to anyone who has survived a totalitarian regime, and anyone who has used a modern toilet, with its /u/-shaped tube that seems to flush waste into another dimension.[31] By realizing that everything we do affects our biosphere, we lose the minimal foreground–background distinction enabling us to think on two different levels at once. We can no longer enjoy things in secret, because we know that (figuratively speaking) Google Earth already has a picture of us doing it, even if no one else sees it. There are no hidden corners, and thus no world as such—"world" is reduced to a merely superficial aftereffect. To have a world is to have a foreground and a background, a hither and a yonder, hidden things and unhidden things. Distance has collapsed. It's no fun when you realize your emissions are messing up people's lives over the horizon. Eco-apocalyptic Jeremiads are far too many to list: this is the dominant mode of ecological discourse. They risk adding to the very problem they address, since "the end of the world"—that is, the end of the concept *world*—has strictly already occurred. By postponing the ultimate crisis into the future, these Jeremiads provide an outlet for genuine ecological anxiety. Yet this end has not abolished the dark side of the thing. It has heightened it.

Ecological awareness means being unable to kid ourselves that there are realms unaffected by our existence. At the same time (and for the same reasons), it means that terms such as *Nature* have now begun to melt, along with the Arctic ice cap and the Antarctic Peninsula. Any attempt to rise above the melting conceptuality results in discovering another level of liquidity. We confront the Lacanian maxim, "There is no metalanguage," which Lacan's student Derrida rephrases as "il n'y a pas de hors-texte" ("there is no outside-text").[32] No philosophical stronghold is exempt from *différance*: it does not supply the comfort of a world. One cannot feel smug about seeing how the "world" trick works—being able to see everywhere all at once with supercomputers that model climate doesn't abolish illusive play. The current environmental emergency requires far more sophisticated mental tools than "world" concepts, including terms such as "surround" that in its tone of virtual reality betrays the inconvenient truth that "world" as such has evaporated.[33] At best, "world," the fantasy of significant depths and surroundings, is inadequate. Deconstruction offers the wisdom of conceptual restraint, even as we struggle to preserve a human-friendly equilibrium state.

Thinking outside the "world" box is desirable beyond the current emergency. Since "world" depends upon establishing distances that ecological thinking doesn't permit, it would be better to imagine ways of undermining "world" than keep on churning out new versions. In particular, "world" is no use for thinking about life forms, because at best we end up with the absurdity of as many "worlds" as there are life forms (Jakob von Uexküll's solution), begging the questions of what counts as a world in the first place, and how these different worlds interact.

Coexistentialism

Worlds have horizons: "here" and "there," inside and outside. Worlds thus imply distance and hierarchy. If all life forms are entangled, no hierarchy is possible without violence. Instead of imagining ourselves part of something bigger (Gaia for instance—and what is Gaia's world?), it would be more helpful to start with the fact of our intimate coexistence with other life forms. We have others—and they have us—literally under our skin. Intimacy might make a better beginning for an ecological ethics than holism.

What happens when you take "world" out of the equation? The beings we misname "animals" emerge, baffling the familiar litany that goes something like this: animals don't have art; don't imagine; don't reflect; don't plan; don't hesitate; have no sense of irony; they just function; are completely absorbed in their environment; are creatures of the here and now. And so they're inferior to us—or superior to us. Why the compulsion to repeat the litany? How come the same ideas prove exactly opposing opinions— that animals are inferior or superior?[34] The litany has to do with concepts of "world." Much philosophy wants to deny worlds to nonhumans. Heidegger claims that nonhumans are lacking in world.[35] Evidence that nonhumans possess worlds often appears anecdotally, as if the exception to our world (in which animals are inferior) proves the rule: a chimp threw a stone, pigeons were found to like Picasso, Derrida's cat looked funnily at him.[36]

Conversely, the environmentalist language of the "more than human" is suggestive but all over the map: Does it mean more human? Or less? Or outside the human? Or surpassing human trajectories?[37] Instead of trying to figure out who or what is more and less, let's begin with the scientific fact of coexistence, which includes symbiosis (and endosymbiosis). The human as such is already nonhuman, insofar as our bodies are colonies of symbionts down to the DNA level (DNA as such is a symbiotic community of code insertions, pieces of viral code, and so on). The oxygen we breathe, the iron we smelt, the oil we burn, the hills we walk on are byproducts of the metabolism of life forms. We need a term like "coexistentialism" to describe what it feels like to be a swarming colony: we contain multitudes.

Perhaps personhood is not a unified whole, but haphazardly bundled sets of unevenly evolved mechanisms for sensing and cognizing. When an ant walks over the sand, maybe she doesn't have a "picture" of the sand, maybe she just walks.[38] Perhaps walking as such is merely trying not to fall. Intelligence may not be a way of picturing a world: then mouse consciousness would not differ much from human consciousness. It's no problem we will never see the world from a mouse's point of view: the mouse herself lacks a sense of mouseness and a mental picture of the world, just as we do (which isn't to say that she doesn't have an "inner life"). Contra Heidegger, we coexist in lacking-a-world.

The discovery of irreducible inconsistency at the signifying level resembles what the mathematician Kurt Gödel revealed concerning logical systems. Every well-defined and consistent system contains at least one theorem that the system itself cannot prove. This insight pertains directly to life and intelligence. All life forms are limited. There exists at least one situation (death) that will quite literally deconstruct them. Life forms are "Gödelizable"—they are subject to Gödel's Incompleteness Theorem, which states that coherent systems are always inconsistent.[39] There is solidarity in our mutual "lameness" (as they say in California). Sentience is also Gödelizable: we can only Gödelize to a certain limit. Our intelligence comes to an end somewhere: it may be very large and we may never find the limit; but in this view, it is necessarily and radically limited by the strangeness of other entities. Finding solidarity by crouching low like a little rodent with a good survival instinct might be better for all beings.

Who are those beings? In the later works of Derrida all kinds of strange entities emerge. Perhaps the most suggestive for ecocriticism is the *arrivant*.[40] Elsewhere I have translated this as "strange stranger."[41] This term is close to Husserl's *das Fremde*. It passes through Heidegger's *Mitsein*: being is always being-with (coexistence), in congruence with basic evolutionary biology. The strange stranger is strange all the way down—there is no way to become fully familiar with him, her, or it (how can we ever fully tell?). If we could anticipate the strange stranger in any way, we would have created a box (such as "world") for them. The strange stranger is the guest to whom we owe infinite hospitality, whose arrival can never be predicted. It would be best to replace the term "animal" with "strange stranger."[42]

"World" is one of the main ways in which Nature manifests. Nature's disappearance is its essence: when looked for, only discrete phenomena appear such as mountains, beech trees, horses. The concept Nature reifies the ambiguous dispersal inherent in the dark side of things. This essentialism provides a safety valve for the runaway machinery of modern life, a holiday in the wilderness. Yet the essentialism is also responsible for the modernity in whose name what is called Nature is destroyed. For the sake of the very life forms for which the term Nature stands, ecological criticism must mobilize a ruthless deconstruction of Nature. Otherwise we are encumbered with the tools of modernity itself, not broken but too disastrously efficient. The trouble with Nature is that it doesn't exist—yet its fantasies grip our minds with hope and fear, imprisoning them in the status quo. The grass is always greener on the other side.

NOTES

1. David Abram, *The Spell of the Sensuous: Perception and Language in a More-Than-Human World* (New York: Pantheon, 1996).
2. Abram, *The Spell of the Sensuous*, 31–72; Maurice Merleau-Ponty, *Phenomenology of Perception*, tr. Colin Smith (London and New York: Routledge & Kegan Paul, 1996), 11, 67–69, 233, 299–345.
3. Graham Harman, *Guerilla Metaphysics: Phenomenology and the Carpentry of Things* (Chicago: Open Court, 2005), 56–58, 177, 187, 214, 245; Graham Harman, *Prince of Networks: Bruno Latour and Metaphysics* (Melbourne: Re.Press, 2009), 15–16, 18–19, 27–28, 35, 75–77, 111–112, 124–126, 135, 137–138, 144–149, 206–207, 210, 215–216.
4. Martin Heidegger, "Language," *Poetry, Language, Thought*, tr. Albert Hofstadter (New York: Harper and Row, 1971), 185–208.
5. Denise Levertov, *Poems 1960–1967* (New York: New Directions, 1983). Copyright © 1961 by Denise Levertov. Reproduced by permission.
6. Wolfgang Iser, *The Act of Reading: A Theory of Aesthetic Response* (Baltimore: Johns Hopkins University Press, 1978).
7. This is just Saussurean linguistics: Ferdinand de Saussure, *Course in General Linguistics*, ed. Charles Bally and Albert Sechehaye, tr. Wade Baskin (New York: McGraw Hill, 1965).
8. Dawkins, *Phenotype*, 45–46, 156. Dawkins himself is a little wary of satisficing, but he is more wary of a teleological approach, which Gould and Lewontin call the "Panglossian paradigm": the idea that adaptation is always the best possible.

9. Tony Duff, *Standard Tibetan Grammar*, 2 vols. (Kathmandu: Padma Karpo, 2009), 1.13–44.

10. Timothy Morton, *The Ecological Thought* (Cambridge, Mass.: Harvard University Press, 2010), 63–66.

11. Bruce Schneider, *Applied Cryotography* (New York: Wiley, 1996), 234; Claude E. Shannon, "Prediction and Entropy of Printed English," *The Bell System Technical Journal* 30 (January, 1951), 50–64.

12. Morton, *The Ecological Thought*, 67.

13. Kwang W. Jeon and James F. Danielli, "Micrurgical Studies with Large Free-Living Amebas," *International Reviews of Cytology*, 30 (1971): 49–89, quoted in *The Extended Phenotype: The Long Reach of the Gene* (Oxford: Oxford University Press, 1999), 160.

14. Jacques Derrida, *The Animal That Therefore I Am*, ed. Marie-Louise Mallet, tr. David Wills (New York: Fordham University Press, 2008), 136.

15. Colin Milburn, "Monsters in Eden: Darwin and Derrida," *Modern Language Notes* 118 (2003), 603–621.

16. Jacques Lacan, *Le seminaire, Livre III: Les psychoses* (Paris: Editions de Seuil, 1981), 48. See Slavoj Zizek, *The Parallax View* (Cambridge, Mass.: MIT Press, 2006), 206.

17. Jacques Derrida, *Dissemination*, tr. Barbara Johnson (Chicago: University of Chicago Press, 1981), 63.

18. See for instance Patrick Curry, *Defending Middle Earth: Tolkien, Myth and Modernity* (New York: Houghton Mifflin, 2004), 13–16.

19. J.R.R. Tolkien, *The Lord of the Rings* (Boston: Houghton Mifflin, 1991), 34, 107, 108, 125.

20. I rehearse, all too briefly, Jacques Derrida's "That Dangerous Supplement," *Of Grammatology*, tr. Gayatri Chakravorty Spivak (Baltimore: Johns Hopkins University Press, 1997), 141–164.

21. Tolkien, *Lord of the Rings*, 48.

22. Tolkien, *Lord of the Rings*, 87.

23. For a suggestive discussion of text as walking, see Roland Barthes, "From Work to Text," *Image/Music/Text*, tr. Stephen Heath (New York: Hill and Wang, 1977), 155–164; Timothy Morton, *Ecology without Nature: Rethinking Environmental Aesthetics* (Cambridge, Mass., and London: Harvard University Press, 2007), 31–32.

24. Affinities between deconstruction and postcolonial studies, inaugurated by Edward Said's *Orientalism* (New York: Vintage, 1979), are strongly in evidence. See Michael Syrotinski, *Deconstruction and the Postcolonial: At the Limits of Theory* (Chicago: University of Chicago Press, 2007).

25. See Cary Wolfe, *What Is Posthumanism?* (Minneapolis: University of Minnesota Press, 2009), chapter 2.

26. For instance, Donna Haraway (see below) and Tim Ingold.

27. Greg Garrard, "Heidegger Nazism Ecocriticism," *ISLE* 17.2 (Spring, 2010), 251–271 (253); see for instance Donna Haraway, *When Species Meet* (Minneapolis: University of Minnesota Press, 2008), 92–93.

28. Peter Jackson, dir., *The Lord of the Rings* (New Line Cinema, 2001–2003).

29. USA for Africa, "We Are the World" (Columbia, 1985).

30. Sarah Palin, "Sarah Palin on the Politicization of the Copenhagen Climate Conference," *Washington Post*, December 9, 2009, available at http://washingtonpost.com/wp-dyn/content/article/2009/12/08/AR2009120803402.html, accessed July 6, 2010.

31. Slavoj Žižek, "Is There a Proper Way to Remake a Hitchcock Film?" available at http://lacan.com/hitch.html, accessed July 6, 2010.

32. Derrida, *Of Grammatology*, 158.

33. Glen Mazis, *Humans, Animals, Machines: Blurring Boundaries* (Albany, NY: SUNY Press, 2008), 14–16, 100–101, 104–109, 188–190.

34. See Greg Garrard, *Ecocriticism* (New York: Routledge, 2011); Garrard develops the terms *mechanomorphism* and *allomorphism* to account for this similarity.

35. Martin Heidegger, "The Origin of the Work of Art," *Poetry, Language, Thought*, tr. Albert Hofstadter (New York: Harper and Row, 1971), 45. See Jacques Derrida, *Of Spirit: Heidegger and the Question*, tr. Geoffrey Bennington and Rachel Bowlby (Chicago and London: University of Chicago Press, 1989, 1991), 47–57.

36. Jacques Derrida, *The Animal That Therefore I Am*, ed. Marie-Louise Mallet, tr. David Wills (New York: Fordham University Press, 2008), 3–11.

37. The term is first used in Abram, *The Spell of the Sensuous*, 8 and passim.

38. Herbert A. Simon, *The Sciences of the Artificial* (Cambridge, Mass.: MIT Press, 1996), 51–53.

39. The best exegesis is found in Douglas Hofstadter, *Gödel, Escher, Bach: An Eternal Golden Braid* (New York: Basic Books, 1999), 17, 101, 265–272, 438–449.

40. Jacques Derrida, "Hospitality," tr. Barry Stocker with Forbes Matlock, *Angelaki* 5.3 (December, 2000), 3–18.

41. Morton, *Ecological Thought*, 38–50, 59–97.

42. Note that there are alternatives: one proposed by Derrida ("animots"), and one by Haraway ("critters"). I am not so fond of the pun in the former or the teleology in the latter (as a derivation of *creature*).

CHAPTER 17

....

QUEER LIFE? ECOCRITICISM
AFTER THE FIRE

....

CATRIONA SANDILANDS

In the opening passage of her 2005 book *In a Queer Time and Place*, Judith Halberstam quotes Michel Foucault: "homosexuality threatens people as a 'way of life' rather than as a way of having sex" (1). For Halberstam, this perceived menace is also a source of political potential: a queer "way of life," including "subcultural practices, alternative methods of alliance, forms of transgender embodiment, and those forms of representation dedicated to capturing these wilfully eccentric modes of being" (1), responds to and calls into question such institutions as the nuclear family, compulsory heterosexuality, rigidly dimorphic gendered embodiments, and normative reproductivity. "Obviously," writes Halberstam, "not all gay, lesbian, and transgender people live their lives in radically different ways from their heterosexual counterparts, but part of what has made queerness compelling as a form of self-description in the past decade or so has to do with the way it has the potential to open up new life narratives and alternative relations to time and space" (1–2).

In this chapter, I consider that queer theory, and especially recent "queer ecological" trajectories that take up questions of biopolitics, hold the potential to open up not only new life narratives but also new narratives *of life*, including understandings of ontology and politics that are more responsive to recent developments in ecological thought than the (largely) uncritically heteronormative versions in which contemporary ecocriticism tends to be steeped. Echoing Lauren Berlant and Michael Warner's formative thoughts in "Sex in Public" (1998), what I propose here are the "radical aspirations" of queer nature building: "not just a safe zone for queer sex, but the changed possibilities" of ecocritical understanding "that appear when the heterosexual couple is no longer the referent or privileged example" (548) in ecological conversation. In order to outline these changed possibilities, the chapter is divided into two major sections. In the first, I will consider briefly two recent articulations of queer ecology in order to draw out their sketch of a "queer life" for ecocriticism; in the second, I will use this sketch as a way of reading Jane Rule's (1989) novel *After the Fire*, which engages directly with both the ontological and the political dimensions of queer ecological thinking.

QUEER LIFE: BECOMINGS[1]

Ontologies

In 1999, Bruce Bagemihl published his monumental book *Biological Exuberance*, which documented extensively that—contrary to popular and scientific understandings—a large number of animal species participated in, as a matter of routine, erotic activities between same-sex participants; his work was followed in 2004 by Joan Roughgarden's equally popular *Evolution's Rainbow*. In these texts and others, as Stacy Alaimo has written, "it is easy to see queer animals as countering the pernicious and persistent articulation of homosexuality with what is unnatural…making sexual diversity part of a larger biodiversity" (55). On the one hand, this "naturalization" of sexual diversity can be (and has been) used relatively uncritically to support a variety of assertions about the biological foundations of sexual preference, the role of sex (including sexual pleasure) in evolution, and most obviously, the apparent naturalness of same-sex activities among human beings (a conclusion that has supported both homophobic and queer positive agendas). As Alaimo also points out, on the other hand, "the multitude of utterly different modes of courtship, sexual activity, childrearing arrangements, gender, transsexualism, and transvestism that Bagemihl and Roughgarden document portray animal lifeworlds that cannot be understood in reductionist ways" (64).

In response, Myra Hird has documented a staggering number and diversity of sexual forms, gendered embodiments, and reproductive possibilities in nonhuman animals and other organisms: "homosexual behaviour," she writes, "occurs in over 450 different species of animals, is found in every geographic region of the world, in every major animal group, in all age groups, and with equal frequency amongst males and females" (2009, 235). Moreover, she argues that stable sexual/gender dimorphism is far from the only possibility for gendered embodiment out there (2008): intersexuality is common in too numerous forms to document; many organisms move from one kind of sexed body to another under different conditions, at different points in their lifespans, and in relation to the gender of other species members; and still other organisms take on specific behaviors or characteristics of other genders in order to fool predators, attract sexual partners, or impress the social competition. What is interesting about this apparent polymorphous perversity and trans possibility is not only the fact of sexual and gender diversity itself; it is also the ways in which "biological queerness" and "animal trans" call into question so many of the arguments about authenticity, embodiment, identity, and even technology on which conventionally human-centered arguments currently rest. For Hird, in other words, queer nature creates new opportunities for posthumanist argument: sex and gender comprise yet another realm in which human behavior is revealed to be not so unique after all, and the line between nature and artifice drawn in mainstream (including some lgbtq) renderings of sexual identity and politics is revealed as ultimately unsupportable. As Elizabeth Wilson adds, referring to the intersex and multipartner lives of many of the species of barnacle that were the subject of Charles Darwin's studies, to think of nonhuman animals as queer in conventional terms is thus "too glib." The point is not to impose human sex/gender order onto the natural world in order to assimilate nonhuman diversity to existent identitarian categories. Rather, the characterization of barnacles as queer "has much more punch if it is used, contrariwise, to render those familiar human, cultural and social forms more curious as a result of their affiliation with barnacle organization. The queerness of Darwin's barnacles is salutary not because it renders the barnacle knowable through its association with familiar human forms, but because it renders the human, cultural and social guises of queer less familiar and more captivated by natural and biological forces" (2002, 284).

Karen Barad has thus extended the meaning of "queer" to render curious still further dimensions of biosocial being; notably, she has deployed the idea of queer *performativity* to develop an account of the co-constitutive materialization of organisms.[2] She writes of a radical reformulation of ontology away from a Cartesian model in which individual organisms (and other entities) pre-exist their interaction, and toward an understanding in which beings are constituted *through* interaction, in other words, performatively: entities do not become themselves as a result of an individual unfolding of internal potentiality against an external environment, but come to rest transitionally in particular configurations of what she calls "spacetimemattering" in their ongoing constitution through others. "Phenomena," she thus writes, "are material entanglements enfolded and threaded through the spacetimemattering of the universe" (146); queer performativity is, then, not simply a matter of the discursive constitution/contestation of power and identity, but of the rendering material of the world itself through chemical, physical, evolutionary, *and* social inter- and intra-actions. As she writes: "ironically, in an important sense, on this account there are no 'acts against nature'.... In this radical reworking of nature/culture, there are only 'acts of nature' (including thinking and language use), which is not to reduce culture to nature, but to reject the notion that nature (in its givenness, its meaninglessness) requires culture as its supplement... and to understand culture as something nature does" (150).

Relatedly, Hird has raised Deleuze and Guattari's notion of "becoming" against this notion of performative co-constitution, noting the generative capacities of sensual/sexual encounter. In their example of the wasp and the orchid, she notes, the sex act that is pollination involves a co-implication of the one with the other: "by pollinating the orchid, the wasp becomes part of its reproductive apparatus, which at the same time becomes a piece of the wasp" (Parisi in Hird 2009, 357), what Deleuze and Guattari would call a "becoming-orchid of the wasp and a become-wasp of the orchid" (357). In addition, Hird points to microbiologist Lynn Margulis's assertion that "new tissues, organs, and species evolved primarily through long-lasting relationships between different species" (357), a radical challenge to textbook accounts of competition, individualism, and selfish genes; sex, as an especially interesting set of inter-agential encounters, suggests particular symbiogenetic fecundity for new bodies and modes of embodiment through diverse kinds of encounters of becoming.[3]

Futures

At a different point on the queer ecological spectrum, Lee Edelman's controversial *No Future* (2004) has generated fierce attention to the ways in which queer material and epistemic specificity offers a critique of what he terms "reproductive futurism"; the work has, not surprisingly, also inspired some queer thinkers to consider the implications of this critique for ecocriticism. Briefly, Edelman's main argument is that contemporary politics are dominated by the figure of the Child in a logic in which the kernel of futurity is seen to reside in the innocent child's wellbeing. The absolute self-evidence of the value of "fighting for the children," in contemporary American family values politics and more broadly, "compels us ... to submit to the framing of political debate ... in terms of ... reproductive futurism: terms that impose an ideological limit on political discourse as such, preserving in the process the absolute privilege of heteronormativity" (2). Insofar as the Child is the unassailable bearer of the value of the future, radical critique is silenced: "for politics, however radical the means by which specific constituencies attempt to produce a more desirable social order, remains, at its core, conservative insofar as it works to ... authenticate a social order, which it then intends to transmit to the future in the form of its inner Child. That Child remains the perpetual horizon of every acknowledged politics, the fantasmic beneficiary of every political intervention (2–3). For Edelman, queerness interrupts the unfolding repetition of the same that inheres in this political logic; as a negative (in his argument, death drive-related[4]) embodiment of the social order's "traumatic encounter with its own inescapable failure" (26) to bind the future to its reproductive fantasy, the queer figures as an explosive troubling of reproductive futurism.

In the midst of the substantial debate that Edelman's text has engendered, several recent authors have considered in detail the implications of his and others' critiques of reproductive futurism for queer ecology and ecocriticism.[5] In a reading of Christopher Isherwood's *A Single Man*, for example, Jill Anderson argues that the novel turns heteronaturativity on its head by staging reproductive futurity as a sort of apocalypse: a sense of the future always already oriented to breeding and to generational continuity sacrifices the present in favor of a perpetually deferred future, and in so doing also justifies the plundering of resources and the devastation of spaces as part of a logic of proliferation. Isherwood is directly critical of postwar fecundity, both of babies and of goods, which he sees as inextricably tied. As Anderson writes, for Isherwood:

> The destruction of the environment directly correlates to the production of children.... [He] infuses the heterosexual act with the power to create a generalized apocalypse, wiping away all life on the planet. At the same time, though, heterosex ... is entirely stripped of any eroticism, making heterosexual acts purely reproductive and not pleasurable in any way. Isherwood is also preoccupied with the

creation of a queer space that overturns heterosexism and homophobia in order to
open up queer erotic possibility, establish zones of safety for queerness, and expose
ecological destruction, particularly through production and consumption. (53)

Although I would want to avoid any simplistic treatment of the relationship between
population and environmental destruction, I would maintain, with Anderson, that the
organization of postwar North American suburbs to facilitate repro-normative time
and space, for example, certainly offers an important opening for a queer ecological critique of reproductive futurism: the figure of the Child, here, facilitates rather than interrupts capitalist proliferation.[6]

Bruce Erickson makes clear the ecological stakes of reproductive futurism by demonstrating that this complex of repro-normative temporal and spatial relations is tied
to what Shannon Winnubst calls a "future anterior," an anticipation of a future state that
establishes the present as a realm of utility, a sacrifice-zone for that which is not yet.
Encompassing the Child whose innocence must be protected from challenge, the future
anterior authorizes an instrumental relation to the present, and especially to the Other
whose present may be seen as a threat to the future of the Same. If the future is the goal
and the present is understood as a condition of "what will have been," then what is—
however horrific—becomes justifiable in light of its necessity of giving rise to the future.
Queer experiences thus indicate a "politics without a future," and demand an uncou-
pling of the present from the future anterior. According to Erickson, then, "thinking
through a politics of nature without a future means rethinking nature such that it is not
bent toward the utility of power. Opening ourselves to the possibilities of history means
addressing the ways in which the ideologies and concrete practices that have formed out
of current understandings of nature represent more about the desired human outcomes
than they do about anything nonhuman" (324).

Nicole Seymour addresses Edelman's implicit challenge to environmentalism even
more directly: given the tendency of the environmental movement, and perhaps especially the environmental justice movement, to be powerfully concerned with the protection of vulnerable groups (e.g., poor people of color and their children), not to mention
with the preservation of biodiversity for future generations, "is there no queer way of
thinking environmentally and ecologically? No environmental or ecological way of
thinking queerly" (3)? Although she clearly believes otherwise, she is also aware of the
complex stakes of the questions: in order to imagine a genuinely queer ecology, any political and ethical narrative in which the projected sanctity of a future nature justifies the
sacrifice of the present needs to be scrutinized carefully. To what extent does the future
Child serve as a naturalizing alibi for a narrowly, even destructively, hetero-reproductive
present? To what extent might a queer negativity facilitate a more profoundly critical
ecology, one in which the future is clearly an ecologically necessary consideration but its
imagination is not exhausted by the hegemonic forms of sociality of the present? There
are, she writes, "ways of thinking about the here and now that are, in fact, crucial: the
belief that environmental devastation is a *possibility*, rather than a current and impending *reality*, or that we have to clean up the planet for *future* generations, rather than for

present ones, allows for the kind of complacency that authorizes such degradation in the first place" (17). Following José Esteban Muñoz, she considers the utopian possibilities of queer ecology, in which radical queer negativity (as expressed in the concrete utopias of art and literature) can potentially give rise to new forms of sociability, new ways of being together—as humans and also among others—that refuse both the heteronormative and the anti-ecological elements of current capitalist relations of production, consumption, and social intelligibility.

Queer Life

Both of these threads, I would argue, demand that ecocriticism consider seriously what it might mean to queer *life*. In a Foucauldian understanding of biopolitics, a central question always circulates: How does power work not only to command death, but also to organize life in particular ways through policies, discourses and institutions that render certain forms of living vital and viable, and others suspiciously toxic to the body and the planet politic? "Saving the earth for the children" is thus always already a biopolitical assertion: saving what, by whom, and for whose children? Why is the future Child the privileged figure around whom environmental ethics and politics are organized, and what about the children—and former children—who might well argue that nothing has ever been saved in their names? What, given non-reproductive forms of generativity, constitutes a child, and where, in this conception, is there space for Others who are not our children, and perhaps not anyone's children in the way we conventionally imagine progeny? In our "saving," what assumptions are we making about the nature of life, the definition of what it means to be "alive," the processes through which life is generated and recedes, the value of living in particular forms and communities, and the institutionalization of particular social and biotic relations designed to understand and cultivate vitality? And not least: what kinds of paternalism or maternalism does the stance of "saving *for*" authorize: if the future is understood to reside in the welfare of beings too young to care for themselves, then what kinds of political practice are we agreeing to in order to secure that particular future in the face of a complex present that happens to be full of wildly diverse Others?

I began this discussion with Berlant and Warner's question: what are "the changed possibilities" of understanding "that appear when the heterosexual couple is no longer the referent or privileged example" (548), in this case, in ecological and ecopolitical understandings of life, generativity, and futurity? Clearly, there are many changes: displacing heteronaturativity in environmental understanding means paying significant attention to the ways in which, biopolitically, we both conceive of and promote particular forms of life, including both organismic understanding and sociopolitical organization.[7] That our concepts of life are heteronormatively organized is abundantly clear: there are direct links, for example, between the evolutionary idealization of heterosexual reproduction and the political idealization of the Child as the bearer, equally teleologically, of a given society's future potential. Despite Foucault's insistence on the difference between a biology of population and a medicine of sex, biological science is, here, borrowed to the task of naturalizing socio-political arrangements of power and privilege; heterosexual nuclear families appear "naturally" paired with heterosexual sex as bearers of life against the ravages of a polymorphously queer perversity. Even if same-sex eroticism has eventually, after a rather long struggle, turned out to be ironically quite articulable with both evolutionary and neoliberal rationalities—in the guise of "sociosexual behaviour" in the one discourse and same-sex marriage in the other—a more self-consciously queer perspective suggests that we should not be at all happy with these articulations for reasons of both ontological expansiveness and political attentiveness. If "queer" is to mean anything at all, it must include a *continual* process of displacing the heterosexual couple at the centre of the ecological universe. That is the ecocritical project to which this chapter now turns.

AFTER THE FIRE: JANE RULE'S QUEER ECOLOGY

In an essay entitled "Stumps" from her 1981 collection *Outlander*, Rule comments on the difficulties of living on her small, "cranky little [Galiano] island" (189): "When we talk, we expect to disagree" (187). The piece, originally published in the gay periodical *The Body Politic* in 1979, is about the need for gay men and lesbians to be part of a diverse public culture rather than to withdraw into protective enclave or invisibility. It is, however, also clearly about the significance fire holds on a rather small island in a dry area of Coastal Douglas Fir-zone forest in southwestern British Columbia: "No matter how much we may quarrel about how to live, no matter how grudgingly we accept each other's company, no matter what conflicting uses we put our forests to," writes Rule, "we know we don't want to burn it down" (189).[8] Rule's essay employs fire as a metaphor: crises craft publics from among dissonant individuals, and gay men and lesbians must be every bit as much a part of those publics as anyone else if our unique perspectives are to be counted in political decision-making. But it also indicates fire as a very particular agent: on Galiano, fire is *fire*, and the particular climatic, biotic and socioeconomic conditions of life in the southern Gulf Islands mean that late summers are times when islanders get worried about cigarette-smoking tourists in their annually summer-droughted forests. I would like to read her novel *After the Fire* in a similar way: the fire of the title is both a metaphor for and a metonym of queer ecology, a sign of the possibility of a queer future in its narrative generation of post-heteronormative relations and temporalities, and also a more materialist gesturing toward the queer potentialities of fire as an agent of ecological change that is demonstrably unfaithful to accustomed narratives of reproductive futurism.[9]

After the Fire is set on Rule's "cranky little" Galiano Island. Her last novel of twelve, it narrates the complex of relationships that develops among five women as they create, after a series of dramatic personal, familial, and corporeal losses, something like a "queer" community: a set of practices of emotional support, intimacy, respect (sometimes grudging), and care that transcends—indeed, that is predicated on the fracturing and/or rejection of—heteronormative kinship bonds of marital or filial obligation. Like all of Rule's novels, however, it is both anti-apocalyptic and anti-utopian; it is, instead, a sort of concentrated biopolitical island microcosm in which even small events have huge and rippling implications. In this respect, Rule's view of Galiano is far more ecologically accurate than politically correct; as ecologist Daniel Botkin notes, islands are actually sites in which the complex biotic facts of constant transformation are most especially apparent, even if idiosyncratically manifest. As Rule is clearly aware, fire is part of that constant movement, no matter how much a given human community might wish to avoid or control it. Here, Botkin offers us further insight: many species, like the Kirtland's Warbler that only nests in the dead branches of "jack-pine woodlands that are between 6 and 21 years old" (69), *require* fire: the jack-pines on which the warblers are entirely dependent germinate *only* in the heat of a fire and grow only when their limbs can reach into full sunlight, as in a fire-produced clearing. I will have more to say about ecologies of fire in a moment; let me suggest here that Rule has intentionally turned away from the dramatic interplay of apocalypse and utopia toward an understanding of fire that is not only more socially complex but also more ecologically observant.

There is no action in the novel before the fire "blooms into the winter night before the fire truck could get there" (1). When they do arrive, the volunteer firefighters can really only watch as the house in which the fire started burns to the ground. As Karen Tasuki, one of the fire fighters, notes: "even if they knew what they were doing, there had never been a chance of saving the house or anyone or anything in it" (2). This fire, echoed by the others that Rule inserts into the narrative periodically as reminders of the thin between the utility of fire and its capacity for devastation, is the fatal event whose after-effects burn through the rest of the novel. Fires in fireplaces and glowing candles speak of warmth, light, and sensuality—a lit match, for example, "restored Karen for a moment to the little illusion she had of fire" (3) as an instrument bent to human pleasure—but "the noise, the heat, the beauty" (2) of *this* fire speak of an event that is much more unpredictable, and much more transformative.

Specifically, the fire acts as both a literal and a metaphoric space-clearing: the five women around and through whom the story moves find their lives transformed by the fire and also by the chains of events that the fire lets loose: as Kirtland's Warblers find a generative space in the low branches of new growth, in *After the Fire* each woman finds a new trajectory in the midst of the events that the fire directly and indirectly causes to occur. The most obvious example of this generative capacity concerns Red, who we discover later is pregnant with the child of the lone man, Dickie John (!), who is killed in the fire: it's his house that is destroyed, his charred body that is later found in the ashes. Red is not in love with Dickie, who has a swaggering reputation for sleeping around, and she does not respond publicly to his death; she had a relationship with him solely to conceive a child and notes wryly that she "just got pregnant before he got bored" (164). She clearly had no intention of co-parenting, let alone of marrying. Although it is doubtful that Dickie would have defended his paternal rights in any case, the fire literally clears the island of any of the heterosexist requirements that might have arisen around the baby's birth. With Dickie's death, Red is free to form the family of her choosing: Red, her dog Blackie, and her baby daughter Blue. Their names defy heteropatriarchy: the cross-species trio is constellated by Red as a set of bruise-like colors, and not according to any patronymy, as we never know Red's surname.

Even beyond Red's post-infernal refusal of heteropatriarchy, the house fire sets loose a cascade of transformative events, each of which also involves the destruction of some type of heteronormative bond. Each of the four other main characters—young Karen, middle-aged Milly Forbes, older Henrietta Hawkins, and elderly Miss James—finds her relationship to Galiano profoundly changed over the course of the novel, changes that are all set in motion by the fire. Henrietta Hawkins has been in a holding pattern for years, visiting her unresponsive husband in a nursing home in Vancouver twice weekly without fail; his eventual death releases a torrent of grief and guilt that threatens to destroy her, but Red and Karen take care of her and help her to return anew to her community, now cared for as well as care giver. Racist and class-obsessed Milly Forbes, deposited on Galiano by her ex-husband to keep her out of the way of his new marriage, festers with bigotry and resentment until she has a hysterectomy (with serious complications, but clearly a delivery from reproductive femininity) and is forced to rely on the other women around her. Ancient Miss James has never married—her sexuality is indeterminate—and had retired to the island after years of globally itinerant teaching; after preparing herself for death, she dies and leaves her tiny, perfect house to Red, clearing the space of her elderly self and carefully defying heteronormative principles of inheritance. And Karen, who retreated to the island in the aftermath of a marriage-like lesbian relationship that seemed predicated on Karen's loss of an independent existence,[10] finds on Galiano both a strong community of women among whom to live and the need—like Miss James before her—to go elsewhere to find out where she "belongs." Using money she inherited from her mother,[11] Karen plans to go to Japan to explore that part of her identity that her father demanded she forget, a clear choice to explore herself anew in the wake of the death of old intimate relationships and demands, both her parents' and her lover's.

For all of these characters, the fire and the changes that echo it throughout the novel are a form of creative destruction. On this island, in this fire, a whole set of calcified, heteronormative patterns of relationship, identity, and belief is set alight, and in the smoking aftermath the loosened seeds of the jack-pines can spread. Specifically, a queer community emerges: this little island is still thoroughly cranky—Karen tolerates but will never love the racist Milly, and Red's ability to choose her bruised family is tightly bound to her general misanthropy—but, once at least a little part of that island is engulfed in flames, it nurtures unthought forms of possibility. Despite Rule's own desires to the contrary, fires happen on Galiano, and in this case, the burning of a dense thicket of over-determined heterosexual conventions allows these women, after the fire, to rethink how they wish to grow in ways that are not part of a heteronormative script. Indeed, we don't know what's going to happen: we are left with Karen's leaving, not with who she becomes once she arrives; Henrietta also adds clearly that "once you stopped thinking of life as something requiring a destiny, you could accept it as the realer miracle it was" (115).

But the largely metaphoric incineration is only part of the queer ecology of this fire; there are also deeply material considerations. In his extraordinary book *Fire: A Brief History*, Stephen Pyne documents that fire is a powerful agent in the midst of a complex set of relationships. Any fire requires three things: ignition, oxygen, and fuel. But that incendiary triumvirate does not begin to describe the intricate dance of factors that goes into the making or flourishing of a blaze, whether it be house fire, industrial fire, or forest fire, and neither does it begin to express the different ways in which species, landscapes, peoples and even inanimate objects are shaped by and participate in fire phenomena. As he writes:

> Around [fire] revolves an ecological triangle, a circulation of biochemicals, species, and communities. It stirs molecules, organisms, landscapes. It kills plants, breaks down ecological structures, sets molecules adrift, shuffles species, opens up niches, and for a time rewires the flow of energy and nutrients. [And in response], plants and animals "adapt" not to fire as a principle but to *particular patterns* of fires [in complex ways]....In brief, fire is one of the Earth's great interactive biotechnologies. (16–17)

The idea that certain species find their ecological niches in the midst of particular fire regimes is not especially new (cf. Kirtland's warblers). What Pyne adds is a much stronger emphasis on the inter-agency and indeterminacy of these relationships. Arguing that fire has "co-evolved" with life and flourishes in different degrees and modes according to highly specific chemical, physical, biological, and anthropogenic constellations, Pyne has us come to understand fire phenomena as bundles of highly contingent processes, conditions, and events in which, at a variety of different levels and in a variety of different temporalities, things do not just "happen" to other things, but molecular, organismic, ecosystemic, and social factors variously invite, repel, prevent, and fail to prevent particular kinds of fire phenomena. At the evolutionary level, for example, some species thrive in the midst of niches opened up by fire and some have developed traits to protect them from fire, but yet others have developed characteristics that, directly and indirectly, may actively welcome immolation: as Pyne writes, "the exquisite choreography that seems to link high intensity burning, in particular, with preferential reseeding suggests strongly" that "organisms...have evolved traits to stimulate fire" (18).

Fires stimulate and are stimulated. Fires demonstrate and create preferences. Fires feed and are fed by different configurations of biological, physical, and social forces. Fires both are and promote flexible opportunists; it is no accident that in so many mythologies, it is a trickster figure who steals the fire, not only because fire is hard to control, but also because it takes advantage of any flammable opportunity to stir up apparent chaos. Fire is constituted responsively; it cannot exist without life forms that speak its language, and indeed, life forms have constituted themselves in particular ways in order to benefit from the conversation. Clearly, these traits indicate that fire exemplifies the intra-agential performativity Barad has described, that it is part of a broadly queer "posthumanist performative account of materialization that does not limit [the question of communicative co-constitution] to the realm of the human" (125). Fire is a thoroughly queer critter in this sense, and perhaps even a particularly revealing example of one: it is an entity that is deeply implicated, in a demonstrably nonteleological way, in the performative transformation of every level of existence from the physical to the biological to the social and back. Fire and stone create and respond to each other; fire adapts jack pines who, when old and dry, offer themselves up for infernal consumption in order to seed; fire is nurtured and organized by human beings, its evolution fostering and fostered by, for example, large cities built of flammable materials. As Pyne documents beautifully, fire is always already relationally constituted, and also comes to exist only in the company of conditions, adaptations, and events that, in a way, invite the kind of incendiary conversation in which fire is required to participate in order to exist.[12] Particular fires converse with and are constituted by particular naturecultures, in which humans are entirely implicated. And even in highly specific conditions, fires do not necessarily respond to or shape their combustible co-conspirators in predictable ways (no wonder fire modeling is such a difficult science[13]).

But to say that fire is a queer critter in this way without locating that understanding in a critique of the social relations of heteronormativity would be to ignore key elements at play in the biopolitical organization of life. Conceiving life as queer opens the world to a reading in which generativity is not reduced to reproductivity, in which the future is not limited to a repetition of a heteronormative ideal of the Same, and in which the heterosexual couple and its progeny—or some facsimile thereof—are not the privileged bearers of life for ecocriticism. And so I turn back to Rule with this question: in the novel, in what way is the fire not only a performatively queer critter, but also a specifically anti-heteronormative one?

Starting with that question, I think we see clearly the *house*, the site of the fire that initiates all the women's transformations. Rule is clear that houses are accoutrements of—literally shelters for—heterosexual relationships. Henrietta and Milly both live alone in single-family homes that were once part of their marital lives; Henrietta comments on being burdened by her possessions in the solid, sensible house her husband had purchased, and Milly's sense of herself as a cast-off wife is clearly partly constituted by the poor quality of her dwelling, "never intended for winter living… [and] in summer, when the water table was low, she didn't flush the toilet more than once a day unless she had company coming. Talk about being put out to pasture" (13)! Karen, conversely, feels inadequate because she is renting a family's summer home and is not able to develop a sense of herself as an autonomous person as she is surrounded by their possessions. Nonetheless, she is clearly aware that the sense of self she might see in a house of her own would be refracted through a heteronormative prism; she comments directly on the heterosexual organization of household properties just after Henrietta's husband dies: "Karen got into her car and drove over to the Hawkinses' house, noticing the sign that marked their drive. *Hen & Hart* over *Hawkins*. Residents had been asked by the fire department to mark their places carefully since there were no house numbers, but the cute heterosexuality of a lot of them irritated Karen, this one included" (119).

The irony that the fire department required this overt demonstration of heterosexuality is not, I think, accidental: it is as if the hetero-household had to proclaim publicly its vulnerability to flame. Indeed, Dickie had built his own house for the express purpose of beginning a life away from his mother, and it was his proudest accomplishment. When it burned down with him in it, his heterosexual place in the world was destroyed in all senses: his paternity of Red's child, his house as a performative declaration of heterosexual territoriality. Along the same lines, is it also important that the thing Miss James gives to Red is a house; against the grain of heteronormative patterns of space, time, and inheritance, Miss James's tiny house with its exquisite collection of singular objects and its orientation to solitude (there is only one comfortable chair) is a subversion of heterosexual spatiality; with her child's father's house destroyed, Red literally receives from Miss James a space outside heteronormativity, through a form of inheritance that is sideways to reproductive futurism. And Rule notices all of these relations: "It struck Henrietta that there could be a pleasure in being childless, that someone with even Miss James' limited resources was free to speculate on generosity, to bestow it where she chose, unlike Henrietta who considered herself in stewardship over what would be Hart Jr.'s and then his children's legacy" (29).

Although Galiano Island is less suburbanized than others of the Southern Gulf Islands, I'd like to think that Rule recognized the ecological implications of her novel in this way: the enactment of reproductive futurism through heteropatriarchal patterns of property ownership creates a situation in which there is so much combustible material that fires are virtually inevitable. Especially in places such as Galiano that experience routine drought cycles, people need to think carefully about not causing fires; that may mean limiting tourist access, but it may also mean thinking very carefully about land use and housing development (I am tempted to say, "thinking like a fire"). In any case, *After the Fire* certainly enacts the articulation of reproductive futurism with combustibility; in order to develop a more sustainable fire regime—at least for human critters—something dry has to burn in order for new forms of life to emerge.

By deploying fire as a more-or-less ecological metaphor in the novel for the generative destruction of a landscape of tinder-dry heteronatural relations, including the organization of matter that facilitates them, Rule suggests that there are important affinities between social and ecological transformation. As with fire's materiality, its metaphoricity is not about some purification of social relationships as much as it is about the radically indeterminate becomings set into motion by the flames. The fire generates a series of dramatic and destructive changes, a coming-apart of a network of heteronormativities; it does not set the stage for a reconstitution of what was there before, and neither does it clear the way for a utopian possibility of something else. The women are altered profoundly by fire and reconstitute themselves as a different kind of community, but in no way is the new landscape impervious to further change: Miss James dies, Karen leaves, Milly is still a racist (if slightly less so), and Red, cherishing her bruises both literally and figuratively, remains deeply suspicious of most human company. Complex fire regimes as a better environmental model for ecocriticism than heteronormative repetitions? Perhaps. But more importantly: fire as a reminder that queer ecology is necessarily a coalitional politics that embraces the contingencies of a material and a metaphoric socioecological queering, in ecocriticism as elsewhere.

Notes

1. For a cross-section of formative writings at the intersections of queer theory and eco-criticism, please compare the following anthologies: Rachel Stein, ed., *New Perspectives in Environmental Justice* (2004); Noreen Giffney and Myra Hird, eds., *Queering the Non/Human* (2008); and Catriona Mortimer-Sandilands and Bruce Erickson, eds., *Queer Ecologies* (2010).

2. I am skeptical of the move by which "performative" comes to be equated with "queer," in this essay of Barad's as elsewhere: there is nothing uniquely queer about the idea that beings are constituted temporarily in and through relations with one another (I prefer Margulis's more descriptive term "symbiogenesis"). But there is something definitely queer in the related displacement of reproductive sexuality from the center of discourses of health and vitality, and especially, from its status as *the* mode of life generation that is understood to bring diversity (in this case, genetic) into the world.

3. Although I cannot include discussion of them here due to space constraints, there are also other broadly queer ecological works that draw from Deleuze and also from Elizabeth Grosz to problematize Cartesian and related understandings of bodies, selves, and desiring subjectivities, but that do not proceed through feminist science studies in the way of Hird, Wilson, Barad, etc. Please see Sandilands 2001; MacCormack 2009; and Scott 2009.

4. See also Leo Bersani's work. Edelman's and Bersani's provocative depictions of queer rela-tions to the death drive are clearly more complex than can be reviewed here. One important point, however, is that "queer" identifies, for Edelman, a structural position (an undoing of the Symbolic) that queer individuals may or may not choose to inhabit (27). For a critique of this queer "anti-social" negativity, see Muñoz's *Cruising Utopia*.

5. Of course, this trajectory is not the only one taken by recent queer ecological thinkers interested in developing a specifically queer ecological politics. See, for example, Stein's and Hogan's (2010) poignant works on the epistemic and political possibilities of thinking ecopolitically from queer subject-positions coded as "against nature."

6. Clearly, queer experience is not somehow inherently antithetical to capitalist relations of consumption (the exact opposite would appear to be the case: childless gay couples and singles in relatively wealthy western countries are a particularly rich market for consumer goods): the vitality of the new gay subject in the world economy is part of what Lisa Duggan (2003) and others refer to as "homonormativity."

7. Again, although space constraints prevent a fuller discussion, I would point to Chris Cuomo's explicitly nonteleological (1998) concept of "flourishing" as a promising ethical term around which to organize this kind of queer ecological rethinking of life.

8. Michele Cantelon, a current Galiano resident, echoes this sense that the fear of fire crafts a qualitatively different public sphere on Galiano: "that fear/concern actually bonds us closer than most anything else. I guess it's because it touches on the most primal physical concerns for survival. But it does seem to bring out the best in people and help them put their baggage aside."

9. In so doing, I am following both Muñoz and Seymour in their Blochian thinking of art and literature as sites for the production/imagination of a concrete utopia (and not simply a queer negativity).

10. Rule was publicly opposed to same-sex marriage.
11. Long divorced from Karen's father, she has killed herself: another image that warps heterosexual inheritance.
12. As he points out, life can exist without fire, but not the reverse.
13. For a taste of the complexities of fire modeling, see Podur and Martell (2009).

Works Cited

Alaimo, Stacy. 2010. "Eluding Capture: The Science, Culture, and Pleasure of 'Queer' Animals." In Catriona Mortimer-Sandilands and Bruce Erickson, eds., *Queer Ecologies: Sex, Nature, Politics, Desire*. Bloomington: Indiana University Press: 51–72.

Anderson, Jill. 2011. "'Warm Blood and Live Semen and Rich Marrow and Wholesome Flesh!' A Queer Ecological Reading of Christopher Isherwood's A Single Man." *Journal of Ecocriticism 31.1*: 51–66.

Bagemihl, Bruce. 1999. *Biological Exuberance: Animal Homosexuality and Natural Diversity*. New York: St. Martin's Press, 1999.

Barad, Karen. 2011. "Nature's Queer Performativity." *Qui Parle 19.2* (Spring/Summer): 121–58.

Berlant, Lauren and Michael Warner. 1998. "Sex in Public." *Critical Inquiry 24* (Winter), 547–66.

Bersani, Leo. 2010. *Is the Rectum a Grave? and Other Essays*. Chicago: University of Chicago Press.

Botkin, Daniel, 1990. *Discordant Harmonies: A New Ecology for the Twenty-First Century*. New York: Oxford University Press, 1990.

Cuomo, Chris. 1998. *Feminism and Ecological Communities: An Ethic of Flourishing*. New York: Routledge.

Duggan, Lisa. 2003. *The Twilight of Equality? Neoliberalism, Cultural Politics, and the Attack on Democracy*. Boston: Beacon Press.

Edelman, Lee. 2004. *No Future: Queer Theory and the Death Drive*. Durham, NC: Duke University Press.

Erickson, Bruce. 2010. "'fucking close to water': Queering the Production of the Nation." In Catriona Mortimer-Sandilands and Bruce Erickson, eds., *Queer Ecologies: Sex, Nature, Politics, Desire*. Bloomington: Indiana University Press: 309–30.

Giffney, Noreen and Myra Hird, eds. 2008. *Queering the Non/Human*. Hampshire: Ashgate Publishing.

Halberstam, Judith. 2005. *In a Queer Time and Place: Transgender Bodies, Subcultural Lives*. New York: New York University Press.

Hird, Myra. 2008. "Animal Trans." In Noreen Giffney and Myra Hird, eds., *Queering the Non/Human*. Hampshire: Ashgate Publishing: 227–47.

Hird, Myra. 2009. "Biologically Queer." In Noreen Giffney and Michael O'Rourke, eds., *The Ashgate Research Companion to Queer Theory*. Hampshire: Ashgate Publishing: 347–62.

Hogan, Katie. 2010. "Undoing Nature: Coalition Building as Queer Environmentalism," in Catriona Mortimer-Sandilands and Bruce Erickson, eds. *Queer Ecologies: Sex, Nature, Politics, Desire*. Bloomington: Indiana University Press: 231–53.

MacCormack, Patricia. 2009. "Queer Posthumanism: Cyborgs, Animals, Monsters, Perverts." In Noreen Giffney and Michael O'Rourke, eds., *The Ashgate Research Companion to Queer Theory*. Hampshire: Ashgate Publishing: 111–26.

Mortimer-Sandilands, Catriona, and Bruce Erickson, eds. 2010. *Queer Ecologies: Sex, Nature, Politics, Desire.* Bloomington: Indiana University Press.

Muñoz, José Esteban. 2009. *Cruising Utopia: The Then and There of Queer Futurity.* New York: New York University Press.

Podur, Justin and Martell, David. (2009). "The Influence of Weather and Fuel Type on the Fuel Composition of the Area Burned by Forest Fires in Ontario 1996–2006." *Ecological Applications* 19.5: 1246–52.

Pyne, Stephen. 2001. *Fire: A Brief History.* Seattle: University of Washington Press.

Roughgarden, Joan. 2004. *Evolution's Rainbow: Diversity, Gender, and Sexuality in Nature and People.* Berkeley: University of California Press.

Rule, Jane. 1989. *After the Fire.* Toronto: MacMillan.

Sandilands, Catriona. 2001. "Desiring Nature, Queering Ethics: Adventures in Erotogenic Environments." *Environmental Ethics* 23.2: 169–88.

Scott, Dayna. 2009. "'Gender-Benders': Sex and Law in the Constitution of Polluted Bodies." *Feminist Legal Studies* 17: 241–65.

Seymour, Nicole. 2013. *Strange Natures: Futurity, Empathy, and the Queer Ecological Imagination.* Champaign: University of Illinois Press.

Stein, Rachel. 2004. *New Perspectives on Environmental Justice: Gender, Sexuality and Activism.* New Brunswick: Rutgers University Press.

Stein, Rachel. 2010. "'The Place, Promised, That Has Not Yet Been': The Nature of Dislocation and Desire in Adrienne Rich's *Your Native Land/Your Life* and Minnie Bruce Pratt's *Crime Against Nature.*" In Catriona Mortimer-Sandilands and Bruce Erickson, eds. *Queer Ecologies: Sex, Nature, Politics, Desire.* Bloomington: Indiana University Press: 285–308.

Terry, Jennifer. 2000. "'Unnatural Acts' in Nature: The Scientific Fascination with Queer Animals." *Gay and Lesbian Quarterly* 6.2: 151–93.

Wilson, Elizabeth. 2002. "Biologically Inspired Feminism: Response to Helen Keane and Marsha Rosengarten, 'On the Biology of Sexed Subjects,'" *Australian Feminist Studies* 17.39: 283–85.

CHAPTER 18

POSTCOLONIALISM

ELIZABETH DELOUGHREY

In the past few years there has been unprecedented scholarly interest and production in the field of postcolonial ecocriticism, including book-length studies on African, Caribbean, and South Asian literatures and the environment.[1] Some critics have interpreted this as a vital and energizing postcolonial turn in the dominant fields of American and British ecocriticism, while others have lamented a lack of ecocritical engagement with the postcolonial methodologies that these studies represent. Although there is a general call for more transnational scholarship in ecocritical studies, national formulations of literary study continue to play an important role in the construction of the field.[2] It remains to be seen whether postcolonial studies and US/UK ecocritical studies will continue in their established, largely separate scholarly worlds connected by an eclectic but growing body of postcolonial ecocritics, or if each respective field will be transformed by the other. The growing concern with the global scope of climate change has given a planetary dimension to both fields of study; thus, both ecocritics and postcolonialists share an interest in theorizing the planet as a whole and in examining literature's part in shaping consciousness of the globe. In this essay I'll explore some of the different mappings of the globe by ecocritics and postcolonalists, and turn to how militarization has been a constitutive part of both globalization and planetary thought, particularly in the Pacific. Moreover I will highlight how postcolonial approaches, which have long theorized the relationship between place and empire, contribute an important critique of universalist modes of globalism.

MAPPING THE GLOBE AND EMPIRE

Since there are different spatial and historical logics to postcolonial and ecocritical theories, there must be a different accounting of their intellectual genealogies. British and American ecocritics have tended to outline a history of "first-wave" and "second-wave" scholarship in which concerns about the impact of empire, race, and gender are thought to have arisen after a primary focus on conservation and wilderness.[3] Postcolonial eco-critics, while often drawing from US ecocriticism, have emphasized their genealogical origins in more rhizomatic terms, drawing from historians of empire, decolonization discourse, geography, Marxism, ecofeminism, political ecology, and environmental justice work.[4] The analytics of place, power, knowledge, and representation are vital to postcolonial studies, which has engaged in an ongoing critique of the homogenization of global space from European colonialism to its aftermath in neoliberal globalization. As a result, postcolonial approaches to environmental thought tend to highlight alter-ity, difference, and rupture, which are vital methods of deconstructing the discourses of Enlightenment universalism. Some of the work of postcolonial ecocriticism includes examining the implications of foundational narratives, problematizing assumptions of a universal subject and of an essentialized nature, and examining how forms of domi-nance are naturalized.

This critique of universal narratives of both history and the subject has been vital to postcolonial theory. This is evident in work that examines the colonial history of map-ping literal and epistemic borders that divide the normative masculine Euro-American subject from its others. The cartographies of empire and their modes of enclosure—whether mapped as colonies, nations, or first, second, third, and fourth "worlds"—have all been important terrain for postcolonial critique. Consequently, postcolonial schol-arship has had a specifically spatial emphasis, even if it has not been especially atten-tive to nonhuman nature beyond questions of resource extraction. While attempting to parochialize European epistemologies and the universal subject of history, postcolonial studies has also been critical of how globalization discourse employs homogenizing nar-ratives that ignore the history of empire and its ongoing legacies of violence. This helps to explain the postcolonial wariness about globalizing narratives in which ecocritical expertise emanates from a "first-world" center and is exported to the peripheries/colo-nies as a second wave.[5] Such a genealogy is all too reminiscent of modernization the-ory of the 1960s in which the industry-based technologies of the North were exported to the global south, upholding a linear model of progress epitomized by the Green Revolution.[6] Activists and scholars around the globe have been understandably criti-cal about the unilateral application of northern technologies of industrial agriculture and environmental policies onto the global south in ways that do not take into account local contexts.[7] As Rob Nixon has argued, generations of activists have fought against an "antihuman environmentalism that too often sought (under the banner of universal-ism) to impose green agendas dominated by rich nations and Western NGOs".[8]

These debates have centered not only on the sovereignty of natural resources but also on access to the global commons, particularly since the Cold War. For example, the United Nations' Convention on the Law of the Sea was catalyzed by the US territo-rial expansion into its coastal seas in the 1950s, which tripled US territory and led to decades of discussion and policy making about fishing and seabed mining rights, as well as the juridical definition of the global commons.[9] A similar remapping took place at the "ends of the earth" in the 1959 Antarctic Treaty, the first nuclear arms treaty in which the southern pole was defined a demilitarized zone and the "province of mankind."[10]

Other international attempts to ensure equitable access to global resources included the United Nations Conference on the Human Environment in Stockholm (1972), which sought to establish a territorial mandate for global environmental sovereignty, and the World Charter for Nature (1982), which critiqued American nuclear militarism and its global environmental impact in particular. The mapping of nationalism and globalism changed radically after World War II; the number of nations doubled and postwar international conferences and treaties reflected a powerful critique from the global south about the expansive role of the hypermilitarized technologies of the North and its regimes for managing global space.

Although ecocritics of all disciplinary backgrounds have been turning to concepts of the globe, they have not been especially attentive to these unprecedented historic events in which world space—from the Earth's oceans and outer space to Antarctica—have been radically remapped. Thus, scholars have critiqued a particular form of northern environmentalism that does not address the cartographic histories of empire and economy.[11] Nevertheless, some American-focused ecocritics have been self-reflexive about the limits of the field and the problems of eco-parochialism. In fact, the recent shift in Americanist circles towards "ecoglobalism" and "eco-cosmopolitanism" has opened up an important bridge to postcolonial approaches. Ecoglobalism is, in Lawrence Buell's words, "a whole-earth way of thinking and feeling about environmentality", while Ursula Heise defines eco-cosmopolitanism as a form of theorizing "environmental world citizenship" that addresses "the challenge that deterritorialization poses for the environmental imagination".[12] Both approaches speak to the need to think in global terms about the environment, as well as to the limitations of this framework. This is an important and welcome shift that encourages us to speak in more complex and historically layered terms about the relationship to place imagined on a global, and perhaps more comparative, scale.

Since the formulations of ecoglobalism and ecocosmopolitanism have been largely separate from postcolonial methodologies, it seems an opportune moment to raise questions about how a *global* approach to environmental literature differs from a *postcolonial* one. Moreover we must ask why, despite decades of postcolonial theorizing about the globe (and its representational limits), most US and UK ecocritics have made a "global turn" without engagement with the work of their postcolonial colleagues who often are working just down the hall. There are many possible reasons for a lack of conversation between postcolonial and mainstream ecocritical approaches to the globe which may include different kinds of disciplinary and regional training as well as varying commitments to critical theory and histories of empire. I suggest the postcolonial critique of the multicultural, humanist model of the world that arose from a specific thread of globalization studies is instructive here.

In his article on ecoglobalism, Buell positions the US as an intellectual origin, writing that "ecocriticism started as an insurgency that located itself explicitly within US literary studies [and that]...spread long since throughout the Anglophone world and beyond."[13] He argues that "the possibility of planetary consciousness" has been prefigured by canonical American texts such as "*Walden, Moby-Dick,* and *Man and Nature,*" positioned as "harbingers of contemporary ecoglobalist imagination".[14] (His assessment contrasts with Bruce Robbins's recent claim that no "worldly" American novels have yet been written.[15]) Certainly ecocritical study has never been the dominant focus for literature departments, and there is a sense that it has been marginalized. Yet as scholars, we must ask what it means to position American ecocritics as a revolutionary "insurgency" and canonical US writers as originary to planetary thought. While I agree with Buell that the recent shift in US ecocriticism has been catalyzed by a general increase in transnational literary approaches and a broadening consciousness of global climate change, we must complicate the privileging of the US and its critics as the origin of ecoglobal consciousness. Susie O'Brien has persistently raised this question about the tautologies of US ecocriticism in which mainstream critics locate the origins of global environmental thought in their own (national) field. Importantly, O'Brien draws on one of the major tenets of postcolonial studies that critiques universalist claims to knowledge by arguing that the American ecocritical desire to "*change* the world," presumes that ecocriticism "might *know* the world".[16] This question about the transparency of the world is one I will return to shortly.

To date, Americanist concerns about global environmental issues sidestep one of the most obvious worldwide ecological threats—the reach of the US military. If, as Buell argues, these nineteenth-century authors write from the center of empire—which gives them a particular insight for critique—we must ask how *contemporary* American ecocritics might use their strategic viewpoints to engage the ongoing military imperialism. Should we privilege the US as a center for planetary environmental consciousness without at the same time addressing its contemporary threats to global sustainability, including consumption, production, and a global military empire? Interestingly, it is the work of postcolonial studies scholars like Rob Nixon that has brought these environmental issues about US imperialism to the foreground. This is not, as Nixon rightly points out, an issue of merely "disciplinary parochialism" but rather a "superpower parochialism," defined as a "combination of American insularity and America's power as the preeminent empire of the neoliberal age to rupture the lives and ecosystems of non-Americans".[17]

There are enormous political stakes in these claims to the globe. Just as Gayatri Chakravorty Spivak and other postcolonial critics have been self-reflexive about the privileges of being located in US academia and the risks of obscuring our own complicity in the very networks of power that we seek to dismantle, a postcolonial critique of ecoglobalism would foreground the political and epistemological implications of being situated in the center of the American empire while positioning it as the origin of ecocritical thought. For instance, most ecocritical scholarship positions Rachel Carson's 1962 *Silent Spring* as an origin or at least catalyst of modern environmentalism that led to the founding of the field of ecocriticism in the 1990s. Yet this American origin story can be complicated by more rhizomatic genealogies of planet-thought. As important as Carson was for shifting public attention towards our toxic environments, the rise of the modern concept of ecology and conservation, as Richard Grove's *Green Imperialism* has shown, can also be attributed to the complex botanical networks of the eighteenth-century European colonial island laboratories, particularly Tahiti, Mauritius, and St. Vincent. The enormous disciplinary system of natural knowledge production cannot be defined as simply European; it was created through the extraction of knowledge and labor from indigenous and colonial subjects. As Grove demonstrates, many of our key ideas about the environment date from these early moments of European empire in which Enlightenment taxonomies and colonial rule were forged. From the ancient Greek and Roman eras to the present, empire was not a supplement to epistemologies of ecology but rather constitutive of them.[18] Thus it should not be a surprise that one of the first ecology journals published in English was the *Journal of the Society for the Preservation of the Wild Fauna of the Empire,* established in 1903 for the benefit of British colonial hunters and published until the end of imperial rule in the 1950s.

Postcolonial ecocritics have argued that colonialism is not a history relegated to the periphery of Europe and the United States, but rather a process that also occurred within and that radically changed the metropolitan center. This is in keeping with scholarship that demonstrates that modernity was not exported to the colonies but rather produced by them in a constitutive relationship to the metropole.[19] A refusal to see the interdependent histories of metropole and colony implicitly relegates postcolonial ecocriticism to the margins of Euro-American discourse. Historians have been more attentive in this regard than literary critics, demonstrating that European Enlightenment knowledge, natural history, conservation policy, and the language of nature—the very sciences and systems of logic that we draw from today to speak of conservation and sustainability—result from a long history of the colonial exploitation of nature, as well as the assimilation of indigenous knowledges from all over the globe. Thus Mary Louise Pratt has pointed out how the Enlightenment taxonomies of appropriated colonial nature could be configured, through the work of Linnaeus and countless plant collectors, into an eighteenth-century "planetary consciousness" that homogenized the world of nature into a binomial taxonomy. At the same time natural "kingdoms" were being inscribed in the language of empire and used to naturalize a racialized and gendered hierarchy of species.[20]

So while Buell has argued that "the 'oldest form of globalization' is environmental rather than economic or political" because species migrate,[21] we need to consider the ways in which claims to a naturalized history of globalization can sidestep the more thorny political formulations, including military ones. While certainly we want to uphold nature's own agency in producing a nonhuman form of globalization, an "environmental" model of globalization, on its own, would be unable to account for the enormous impact of other moments of globalization that include: the first circumnavigation of the earth which in the sixteenth century brought the Pacific under European domain; the eighteenth- and nineteenth-century forcible trade of people and plants across the globe by western European empires; the centralization of British (Greenwich) space/time at the International Meridian Conference (1884) that, according to Denis Cosgrove, "inscribed Eurocentric assumptions into a hegemonic global image"; and the laying of nineteenth-century cable and other communication technologies instigated first by the British empire and then by what Cosgrove calls "the competitive reach of commercial, industrial, and finance capital".[22] These are only a few examples of any number of events that might be claimed to usher in the moment of globalization. In short, one cannot pinpoint an *original* moment of globalization or a people especially imbued with "ecoglobalist affects," and we might even question, following Bruno Latour, whether we have ever really been global. Perhaps the turn to globalism is way of touching on different historical nodal points in order to better understand our own contemporary entanglements.

REPRESENTATIONS: WORLD(ING) AND PLANETARITY

Postcolonial approaches to the environment have emphasized the mediating role of representation in order to destabilize the universal subject, ranging from debates on the construction of the "native informant" to whether the "subaltern can speak."[23] In troubling transparent representations of the human, postcolonialists have traced out how the colonial process naturalized a hierarchy of species and codified myths of biological and climactic determinism.[24] In its deconstruction of the normative masculine human subject, the field has largely been concerned with highlighting alterity and the limits of representation. As "ecomaterialists" who share much with a previous generation of social ecologists,[25] postcolonial ecocritics have on the one hand highlighted the contingency of the representation of the human subject while on the other firmly placing the human *in* nature, as distinct from the body of ecocritical work that upholds a nature/culture divide by seeking to protect the purity of wilderness areas. As Ramachandra Guha pointed out over twenty years ago, the Deep Ecology and US environmental movement harnessed universal discourses of nature conservation that, in certain instances, displaced humans in the global south in the name of wilderness conservation. Guha also pointed out the ecological threats of both global militarism and overconsumption by the industrialized elite, both at home and abroad.[26] Likewise Deane Curtin has challenged the universal claims of some strains of western ethics, calling attention to their reliance on an unmarked individualism and upon narratives of progress and development.[27] In the flurry of postcolonial ecocriticism to follow, scholars have emphasized that empire is constitutive to knowledge of place and its representation, and that the histories of empire have contributed to the hybridization and creolization of plants, peoples, and place in ways that profoundly denaturalize absolute ontological claims, particularly in places of settler colonialism. Postcolonial ecocriticism has brought forward critiques of capitalism, consumption, technology, neoliberalism, modernization and biopiracy in the former British colonies and beyond.[28]

Until the late 20th century the sun never set on the British empire, so for all its critiques of universalism and globalism, postcolonial scholarship continues to engage an

enormous geographic expanse, examining national, regional, and global literary studies. This has generated a productive tension in the field, in which representation has
been deeply entangled with these questions of the globe, the world, and the worlding
process. These questions about the ecocritical claim to the globe have been raised by
O'Brien's early essays as well as by Graham Huggan. The latter turns to Spivak's theory of "worlding" the Third World, in which she examines how colonies such as India
were thought to enter the world only via the universalizing discourse of empire which
simultaneously alienated the colonial subject in his or her home. Thus the violence of
"worlding" is waged in material and ontological terms. Huggan reminds us of the critic's
implication in this process, reiterating Ania Loomba's concern that postcolonial studies
is "overworlding" the Third World by situating it as a "locus of anti-imperialist resistance, the overpowering rhetoric of which risks silencing the very masses on whose
behalf it claims to speak".[29] As such, both postcolonial and ecocritical scholarship are
implicated in this critique. As is clear, there is a history of resistance to the ways in which
environmental narratives emanating from the metropole become universalized, as
much as there has been a critique of the "overworlding" of postcolonial difference. Both
have implications for our acts of reading the environment. This is not to suggest that
scholars and environmentalists in the global south are not also complicit or implicated
in these complex relations. As Anna Lowenhaupt Tsing has pointed out, postcolonial
subjects may use a "strategic universalism" when engaging the discourse of northern
environmental movements.[30]

There are multiple ways of theorizing the world in postcolonial studies. Vandana
Shiva has argued for an "earth democracy," which is not derived from moments of crisis
but rather the every day, arguing that "we [must] base our globalization on ecological
processes and bonds of compassion and solidarity, not the movement of capital".[31] As
George Handley and I have argued, Édouard Glissant's work has been vital to thinking alternative modes of globalization. In an effort to maintain diversity in the globalizing wake of sameness, Glissant proposes a theory of "tout-monde," or "worldness."[32]
He describes an "aesthetics of the earth;" an "ecology" that criticizes homogenizing
modes of globalization, monolingualism, consumption, "exclusiveness," and "territorial
thought". In making an argument against discourses of universalism he poses an "aesthetics of disruption and intrusion" into sacred claims to legitimacy and into the homogenizing market of consumption itself.[33] Building upon this work, O'Brien observes that,
being "wary, with good historical reason, of the ideological and material implications of
globalizing impulses, postcolonialism admits the force of the global in a way that explicitly prohibits its recuperation into a formula that confirms the place of the individual in
a universal order, either of nature or culture. The global and the local come together, not
by way of simple synecdoche, or the relationship between macrocosm and microcosm,
but in a way such that each interrupts and distorts the other".[34] As such, these theories of
the globe are often marked, productively I think, by the tensions between alterity, totality, and representation.

In writing against the homogenizing and universalizing thrust of globalization,
Spivak offers the term "planetarity" as a useful way of theorizing a process in which if we

"imagine ourselves as planetary subjects rather than global agents, planetary creatures rather than global entities, alterity remains underived from us." In her view, "to think of it is already to transgress" because it recognizes that our metaphors of "outer and inner space," or human and nonhuman, are neither "continuous with us" nor "specifically discontinuous". Her argument addresses Loomba's critique in that planet-thought, a mode of reading, refuses to "authorize itself over against a self-consolidating other",[35] foregrounding an ecological model of thinking of the planet as "a species of alterity". In *Death of a Discipline,* Spivak claims that planet-thought "opens up to embrace an inexhaustible taxonomy" of alterity often read in terms such as "mother, nation, God, nature".[36] For Spivak and Glissant, opacity, alterity, and *not knowing* are vital methods of thinking the planet. Both are careful to pose a model of planet-thought that attempts to avoid the epistemological and ontological violence of colonization, militarization, and the structural adjustments of neoliberalism. Yet the turn to these impossibly articulated modes of thinking the planet has also drawn criticism. As Djelal Kadir warns, Spivak's validation of the planetary potential of comparative literature overlooks a "planet whose every inch is already plotted on universal global positioning systems, whose interplanetary space is thoroughly weaponized, and whose planetarity, rather than 'undivided "natural" space'... is already naturalized into martial containment."[37] It is this relationship between worlding and militarism that I take up in this next section.

MILITARISM AND THE ENVIRONMENT

Most mainstream genealogies of ecocriticism trace founding moments of environmental thought to the publication of Rachel Carson's *Silent Spring* (1962), the first Earth Day in 1970,[38] and the *Apollo* space mission images (1968–69) which are thought to be key to catalyzing global consciousness. In fact, Buell observes that "the whole earth image taken from the moon a third of a century ago has long since become a logo, a cultural cliché".[39] While it's true that most ecocritics invoke the *Apollo* images, none to my knowledge have tied them to a particular kind of global consciousness derived from American militarism in the Cold War. Denis Cosgrove has explained that the global view grew out of the aerial perspective of military aircraft and that "the idea that *vision* in the form of a mastering view across space and time was uniquely available to an aviator disengaged from ... earthbound mortals became a recurrent feature of geopolitical discourse at mid-century".[40] While the *Apollo* space mission photos were certainly influential, they were part of a context in which *National Geographic* and other popular magazines utilized wartime cartography in ways that naturalized nationalism, militarism, and American empire under the guise of a unifying gaze of the globe. As Tim Ingold has observed in his discussion of how classroom globes map territory, "the image of the world as a globe is ... a colonial one". Aerial military technologies in turn catalyzed American initiatives to expand their commercial aviation reach, evident in air space treaties and a rise in concepts of global connectivity, epitomized as Cosgrove points out in the branding of airlines like "Trans World Airways" (TWA). Thus "global thinking was explicitly connected to air travel", which began with the airplane and culminated in the astronaut's gaze. The 1969 *Apollo* picture represents "an American image of the globe that has come to dominate late twentieth-century Western culture", and is not necessarily a *global* image but an American image *of* the globe.[41] Here I'd like to bring together two parallel discourses about the *temporal* depth of global ecological thought on the one hand, and the globalizing *spatial* compression created by American militarism since WW2.

While it has been the norm for ecocritical publications to gesture towards a universal environmental crisis that threatens human existence on earth, the claim for the protection of a global ecology has not been tied directly to the globalizing reach of US militarism and its environmental consequences. There are a number of explanations for this silence. The first is a dearth of critical scholarship on militarization itself, despite an enormous American military build-up in the past decade with vast environmental consequences.[42] As Cynthia Enloe reminds us, US militarization is so ubiquitous that it becomes hidden in plain sight and deeply naturalized.[43] Second, a particular thread of globalization studies has perpetuated a largely historical approach to cosmopolitanism in ways that understate the ongoing power of the state and implicitly deflect attention away from forms of state violence such as colonialism and militarism. Yet war, which has largely been neglected by globalization studies, is constitutive of the globalization process. Tarak Barkawi observes, "in focusing on global flows held to be corrosive of territorially defined entities, globalization studies lost sight of war. Implicitly, war here is misconceived as a breakdown of communication and interchange, rather than as an occasion for circulation".[44] Finally, the majority of ecocritical scholarship focuses on national and bioregional concerns like energy and natural resource use, consumption, foodways, state conservation, and population, and has not, with a few exceptions, engaged forms of militarism.

Huggan and Tiffin's book *Postcolonial Ecocriticism* has been one of the few to position the United States as a global ecological threat, "a country that has actively and aggressively contributed to what many now acknowledge to be the chronic endangerment of the contemporary late-capitalist world".[45] Although they do not develop this point specifically in relation to militarism, their work continues an important postcolonial critique of structural adjustment policies in an extended discussion of concepts of development.[46] Anthony Carrigan has usefully examined the ways in which "militourism," to borrow a term from Teresia Teaiwa about the suturing of the military to tourist spaces, has been constitutive to representations of the environment in postcolonial literature. Rob Nixon's *Slow Violence and the Environmentalism of the Poor* (2011) is perhaps the most extended discussion in ecocriticism as to the complex issues posed by what he terms "slow violence," which he defines as damage that "occurs gradually and out of sight ... dispersed across time and space." He highlights Carson's concern with "the complicity of the military-industrial complex in disguising toxicity" and, following in her wake, is one of the few ecocritics who turns to US militarization, examining the "fatal environmental imprecision" created by American so-called precision warfare in the Gulf and its appalling legacy of poisonous depleted uranium, with a radioactive half-life of over 4 billion years. The 1991 Gulf War was, according to one scientist, "'the most toxic war in Western military history.'"[47]

The legacy of the Cold War has not, strangely enough, been a major concern to US ecocritics but it certainly has played a vital part in contemporary understandings of both ecology and environmentalism itself. Donald Worster has written that "the Age of Ecology began on the desert outside Alamogordo, New Mexico on July 16, 1945, with a dazzling fireball of light and a swelling mushroom cloud of radioactive gases."[48] He has suggested that nuclear militarism catalyzed public consciousness about the invisible pollution of the global environment, a new understanding of interconnected geographies that helped Carson redirect widespread fears of radioactive fallout towards contamination by pesticides.[49] Although it is not often noted, Carson's concern with the chemical fallout of industrial agriculture had built upon a decade of global protest against the material, social, and political fallout of American militarism. Thus, while Carson represents a vital turning point in thinking about the global environment, her work, rhetorically speaking, was deeply tied to the anti-nuclear, "one world or none" movement.[50] In this way the globe became connected discursively, as Heise points out, as "a world at risk".[51]

As I have written elsewhere, the historical connection between ecological thought and radioactive militarism is not as distant as it might seem. Ecosystem ecology, as it was organized by Eugene Odum, the field's "founding father", was in part facilitated by the rapid expansion of nuclear testing in the Pacific Islands and the subsequent radiological contamination of the planet.[52] The field of radiation ecology began in the Pacific with Odum's study of the Marshall Islands, and as a result, AEC-funded research laboratories and programs in radioecology were organized in universities and nuclear power sites all over the United States, catalyzing the institutional development of ecosystem ecology.[53] This was in response to a global public outcry about the dangers of nuclear fallout and a worldwide movement against US militarism, which created some of the first modern conceptions of a globalism linked by the internalization of militarized radiation (fallout)—as well as the threat of nuclear apocalypse. So while there is much to say about the contributions the US has made to ecological thought, the role of American militarism has not factored enough in these discussions, whether we speak in terms of how the AEC helped establish the field of ecology, or the role of US imperialism, past and present.

PACIFIC WARS OF LIGHT

Discourses of alterity and difference have been at the forefront of postcolonial ecocriticism, which has done much to call attention to the material histories of nature and their representational affects and aesthetics.[54] This concern with alterity has been an important methodology for addressing the history of colonialism and its neoliberal and neocolonial legacies. In the indigenous literature of the Pacific Islands, representations of globalization, planetarity, and *te ao marama,* the world of light (in Maori), have been tied closely to the militarization of the region. One might locate the region's globalization in the history of ancient voyaging traditions, as does Epeli Hau'ofa, as well as in the long history of European and US colonialism in the region. While the earliest Pacific literary texts engaged the cultural and political legacy of World War II such as Florence Johnny Frisbie's autobiography *Miss Ulysses from Puka-Puka* (1948) and Vincent Eri's novel *The Crocodile* (1971), the region's literature did not specifically connect militarism and the environment until the United States, the United Kingdom, and France began using the region as a nuclear testing zone, exposing the Pacific Islands to threatening levels of nuclear fallout. The global implications of atmospheric weapons testing became especially severe with the 1954 *Bravo* test, which covered the surrounding islands and a Japanese fishing vessel with radioactive strontium, cesium, and iodine, killing Japanese sailors and exposing hundreds of Marshall Islanders to nuclear fallout, which resulted in miscarriages, leukemia, thyroid cancers, genetic defects, and death. Designed to maximize the spread of fallout and estimated at 1,000 times the force of the bombs dropped on Hiroshima and Nagasaki, *Bravo* has been called the worst radiological disaster in history; fallout was detected in the rain over Japan, in the lubricating oil of Indian aircraft, in winds over Australia, and in the sky over the United States and Europe.[55] *Bravo* and the subsequent 2,000 or so nuclear tests on this planet, Eileen Welsome observes, "split the world into 'preatomic' and 'postatomic' species".[56] Radioactive elements produced by these weapons were spread through the atmosphere, deposited into water supplies and soils, absorbed by plants and subsequently absorbed into the bone tissue of humans all over the globe. The body of every human on the planet is now thought to contain strontium-90, a man-made byproduct of nuclear detonations.[57] Indeed, forensic scientists use the traces of militarized radioactive carbon in our teeth to date human remains.

Due to the decades of nuclear testing in the region, Pacific sovereignty discourse and literature has a profound relationship to what Paul Virilio calls the "wars of light,"[58] demarcating them from the ways in which other postcolonial regions have engaged militarization and colonial violence. The Pacific literary response to the militarized radiation has been substantive, beginning with Maori poet Hone Tuwhare's well-known poem "No Ordinary Sun," written after the *Bravo* test and an elegy to the globalizing impact of the Cold War and its scorching implications for life on earth. Tuwhare was stationed in Japan in 1946 and witnessed firsthand the impact of atomic devastation on Hiroshima.[59] In this five-stanza poem, he repeatedly negates the natural metaphors accorded to the nuclear bomb by the AEC that liken weaponry to the sun. Elsewhere I have written of the heliographic focus of anti-nuclear literature in the Pacific and the ways in which authors like Tuwhare have turned to allegories of the sun and light to deconstruct the Cold War naturalization of militarized radiation.[60] The poem's allegorical mode has turned "No Ordinary Sun" into a rallying point for the peace movement across the Pacific. It has been reproduced in stone in the Wellington Peace Flame Garden, has been set to music, and has been adapted in a series of anti-nuclear paintings by New Zealand's well-known visual artist, Ralph Hotere.[61] Part of the poem's effectiveness is its refusal to visualize the spectacular effects of nuclear detonations and their apocalyptic impact. Thus the poem ends: "O tree/in the shadowless mountains/the white plains and/the drab sea floor/your end at last is written." In concluding with a "drab" landscape, Tuwhare avoids the apocalyptic temporality of "the end is near" and substitutes it with the authorial claim to representation: "the end at last is written."

The poem concludes, not with the visual destruction of the globe, but with its oppo-site: its total illumination in a "shadowless" landscape. If, like Spivak and Glissant, we define globalization by its will to homogenize and to know the planet, we can see in Tuwhare's poem how he critiques the way military globalization erases alterity and shadow. Tuwhare visualizes how the violence of heliocentric modernity illuminates the ends of the Earth—mountains, sea floors, shadows—without allowing the space for alterity or the space for *not knowing*, not seeing. He offers a vital counter to colonial and militarist mappings of the Pacific, particularly by highlighting those spaces that are understood as beyond human habitation—the mountains, deserts, and sea floors fully illuminated by this "monstrous sun." Hence, in this poem the shift to universalism (at the cosmic level) suggests a "drab" place without difference, something that should not be desired or normative, even if it is "not ordinary."[62]

Tuwhare's shift from the landscape of trees and birds to those spaces of planetary otherness to suggest extraterrestrial difference on our own planet has also been shared by Maori author James George in his novel about the impact of the Cold War, *Ocean Roads*. This remarkable text maps the globalizing process of Cold War militarism in a way that, to borrow from Barkawi, "theorize[s] war as a pervasive and historically sig-nificant form of international interconnectedness, as a *globalizing force*".[63] Thus the protagonist Isaac Simeon, a British physicist employed by the Manhattan Project who helped design the first plutonium weapon, travels from Los Alamos Laboratories and the Trinity site to Nagasaki to witness the aftermath of the atomic attack, while his New Zealand photographer-wife travels throughout Vietnam during the war and then to military memorial sites such as the Trinity and Pearl Harbor monuments. Yet the space given textual prominence for this couple is Antarctica, a place where Isaac has a mental breakdown that leads to his institutionalization in 1959. In militarized Antarctica, where "the only green for a couple of thousand miles is that of military fatigues", he observes, "I spent a decade there without even knowing it. Every empty mile, every breath of grave-yard wind had my name on it. A name like mine, arrogance like mine. I just never real-ized it until I stood on it, set my foot with my flesh instead of my mind, my imagination". In wandering in the Antarctic desert he finds "phantom footprints" and total silence, replicating his experience in post-atomic Nagasaki. It's curious that of all the military landscapes he has mapped, George turns to Antarctica to set the scene for his protago-nist's realization of his complicity in nuclear violence, an awareness that renders him speechless for a decade. But Antarctica, like Tuwhare's "sea floor," represents the limits of human habitation on earth, and a space of the planet's alterity. It is a place of "endless twilight", a desert where there has been no rain in a million years, where "'even the ash from burned human excrement lasts forever'". Antarctica, Isaac determines, is extrater-restrial: "I might as well have been on Mars".[64] Thus it is, like planetarity, an uncanny place, of our earth home and also a place of not knowing, of not belonging, a profound lack of embedded or place-based consciousness. Isaac is not the only one to interpellate the poles as extraterrestrial—NASA used the Antarctic Dry Valleys (the same ones inscribed in the novel) as testing areas for their Mars space probes.[65] As such, the climatic ends of the Earth provide an imaginary locus for thinking through earthly and extraterrestrial globalism.

As befitting someone inhabiting a space of alterity, Isaac becomes lost in the landscape, "reciting mathematical conundrums in his mind", his own way of ordering the world. In a panic "he begins to run, knowing that his tiny figure is covering in seconds what the glacier covers in a century," and he then sleeps, dreaming of houses "far below, like a Lillliput landscape". It's significant that George attributes an aerial view to his protagonist in his moment of crisis; Isaac becomes detached from his own human scale, imagining himself from above even as he becomes subject to the immensity and alterity of Antarctica. There he dreams of the lights of a city below and of himself as the plutonium-239 "implosion bomb" that he created, the "Fat Man" dropped on Hiroshima in 1945. Interestingly, it is the anthropomorphism of these first weapons of mass destruction (the bomb dropped on Hiroshima was termed "Little Boy") that allows Isaac to merge with the other that he has created, to set "foot with (his) flesh instead of (his) mind." Hence he describes a dream in which the B-52 bomber's doors open and he "slip(s) away," his head and body "encased in their metal sarcophagus," which represent "two separate nuclear weapons". It is in this fusion process, he explains, that "I have begun." But even in the increasing heat, pressure and process of becoming an exploding plutonium weapon dropping on an unaware city, Isaac imagines a second, larger aerial gaze: "someone shadowing my flight might glimpse my skin buckling, cracking, the first rip sending searing light into the last picoseconds of blue sky". The merger with that weapon of alterity (in that its destructive power cannot be fully comprehended), is not in Isaac's dream a merger with the environment but rather an always Apollonian view of detachment. Thus while a nuclear weapon at detonation will violently merge with its environment even as it destroys it, Isaac does not imagine this merger and he maintains his alterity and his aerial vision. He descends to Nagasaki and his dream concludes: "beneath me, skin peels, eyeballs melt, bones become liquid". As someone who refers to himself elsewhere as a "disciple...of light", Isaac believes himself to be "more a child of the sun than the earth" and thus a sign of both global nuclear militarization (its homogenization) and planetarity (its alterity).[66]

Cosgrove has argued that in on our global vision, the arctic poles "represent the final ends of the earth, global destinations of ultimate inaccessibility. Their 'conquest' offered individuals and nations a competitive sense of global mastery comparable only to circumnavigation by sea or air or the ascent of high mountains".[67] So while Isaac might have experienced the realization of his own complicity in the violence of global militarism in the aftermath of visits to Trinity and Nagasaki, George deliberately locates his breakdown in Antarctica, a depopulated "end of the earth" which in its continual illumination throughout the austral summer, its lack of green flora and normative models of time tied to our perception of the setting sun, becomes the figure for a post-apocalyptic planetarity (difference) that renders human time and, given Isaac's breakdown, even articulation impossible.

   While postcolonial ecocritics have focused on the populated regions of the Earth, Cosgrove reminds us that the colonizing reach of military globalization also entails "the Enlightenment vision of global encirclement", which becomes possible through the conquest of the poles. Consequently the "*cold* war was aptly named" because of the militarization and nuclearization of the Arctic and Antarctic: "The militarization of the North Pole redirected competitive research toward Antarctica ... and American detonation of hydrogen bombs to examine auroral effects. There is a direct line of descent from this work to the discovery of the Antarctic ozone deficit and fears of global climatic catastrophe". As such, contemporary fears of "the end of the Earth" created by rapid climate change can be traced back to an earlier discourse of the nuclear annihilation of the planet. Importantly Isaac's institutionalization occurs in February 1959, shortly after his trip to Antarctica where it seems he was a scientific researcher for the International Geophysical Year (IGY), a global research project that Cosgrove calls "a defining moment for twentieth-century globalism". The IGY included extensive research in Antarctica and resulted in the USSR and US launching the first artificial satellites, *Sputnik* (1957) and *Explorer* (1958).[68] George's decision to place Isaac's breakdown in Antarctica amidst the IGY raises important questions about how Cold War science produced at the literal "end of the Earth" was made possible by our planet's own polar spaces of alterity, transforming what were understood to be spatial limits of the earth into temporal ones.

   On one hand we might interpret Isaac's incorporation of the omniscient eye into his dream ("someone shadowing") as yet another visual logic in a novel whose form has been constituted by its engagement with such technologies of light as such as nuclear and medical radiation, fire and napalm, as well as photography and film.[69] On the other hand, George's decision to locate this dream and transformation of his character in Antarctica suggests his invocation of the ways in which Cold War militarization created another spatial logic for understanding the planet. The "scramble for the seas" that constituted much of the 1950s was also tied to a "scramble for outer space" as the Soviet Union and United States rushed to produce both artificial satellites and intercontinental ballistic missiles (ICBM). The 1954 *Bravo* test in fact demonstrated the general portability of hydrogen weapons and thus the US Department of Defense gave top priority to developing the significantly named *Atlas* ICBM series. Moreover their experiments at the southern pole, where the earth's magnetic field is the lowest, led to a short but controversial nuclearization of the ionosphere, in which they detonated a number of high altitude weapons, so-called rainbow bombs, that created a broader distribution of radiation and involved the deliberate disruption, sometimes for weeks, of radio and radar communications.[70]

   Cosgrove observes that the poles "remain eschatological ends of the earth, whence ozone depletion or ice-sheet meltdown threatens life across the globe".[71] It is significant that George positions one of major climax points of the novel here, one that far exceeds the momentary appearance in the novel of the *Apollo* space mission to the moon, which produced our iconic photographs.[72] While Etta witnesses the televised moon landing from her hotel in Saigon and remarks on the differences in experiences of distance from the earth, the personally transformative moment in the novel is associated with Antarctica. Elsewhere I've argued that George's novel represents the alterity of the planet through metaphors of light and radiation.[73] Fittingly, that experience of the total light of nuclearization, while it cannot be experienced without the death of the subject, is displaced onto Antarctica, a place—during the austral summer—of total light which is not disconnected from the homogenizing reach of global militarism. Thus it is, like Spivak's theory of planetarity, an uncanny place of our earth home and also a place of not knowing, of not belonging, a profound lack of embedded or place-based consciousness.[74]

Noël Sturgeon has commented that the end of the Cold War in the 1980s was simultaneous with the rise of global environmentalism, the discursive and political implications of which have not been fully explored. While ecocriticism is largely concerned with terrestrial matter, such as the trees and soil that are thought to "root" human relationships to the land, it has not engaged enough with the ways in which our images of the Earth arise from Cold War militarism as well as with how modes of imagining the Earth might contribute to the naturalization of the military surveillance that has expanded since the era of *Sputnik* and justified first by the war against communism and later by a war against that ubiquitous enemy, "terror." If the concept of the literary hero has military roots, as Catharine Savage Brosman argues, we might better examine the ways in which literary forms might naturalize military violence.[75] Moreover, American ecocritics might engage the present history of US militarism to better theorize an ecoglobalism without universalism, an acknowledgment of the violence of American empire as much as its necessary parochialization. This is one vital method of planet-thought, in which militarism and environmentalism are paradoxically continuous and discontinuous. Moreover, this approach to planet-thought would recognize our own attempts, as academics, to dismantle the homogenizing networks of power in which we are enmeshed.

Cosgrove suggests the ends of the Earth, whether imagined as Antarctica or outer space, reflect the closure of open space, and the end of a frontier.[76] Postcolonial approaches to ecocriticism insist on examining the shifting concept of the frontier, in both material and disciplinary terms. The newness of ecoglobal models provide a welcome opportunity to create a vital dialogue between postcolonial and ecocritical thought, but claims to the globe might be tempered by critiques of totality and universalism. Moreover, the frontiers of literary study are not necessarily outside of the legacies of colonial violence or the ongoing reach of US militarism. These are some of the thorny entanglements to consider as we witness the expansion of US-based ecocriticism and its recent shift into the environmental humanities.

NOTES

1. The most recent works include: Graham Huggan and Helen Tiffin, eds., "Special issue: Green Postcolonialism," *Interventions: International Journal of Postcolonial Studies.*, 9 (2007); Helen Tiffin, ed., *Five Emus to the King of Siam.* (Amsterdam, New York: Rodopi, 2007); Special issues of *ISLE: Interdisciplinary Studies of Literature and the Environment* 14 (Winter

2007); and *Modern Fiction Studies* 55 (2009); Bonnie Roos and Alex Hunt, eds. *Postcolonial Green: Environmental Politics & World Narratives* (Charlottesville: University of Virginia Press, 2010); Graham Huggan and Helen Tiffin, *Postcolonial Ecocriticism: Literature, Animals, Environment* (New York: Routledge, 2010); Upamanyu Mukherjee, *Postcolonial Environments: Nature, Culture & Contemporary Indian Novel in English* (London: Palgrave Macmillan, 2010); Rob Nixon, *Slow Violence and the Environmentalism of the Poor* (Cambridge: Harvard University Press, 2011); Anthony Carrigan, *Postcolonial Tourism* (New York: Routledge, 2011); and Elizabeth DeLoughrey and George B. Handley, eds. *Postcolonial Ecologies: Literature of the Environment* (New York: Oxford University Press, 2011).

2. See Lawrence Buell, "Ecocriticism: Emerging Trends" in *Qui Parle* 19 (Spring/Summer 2011), 87–115 on ecoglobalism and Ursula Heise, *Sense of Place and Sense of Planet* (Oxford: Oxford University Press, 2008) on eco-cosmopolitanism.

3. Critics have generally agreed that mainstream formulations of ecocriticism have largely been concerned with tropes of wilderness conservation, pastoralism, the individual's relationship to non-human nature, the sublime, pollution, and apocalypse. See Jonathan Bate, *Song of the Earth* (Cambridge: Harvard University Press, 2002); Buell *The Future of Environmental Criticism: Environmental Crisis and Literary Imagination* (Malden: Blackwell Publishing, 2005); and Greg Garrard, *Ecocriticism* (New York: Routledge 2011) for a representative few.

4. Compare Buell "Ecocriticism: Emerging Trends" to DeLoughrey and Handley's "Introduction" Postcolonial Ecologies (2010). The "wave" narrative often erases the important contributions of ecofeminists and environmental justice scholars who were publishing in the earliest issues of the foundational journal ISLE. Examples of some earlier ecofeminist and environmental justice literary approaches include Joni Adamson, Mei Mei Evans and Rachel Stein (eds) *The Environmental Justice Reader: Politics, Poetics, and Pedagogy*. Tucson: The University of Arizona Press, 2002; Joni Adamson *American Indian Literature, Environmental Justice, and Ecocriticism: The Middle Place*. Tucson: The University of Arizona Press, 2001; Stacy Alaimo *Undomesticated Ground: Recasting Nature as Feminist Space*, Cornell University Press, 2000; Gaard, Greta & Murphy, Patrick *Ecofeminist Literary Criticism: Theory, Interpretation, Pedagogy* University of Illinois Press 1998; and Gaard, Greta. Ed. *Ecofeminism: Women, Animals, Nature*. Philadelphia: Temple University Press, 1993.

5. See critiques in Ramachandra Guha, "Radical American Environmentalism and Wilderness Preservation: A Third World Critique," *Environmental Ethics* 11 (1989); Rob Nixon, "Postcolonialism and Environmentalism," in *Postcolonialism and Beyond*, ed. Ania Loomba et al. (Durham, NC: Duke University Press, 2005); and Susie O'Brien, "Articulating a World of Difference: Ecocriticism, Postcolonialism and Globalization." *Canadian Literature* 170–171 (Autumn/Winter 2001).

6. See Vandana Shiva, *The Violence of the Green Revolution: Third World Agriculture, Ecology and Politics*. (New York: Zed Books Ltd., 2001) and Huggan and Tiffin, "Development" (2010).

7. This is apparent in critiques of a Green Revolution that was deliberately intended, according to USAID director William Gaud, to displace and delegitimize the "red revolution" arising from recently decolonized nations. William S. Gaud, "The Green Revolution: Accomplishments and Apprehensions," *AgBioWorld*. March 8, 1968. http://www.agbioworld.org/biotech-info/topics/borlaug/borlaug-green.html

8. Rob Nixon, *Slow Violence*, p.5.

9. In 1945 President Truman violated the freedom of the seas doctrine with his proclamation that the fisheries and maritime mineral resources contiguous to the US coasts were national territory, greatly extending the littoral (coastal) state to 200 miles out to sea. Two years later Truman violated international law by annexing Micronesia, a "sea of islands" as large as the north Atlantic Ocean, an acquisition that more than doubled US territory. When we factor in the 3.9 billion acres of submarine land and resources, 1.7 times the size of onshore territory, Truman tripled the territorial size of the United States. See Elizabeth DeLoughrey, *Routes and Roots: Navigating Caribbean and Pacific Island Literatures* (Honolulu: University of Hawai'i Press), pp.31–37.

10. Seyom Brown, Nina Cornell, Larry Fabian and Edith Weiss, *Regimes for the Ocean, Outer Space, and Weather; Resource Management at the International Level: The Case of the North Pacific*, (Washington, D.C.: Brookings Institution, 1977), p.128.

11. See Shiva, Violence, and Richard Peet and Michael Watts, eds., *Liberation Ecologies* (London; New York: Routledge, 1996).

12. Buell, 'Ecoglobalist Affects: The Emergence of U.S. Environmental Imagination on a Planetary Scale', in Wai-Chee Dimock and Lawrence Buell, eds. *Shades of the Planet: American Literature as World Literature* (London: Princeton University Press, 2007), pp.227–248 (p.227); Heise, p.10. See also Timothy Morton, *The Ecological Thought* (Cambridge; London: Harvard University Press, 2010): "Small is beautiful...The local is better than the global. These are some of the slogans of environmental movement since the late 1960s. I'll be proposing the exact opposite...In my formulation, the best environmental thinking is thinking big—as big as possible, and maybe even bigger than that, bigger than we can conceive." (20).

13. Buell, p.228. O'Brien argues that Cheryll Glotfelty's introduction to the *Ecocriticism Reader* makes a similar claim for extending US ecocriticism to the world in Susie O'Brien, "Back to the World: Reading Ecocriticism in a Postcolonial Context," in *Five Emus to the King of Siam*, ed. Helen Tiffin. (Amsterdam, New York: Rodopi, 2007), pp.177–199.

14. Ibid., 242.

15. Robbins, Bruce. "The Worlding of the American Novel," in *The Cambridge History of the American Novel*, ed. Leonard Cassuto. (Cambridge: Cambridge UP, 2011), pp.1096–1106.

16. O'Brien, 'Back to the World', p.181.

17. Nixon, *Slow Violence*, p.34.

18. See Antonello Gerbi, *The Dispute of the New World* (Pittsburgh: Pittsburgh University Press, 1973) and *Nature in the New World* (Pittsburgh: Pittsburgh University Press, 1985); Richard Grove, *Green Imperialism* (Cambridge: Cambridge University Press, 1995); Richard Drayton, *Nature's Government* (New Haven: Yale University Press, 2000); Nancy Stepan, *Picturing Tropical Nature* (Ithaca: Cornell University Press, 2001); Donald Moore, Jake Kosek, and Anand Pandian, eds., *Race, Nature, and the Politics of Difference* (Durham: Duke University Press, 2003); William Beinart and Lotte Hughes, *Environment and Empire* (Oxford: Oxford University Press, 2007); Elizabeth DeLoughrey, Renée Gosson and George Handley, eds, *Caribbean Literature and the Environment* (Charlottesville: University of Virginia Press, 2005); and DeLoughrey and Handley, eds., *Postcolonial Ecologies* (Oxford: Oxford University Press, 2011).

19. Sidney Mintz, *Sweetness and Power* (New York: Penguin Books, 1985).

20. Mary Louise Pratt, *Imperial Eyes* (London, New York: Routledge, 1992), p.15.

21. Buell, 'Eco-globalist Affects', p.227.

22. Denis Cosgrove, *Apollo's Eye: A Cartographic Genealogy of the Earth in the Western Imagination* (Baltimore, MD: Johns Hopkins University Press, 2001), p.221.

23. The literature on this is enormous, but good starting points are Gayatri Chakravorty Spivak, "Can the Subaltern Speak?" in *Wedge*, 7/8 (Winter/Spring 1985); and Graham Huggan, *The Postcolonial Exotic* (New York: Routledge, 2001).

24. See DeLoughrey, Gosson, and Handley, *Caribbean Literature*. In Una Chaudhuri, "There Must Be a Lot of Fish in That Lake: Towards an Ecological Theatre," *Theatre* 25 (1995), 23–31, Chaudhuri argues, "Along with other discourses born of the age of industrialization, nineteenth-century humanism located its shaky foundations on the growing gap between the social and natural worlds, constructing a fragile edifice that could sustain itself only at the cost of actively ignoring the claims of the nonhuman."

25. See Mukherjee, *Postcolonial Environments*; and Carrigan, *Postcolonial Tourism*.

26. Guha, 'Radical American Environmentalism'. He contended that deep ecology demonstrated a "lack of concern with inequalities *within* human society," dehistoricized nature (72), and overlooked more pressing environmental issues such as global militarization and the growing "overconsumption by industrial nations and by urban elites in the Third World" (74).

27. Deane Curtin, *Chinnagounder's Challenge: The Question of Ecological Citizenship* (Bloomington, IN: Indiana University Press), 1999. On individualism and universalism, see also Noël Sturgeon, *Ecofeminist Natures* (New York, London: Routledge, 2007) and O'Brien, "Back to the World".

28. See Vandana Shiva, *Earth Democracy* (Boston: Boston South End Press, 2005); Carolyn Merchant, *Death of Nature* (San Francisco: Harper Collins, 1983); Elizabeth DeLoughrey, Renée Gosson and George Handley, *Caribbean Literature and the Environment: Between Nature and Culture* (Charlottesville, University Press of Virginia, 2005).

29. Graham Huggan, "Greening' Postcolonialism: Ecocritical Perspectives," *Modern Fiction Studies* 50:3 (2004), 701–733 (p.704). See Ania Loomba, "Overworlding the Third World," in *Colonial Discourse and Post-Colonial Theory: A Reader*, ed. Patrick Williams and Laura Chrisman (New York: Columbia University Press, 1994), pp.305–323. Also Gayatri Chakravorty Spivak, "The Rani of Sirmur," *History and Theory* 24:3 (1985), 247–272; and Bill Ashcroft, Gareth Griffiths and Helen Tiffin, *Postcolonial Studies: The Key Concepts* (New York, London: Routledge, 2000).

30. Anna Lowenhaupt Tsing, *Friction: An Ethnography of Global Connection* (Princeton, NJ: Princeton University Press, 2011).

31. Shiva, Earth Democracy, 4.

32. Handley and DeLoughrey, *Postcolonial Ecologies*. Édouard Glissant, "The Unforeseeable Diversity of the World," trans. Haun Saussy, in *Beyond Dichotomies: Histories, Identities, Cultures, and the Challenge of Globalization*, ed. Elisabeth Mudimbe-Boyi (Albany: State University of New York Press, 2002), pp.287–295.

33. Édouard Glissant, *The Poetics of Relation*, trans. Betsy Wing (Ann Arbor, MI: University of Michigan Press, 1997), 146, 151.

34. O'Brien 2001, p.143. See also Susie O'Brien, "The garden and the world: Jamaica Kincaid and the cultural borders of ecocriticism," *Mosaic: a Journal for the Interdisciplinary Study of Literature* 35.2 (2002): 167–185; and Rajagopalan Radhakrishnan, "Worlding, by Any Other Name," in *History, the Human, and the World Between* (Durham, NC: Duke University Press, 2008), pp.183–248.

35. Gayatri Chakravorty Spivak, "World Systems and the Creole," *Narrative* 14.1 (2006): 102–112 (pp.107–8, 107).

36. Gayatri Chakravorty Spivak, *Death of a Discipline* (New York: Columbia University Press), p.72, 73.

37. Kadir Djelal, "Comparative Literature in an Age of Terrorism," *Comparative Literature in and Age of Globalization*, ed. Haun Saussy (Baltimore: Johns Hopkins University Press, 2006), pp.68–77 (p.72).

38. See Heise, Garrard and Mukherjee.

39. Buell, 'Eco-globalist Affects', p.227. Wolfgang Sachs, *Planet Dialectics: Explorations in Environment and Development* (London: Zed Books, 1999); Denis Cosgrove, *Apollo's Eye: A Cartographic Genealogy of the Earth in the Western Imagination* (Baltimore: Johns Hopkins University Press, 2001); and Heise have all demonstrated how new technologies from the internet to satellites have provided new ways of imaging the earth.

40. Cosgrove, p.242.

41. See Tim Ingold, "Globes and Spheres: The Topology of Environmentalism," in *Environmentalism: The View from Anthropology*, ed. K. Milton (London: Routledge, 1993), pp.31–42 (p.38).

42. For an account of the US military's holdings and operations in forty-six countries and territories, see "The Department of Defense Base Structure Report: Fiscal Year 2011 Baseline Report," http://www.acq.osd.mil/ie/download/bsr/bsr2011baseline.pdf. There have been many articles documenting the US military's impact in Vietnam, Bikini and Enewetak Atolls, Okinawa, Hawai'i, and Guam in particular—too many to list here. Interestingly, recent articles have turned to the military's excessive contribution to carbon emissions, such as work by University of Nebraska's Adam J. Liska and Richard K. Perrin's "Securing Foreign Oil: A Case for Including Military Operations in the Climate Change Impact of Fuels," *Environment Magazine* (July/August 2010), http://www.environmentmagazine.org/Archives/Back%20Issues/July-August%202010/securing-foreign-oil-full.html

43. Enloe, Cynthia. *Bananas, Beaches and Bases*, UC Press, 2001.

44. Barkawi, Tarak. "Connection and Constitution: Locating War and Culture in Globalization Studies." *Globalizations* 1.2 (2004): 155–170. (p.155).

45. Huggan and Tiffin, p.1.

46. See also Gustavo Esteva, "Development," in *The Development Dictionary: A Guide to Knowledge as Power* (London: Zed Books, 2010), pp.1–23.

47. Nixon, p.xi, 201, 204.

48. Donald Worster, *Nature's Economy: A History of Ecological Ideas*, 2nd edn. (Cambridge: Cambridge University Press, 1994), p.342.

49. See also Ralph H. Lutts, "Chemical Fallout: Rachel Carson's *Silent Spring*, Radioactive Fallout, and the Environmental Movement" in *No Birds Sing: Rhetorical Analyses of Rachel Carson's Silent Spring*, ed. Craig Wadell (Carbondale: Southern Illinois University Press, 2000), pp.17–42.

50. For more on the "one world or none" see Paul Boyer, *By the Bomb's Early Light: American Thought and Culture at the Dawn of the Atomic Age* (Chapel Hill and London: University of North Carolina Press, 1994).

51. Heise, p.27.

52. Joel Bartholomew Hagen, *An Entangled Bank: The Origins of Ecosystem Ecology* (Piscataway, NJ: Rutgers University Press, 1992), p.101.

53. Hagen, p.112. Discussed in Elizabeth DeLoughrey, "Heliotropes: Solar Ecologies and Pacific Radiations" in *Postcolonial Ecologies: Literatures of the Environment*, eds. DeLoughrey and George Handley (Oxford: Oxford University Press, 2011), pp.235–253.

54. On domination, Max Horkheimer and Theodor Adorno, *Dialectic of Enlightenment* (New York: Herder & Herder, 1972) has been foundational. See Carolyn Merchant, *Ecology: Key Concepts in Critical Theory* (New York: Humanity Books, 1999); Val Plumwood, *Feminism and the Mastery of Nature* (New York and London: Routledge, 1993), Karen J. Warren, *Ecofeminist Philosophy: A Western Perspective on What It Is and Why It Matters* (New York: Rowman and Littlefield Publishers, Inc., 2000), and DeLoughrey and Handley, *Postcolonial Ecologies*. As O'Brien has argued in 'Articulating a World of Difference', postcolonial ecocritical literature 'reject(s) hierarchies of colonialism and nationalism', and 'reimagines identity as the product of an ongoing engagement with the alterity of the world' (147).

55. Jungk, Robert. *Brighter than a Thousand Suns: A Personal History of the Atomic Scientists* (New York, NY: Harcourt Brace, 1958), p.310.

56. Welsome, Eileen. *The Plutonium Files: America's Secret Medical Experiments in the Cold War* (New York, NY: Dial Press, 1999), p.30.

57. Caufield, Catherine. *Multiple Exposures: Chronicles of the Radiation Age* (Toronto, CA: Stoddard Publishing Co., 1988), p.132.

58. Virilio, Paul. *War and Cinema: the Logistics of Perception* (London: Verso, 1989), p.68.

59. Hunt, Janet. *Hone Tuwhare: A biography*. Auckland: Godwit Press, 1998, p.49.

60. DeLoughrey, "Heliotropes".

61. A bibliography of written and musical works on Tuwhare can be found here: <http://www.library.auckland.ac.nz/subjects/nzp/nzlit2/tuwhare.htm>

62. Hone Tuwhare, "No Ordinary Sun" <http://honetuwhare.org.nz/more-poems/> [Accessed 22 December 2013].

63. Barkawi, p.156.

64. George, James. *Ocean Roads* (Wellington, NZ: Huia Publishers, 2006), p.65, 342, 66, 336, 66, 336, 336.

65. May, John. Greenpeace Book of Antarctica: A New View of the Seventh Continent. (London: Dorling Kindersley, 1988), p.51.

66. George, p.338, 338, 339, 340, 340, 61, 340.

67. Cosgrove, p.217.

68. Cosgrove, p.220, 220, 219.

69. See Elizabeth DeLoughrey, "Radiation Ecologies and the Wars of Light" in *Modern Fiction Studies* 55 (2009), 468–495.

70. *Nukes in Space: The Rainbow Bomb*. Film. Dir. Peter Kuran (CMV Laservision, 1999).

71. Cosgrove, p.220.

72. George's chapter "Astronaut's Eyes" in *Ocean Roads* is a reference to the ways in which the New Zealand protagonist Troy Henare, a sharp-shooter in the Vietnam War, has a gaze that "always inhabited a different orbit, a distant orbit" (112). His mother Etta realizes this as she watches the 1969 *Apollo* moon landing in her Saigon hotel room, allowing her for the first time to articulate the distance in her son's gaze as "astronaut's eyes" (111). As a war photographer, Etta makes the connection between militarization of space and of Vietnam, calling attention to the ways in which their shared technologies and media produce different public responses. Thus when a few days later she sees on the television a parachute landing with a "large cocoon" that looked like "the shape of a Vietnamese peasant's hat" she

is surprised to see none of the helicopters "shot at it" (89). Instead they are provided "the softness of a life raft" and she recognizes the three faces of the astronauts (89). Later she ponders the situation of the third astronaut, who never landed on the moon "to have his tourist photos taken among the craters and deserts like the others," (89) to participate in this form of "militourism."

73. DeLoughrey, "Radiation Ecologies."
74. One could also be more critical of the representation of Isaac's experience. Cosgrove writes, "Devoid of disturbing human presence, [the poles] were silent stages for the performance of white manhood" (217).
75. Catharine Savage Brosman, "The Functions of War Literature," *South Central Review* 9.1 (1992): 85–98.
76. Cosgrove, p.221.

CHAPTER 19

....

EXTINCTIONS

Chronicles of Vanishing Fauna in the Colonial and Postcolonial Caribbean

....

LIZABETH PARAVISINI-GEBERT

> For one species to mourn the death of another is a new thing under
> the sun.
>
> Aldo Leopold, *A Sand County Almanac* (1949)

IN 2008, the Caribbean monk seal (*monachus tropicalis* or West Indian seal)—the only subtropical seal native to the Caribbean Sea and the Gulf of Mexico—was declared officially extinct by the International Union for Conservation of Nature and Natural Resources (IUCN). The last recorded sighting of this gentle creature—which once lived in large pods of between 50 and 500 on beaches throughout the region—was in 1952, when "a small colony" was spotted at the Seranilla Bank between Jamaica and the Yucatan Peninsula. Despite reports a year later of "remnants of this species" still living "somewhere within their former range" (King 218), and after five years of futile efforts to find or confirm sightings, in June 2008 the monk seal finally joined the growing list of victims of ecological changes unleashed by colonialism and postcolonial tourism development in the Caribbean basin. It has gone the way of the dodo of Mauritius and has become in the process the only seal in recorded history to vanish due to human exploitation and unrelenting encroachment even in its remotest habitats. Its disappearance sent a minor ripple throughout the conservationist world, where the seal is now mourned as a symbol of the fate of animals that fall victim to human predatory behavior and unchecked coastal development.[1]

Given the Caribbean monk seal's cameo role in one of the earliest texts about the conquest and colonization on the region, its disappearance is a natural point of departure for my analysis of the meanings of extinction for a postcolonial Caribbean as chronicled in our literatures. The seal enters literary and recorded history in Christopher Columbus's diary of his second voyage to his newly discovered territories. At the end of August 1494, with his ship anchored by the rocky islet of Alta Vega off the southern coast of Haiti, the men he sends ashore kill eight of what the Admiral called "sea wolves" to feed the crew (Columbus 69; King 215). Less than ten years later, in 1513—as Antonio de Herrera y Tordesillas will record in his *Historia general de los hechos de los Castellanos en las islas y tierra firme del Mar Oceano* (History of the deeds of the Castilians in the islands and mainland of the Ocean Sea, 1601–1615)—Juan Ponce de León, having just discovered the Dry Tortugas Islands, sent a foraging party that returned with fourteen dead seals. So begins the narrative of the relentless slaughter of the mellow and slow-moving creatures, which at its peak approached a hundred deaths per night (King 215–216).

The killings of Caribbean Monk Seals recorded in some of the region's oldest proto-literary texts represent one of the earliest indications of how quickly the Columbian encounter would evolve into an ecological revolution, a concept that Elinor Melville describes in her book about the environmental consequences of the conquest of Mexico, *A Plague of Sheep*, as "an abrupt and qualitative break with the process of environmental and social change that had developed in situ" (Melville 12). In the face of catastrophic habitat collapse, small island ecologies experienced "substantial species loss" from the earliest stages of European colonization (Miller 61). This ecological revolution can be measured in terms of biodiversity losses that have led to the disappearance of thousands of flora and fauna species in the region, some dating back to the earliest decades of the colonization and conquest of the Indies.

Barbados, one of the earliest plantation settlements in the Caribbean, is perhaps the best example of the impact of habitat collapse in the region in the first centuries of the European conquest. Colonized by English Royalists sent "beyond the sea" by a victorious Oliver Cromwell in the early seventeenth century, it was completely deforested in a little over twenty years as planters submitted nearly 80 percent of the landmass to sugar cultivation—a fate that the small colony would quickly share with neighboring islands (Miller 85). As Shawn Miller explains in *An Environmental History of Latin America*:

> Scores of plants, mammals, reptiles, and birds were unique to each island, and an uncounted number of species, possibly ranging in the thousands, without their forest habitats, disappeared forever without the slightest human notice. On Barbados, a few deletions were noted: the palmito palm, the mastic tree, the wood pigeon, a few species of conures, the yellow-headed macaw, and one variety of hummingbird—all vanished. No monkey species survived sugar's colonization, and of the 529 noncultivated species of plants found on Barbados today, only 11 percent are native to the island. (Miller 85)

Throughout the Caribbean, deforestation to clear the land for sugar plantations led to the loss of a variety of unusual native rodents like the *hutía* and shrew-like insectivores, many of them ancient species that have now not been seen for several centuries. The Martinican Amazon parrot became extinct due to habitat loss as the island was cleared for agriculture in the seventeenth century; it has not been recorded since 1722. In 1699, Père Labat, in the memoir of his voyage to the Caribbean (*The Memoirs of Père*

Labat 1693–1705), described a large population of small parrots living in Guadeloupe, named *Arantiga labati* in his honor, of which no specimens have been recorded since the mid-eighteenth century. Fifteen mammals have become extinct in Hispaniola— the highest number of mammal extinctions of any Caribbean island—due to the severe deforestation of Haiti. Jamaica was home to a monkey, the *Xenothrix mcgregori*, lost when its forest habitat was cut by European colonists. It died out in the 1750s. The Cuban Red Macaw was reasonably common around 1800 in Cuba. Human encroachment in its habitats increased dramatically in the early nineteenth century, when Cuba intensified its sugar production to meet the demand created by the collapse of the St. Domingue sugar mills after the Haitian Revolution. The bird was hunted for food and nests were plundered or disturbed to acquire young birds to keep as pets. The last one is believed to have been shot in 1864 at La Vega in the vicinity of the Ciénaga de Zapata swamp, which seems to have been the last stronghold of the species. Nine species of Antillean iguanas and snakes became extinct after Europeans introduced mongoose and rats to protect sugar cane workers in the nineteenth century, joining the uncounted species that have disappeared due to the introduction of invasive alien species ("Sharing the Same Dream"). The current invasion of the Caribbean Sea by lionfish released accidentally in Florida, it is feared, will account for a number of future extinctions.[2]

Should we be troubled by the fact that, until efforts were made recently to reintroduce parrots to Martinique, there were no endemic species left on the island? How much should we grieve for the Cuban Red Macaw? Should we mourn the Caribbean monk seal? These lost creatures are the closest the Caribbean region has come to having the "charismatic megafauna" that attracts worldwide attention—Polar bears, American Eagles, Panda bears, Bengal tigers, in short, those animals whose endangerment was " 'foremost in the minds' of those who drafted the Endangered Species Act" (Boudreaux 773). The loss of these proto-charismatic Caribbean megafauna, however, are just the proverbial tip of the iceberg, harbingers of more serious—albeit perhaps less dramatic— biodiversity losses threatening the diverse island ecologies dotting the region.

The Caribbean is (alas!) one of the world's hotspots, a concept developed by conservation biologists to identify "particular areas of the world that contain high levels of endemic species that are highly threatened or endangered" (Bernau 617). With around 7,000 species of plants and 160 bird species found nowhere else in the world, the Caribbean is a critical area for intervention to preserve "not only the number of species but also the number of individuals within that species, and all the inherent genetic variations" (Whitty May/June 2007). Biodiversity, which Julia Whitty defines as "the sum of an area's genes (the building blocks of inheritance), species (organisms that can interbreed), and ecosystems (amalgamations of species in their geological and chemical landscapes)" (Whitty April 2007), is a critical element in maintaining ecological viability, particularly in threatened small island ecologies ("Sharing the Same Dream"). A rich biodiversity—"life's only army against the diseases of oblivion" (Whitty May/June 2007)—is the key to the "tough immune system" needed for maintaining Caribbean flora, fauna, peoples and cultures.[3]

Environmentalism has brought much-needed attention to the problems biodiversity losses pose to human survival on the planet. As a recent poll by the American Museum of Natural History revealed, "7 in 10 biologists believe that mass extinction poses a colossal threat to human existence, a more serious environmental problem than even its contributor, global warming, and that the dangers of mass extinction are woefully underestimated by most everyone outside of science" (Whitty April 2007). In the small island developing states of the Caribbean, the biological diversity is "extremely fragile" and is particularly threatened "by a combination of natural and anthropogenic factors" (UNEP). Exacerbating that threat is the reality that, globally, 80 percent of post-1600 extinctions have happened, disproportionately, on islands ("Sharing the Dream"). In the Caribbean, the threat of extinction looms even over the coral reefs so crucial to the health of the surrounding environment. As Fred Pearce argued in a *New Scientist* article in 2003, "the coral reefs of the Caribbean are close to extinction," due to disease, over-fishing, "sewage pollution, damage from cruise ships and divers, topsoil washing into the sea following deforestation, and record sea temperatures caused by global warming and El Niño" (Pearce 9).

Central to my concerns about biodiversity is an understanding of how the Caribbean region's subordinate entry into global mercantilism in the sixteenth century continues to haunt us. As the Caribbean islands—and to a lesser degree the continental territories of the Caribbean basin—adapted to their new realities after the start of the conquest, their roles were defined as bound with the extraction of natural resources and the production of commodities for metropolitan consumption. With scant care for the welfare and development of the local population, the territories fell into patterns of exploitation that paid little attention to their impact on local inhabitants or environments. As many plants and animals fell victim to earlier forms of environmental misuse (the plantation, mining, deforestation, overfishing), the region's newest form of resource exploitation—tourism development, particularly on our coasts—threatens mangroves and other coastal fisheries, coral reefs, seagrasses and their dependent species, turtles who have seen significant losses in access to former nurseries, marine mammals like the West Indian manatee dependent on coastal habitats, migratory birds dependent on disappearing coastal watersheds, and countless remaining species.

Extinctions—past and threatening ones alike—pose a large number of questions: biological, environmental, cultural, literary, and national. Here, I look at one of these questions, that of the ways in which these biological losses have impacted the ways in which the Caribbean region has been imagined and reimagined textually as writers have begun to ponder the extinction of Caribbean islands and peoples as the ultimate result of global warming, continued deforestation, galloping desertification, and rising sea levels. Ultimately such threats should prompt us to reconsider what it means to be postcolonial in the twenty-first century.

Derek Walcott poignantly ponders the apocalyptical question of whether the destruction of the Caribbean's ecosystems could signal the loss of the people who inhabit them—the end of island nations and their peoples—in his essay "Antilles: Fragments of Epic Memory":

> The Caribbean is not a [tourist] idyll, not to its natives. They draw their working strength from it organically, like trees, like the sea almond or the spice laurel of the heights. Its peasantry and its fishermen are not there to be loved or even photographed; they are trees who sweat, and whose bark is filmed with salt, but every day on some island, rootless trees in suits are signing favorable tax breaks with entrepreneurs, poisoning the sea almond and the spice laurel of the mountains to their roots. A morning could come in which governments might ask what happened not merely to the forests and the bays but to a whole people. ("Antilles" 83)[4]

The concern for the impact of biodiversity losses in writings about the Caribbean can be found in some of the earliest literary and proto-literary texts written about the region. Aphra Behn, in her novel *Oroonoko*, published in 1688, already pondered what the increasingly intense clearing of the Caribbean forests would mean for the indigenous peoples and animals relegated to the diminishing woods. Behn's sojourn in Suriname in 1653 coincided with what has been called "The Great Clearing," the period between 1650 and 1665, marked by devastating deforestation throughout the British and French Caribbean that resulted in significant soil erosion and "the scarcity and high price of timber for construction and fuel wood, particularly for refining the sugar" (Williams 102–3). The geography of Behn's novel—which reflects the history of the development of the plantation economy in British-held territories in the first half of the seventeenth century—is built on the social and economic separation between the cleared land of the sugar plantation to which the narrator belonged as an Englishwoman and the dense woods that are the domain of the indigenous inhabitants. It is a division that forces the planters—already dependent on food importations for their survival—to rely on the indigenous forest dwellers who "supply us with that 'tis impossible for us to get: for they do not only in the woods, and over the savannahs, in hunting, supply the parts of hounds, by swiftly scouring through those almost impassable places, and by the mere activity of their feet run down the nimblest deer and other eatable beasts" (12). Behn's text alludes repeatedly to the increased pressure placed on the forest fauna by the demand to help feed the growing plantation population, recognizing the forests as an endangered liminal terrain. Implicit in her query about the fate of the forests is the question of where the natives will go if the clearing of the forests continues at the established accelerated pace and how the colony will fare without access to forest animals as food. Writing in 1701, just a few decades after Behn's departure from Suriname, German entomologist Maria Sibylla Merian will echo similar concerns in her *Insects of Surinam*, pointing to the planters' errors in eschewing food security in their obsession with sugar cultivation. Wishing that the colony "were inhabited by a more industrious and less selfish population" (93), she offers a number of crops that would lay the foundation for sustainability, only to be mocked "for seeking anything but sugar in the country" (Merian 117).[5]

Behn's Creole contemporary, Cuban writer José Martín Félix de Arrate y Acosta, celebrates the island's biodiversity while recording one of the earliest acknowledgments of creeping extinctions. In his *Llave del Nuevo Mundo* (Key to the New World, published in 1666), one of Cuban literature's most important early foundational texts, he offers an implicit Creole-led project for the conservation of Cuba's remarkable biodiversity against the forces of the Spanish empire, which, as the eighteenth century opens, seek to move towards a mono-crop system, following the successful example of the French and British Caribbean colonies. Cuba's mountains, Arrate writes, "abound with rich and wild fruit, precious woods—cedar, mahogany, passion-fruit trees, *guayacos*, lingum vitae—and other broad and valuable trees" (Arrate, n.p.). The focus of his text, which he expects will be read by Crown officials in Spain, is to underscore the difference, diversity, and implied self-sufficiency and sustainability of the island as an environmental system different from that of Spain. His text is a narrative of an enviable abundance that is the foundation for a proto-national identification, of an expression of an incipient *cubanía* that will begin the separation (of which twentieth-century Cuban anthropologist Fernando Ortiz will write in *Cuban Counterpoint*) between producers of sugar living in the deforested plains and those able to plant and profit—yet still conserve and live— on the edge of the abundance and protection of the forests, planting cacao, coffee, and tobacco. Arrate, in his effort to emphasize this difference, writes of the "beautiful variety of flowering trees in the countryside, of fragrant herbs and plants," of the abundance of singing birds—nightingales, mockingbirds, manakins, bellbirds, and cotingas—of game birds like ring doves, quail, partridges, of the diversity of ducks in rivers and lagoons, and of the "birds of flashy and varied feathers, such as the flamencos, tanagers, parrots, and parakeets" (Arrate, n.p.). He establishes a clear distinction between these lands of natural abundance and the "tierras de labor" (literally, "lands of labor" or plantations that require a labor force) that produce "besides tobacco and sweet cane, which are the most useful crops, a profusion of manioc, sweet potatoes, ginger, corn, rice, cocoa and coffee" (Arrate, n.p.). Amid this abundance, he also records noted extinctions, writing that "before the Spaniards populated the island there were no more quadrupeds than certain *hutías* and certain types of mute dogs, which are now extinct" (Arrate, n.p.).

At the dawn of the eighteenth century, Père Labat, in his extensive report of his visit to the Caribbean, written at a time of fast plantation development in Martinique and Guadeloupe, writes of his concerns with the loss of biodiversity. In Guadeloupe he had encountered the *diablotin*, an ungainly bird the size of a pullet that lived in "hole in the mountains, like rabbits." Their flesh is dark, with a "rather fishy flavor," but "good and nourishing." Their trajectory as a species has already been inexorably derailed by colonial agricultural expansion:

> These birds are a veritable manna sent by God every year for the settlers and negroes, who live on little else during the season. It is only the difficulty of getting them which preserves the species, and these birds would be killed out completely in a few years owing to the bad custom of the French, were it not for the fact that they choose the most inaccessible places for their homes. (65)

His concern, ironically, does not impede his going out with a hunting party into the volcanic area that is the birds' habitat and killing 150 of them, which they ate on the spot. Enhancing the irony is Labat's juxtaposition of the tale of this threatened extinction with a chapter on "A Carib Carbet in Martinique," which relates his visit to the "last carbet remaining in Martinique," the last sad stronghold of the indigenous Martinican Caribs.

Their habitat destroyed, the forests on which they depended for their livelihood cleared, Labat describes them as they prepare to abandon the island and join equally dwindling groups in St Vincent and Dominica—becoming, in the process, one of the earliest environmental exiles whose plight is captured in the region's literature.

US naturalist Frederick Ober, looking for a specimen of the diablotin nearly 200 years later, has to return home empty handed. Following in the steps of Père Labat, whose book he uses as a guide in his own travels through the Caribbean (which result in his 1907 book *Our West Indian Neighbors*), Ober writes:

> My first hunt for the bird was in the island of Dominica, which has a mountain about 5000 feet in height; but I did not find it, because, as I was told, it had been exterminated by the manacou, a native possum which had sought it out in its holes and devoured its eggs. Neither was I successful in Guadeloupe…The bird I never saw— or, at least, never knew it if I saw it—was the impelling motive for many a hard climb up the steep sides of those Caribbean volcanoes, and in my search I ascended them all…I passed a night one time on the brim of Saint Eustatia's perfect crater-cone for the sole purpose of observing the nocturnal sounds, and if possible scenes, as I lay wrapped in my blanket, with the fierce winds whistling around me. I thought I heard the voice of the little devil, in the air above me, and anxiously peered into the darkness, gun a-poise; but no form of bird rewarded my vigil, and in the morning I returned empty handed to the coast. (328)

Ober's is not the only echo of Père Labat's concern with the losses the plantation would bring to Martinique and Guadeloupe. In Maryse Condé's novel *Traversée de la Mangrove* (*Crossing the Mangrove* 1989)—a text that looks at a community's continued efforts to live in harmony with the rhythms of a life between mangrove and forest— a father speaks to his son of "a time before jealousy and hatred poisoned the world" around them, "before the brutal hand of man had deflowered the trees and the forests of Guadeloupe were bursting with all sorts of birds" (70). Condé's community is imagined as grounded in the peasantry's "natural" relationship with the forest, as we see in her character Aristide's description of the sense of peace he finds in the forest: "It was only among the big trees that he felt a sense of well-being, among the *marbri*, the big-leafed chestnut, the *gommier blanc*, the burwood, the *bois la soie* bush. He glided among their serene and silent shadows, barely pierced by the chirping of the birds" (70). Poignantly, Aristide knew about these birds only from the pages of a book his father often perused with him, Père Labat's *Nouveau voyage aux Isles de l'Amerique*. Condé acknowledges, through his reference to Labat's seminal text, the priest's early realization of the losses the plantation system would bring to Guadeloupe as measured in deforestation and habitat destruction, and builds her fictional community as one anchored by the notion of a possible return to that idealized pre-plantation time.[6]

The intertextual dialogue between these three writers—Père Labat, Ober, and Condé—is characteristic of how biodiversity concerns have been articulated in the literature of the region. These writers' preoccupation with expressing through writing the threat to endangered species posed by habitat encroachment gives us but a glimpse of a rich vein of similar "conversations" open for further critical exploration. The thematic continuity between earlier writers and contemporary works is a critical element in the development of a regional literature that has always been aware of the fragility of environments that are both finite and easily disrupted. These anxieties about the impact of habitat destruction naturally shift to concerns with the displacement and potential extinction of the living things (flora, fauna, and human beings) dependent on those habitats for their survival. In Jamaica Kincaid's *A Small Place*, for example, she bemoans how a "big new hotel ... with its own port of entry" has been built on a bay that "used to have the best wilks [*Cittarium pica*, a West Indian snail] in the world"; their habitat destroyed, she ponders the question of "where did they all go?" (57). Of these more recent texts I want to look at two examples of how they approach issues of extinction—V. S. Naipaul's *The Loss of El Dorado* and Mayra Montero's *In the Palm of Darkness* before moving on to Haiti's Creole pig and its sad extinction tale.

In an essay entitled "V.S. Naipaul and the Interior Expeditions," Sandra Pouchet Paquet argues "that in respect to the way he shapes the history and character of indigenous peoples over a span of some thirty-nine years, Naipaul moves away from the traditional imperial models of cross-cultural exploration he identifies in the travel narratives of Aldous Huxley, D.H. Lawrence, and Evelyn Waugh, through a more rigorous imaginative inquiry into history, to something approaching what Wilson Harris might describe as 'an art of compassion' ("Interior of the Novel" 140) that unravels the blocked formations of a colonial relationship" (Paquet n.p.). Her study looks at various texts by Naipaul, teasing out the changing nature of his approach to indigeneity and its disappearance, but I would like to focus here more narrowly on how he uses the disappearance (shall we say "extinction") of the Chaguanes Indians in *The Loss of El Dorado* (1969) and his Nobel Prize lecture.

Naipaul narrates his seminal encounter with the history of the Chaguanes, to whom he returns again and again his writings, in the first pages of *The Loss of El Dorado*, where he describes coming across a letter from the King of Spain to the governor of Trinidad dated 12 October 1625 asking for "some information about a certain nation of Indians called Chaguanes, who you say number above one thousand, and are of such bad disposition that it was they who led the English when they captured the town" (11–12). Intrigued by this moment in which the colony of Trinidad was touched by "history," he ponders the erasure of these Indians who "acknowledge no master save their own will" (12) but who have vanished from subsequent historical records. He will return to the tale—with slight but important variations in the telling of the story—in his Nobel Prize acceptance speech in 2001:

> What the governor did I don't know. I could find no further reference to the Chaguanes in the documents in the Museum.... What is true is that the little tribe of over a thousand—who would have been living on both sides of the Gulf of Paria—disappeared so completely that no one in the town of Chaguanas or Chauhan knew anything about them. And the thought came to me in the Museum that I was the first person since 1625 to whom that letter of the king of Spain had a real meaning. And that letter had been dug out of the archives only in 1896 or 1897. A disappearance, and then the silence of centuries. (*The Loss of El Dorado*, 12; "Nobel Prize Lecture," n.p.)

In his Nobel Prize acceptance speech, Naipaul pauses to lament this erasure of the Chaguanes from the consciousness of those who succeeded them in the land they had occupied, referring to them as a "dispossessed" people whose particular relationship to the landscape had been "obliterated":

> The people who had been dispossessed would have had their own kind of agriculture, their own calendar, their own codes, their own sacred sites. They would have understood the Orinoco-fed currents in the Gulf of Paria. Now all their skills and everything else about them had been obliterated. ("Nobel Prize Lecture," n.p.)

This obliteration, whose importance is marked by the loss of a specific kind of familiarity with the surrounding landscape and its currents and cycles, separates these "natural" inhabitants from the immigrants who have replaced them. The latter—like the Indian community to which Naipaul belonged—are described as alienated from that landscape, pretending that they had brought "a kind of India with us, which we could, as it were, unroll like a carpet on the flat land" ("Nobel Prize Lecture," n.p.). With no familiarity with the surrounding landscapes, they are also dispossessed from a land that has been given over to "sugar-cane, estate land up to the Gulf of Paria" and to a soap factory whose pervasive smell erases all other scents.

Naipaul's concern with indigenous erasure—later in his speech he will use the word "extinction"—is emblematic of how writers in the Caribbean imagine postcoloniality in an environmentally endangered world. Postcolonial theory is, by definition, an optimistic approach to the problems posited by Caribbean history: it assumes recovery from an affliction of sorts, hence the vocabulary of empowerment that it brings to cultural analysis in the region. In a postcolonial state—under certain circumstances, given certain conditions, if some actions can be taken—we can transcend the negative impacts of colonialism; we can redefine our identities, reframe our institutions, empower our people. (This is the approach against which Naipaul rallied with his pessimistic assessment of a West Indies in which nothing was created, which made him the understandable *bête-noire* of postcolonialists.) The narrative of extinction, on the other hand, presents obstacles to this kind of postcolonial thinking, as the silence of absence—as in the disappearance of the Chaguanes—represents a foundational void, which Naipaul fully recognizes in *The Loss of El Dorado* when he writes that the disappearance of the Chaguanes was "unimportant…part of nobody's story" (12). The fundamental difference between the tale as told in *The Loss of El Dorado* in 1969 and his 2001 Nobel Prize account is that of the transformation of that "unimportant" loss into the "unbearably affecting story" that tells of how

> …at certain times aboriginal people came across in canoes from the mainland, walked through the forest in the south of the island, and at a certain spot picked some kind of fruit or made some kind of offering, and then went back across the Gulf of Paria to the sodden estuary of the Orinoco. The rite must have been of enormous importance to survive the upheavals of 400 years, and the extinction of the aborigines in Trinidad. Or perhaps—though Trinidad and Venezuela have a common flora—they had come only to pick a particular kind of fruit. I don't know. I can't remember anyone inquiring. And now the memory is all lost; and that sacred site, if it existed, has become common ground. ("Nobel Prize Lecture," n.p.)

This tale of the loss of the sacred is—despite its disjointed articulation in the text—a narrative that links the puzzling disappearance of the Chaguanes to the destruction of Trinidad's primeval forest, an event that deprived nature of the capacity for hierophany—of the power to produce, as Mircea Eliade describes so eloquently in *The Sacred and the Profane* (1961), a manifestation of the sacred through sensory experience. Naipaul, whose focus is primarily historical and not ecological, does not conceive of the elements of his story as a narrative of environmental loss and its consequences. Yet the ecological foundations of this historical tragedy are clearly there to be read in Naipaul's chronicle of an indigenous community that disappeared from the land after its forest habitats were destroyed to plant sugar cane and which was replaced in turn by an immigrant population of the dispossessed who can no longer experience (see, feel, smell or taste) any manifestation of the sacred in the surrounding nature.

Naipaul's mourning for the loss of the sacred in a land degraded by colonial exploitation finds an unlikely echo in Mayra Montero's *In the Palm of Darkness*, the Caribbean region's first avowedly environmentalist novel. It narrates the tale of American herpetologist Victor Grigg who, with the aid of his Haitian guide, Thierry Adrien, a devout Vodou practitioner, is on a quest for an elusive and threatened blood frog, *eleutherodactylus sanguineus* or *grenouille du sang*, extinct everywhere but for a mountain near Port-au-Prince. In the volatile and bloody setting of the Haitian mountains Montero uncovers a haunted postcolonial space in the interstices between Griggs scientific perspective and Adrien's animistic Vodou-inspired worldview. Montero uses this binary to unveil how the extinction of species is the direct outcome of an environmental collapse as the forests that were the frogs' habitat disappear. She shows, concomitantly, how the troubled landscape of Haiti—and the very environment on which the Haitian people depend for survival—has decayed precipitously due to colonial exploitation, postcolonial political corruption, violence, institutional terror, and religious turmoil—conditions now exacerbated by the aftermath of the deadly January 2010 earthquake.

In the Caribbean imaginary, Haiti has emerged as despoiled terrain, a warning of the direst consequences facing those Caribbean nations that do not make a concerted effort to reverse ecological degradation and biodiversity collapse. In spaces as small as many Caribbean island-nations, the ecological balance is fragile, the level of vulnerability very high. As a result, the viability of the nation itself and the survival of its people are marked by an unimaginable urgency. Nowhere in the Caribbean is this revealed more heartrendingly than in Haiti. The devastation brought upon the Haitian landscape by continued deforestation, desertification, failed tourism development, and the collapse of agro-business amidst governmental corruption, has become the country's most glaring socio-economic and political problem, bringing it to the very edge of environmental despair.[7] Ironically, these developments had been already identified in the eighteenth century by Médéric Moreau de St. Mery, who, in *A Topographical, Political Description of St. Domingo*, had already noted the impact of heedless deforestation on Haiti's rain patterns and on the disappearance of once-common fauna. Today, with only 4 percent of the Haitian territory covered in forests, previously fertile fields are now desert-like. Most of the topsoil has been washed to sea, where it has contributed to the destruction of breeding habitats for marine life. The resulting decreases in rainfall have significantly reduced agricultural production.

In *In the Palm of Darkness*, Montero posits the possibility of the extinction—not only of the frogs whose last specimen dies in the final pages of the novel—but of a nation and its people:

> You want to know where the frogs go. I cannot say, sir, but let me ask you a question: Where did our fish go? Almost all of them left the sea, and in the forest the wild pigs disappeared, and the migratory ducks, and even the iguanas for eating, they went too. Just take a look at what's left for humans, just take a careful look: You can see the bones pushing out under our skins as if they wanted to escape... to leave behind that weak flesh where they are so battered, to go into hiding someplace else. At times I think, but keep it to myself, I think that one day a man like you will come here, someone who crosses the oceans to look for a couple of frogs, and when I say frogs, I mean any creature, and he will find only a great hill of bones on the shore, a hill higher than the peak of Tête Boeuf. Then he will say to himself, Haiti is finished, God Almighty, those bones are all that remains. (p. 11)[8]

Haiti, scientists tell us, is "on the brink of an era of mass extinctions similar to the time when dinosaurs and many other species suddenly disappeared from Earth" ("Haiti's Wildlife"). Blair Hedges, a member of a group of biologists engaged in the development of a species-rescue program for Haiti's endangered frogs, has argued that

> ...during the next few decades, many Haitian species of plants and animals will become extinct because the forests where they live, which originally covered the entire country, are nearly gone. The decline of frogs in particular, because they are especially vulnerable, is a biological early-warning signal of a dangerously deteriorating environment, just as a dying canary is an early-warning sign of dangerously deteriorating air in a coal mine.... When frogs start disappearing, other species will follow and the Haitian people will suffer, as well, from this environmental catastrophe. ("Haiti's Wildlife")

Montero's novel envisions precisely that suffering of the Haitian people against which Hedges warns us through the specific links it establishes between the fate of the beleaguered frogs in their dwindling habitats and the possibilities of survival for a population adrift between a despoiled environment and the political brutality of the *tonton macoutes* and their battles for territorial control. Her tale is that of a postcolonial nightmare marked by state corruption, institutionalized brutality and almost casual and senseless violence. Mired in violence, Thierry's life is as endangered as that of the elusive frog, as Victor comes to understand after he listens to his guide's own life story:

> Thierry sat looking at me and began a sad monologue, it was like a confession, he talked about the man he had stabbed to death and about his entire family. I realized that he too was a dying species, a trapped animal, a man who was too solitary. (178)

Montero's assessment of Haiti's postcolonial quandary points to colonialism as an irreversible ill, as a force that once unleashed onto the region becomes like a dormant infection—ready to strike at any instance of a weak immune system. It posits a different concern with postcoloniality, one that runs counter to the possibilities of recovery at the heart of postcolonial theories. Haiti—despoiled by colonial greed and prey to a legacy of violence and exploitation—emerges from Montero's narrative as a place where the gods have asked the animals to flee, a space in which a religious faith rooted in nature does not trust itself to be able to continue to sustain life:

> They say that Agwé Taroyo, the god of waters, has called the frogs down to the bottom. They say they have seen them leave: Freshwater animals diving into the sea, and the ones that don't have the time or strength to reach the meeting place are digging holes in the ground to hide, or letting themselves die along the way. (95)

The flight of the frogs into the depth of the waters where the ancestors live—their fleeing to the region known *en bas de l'eau* or *anba dlo* in Vodou—signals a retreat to waters that are still capable of the hierophany the land has lost through abuse and mismanagement. As the space from which the power and blessing of the ancestors can be reclaimed for the benefit of the living—as it is done in the *retirer d'en bas d'leau* ceremony performed a year and a day following a person's death—the sea stands in opposition to the deforested mountains that used to shelter the sacred *mapou* trees and the depleted and often abandoned family land that included the *heritaj* where the ancestors are buried. In Montero's rendition—which echoes Naipaul's concerns with the loss of sacred spaces in Trinidad—Agwé claims not only the frogs (among them the last remaining species of the *grenouille du sang*), but also Victor Grigg and Thierry Adrien, lost in the shipwreck of the boat taking them from Jérémie to Port-au-Prince, their bodies never recovered from the shores of Grand Goave, where their spirits await reclamation.

The history of fauna extinctions as recorded in the literature of the Caribbean region chronicles the impact of what Rob Nixon has called "slow violence...a violence that occurs gradually and out of sight, a violence of delayed destruction that is dispersed across time and space, an attritional violence that is typically not viewed as violence at all" (2). Hostages to the economic demands of metropolitan centers not always aware of the environmental damage caused by their policies and production expectations, the islands of the Caribbean have experienced successive waves of ecological assault chronicled in fiction and nonfiction alike through countless narratives of extinction. Rob Nixon argues in *Slow Violence and the Environmentalism of the Poor* (2011) that we need to rethink "conventional assumptions about violence as a highly visible act that is newsworthy because it is event focused, time bound, and body bound ... and devise arresting stories, images, and symbols adequate to the pervasive but elusive violence of delayed effect" (3). The stories I have discussed here belong among those much-needed chronicles of slow violence. I would like to conclude my discussion, however, with the story of the quick extermination of Haiti's Creole pig, a tale more easily recognized as "violent" and which points to the continued impact of colonialism and new forms of neocolonial oppression on threatened species and the peoples whose very lives depend on them.

The 1982–83 "eradication" of Haiti's creole pig, which responded to USAID/Haiti fears that an outbreak of swine flu in Hispaniola could spread from the Dominican Republic through Haiti to the United States, has been described by former Haitian President Jean-Bertrand Aristide as "a classic parable of globalization" (Aristide). Haiti's extremely hearty black pigs were "at the heart of the peasant economy," contributing on the one hand to the preservation of the fertility of the soil while functioning as literal "piggy banks" for the Haitian peasantry, allowing for the accumulation of small savings to pay for weddings, seed, medical emergencies, and children's schooling. The eradication of the Creole pig was, in Aristide's words, "a moment of neo-colonial trauma" for Haiti as a nation. The pigs, although not indigenous to the island, had evolved a working ecological accommodation with the landscape since being dropped by Columbus on the island to feed Spanish colonizers. Well adapted to Haiti's despoiled terrain, sparse vegetation and scarcity of fresh water, the history of their eradication was unique in its effectiveness and devastating impact: "With an efficiency not since seen among development projects, all of the Creole pigs were killed over a period of thirteen months" (Aristide).

The deliberate, forced extinction of the Creole pig brought incalculable loss to Haiti's already embattled peasantry. It was an extinction that could not easily be withstood by the survival economy that characterizes Haiti's rural realities. In Aristide's own assessment,

> ...in monetary terms Haitian peasants lost $600 million dollars. There was a 30 percent drop in enrollment in rural schools, there was a dramatic decline in the protein consumption in rural Haiti, a devastating decapitalization of the peasant economy and an incalculable negative impact on Haiti's soil and agricultural productivity. The Haitian peasantry has not recovered to this day. (Aristide)

Compounding the irony of the Creole pig calamity was the farce of the United States' efforts to repopulate the Haitian countryside with "better pigs" from Iowa that "required clean drinking water (unavailable to 80 percent of the Haitian population), imported feed (costing $90 a year when the per capita income was about $130), and special roofed pigpens" (Aristide). Christened *les princes aux quatre pieds*, they were ill suited for the realities of Haiti's degraded environment and survival economy. As a peasant told Colin Dayan, "they have soft stomachs, delicate feet, and thin skin" (Dayan). Recently, through a joint repopulation effort, Haitian and French agronomists have bred a new variety of pig that closely approximates the environment-suitable characteristics of the extinct Creole pig. The impact on Haiti's wildlife of the extirpation and reintroduction of pigs is not yet clear.

What is the importance—in my context—of the extinction of the Creole pig? It is one in a long line of past and future extinctions that, like the demise of frogs worldwide, and the aggressive invasion of the Caribbean Sea by lionfish, signal that (environmentally) all is not well with our small corner of the world. In the case of the Haitian Creole pig, however—a planned and efficiently managed eradication of an introduced semi-domestic species—we see the transparency of colonial presuppositions still at work. The possibility of infection coming out of the Caribbean region may have seemed an intolerable risk to a larger and stronger economy such as that of the United States. The potential for infection represented by the pigs, coincidentally, came at a time when Americans feared that the AIDS epidemic had its origin in Haiti—these where the times when AIDS was believed to be cause by the four Hs: homosexuals, heroin addicts, hemophiliacs, and Haitians. The costs of extinction—in this very quick and neocolonially engineered incident—show a specific type of vulnerability for a population overly dependent on one species for their well-being. It shows, in a fast, "violent" instance, the damage that the slow violence of habitat destruction and species extinctions has and continues to inflict on the Caribbean region.

The loss of the Creole pig, like the vanishing of the Caribbean Monk Seal that opened this discussion and the losses of so many species that writers have chronicled since the fifteenth century—in short, "the disappearance[s], brought about by natural or unnatural means, of entire species" (Whitty May/June 2007)—are instances of environmental trauma that remains as cautionary tales of what environmental mismanagement has wreaked in Caribbean societies. With them we have lost their natural habitats, their contributions to biodiversity, their specific roles in island ecologies, their quirks and idiosyncrasies, their particular beauty, their capacity for hierophany.[9] As the Haitian peasantry awaits some form of environmental justice that will restore to them their extinct pigs—needed more than ever now, as Haiti struggles to recover from its devastating earthquake—so does the region await environmental reparations, apologies, oil spill and cruise ship garbage cleanups or someone to take responsibility for the lionfish debacle. Some reparation, indeed, for the havoc wreaked on their ecologies through centuries of exploitative colonialism and its main manifestation—the deforesting plantation and the equally destructive massive tourism development. The Caribbean's path to environmental justice reveals, indeed, that environmental problems are a manifestation of other, larger problems endemic to culture, society, and economic structures in colonized societies struggling to continue to exist in a globalized world—and so our writers have been telling us, for a few hundred years.

NOTES

1. The idea of environmental mourning has been discussed very movingly by Catriona Mortimer-Sandilands in "Melancholy Natures, Queer Ecologies," in *Queer Ecologies: Sex, Nature, Politics, Desire* (2010) and by Scott Slovic in *Going Away to Think: Engagement, Retreat, and Ecocritical Responsibility* (2008).
2. For more on the Caribbean's lionfish invasion's threat to other marine species see Freshwater, Wilson, Hines, Parham, Wilbur, Sabaoun, Woodhead, Akins, Purdy, Whitfield, Paris "Mitochondrial Control Region Sequence Analyses Indicate Dispersal from the US East Coast as the Source of the Invasive Indo-Pacific Lionfish Pterois volitans in the Bahamas" (2009) and "Lionfish Decimating Other Tropical Fish Populations, Threaten Coral Reefs (2008).
3. For more on the environmental health metaphor see Greg Garrard, "Nature Cures? or How to Police Analogies of Personal and Ecological Health," *Interdisciplinary Studies in Literature and Environment* 19:3(Summer 2013): 494–514.

4. In "Antilles," as in other writings and interviews on environmental issues in his native St Lucia and the rest of the Caribbean, Walcott proposes the "rootless tree" as emblematic of Caribbean residents (particularly government officials and entrepreneurs) who consistently choose economic development over the preservation of local environments and cultures. The metaphoric possibilities of the notion of rootlessness allows Walcott to engage political, economic, cultural and environmental critiques simultaneously.

5. The multilayered nature of Merian's commentary in *Insects of Surinam* underscores her assessment of the colony as a beleaguered space in which the symbiosis between insects and the plants they feed upon—extended to the relationship between indigenous and African populations and nature—is ruptured by the plantation's unsustainable approach to the environment. Merian's binary depiction of the stress between the "natural" symbiotic relationships between insects and plants and the planters' refusal to engage sustainably with the landscape mirrors the racial and class tensions intrinsic to the plantation system. For a fuller discussion of this rupture see Paravisini-Gebert's "Maria Sibylla Merian: The Dawn of Field Ecology in the Forests of Suriname, 1699–1701."

6. One wonders if John James Audubon (1785–1851)—that would-be preserver of birds through art—had learned the urgency of recording the existence of threatened birds from the plight of the birds of his childhood in his increasingly deforested native Haiti.

7. For an overview of Haiti's environmental crisis (including an enlightening comparison with the neighboring Dominican Republic), see Jared Diamond's "One Island, Two Peoples, Two Histories: The Dominican Republic and Haiti," from his book *Collapse: How Societies Choose to Fail or Succeed* (Penguin, 2011).

8. The disappearance of frogs throughout the world is presented by Montero in this novel as a phenomenon beyond the comprehension of both faith (Thierry) and science (Victor). Here, through Thierry's words, we can see—implicit in his Vodou practitioner's approach to life and death, magic and rationality—an implicit critique of the Judeo-Christian belief in the subordination of other species to man. Haiti's endangered species emerge from the text as conscious of the deterioration of their habitats and authorized by the Vodou lwa or spirits to depart before their annihilation is accomplished by humans.

9. For in-depth looks at island biogeography, see David Quammen's *The Song of the Dodo: Island Biogeography in an Age of Extinction* (1997).

References

Aristide, Jean Bertrand. "Haitian Pigs Meet Globalization." *Haiti Action* Committee. http://www.haitisolidarity.net/article.php?id=240. Accessed on 11 June 2009.

Arrate, José Martín Félix de. *Llave del Nuevo Mundo, antemural de las Indias Occidentales: La Habana descripta* [1761]. http://www.cervantesvirtual.com/servlet/SirveObras/01362845434592728987891/index.htm. Accessed on 10 August 2009.

Behn, Aphra. *Oroonoko*. London: Penguin Classics, 2003.

Bernau, Bradley M. "Help for Hotspots: NGO Participation in the Preservation of Worldwide Biodiversity." *Indiana Journal of Global Legal Studies* 13: 2 (Summer 2006): 617–643.

Boudreaux, Paul. "Understanding 'Take' in the Endangered Species Act." *Arizona State Law Journal* 34 (2002): 733–775.

Columbus, Christopher. *The journal of Christopher Columbus and documents relating the voyages of John Cabot and Gaspar Corte Real*. Translated by Sir Clements Robert Markham. London: The Hakluyt Society, 1893.

Dayan, Colin (Joan). "A Few Stories about Haiti, or, Stigma Revisited." *Research in African Literatures* 35: 2 (Summer 2004).

Diamond, Jared. *Collapse: How Societies Choose to Fail or Succeed*. New York: Penguin, 2011.

Freshwater, D. Wilson, Andrew Hined, Seth Parham, Ami Wilbur, Michelle Sabaoun, Jennifer Woodhead, Lad Akins, Bruce Purdy, Paula E. Whitfield, Claire B. Paris "Mitchondrial central region sequence analyses indicate dispersal from the US East Coast as the source of the invasive Indo-Pacific linonfish Pterois volitans in the Bahamas". *Marine Biology* 156: 6 (May 2009): 1213–1221.

Garrard, Greg. "Nature Cures? or How to Police Analogies of Personal and Ecological Health," *Interdisciplinary Studies in Literature and Environment* 19: 3 (Summer 2012): 494–514.

Hairr, John. *Caribbean Monk Seals: Lost Seals of the Gulf of Mexico and Caribbean Sea*. Landisville, PA: Coachwhip Publications, 2011.

Kincaid, Jamaica. *A Small Place*. New York: Farrar, Straus and Giroux, 1988.

King, J. E. The Monk Seals (*genus Monachus*). *Bulletin of the British Museum (Natural History) Zoology* 3 (1956): 201–256. http://biostor.org/reference/1297. Accessed on 29 August 2011.

Labat, Jean Baptiste. *The Memoirs of Père Labat 1693–1705*. Translated and abridged by John Eaden. London: Frank Cass & Co, 1970.

Leopold, Aldo. *A Sand County Almanan and Sketches Here and There*. New York: Oxford University Press, 1968.

US Federal News Service, "Lionfish Decimating Other Tropical Fish Populations, Threaten Coral Reefs", 17 July 2008.

Melville, Elinor G. K. *A Plague of Sheep: Environmental Consequences of the Conquest of Mexico*. Cambridge: Cambridge University Press, 1994.

Merian, Maria Sibylla. *Metamorphosis insectorum Surinamensium*. London: Pion, 1980–1982.

Miller, Shawn William. *Environmental History of Latin America*. Cambridge: Cambridge University Press, 2007.

Montero, Mayra. *In the Palm of Darkness*. New York: Harper Perennial, 1998.

Moreau de Saint-Méry, Médéric Louis Elie. *A Topographical, Political Description of St. Domingo: Its Climate, Population, Character, Manners of the Inhabitants, and Government*. Boston: J. Bumsteadm, 1808.

Mortimer-Sandilands, Catriona. "Melancholy Natures, Queer Ecologies." in *Queer Ecologies: Sex, Nature, Politics, Desire*. Edited by Catriona Mortimer-Sandilands and Bruce Erickson. Bloomington: Indiana University Press, 2010, pp. 331–358.

Naipaul, V. S. *The Loss of El Dorado*. New York: Vintage, 1973.

——. "Nobel Lecture." Nobelprize.org. 24 Oct 2011. http://www.nobelprize.org/nobel_prizes/literature/laureates/2001/naipaul-lecture.html. Accessed on 10 May 2011.

Nixon, Rob. *Slow Violence and the Environmentalism of the Poor*. Cambridge, MA: Harvard University Press, 2011.

Ober, Frederick. *Our West Indian Neighbors*. New York: James Pott and Co., 1907. http://www.archive.org/stream/ourwestindianneooobergoog#page/n5/mode/2up

Paquet, Sandra Pouchet. "V.S. Naipaul and the Interior Expeditions: 'It is Impossible to Make a Step without the Indians.'" *Anthurium* 5: 2 (Summer 2007). n.p. http://anthurium.miami.edu/volume_5/issue_2/paquet-vs.html. Accessed on 6 June 2010.

Paravisini-Gebert, Lizabeth. "Maria Sybilla Merian: The Dawn of Field Ecology in the Forests of Suriname, 1699–1701." *Review 84* 45: 1, 10–20.

Pearce, Fred. "Extinction looms for Caribbean 'rainforest of the oceans.'" *New Scientist 179*. 2405 (July 26, 2003): 9.

Quammen, David. *The Song of the Dodo: Island Biogeography in an Age of Extinction*. New York: Scribner, 1997.

Reaser, Jamie, Laura A. Meyerson, Quentin Cronk, Maj de Poorter, L. G. Elrege. "Ecological and Economic Impacts of Invasive Alien Species in Island Ecosystems." *Environmental Conservation 34*: 2: 98–111.

"Rescue Missions Under Way to Save Haiti's Species from Mass Extinction." *US Fed News Service, Including US State News* [Washington, D.C] *17 Nov* 2010.

"Sharing the Same Dream: Paying for Caribbean Diversity." *Economist* (5 May 2008). http://www.economist.com/node/11318390. Accessed on 10 July 2009.

Slovic, Scott. *Going Away to Think: Engagement, Retreat, and Ecocritical Responsibility*. Reno: University of Nevada Press, 2008.

UNEP (*United Nations Environmental Programme*), "*Progress in the Implementation of the Programme of Action for the Sustainable Development of Small Island Developing States.*" *Commission on Sustainable Development, Sixth session, 20 April–1 May 1998. E/CN.17/1998/7/ Add.5 of 12 February 1998.*

Walcott, Derek. Walcott, Derek. "The Muse of History." In *The Routledge Reader in Caribbean Literature*. Ed. Alison Donnell and Sarah Lawson Welsh. London: Routledge, 1996, pp 354–358.

—— *The Prodigal*. London: Faber and Faber, 2005.

Whitty, Julia. "Animal Extinction—the greatest threat to mankind." *Independent* (London). Monday, 30 April 2007 http://www.independent.co.uk/environment/animal-extinction--the-greatest-threat-to-mankind-397939.html

——. "Gone: Mass Extinction and the Hazards of Earth's Vanishing Biodiversity." *Mother Jones*. May/June 2007 http://motherjones.com/environment/2007/05/gone?page=2

PART III

GENRE

....

CHAPTER 20

ECOCRITICAL APPROACHES TO LITERARY FORM AND GENRE
Urgency, Depth, Provisionality, Temporality

....

RICHARD KERRIDGE

THIS essay is about ecocriticism as a critical practice: a way of reading and evaluating texts. I will look mainly at literary ecocriticism, but many of the questions raised here apply across the range of artistic forms. My aim is to explore the criteria by which ecocritical judgements about texts are reached—the criteria involved in ecocritical close reading and attention to literary form and genre. Necessarily, the essay is also about the hopes ecocritics have for what literature can achieve, since ecocritical reading must take its criteria from those hopes.

The fundamental task for ecocritics is to evaluate texts from the viewpoint of environmental concern, and by doing so introduce environmental criteria into general cultural debate. How good is this novel, poem, play or work of non-fiction from the viewpoint of environmental priorities? What *makes* a work good or bad in ecocritical terms? The basic hope is that environmental criteria will become an expected part of debate about all kinds of new artistic work, and that this will be a sign of a general shift in cultural values and—most importantly—in everyday behavior. Ecocritics hope to influence readers and writers, so that works concerned with environmental values will become more popular, and new works will emerge to inspire change. But ecocritical criteria pull in different directions, reflecting the contradictory demands made by the environmental crisis itself. Part of the ecocritic's task is to assess these conflicting pressures as they come to bear in each context.

An important example is the relationship between urgency and depth. Many environmental dangers call for very rapid action. Global warming is an obvious example. The Intergovernmental Panel on Climate Change (IPCC) report of 2007 predicted a probable rise in average global temperatures in the next century of between 2 and 4.5 degrees centigrade. In September 2009, the Hadley Centre at the United Kingdom's Met Office reported that a global increase of 4 degrees by the end of the century was likely, with some areas experiencing rises as high as 10 degrees. At the UN Climate Change Conference at Cancun in 2010, 194 nations agreed to the target of limiting global average warming to an increase from pre-industrial levels of less than 2°C. Some countries argued that even warming limited to 2° would be catastrophic in many places, and that 1.5° was the highest acceptable target, a view supported in 2011 by Christiana Figueres, executive secretary to the UN framework convention on climate change: "Two degrees is not enough—we should be thinking of 1.5C. If we are not headed to 1.5C we are in big, big trouble."[1]

The message from these agencies and nearly all climate scientists is that if there is to be any chance of limiting the increase to 2°, let alone 1.5, there must be substantial global cuts in carbon emissions, achieved quickly. Severe climate change will probably occur unless we mobilize every kind of effort to stabilize global CO_2 emissions and then, in the developed world, bring them into steep decline, and do all this in a very short period. In 2008, the former chief science adviser to the British government, Sir David King, said fifteen years, and Andrew Simms of the New Economics Foundation said one hundred months[2]—nearly half gone as I write. The environmental writer Bill McKibben cites scientific opinion that to have a chance of achieving the 2° limit, we must release no more than 565 gigatons of CO2 between now and 2050. At the present rate, we will exceed that amount by 2028. Fossil-fuel corporations already count 5,795 gigatons at present unused as existing assets whose value they will lose unless the fuel is extracted and sold. McKibben writes of our "our precarious—our almost-but-not-quite-finally hopeless—position" (McKibben 2012: 1).

Progress is terribly elusive, whether in reaching international agreements or changing the everyday priorities of individuals. Many other environmental problems, such as the threat to biodiversity, present us similarly with time rapidly running out. Mark Lynas, in *The God Species* (2011), analyses nine "planetary boundaries" identified by a team of 29 scientists in 2009—threshold figures that we cannot exceed for long without globally catastrophic consequences. Three of these boundaries have already been crossed (number of species per million becoming extinct each year, atmospheric CO_2 parts per million, and quantities of reactive nitrogen introduced annually to the biosphere). Three others are approaching quickly, and for two the measurements are not yet available (see Lynas 2011: 235–36).

In the face of warnings like these, many ecocritics feel that their work has an activist mission. They are searching for ways of getting people to care. That is the fundamental aim of their criticism of culture. They hope their arguments will directly persuade people to care, and will influence new creative works that will move people to care. In any academic school of political criticism, this activist sense of urgent purpose co-exists with a more detached analytical approach that seeks to understand the cultural and material interactions at work. There need not be a wide gulf between these versions of ecocriticism: often the more detached analysis is implicitly concerned to provide a stronger basis for activism, and the two approaches can lead into each other. For ecocriticism, however, there is an exceptional sense of urgency, produced by those "ticking clock" warnings. Definitions of ecocriticism usually start by linking the literary movement to the global crisis. The link implies that the fundamental purpose of the work is to be part of an attempt to change culture, and through culture change policy and behaviour. Taking the crisis seriously entails this commitment (though it does not necessarily entail an apocalyptic tone).

Ecocritical literature is full of statements to this effect. Glen A. Love, one of the first US ecocritics, said in 1990 that "The most important function of literature today is to redirect human consciousness to a full consideration of its place in a threatened natural world [...] Because of a widely shared sense—outside the literary establishment—that the current ideology which separates human beings from their environment is demonstrably and dangerously reductionist" (Glotfelty and Fromm 1996: 237). Lawrence Buell, one of the most influential ecocritics, wrote in 2005 that "many nonhumanists would agree—often more readily than doubt-prone humanists [that is, scholars in the academic 'humanities'] do—that issues of vision, value, culture and imagination are keys to today's environmental crises at least as fundamental as scientific research, technological know-how, and legislative regulation" (Buell 2005: 5). Buell rejects the notion that the humanities are impractical, and sees ecocriticism as having been conceived from the beginning as "an alliance of academic critics, artists, environmental educators, and green activists" (6). Scott Slovic, who has assisted the emergence of ecocriticism in many parts of the world, wants ecocritics to "help those toiling in the realms of politics, economics, law, and public policy to move beyond the constraining discourse of those fields and appreciate the values-rich language of story and image" (Slovic 2008: 134–35). Stacy Alaimo, one of the leading ecofeminist and "New Materialist" voices in ecocriticism, hopes that by emphasizing and exploring "the material interconnections of human corporeality with the more-than-human world," ecocritics will be able "to forge ethical and political positions that can contend with numerous late twentieth- and early twenty-first-century realities in which 'human' and 'environment' can by no means be considered as separate" (Alaimo 2010: 2).

Each of these writers speaks from a different ecocritical position, but their common hope is to reach beyond their specialist academic audiences and contribute to a transformation of culture and behavior in response to the urgent environmental crisis. They want to do whatever can be done in the literary sphere to assist the emergence of a sustainable culture, and like all kinds of environmentalists they wait anxiously for signs of that emergence; signs in literary culture and elsewhere. The word I use for the change they are seeking is "care," because the word must encompass feeling and action as well as awareness. Many commentators have identified our social predicament about climate change not as a lack of knowledge but as a disconnection between what we know and how we act. We do not behave as if we knew what we know; our behavior implies a different state of knowledge.

Nicole Seymour, for example, in an interesting and troubling essay, has recently suggested that "the political-intellectual Holy Grail of 'awareness' might not actually be the measure of success" (Seymour 2012: 60). Awareness is not producing change. Instead, we face a "deeply weird current moment—in which reports of immanent collapse inspire not robust environmentalist action but doomsday fatigue" (57). Seymour's

recommendations are that ecocritics should "more deeply consider questions of disposition, feeling, and affect," and that they should experiment in their work with a greater
range of moods. Specifically, "instead of remaining serious in the face of self- doubt,
ridicule, and broader ecological crisis," we should "embrace our sense of our own absurdity, our uncertainty, our humor, even our perversity" (57):

> A turn to affect in ecocriticism, then, would have us ask how we really feel about
> what we know, and what we really know about how we feel. Such explorations matter
> because, as I have suggested, the ecocritic at this particular point in time faces unique
> emotional and conceptual pressures: to be teacherly, to be somber, to be ecologically
> correct, to be useful; all at a time at which we particularly fear being useless. [...] If
> we can laugh at ourselves, be less sure of ourselves, we might be able to approach our
> object differently, and invite others to approach our object differently. We might be
> able to understand why we can't make *others* understand. (61–62)

Seymour's starting point for these suggestions is her perception that the environmental
crisis has opened an unusual gap between what we know and what we feel and do, giving
us a sense of absurdity: our knowledge and our behaviour cannot both be authentic, can
they?

Others see this gap too. The novelist John Lanchester has said memorably that "I suspect we're reluctant to think about it [climate change] because we're worried that if we
start we will have no choice but to think about nothing else" (Lanchester 2007: 3). That
is, he can just about begin to imagine what really thinking about it would be like, but
cannot do that thinking yet. He has to shy away, because to think about climate change,
really, would be transformative, and the conditions of palpable emergency that would
force the transformation have not yet arrived.

In psychoanalytical terms (though one need not be committed to the full psychoanalytical explanation to accept the point), this "gap" is the manifestation of a defensive
response called "splitting," which enables one to know the traumatic truth, yet simultaneously not know it. Part of us knows and part does not. Joseph Dodds explains that one
form of splitting is the sort of "intellectualization" that separates "abstract awareness of
the crisis from real emotional engagement" (Dodds 2011: 52). Individuals use splitting as
a coping-response, while the public culture of industrial society uses it to suppress our
awareness of material connections: "We get our food pre-wrapped in the supermarket,
and though we may occasionally intellectually grasp the complex networks behind it,
phenomenologically food is just there, appearing on the shelves and waiting for us to
consume it" (50).

Dodds' analysis suggests that the aim of ecocriticism and the literature it seeks to
encourage should be to overcome splitting and reveal these hidden connections. The
idea of the single moment that is revelatory, unifying and saving, the Pauline conversion, will undoubtedly be attractive here. It is an idea that goes with the notion of the
great transformative artistic work, and with our most familiar literary forms: the novel
whose plot builds towards a climactic confrontation, and the poetry of concentrated
revelatory lyric intensity. Yet ecocritics must be concerned with whether a concentrated

revelatory moment is also an isolated moment, itself split off from practical daily life. How will the moment continue to reverberate? Should ecocritics think rather in terms of slow incremental process, integrated with other areas of life, and of less climactic literary forms? Ecological crisis may expose the divisions between art and life, or work and leisure, as another form of evasive "splitting."

Slavoj Žižek, too, finds a disastrous gap between knowledge and belief: "we *know* the (ecological) catastrophe is possible, probable even, yet we do not believe it will really happen" (Žižek 2011: 328). At the moment that gap seems impassable for most of us in rich societies, which is why the conspiracy theories put about by deniers—the claim that the whole thing is a "scam" perpetrated by the entire international community of climate scientists—gain some public traction, absurd though they are. The gap identified by Seymour, Lanchester and Žižek makes environmentalists themselves behave as if they do not really believe their own message.

"We do not believe it will really happen." Žižek means belief of an existential kind, consisting in actions, emotions and intellectual convictions. "Belief" in this sense might be an alternative word to the "care" I use above, except that perhaps "belief" is too all-or-nothing, too suggestive of instantaneous and complete conversion. Žižek seems to mean it that way: "The turn to an emancipatory enthusiasm takes place when the traumatic truth is not only accepted in a disengaged way but is fully lived" (xii). I use "care" in preference to Žižek's "believe" in order to have alternative models to the idea of abrupt and absolute conversion. Again, the idea of some sort of cultural and emotional tipping-point, bringing about a sudden and dramatic general conversion to the cause, is a beguiling idea for environmentalists, because of the urgency, but a dangerous idea if it leads to despair at anything less. Searching for works that can convert us in a single transformation, a fantasy that mimics the climactic plot-points of thrillers, we may miss the possibility of the more complex, unresolved, exploratory and human tones desired by Seymour.

"Care" preserves the range of possibilities, from incremental and gradually spreading change to abrupt social revolution. The word encompasses feeling ("care about") and action ("take care of"). It can be interpreted in a way that gives us both active, vigilant policy and the range of phenomena indicated by the word "affect," including personal emotion, bodily reaction and collective, communicated mood. That is the combination I want to indicate with the word, rather than the "caring" nature traditionally and normatively attributed to women, and sometimes made the basis of ecofeminist accounts of ethics. Seymour observes that "affect is located variously—in the subject, outside the subject, between the subject and an object" (Seymour 2012: 61). For ecocritics, the hope is that people will begin to care in a way that is not sealed off in certain cultural spaces, types of activity and psychological spaces, but spreads throughout our working lives, home lives, recreational lives and political lives, making a difference.

Confronting this care, all the time, are questions that require technical expertise and will only be answered gradually, with frequent readjustment. We know that we are beginning to care, because the care is making a difference to our behaviour. But how far must that difference consist of restraining accustomed desires and finding non-consumerist pleasures? How far can it consist of searching for technological solutions that will allow "green" growth and consumerism? Literary ecocritics can have little input into the technical debates that set and shift the parameters of what seems practical. The most an ecocritic can hope to do with these debates is watch them and hold literary discussion accountable to questions of scientific accuracy, recognizing the shifts in the arguments and exploring the human implications of each turn. Observing this fine line between what must responsibly be accepted as the domain of technical experts and what should be a matter for open debate is one of the most difficult disciplines of ecocriticism. But getting people to care and make the environment a real, practical priority—that is a cultural matter, and a desperately urgent one if we take these warnings seriously.

That is the urgency. What about the depth, and why might it conflict with the urgency? We are talking about huge changes to our priorities, changes that go against established habit and much traditional culture—perhaps even against our evolved dispositions, since we are called upon to be willing to transform our lives in order to avert a threat that in most places is not yet tangible. McKibben says that "Given a hundred years, you could conceivably change lifestyles enough to matter—but time is precisely what we lack" (McKibben 2012: 3). Much ecocritical theory has been preoccupied with the idea that fundamental philosophical change is needed for practical change to occur.

From the beginning, a strong theme in ecocriticism has been the need to depart from the Cartesian tradition of dualism that separated mind from body and humanity from nonhuman nature. It was necessary to reject these dualisms in order to discover an ecocentric and "embodied" perspective, which would build up our perception of the human self as constituted and maintained by the ecosystem. For the ecofeminist philosopher Val Plumwood, for example, the break with this dualistic tradition and the form of reasoning it produced was the most important intellectual step that environmentalists needed to take. Plumwood argued that "developing environmental culture involves a systematic resolution of the nature/culture and reason/nature dualisms that split mind from body, reason from emotion, across their many domains of cultural influence" (Plumwood 2002: 4). In *The Spell of the Sensuous* (1996), David Abram drew on the phenomenological ideas of Maurice Merleau-Ponty to advocate a re-immersion in nature by means of a reawakening of the bodily perceptions of the natural world that modernity had suppressed. More recently, ecocritical theorists have developed the anti-dualist theme in a variety of ways, drawing on different schools of philosophical and scientific thought.

Some, such as Stacy Alaimo, Susan Hekman, Catriona Sandilands, Serenella Iovino, and Serpil Opperman, are New Materialists, seeking to shift emphasis from the idea of the unitary self, and of agency as exclusively a human attribute, to perceptions of human individuals and societies as embedded parts of larger material processes of exchange and flow. The physicist and cultural theorist Karen Barad has provided some influential terms, proposing, for example, that we should turn from the familiar term "inter-actions," implying the relatively separate engagement with each other of separate entities, to "intra-actions," a term that situates the action as always already inside a larger flow. This shift constitutes a recognition that "relata do not pre-exist relations" (Alaimo and Hekman 2008: 133). Wendy Wheeler arrives at a similar account of selfhood-in-system by concentrating on biosemiotics—the continuing transmission of material signs, from the genetic level upwards, that constitutes natural life. Timothy Morton asks us to think in terms of the "mesh" of exchange and interdependency. The idea that there are clear boundaries between self and external world, humanity and nature, or conscious and unconscious beings, is challenged by an array of alternatives: co-evolution, shared ancestry, hybridity, system, process, energy flow, symbiosis, biosemiotics, the mesh. What these thinkers have in common is the perception that the environmental crisis necessitates a transformation of many of the bedrock assumptions on which our daily lives are led—assumptions about action, responsibility and the limits of selfhood. The implication is that only these deep conceptual changes can provide a way out of the impasse identified by Seymour, Lanchester, Dodds, and Žižek.

Such changes face a lot of obstacles to their spread throughout consumerist culture, to put it mildly—especially when their practical implication is unclear. The proposal is that we should move from traditional ideas of agency as an exclusively or predominantly human attribute to a concept of "agentic assemblage," in which human agency is bound up with that of "microbes, animals, plants, metals, chemicals, word-sounds, and the like," as Jane Bennett, one of the leading New Materialists, puts it (Bennett 2010: 120–21). This proposal does not necessarily weaken the demands that can be made of that human agency, since, arguably, the recognition that agency is distributed in these assemblages and across whole ecosystems points not to determinist fatalism but to a subtler and more realistic sense of responsibility: one that does not rebound between extremes of hubris and resignation. "Sometimes," Bennett says, "ecohealth will require individuals and collectives to back off or ramp down their activeness, and sometimes it will call for grander, more dramatic and violent expenditures of human energy" (122). She suggests that the outcome of her New Materialism can be a flexible approach capable of turning either to anti-consumerist values or to technological solutions.

Still, there does seem to be something paradoxical about dispersing and qualifying our notion of human agency at the very moment we need to make an unprecedented demand upon that agency. For this risky approach to be justified, we must be very convinced that less, in this case, really can be more, and that we have not too much to lose, as traditional ideas of responsibility cannot save us from ecological disaster. Bennett deplores the "hubristic demand that only humans and God can bear any traces of creative agency," and our habit of grasping "for that special something that makes *human* participation in assemblages radically *different*" (121). "Why," she asks, "are we so keen to distinguish the human self from the field?" To which the environmentalist answer might be: because, as far as we can see, human beings are the only creatures able to perceive the global relationships that constitute the crisis, and the likely future consequences; probably the only creatures, too, who might on the basis of that information act to restrain evolved and habitual desires. Other species do not, on the evidence, make self-denying interventions to save each other from extinction. Perceptions of human exceptionality may emerge from cultural traditions heavily responsible for the crisis, but it is hard to think of the rapid transformations we need as anything other than increases in human responsibility.

Bennett acknowledges that the conceptual change she is advocating requires people to "rewrite the default grammar of agency, a grammar that assigns activity to people and passivity to things" (119). The task "seems necessary and impossible." Such an approach will have to proceed by deconstructing the language of ordinary assumptions. It cannot work with the forms of narrative with which we generally try to make sense of our lives. Ecocritics who advocate this deconstructive approach are placing themselves in the traditional position of an avant-garde, preparing ideas for a later time. The term "avant-garde" recovers its original aspiration here: its vision of a future in which what is now startlingly experimental has become normal. But how long have we got? The ecocritical avant-garde cannot be content with marginal bohemian space, but must aim for rapid normalization: hence the conflict between the depth of this strategy and the urgency of a crisis that asks deep cultural questions but requires rapid answers.

The New Materialist ecocritics are aligning ecocriticism with post-structuralism's general critique of the concept of the unified self. They seek to banish early ecocriticism's hostility to "theory," and to apply post-structuralist insights to material ecological relationships, rescuing post-structuralism from an exclusive concern with cultural constructionism. But in doing this, they risk entrapping ecocriticism in one of post-structuralism's greatest disadvantages: its need to deconstruct ordinary language, and thus its dependency on forbiddingly dense, technical and alien linguistic formations, far removed from the idiom and conventional narrative structure of personal experience.

For political post-structuralism, conventional narrative subjectivity is beyond positive use, so deeply is it implicated in the production of oppressive ideology. But to be confined to the theoretical level (a particularly ironical fate for theories of "embodiment") is a serious disadvantage when entry into public culture is the priority (and in teaching that values the narrative self-expression of students). Explanations of "theory" frequently lack particular examples drawn from experiential life, and as a result have difficulty in exploring the affective dimension. Some eloquent "narrative scholarship" produced by the New Materialist critics begins to find powerful answers to this problem (see, especially, Catriona Sandilands's essay on her mother's Alzheimer's, in Alaimo and Hekman 2008), but, nevertheless, the question, in the context of the urgent crisis, is how rapidly can New Materialist and Deep Ecological ideas move beyond the academic domain.

A philosophy that dissolves unitary selfhood must expect to have difficulty in finding expression in conventional narrative. Who is the protagonist? What is the narrative point of view? Literary forms in the Modernist tradition—dispersed, ventilated, fragmented, multivocal, dialogical forms without stable narrative viewpoint, or impersonal forms replacing the single narrative or lyric voice with cut-up and collage—would seem more adaptable to ecocentric and New Materialist approaches. Sandilands, writing about Walter Benjamin, identifies literary montage as a critical-artistic practice "that seeks to transform the obsolescent fragments of commodity capitalism into 'dialectical images,' groupings of things that reveal elements of the experience of capitalist modernity obscured in everyday existence" (Goodbody and Rigby 2011: 31): a form to counteract "splitting," in other words. Ursula Heise suggests that the Modernist tradition of narrative collage, with its breaks, interruptions and switches of viewpoint and register, offers possibilities for the representation of ecological relationships that go beyond the range of local place and individual perception—with the advantage that these forms are already quite widely familiar and have passed into popular genres such as Science Fiction; they are no longer purely avant-garde (see Heise 2008: 76–77).

The poet Harriet Tarlo argues that "found poetry"—poems consisting largely or entirely of pieces of quoted text from a variety of sources—is a genre especially suited to environmental concerns. Not only is this kind of poetry not restricted to the locality of the particular dramatized viewpoint and to certain kinds of "poetic" language, but the use—or, as Tarlo not entirely whimsically calls it, the "recycling"—of found text introduces questions about ownership and public space. For Tarlo, the method of "found" poetry foregrounds the question of whether literary culture can be regarded as a public commons, like the atmosphere, or like the biosphere as an interconnected global ecosystem (see Tarlo 2009: 125). Such poetry "confronts us with our complicity as users of the common cultural coinage of our own everyday language" (123). Tarlo cites the work of Jack Collom, Rachel Blau DuPlessis, Harryette Mullen, Peter Reading, Dorothy Alexander, and Tony Lopez, all of whom have used cut-up and collage techniques with direct reference to the ecological crisis.

Does ecocriticism have to choose between these still, for the most part, avant-garde literary strategies and those able to reach larger audiences and deploy more familiar narrative and lyrical forms, connecting with the personal stories we tell ourselves? A parallel presents itself. At the end *The Revenge of Gaia*, his most pessimistic book about global warming, James Lovelock, the originator of the Gaia hypothesis, argues that our urgent need is for a combination of two things in deep tension with each other (see Lovelock 2006: 142, 153–54). We need emergency technological measures, including new nuclear power stations, to make sure that civil order survives the first shock of climate change, and we also need a shift of social and personal values in the direction of Deep Ecology, to give us a chance of stabilising the global ecosystem and living peaceful, fulfilled lives as we do so. Lovelock asks us to think in two ways that are normally fiercely opposed to each other. The urgency changes the meaning of these different options.

For literary ecocritics, Lovelock's proposal suggests that we might allocate different tasks to different literary forms and genres. Prompted by Lovelock, we might say that we need all the different literary forms to do different jobs: realistic novels and lyric poems, action thrillers, realist and Brechtian theater, avant-garde forms in the Modernist tradition. Analogies between ecosystems and the way culture works are a strong tradition in ecocriticism. Felix Guattari delineated what he called the three ecologies: physical, psychological, and cultural. Hubert Zapf has advanced a theory of imaginative literature's place in a functioning cultural ecosystem. One does not have to take this sort of analogy too far, looking at the present array of literary genres, to recognize that these genres have all "evolved" in relation to various needs, pressures and desires, and continue to evolve. If the fundamental aim of literary ecocriticism is that environmental care should become stronger and more pervasive throughout literary culture, ecocritics will not be looking for a single form of literature that meets all the criteria at once; nor will they search only for a small number of new forms or genres specially adapted to environmental priorities. Rather, they will want to address all these various needs and audiences, and to bring environmentalism into all the influential forms of literature. Nor can they say, "I go to avant-garde poetry and literary fiction for intellectual satisfaction, and to thrillers for leisure entertainment and a certain emotional release"—or they can't leave it at that, without perpetrating another kind of "splitting."

If we try to assign literary genres to Lovelock's two strategies, then, an obvious impulse is to link realist narrative, and lyric poetry with a conventional dramatic speaker, to the pragmatic emergency responses, and avant-garde Modernist forms to the Deep Ecological (and New Materialist) shifts in culture. That would be too neat and simple. Extended literary analysis would find other possibilities in both forms. But as a crude starting-assumption, this initial impulse reveals something important: the emergency does not give us leeway to entrench ourselves in our taste for one literary genre or another. Ecocritics must continually look at the need to reach a variety of audiences, and to address different emotional reactions to the crisis, and to accommodate conflicting tactics. The crisis makes us twist and turn.

Also, it becomes clear that ecocritical literary judgments must have an exceptional degree of temporality and provisionality. Because of the scale, complexity and urgency of this crisis, questions of what makes a particular text good or bad in ecocritical terms have to be answered in terms of the needs of the particular moment. Ecocritical assessments of literary quality are not reducible to questions of what might make people care, but, under such exceptional pressure, they seem inextricable from those questions. The provisionality arises also because literary ecocritics must react, continuously, to scientific and technical debates in which they can play no part. Much uncertainty surrounds the threat, not so much about the basic mechanism as about the precise degree of warming that is likely, and the regional consequences of that warming.

Will feedback effects intensify the change or reduce it? How far will sea levels rise? Has the rate of warming in the last ten years been slower than projected? If so, is this because aerosols—solid particles and droplets in the atmosphere, produced, like the warming, by industrial emissions—are "masking" the warming trend by reflecting some of the sun's heat and temporarily delaying the really dramatic increase? Do controversies about the methods of collecting some of the data genuinely cast any doubt upon the climate change warnings? If so, how much doubt? Is "peak oil" a reality? Which of the new sustainable energy technologies stands the best chance of success?

Literary ecocritics cannot answer such questions for themselves. Yet if literary culture has any broad social influence—and ecocriticism, like all political criticism, is founded on the hope that it does—then any literary critic writing about these things must feel a disconcerting sense of responsibility. So much may be at stake. In writing the paragraph above, I was troubled by numerous questions. Was I summarizing the position fairly, or overstating the uncertainty and thus conceding too much to those who would dismiss the warnings? I can't be sure. I must respect the consensus of the experts, but continue to watch new developments. A special discipline is required of ecocritics here, a peculiar form of intellectual and moral precision, and scruple.

Responding to the expert opinion, we must try to take into account a variety of factors: the high stakes, the urgency, the difficulty and depth of the transformation required, and the risks involved in delaying action. The threat itself, and all these factors, must be considered in terms of probabilities rather than certainties. I don't mean by this that literary ecocritics can professionally assess the scientific probabilities, but that, from the layman's standpoint, the existence of a scientific consensus for a view must itself constitute a probability that the view is more accurate than opinions for which there is no consensus. There is a necessary modesty in this approach, to which literary theorists may be unaccustomed. They are called upon to commit everything to a probability that will be determined elsewhere. If the probability changes, they must change accordingly, and not feel they were wrong, since the only right thing they can do is take account of present probability. Hugely transformative action is required because of a probability that may change. No part of this statement can be avoided.

In the 1960s and 1970s, several explicitly political schools of literary criticism emerged to challenge the Arnoldian and Leavisite liberal humanist tradition. Ecocriticism came later, and doesn't neatly fit the pattern of these other schools, but ecocritics have followed their example in many ways. A feature they all had in common was a rejection of liberal humanism's idealist search for classics whose literary quality was separable from their historical moment or particular political cause. Matthew Arnold had argued that the critic's task was to identify "on all the matters which most concern us, the best which has been thought and said in the world" (Arnold 1994: 5). F. R. Leavis and his followers saw critical debate as the continuing process of revaluation that assessed a work's fitness to be included in the "great tradition." The new political critics—New Left Marxist, Feminist, Postcolonial and Queer—rejected this idealist tendency. They saw, in this degree of generalization of human experience, a device for masking differences of wealth and power that would be revealed by the study of particular historical moments. The radical literary criticisms therefore placed more emphasis on literary value conceived as relative—as defined in relation to the needs and priorities of particular groups and struggles at particular moments. This is a matter of emphasis, since a superb response to a particular set of circumstances becomes inspiring and admirable beyond those circumstances. Ecocriticism, though, is under special pressure not to distance the specific political challenge.

To a substantial extent, for these radical criticisms, what was needed, and therefore "good," at one moment was different from what was needed at another. Different readerships had different needs, even when the desired result was collective cultural change. However, these new criticisms did not entirely relinquish the idea of more generalised standards of literary quality, and in all the critical schools a tension remained between the two kinds of quality: relative and general, or political and artistic. Crudely, there is the question of *what* a text is doing—is it doing what is needed now?—and the question of *how well* the text is doing it. Neither question can be relinquished, yet neither is sufficient to determine literary quality. The second question may be answered in aesthetic terms, by a criticism that looks for inspired artistic control of literary form, while the first must be answered in ethical and political terms, but attempts to keep these sets of terms separate are notoriously problematical, like attempts to separate form and content, or the ethical and the practical. Judgments about how "good" a work is must be a compound of both questions; for ecocriticism especially so.

Here are some things literature can do now, tentatively matched with the genres that seem best suited:

1. Literature can provide an all-out apocalyptic vision of catastrophe, to shock and scare us deeply. Three overlapping genres already attempting to do this in novel and film are Science Fiction, Horror and The Road Novel/Movie. A crucial factor for ecocritics is the extent to which the apocalyptic plot is combined with elements of literary realism, giving us characters and events that seem consistent with real possibility ("yes, this is how that person would react"). Another is the degree of compatibility with what is scientifically understood to be possible. One can imagine a revived Epic Poetry presenting the apocalyptic scenario too.

2. An important role for culture could be the advocacy of a pragmatic willingness to accept interim measures that are undesirable in the long term, such as the ones Lovelock sees as likely to be necessary. Science Fiction (or what Margaret Atwood calls "speculative fiction," depicting future scenarios in which nothing happens that is not already possible) and Literary Realism are the relevant genres.

3. The environmental problems already developing fast call for stark realist representation, in works exploring particular instances of damage and the ecological and human consequences. These topics need writing that combines ecological, social, and individual perspectives, showing us the costs and consequences of different choices. This is clearly a task for realistic fiction and poetry, and perhaps for forms of epic realism that combine long perspectives with zooms into intensely realized local settings.

4. Literature can also provide poetic engagement with the natural environments we are losing or at risk of losing. The love of wild nature takes many cultural forms in different parts of the world, and for many environmentalists is a powerful motivating force, led by passionate pleasure as well as fear. Nature writing and television nature documentaries are enduringly popular genres, often associated with practical conservation campaigns and with ecotourism that, at its best, gives communities an economic motive to protect their wild nature. In the non-fiction genre, and also in poetry and novels, nature writing is able to integrate personal stories into the wider picture provided by science and cultural history. If a new commitment to environmental care does spread through modern culture, it seems likely that an essential part will be a renewed willingness in industrialized societies to find social and personal meaning in seasons, landscapes, and the drama of life and death in nature.

5. Ursula Heise has called for forms of literature capable of representing the global and futuristic perspectives that enable us to "see" climate change—spatial and temporal perspectives reaching beyond the narratives of individual lives. Rather

than the cohesive narratives of episodes in the lives of small numbers of characters that are the main territory of Literary Realism, Heise suggests that Modernist traditions of cut-up and collage may have more potential, as may digital texts using "Google Earth"–style zooming and incorporating graphs and databases. Timothy Morton argues similarly. Climate change, he says, is a "hyperobject," so extensive in time and space as to be practically unlimited. We are always already inside it and cannot exit. Forms of art and literature should therefore be found that suggest this unboundedness: forms that remain ostentatiously incomplete, not permitting a sense of closure. These ideas point to poetry and cut-up narrative in the Modernist "open field" traditions recommended by Harriet Tarlo. As we have seen, cut-up and collage offer possibilities also to ecocritics seeking literary forms for ecocentric and New Materialist ideas: forms that depart from familiar subjectivity in order to represent the decentred, continuous and unbounded flow in which creatures and things continually produce each other.

6. Utopian eco-fiction—again, needing a strong element of literary realism within its utopian setting—can attempt to demonstrate the possibility of a society founded upon environmental care.

7. Realistic novels and confessional lyric poetry seem to be the genres best equipped to explore people's current reactions and evasions (such as "splitting") and the emotional and behavioral shifts that would occur if we began to change.

The purpose of this list is to identify the main demands that ecocritics can most pertinently make of different genres of writing (rather than performance, though there is much overlap), and therefore the criteria that will be involved in ecocritical judgments of particular works—the provisional and temporal judgments I have been discussing.

Sadly, it is hard to find any examples of number seven. Where are the rigorously realist novels, with present-day settings, dealing with people's emotional responses to the threat of climate change? *Solar* (2010), the much-heralded climate-change novel by Ian McEwan, turned out to be a bleakly comic allegory rather than a work of literary realism, and some of McEwan's comments seemed to suggest that he'd considered a realist approach but found it untenable. Confessional lyric poetry dealing directly with the subject is also scarce, but there are some notable examples (Ruth Padel's "Slices of Toast," for one). Perhaps the difficulty realism encounters in dealing with this subject is symptomatic of the broader cultural impasse discussed above. Until there is movement, novels on the subject can find no plot development. Lyric poetry does not have quite this problem because, tellingly, plot development is not what it requires; it can inhabit the impasse.

For the novel, deprived thus of plot, one response is ultimatum. I will not co-operate with your splitting. Until you begin to move, I will not give you the satisfactions you expect from me, the stories that imply a continuing normality. This seems to me to be the single terrible gesture made by Cormac McCarthy's *The Road* (2006), the most uncompromising of the apocalyptic Road Novels, described by the environmental writer George Monbiot as "the most important environmental book ever written." For

Monbiot, *The Road* shows "what would happen if the world lost its biosphere, and the only living creatures were humans, hunting for food among the dead wood and soot" (Monbiot 2007).

In many respects, Monbiot's view seems highly questionable. The novel's dreadful scenario, in which an unspecified catastrophe has abruptly destroyed the earth's ecosystem, killing plant-life and animal-life but not human life, does not conform to any scientifically conceivable possibility. Society has collapsed. Survivors either scavenge tinned food or form cannibal gangs, some farming children for eating. Like all of McCarthy's work, the novel seems fascinated by ruthless violence, as if that were the only deep truth, and the main purpose of the implausible ecological scenario seems to have been the contrivance of a "survivalist" setting in which the traditional masculine frontier values of taciturn toughness are the only effective form of virtue. A father travels with his son through the ruined landscape, using his resourcefulness and resilience to evade the cannibals, while having to hold at bay his emotional reaction to what has happened to their lives, a reaction that has great implied depth but finds little direct expression. The mother committed suicide soon after the catastrophe, unable to face this new life. In one place—when father and son stumble upon a cellar of captives waiting to be butchered— the novel flashes a voyeuristic glimpse reminiscent of sadistic slasher movies.

So there is much to object to, on ecocritical grounds and others. But this novel does one big thing that is highly instructive. The scenario it depicts is so cruelly hopeless, so terminal in its account of both the global ecosystem and human civilization (it gives us several familiar genres, such as the road novel and the Proustian reminiscence of childhood, in a kind of defeated and terminal form), and so sickening to anyone who feels responsibility for handing on the world to children, as to amount to the ultimatum I mention above. All consolation is withheld. When the man dimly and with bafflement recalls his childhood before the catastrophe, he seems for a moment to confront the reader, making us feel our own pre-catastrophic position. This strategy of insufferability, if strategy it is, says to the reader: here is something that gives you no option of reacting just a little. You must either face the scenario, or turn away from it unable to pretend you are doing anything else.

I will conclude with one more example, better yet worse than *The Road*, to illustrate how ecocriticism must always ask what a work is doing to move us out of this impasse. In 2012, the poet Jean Sprackland published *Strands*, a work of prose non-fiction about the objects she had found while regularly walking on a beach near Liverpool. The book is in the nature writing tradition of the almanac—the yearbook of meditations upon local sights. But this is an example of "the new nature writing," concerned with the disorderly and dirty "edgelands" between human society and the natural wild, rather than with wilderness as separate space. A beach near a big city is a good example. The characteristic feature of this genre is that a single familiar object, near at hand, prompts questions about its origin that take us right across the world and into philosophy, history, politics, and science: the genre is an apt one for ecocriticism. One chapter in *Strands* concerns plastic, starting with commonplace litter on the beach, taking us back to the startlingly recent invention of the material (such global transformation in so short a time), and carrying us out to the famous Great Pacific Garbage Patch, "said by some observers to cover an area twice the size of Texas" (Sprackland 2012: 106).

Some of the items Sprackland finds are endearingly outmoded things she remembers from childhood, which gives us a jarring sense of both the recentness and the irrevocability of the changes brought by plastic. On the beach, the natural sublime can be encountered in a form that is contained by the allotted hours of leisure and the ease of moving in and out of this world—its proximity to social space, work space and home space. But the sense of security here is menaced by statements that place us in the mesh of global relations, much larger than our familiar territory, yet frighteningly finite: "there are, on average, forty-six thousand pieces of plastic floating on or near the surface of every square mile of ocean in the world" (104). Vertigo is produced by this sudden opening-out—this loss of proportionality, this leap from the small to the vast, with no gradation. What have we done, with our little Lego bricks and toothbrushes?

But ecocritics must ask what the text then does with this vertigo. Do we merely glimpse the impasse and turn away, back to normal affairs? The reviewer of *Strands* in *The Guardian*, Laurence Scott, complained about the occasional solemnity of tone:

> Her diligent research finds new ways to trigger that increasingly familiar sense of dismay over our toxic planet: shrimp have grown drunk on the residue of anti-depressants from our urine; to eat fish is to eat plastic; there seems to be either too many or too few of every creature under the sun. But here we arrive at Sprackland's eco-solemnity, a problem of tone, and a tendency to employ truisms, that interferes with her otherwise absorbing narrative. (Scott 2012)

This is fatuous. We are menaced by impending ecological disaster, but God forbid we should be solemn about it. Nothing, not even impending catastrophe, must be allowed to disturb our cool lightness of tone. This attitude is a familiar manifestation of "splitting." Yet, unfortunately, there is a real, unresolved incommensurability between the different tones and scales in Sprackland's book, which gives Scott's trivialising objection an opening. *Strands* is otherwise admirable in ecocritical terms, but the episodic structure—the way each chapter frames a particular walk without narrative continuities, consequences—enables us to turn away too easily, and return to normality after the space for reflection afforded by an afternoon walk or an hour of reading. For literature to be more profoundly disruptive than this is a lot to ask. Perhaps it is an unrealistic demand, but it is one ecocritics must make, if they are to begin to leave the condition of not really believing what they know.

NOTES

1. See Fiona Harvey, 'UN chief challenges world to agree tougher target for climate change.' *The Guardian*, June 1, 2011. Available at http://www.guardian.co.uk/environment/2011/jun/01/climate-change-target-christiana-figueres
2. Andrew Simms, "The Final Countdown." *The Guardian*, August 1, 2008. Available at http://www.guardian.co.uk/environment/2008/aug/01/climatechange.carbonemissions

Works Cited

Abram, David, *The Spell of the Sensuous*. New York: Vintage, 1996.

Alaimo, Stacy, *Bodily Natures: Science, Environment and the Material Self*. Bloomington: Indiana University Press, 2010.

Alaimo, Stacy, and Hekman, Susan, eds, *Material Feminisms*. Bloomington and Indianapolis: Indiana University Press, 2008.

Arnold, Matthew, *Culture and Anarchy (1869)*. New Haven: Yale University Press, 1994.

Bennett, Jane, *Vibrant Matter: A Political Ecology of Things*. Durham and London: Duke University Press, 2010.

Buell, Lawrence, *The Future of Environmental Criticism: Environmental Crisis and Literary Imagination*. Malden: Blackwell, 2005.

Dodds, Joseph, *Psychoanalysis and Ecology at the Edge of Chaos: Complexity theory, Deleuze/Guattari and Psychoanalysis for a Climate in Crisis*. London: Routledge, 2011.

Glotfelty, Cheryll, and Fromm, Harold, eds, *The Ecocriticism Reader*. Athens: University of Georgia Press, 1996.

Goodbody, Axel, and Rigby, Kate, eds, *Ecocritical Theory: New European Approaches*. Charlottesville and London: University of Virginia Press, 2011.

Heise, Ursula, *Sense of Place and Sense of Planet: The Environmental Imagination of the Global*. Oxford and New York: Oxford University Press, 2008.

Lanchester, John, "Warmer, Warmer" *London Review of Books*, March 22, 2007, 3–9.

Lovelock, James, *The Revenge of Gaia: Why the Earth is Fighting Back—and How We Can Still Save Humanity*. London: Allen Lane, 2006.

Lynas, Mark, *The God Species: How the Planet Can Survive the Age of Humans*. London: Fourth Estate, 2011.

McCarthy, Cormac, *The Road*. London: Picador, 2006.

McEwan, Ian, *Solar*. London: Jonathan Cape, 2010.

McKibben, Bill, "Global Warming's Terrifying New Math." *Rolling Stone* Issue 1162, August 2, 2012: http://www.rollingstone.com/politics/news/global-warmings-terrifying-new-math-20120719#ixzz21pbre6yz

Monbiot, George, "Civilisation ends with a shutdown of human concern. Are we there already?," *The Guardian*, October 30, 2007: http://www.guardian.co.uk/commentisfree/2007/oct/30/comment.books

Morton, Timothy, *The Ecological Thought*. Cambridge: Harvard University Press, 2010.

Plumwood, Val, *Environmental Culture: the Ecological Crisis of Reason*. London: Routledge, 2002.

Scott, Laurence, "Strands—A Year of Discoveries on the Beach by Jean Sprackland—review," *The Guardian*, July 27, 2012: http://www.guardian.co.uk/books/2012/jul/27/strands-year-discovery-jean-sprackland-review

Seymour, Nicole, "Toward an Irreverent Ecocriticism." *Journal of Ecocriticism* 4 (2), July 2012, 56–71.

Slovic, Scott, *Going Away to Think: Engagement, Retreat and Ecocritical Responsibility*. Reno: University of Nevada Press, 2008.

Tarlo, Harriet, "Recycles: the Eco-Ethical Poetics of Found Text in Contemporary Poetry." *Journal of Ecocriticism* 1(2), July 2009, 114–130.

Wheeler, Wendy, *The Whole Creature*. London: Lawrence and Wishart, 2006.

Žižek, Slavoj, *Living in the End Times*. London: Verso, 2011.

CHAPTER 21

....

ARE YOU SERIOUS? A MODEST PROPOSAL FOR ENVIRONMENTAL HUMOR

....

MICHAEL P. BRANCH

IN a recent essay called "A Climatologist Walks into a Bar...," Robert Butler observes despairingly that *Man Walks into a Bar*, the self-proclaimed "biggest joke book in the world," contains among its 6,000 entries not a single joke about the environment or environmentalists, about climate change or biodiversity loss or even about the planet itself. "This is the future we face," laments Butler, "rivers dry up, sea levels rise, animals become extinct and there won't be a single blonde joke, or lightbulb joke, or three-men-walked-into-a-bar joke about any of it." No doubt there are those for whom the dearth of global warming one-liners is not a major concern, but doesn't it seem odd that a 550-page joke book can't spare a few lines to engage with nature and those who work to protect it, if not also with those who study the arts by which its grandeur and complexity are expressed? I confess that I feel left out. What is so appallingly unfunny about nature writers, ecocritics, and environmental activists? Can we be so utterly irrelevant as to not even be worth laughing at, let alone laughing *with*?

Before I address these questions, I'd like immediately to correct this abhorrent condition of jokelessness in which we reportedly find ourselves. Since blonde jokes are passé and many scholars of environmental literature have never walked into a bar (especially not with *two* men), I thought it best to compose a light bulb joke—also an obvious choice given the urgent need to replace conventional bulbs with compact fluorescents. So, for my fellow ecocritics and those who would seek to understand us, I offer this opening salvo...

How many ecocritics does it take to screw in a light bulb?
Answer: Ten.

(1) One to claim that "75 watt" constitutes a textual utterance characteristic of a genre that has been unjustly marginalized and is thus in urgent need of scholarly recovery;

(2) One to argue that measuring illumination by the archaic unit of "candlepower" is a naïve form of undertheorized, romantic pastoralism that shows precisely what's been wrong with ecocriticism all along;

(3) One to lament the painful irony that although we ecocritics love nature, we actually spend most of our time indoors, screwing in light bulbs;

(4) One to offer a penetrating analysis of the patriarchal, phallocentric implications of "screwing" in the light bulb;

(5) One to hold the ladder and thus feel complicit, causing a sense of guilt that the lightbulb's contribution to global warming will ultimately result in a polar bear stranded helplessly on one of those really small chunks of floating ice;

(6) One to calculate whether screwing in light bulbs will even be valued by the senior faculty when their tenure case comes up for consideration;

(7) One to point out that if our professional lives weren't so alienated from our environmentalist practice, we would be *unscrewing* light bulbs;

(8) One to observe that although we've always screwed in light bulbs, we could secure more grant funding if we rebranded the bulb replacement as a "sustainability initiative";

(9) and (10) Finally, two to argue about whether the light emitted by the bulb is first-, second-, or third-wave.

Shakespeare wrote in *Love's Labour's Lost* that "A jest's prosperity lies in the ear/Of him that hears it, never in the tongue/Of him that makes it," which is a fancy, Elizabethan way of saying that you may not find that joke funny. Whether you do will depend not only upon your sense of humor, but also upon whether you perceive yourself as the butt of the joke. Ecofeminist scholars may be insulted by #4, for example, while climate activists may find #5 tasteless, fair-minded departmental administrators may be upset by #6, and those engaged in shaping the future of ecocriticism may feel that #9 trivializes productive critical debates. A joke may be offensive because it is compact and unqualified in its assertions, and thus inherently reductive and essentializing. While it must risk offense, though, humor also functions as a mirror: however distorted its reflection, it offers a salutary opportunity to momentarily transcend the limits of our usual vision, to view ourselves in a new way—to see ourselves, perhaps, as others might see us. Whether we are able to laugh as we stand before the mirror is another matter.

* * * * *

In this essay I offer a modest proposal for environmental humor, and I'll say up front that it does not involve ecocritics eating poor Irish children—though that would be a substantial improvement over the food we're served at academic conferences. Before making my case, though, I want to launch a preemptive rhetorical strike by stating exactly what I do not intend to advocate. Unfortunately this is necessary because of the perennially low cultural status of humor since about the time they shoveled dirt onto Horace in 8 BC, and because hyperbolic claims for the universal efficacy of humor have been as common as the American tall tale.

I first separate myself from most writers on humor by refusing to make claims regarding the health benefits of humor. It is demonstrable that laughing raises your heart rate, blood pressure, and pulmonary ventilation; increases brain activity and alertness; stimulates the production of endorphins from the ventromedial prefrontal cortex; reduces the perception of pain; and leads to relaxation—but so do having sex, playing racquetball, or crashing your truck, and I say this even as a person who has given up racquetball. As for broad claims regarding the healing power of laughter—claims whose intolerable ubiquity date to 1979, when Norman Cousins wrote a bestselling book explaining how he cured his own cancer by watching Marx Brothers movies (yes, really)—there is virtually no scientific evidence to support them. We do, on the other hand, have incontrovertible evidence that the lack of scientific evidence is of absolutely no concern to people who already know what they believe.

Which leads, indirectly, to the second argument I would like to not make: that we environmental writers, scholars, and activists should enter the New Age by joyfully embracing the nurturing, healing power of humor. For those of you preternaturally fortunate enough to have avoided exposure to the "positive humor movement," a glance at the homepage of the Humor Project, a typical purveyor of this giggling brand of snake oil, will speedily bring your good fortune to an end. Here you will discover evangelical pronouncements regarding the panacea of humor, including a series of remarkably cloying daily "laffirmations," the innovative suggestion that you should wear a red clown nose to work, and the astonishing proposal that you "Have fun with your fellow workers by giving out every now and then a PMS Award (Positively Motivating Smile)." You will also find "1,001 Ways to Add Humor to Your Life and Work" (apparently 1,000 wasn't sufficient), information about the "laughter-fueled" 53rd International Humor Conference (which attracted over 21,000 participants, and that's no joke), and links to a vast gaggle of laughter therapy hucksters who will come to your place of business, tell you and your colleagues to be funnier, and then head to the bank with your $6,000 speaker's fee (who's laughing now?). I agree that ecocritics provide no exception to the rule that academics are in desperate need of therapy—only some of which we find it possible to obtain at the expense of our students—but I draw the line at therapy of the red nose variety; if you want a red nose, better to choose the simpler and more sanative approach of drinking more whiskey.

Finally, I would like very much to not argue for a new scholarly interest group devoted to the examination and promotion of environmental humor—and, in particular, to not argue in the strongest possible terms that I should be appointed an officer of such a group. Humorist Roy Blount Jr. has observed that "nothing is less humorous than a good faith effort to define and explain humor," and I likewise admonish that the surest way to kill humor is to let scholars get organized and start exegesisizing all over it. We find proof of this hazard in the penumbral corner of academia called "humor studies," where the mind-numbing pedantry of scholarly analyses of the comic has proliferated to an alarming degree. These studies so thoroughly murder to dissect that formal charges might well be brought against them, and an afternoon spent in perusal of such books brings to mind not only Mark Twain's complaint that "the more you explain it, the more I don't understand it," but also his helpful recommendation that we should all "make a special effort to stop communicating with each other, so we can have some conversation." All of this omits mention of the humor studies scholars themselves, who are so dour a lot that it might be imagined they chose to study humor in the futile hope that some might rub off on them. Let ecocritics recognize, with Lear, that that way madness lies.

* * * * *

Having cleared the air, let's return to my opening question: Why aren't we environmental writers, scholars, and activists funnier? Why don't we see more humor in the subject of our studies, and why don't we employ more humor in our scholarly and creative work?

One reason is suggested by nature essayist David Gessner, who uses his provocative essay "Sick of Nature" to rail against the earnestness of nature essayists—individuals who, if gathered together, would resemble "a reunion of Unabombers." The problem with nature writing, according to Gessner's delightfully self-loathing rant, is that reading in this genre is "like going to Sunday School." "[S]uddenly, I realized that I hated nature, or at least hated writing about it in a quiet and reasonable way," he writes. "Why? Because the whole enterprise struck me as humorless, which in turn struck me as odd, given that comedy often draws on a strain of wildness." The problem with nature, Joyce Carol Oates argued in her snide essay "Against Nature," is that it "inspires a painfully limited set of responses in "nature writers" ... reverence, awe, piety, mystical oneness." But the problem, silly Joyce Carol Oates, lies not in nature itself, but rather in the constrained imagination of the writer—who, as Gessner's confessional self-accusation suggests, too often allows himself to be defined by the circumscribed conventions of a genre and the preconceived expectations of its readers. Gessner is right, though, that we've left little room for humor in environmental writing in part because the genre has evolved as a vehicle for the expression of piety and reverence. But, as I'd like to contend here, where reverence rules irreverence must soon challenge.

There is also the matter of the importance and seriousness of our work. For those who believe, as I do, that the global environmental crisis is real and urgent, that it requires a moral as well as a strategic response, and that our teaching, writing, and scholarship should contribute to the amelioration of this crisis, it may be difficult to imagine what's funny about any of this. Those of us engaged in literary studies also know that, since about the time poor Gulliver returned from his travels, we have had to be serious if we wished to be taken seriously. "The world likes humor, but treats it patronizingly," wrote E. B. White. "It feels that if a thing is funny it can be presumed to be something less than great, because if it were truly great it would be wholly serious." I disagree adamantly with the proposition that "wholly serious" forms of environmental writing and scholarship are more engaging or effective than a practice that includes the creativity, spontaneity, flexibility, playfulness, and enjoyment that humor brings. I similarly reject the assumption, largely an invention of the Victorian period, that humor contaminates and subverts serious work, and must for that reason be kept strictly separated from it. If humor is vitally important to our happiness and mental health, our friendships and social relations, our professional collaborations and teaching, if it is energizing and restorative and pleasurable, how then can we rationalize its banishment from our most important work?

∗ ∗ ∗ ∗ ∗

So what good might come of a greater openness to humor in our critical and creative practice? What new perspectives might humor provide, what new insights might it produce, what new pleasures might it enable?

First, the ecocritical hesitancy to laugh has caused us to miss some very interesting texts, and to miss opportunities to recognize and enjoy humor in many of the texts we do study. A few brief examples from my own experience as a student of earlier American literatures may be helpful. When teaching seventeenth-century American literature, we tend to focus on theocrats like John Winthrop, whose idea of the city on the hill is widely celebrated, while failing to notice natural history writers like William Wood and Thomas Morton, for whom the hill itself was most important, and for whom humor was indispensible. Morton's *The New English Canaan* (1637), for example, is a book that contains one of the most important natural history catalogs of the early colonial period, and also one of the most amusing satires ever written on the hypocrisy and sanctimoniousness of Puritan culture. In the eighteenth century, we are more likely to teach the statesmanly verities of James Madison than the bawdy foibles of Benjamin Franklin, who was a gifted natural science writer and also a preeminent Enlightenment humorist—a man who, in the guise of Poor Richard, used comedy to proffer his most important lessons, such as "Fish and Visitors stink after three days," and "In Rivers and bad Governments, the lightest things swim at top" (note to readers with indoor plumbing: for "things" read "feces"). And we hardly know what to make of a character like William Byrd, who was enough of a naturalist to win membership in the Royal Society and yet whose diaries, which report candidly and enthusiastically on the "rogering" and "flourishing" of wives (both his own and other people's) include gems like this one: "I read a sermon in Dr. Tillotson and then took a little nap. I ate fish for dinner. In the afternoon my wife and I had a little quarrel which I reconciled with a flourish. Then she read a sermon in Dr. Tillotson to me. It is to be observed that the flourish was performed on the billiard table." If sermons in my neighborhood were as stimulating, I might consider returning to church.

Among canonical American writers of the nineteenth century, humor is practically universal. Washington Irving, whose comic characters Ichabod Crane and Rip Van Winkle remain cultural staples today, was America's first professional writer and one for whom landscape was vital to literary art; he launched his career as a Knickerbocker humorist associated with *Salmagundi*, a magazine that in many respects prefigures *The Onion*. We teach Harriet Beecher Stowe's *Uncle Tom's Cabin* for its abolitionist message, but in her own day Stowe was also known for the vernacular landscapes and language she used in humorous stories like "The Minister's Wooing." The Down East humorists made possible the place-based focus of such late nineteenth-century texts as Sarah Orne Jewett's *The Country of the Pointed Firs*, just as the early Southwest humorists pointed the way for Mark Twain's great picaro, Huck Finn, to light out for the territory. Nathaniel Hawthorne, who composed lyrical nature essays including the gorgeous "Buds and Bird-Voices," also wrote *The Scarlet Letter*, the first American novel to contain the term "sense of humor." Hawthorne's greatest admirer, Herman Melville, peppered *Moby-Dick* with jokes, and while many are straight-ahead penis jokes worthy of any forecastle locker room, the depth of Melville's cosmic humor is suggested by the opening sentence of the chapter entitled "The Hyena": "There are certain queer times and occasions in this strange mixed affair we call life when a man takes this whole universe for a vast practical joke, though the wit thereof he but dimly discerns, and more than suspects that the joke is at nobody's expense but his own." Even that most sober philosopher of nature, Ralph Waldo Emerson, whose Harvard class of 1821 must certainly have voted him "Least Likely To Ever Get a Laugh," published an essay called "The Comic," in which he asserted that "The perception of the Comic is a tie of sympathy with other men, a pledge of sanity, and a protection from those perverse tendencies and gloomy insanities in which fine intellects sometimes lose themselves."

We arrive inevitably at the pondside shack of our ornery old uncle, Henry Thoreau, whose *Walden* has remained central even as the territorial wrangling of the culture wars has unseated a host of once canonical writers. Since April Fools' Day in 1900, when *The Dial* published an essay on "Thoreau as Humorist," scholars of Thoreau's work have exhumed, elucidated, and occasionally even enjoyed Thoreau's wry humor, which is everywhere apparent in *Walden*. From punning (he thrills in trampling his neighbors' "premises"—that is, both their woodlots and their assumptions), to linguistic play ("I have watered the red huckleberry ... which might have withered else in dry seasons" is American literature's most lyrical euphemism for pissing in the woods), to satirical attack (as in his deathbed essay, "Walking," where he comments that "When sometimes I am reminded that the mechanics and shopkeepers stay in their shops not only all the forenoon, but all the afternoon too ... I think that they deserve some credit for not having all committed suicide long ago."), Thoreau is a writer whose engagement with nature and culture is inseparable from his use of humor.

Indeed, Uncle Henry's humor does not relieve or season his social critique but brilliantly enables it. Consider, for example, both the moral force and the delightful comedy of his account, in *Walden*, of trying to give instructions for the fabrication of a pair of pants that happens then to be out of fashion:

> When I ask for a garment of a particular form, my tailoress tells me gravely, "They do not make them so now," not emphasizing the "They" at all, as though she quoted an authority as impersonal as the Fates, and I find it difficult to get made what I want, simply because she cannot believe that I mean what I say, that I am so rash. When I hear this oracular sentence, I am for a moment absorbed in thought, emphasizing to myself each word separately that I may come at the meaning of it, that I may find out by what degree of consanguinity *They* are related to *me*, and what authority they may have in an affair which affects me so nearly; and, finally, I am inclined to answer

her with equal mystery, and without any more emphasis of the "they,"—"It is true, they did not make them so recently, but they do now."

Such delicious sarcasm must certainly rank Thoreau among the greatest of literary smart asses, but it is also crucial to observe how his comic move here underwrites and ampli- fies *Walden*'s serious argument that slavish conformity to fashion has devastating intel- lectual and moral consequences. While *Walden* and Thoreau's other works are laced with comic rhetorical thrusts, however, ecocritics have tended not to relish Thoreau's humor, instead celebrating Saint Henry of the Pond for his spiritual and aesthetic sen- sibilities, as if his appreciation of nature and his keen social critique could somehow be extricated from the striking playfulness, depth, and power of his comic sensibility.

* * * * *

I should add at this point that a few stalwart ecocritics have indeed attempted liter- ary analyses emphasizing humor. The most focused of these is Katrina Schimmoeller Peiffer's 2000 book *Coyote at Large: Humor in American Nature Writing*, which includes chapters on Simon Ortiz, Edward Abbey, Ursula Le Guin, Lousie Erdrich, Sally Carrighar, Wendell Berry, and Gary Snyder. This is an intelligent, helpful study, and while I don't find the writers under consideration to be as funny as Peiffer does—I love Berry's work, for example, not for the laughs but rather for putting me in touch with my Inner Curmudgeon—I concur with her core objection that ecocriticism has "conspired to train us to perceive only the solemnity and seriousness in nature writing." A prob- lem with Peiffer's analysis, one common to humor studies generally, is its indulgence in extravagant claims on behalf of the efficacy of humor—in this case the blithe assertion that "humor routes us into a nondualistic animist spirituality."

In exaggerating its claims on behalf of environmental humor, though, Peiffer's book only follows a better known and much earlier study, Joseph Meeker's seminal 1974 work *The Comedy of Survival*. Here Meeker advances not only the happy argument that liter- ary comedy values resilience, flexibility, and endurance, a proposition I embrace whole- heartedly, but also the dubious contention that a comic outlook has been specifically selected for by evolutionary processes precisely because of its survival value. Perhaps so, but it is hard for me to view Jim Carrey, Jeff Foxworthy, or Lisa Lampanelli as the pinna- cle of evolution. Better had Meeker stopped with his elegant, humane, and lucid asser- tion that "Comedy demonstrates that humans are durable, although they may be weak, stupid, and undignified." The more damning problem with *The Comedy of Survival* is the stunning production design of the widely available 1980 paperback reprint, which not only features a cover as chartreuse as a fishing lure, but, much worse, is adorned with many explicit drawings of a naked lady—I'm talking graphic, full-frontal nudity—danc- ing rather erotically with a very large moose. Please don't mistake my point here. I'm extremely fond of both naked ladies and moose (I do credit Meeker with helping me to imagine them *together*), but I worry this sort of thing gives people the wrong impres- sion about the ecocritical enterprise. Despite my skepticism regarding Meeker's comic biological determinism, however, I've always loved this inventive and engaging book—though perhaps I've been swayed less by its argument than by the titillating images of the nude moose.

While the studies I've mentioned are not themselves humorous (naked moose notwithstanding), I do believe that a fuller engagement of humor in environmental writing has the potential to energize our critical analyses and the liveliness of the prose in which they are offered. Many humor scholars begin their critical books by explaining defensively that although they will analyze humor, they shouldn't be expected to produce any. This is fair enough, but I want to point out that it is indeed possible to generate critical insights that are both humorous and incisive, just as Thoreau's prose is simultaneously funny and serious. I've mentioned David Gessner's comic complaint against nature writing, which both amuses us and, in useful ways, turns our laughter toward a redemptive form of critical self-recognition. However, much earlier examples also come to mind. Among my favorites is D. H. Lawrence's 1923 pearl, *Studies in Classic American Literature*, which I consider an indispensible work of ecocriticism and also a monumentally witty and perceptive book. Beginning with a chapter entitled "The Spirit of Place," Lawrence proceeds to comment on the work of canonical American authors, often exposing brilliantly the mythic constructions of nature upon which they depend for their effects. In writing about Crevecoeur, for example, Lawrence not only relishes the paradox of Crevecoeur retreating to French salons while trying to sell the reader on the nobility and purity of his fabricated identity as the "American farmer," but also offers a wry gloss on the farmer's wife and child, who are so thoroughly idealized as to be denied names:

> The Farmer had an Amiable Spouse and an Infant Son, his progeny. He took the Infant Son…to the fields with him, and seated the same I.S. on the shafts of the plough whilst he, the American Farmer, ploughed the potato patch. He also, the A.F., helped his Neighbours, whom no doubt he loved as himself, to build a barn, and they labored together in the innocent Simplicity of one of Nature's Communities. Meanwhile the Amiable Spouse, who likewise in Blakean simplicity has No Name, cooked the dough-nuts or the pie, though these are not mentioned.

If the sarcasm here is wonderful, what it exposes is vitally important to an understanding of Crevecoeur's pastoral devices and techniques. The more one reads Crevecoeur, the funnier and more incisive Lawrence's analysis appears, and the more useful and enjoyable it thus proves.

Or, go back still further, to another demythologization of an American writer whose work has profoundly influenced the American imagination of nature: Mark Twain's delightful and exhaustive enumeration of "Fenimore Cooper's Literary Offenses." Here Twain observes that Cooper's much beloved wilderness mystique boils down to a number of rather cheap tricks:

> Another stage-property that he pulled out of his box pretty frequently was the broken twig. He prized his broken twig above all the rest of his effects, and worked it the hardest. It is a restful chapter in any book of his when somebody doesn't step on

a dry twig and alarm all the reds and whites for two hundred yards around. Every time a Cooper person is in peril, and absolute silence is worth four dollars a minute, he is sure to step on a dry twig. There may be a hundred other handier things to step on, but that wouldn't satisfy Cooper. Cooper requires him to turn out and find a dry twig; and if he can't do it, go and borrow one.

As with Lawrence's comic excoriation of Crevecoeur, we laugh at Twain's send up of Cooper precisely because we recognize its accuracy. As literary critics, Lawrence and Twain understand perfectly the Horatian dictum *utile et dulce*, which although sometimes mistranslated as "candy is useful," actually proposes that our writing should seek to teach and to delight. As my essay is *modest* proposal, I do not intend to suggest that ecocritical analyses be punctuated by rimshots or laugh tracks (though I should perhaps note that Charles Douglass, inventor of the laugh track, is an alumnus of my university). I wish only to observe that the engaging playfulness and humor we find in a great deal of literature is often lacking in the work of those who study that literature.

*****

For those of us who are environmental writers, there is an even better reason to deploy the comic mode, and that is the tremendous value of humor in our fight against exploitation of the natural environment. I do not assume that all environmental writers consider themselves activists (though certainly many of us do), but I think most would self-identify as environmentalists, and as people who view their work as part of a larger cultural response to the conditions of environmental degradation that mark our age. In advancing our causes, however, we have usually overlooked the strategic value of humor. As activist-writer Rick Bass observes, "One of the worst things about environmentalists, as has been noted often, is a growing humorlessness that afflicts them—us—and that can grow a little more intense, a little more bitter, year by losing year." I find that the more of these losing years I live—the more damage and loss I register emotionally, the more unjust or misguided the systems of power appear to me, the more angry I become— the more desperately am I in need of humor as one of the arrows in my quiver. In *The Mysterious Stranger*, Twain averred that "Against the assault of laughter nothing can stand." "You are always fussing and fighting with other weapons," he writes. "Do you ever use that one [humor]? No, you leave it lying and rusting. As a race, do you ever use it at all? No, you lack sense and the courage." These may be biting words from a man advocating humor, but I believe they offer a salutary challenge to environmental writers.

Environmental rhetoric has been dominated by the jeremiad—the fuming tirade aimed at those perceived as environmental backsliders—and the elegy—the self-indulgent expression of grief and mourning in the face of loss. I would argue not only that these two highly stylized rhetorical modes have inherent limitations that compromise their effectiveness, but that much of the efficacy they once possessed has been exhausted through overuse. We desperately need the jeremiad and elegy to communicate our moral outrage and our justifiable anguish at the environmental violence to which we must bear witness, but we must also admit that the conventions of nature writing in these modes have begun to ossify, limiting their power to surprise the reader or provoke change in the reader's assumptions or attitudes. How long will a substantial readership continue to turn the pages of another brittle eco-rant, or tacitly agree to suffer the misery registered in writing that functions primarily as tombstone? Already we live in a moment when a popular novelist like T. C. Boyle can easily parody nature writing, as he does so effectively in the "Pilgrim at Topanga Creek" sections of *The Tortilla Curtain* (which parodies Annie Dillard's *A Pilgrim at Tinker Creek* specifically and critiques the solipsism of nature writing generally), or when a television and film comedian like Chris Elliot can turn author and write a book like *Into Hot Air: Mounting Mount Everest*, a boisterous parody of Jon Krakauer's bestselling *Into Thin Air*. Perhaps, then, we should seek an alternative approach that allows us to break free from the stultifying conventions of environmental discourse—that permits us to return some of the pleasure to our project, without compromising the fierce moral seriousness of its aims.

One possibility is to open our minds to the potential environmental efficacy of satire—a form venerable long before Aristophanes satirized Socrates in *The Clouds*. And in proposing satire I want to emphasize the importance of Juvenalian satire as well as Horatian, the former of which is as jugular as the latter is jocular. A satirical text need not be a tissue of effete witticisms, but rather may be constructively abrasive; wielded as a cudgel, it may function as a means of exposing injustice. And while public ridicule has remained unfashionable in the academy—except, of course, in book reviews published in academic journals—we still have plenty to learn from Swift and Johnson, Bierce and Twain, Orwell and Huxley, Heller and Burroughs (William, not John). In our own day, anyone who has watched the satirical television programs *The Simpsons* or *South Park* knows how effectively satire can strike a wide range of cultural targets. Consider in the same vein the work of television comedian Stephen Colbert, or that of my old college dorm mate Jon Stewart, whose *The Daily Show* regularly exposes the absurdity and hypocrisy of American political, corporate, and media cultures. While you may not be an enthusiast of such programs, you hardly need be a fan to admit the extraordinary power of this brand of satire to expose contemporary vice and folly. Satire is not only funny but also enormously forceful and effective—and, human nature being what it is, the comic exposure of vice and folly has the added benefit of offering a great deal of job security.

As writers and environmentalists, it seems we are perpetually on the defensive: even as we try to inspire, persuade, and reform, we secretly fear that we are *Vox Clamantis in Deserto*: well-intentioned but largely ineffectual players whose power is dwarfed by corporate influence, retrograde government, or even by our local real estate developer—who, in my own case, appears increasingly less concerned about my resistance each time he climbs out of bed with the mayor. By night we dream of blowing up Glen Canyon Dam, but by day we write letters to the editor. The satirist, by contrast, is ever on the offensive, and while he is likely to be viewed as transgressive and caustic, he effectively challenges established power structures, exposing their absurdity or violence, forcing villains to account for themselves. Orwell had it right when he declared that "Every joke is a tiny revolution," for satirical humor is inherently inimical to established power, including structures of power lacking the moral leadership necessary to respond to the environmental crisis. As Malcolm Muggeridge, mid-twentieth-century editor of the satirical magazine *Punch*, put it, "by its nature humor is anarchistic, and implies when it does not state, criticism of existing institutions, beliefs, and functionaries." As the title of Muggeridge's magazine reminds us, we don't call them "punch" lines for no reason.

There are many theories of humor, chief among them Freud's "relief" theory, which posits that humor is an unconscious discharge of repressed energy, and Hobbes's "superiority" theory, which follows Aristotle in worrying that the wellspring of laughter is our cruel assumption of supremacy over others (this sympathetic insight comes to you from a man whose *Leviathan* declares unconditionally that life, much like my brother-in-law, is "solitary, poor, nasty, brutish, and short"). But perhaps the most useful major theory of humor, promulgated by Kant, Schopenhauer, Kierkegaard, and others, is "incongruity" theory, which posits laughter as a response to the gap between expectation and reality, between what it seems should happen and what actually happens. In the American context the most helpful exponent of this theory is Louis D. Rubin Jr. who invokes the compelling term "the great American joke" to refer to the excruciating breach between the promise of American democracy and its (perhaps inevitable) failure to fulfill that promise.

Although humor may be generated through the sorts of trivial incongruities that are the fodder of television sitcoms, the satirist is instead interested in the serious business of addressing the troubling gap between what our ideology promises and the often disappointing outcomes that our policies and practices actually produce. As an example, consider the cultural work of such innovative, influential stand-up comedians as Lenny Bruce, Richard Pryor, and George Carlin, who methodically deconstructed languages of power and used humor to shine a light on America's hypocritical unwillingness to promote racial equality and protect individual freedom. Or, think of the courage and effectiveness of filmmakers who used humor as the vehicle of penetrating social critique: Charlie Chaplin, whose *The Great Dictator* (1940) bravely satirized Hitler on the eve of the US entry into World War II, or Stanley Kubrick, whose Cold War classic, *Dr. Strangelove or: How I Learned to Stop Worrying and Love the Bomb*(1964), used black humor to expose the terrifying absurdities of the nuclear arms race. The incongruities these comics and filmmakers exposed were painfully real, and there was consequently a sense in which every laugh they produced was one small blow to the *status quo*. This is why Kenneth Rexroth, in his excellent 1957 essay "The Decline of American Humor," asserted that comedy is essentially a radical force for change, and that as a result of this important cultural function, "Great humor has a savagery about it." The genius of humor that exposes incongruity, Rexroth maintained, is that it prompts "The realization that the accepted, official version of anything is most likely false and that all authority is based on fraud," while also inspiring in us "The courage to face and act on these two conclusions."

Disappointingly few environmental writers have taken up the satirist's sword, but one who did, Edward Abbey, makes sufficiently clear the potential power of this approach.

Abbey was deliberate and strategic in envisioning humor as a weapon, even paraphrasing Whitman's benediction in advising his readers: "This is what you shall do: Be loyal to what you love, be true to the Earth, and fight your enemies with passion and laughter." In "Why I Write," Abbey described his motivations as a writer this way: "Not so much to please, soothe or console, as to challenge, provoke, stimulate, even to anger if necessary—whatever's required to force the reader to think, feel, react, make choices.... I write to amuse my friends, and to aggravate—exasperate—ulcerate—our enemies." Far from imagining humor as mere entertainment, Abbey falls squarely in the venerable tradition of satirists who employ laughter as a tool of battle. And if Cactus Ed's humor is occasionally more juvenile than Juvenal, he does use comic strategies to make good on his own charge that "The artist in our time has two chief responsibilities: (1) art; and (2) sedition." Or, to quote from Wendell Berry's graceful appreciation of Abbey in *What Are People For?*, "Humor, in Mr. Abbey's work, is a function of his outrage, and is therefore always answering to necessity."

Hopeful signs of the efficacy of environmental satire are certainly present in a book like *Desert Solitaire*, which regularly employs humor to fire at its targets, which it rarely misses. The administrators of the National Park System are said to be "distinguished chiefly by their ineffable mediocrity," while the operatives of the local Chamber of Commerce "look into red canyons and see only green, stand among flowers snorting out the smell of money, and hear, while thunderstorms rumble over mountains, the fall of a dollar bill on motel carpeting." Those who would "develop" the wilderness of the American West with roads and dams simply because development conforms to their myopic and environmentally destructive concept of "progress" receive a serious roasting throughout the book. The humor here is profoundly anti-authoritarian, as in this derision of how uncivilized American culture actually is: "Civilization is tolerance, detachment, and humor, or passion, anger, revenge; culture is the entrance examination, the gas chamber, the doctoral dissertation and the electric chair." Amidst his scathing anti-institutional polemic against industrial ecotourism, Abbey reserves a lighter treatment for the benighted visitors to Utah's Arches "Natural Money-Mint," as in his gentle ribbing of the Cleveland man who informs Abbey that the desert would be a decent place, "if only you had some water."

While the desert of the Colorado Plateau is sacred to Abbey, nothing else is. Abbey would surely agree with seventeenth-century English critic John Dennis that "the design of Comedy is to amend the follies of Mankind, by exposing them." Abbey's humor strikes at government, religion, the military, capitalism, education, and many other targets that he feels disseminate an ideology of "progress" resulting in the destruction of the Earth. But even in his most sweeping attacks Abbey maintains the equanimity of the satirist, as in his wry insistence that "In social affairs, I'm an optimist. I really do believe that our military-industrial civilization will soon collapse." Whether the nettlesome Cactus Ed is ultimately remembered as the Juvenal, Swift, or Twain of the environmental movement remains to be seen, but it is clear that his aggressive use of humor offers one useful model of how the comic mode might be deployed to transform our outrage into an animated, potent form of cultural critique. In the meantime, we might at least say of environmental humor what Abbey himself said of human reason, that it "has seldom failed us because it has seldom been tried."

* * * * *

Even those who prefer not to take up humor as a sword, however, might wish to raise it as a shield, to accept a modest dose of it as inoculation against the diseases of fatigue, frustration, and failure that are epidemic among environmentalists. Because we love the world so deeply and yet are forced to watch it burn—or melt—we find in our love for nature not unalloyed joy but rather a bittersweet affection shot through with grief. At the etymological root of the word "compassion" is the idea that we "suffer with," and in our compassion for the suffering of the earth and its creatures we experience a kind of trauma that often strips us of energy and hope.

Because it is so dynamic and flexible, humor can not only "aggravate—exasperate—ulcerate—our enemies," but also function as a coping mechanism to help us preserve the resilience upon which our own creativity and courage depend—even if, as bluesman Big Bill Broonzy crooned, "When you see me laughing/I'm laughing just to keep from crying." Humor may in fact be the *product* of suffering, and our laughter in some deep sense a direct response to grief. It can also function as a form of sympathy. Since the late eighteenth century, it has been thought that the appreciation of humor requires a sympathetic imagination, a sense of "fellow feeling" characterized by acceptance, flexibility, perhaps even the capacity to forgive oneself or others. As Henri Bergson observed, humor can also bind people together, causing them to be more resilient, and ultimately helping them to examine and revise their shared identity and sense of common purpose. And while a sense of humor remains impossible to define precisely—as the term "sense" implies—we are for good reasons deeply suspicious of those who lack this sense, for we consider the ability to laugh fundamental to our humanity. Indeed, this notion that a sense of humor is a demonstration of our humanity is a primary reason most US presidential campaigns of the modern era have had joke writers on their payroll.

Since the nineteenth century, the sense of humor has also been strongly correlated with the idea of self-knowledge. Humor enables us to engage in a useful process of self-reflection because it provides a form of detachment allowing us to admit, examine, and then correct or forgive our faults and failures. This power of humor to produce humanizing insight and self-knowledge prompted progressive educational reformers of the 1930s and 1940s to argue that humor should become part of the school curriculum; it also inspired the Mark Twain Association's attempts to endow a chair in humor to rotate among universities, professing the sort of humanizing levity that might make students more humane and the academy less grim.

It seems to me that, especially for environmental writers and activists, an inability or unwillingness to engage in this kind of self-reflexive humor is potentially debilitating. If we refuse to laugh at ourselves, we reinforce the unhappy stereotype of the environmentalist as solemn, didactic, or smug. Much worse, we deprive ourselves of the opportunity to see ourselves as others might see us, to momentarily transcend our entrenched assumptions and ideological positions, to stand before the mirror of humor and gain a fresh perspective on who we are and what we do. As Mikhail Bakhtin expressed it in his book on Rabelais, laughter is "one of the essential forms of the truth concerning the world as a whole, concerning history and man; it is a peculiar point of view relative to the world." Through humor, writes Bakhtin, "the world is seen anew, no less (and perhaps more) profoundly than when seen from the serious standpoint." And in this broadened perspective on ourselves and the world there is the potential for a necessary acceptance of ourselves and each other, of conflicting points of view, of the abhorrent contradictions and disheartening failures which must not prevent us from doing our work.

"Sustainability," as I suggest in #8 of the light bulb joke with which I opened this essay, is a term we use a great deal—and that we demand convey a range of meanings and advance a number of causes with a variety of audiences. The core insight of the sustainability revolution, though, is that before making choices we should ask whether our actions can be perpetuated over time without causing excessive harm to the natural environment. My suggestion is that we should also apply this helpful standard to ourselves and our work, asking whether our current approach to environmental writing, scholarship, teaching, and activism can be sustained, or whether perhaps our unremitting earnestness and the inflexible rhetorical forms it has engendered now threaten to become a liability to our cause. It is precisely because we *are* serious—because our tasks are difficult and the stakes are high—that I propose (modestly, of course) that we recognize the value of humor as both sword and shield. Enjoying our image as it appears reflected in a light bulb joke will not solve all our problems, but it is—much like a hundred oil company executives at the bottom of the sea—a damned good start.

··

CHAPTER 22

IS AMERICAN NATURE
WRITING DEAD?

··

DANIEL J. PHILIPPON

EVERY day, all over the world, seven billion people wake up and go about their lives. Many struggle in dire poverty, unable to afford even the first meal of the day. Others dwell in relative comfort, stopping at their local breakfast spot for a sausage, egg, and cheese biscuit and a tall vanilla latte to go. Then, wherever they are, they go to work, or go looking for work, or try merely to survive, producing goods and providing services if they can, residing in cities, towns, and countrysides, and behaving in ways shaped by a host of intersecting factors, from race, class, and gender to biology, culture, and religion. In the process, they use the Earth's resources at vastly different rates, generate waste in vastly different ways, and transform vastly different aspects of the planet: its atmosphere, waters, and soils, its genes, species, and ecosystems. And they do this again and again, every day, all over the world.

Of what value is nature writing in such a world?

It's a crucial, potentially painful, question, and one that gets to the heart of the genre's dilemma, particularly in terms of its U.S. variant. After some three centuries of American nature writing, give or take a century or so, has the genre of Henry David Thoreau, Aldo Leopold, and Rachel Carson outlived its usefulness? Does it have anything helpful to say in the face of the sustainability challenges of the twenty-first century? With the end of nature now at hand, and environmentalism left for dead according to some commentators, can the genre of nature writing be far behind? Is it time not merely to espouse "ecology without nature" or extend our reading "beyond nature writing" but to declare the death of nature writing?

Answering this question will require some ecocritical soul-searching, and a willingness to confront literary pieties, for American nature writing has been a central concern of ecocriticism since its inception in the 1990s. Without nature writing, whither ecocriticism? Can a critical movement survive the passing of its signature genre?

To address these questions, this chapter will review several attempts to define nature writing as a genre; explore some recent critiques of nature, nature writing, and environmentalism; reexamine a few canonical works in the genre; and consider the attempts by some contemporary writers to address issues of sustainability in an age of climate disruption. Throughout these investigations, I will argue that while the generic label "nature writing" may now be more trouble than it's worth, the expansive sensibility expressed in much traditional nature writing still remains a useful tool with which to address the various humanistic challenges associated with sustainability. While "nature writing" may well be dead, in other words, its spirit unquestionably lives on.

ATTEMPTS AT DEFINITION

Recognition of "nature writing" as a distinct genre dates to at least the beginning of the twentieth century. The earliest entry for "nature-writing" in the *Oxford English Dictionary* is from the June 1901 issue of the *Atlantic Monthly*, in which Paul E. More compares "Thoreau's attitude of mind with that of Wordsworth and the other great poets of the century who have gone to Nature for their inspiration, and have made Nature-writing the characteristic note of modern verse" (860). Read in isolation, More's use of the term seems to suggest that nature appreciation transcends genre rather than defines it, but in the remainder of the article ("A Hermit's Notes on Thoreau") More in fact argues that "Thoreau was the creator of a new manner of writing about nature" (860). Although he acknowledges that Thoreau shares with previous writers an interest in observation, classification, and description, as well as a personal experience of the natural world, More nevertheless finds Thoreau's interest in "the moral significance of nature" to be his distinctive quality (861).

More's desire to identify Thoreau's "characteristic traits" is an impulse shared by several subsequent critics who also express an interest in the structural components of the genre. Joseph Wood Krutch, for instance, in the prologue to his landmark 1950 anthology, *Great American Nature Writing*, argues that nature writing is "an emergent literary form," which exhibits a "recognizably modern" attitude of fellowship with nature that began with Thoreau. Expression of this fellow feeling, according to Krutch, cannot be found in "accounts of discovery, exploration, and adventure," nor in "purely subjective musing on the one hand, and purely objective scientific observation on the other" (2). "Only literary artists with the artist's determination to communicate personal experience could create the genre," Krutch explains; "though such artists would have to absorb part of what the scientist and philosopher were teaching" before they could do so (21). Thirty years later, Paul Brooks echoed Krutch's view of the genre in *Speaking for Nature* (1980), the first book-length study of nature writing to appear after the birth of environmentalism in the 1960s and 1970s. Since Thoreau's time, Brooks observes, "there has grown up a literature of nature in America that has opened the eyes of millions of readers, leading to a widespread feeling of kinship with the other forms of life with which we share the earth" (xiv). Yet Brooks sees literature and culture as more interactive than Krutch, perhaps due to his role as Rachel Carson's editor at Houghton Mifflin. Both Thoreau and Carson, Brooks declares, "were part of a literary as well as a scientific tradition, influenced by their contemporaries and by the climate of the age" (xii–xiii).

The tension between a taxonomic approach to nature writing (which attempts to codify the essential characteristics of a genre, to which texts belong) and a rhetorical one (which sees genres as typified responses to rhetorical situations, and texts as instances of these) can be seen most clearly in Thomas J. Lyon's *This Incomparable Land* (2001), which remains the most popular guide to the genre. On the one hand, Lyon is nothing if not taxonomic, titling one of his chapters "A Taxonomy of Nature Writing," and agreeing with previous commentators that "the literature of nature has three main dimensions to it: natural history information, personal responses to nature, and philosophical interpretation of nature" (20). Likewise, Lyon builds on prior claims of nature writing's distinctiveness in observing that its crucial point is "the awakening of perception to an ecological way of seeing," by which he means "the capacity to notice pattern in nature, and community, and to recognize that the patterns radiate outward to include the human observer" (x). Yet, almost in spite of himself, Lyon repeatedly acknowledges the ways that nature writing is both shaped by history and society and shapes them in return. He notes that the genre was born in the age of romanticism and science, influenced by Darwin and mid-twentieth-century ecologists, and motivated by the negative effects of technological and industrial progress (30–35). He cites Brooks's argument that these writers had a notable effect on national policy (77), and he agrees with Barry Lopez that nature writing has provided "the foundation for a reorganization of American political thought" (121). And while he claims that "the main outlines of the genre… have not changed an iota" in the twentieth century, he nonetheless recounts the ways that the century "required of nature writers a depth of response that was fundamentally new," as they wrestled with the explosion of scientific knowledge, the continuing degradation of the environment, and the transformational effect of feminism (99).

This tension in Lyon's account likely results from his desire in the book's first edition (published in 1989) to defend nature writing as a distinct genre and to publicize its virtues to an audience unfamiliar with its provenance. This exigence has changed as ecocriticism has developed in the intervening decade, but studies of nature writing have nevertheless continued to employ these divergent understandings of genre—although they have done so to different degrees and for different ends. Peter Fritzell, on the one hand, in *Nature Writing and America* (1990) offers a highly circumscribed taxonomy that is both nationalistic and Arnoldian in its attempt to identify the traits that distinguish the "best" American nature writing from the unexceptional. Lawrence Buell, on the other hand, declines the apologist's role in *The Environmental Imagination* (1995), the most searching scholarly exploration of the genre to date. Describing nature writing as an "enclave" canon ("so-called with enthusiasm by partisans, but with condescension by most professional students of literature"), Buell opts to abandon the term altogether, preferring instead "environmental nonfiction" as a more inclusive moniker for what he believes to be a multigeneric field (8, 397). Most significantly, he sees this field as both aesthetic and rhetorical, given that it has "played a part in shaping as well as merely expressing" the emerging culture of environmental concern (3).

Since Buell's landmark work, other critics have continued to explore the contours of the genre in distinctive ways. Don Scheese and Randall Roorda have focused on its motif of pastoral retreat, also a major concern for Buell. Daniel G. Payne and Daniel J. Philippon have built on the work of Paul Brooks and explored the genre's political efficacy. And many writers and scholars have followed in the footsteps of Krutch and Lyon, producing anthologies that have remapped the canon of nature writing along a range of diverse coordinates: by comparing it to other genres, juxtaposing British and American texts, celebrating the contributions of women writers, and emphasizing the nature writing of various states and regions.

The major attempt at taxonomizing the genre since *The Environmental Imagination* has been Patrick Murphy's *Farther Afield in the Study of Nature-Oriented Literature* (2000), which contains several chapters devoted to identifying and analyzing the structural features of environmental representation in poetry, fiction, and nonfiction. Murphy distinguishes between a *genre*, which he defines according to style or structure, and a *mode*, which he says constitutes a philosophical or conceptual orientation. He thus sees nonfiction nature writing as but one genre within the larger mode of "nature literature," which also includes poetry and fiction about the natural world. Similarly, he identifies nonfiction environmental writing as one genre within the larger mode of "environmental literature," which also includes poetry and fiction about environmental issues and problems. Both of these modes constitute subdivisions of Murphy's overarching category of "nature-oriented literature," which he sees as encompassing any kind of literature that "reveals ecological sensibilities and nature sensitivities" (10). Given the lengths he goes to bring neatness to what Lyon admits "is not, in truth, a neat and orderly field," Murphy could certainly be accused of splitting hairs (20). But his taxonomy is admirable not only for its ambition but also because it calls attention to the problematic nature of the terms "nature" and "environment" when defining nature writing, not to mention the relationship this kind of writing has had to the social movement known as "environmentalism." The weakness of the taxonomic approach is not, therefore, that the categories it uses to organize the world of literary production are in dispute; rather, it is that taxonomies give the appearance of stasis to a world in constant motion. They miss the fundamentally rhetorical nature of generic categories, which concern the interaction of author, audience, text, and context as much as they do the thematic or formal features of any one text. We would thus do well to ask not simply "what is nature writing?" but also "how has nature writing shaped and been shaped by environmental discourse over time?" Doing so may also help us recognize that the distinctions between nature writing and environmental writing may no longer be valid, if they ever were, and that the time may have come to declare nature writing dead and get on with the business of building a sustainable world.

RECENT CRITIQUES

If it is indeed the case that the genre of nature writing might better be seen as a set of pragmatic responses to environmental change, it may be hard at first glance to see why the genre might be dying, much less dead, for the twenty-first century has seen environmental changes at a pace and scale unprecedented in human history. But the death of nature writing is a question not merely of genre but also of context: a context in which "nature" is said to have ended; nature writing has been criticized for being androcentric, ethnocentric, and restrictively lococentric; and environmentalism has been declared dead. Should all of the above hold true, it would be retrograde to say the least to cling to a category of texts whose reason for being has been so thoroughly undermined.

To say that the idea of "nature" has been contested of late is an understatement. One of the first modern critics to identify problems with the term was Raymond Williams, who noted in 1976 that *nature* is "perhaps the most complex word in the language" and later in 1980 that "the idea of nature contains, though often unnoticed, and extraordinary amount of human history" ("Nature" 184; "Ideas" 67). Another early commentator was the environmental historian Carolyn Merchant, who argued in *The Death of Nature* (1980) that the idea of "nature" as a living being was killed in the sixteenth and seventeenth centuries, when capitalism and the scientific revolution began to imagine both women and nature as passive dependents in need of control. But the most popular expression of the belief that nature has ended can be traced to Bill McKibben, whose *The End of Nature* (1989) was the first mass-market book to publicize the phenomenon of global warming. While *The Death of Nature* illustrated that ideas of nature have been changing for centuries, *The End of Nature* maintained that the present shift in understanding is unique in its material and global foundations: "We have changed the atmosphere, and thus we are changing the weather. By changing the weather, we make every spot on earth man-made and artificial. We have deprived nature of its independence, and that is fatal to its meaning. Nature's independence *is* its meaning; without it there is nothing but us" (58).

McKibben's argument reflects only one side of the debate, however, because while some forms of environmental protection depend on a romantic understanding of "nature as other," other forms rest on an evolutionary understanding of nature as coterminous with humans. Indeed, the "nature as other" perspective found its most prominent critic in William Cronon, whose 1996 essay, "The Trouble with Wilderness; or, Getting Back to the Wrong Nature," angered many environmentalists by calling the idea of wilderness (the ultimate symbol of American nature) a cultural construction: "the creation of very particular human cultures at very particular moments in human history" (144). Wilderness, Cronon argued, "embodies a dualistic vision in which the human is entirely outside the natural" (149). In place of this fantasy—the "dream of an unworked natural landscape"—Cronon suggested that "we need to embrace the full continuum of a natural landscape that is also cultural, in which the city, the suburb, the pastoral, and the wild each has its proper place, which we permit ourselves to celebrate without needlessly denigrating the others" (149, 151). While Cronon's opponents argue that his constructionist view could be used to justify unrestrained human action (for if humans are indeed "part of nature," then every human activity is as natural as every other), this is not a necessary conclusion, because the opposite could also hold true (since whatever we do to nature, we do to ourselves). Increasingly, these battles over the idea of "nature" have caused a number of critical theorists to suggest that the term has so many complexities and contradictions that we would do well to abandon it altogether. Timothy Morton, for example, has argued that "the idea of nature is getting in the way of properly ecological forms of culture, philosophy, politics, and art" (1).

When Karla Armbruster and Kathleen Wallace encouraged ecocritics to explore the boundaries of their methodology "beyond nature writing" in 2001, they were arguing for an extension of ecocriticism into other genres and texts, not for abandoning nature writing altogether (3). But if nature writing faces the same conceptual problems that "nature" has—namely, its reliance on the romanticized "otherness" of nature—perhaps that time has now come. Although Thomas J. Lyon wrote in 2001 that "[n]o one, to my knowledge, has spoken of the death of the nature essay," Moira Farr had in fact made that argument eight years earlier in her 1993 essay "The Death of Nature Writing." Farr became unnerved by climate change during the summer of 1988 in the same way Bill McKibben was, and she concluded that not only had nature died that summer but so had nature writing. Annie Dillard, she came to believe, was "arguably the last human being who could, in any convincing way, write about nature as though it were wholly clean (even in [sic] its most horrific) and inspirational." And *Pilgrim at Tinker Creek*, Farr said, "might well be the book that takes its place in history as nature's last will and testament" (19).

Since then, many other writers and critics have weighed in on the various blind spots that stem from the genre's romantic roots. Some of the earliest such critiques came from ecofeminists, who observed that although women have been as active as men in writing about nature since the nineteenth century, they have often written in unheralded forms—such as the letter or diary—and have approached their subject in unconventional ways—emphasizing, for instance, the neighborliness of the backyard garden over the rugged individualism of the "untamed" frontier. More recently, critics have pointed to the ways in which the Anglo-American tradition of nature writing, best represented by Robert Finch and John Elder's *Norton Book of Nature Writing*, fails to represent the diversity of ways people engage with nature in the evolutionary sense (defined as the entirety of the physical world, including humans and our cultures) rather than just the romantic sense.

These critiques all speak to the emergence of an environmental justice ecocriticism concerned with multiculturalism and social justice, but they have also emerged alongside related attempts to address further limitations of traditional nature writing (Adamson, Evans, and Stein). In *The Truth of Ecology* (2003), for example, Dana Phillips accuses contemporary nature writers of being "too selfish," inclined to mysticism and individual epiphany at the expense of natural history and moral agency (195). As a result, Phillips claims, "today's nature writers are forced to overlook the actuality of the landscape we have made for ourselves, so that they can fix their sights on more ideal terrain, which they hope to conquer and settle in spirit" (234). In a related line of reasoning, other critics have argued that nature writing's pastoral impulse (in which the rural retreat functions as a refuge from modernity) not only obscures the genre's urban roots but also diverts attention from the city as both a unique environment in its own right and a powerful force affecting other environments. "What the crisis of nature writing amounts to, in a few words," says Jenny Price, "is that Thoreau really, really needs to Get on the Bus" (223). And once on the bus, the argument goes, Thoreau is only a few stops away from acknowledging that every place is inextricably linked to a network of global cultural and economic processes that once appeared to end at the city limits.

Among the critics emphasizing this recognition are those concerned with postcolonial literature, who are less interested in finding fault with nature writing for its historical role in the process of ecological imperialism than in moving beyond modes and genres altogether. "What actually counts as 'environmental literature' is moot," according to Graham Huggan and Helen Tiffin, in part because postcolonial ecocriticism is more interested in activism, "in the undoing of the epistemological hierarchies and boundaries—nowhere more apparent than under historical and/or contemporary conditions of colonization—that have set humans against other animals, and both against an externalised natural world" (23 n. 2). Similarly, while critics interested in issues of globalization acknowledge the limits of both the localist emphasis of nature writing and the nationalist frames through which the genre has usually been studied, their more significant goals are to attend to the function of spatial scale in all forms of environmental discourse and, as Ursula Heise observes, to "the emergence of new forms of culture that are no longer anchored in place" (10). A similar post-Foucauldian desire to illuminate how structures of discourse are tied to structures of power shapes the emerging fields of posthumanism, critical animal studies, and queer ecocriticism.

While not all nature writing has had an explicitly political agenda, much of it has contained at least an implied desire to reorder individual and societal priorities, and so to some extent the genre shares the activist bent of its critics. Differences exist, of course, in the kind of politics being advocated and the degree to which those politics are manifest in a text. In an important article on "Epistemology and Politics in American Nature Writing" (1996), Scott Slovic distinguishes between two dimensions of nature writing: the rhapsodic, epistemological mode (in which writers explore and celebrate "the nature of the universe and the relationship between human beings...and the natural world") and the mode of the political jeremiad (in which writers seek to persuade their audience "to adopt a new perspective by pointing out problems with readers' current way of thinking"). While no text can be wholly apolitical, perceptions of where nature writing falls on this spectrum depend in part upon whether a writer's persuasive rhetoric is "embedded" or "discrete"—that is, whether a writer tries to embed both of these modes in one text or work discretely in one mode or the other in different texts (84–86).

If Slovic is correct that "all literature, all language, is values-oriented and, by extension, political," and if the idea of "nature" has indeed reached the end of its useful life, then it might appear we would do well simply to call all nature writing "environmental writing" and be done with it (108). Such is Lori Lichtman's conclusion when she writes that "the environmental writer has emerged as the final product of the American nature writer." Yet this merely exchanges one set of problems for another, given that "environment" is no less troublesome a term than "nature," and that environmentalism may be transforming into a broader-based social movement under the banner of "sustainability." In *American Literary Environmentalism* (2000), David Mazel explores the concept of "the environment" in detail, arguing that it is a discursive construction that "depends upon an *exclusion* that separates the environment from the speaker who is environed," much like Cronon's claim about the idea of wilderness (xvi). Mazel ultimately argues for a kind of strategic essentialism, claiming that "the term will serve in a postmodern environmentalism as a sort of useful fiction, necessary but necessarily *revisable*," and that seems to be precisely what has been occurring (xv). For instance, Ted Nordhaus and Michael Shellenberger—writing in their book *Break Through* (2007), which was inspired by their 2004 essay "The Death of Environmentalism"—proclaim that "if we are to overcome ecological crises, we must no longer put concepts like nature or 'the environment' at the center of our politics" (17). Instead, they propose a "politics of possibility" to counter the "politics of limits" that defines traditional environmentalism; theirs is "an explicitly pro-growth agenda that defines the kind of prosperity we believe is necessary to improve the quality of human life and to overcome ecological crises" (15).

The specifics of Nordhaus and Shellenberger's conclusion are less important than their premise: that even the useful fiction of "the environment" no longer seems very productive in an age of globalization and climate change. Indeed, the context for nature writing has changed so drastically since Paul More's use of the term in 1901 that to speak of contemporary writing about the human-nature relationship as "nature writing," as if such writing could occur without addressing the relationship of ecological health, social justice, and economic viability (or, in a word, "sustainability"), seems dangerously nostalgic. Cultural change often occurs slowly, however, and so it may be best to describe this as a period of transition, not merely from nature writing to environmental literature, but from environmental literature to something yet to be named. At the same time, to imagine that writing from previous eras has nothing to contribute to the present is as reductive as nostalgia is dangerous, and so we must look back before we can move forward.

CANONICAL TEXTS

Exactly what the so-called "canonical" texts of nature writing have to offer twenty-first century readers is an interesting question, given that much sustainability discourse tends to valorize technical fixes and public policy solutions—and understandably so, given the scale of the problems we face. One important answer comes from John Elder, writing in the introduction to his two-volume encyclopedia, *American Nature Writers*, published in 1996. According to Elder, "Recognizing limitations in the genre as we have understood it until now is by no means intended to disparage this form of writing. On the contrary, nature writing remains a distinctive and prophetic voice in our American tradition, and one of the chief antagonists of the materialism that continually threatens our national soul" (Elder, "Introduction" xviii). Nature writing, in other words, even in its most traditional forms, could be said to have laid the foundation for sustainability by playing an oppositional role in American culture, and it has achieved this jeremiadic function not only by rhapsodizing about the natural world but also by celebrating values *other* than economic growth, such as beauty, ecological health, and scientific inquiry. What follows are examples of how three classic texts address these values, and while all of these texts contain some romantic understandings of nature-as-other, what makes them interesting is that they also display evolutionary understandings of nature— appreciations for the kind of wildness that Paul Wapner has argued will prove central to a more sustainable, "postnatural" world (133–66).

Paul More, as we have seen, believed Thoreau's unique contribution to the emerging literature of nature was his interest in "the moral significance of nature." But Thoreau's understanding of nature's moral significance was inseparable from his appreciation of its beauty, and his appreciation for nature's beauty was also tied up with his comprehension of nature as a process. Perhaps no section of *Walden* (1854) better illustrates this than the lengthy "deep cut" portion of the book's penultimate chapter, "Spring," in which Thoreau observes a thawing bank of sand and clay through which the Fitchburg railroad runs. Watching this scene, Thoreau says, "I am affected as if in a peculiar sense I stood in the laboratory of the Artist who made the world and me,—had come to where he was still at work, sporting on this bank, and with excess of energy strewing his fresh designs about" (306). No mere apostle of natural theology, Thoreau builds on Jeremiah's analogy of God as potter (Jer. 18: 1–6) first to compare the earth to a leaf and then to compare humans to both organic forms (complete with Thoreau's distinctive punning): "What is man but a mass of thawing clay?... Is not the hand a spreading *palm* leaf with its lobes and veins?" (307–8). In the end, Thoreau realizes, "There is nothing inorganic.... The earth is not a mere fragment of dead history, stratum upon stratum like the leaves of a book, to be studied by geologists and antiquaries chiefly, but living poetry like the leaves of a tree, which precede flowers and fruit,—not a fossil earth, but a living earth.... And not only it, but the institutions upon it, are plastic like clay in the hands of the potter" (309). The significance of the world, for Thoreau, is found not in its market value but rather in the beauty of its complexity and fluidity: the artistry and poetry of its natural forms, which are themselves intimately intertwined with social institutions like the railroad (Buell, *Future* 42–44).

Like Thoreau's moral understanding, Aldo Leopold's "Land Ethic" also depends upon a geological perspective of the living earth. "A sense of time lies thick and heavy on such a place," writes Leopold near the start of "Marshland Elegy," one of the finest chapters in *A Sand County Almanac* (1949), a book frequently described as "the Bible of the environmental movement" (96). Watching the cranes descend to their feeding grounds on a glaciated Wisconsin marsh, Leopold observes that "our appreciation of the crane grows with slow unraveling of earthly history.... When we hear his call we hear no mere bird.

We hear the trumpet in the orchestra of evolution. He is the symbol of our untamable past, of that incredible sweep of millennia which underlies and conditions the daily affairs of birds and men" (96). Adding the emerging, mid-century science of ecology to this evolutionary outlook, Leopold developed his Land Ethic, which is often rendered in the form of a moral maxim: "A thing is right when it tends to preserve the integrity, stability, and beauty of the biotic community. It is wrong when it tends otherwise" (224–25). What makes the Land Ethic especially notable is that it emerges out of a narrative, rather than an argument. Thus when Leopold encourages his readers in the final section of *A Sand County Almanac* to "examine each question in terms of what is ethically and aesthetically right, as well as what is economically expedient," his appeal for the ecological health of the land rests on dozens and dozens of examples of Leopold's own "love, respect, and admiration for land" and his "high regard for its value… in the philosophical sense" (223–24).

By the time Rachel Carson came to write *Silent Spring* (1962), she, too, had already laid the groundwork for her argument, in three previous books of bestselling nature writing that described the beauty and wonder of the sea: *Under the Sea Wind* (1941), *The Sea Around Us* (1951), and *The Edge of the Sea* (1955). As a result, Carson was able to dwell more on the science behind a pressing public policy issue: the long-term effects of misusing synthetic chemical pesticides, which she saw as a symbol of human arrogance. *Silent Spring* is often mischaracterized as offering only an apocalyptic vision of the future, a claim based mainly on "A Fable for Tomorrow," the frightening portrait of a spring without bird song that opens her book. Yet Carson's points are more nuanced than this—and ultimately more hopeful. Like Leopold, she argues for a change in the way humans view the world: "Man, however much he might like to pretend the contrary, is part of nature," she asserts (188). But she takes Leopold a step further, linking ecological science to the human health sciences of toxicology and epidemiology and observing that "there is also an ecology of the world within our bodies" (189). *Silent Spring* is ultimately not a condemnation of science or technology but rather a questioning of how science is applied and which technologies are appropriate to use, especially when the long-term consequences of their use are uncertain. Building on the aesthetic and ethical values of Thoreau and Leopold, Carson develops a stirring call for democratic involvement in questions of hazard and risk, in order to ensure a public policy of precaution: "Who has decided—who has the *right* to decide—for the countless legions of people who were not consulted that the supreme value is a world without insects, even though it be also a sterile world ungraced by the curving image of a bird in flight?" (127).

As we consider how traditional forms of nature writing might contribute to a more sustainable world, it is notable that Leopold and Carson are both singled out as foundational figures in Simon Dresner's landmark book, *The Principles of Sustainability* (21–30). Yet at the same time, Lawrence Buell cautions us not to generalize too much from what may be "a limited number of exceptional cases" ("Literature" 22). The temptation "to extract from works of art or map them onto paradigms of environmental value," Buell admits, can be dangerous, because art ultimately resists the reduction to instrumentalism (24). Art and literature, Buell observes, "script environmental-ethical concern … in exploratory, often tentative ways complicated by multiple agendas and refusal to take fixed positions" (25). And indeed none of these authors are without complexity or contradiction: Thoreau found himself "refreshed and expanded" by the trains that carried their commercial freight by Walden Pond (119); Leopold said that "every time I turn on an electric light ... I am 'selling out' to the enemies of conservation" ("Game" 165); and Rachel Carson's claim that "the 'control of nature' is a phrase conceived in arrogance" seems to leave little room for humans to act in the world, especially to control a disease as deadly as malaria (297).[1]

Despite these limitations, it remains the case that these writers' detailed illustration and spirited defense of nonmarket values are a crucial component of what I have termed their *expansive sensibility*. Indeed, as Scott Slovic and Terre Satterfield have shown, nature writers could be said to function as "lay ethicists" who express their values through stories—stories that allow for nuance, provide a space for emotion, and capture the clarity and quality of values in ways that other methods of valuation do not (282–85).

SUSTAINABILITY AND CLIMATE DISRUPTION

This is all well and good, of course, except that the world has changed a great deal since 1962, not to mention 1854, and with each passing day the apocalypticism for which Rachel Carson has been criticized seems more and more justified by the facts. Moreover, the challenges of sustainability stem not so much from an absence of nonmarket values but from the problem of competing goods in an era of limited resources. Defining sustainability in terms of the "critical limits" involved in reaching ecological carrying capacity, rather than the "competing objectives" of social, economic, and ecological goals, only postpones the problem of how to reconcile those limits with human needs and desires (Farrell and Hart). Despite these difficulties, contemporary writers have shown that they still have a vital role to play in addressing the challenges of sustainability, including the pressing concern of climate change.

Although a full review of what might be called the "literature of sustainability" is beyond our purview, it is clear that coming to terms with these issues has required writers to extend the expansive sensibility of traditional nature writing even further than before. And while our focus here will remain on U.S.-based nonfiction prose writers, it is worth acknowledging that attention to sustainability has taken place in a wide range of genres around the world, including poetry, fiction, films, images, music, and other forms of popular culture. In addition, where critics of nature writing have faulted the genre for what they see as its naïve realism (Phillips), the emphasis of sustainability discourse has been less mimesis than politics, in the widest sense of the term: that is, the ways we organize our social lives together, for the benefit of ourselves and the wider world.

We might also see these developments less as a sharp break from the past than as a co-evolutionary response to and with broader changes in environmental thought. Thus while the signature elements of Thomas Lyon's taxonomy are still present, they, too, have expanded to involve personal experience, scientific information, and philosophical interpretation of our varied selves and cultures as they intertwine with a multiplicity of nonhuman natures, whatever and wherever they may be. As Jenny Price has written of the ways that nature writing may change in response to critiques of "nature": "The literature's powering question will become, rather, what nature is it? And then—how do we use nature? how do we change nature? how does nature react? How do we react back? how do we imagine nature? who uses and changes and imagines nature? and often the most important questions of all: how sustainably? how fairly? how well?" (230–31). Or, as Jason Cowley wrote in his editor's letter for the "New Nature Writing" issue of *Granta* (2008), the writers in this new generation "share a sense that we are devouring our world, that there is simply no longer any natural landscape or ecosystem that is unchanged by humans. But they don't simply want to walk into the wild, to rhapsodize and commune: they aspire to see with a scientific eye and write with literary effect" (9). That Houghton Mifflin Harcourt bundles "The Best American Science and Nature Writing" in one yearly package is but one more indication of how significant the findings of science have become to this literature.

Three broad areas seem to mark the terrain that interests these writers: rethinking our connection to the rest of the living world, rethinking our ideas of space and time, and rethinking the relationship of the individual to the community. Given that the defining motive of sustainability discourse is a concern for future generations, some of the most powerful book-length writing in this area has come from women who use their identity as mothers to inform, convince, and persuade their readers about the need for change. By exploring three of these works, I mean not to privilege heterosexual reproduction, nor to deny the significance of other perspectives on sustainability—whether male, non-white, queer, or differently abled—but simply to identify one common theme in the search for a more sustainable world.

In an age of invasive species, genetically modified organisms, and global pandemics, rethinking our connection to the rest of the living world could not be more urgent, and few writers have tackled this subject with more depth and elegance than Sandra Steingraber. Particularly in *Having Faith: An Ecologist's Journey to Motherhood* (2001)— her account of the pregnancy and birth of her daughter, Faith—Steingraber demonstrates the intricacy of what Stacy Alaimo calls our "trans-corporeality" (Alaimo 2010) by documenting our myriad connections to the biosphere. "When I became pregnant at age thirty-eight," Steingraber writes, "I realized, with amazement, that I myself had become a habitat. My womb was an inland ocean with a population of one" (ix). Exploring the effect of toxic chemicals on her developing fetus, the challenges of regulating these chemicals, and the limitations of a lifestyle approach to risk, Steingraber shows not only how "a woman's body is the first environment" but also that "if a mother's body is contaminated, so too is the child who inhabits it" (x). Interweaving poetic, character-driven scenes with her interpretation of scientific information for a non-specialist audience, Steingraber builds on the work of Rachel Carson and urges a precautionary approach to risk, in which the burden of proof "should rest with those seeking to conduct possible harmful activities—not with the public in demonstrating that harm has already occurred" (285).

In addition to exploring connections with the world outside of our bodies, contemporary writers have been rethinking ideas of space and time: expanding what constitutes "place" to include not merely wilderness landscapes, but urban, suburban, and even oceanic environments, as well as considering how global concerns, such as climate change, modify our sense of temporal continuity. Of the attempts by literary nonfiction writers to come to terms with climate change, Amy Seidl's *Early Spring: An Ecologist and Her Children Wake to a Warming World* (2009) stands out for its desire to make sense of these changes on a local, personal level. Unlike the globe-trotting journalism of Elizabeth Kolbert's *Field Notes from a Catastrophe* (2006) or the road-tripping travel writing of Bruce Stutz's *Chasing Spring: An American Journey Through a Changing Season* (2006), Seidl's approach is to stay home and watch for signs of temporal confusion in her Vermont backyard. While her title and structure explicitly echo those of Carson and Steingraber, Seidl's intentions are more modest: to stand witness to these changes, in the hope of inspiring action. Her conceit is that Carson's spring has turned out less silent than unseasonable: it now arrives several weeks early in New England. Acknowledging that her concerns "do not compare to the concerns of others whose lands have clearly crossed environmental thresholds," Seidl nevertheless seeks to map her own perceptions in the service of hastening the transition to a post-carbon world (157). "And given what I know about the world," Seidl adds, speaking of her daughter Celia, "my life also includes the responsibility of seeing that hers has a chance to unfold. For that to happen I must work to guarantee that the living systems she and I depend on are healthy, functioning, and thriving" (159).

Expanding our ideas of self, space, and time in these ways leads not only to a deeper sense of connectedness with the rest of the world but also to a richer understanding of what protecting "living systems" might entail. "Systems thinking" of this sort—making sense of what the National Science Foundation calls "coupled natural and human systems"—is one of the hallmarks of the sustainability movement, and writers in search of sustainability have also approached this subject by rethinking their relationship to the overlapping communities of which they are a part. This has involved a reconsideration of such ideas as the "ecological citizen," the "commons," and the "working landscape." Moreover, it has required an acknowledgment, as Kimberly N. Ruffin has written, of "gross differences in the human experience of citizenship" and "the ways in which the exploitation of humans and nonhumans are intertwined" (159).

One subject that has brought many of these themes together has been food, which requires us to see landscapes as having people in them, to attend to the role of work and class in producing our daily bread, and to recognize how politics and history have shaped all of these agricultural relationships. Food writing has a long history, of course, but its recent resurgence has everything to do with the rise of the sustainable food movement, which has been underway since at least the publication of Eric Schlosser's *Fast Food Nation* in 2001 (Pollan, "Food"). Barbara Kingsolver's *Animal, Vegetable, Miracle: A Year of Food Life* (2007), one of the many recent attempts to examine sustainable food from a first-person perspective, follows Kingsolver and her family as they attempt to eat locally for an entire year. Similar to Alisa Smith and J. B. MacKinnon's *Plenty: Eating Locally on the 100-Mile Diet* (2007), *Animal, Vegetable, Miracle* is notable for its humor and irony as much as for its fact-filled warnings about the dangers of industrial food production. As if in response to critics who have faulted nature writing for its "boundless purity and bloodless prose" (Zakin x), Kingsolver is both self-deprecating in admitting her own failings and amusing in describing such subjects as the challenges of turkey sex. Equally striking is the form of the book, in which Kingsolver's personal experiences and social reflections are interlaced with factual and scientific sidebars by her biologist husband, Steven L. Hopp, and chapter-ending meditations and recipes by her college-age daughter, Camille Kingsolver. As much homesteading handbook as food memoir, *Animal, Vegetable, Miracle* seeks ultimately to do the work all such writing attempts in the world: to help readers live in accord with ecological principles, seek justice in their dealings with others, and create truer forms of wealth, wherever their communities may be.

Such writing is not without its challenges, however, in both content and style. In terms of content, while it is easy to embrace the idea of sustainability, it is difficult to know exactly what actions will bring about a more sustainable future, given the complexities of global change. Should these relatively privileged authors have reduced their own environmental impacts by not having children, for example, rather than urging others to consume differently for the sake of their own offspring? Should they have focused their attention more on collective action rather than on changes to individual behavior? Should they have put more emphasis on market forces or technological solutions rather than on government reforms? In addition, for those cases in which we generally *can* agree on what to do, such as using less fossil fuel, even the most eloquent essayist may still have difficulty convincing readers to make the necessary changes, given the large number of barriers to action that exist, whether they be psychological, cultural, political, or economic.

Writing about sustainability also poses a host of stylistic questions. How much science can Steingraber include without putting her readers to sleep? How much emotion can Seidl provide without romanticizing her life? How much moralizing can Kingsolver advance without becoming insufferable? Of all of these writers, Kingsolver seems the most self-aware of her predicament, though that does not prevent her from sounding preachy at times. But while she doesn't shy away from promoting changes on both a national or global scale, such grand gestures are not her principal concern. As she writes in the concluding chapter of her book: "It's the worst of bad manners—and self-protection, I think, in a nervously cynical society—to ridicule the small gesture. These earnest efforts might just get us past the train-wreck of the daily news, or the anguish of standing behind a child, looking with her at the road ahead, searching out redemption where we can find it: recycling or carpooling or growing a garden or saving a species or *something*. Small, stepwise changes in personal habits aren't trivial. Ultimately they will, or won't, add up to having been the thing that mattered" (346). Whatever challenges remain for such writing, and no matter what it ends up being called, it remains of inestimable value to our world, if for no other reason than because it continues to challenge *us*.

NOTE

1. DDT is still used in the tropics to kill malarial mosquitoes. Its value, when impregnating mosquito nets for example, lies in the quality that alarmed Carson: its chemical stability.

WORKS CITED

Adamson, Joni, Mei Mei Evans, and Rachel Stein, eds. *The Environmental Justice Reader: Politics, Poetics, and Pedagogy*. Tucson: University of Arizona Press, 2002.

Alaimo, Stacy. *Bodily Natures: Science, Environment, and the Material Self*. Bloomington: Indiana University Press, 2010.

Armbruster, Karla, and Kathleen R. Wallace, eds. *Beyond Nature Writing: Expanding the Boundaries of Ecocriticism*. Charlottesville: University Press of Virginia, 2001.

Brooks, Paul. *Speaking for Nature: How Literary Naturalists from Henry Thoreau to Rachel Carson Have Shaped America*. Boston: Houghton Mifflin, 1980.

Buell, Lawrence. *The Environmental Imagination: Thoreau, Nature Writing, and the Formation of American Culture*. Cambridge, MA: Harvard University Press, 1995.

——. *The Future of Environmental Criticism: Environmental Crisis and Literary Imagination*. Malden, MA: Blackwell, 2005.

——. "Literature as Environmental(ist) Thought Experiment." *Ecology and the Environment: Perspectives from the Humanities*. Ed. Donald K. Swearer. Cambridge, MA: Center for the Study of World Religions, 2009. 21–36.

Carson, Rachel. *Silent Spring*. 1962. Intro. Al Gore. New York: Houghton Mifflin, 1994.

Cowley, Jason. "Editor's Letter: The New Nature Writing." *Granta 102* (2008): 7–12.

Cronon, William. "The Trouble with Wilderness; or, Getting Back to the Wrong Nature." *Uncommon Ground: Rethinking the Human Place in Nature*. New York: W. W. Norton, 1996. 69–90.

Dresner, Simon. *The Principles of Sustainability*. 2nd ed. Sterling, Va.: Earthscan, 2008.

Elder, John, ed. *American Nature Writers*. 2 vols. New York: Charles Scribner's Sons, 1996.

Farrell, Alex, and Maureen Hart. "What Does Sustainability Really Mean? The Search for Useful Indicators." *Environment 40.9* (Nov. 1998): 4–9, 26–31.

Farr, Moira. "The Death of Nature Writing." *Brick 47* (Winter 1993): 16–27.

Finch, Robert, and John Elder, eds. *The Norton Book of Nature Writing*. College edition. New York: W. W. Norton, 2002.

Fritzell, Peter A. *Nature Writing and America: Essays Upon a Cultural Type*. Ames: Iowa State University Press, 1990.

Heise, Ursula K. *Sense of Place and Sense of Planet: The Environmental Imagination of the Global*. New York: Oxford University Press, 2008.

Kingsolver, Barbara. *Animal, Vegetable, Miracle: A Year of Food Life*. New York: HarperCollins, 2007.

Kolbert, Elizabeth. *Field Notes from a Catastrophe: A Frontline Report on Climate Change*. London: Bloomsbury, 2012.

Krutch, Joseph Wood, ed. *Great American Nature Writing*. New York: William Sloane Associates, 1950.

Leopold, Aldo. *A Sand County Almanac and Sketches Here and There.* Illus. Charles W. Schwartz. New York: Oxford University Press, 1949.

Leopold, Aldo. "Game and Wildlife Conservation." *The River of the Mother of God and Other Essays.* Ed. Susan L. Flader and J. Baird Callicott. Madison: U of Wisconsin P, 1991. 164–68.

Litchman, Lori. "The Metamorphosis of the Nature Writer: The Movement of American Nature Writing from Pastoral to Environmental." *The Writer's Chronicle*, December 2009. Web.

Lyon, Thomas J. *This Incomparable Land: A Guide to American Nature Writing.* Minneapolis: Milkweed Editions, 2001.

Mazel, David. *American Literary Environmentalism.* Athens: University of Georgia Press, 2000.

McKibben, Bill. *The End of Nature.* New York: Random House, 1989.

Merchant, Carolyn. *The Death of Nature: Women, Ecology, and the Scientific Revolution.* San Francisco: Harper and Row, 1980.

More, Paul E. "A Hermit's Notes on Thoreau." *The Atlantic Monthly* 87.524 (June 1901): 857–64.

Morton, Timothy. *Ecology without Nature: Rethinking Environmental Aesthetics.* Cambridge, MA: Harvard University Press, 2007.

Murphy, Patrick D. *Farther Afield in the Study of Nature-Oriented Literature.* Charlottesville: University Press of Virginia, 2000.

Nordhaus, Ted, and Michael Shellenberger. *Break Through: From the Death of Environmentalism to the Politics of Possibility.* New York: Houghton Mifflin, 2007.

Phillips, Dana. *The Truth of Ecology: Nature, Culture, and Literature in America.* New York: Oxford University Press, 2003.

Pollan, Michael. "The Food Movement, Rising." *The New York Review of Books* 57.10 (10 June 2010). Web. http://www.nybooks.com/articles/archives/2010/jun/10/food-movement-rising/

Price, Jennifer. "Thirteen Ways of Seeing Nature in LA." *Land of Sunshine: An Environmental History of Metropolitan Los Angeles.* Ed. William Deverell and Greg Hise. Pittsburgh: University of Pittsburgh Press, 2005. 220–44.

Ruffin, Kimberly N. *Black on Earth: African American Ecoliterary Traditions.* Athens: University of Georgia Press, 2010.

Satterfield, Terre, and Scott Slovic, eds. *What's Nature Worth: Narrative Expressions of Environmental Values.* Salt Lake City: University of Utah Press, 2004.

Schlosser, Eric. *Fast Food Nation: The Dark Side of the All-American Meal.* New York: Houghton Mifflin, 2001.

Seidl, Amy. *Early Spring: An Ecologist and Her Children Wake to a Warming World.* Boston, MA: Beacon Press, 2010.

Slovic, Scott. "Epistemology and Politics in American Nature Writing: Embedded Rhetoric and Discrete Rhetoric." *Green Culture: Environmental Rhetoric in Contemporary America.* Ed. Carl G. Herndl and Stuart C. Brown. Madison: University of Wisconsin Press, 1996. 82–110.

Smith, Alisa, and J. B. MacKinnon. *Plenty: Eating Locally on the 100-Mile Diet.* New York: Three Rivers Press, 2007.

Steingraber, Sandra. *Having Faith: An Ecologist's Journey to Motherhood.* New York: Berkley Books, 2001.

Stutz, Bruce. *Chasing Spring: An American Journey Through a Changing Season.* New York: Scribner, 2008.

Thoreau, Henry David. *Walden.* 1854. Ed. J. Lyndon Shanley. Princeton, NJ: Princeton University Press, 1971.

Tiffin, Helen, and Graham Huggan. *Postcolonial Ecocriticism: Literature, Animals, Environment.* New York: Routledge, 2010.

Wapner, Paul. *Living Through the End of Nature: The Future of American Environmentalism*. Cambridge, MA: MIT Press, 2010.

Williams, Raymond. "Nature." *Keywords: A Vocabulary of Culture and Society*. New York: Oxford University Press, 1976.

Williams, Raymond. "Ideas of Nature." *Problems in Materialism and Culture: Selected Essays*. London: NLB, 1980. 67–85.

Zakin, Susan, ed. *Naked: Writers Uncover the Way We Live on Earth*. New York: Four Walls Eight Windows, 2004.

CHAPTER 23

....

ENVIRONMENTAL WRITING FOR CHILDREN

A Selected Reconnaissance of Heritages, Emphases, Horizons

....

LAWRENCE BUELL

STORIES for children about encounters with the physical environment surely long pre-date the invention of childhood itself as a distinct life-stage in the post-Enlightenment West, judging from what can be pieced together about ancient storytelling practices. In the twenty-first century, oral storytelling cultures continue to thrive worldwide, in (sub)urban bourgeois families as well as more traditional cultures, but they have been supplemented increasingly by print and other media. The field is so vast that no one can pretend to know more than a fraction of it. For ecocriticism the challenge is compounded by the glaring asymmetry between the inherent importance and richness of the archive and the movement's overwhelming emphasis thus far on for-adult genres. Happily the prospect looks much brighter than it did a dozen years ago (e.g., Dobrin and Kidd, Gaard, Leznik-Oberstein, Sigler, Wagner-Lawlor, among others), but the archive as a whole is still largely *terra incognita*.

The broad-brushstrokes reconnaissance attempted here falls into two unequal parts. The first and longer section identifies selected representative topoi or traditions emanating from the so-called golden age of children's writing in the late Victorian era. Then follows a briefer review of trend-lines during the past half-century or so.

1

....

As an admittedly schematic but I hope sufficiently flexible way of charting in short form the rise of modern (Western) environmentally oriented children's literature, this section focuses on the permutations of two overlapping topoi that have served as carriers of environmental concern since the late nineteenth century. That my examples are almost exclusively Anglophone is, I hope, more a comment on the limits of my expertise than an overstatement of the pervasiveness of the formations described.

The first body of writing I'll discuss purports to imagine nonhuman life-worlds from the standpoint of the creatures themselves, generally not as a realm of absolute difference but as a parallel universe reflecting back upon the human, often featuring interaction with human actors. Such writing leans heavily on the ancient talking animal convention and other stratagems that semi-anthropomorphize its fictive nonhumans but in the process also at least implicitly chides human insouciance and cruelty toward other creatures, lodging thereby a moral extensionist claim that humans should take the interests and welfare of other creatures more greatly into account, sometimes to the point of envisioning human (children) themselves as fellow animals (v. Lesnik-Oberstein, Morgenstern). Well-known examples include Anna Sewell's *Black Beauty* (1877)—the "Uncle Tom's Cabin of the horse" as it was called in its own day (Dingley 290); Beatrix Potter's *Tale of Peter Rabbit* (1902); Kenneth Grahame's *Wind in the Willows* (1908); Felix Salten's *Bambi* (1923) and the Disney films thereof; E. B. White's *Charlotte's Web* (1952); and Richard Adams's *Watership Down* (1972).

The second body of writing I'll take up constellates around the discovery or construction of special, often hidden outdoor places by children that are shown to have catalytic significance in bonding them to the natural environment and beyond that, by implication at least, in identity-formation over the long run, such that natural environment comes to feel a catalytic agent and crucial ingredient of personal being. Early examples include Ernest Thompson Seton's *Two Little Savages* (1903), whose lonely immigrant boy protagonist, first alone and then with a companion, becomes increasingly at home and proficient in woodsy ways, in tandem with which the episodic plot is made to do double duty as a kind of ancillary Boy Scout manual, with lessons in camping and woodcraft that include illustrated directions on how to build, hunt, recognize species, prepare food, and so on. (Seton was a co-founder of the movement who eventually resigned in protest against its increasingly paramilitary character.) More enduringly famous have been the Mowgli stories in Kipling's *The Jungle Book* (1994), Romulus-and-Remus tales about a lad nurtured as a wolf-cub, indeed perhaps the single most influential text of the Euro-colonial era in transposing Enlightenment-era fascination with the figure of the "wild child" to the imperial periphery; and Frances Hodgson Burnett's *The Secret Garden,* in which the *hortis conclusis* tradition—the enclosed garden as sacred and/or amatory space—meets the Brontë sisters, as it were. (Two unloved and deeply neurotic young cousins achieve psychic and physical healing through the delights of discovering and helping to regenerate the walled garden on a lonely Yorkshire estate locked up for a decade after the boy's mother's death, partly through the kindly ministrations of a local third child, an innocently Pan-like liminal figure with uncanny powers of rapport with wildlife and plants.) Maurice Sendak's *Where the Wild Things Are* (1963), which transports little Max from bedroom tantrum to an exotic jungly setting for a "wild rumpus" with a troupe of ferocious-looking but convivial beasties whom he subdues, seems a direct descendant of *The Jungle Book* and other colonial-era narrative sorties into faraway places. Two latter-day descendants of *The Secret Garden*—also including poignant themes of trauma and grieving for death of loved ones–are Katherine Paterson's *Bridge to Terabithia* (1978), which turns on a young boy and girl creating a Narnia-like kingdom in the woods near home, and Bev Doolittle/Elise Maclay's *The Earth Is My Mother* (2000), a more explicitly environmental-*ist* fiction in which an eleven-year old girl helps to preserve from being developed into a resort her own special place, which was also her late mother's special place, a pristine nearby canyon.

By singling out these two constellations or topoi, I do not mean to suggest that they are hermetically self-contained or homogenous or that they provide a comprehensive taxonomy of the juvenile environmental imaginary during the century in question. The whole expanse of literature for children with some sort of environmental tinge to it is more accurately conceived in terms of multiple projects with porous borders that allow for interpeneration more often than not. Nor is this whole domain more amenable to tidy demarcation *qua* "children's writing" than the categories of "juvenile" and "adult" literature in general. Ever since its 1884 publication, readers have debated whether Mark Twain's *Huckleberry Finn* should be thought of as a book for children; and such texts as Daniel Defoe's *Robinson Crusoe* and James Fenimore Cooper's *The Last of the Mohicans* written for the adult market later became for a long time mainly devoured by youth, only to become *de facto* reclassified again as they became *passé* for the common reader and fell increasingly to the custody of literary academics. Indeed even the vast body of literature unmistakably targeted to juvenile readership criss-crosses generational lines in being adult-world refractions of what grownups suppose children are, want, need, as Jacqueline Rose has shown in *The Case of Peter Pan*, whose various excerptings and retellings make it an especially tangled *exemplum* of both authorial intent and readerly desire.

At all events, the two constellations here identified may make a serviceable base of operations for closer examination of some key emphases in more or less environmentally oriented children's writing in its early modern stages of development in the Europhone west, and all the more so because of the ostensible contrast they showcase between texts featuring animal protagonists and texts featuring human ones.

These hedging qualifiers "more or less environmentally oriented" and "ostensible contrast" are chosen advisedly in order to anticipate two complications. First, few of these books pursue overtly environmentalist agendas as primary concerns; and, relatedly, the other-than-human domains most of them conjure up are easily read as allegories of the human estate—indeed quite understandably so, to the extent that all of them, like the great majority of all expressive art directed at children both modern and ancient, have strong didactic thrusts. Consider those two rabbit books. *The Tale of Peter Rabbit* is transparently construable as a bad-boy story in animal drag, and as such a slightly more indulgent avatar of Mother Goose ditties like "The Three Little Kittens"—a droll affectionate-cautionary tale about the mishaps that befall wayward children who stray from the dictates of maternal prudence. Potter's illustrations, which show Peter in his panicky escape from Mr. McGregor's garden having to shed his human clothes and revert, as it were, to the bestial state, reinforce the suspicion that this story isn't really about animals but rather an animal fable: that the prototype for Peter is the boy who naughtily goes feral. If animal stories have been a staple of children's eco-writing partly in reflection of adult propensity to see little children as animal-like, then one might expect them also to build in takeaway warnings against being or remaining too much so. So understood, *The Tale of Peter Rabbit* recalls the dictum of Canadian animal-story writer Charles G. D. Roberts that such stories appeal to interest in "the field of animal psychology" to the end of freeing readers from "the mean tenement of self of which we do well to grow weary" without "requiring that we at the same time return to barbarism" (28, 29). Roberts here presupposes an *adult* audience, of course, but that he commends literary enlistment of scientific empiricism in such a way as to re-draw the line of separation between human and animal "barbarism" is telling for Potter as well. Both her barnyard tales and his *Kindred of the Wild* (1902) follow Charles Darwin's analyses of human-animal kinship in *The Descent of Man* and *The Expression of the Emotions in Man and Animals* so as partially to compensate for *Origin of Species*'s unsettling deliquescence of species borderlines, by contending both for the presence of emotion and cognition among higher animals and for the superiority of even the least advanced human races (Crist 11–50).

Our other rabbit saga, Richard Adams's *Watership Down,* offers a fuller immersion in lapine natural history than Potter's short-form cottage-garden yarn. Although she had far and away the more rigorous formal training in natural science than he, Adams makes much more of a show of documenting—however accurately—rabbit sociology at ground level: how they feed; how they negotiate darkness, rain, cold, animal predators, and human encroachments; how they oscillate between passive and aggressive, between focus and feckless distraction; their sense of distance and perspective, and so forth. Yet it also makes perfect sense that critics have tended to treat the ordeal of the fugitive rabbit band's trek from its soon-to-be-destroyed original warren through the ordeal of establishing a new, safer, and thriving one less as an attempted rendition of the life-world of rabbitry than as Tolkeinesque fantasy and/or morphed rendition of traditional epic or saga (e.g., Kitchell, Bridgman). In many ways, the novel positively begs to be read allegorically: through its chapter epigraphs—most of them from canonical literature, philosophy, and religion; then by scripting the plot as quest narrative, in which the score of main actors all have proper names and highly individuated personalities; and by endowing rabbit culture with a sense of cultural tradition, complete with a complex body of myth and legend that several of the band are adept at spinning into trickster tales at crucial points.

But none of the anthropomorphizing in either rabbit tale, keeps either from successfully creating a counter-space for dramatizing the threat posed to animals by human incursion. As such, even *Peter Rabbit,* though *Watership Down* to a much greater extent, reads like an anticipatory response to nature writer Barry Lopez's call in 1983 to "renegotiat[e] the contracts" between modern humankind and animals. Lopez not only mourns the attenuation of existential contact between modern westerners and animals that historian Keith Thomas chronicles in *Man and the Natural World* but also argues further that such loss of intimacy has diminished the horizon of human possibility itself, by which he means both the sense of "awe and mystery that animals excite" and the sense of the plurality of other life-worlds beyond just the human that coexist "as part of a coherent and shared landscape" and might—if only modern humans again paid proper attention and respect to their complexities—help to "revive us as a species" (Lopez 384, 386). The increasingly respectful attention paid during the quarter century since this essay appeared to the significance of the mental and also ethical capacities of animals in a range of fields from primatology and philosophy shows that "Renegotiating the Contracts" was much more than the pipe dream of one solitary freelance literary neoprimitivist.

The counter-model Lopez specifically had in mind is First Peoples' greater existential proximity to animal worlds and how that sense of coexistence and reciprocity enriches their vision of what it means to exist humanly, as shown in their place-based storytelling practices. So arguably the neo-aboriginal children's writing of which I take brief note in the next section—drawing *inter alia* upon the Afro-diasporic tales of trickster rabbits that Joel Chandler Harris pilfered for his Uncle Remus tales (*v.* Mungoshi 7–25)—makes a better fit for his diagnostic than the two books I have been discussing. But it's all the more important on that account not to stint the import of even nominal attempts like *Peter Rabbit* to renegotiate the human-animal contract by table-turning. *Bambi* makes a particularly striking analogue. Both the Felix Salten novel and the Disney film adaptations rest on egregiously *faux* natural history. Yet *Bambi*'s melodrama of creatures of the forest as noble savages besieged by human predator-destroyers has made an impact on the Western cultural imaginary hardly short of Rachel Carson's *Silent Spring* (Mittman). Witness the phobic reaction of the sport-hunting industry, which in the mid-twentiethth century and maybe still today looks on *Bambi* as the worst disaster that ever befell it (Cartmill).

Among the early literature that keeps its eye most resolutely on the issue of animal ethics even as it makes free use of fantasy elements is Anna Sewell's *Black Beauty*. This is the first enduring classic of "humanitarian" reform, which gave rise to the Society for the Protection of Cruelty to Animals and other like organizations, and as such is a forerunner both of contemporary animal rights advocacy and the pro-animal fictions of which J. M. Coetzee's *The Lives of Animals* and *Elizabeth Costello* stand out as perhaps the most-discussed texts in world literature today. *Black Beauty* is a shrewd rewriting of the then-fashionable declensionary plot of Zola-esque naturalist fiction *à la* Upton Sinclair's *The Jungle* or Frank Norris's *Vandover and the Brute,* which turns on the fall of a precariously secure person or family into a vortex of animal misery usually leading to death. *Black Beauty* undertakes the analogous thought experiment of imagining how literal beasts might experience their own bestialization as they become exploited as playthings or work slaves. Admittedly, this early chapter of animal rights history involved some distinctly problematic ideological compromises. The good faith of the whole Victorian humanitarian movement itself has been questioned by historians who read it as a displacement of gentry-class fears about the much more socially explosive immiseration of human underclasses that often involved a blame-the-victim strategy in the form of stigmatizing drovers and other working class abusers of domestic animals as uncivilized brutes (Turner). *Black Beauty* exemplifies this in its longish section deploring abusive hackney drivers. Yet it offsets this classism both by putting rich and poor humans pretty much on the same level overall in respect to sensitivity or lack thereof to equine feelings and welfare, and by subjecting class hierarchies themselves to intermittent critique, as by having the noblest of all the book's working poor killed off by his own generosity toward an unworthy patron—thereby consigning Black Beauty to a series of increasingly dreadful masters who nearly do him in as well.

What clinches a secure and happy ending for him is especially telling in present context. The mentee of the groom previously established as the human character who best understands horses just happens to cross paths with Black Beauty and recognizes him despite his almost-fatally degraded condition. As a plot device, it's the flimsiest of Dickensian coincidences, but as a thematization of how intimate knowledge of and acculturation to the lives of animals can pay off crucially at the level of environmental memory it showcases the promise of renegotiating the contracts, in Lopez's phrase, across species lines. The now-grown-up little Joe Green, who as an inexperienced stable boy had mistreated Black Beauty at first, now confirms his mature humanity through this scene of recognition. The act of recognition is the outward sign of the fruits of an adult lifetime of commitment to grasping the ways of horses so as to be able to distinguish even after many years and despite drastically changed appearances the individual creature from the rest of the species. Just as with *Uncle Tom's Cabin, Black Beauty* seeks to enlist its readers as secondary witness to the protagonist's trauma narrative, so as to instill in them by force of sympathy a kind of surrogate memory of how animals experience suffering.

The redemption of little Joe Green anticipates our second constellation: literature that turns on crucial episodes of children bonding to cherished outdoor niches. Books of such kind highlight a type of experience that developmental psychologists have confirmed as being formative of adult identity. Edith Cobb's *The Ecology of Imagination in Childhood* (1977), which argued for a correlation between exceptional adult creativity and reported experiences of having bonded to special outdoor play-spaces during middle childhood (between infancy and adolescence), has been broadly if not uniformly confirmed by the more empirical research of such recent psychologists as Louise Chawla (Chawla 1986, 1990) and Peter Kahn, Jr. Kahn's fieldwork is additionally remarkable for its discovery of broadly similar biophilic receptivity across different habitats and cultures: African American kids in Houston, Lusophone kids both in Lisbon and the Brazilian outback, white middle-class children in the United States. The vast archive of post-romantic autobiographical literature for adults from Wordsworth to Thoreau to Mary Austin and John Muir down to latter-day fiction and life-writing by men and women across color and country lines further testifies to this, even in cases where the special place in question is far from pristine but, on the contrary, almost overshadowed by urban encroachment or even toxified.

Children's literature of this kind maps almost perfectly onto both the canonical-literary and the psychological archives. David Sobel's *Children's Special Places: Exploring the Role of Forts, Dens, and Bush Houses in Middle Childhood* (1993) makes no mention of Ernest

Thompson Seton, but it provides an uncannily precise retrospective gloss on the delight shown by Yan and (later on) also his friend Sam in sleuthing out, camping, and building huts and wigwams in secret outdoor near-home niches.

As with our first constellation, it's possible to read this literature in less environment-centric terms than I propose here, as incipient *Bildungsroman*, such that the dimension of environmental bonding seems ancillary to the main business of growing up and presumably away from the intense bonding-with-nature phase. Even though the plot of *The Secret Garden* centers on the discovery of the garden and the transformative delight and healing (both physical and psychic) that accrues to the children through their connection with it, it can be read as directed rather in the long run more toward the socialization of Mary and Colin into proper Victorian/Imperial gentlefolk, especially as Colin emerges toward the end of the novel to assert his place as inheritor of the estate (*v.* Phillips). From this standpoint, the garden diminishes into a symbolic transitional object that brings Mary, Colin, and his equally wounded father together in family solidarity *via* their mutual bond around the memory of the lost mother whose own favorite place this was. Garden cultivation equals retrieval of the lost mother-figure. All this comports with earlier eighteenth- and nineteenth-century moral tales for children where gardens figure prominently as scenes of instruction (Smith), tales that typify more broadly the difference between the (even) more strongly didactic, often tractarian, cast of pre-Romantic writing for children—much more committed than the texts this essay discusses to conceiving children as adults-to-be than in childhood as a distinct life-stage with its own special claims and privileges. So too the most explicitly environmentalist text named so far: *The Earth Is My Mother*. It goes way beyond *The Secret Garden* in identifying eleven-year old Sarah Stewart's late mother flatly with Mother Earth and culminates in her receiving the first-ever presidential "Eco-Hero" award for efforts on behalf of wilderness protection. Yet *The Earth* scripts the president's message at the award ceremony not as a call to save the earth but rather as a much more generalized tribute to heroic persistence: individual people, including kids "can make a difference" and that it's "important not to give up" in the face of "failure and disappointments" (Doolittle and MacKay 174–75).

On the other hand, the story also makes it quite clear that Sarah's perspective is much more place-connected than is the president's. So we side at our peril with his version—and with a generic *Bildungsroman* reading of the book as a whole. The same claim might be lodged in different measure for the other books in this constellation as well. If you try to read through or against the emphasis on environmental construction of personal identity, you do so at peril. To return to *The Secret Garden*, the garden's uncanny charisma cannot be reduced to the ghost of the missing mother, or to some generic theory of the lure of secrecy or uncanniness, or to a symbolic inner sanctum of class privilege that unlocks Colin's realization of what it means to be the Young Rajah. Whether you take environment as the decisive factor or as part of an eclectic mix, *Secret Garden* is irrepressibly a book about biophilia—the power of active interaction with the living earth (birds, flowers, trees, and animals) to reshape human being, particularly at the impressionable life-stage of the two cousins, both aged ten. This gets dramatized not only by the sheer delight they take in the garden and its effect of that on their mental and physical health, but by showing them upfront in a pre-garden default stage of ecophobic hostility to the landscape of the Yorkshire moors that's symptomatic of their extreme self-centeredness, and then later on by putting them both–especially Mary–in fascinated awe of the slightly older local lad, Dickon, who models a magically intimate relation with the natural world, as if he were "a sort of robin without beak or feathers" (Burnett 152).

Burnett's *ex cathedra* pronouncements suggest that the novel congealed from an array of different biographical strands that included mourning for a son who died young, flirtation with the mind-cure doctrines of Christian Science, and a Dickon-like personal experience of summertime rapport with a particular English robin. Especially salient, however, was a lifelong passion for gardens that began, tellingly, in her own middle childhood with "a small bed in the centre of the few yards of iron-railed front garden before a house in an old square in the ugliest, smokiest factory town to be found anywhere in all the North of England" (Burnett 209).

The juvenile literature of middle childhood encounters with special outdoor places is too diverse to permit unitary generalization about the degree of importance accorded the E-factor in their relative conceptions of child development. Sendak's *Where the Wild Things Are* implies that if little Max is not to be eaten up by those wild beasties that love him so, they must eventually be exorcised. As such it reads almost like a textbook exemplification of Freud's theory of the relation between *poesis* and daydreaming: through the vicarity of imagination you can indulge, as in dreams, the lure of the impossible, the dangerous, the forbidden, but in a harmless fashion that leaves you in your armchair and concealed from public view. Kipling's composition of the Mowgli stories for the *Jungle Book* performed the obverse, in that the author's vision for the boy-protagonist evidently began with an earlier tale about him being absorbed as a young man into colonial society. "As Kipling wrote his way 'backward' into Mowgli's infancy and development," notes one scholar, the trope of the wild child takes over and "steers the narrative toward disruption" of that anterior closure (Hotchkiss 436). In *Two Little Savages*, the episodes, yarns, and woodcraft lore keep accumulating and the boys never do mature. But such divergences—only to be expected from individual tales that build from a very general template—hardly undermine these stories' aggregate testimony to the generative, or regenerative, impact of imagined contact with outdoor places in the fashioning of personal identity.

With ever-larger percentages of earthlings dwelling in metropolitan areas and with increasingly strict controls being put–for middle class children, anyhow–on foraging at will in the outdoors, an increasing concern being voiced in public discourse is fear of what environmental journalist Richard Louv calls "nature-deficit disorder," or malformation of adult identity arising from curtailment of children's roaming about and exploration of wild places, such as this author and his peers allegedly did with much greater freedom. Literature for children that turns on the crucial impact of bonding to outdoor places in middle childhood, presents itself as an anticipatory response to such concern by providing a kind of "prosthetic memory" (cf. Landsberg) that might partway offset the effects of what Peter Kahn, Jr., terms "generational environmental amnesia" (Kahn 2002: 113 and *passim*). Conceivably this mordant diagnosis of generational slippage under the regime of industrial modernity–each generation starts with more diminished expectations of environmental salubrity that become the new "normal"—may be skewed by a certain nostalgia factor, such as Raymond Williams identifies at the start of *The Country and the City,* that is, the chronic assumption that the last generation lived closer to nature than the one before, traced by Williams all the way back to the time of the Norman conquest. Nor, so far as I know, have experimental psychologists thus far empirically measured the long-term impact of outdoor contact on a child's psychic development as precisely as (for example) it *has* been empirically demonstrated that convalescence from illness or surgery is facilitated by contact with nature, or even images thereof (Ulrich, Sternberg). But the evidence for biophilia, — that is, human responsiveness to nonhuman beings—and for middle childhood's susceptibility to this and to place imprints generally, does seem increasingly probable (Kellert), suggesting that the persistence of the theme in children's environmental writing is no fluke. So there would seem to be truth as well as poetry to Wallace Stegner's insistence that if you "expose a child to a particular environment" between the ages of five and twelve and "he will perceive in the shapes of that environment until he dies" (Stegner 21).

To dwell so long on my two chosen constellations of practice and to treat them as persisting over time is to risk legitimate objection to my own ethics of critical practice. I threaten to leave a false impression that the basic structural templates for children's environmental literature were permanently forged by western (specifically Anglo-American) writers over a century ago and to misrepresent the variegation and internal dissonances of practice and of environmental(ist) ideology, especially during the past half century. The next, briefer section will briefly attempt to begin to redress that imbalance.

Any impression given above of sustained ideological homogeneity, even within Europhone children's environmental literature, will be quickly dispelled with another pair of well-known examples: Kenneth Grahame's *The Wind in the Willows* (1908)—like *The Secret Garden* a text of the Edwardian era–and *The Lorax* (1970) by Theodore Geisel (aka Dr. Seuss), the first significant expression in children's literature of the radicalization of the U.S. environmentalist agenda in the 1960s.

Both books actually share a common project: to confront the disruptions of industrial modernization and attendant seductions of consumer culture at their respective historical moments, though their executions of that project starkly differ. For *Wind in the Willows,* published at the dawn of the automotive age, the disruptions take the form of the seriocomic mishaps of Mr. Toad's motor mania and his capricious, out-of-control spendthrift propensities as unworthy scion and heir. *The Lorax* does so far more soberly, through the Once-ler's rueful story of his rapacious deforestation and pollution of what had once been a pristine environment, and moralistic denunciations by the Lorax, who looms up as a far more monitorial superego than his closest counterpart in *Wind in the Willows,* Mr. Badger. The telltale mark of the stark contrast between the Edwardian and post–Rachel Carsonish *epistèmes* is of course that *Wind in the Willows* can see its way toward the unambiguous restitution of an even more idyllic order than it evokes at the start by keeping runaway modernization at bay on the one side and on the other side the threat to the appealingly civil animal protagonists posed by the more feral denizens of the wildwood. The "simple pastoral" myth of an unruffled middle landscape of coun-tryside nestled between city and wilderness gets unequivocally reaffirmed (Marx). *The Lorax,* by contrast, offers no more than the faintest ray of hope that the devastation of *its* once-idyllic landscape can be reversed. The rhetoric of *Willows* works to gratify the desire for a felicitous space into which the reader can settle snugly, like Mole delightedly rediscovering his old burrow with the aid of Rat's ministrations. *The Lorax* really sticks it to its readers, especially in the final twist of having the Once-ler throw the burden entirely on the child-listener to solve the world's environmental problems by planting the very last Truffula seed in existence.

This rhetorical shift might be construed in part merely as a more extreme than average variation to be expected within modern children's writing generally between entertain-ment and instruction. (Both books have been chided for going to extremes, Grahame for complacent embrace of a classist *status quo,* Seuss for gratuitous doom-crying) (*v.* Grahame, Lerer introduction; Marshall).But *The Lorax*'s militant environmentalism, though atypical of Seuss—it's by far the most preachy of his books—is also historically symptomatic in auguring a greater pervasiveness of overt environmentalism in sub-sequent children's writing, especially during the past two decades. "New and increas-ingly activist books that reflect environmental concerns are published yearly," one critic noted in 1994 (Sigler 151), probably by no coincidence on the eve of the first major con-ference (1995) of the then-new Association for the Study of Literature and Environment (ASLE). Today, children's literature looks more green-conscious than ever. Since 2005, for instance, the Newton Marasco Foundation has been issuing annual Green Earth Book Awards in three categories: picture book, children's fiction (middle child-hood), and young adult (http://www.newtonmarascofoundation.org). The 2010 win-ners include S. Terrell French's novel *Operation Redwood*—in which an urban biracial (Chinese/American) boy and his Chicano friend team up with the daughter from a backcountry farming family to conduct a (successful) children's tree-sitting cam-paign to save the neighboring grove that his nasty businessman uncle has targeted for clear-cutting; and Saci Lloyd's *Carbon Diaries: 2015,* a London-based global warming fiction featuring a teenage girl's struggles to cope with the extreme weather and dra-conian carbon rationing regime that threaten to destroy her dysfunctional family and unstable neighborhood.

The surge of new environmentally concerned writing for children would take a book in itself to itemize, let alone appraise. Yet some generalizations can be ventured. First, environmental(ist) agenda by no means automatically equates to counter-hegemonic position-taking across the board. *Operation Redwood* for instance invokes the mem-ory of Earth First! and condones lawbreaking in selected circumstances; but closure comes when Julian's granny, the fairy godmother–like alpha-matriarch parent of the evil uncle, intervenes to forestall and reengineer the board of directors' fateful plan.

An environmentalist agenda, whether traditionally preservationist as here, or futur-
ologically apocalyptic as in *Carbon Diaries 2015,* or responsive to (say) animal rights
or environmental justice concerns as in Dav Pilkey's kids-save-the-turkeys picture
book *'Twas the Night Before Thanksgiving* (1990) and Abenaki writer Joseph Bruchac's
Trail-of-Tears novel *The Journal of Jesse Smoke: A Cherokee Boy* (2001), will often
incorporate some quite conventional elements, such as affirmation of heteronormative family values (first three books especially, despite salience of a major gay character
in *Carbon Diaries* and "blended"-family tension in *Operation Redwood*) or the virtues
of individual striving and gumption (books one, two, and four). Second, and related,
the sense of urgency surrounding eco-didactic agendas of whatever sort in contemporary children's literature may easily be contained by such pleasurable elements as
adventuresome plotlines, enticing illustrations, and upbeat closure. In taking note of
such matters, ecocritics have by turns deplored the containment of ecocritique within
normalizing constraints (e.g., Sturgeon) and taken a more hopeful view of the positive
potential of its progressive elements fora positive "ecopedagogy" (e.g., Gaard). Both
the characteristically strong didactic cast of much children's literature, environmental
or otherwise, and differences of critical opinion about what both environmental and
ecocritical agendas should be, we may expect such divergent assessments to continue
indefinitely.

Third, the likelihood that some tempering of nonnormative eco-dissidence in children's literature will continue to persist seems confirmed by another development
that deserves far more discussion than I can give it here: the rise of what might be
called cultural survival literature for children around the theme of intimacy between
humans and the natural world by first peoples and other postcolonial authors around
the world: for example, the late Oodgeroo Nunukul's *Dreamtime* (1972), a collection of Australian aboriginal stories by one of the major figures in the contemporary
aboriginal literary renaissance; *The Girl Who Married the Moon: Tales from Native
North America* (1994), a collaboration between Bruchac and Cherokee storyteller
Gayle Ross; *The Story of Colors (La historia de los colores)* by Zapatista Subcomandante
Marcos; Zimbabwean Charles Mungoshi's *One Day, Long Ago: More Stories from a
Shona Childhood* (1991); and *The People Who Hugged Trees* (1990), by Deborah Lee
Rose, an adaptation of the Indian folktale that stands behind the grassroots Chipko
movement instigated by Indian activists in modern times (*v.* Platt). All these texts
in one way or another both seek to displace the baleful legacy of the Eurocentric
speaking-for-the-native tradition in which several of the texts discussed in section one
are complicit. The potential difference such emergent writing can sometimes make
is made clear by such works of comparative diagnostic appraisal as Clare Bradford's
Unsettling Narratives: Postcolonial Readings of Children's Literature (2007) and Doris
Seale and Beverly Slapin's *A Broken Flute* (2005). Seale and Slapin offer a cornucopia of
meticulous and pointed reviews of recent texts about Native American experience by
both white and Native writers, emphasizing in no uncertain terms that Native-written
works have generally addressed specific episodes in the shocking history of genocide,
displacement, forced assimilation, and the like much more candidly and accurately

(29–83 and *passim*). Yet contemporary indigenous and other postcolonial children's writing is by no means a protest literature unequivocally. In the aforementioned works by Oogderoo, Marcos, and Mungoshi, enchanting stories of animal agents and traditional human lives led close to nature combine with enticing illustrations to produce neoprimordialist effects that cater to exoticist wish-fulfillment more than they unsettle. In these and many other books like them, the demands of the global book market together with a predictable prudence about immersing juvenile readers in too many gory details make for considerably more euphemized presentations than, say, the *Märchen* sanitized in the fairy tales of the brothers Grimm (which later retellings have tended to euphemize further for polite consumption).

Fourth and finally, as the contrast between the landscapes of *The Wind and the Willows* and *The Lorax* indicates, the continued evocation of premodern community and relatively natural landscapes in children's literature by first worlders and first peoples alike must also be understood against the background of the accelerating (sub)urbanization during the past hundred years, as the majority of the world's human inhabitants have come to live in metropolitan areas. This has left its own mark on the represented environment(s) of children's literature, tilting it in a more urbanized and increasingly also downright pro-urban direction. This story begins with urban sprawl books of the mid-twentieth century, such as Virginia Lee Burton's *The Little House* (1942), about a cute little cottage in the country that gradually gets engulfed by the encroaching city but at the end gets happily moved back into the country again. This kind of story is still being reprised, as in Jeannie Baker's Australian counterpart, *Window* (1991), which features a family driven to relocate to a more rustic spot after their countrified dwelling gets engulfed, only to find the whole process starting over again. But arguably more fitting for the twenty-first century are texts like *Popville*, by Anouck Boisrobert and Louis Rigaud (2010), a pop-up book that tracks urban growth in an inviting reader-friendly manner; or Christoph Niemann's *Subway* (2010), another book for the very young designed make the potentially scary experience of underground travel appealing to kids. Altogether, children's literature of the future seems at least as likely to treat cityscape as livable habitat as in the dystopian terms of *Carbon Diaries 2015* and its still more frightening sequel *Carbon Diaries 2017.* At the same time, it seems no less certain that the proportion of future eco-writing for children, whatever its tradeoffs between anodyne soothing and provocative ecoconsciousness-raising, will continue to build upon the intensified self-consciousness of the expanding menu of contemporary environmental *problems* that such books as *The Little House* and especially *The Lorax* first sought to bring to consciousness.[1]

NOTE

1.   Previous versions of this paper were presented at fora at the University of Toronto and Indiana University, whose members I thank for their candid and illuminating comments. My sincere thanks to Rachel Levy for indispensable research assistance throughout the process of writing and revision.

Works Cited

Adams, Richard. *Watership Down*. New York: Macmillan, 1972.

Baker, Jeannie. *Window*. New York: Greenwillow, 1991.

Boisrobert, Anouck, and Louis Rigaud. *Popville*. New York: Roaring Brook, 2010.

Bradford, Clare. *Unsettling Narratives: Postcolonial Readings of Children's Literature*. Waterloo, Ont: Wilfrid Laurier UP, 2007.

Bridgman, Joan. "The Significance of 'Myth' in Watership Down," *Journal of the Fantastic in the Arts*, *6.1* (21): 7–24.

Bruchac, Joseph. *The Journal of Jesse Smoke: A Cherokee Boy: The Trail of Tears, 1838*. New York: Scholastic, 2001.

Bruchac, Joseph, and Gayle Ross. *The Girl Who Married the Moon: Tales from Native North America*. Golden, CO: Fulcrum, 1994.

Burnett, Frances Hodgson. *The Secret Garden*. (1911) Ed. Gretchen Holbrook Gerzina. New York: Norton, 2006.

Burton, Virginia Lee. *The Little House*. Boston: Houghton, 1942.

Caduto, Michael J., and Joseph Bruchac. *Keepers of the Earth: Narive American Stories and Environmental Activities for Children*. Golden, CO: Fulcrum, 1988.

Cartmill, Matt. *A View to Death in the Morning: Hunting and Nature Through History*. Cambridge MA: Harvard UP, 1993.

Chawla, Louise. "The Ecology of Environmental Memory," *Children's Environments Quarterly*, 3.4 (1986): 34–42.

——. "Ecstatic Places," *Children's Environments Quarterly*, 7.4 (1990): 18–23.

Crist, Eileen. *Images of Animals: Anthropomorphism and Animal Mind*. Philadelphia: Temple UP, 1999.

Cobb, Edith. *The Ecology of Imagination in Childhood*. NY: Columbia UP, 1977.

Dingley, Robert. "A Horse of a Different Color: Black Beauty and the Pressures of Indebtedness," *Victorian Literature and Culture*, 25 (1997): 241–51.

Dobrin, Sidney I., and Kenneth B. Kidd, ed. *Wild Things*. Detroit: Wayne State UP, 2004.

Doolittle, Bev, and Elisa Mackay. *The Earth Is My Mother*. Shelton, CT: Greenwich Workshop, 2000.

Freud, Sigmund. "Creative Writers and Day-Dreaming." (1908). *The Standard Edition of the Complete Psychological Works of Sigmund Freud*. Trans. and gen ed. James Strachey. London: Hogarth Press, 1959. 9: 141–53.

French, S. Terrell. *Operation Redwood*. New York: Amulet Books, 2009.

Gaard, Greta. "Toward an Ecopedagogy of Children's Environmental Literature," *Green Theory and Praxis: The Journal of Ecopedagogy*, 4.2 (2008): 11–24. Rpt. as "Children's Environmental Literature: From Ecocriticism to Ecopedagogy," *Neohelicon*, 36 (2009): 321–34.

Grahame, Kenneth. *The Wind in the Willows: An Annotated Edition*. Ed. Seth Lerer. (Orig. 1908). Cambridge MA: Harvard UP, 2009.

Hotchkiss, Jane. "The Jungle of Eden: Kipling, Wolf Boys, and the Colonial Imagination," *Victorian Literature and Culture*, 29 (2001): 435–49.

Kahn, Peter H., Jr. "Children's Affiliations with Nature: Structure, Development, and the Problem of Environmental Amnesia." *Children and Nature: Psychological, Sociocultural, and Evolutionary Investigations*. Ed. Kahn and Stephen Kellert. Cambridge MA: MIT Press, 2002. 93–116.

——. "The Development of Environmental Moral Identity." *Identity and the Natural Environment: The Psychological Significance of Nature*. Ed. Susan Clayton and Susan Opotow. Cambridge MA: MIT Press, 2003. 113–34.

Kellert, Stephen R. "Experiencing Nature: Affective, Cognitive, and Evaluative Development in Children." *Children and Nature: Psychological, Sociocultural, and Evolutionary Investigations*. Ed. Peter H. Kahn, Jr., and Kellert. Cambridge MA: MIT Press, 2002. 117–51.

Kitchell, Kenneth F., Jr. "The Shrinking of the Epic Hero: From Homer to Richard Adams's WatershipDowb," *Classical and Modern Literature, 7* (Fall 1986): 13–30.

Landsberg, Alison. *Prosthetic Memory: The Transformation of American Remembrance in the Age of Mass Culture*. New York: Columbia UP, 2004.

Leznik-Oberstein, Karin. "Children's Literature and the Environment." *Writing the Environment: Ecocriticism and Literature*. Ed. Richard Kerridge and Neil Samuels. London: Zed, 1998. 208–17.

Lloyd, Saci. *The Carbon Diaries 2015*. New York: Holiday House, 2008.

Lopez, Barry. "Renegotiating the Contracts," *Parabola, 8* (Spring 1983): 381–88.

Lopez, Barry. *Crow and Weasel*. San Francisco: North Point, 1990.

Louv, Richard. *Last Child in the Woods: Saving Our Children from nature-Deficit Disorder*. Chapel Hill, NC: Algonquin Books, 2005.

Marcos, Subcomandante. *The Story of Colors/La historia de los colores*. Trans. Anne Bar Din. El Paso, TX: CincoPuntos Press, 1996.

Marshall, Ian, "The Lorax and the Ecopolice," *ISLE: Interdisciplinary Studies in Literature and Environment, 2.2* (1996): 85–92.

Marx, Leo. *The Machine in the Garden: Technology and the Pastoral Ideal in America*. New York: Oxford UP, 1964.

Mittman, Greg. *Reel Nature: America's Romance with Wildlife on Film*. Cambridge MA: Harvard UP, 1999.

Monhart, Rebecca, and Leigh Monhardt, "Children's Literature and Environmental Issues: Heart Over Mind?" *Reading Horizons, 40.3* (2000): 175–83.

Morgenstern, John. "Children and Other Talking Animals," *The Lion and the Unicorn, 24* (2000): 110–27.

Munghosi, Charles. *One Day, Long Age: More Stories from a Shona Childhood*. Harare: Baobab, 1991.

Niemann, Christoph. *Subway*. New York: HarperCollins, 2010.

Oodgeroo Nunukul. *Dreamtime: Aboriginal Stories*. (1972). New York: Lothrop, Lee, and Shepard, 1994.

Paterson, Kathleen. *The Bridge to Terabithia*. New York: HarperCollins, 1977.

Phillips, Jerry. "The Mem Sahib, the Worthy, the Rajah and His Minions: Some Reflections of the Class Politics of *The Secret Garden*." (1993). *The Secret Garden: Norton Critical Edition*. Ed. Gretchen H. Gerzina. London: W.W. Norton, 2006. 342–66.

Pilkey, Dav. '*Twas the Night Before Tranksgiving*. New York: Orchard, 1990.

Platt, Kamala. "Environmental Justice Children's Literature: Depicting, Defending, and Celebrating Trees and Birds, Colors, and People." *Wild Things: Children's Literature and Ecocriticism*. Ed. Sidney I. Dobrin and Kenneth B. Kidd. Detroit: Wayne State UP, 2004. 183–97.

Potter, Beatrix. *The Tale of Peter Rabbit*. London: Frederick Warne, 2901.

Roberts, Charles G. D. *The Kindred of the Wild: A Book of Animal Life*. Boston: Page, 1902.

Rose, Deborah Lee. *The People Who Hugged the Trees*. Niwot, CO: Roberts Rinehart, 1990.

Rose, Jacqueline. *The Case of Peter Pan; or the Impossibility of Children's Fiction.* London: Macmillan, 1984.

Seale, Doris, and Beverly Slapin, eds. *A Broken Flute: The Native Experience in Books for Children.* Walnot Creek, CA: Altamira, 2005.

Sendak, Maurice. *Where the Wild Things Are.* New York: Harper, 1963.

Seton, Ernest Thompson. *Two Little Savages.* New York: Grosset and Dunlap, 1902.

Seuss, Dr. [Theodore Geisel.] *The Lorax.* New York: Random House, 1971.

Sewall, Anna. *Black Beauty: The Autobiography of a Horse.* New York: Grosset and Dunlap, 1945.

Sigler, Carolyn. "Wonderland to Wasteland: Toward Historicizing Environmental Activism in Children's Literature," *Children's Literature Association Quarterly,* 19.4 (1994): 148–53.

Smith, Elise L., "Centering the Home-Garden: The Arbor, Wall, and Gate in Moral Tales for Children," *Children's Literature,* 36 (2008): 24–48.

Sobel, David. *Children's Special Places: Exploring the Role of Forts, Dens, and Bush Houses in Middle Childhood.* Tucson: Zephyr Press, 1993.

Stegner, Wallace. *Wolf Willow: A History, a Story, and a Memory of the Last Plains Frontier.* New York: Viking, 1962.

Sternberg, Esther M. *Healing Spaces: The Science and Place and Well-Being.* Cambridge MA: Harvard UP, 2009.

Sturgeon, Noel. "'The Power is Yours, Planeteers!': Race, Gender, and Sexuality in Children's Environmental Popular Culture." *New Perspectives on Environmental Justice: Gender, Sexuality, and Activism.* Ed. Rachel Stein. New Brunswick: Rutgers UP, 2004. 262–276.

Thomas, Keith. *Man and the Natural World: Changing Attitudes in England, 1500–1800.* London: Allen Lane, 1983.

Turner, James. *Reckoning with the Beast: Animals, Pain, and Humanity in the Victorian Mind.* Baltimore: Johns Hopkins UP, 1980.

Ulrich, Roger S. "Biophilia, Biophobia, and Natural Landscapes." *The Biophilia Hypothesis.* Ed. Stephen Kellert and Edward O. Wilson. Washington, DC: Island Press, 1993. 73–137.

Wagner-Lawlor, Jennifer A. "Advocating Environmentalism: The Voice of Nature in Contemporary Children's Literature," *Children's Literature in Education,* 27.3 (1996): 143–52.

Williams, Raymond. *The Country and the City.* New York: Oxford UP, 1973.

....

CHAPTER 24

THE CONTEMPORARY ENGLISH NOVEL AND ITS CHALLENGES TO ECOCRITICISM

....

ASTRID BRACKE

CONTEMPORARY ecocriticism is characterized by a paradox that is rarely remarked on: despite its insistence that human–nature relations and environmental crisis are important, pervasive and worthy of critical study, the majority of ecocritical scholarship has historically been concerned with a limited set of nature-oriented or environmentally inflected texts. To put it differently, even though ecocriticism is clearly thriving in terms of geographical expansion, publications, and conferences, the cultural ubiquity of environmental issues is still not reflected in its relatively narrow canon.

Ecocriticism is founded on the belief that literary criticism can somehow contribute to the alleviation of environmental crisis, if only by raising awareness about human–nature relations. The question is, however, how much consciousness-raising can be done if ecocritical practice—*what* and *how* ecocritics read—remains as conservative as it is now? Of course, focusing on nature-oriented and environmentally inflected literature has served ecocriticism well in the past: it has led to the canonization of previously forgotten works and has given the field a signature focus and made it recognizable. At the same time, its canon is hardly representative of literature in general and, more importantly, does not do justice to the possibilities of ecocritical analysis. In this essay, I argue that a broadening of ecocriticism is needed if it wants to develop as a critical practice and continue to raise awareness about environmental concerns. Such an expansion requires both including a wider variety of texts for ecocritical study and broadening ecocritical practice—in other words, a shift in *how* and *what* ecocritics read.[1]

In particular, I will focus on the contemporary English novel, which—for a variety of reasons—has been largely ignored by ecocritics, yet also offers numerous possibilities for analysis.

CHANGING HOW AND WHAT
ECOCRITICS READ

Much ecocriticism is evaluative, if not in theory, then at least in practice. Richard Kerridge's 1998 definition is an apt example of this: ecocriticism, he proposes, "seeks to *evaluate* texts and ideas in terms of their coherence and usefulness as responses to environmental crisis" ("Introduction" 5, emphasis mine). Although arguably to some extent the task of the critic is always to assess a text, evaluating works on their environmental merits has excluded the majority of contemporary works from ecocritical analysis, as a comment by Serpil Oppermann shows. She has claimed that "[ecocritics] *expect* of writers that they inscribe ecological viewpoints in their work" ("Ecocentric Postmodern Theory" 230, emphasis mine), implying a fairly limited ecocritical canon, as well as a high risk of prescriptiveness. In addition to being overtly evaluative, ecocritical reading practices have also tended to avoid certain aspects that are an established part of literary criticism, such as textual form: for instance, genre and structure, focalization and narrative perspective. Ecocritics have focused primarily on *what* is described or presented in a work rather than on *how* it is presented. Consequently, the more formal or narratological aspects of literary works have received relatively little ecocritical attention.[2] In particular, contemporary novels that draw attention to their form—for example through their experimental structure—have been ignored almost entirely, despite the insights they might yield about human–nature relations.

The novel itself has also proven to be an obstacle to ecocriticism: of all genres, it is most frequently judged to be unsuitable, or at least problematic, for ecocritical analysis. Dominic Head has repeatedly discussed the (im)possibility of reading novels ecocritically.[3] He suggests that the novel's audience may not be receptive to environmental themes, since, unlike nature writing, the novel "is a mode of discourse which speaks to an increasingly urbanized population whose concerns appear to have no immediate connection with the non-human environment" ("Problems" 66).[4] Another issue that ecocritics tend to have with the novel is that traditional novelistic plots may provide insufficient scale, for instance when it comes to representing environmental crisis. Greg Garrard has argued that "[n]one of the traditional forms in literature, film, or television documentary is unproblematically suited to capturing the geographical and temporal scale, and uncertainty of climate change in particular" ("Ian McEwan's Next Novel" 709). Furthermore, the sheer anthropocentrism of the genre may be another possible impediment to ecocritical analysis, as Head proposes: "[t]he tendency of the novel to focus on personal development, and on social rather than environmental matters (and on time rather than place) is sometimes said to create an impression of alienation from the natural," and the textuality of novelistic discourse is feared by some to draw attention away from the natural world ("(Im)Possibility" 64–5). Thematically, the novel has presented difficulties to more traditional ecocritics: the settings of novels often subvert attempts at referentiality, describing environments that are frequently (sub)urban, or even wholly fictional, and not striving for the kinds of factuality that nature writings and environmentally inflected texts demonstrate.

Yet ecocritical issues with the novel go beyond anthropocentricism, matters of audience or plot. In their introduction to *The Good of the Novel* (2011), Liam McIlvanney and Ray Ryan suggest that the novel "does" character and interiority (xiii)—two aspects that particularly conservative ecocritics may fear distracts from representations of nature. Furthermore, and importantly for ecocriticism, "[t]he novel's truths are not reducible to a formulation, a proposition. They are partial, provisional. The novel represents a distinctive kind of ontology. The novel's wisdom is the 'wisdom of uncertainty' " (ibid.). This final element—the "wisdom of uncertainty"—is where the majority of ecocriticism's problems with the contemporary novel lie. Ecocritics are traditionally inclined to "read for the message," analyzing works for an environmental dimension or moral, whereas the novel often avoids conclusive messages. At the same time, epistemological uncertainty suits contemporary circumstances particularly well: in a world dominated by mass media, issues such as climate change are continually challenged, and views of nature varied and frequently ambiguous.

Of course, the case for the expansion of ecocritical practice has been made before. The best-known example to date is the collection *Beyond Nature Writing* (2001), edited by Karla Armbruster and Kathleen Wallace, which developed out of the question how "productive … an ecocritical approach [can] be when used with texts as far 'beyond nature writing' as [for example] the works of Henry James would seem" ("Introduction" 7). Patrick D. Murphy has over the years similarly advocated the expansion of ecocriticism beyond nature writing, for instance, in *Ecocritical Explorations in Literary and Cultural Studies* (2009), which includes a chapter on the contemporary American novel, as has Oppermann in her articles on contemporary fiction.[5] Yet whereas both critics demonstrate a generic broadening of the ecocritical canon, it is a broadening *within* the larger category of nature-oriented or environmentally inflected literature. While a decade after the publication of *Beyond Nature Writing*, ecocriticism has indeed moved "beyond nature writing," this does not necessarily mean that it has also moved beyond explicitly nature-oriented or environmental(ist) texts.

READING CONTEMPORARY ENGLISH NOVELS ECOCRITICALLY

Even though much contemporary English fiction has defied ecocritical analysis— being too anthropocentric, too experimental, too textual, or simply, too little concerned with nature—reading contemporary English novels from an ecocritical perspective requires little else than a shift in reading practices. The resulting expansive and broad ecocritical approach is founded on at least two elements: an inclusive definition of ecocriticism, and the assumption that a work does not have to be environmental(ist) or nature-oriented to merit an ecocritical reading.

Most definitions of ecocriticism suggest a broad scope and enable diverse readings. Cheryll Glotfelty's, for instance—"ecocriticism is the study of the relationship between literature and the physical environment" ("Introduction" xviii)—allows for both ecocritical approaches of the more traditional kind and ecocritical analyses of texts that at first sight do not invite them, like certain contemporary English fictions. Even if a novel is not explicitly nature-oriented, it can still provide insights on contemporary human–nature relations; even in the most experimental novels, structure, focalization, and genre may influence the representation of nature. The majority of the works that I will examine in the remainder of this essay have dissuaded ecocritical readings, apart from *Solar*, which is especially interesting because of the responses it did elicit, and what these say about contemporary ecocriticism.

URBAN ECOCRITICISM? *IF NOBODY SPEAKS OF REMARKABLE THINGS* AND THE POSSIBILITIES OF ECOCRITICISM

Jon McGregor's debut novel *If Nobody Speaks of Remarkable Things* (2002) is set in a fictional, industrial town somewhere in Britain. The novel consists of two narrative strands, and two narrators: an omniscient narrator describes a city, and in particular one street, on August 31, 1997, and a female first-person narrator looks back on that day a few years later. Whereas many Brits remember August 31, 1997, mainly as the day on which Princess Diana died, the major event that takes place on the street, and to which the entire omniscient narrative builds up, is an accident at the end of the afternoon when a child is hit by the car of one of his neighbours.

Ecocritical readings of urban novels remain rare: at most, ecocritics discuss natural spaces within cities, such as parks or community gardens, rather than cities as naturalcultural spaces in themselves. Of course, this makes some sense given the field's inherent focus on representations of nature. Yet this bias is not only an effect of ecocriticism's ideological and political roots: Michael Bennett has proposed in *The Nature of Cities* that the texts ecocritics study tend to reflect the environments in which they live. Since, in the United States at least, the majority of ecocritics prefer to live in non-urban areas, texts about rural areas are examined most often (38). If there is indeed a correlation between the environments in which ecocritics live and work, and the kinds of texts they analyze, ecocriticism is bound to become more concerned with the city as the field develops and spreads towards more urban areas within and outside of the United States. As a critical practice, however, ecocriticism is not yet ready for this influx of the urban and first needs to find ways of coming to terms with those areas that it had previously avoided.

Bennett advocates more ecocritical engagement with cities through "social ecocriticism," which draws on social ecology and focuses on "how the social, political, and economic decisions made by humans effect [sic] our interaction with the environment" (33). Social ecocriticism, however, has been explored by few other ecocritics, most likely because it intersects—and seems to have merged—with the environmental justice movement, which has established itself as a more productive subfield of ecocriticism. Another concept that attempts to bring together nature and cities is "urban ecology," in which ecology and ecological metaphors are used to describe or "read" cities. Urban growth, for instance, has been examined in terms of ecology—for example, the concentric growth of a tree stem may be compared to the equally concentric growth of a certain city.[6] Nonetheless, readings of cities need not be limited to social ecocriticism or urban ecology, as an analysis of McGregor's novel shows.

The few references to nature in *If Nobody Speaks* fall into to one of two categories: dualistic descriptions, which present nature as distinctly other and not really belonging to the city, and what I call instances of "urban nature," in which natural elements are described as truly part of the city. In the first-person narrative, the narrator gives an example of the former when she remembers how on August 31, 1997, she contemplated going inside after breakfast, opening a window in her bedroom, and smelling "the flood of fresh summer air that had come sweeping in, the sweetness of a rolling wind that was *still clean* from the countryside" (63, emphasis mine). She draws on and enforces the binary opposition between the countryside and the city here by assuming that the air is *still clean*—juxtaposing the country with the city. Other instances of dualistic representations of nature in the novel use light and darkness to create a contrast. The omniscient narrator describes the early morning of August 31 when the woman living at number nineteen—almost all characters remain unnamed, and are only referred to by their house number—wakes up to go to the toilet. There, she watches "the shadows of pigeons flap across the bathroom wall" (15). Roughly at the same time, bird shadows flit across the face of a girl sleeping at number eleven (16). These asides, although brief and hardly registered by the characters, express a certain oppositional relation between nature and culture, in which nature is seen as that which is not really part of city life: it either belongs to the country or is just a shadow.

Yet there are also instances in *If Nobody Speaks* when nature is not conceived in dualistic terms, but as part of the city. While on the phone with her mother, for example, the first-person narrator opens a window: "a burst of noise rushes in. Traffic, and shouting, and music. And birdsong, from somewhere up on the roof, a thin twitter that creeps and tangles in with all the other sounds" (80–1). Although she distinguishes the birds chirping, this sound is part of a larger tangle of sounds, just as the sounds of cars, people and music are. Rather than presenting the birdsong as something different from these other city sounds, it is placed in the same category: it is urban nature, something that is generally perceived as natural yet has become part of—enmeshed with—the same whole that is the city, which consists of natural and nonnatural components.

Another example of urban nature in the novel is the rain shower that interrupts life in the street in the afternoon, forcing people into their houses. Put like this, it seems as if another binary opposition is presented: the rain—"nature"—is affecting the people living on the street—"culture." Yet a closer look at the passage shows that the case is not quite as black and white as that. The approaching rain is described in terms of scent: "there's a smell in the air, swelling and rolling, a smell like metal scraped clean of rust, a hard cleanness, the air tight with it, sprung, an electric tingle winding from the ground to the sky, a smell that unfurls in the back of the mouth, dense, clammy, a smell without a name but easy to recognize … it smells like rain" (208). Notably, the rain is not described in natural terms—no mention is made of the rain's earthy smell—but the omniscient narrator uses terms that are associated with industry: "metal scraped clean of rust," "an electric tingle." This conflation of a natural phenomenon and nonnatural associations signals just how ambiguous rain really is or has become: it is neither nature nor culture. Since the Industrial Revolution, and particularly since the first nuclear tests, rain has come to illustrate what Bill McKibben calls "the end of nature." Nature has ended because it is no longer a force separate from humanity, but influenced and shaped by it, which is quite different from the way things used to be, when humans only changed those places in which they lived: "Beginning with the invisible releases of radiation, and then the toxic pollutants like DDT, and then the by-products of large-scale industrialization like acid rain … we began to alter even those places where we were not" (McKibben xix). In *If Nobody Speaks*, then, nature is sometimes much more ambiguous than it seems at first sight: neither nature nor culture, it is an example of urban nature.

The passage is also interesting because of how punctuation—form—works to represent the rain. When it is just a drizzle, this is emphasized through the use of commas: "One, two, three drops at a time, a slow streak down a bedroom window, a wet thud on a newspaper page, a hiss onto barbecue coals" (209). Once it is really pouring, the rain is described in one long sentence, spread over four paragraphs, each beginning with the phrase "the rain falls," and running on for thirty-two lines before arriving at a full stop (211–13). Whereas the delayed full stop underlines the momentum of the rain, the few commas used in this sentence illustrate its force: "the rain falls and seeps through the cracks in the felt roof of the attic at number twenty-two, the girl with the short hair and the glasses repositioning an empty icecream tub for the last time, watching the pond-ripples slipping back and forth as each invading drop falls from the stained ceiling" (211). The consonance of s-sounds—*falls, seeps, ripples, slipping*—and the word "invading" all add to the reader's sense of the rain's power.

Once the rain begins to slow, more commas—and punctuation in general—are used, recalling how individual drops become more distinguishable as rain lets up: "the rain falls, gently now, past the small window of the attic flat of number twenty-one, the man with the tattoo is in bed again, smoking, and the woman with the henna-red hair is scooping up fallen petals from a vase of roses she has already kept longer than they were intended to be kept, she takes the fallen petals and stuffs them into an empty jamjar" (213). In the next paragraph, the rain has almost completely stopped: "as the rain fades away there is stillness and quiet, light flooding rapidly into the street and through windows and open doors, the last few drops falling conspicuously onto an already steaming pavement, there are streams and dribbles and drips from gutters and pipes in various states of disrepair" (ibid.), before the storm passes across the rest of the city and into the hills surrounding it. Just as in the earlier passage, consonance recalls the sounds of the rain, and as the rain slows, the pace of the sentences also slows down.

Urban novels like *If Nobody Speaks*, then, certainly pose a challenge to ecocriticism, yet it is a challenge that needs to—and can—be met. Even though nature is effectively marginal for much of the work, the novel describes experiences of the human and nonhuman environment that are also part of Western contemporary life—perhaps more so than those presented in traditional nature writing. An ecocritical reading of *If Nobody Speaks* is productive particularly because I focus not primarily on depictions of nature—although I do look at those as well—but rather on the way in which nature is represented. Consequently, a relatively short passage becomes significant when it is analyzed in terms of word use and punctuation which highlight, in this case, the force of the rain. To put it differently, rather than distracting from representations of nature, such a close textual reading actually serves to foreground them.[7] A similar effect can be achieved when examining novels with experimental structures, such as David Mitchell's *Cloud Atlas* (2004).

A SEXTET FOR OVERLAPPING SOLOISTS: THE STRUCTURE OF *CLOUD ATLAS*

Cloud Atlas consists of six different narratives, written in six different genres, set in six different periods, and featuring six different main characters.[8] All of the stories—ranging from an eighteenth-century travel journal to an oral story told in a post-apocalyptic future—deal in some way or another with the collapse of social, cultural, and political systems, as well as the destruction of the natural environment. These apocalypses include the annihilation of tribes in the Pacific in the eighteenth century; World War I; feared nuclear apocalypse in the 1960s; and a future, worldwide dystopian "corporacy," in which everything—humans, souls, and nature—is commercialized. Although to date little ecocritical work has been done on Mitchell, *Cloud Atlas* offers numerous points of entry for an ecocritical reading.[9] The eighteenth-century journal of Adam Ewing—the first narrative—invites an analysis of environmental colonialism, whereas in the narrative describing corporacy, the fifth story, widespread environmental destruction is placed side-by-side with the complete breakdown of boundaries between humans and nonhumans. Individually, then, the six narratives can well be read ecocritically—even quite conventionally, focusing solely on the content. However, *Cloud Atlas* is not a collection of short stories, but a novel, and as such its structure is significant.

The six narratives are arranged according to a "two-two-two formation": two stories are set in the past, two more or less in the present, and two in the future. Apart from the sixth, all stories are interrupted halfway through and concluded in reverse order in the second part of *Cloud Atlas*. This design allows the novel to bypass the limited timescale of most novels, which, according to Kerridge, has kept them from adequately engaging with apocalypse: "conventional plot structures require forms of solution and closure that seem absurdly evasive when applied to ecological questions with their extremes of timescale and complexities of interdependency" ("Narratives of Resignation" 99). Yet the scope of (environmental) apocalypse is not merely represented by means of themes recurring in different historic periods, but through the way in which the six narratives of *Cloud Atlas* are arranged as well. Particularly the first—"The Pacific Journal of Adam Ewing"—and sixth—"Sloosha's Crossin' and Ev'rythin' After"—narratives are relevant in this respect.

Ewing's narrative begins the novel and as such introduces themes—colonization, human greed—that are further explored in the rest of the work. Given the structure of *Cloud Atlas*, "Adam Ewing" also brings the novel to a close as the second half of the narrative is told. Comments made by Ewing in the final pages of *Cloud Atlas* are consequently both a prophecy and a conclusion. For instance, towards the end of his journal, he contemplates the fate of humankind: "one fine day, a purely predatory race *shall* consume itself ... Is this entropy written in our nature?" (528, emphasis in original). Since Ewing's story is chronologically earliest, it predicts the events of the five other narratives of *Cloud Atlas* that take place at a later date. Yet his remark on the human race also sums up everything that happened in between the two parts of Ewing's narrative.

"Sloosha's Crossin'" is the only story that is narrated without interruption. Set furthest into the future of all the narratives, it seems as if the other stories build up to it. Structurally, however, it is not the last but the middle narrative, which allows it to comment on both the five half narratives preceding it, and refer to the halves following it. One of the characters in "Sloosha's Crossin'," Zachry, illustrates the position of the story in the larger novel particularly well. Zachry's tribe is regularly visited by a mysterious group of people called the Prescients, the only ones to have retained some knowledge from before "the Fall," an apocalyptic event in the past. Zachry asks one of them, Meronym, what caused the Fall. She tells him that the "Old'uns"—those living before the apocalypse—"tripped their own fall" with their "hunger for more" (286), just as the apocalyptic events in the five other narratives are caused by human greed. Therefore, Meronym's remark, because it appears in a central place in the novel, comments on the past within the story and the stories preceding it, as well as proleptically enframes the as-yet-unread second halves of the stories.[10]

Cloud Atlas's structure, then, points to two possible futures for the human race that have environmental ramifications: entropy or survival. Essentially, the novel asks the question whether the harm humanity has done can still be reversed, or whether in harming its natural environment it is effectively killing itself. Peter Childs and James Green have suggested that "Sloosha's Crossin'" signals a change in humanity's fate: "If, during the first half of the text, humanity appears to be shackled to its apocalyptic destiny ... the reversal of this forward momentum opens up an alternative perspective" (35): a future that is not as bleak as the first five half narratives of *Cloud Atlas* imply, since "the novel argues the case for ethical choices made by individuals and societies reasserting the potential for enlightened political agency" (ibid.). In other words, they propose that Zachry and his tribe have learned from Meronym to make better choices in the future and, essentially, save humankind. This view makes *Cloud Atlas* a narrative of progress, similar to the kinds advocated by Ewing's eighteenth-century contemporaries. Hélène Machinal argues along similar lines, and perceives "Sloosha's Crossin'" as a story in which certain ethics and values—perhaps even a sense of humanity—is restored: "the central tale is that in which the necessity of a collective vision is reasserted" (134). Yet none of these critics takes into account that although "Sloosha's Crossin'" is indeed the central tale and the only story told in full, it is not in fact the *final* narrative of the novel. Once the reader has finished Zachry's narrative, five other half narratives still await in which yet more destruction and apocalypse is described. And, while Zachry survives tribal warfare long enough to father a son, the Prescients are killed by a mysterious disease which is wiping out the remaining population of the Earth. Consequently, even if "Sloosha's Crossin'" indeed shows the reinstatement of humanity and a turnaround for humankind, the epidemic may prevent the rosier future that Childs, Green, and Machinal sketch out.

One of the reasons that experimental novels such as *Cloud Atlas* have been neglected by ecocritics is that contemporary literature's concern with textuality, as Head suggests, "might lead readers away from an engagement with representations of the natural" ("Problems" 64). *Cloud Atlas*, however, achieves quite the opposite: its complex recursive structure does not lead attention *away* from its environmental dimension, but *foregrounds* and *emphasizes* it. The novel places contemporary environmental, social, cultural, and political issues in a larger context that a more conventional work cannot provide. Contemporary English novels such as *If Nobody Speaks* and *Cloud Atlas* therefore engage with precisely those issues that have been deemed problematic by ecocritics, yet nonetheless invite ecocritical analysis. In fact, in both cases, an approach that focuses on narrative form highlights representations of nature that a reading aimed solely at the novels' content may not have revealed. Yet contemporary novels do not merely challenge ecocritics to question or revise their reading practices, but also inspire them to critique the premises that ecocriticism is founded on. The same is true of *Solar* (2010) by Ian McEwan, a novel much anticipated by ecocritics that did not quite live up to their expectations.

SOLAR'S CHALLENGES TO ECOCRITICAL PREMISES

Hailed as the first novel on climate crisis by a major British author, *Solar* revolves around the personal and professional life of Nobel laureate Michael Beard, a scientist working at the National Centre for Renewable Energy. The ruins of his private life—multiple divorces and problematic relationships with women, an ever-expanding waistline, and his continual desire for more food, drink, and sex—are set off by the success of his career. When his postdoctoral researcher dies in a freak accident, Beard appropriates the young man's research and becomes an expert on solar energy. In the final pages of the novel, Beard seemingly has a heart attack at the moment that his long-term girlfriend catches him with his mistress, and hours before his latest project, a solar energy plant, is revealed.

The novel was long awaited and eagerly anticipated by British ecocritics such as Garrard and Kerridge. In an article written before *Solar* was published, Garrard uses themes in McEwan's oeuvre to predict the impact this new novel may have on environmentalism and specifically ecocriticism. His expectations were high: he anticipated it to "rapidly become a key text in any ecocritical reading list" ("Ian McEwan's Next Novel" 696) and to "provoke a fundamental shift in ecocritical assumptions, from moral idealism to pragmatism" (718). Indeed, comments made in the press about *Solar* and articles such as Garrard's suggest that it would be the kind of novel that Kerridge, writing in 1998, was waiting for when he claimed that "[a]n environmentalist novel, approaching other areas of experiences from an ecological sensibility, is still to come" ("Nature in the English Novel" 155). Once *Solar* was published, however, it soon became clear that it was not the environmental(ist) novel that ecocritics had been hoping for: although dealing in a secondary fashion with climate crisis, this theme is always made subservient to Beard's messy private life and moral failings. The only character in the work that shows any kind of promise as a possible environmental hero, Beard's postdoctoral researcher Aldous, dies in the first part of the novel after sleeping with Beard's wife.

Consequently, some ecocritics were disappointed with *Solar*. Axel Goodbody, for example, noted that "Beard is indeed on the one hand a gifted physics scholar and takes responsibility for saving humankind, [but] on the other, he is lazy, cowardly and chaotic. In McEwan's schematic representation, his personality remains split and without psychological plausibility. There are also no other characters in the novel which represent a more complex view of the contradictions and tensions inherent to his contemporaries" (145).[11] Kerridge similarly suggests that McEwan does not acknowledge the full potential of climate crisis: "He does not explore the emotional complexity of our responses to the threat. And if it is true that we are, collectively, evading its emotional import,... then McEwan avoids the task of imagining for us, and showing us in artistic form, the feelings we do not yet dare to have" ("Single Source" 159–60). The disillusionment of these critics may very well be caused by the novel's genre—satire—and the way in which it prevents the kind of reading for the message that is part of much ecocritical scholarship. Although satire as a genre is by no means "anti-ecocritical"—I doubt there are any such genres at all—*Solar*'s satire is all-encompassing, and none of the (moral) standpoints on the environment presented in the novel is spared. Instead of—or, in addition to—remarking on the novel's environmental(ist) shortcomings, ecocriticism might do better to acknowledge the opportunities *Solar* offers to examine some of the field's assumptions, such as the importance of environmental crisis and the belief that art can play a role in alleviating this crisis.

The undeniable existence of environmental crisis is one of the foundational premises of ecocriticism, as Kerridge notes: "The starting point for the ecocritic is that there really is an unprecedented global environmental crisis, and that this crisis poses some of the great political and cultural questions of our time" ("Introduction" 5). Beard, however, consistently denies climate crisis and belittles its importance: he has "other things to think about [and is] unimpressed by some of the wild commentary that suggested the world was in 'peril'" (15). Yet rather than dismissing this as a failure on the author's part to create a character competent—or complex—enough to deal with climate crisis, Beard's unwillingness or inability to be fully aware of environmental crisis reflects some of the sentiments that exist about human–nature relationships in contemporary Western culture. In fact, Beard's feelings are hardly uncommon, as John Lanchester shows: he admits experiencing a "strong degree of psychological resistance to the whole subject of climate change. I just don't want to think about it" (par. 2), and believes that "we're reluctant to think about it because we're worried that if we start we will have no choice but to think of nothing else" (par. 3). This notion is echoed by Beard's girlfriend Melissa: "to take the matter seriously would be to think about it all the time. Everything else shrank before it. And so, like everyone she knew, she could not take it seriously, not entirely. Daily life would not permit it" (165). In this respect, *Solar* illustrates a pluriformity of views on nature: through a combination of characters—Beard, Melissa, and the idealistic Aldous—the novel shows the many dimensions of contemporary debates on environmental crisis and climate change, which cannot be caught in the simplistic opposition between deniers and activists. The complexity that Goodbody and Kerridge seek, then, is not to be found in the main character, but in the novel as a whole and its satire.

A second premise of ecocriticism, voiced by Scott Slovic among others, is that art can make a difference in a time of environmental crisis: language and literature are "crucially important in exploring and even *shaping* our sense of personal values and in communicating these values" (118, emphasis in original).[12] In *Solar*, however, any contribution that art can make to the alleviation of climate change—or even merely to raising more awareness of the subject—is persistently mocked. The most striking example of this satire of the arts is Beard's stay aboard a ship in the Arctic with a group of artists who all seem to be "seized by the same particular assumption, that it was art in its highest forms, poetry, sculpture, dance, abstract music, conceptual art, that would lift climate change as a subject, gild it, palpate it, reveal all the horror and lost beauty and awesome threat, and inspire the public to take thought, take action, or demand it of others" (77).[13] The narrative further mocks the artists in its descriptions of their projects, which seem ineffectual at best and futile at worst. In an attempt to address increased consumerism and capitalism, for instance, one of them creates a life-sized Monopoly set that inadvertently becomes a huge commercial success for the makers of the game (51). A Spanish artist makes ice sculptures that rapidly melt in the hot climate of southern Europe (64), and a novelist uses scientific principles in his work—much like McEwan himself in fact—only to have his understanding of them ridiculed by Beard, the only scientist on board (76). Art, *Solar* suggests, has very little to offer at this point in history—a sentiment that completely runs counter to much ecocritical scholarship. Of course, *Solar*'s satire of these two ecocritical premises does not mean that ecocriticism should just abandon these assumptions: challenging certain beliefs is not the same as denying them. Nevertheless, a more sceptical attitude towards its own assumptions will aid rather than hinder the field's development.[14]

Ecocriticism and The Contemporary English Novel

Contemporary English fiction remains a largely unexplored territory for ecocritics, a focus that, as I discussed, is caused partly by elements inherent to much contemporary literature: self-referentiality, anthropocentrism, an urban audience, and other concerns seem to have put many ecocritics off the contemporary English novel altogether. Yet ecocriticism itself, and the reading practices it has developed over the years, also plays a role in this respect. Ecocritical practice—which I examined earlier mainly in terms of reading for the message and a preference for nature-oriented literature—has kept ecocritics from coming to terms with certain themes, such as the urban. A final point to be explored is the tension between actual environmental circumstances and how nature is presented in literature, advertising, films, photography, and so on. Ecocritics aim to analyze representations of nature wherever they appear, but what if certain nature descriptions are consistently idealizing or escapist? To put it differently, what should be the ecocritic's response if a contemporary English novel consistently presents a natural landscape in idealizing terms and tropes, instead of acknowledging the actual environmental circumstances in Britain or the world? At the moment, it seems that this discrepancy between reality and representation enforces ecocriticism's focus on nature-oriented literature and confirms many ecocritics' suspicions of the contemporary novel.

For decades—more or less right up until the turn of the present century—critics analyzed tropes of nature not in terms of how accurate they were, but merely as ways of thinking about or conceiving of certain landscapes. Leo Marx, for instance, notes that the Elizabethans used two contrasting tropes to describe America: the wilderness and the garden. He uses this dissonance to illustrate two different views of nature and the American landscape, instead of examining whether these tropes corresponded with historical environmental circumstances.[15] Over the past decades, however, ecocritics have, rightly, become more critical towards tropes of nature, particularly pastoral. Early ecocriticism was heavily indebted to pastoral—both the trope itself as well as the genre—because it provided the context for the individual's experience of nature that was central to nature writing. More recently, however, pastoral has become something of an ecocritical black sheep, best avoided altogether. In his discussion of the trope, for instance, Dana Phillips proposes that it is wholly unsuitable to the present age: "I doubt that the pastoral (as conceived along traditional lines) will help us confront the environmental crisis head on" (146). Similarly, Garrard has argued that the use of pastoral is counterproductive to environmental aims, since it is premised on mistaken views of "nature as a stable, enduring counterpoint to the disruptive energy and change of human societies" (*Ecocriticism* 63). Instead, he suggests, we ought to use tropes of nature that are "profoundly shaped by scientific thought" such as the human animal and the whole Earth (ibid. 202)—just as both Terry Gifford and Lawrence Buell have proposed other concepts or tropes to replace pastoral: "post-pastoral" and "naturism," respectively.[16]

Yet arguing that pastoral should not be used— by writers, advertisers, filmmakers— has not benefited ecocriticism at all, particularly because literary critics have little say in what representations authors and other artists should or should not employ. Although it is perhaps valid to suggest that tropes such as pastoral are not environmental, this evades the central question: Why does contemporary Western culture continue to rely so much on "anachronistic" tropes such as pastoral?[17] In trying to avoid this question, ecocritics have also avoided the majority of texts that pose it—including much contemporary English fiction. A. S. Byatt, for instance, consistently uses paradise as a variety of pastoral in her work, and many of John Fowles's novels draw on pastoral motifs,[18] as does Adam Foulds's Booker-shortlisted *The Quickening Maze* (2009) on the poet John Clare.

A more constructive and productive approach than arguing against their use is to replace an evaluative with a diagnostic approach: examine the ways in which these tropes are employed and what this says about human–nature relations, and in particular explore the many examples in which novels do not merely reproduce but reconceptualize them. The pastoral, for example, has been primarily understood by ecocritics and other scholars as representing an escapist, idealized image of nature. However, the escape or retreat is only one part of the trope, which is characterized by the movement of retreat *and return*. Consequently, the desire to retreat or escape to an untouched or unspoilt natural space is always countered by the necessity of return to a less-than-ideal space, such as the city. This contrasting movement is particularly suitable to contemporary Western circumstances and views of nature, in which a longing for "real" nature is always necessarily overshadowed by the awareness of actual environmental circumstances.

Much contemporary English fiction draws on and plays with the pastoral contrast of retreat and return. In Gerard Woodward's novel *August* (2001), a London family seeks their own retreat in the Welsh countryside. Their experiences of the landscape are contrasted with an omniscient narrator's perspective on the hardships that the farmers suffer, as well as the pastoral space that the family "escapes" from: their London garden, a lush, green space. Another example is Julian Barnes's use in *England, England* (1998) of hyperspaces as pastoral spaces which are continually defined in contrast to each other. Consequently, what serves as a retreat in one part of the novel, is a place to escape from in the next.

Reading the contemporary English novel ecocritically, then, does not merely mean reading the individual works differently, but also approaching the tropes and themes explored by them differently. Yet the study of novels in general also benefits from increased ecocritical interest in contemporary English fictions. Ecocriticism is not merely another modish -ism, but a critical approach grounded in an age-old concern with nature, which has been revitalized by environmentalism and environmental crisis, providing a unique perspective on literature. The time has come for ecocritics to shake off old concerns about the novel and embrace the possibilities it has to offer the field, particularly since the continued success of ecocriticism depends on the ways it can prove its relevance to the academic and critical community at large, and its broad and open take on representations of nature wherever they appear. Therefore, expansion of ecocritical practice, not merely increased methodology or more "theory," as others have suggested,[19] is where ecocriticism should next be headed.

NOTES

1. I also explore this subject in "Redrawing the Boundaries of Ecocritical Practice", and, in more depth, in my forthcoming dissertation, *Ecocriticism and the Contemporary British Novel*.
2. For critics arguing the generic expansion of ecocriticism, see Patrick D. Murphy and Adeline Johns-Putra.
3. See in particular his articles "Problems in Ecocriticism and the Novel," "The (Im)Possibility of Ecocriticism," and his *Cambridge Introduction to Modern British Fiction*.
4. Such arguments often seem unaware that one of the oldest modes used to describe nature—pastoral—was aimed at urban audiences. See Simon Schama, who, in his discussion of Hampstead Heath, notes that "*both* kinds of arcadia, the idyllic as well as the wild, are landscapes of the urban imagination" (525, emphasis in original).
5. See particularly "Seeking Environmental Awareness in Postmodern Fiction" and "Ecocentric Postmodern Theory."
6. See Andrew Ross who explains that urban ecology also provided "a biological gloss... for the experience of social conflict within cities" (Ross 17).
7. See also Cantrell, Walker, and Westling for ecocritical readings that similarly draw attention to the effect of style (in this case, Woolf's).
8. One of the characters of *Cloud Atlas*, Robert Frobisher, describes the musical piece he is composing—the Cloud Atlas Sextet—as a "sextet for overlapping soloists" (463), a phrase that aptly describes the six narratives of the novel and their relation to each other.
9. Nonetheless, none of the essays in a recent collection on David Mitchell's fiction explores the environmental dimensions of his work (see David Mitchell, *Critical Essays*, edited by Sarah Dillon).
10. Childs and Green note that in linguistics, the term "meronym" "denotes a constituent part of a whole," much as in Mitchell's fiction, "everything seems to be demonstrably part of the larger whole. Each character is a meronym of the web of relations entangling all the others" (32).
11. "In der Tat ist Beard einerseits physikalisch begabt und verantwortungsvoll um die Rettung der Menschheit besorgt, andererseits ein fauler, feiger Chaot. Seine Persönlichkeit bleibt in McEwans schematischer Darstellung gespalten und ohne psychologische Plausibilität. Der Roman stellt auch keine anderen Personen vor, die eine komplexere Sicht auf die Widersprüche und Spannungen im Leben der Zeitgenossen hergäbe" (145, translation mine).

12. This sentiment is echoed by Kerridge, who suggests that inventing or helping artists to invent new forms for environmental crisis is one of the tasks of ecocritics ("Environmentalism and Ecocriticism" 534).

13. The episode was inspired by McEwan's own stay on a ship in the Arctic as part of the Cape Farewell project in 2005.

14. Garrard similarly identifies a development in ecocriticism's treatment of its primary object of study—nature: "ecocriticism is in the process of shifting from a predominantly 'nature-endorsing' position to a 'nature-sceptical' one" ("Ecocriticism" 16).

15. See *The Machine in the Garden* (1965), 42ff.

16. Post-pastoral texts, as Gifford defines them, are "aware of the anti-pastoral and of the conventional illusions upon which Arcadia is premised, but...[find] a language to outflank those dangers with a vision of accommodated humans, at home in the very world they thought themselves alienated from by their possession of language" (*Pastoral* 149). In an endnote on his use of the term "pastoral ideology," Buell mentions, between brackets, that he favours the term "naturism," over pastoralism "as having less ideological and aesthetic baggage and as referring unequivocally to the material nonhuman environment" (*The Environmental Imagination* 439 n.4).

17. Garrard notes the risk of anachronism in the use of tropes such as pastoral, dwelling and apocalypse (*Ecocriticism* 202).

18. See Tom Wilson's discussion of Fowles's oeuvre in *The Recurrent Green Universe of John Fowles*.

19. In recent years, many ecocritics have suggested that ecocriticism lacks a methodology and have consequently sought to promote their own. See for instance Simon Estok's "Theorizing in a Space of Ambivalent Openness: Ecocriticism and Ecophobia," *ISLE 16.2* (2009), S. K. Robisch's virulent response "The Woodshed," *ISLE 16.4* and Garrard's overview in *The Year's Work in Critical and Cultural Theory* Vol. 19, 2011. A number of contributors to the 2010 *ISLE* forum on ecocriticism and theory similarly proceed from the belief that ecocriticism as yet lacks a methodology or theory. See, for example, Serenella Iovino's contribution; Oppermann's "Ecocriticism's Phobic Relations with Theory"; and Helena Feder.

WORKS CITED

Armbruster, Karla and Kathleen Wallace. "Introduction". *Beyond Nature Writing. Expanding the Boundaries of Ecocriticism*. Eds. Karla Armbruster and Kathleen Wallace. Charlottesville and London: University of Virginia Press, 2001. 1–25. Print.

Barnes, Julian. *England, England*. London: Picador, 1998. Print.

Bennett, Michael. "From Wide Open Spaces to Metropolitan Places." *Interdisciplinary Studies in Literature and Environment* 8.1 (2001): 31–52. Print.

Bracke, Astrid. "Redrawing the Boundaries of Ecocritical Practice." *Interdisciplinary Studies in Literature and the Environment* 17.4 (Autumn 2010): 765–68. Print.

——. *Ecocriticism and the Contemporary British Novel*. Diss. Radboud University Nijmegen (2013).

Buell, Lawrence. *The Environmental Imagination*. Cambridge MA: Harvard University Press, 1995. Print.

Cantrell, Carol H. "'The Locus of Compossibility': Virginia Woolf, Modernism and Place." *Interdisciplinary Studies in Literature and Environment* 5.2 (1998): 25–40. Print.

Childs, Peter, and James Green. "The Novel in Nine Parts." *David Mitchell. Critical Essays*. Ed. Sarah Dillon. Canterbury: Gylphi, 2011. 25–47. Print.

Dillon, Sarah, ed. *David Mitchell. Critical Essays*. Canterbury: Gylphi, 2011. 3–23. Print.

Estok, Simon. "Theorizing in a Space of Ambivalent Openness: Ecocriticism and Ecophobia." *Interdisciplinary Studies in Literature and Environment* 16.2 (2009): 203–25. Print.

Feder, Helena. "Rethinking Multiculturalism: Theory and Nonhuman Cultures." *Interdisciplinary Studies in Literature and Environment* 17.4 (2010): 775–77. Print.

Foulds, Adam. *The Quickening Maze*. London: Jonathan Cape, 2009. Print.

Garrard, Greg. "Ian McEwan's Next Novel and the Future of Ecocriticism." *Contemporary Literature* 50.4 (2009): 695–720. Print.

——. "Ecocriticism." *The Year's Work in Critical and Cultural Theory* 18 (2010): 1–35. Print.

——. "Ecocriticism." *The Year's Work in Critical and Cultural Theory* 19 (2011): 46–82. Print.

——. *Ecocriticism*. 2nd ed. London and New York: Routledge, 2011.

Gifford, Terry. *Pastoral*. London and New York: Routledge, 1999. Print.

Glotfelty, Cheryll. "Introduction." *The Ecocriticism Reader*. Eds. Cheryll Glotfelty and Harold Fromm. Athens and London: University of Georgia Press, 1996. Xv–xxxvii. Print.

Goodbody, Axel. "*Die Ringe des Saturn* und *Solar*. Sinnbilder und Schreibstrategien in Literarischen Stellungnahmen zur Ökologischen Krise von W.G. Sebald und Ian McEwan." *Ökologische Transformationen und Literarische Repräsentationen*. Eds. Maren Ermisch, Ulrike Kruse, and Urte Stobbe. Göttingen: Universitätsverlag Göttingen, 2010. 131–48. Print.

Head, Dominic. "Problems in Ecocriticism and the Novel." *Key Words 1* (1998): 60–73. Print.

——. "The (Im)Possibility of Ecocriticism." *Writing the Environment*. Eds. Richard Kerridge and Neil Sammells. London: Zed Books, 1998. 27–39. Print.

——. *The Cambridge Introduction to Modern British Fiction*. Cambridge: Cambridge University Press, 2002. Print.

Iovino, Serenella. "Ecocriticism, Ecology of Mind and Narrative Ethics: A Theoretical Ground for Ecocriticism as Educational Practice." *Interdisciplinary Studies in Literature and Environment* 17.4 (2010): 759–62. Print.

Johns-Putra, Adeline. "Ecocriticism, Genre, and Climate Change: Reading the Utopian Vision of Kim Stanley Robinson's Science in the Capital Trilogy." *Ecocriticism and English Studies*. Spec. issue of *English Studies* 91.7 (2010): 744–60. Print.

Kerridge, Richard. "Introduction." *Writing the Environment*. Eds. Richard Kerridge and Neil Sammells. London: Zed Books, 1998. 1–9. Print.

——. "Nature in the English Novel." *Literature of Nature*. Ed. Patrick D. Murphy. Chicago: Fitzroy Dearborn, 1998. 149–57. Print.

——. "Narratives of Resignation: Environmentalism in Recent Fiction." *The Environmental Tradition in English Literature*. Ed. John Parham. Burlington: Ashgate, 2002. 87–99. Print.

——. "Environmentalism and Ecocriticism." *Literary Theory and Criticism*. Ed. Patricia Waugh. Oxford: Oxford University Press, 2006. 530–41. Print.

——. "The Single Source." *Ecozon@ 1.1* (2010): 155–61. Web. January 9, 2012. <http://www.ecozona.eu/index.php/journal/article/view/36>.

Lanchester, John. "Warmer, Warmer." *London Review of Books*, March 22, 2007. Web. January 9, 2012. <http://www.lrb.co.uk/v29/n06/john-lanchester/warmer-warmer>.

Machinal, Hélène. "*Cloud Atlas*. From Postmodernity to the Posthuman." *David Mitchell. Critical Essays*. Ed. Sarah Dillon. Canterbury: Gylphi, 2011. 127–54. Print.

Marx, Leo. *The Machine in the Garden*. Oxford: Oxford University Press, 1965. Print.

McEwan, Ian. *Solar*. London: Jonathan Cape, 2010. Print.

McGregor, Jon. *If Nobody Speaks of Remarkable Things*. London: Bloomsbury, 2002. Print.

McIlvanney, Liam, and Ray Ryan. "Introduction." *The Good of the Novel*. Eds. Liam McIlvanney and Ray Ryan. London: Faber and Faber, 2011. vii–xiv. Print.

McKibben, Bill. *The End of Nature*. New York: Random House, 1992. Print.

Mitchell, David. *Cloud Atlas*. London: Sceptre, 2004. Print.

Murphy, Patrick D. *Ecocritical Explorations in Literary and Cultural Studies*. Lanham, MD: Lexington Books, 2009. Print.

Oppermann, Serpil. "Seeking Environmental Awareness in Postmodern Fictions." *Critique* 49.3 (2008): 243–53. Print.

——. "Ecocriticism's Phobic Relations with Theory." *Interdisciplinary Studies in Literature and Environment* 17.4 (2010): 768–70. Print.

——. "Ecocentric Postmodern Theory: Interrelations between Ecological, Quantum, and Postmodern Theories." *Ecocritical Theory. New European Approaches*. Eds. Axel Goodbody and Kate Rigby. Charlottesville and London: University of Virginia Press, 2011. 230–42. Print.

Phillips, Dana. *The Truth of Ecology*. Oxford: Oxford University Press, 2003. Print.

Ross, Andrew. "The Social Claim on Urban Ecology." Interviewed by Michael Bennett. *The Nature of Cities. Ecocriticism and Urban Environments*. Eds. Michael Bennett and David W. Teague. Tucson: The University of Arizona Press, 1999. 15–30. Print.

Schama, Simon. *Landscape and Memory*. London: HarperCollins, 1995. Print.

Slovic, Scott. *Going Away to Think*. Reno: University of Nevada Press, 2008. Print.

Walker, Charlotte Zoë. "The Book 'Laid Upon the Landscape': Virginia Woolf and Nature." *Beyond Nature Writing. Expanding the Boundaries of Ecocriticism*. Eds. Karla Armbruster and Kathleen Wallace. Charlottesville and London: University of Virginia Press, 2001. 143–61. Print.

Westling, Louise. "Virginia Woolf and the Flesh of the World." *New Literary History* 30.4 (1999): 855–75. Print.

Wilson, Thomas M. *The Recurrent Green Universe of John Fowles*. Amsterdam and New York: Rodopi, 2006. Print.

Woodward, Gerard. *August*. London: Chatto & Windus, 2001. Print.

CHAPTER 25

···

"A MUSIC NUMEROUS AS SPACE"

Cognitive Environment and the
House that Lyric Builds

···

SHARON LATTIG

... to move things is all that mankind can do, for such the sole executant is
muscle, whether in whispering a syllable or in felling a forest.

> —Charles Sherrington, 1924

The Birds begun at Four o'clock—
Their period for Dawn—
A Music numerous as space—
But neighboring as Noon—

> —Emily Dickinson, Poem 783

DWELLING AT THE BREAST

In the first of his pantheistic natural histories, the 1856 tract, *L'Oiseau*, historian Jules
Michelet depicts the building of a bird's nest:

> On the inside... the instrument that prescribes a circular form for the nest is noth-
> ing else but the body of the bird. It is by constantly turning round and round and
> pressing back the walls on every side, that it succeeds in forming this circle.... The
> house is a bird's very person; it is its form and its most immediate effort, I shall
> even say, its suffering. The result is only obtained by constantly repeated pressure
> of the breast. There is not one of these blades of grass that, in order to make it curve
> and hold the curve, has not been pressed on countless times by the bird's breast, its
> heart, surely with difficulty in breathing, perhaps even, with palpitations.[1] (qtd. in
> Bachelard 101)

This passage is taken up a century later by Gaston Bachelard, who explicates it in his phenomenology of intimate enclosure, *The Poetics of Space*. In his view, Michelet's bird illustrates what Victor Hugo calls "the function of inhabiting" (Bachelard 90), which is enabled in turn by "the strange, symmetrical, immediate, almost consubstantial flexibility of a man and an edifice" (Bachelard 91). In writing *The Hunchback of Notre Dame,* Hugo had conceived of the soul and physiognomy of Quasimodo as formed by his in habitation of the alcoves and niches of Cathédrale Notre Dame de Paris. Michelet's account of nest-building—a visionary architecture as much as it is an ornithological report—suggests that the libido of the creature-builder flows outward and into a dwelling that is consequently infused with its being. Yielding to the contours of the breast, the nest becomes both extension of, and complement to, the bird's physicality. In the course of home-making, the outward pressure exerted by the animal (its *ex-pression,* if you will) organicizes what is expressed; in Bachelard's words, "[t]he nest" becomes "a swelling fruit, pressing against its limits" (101). The envisioning of the ontology of tenant and home as "almost consubstantial" by all three thinkers serves to recast the spiritual continuity and unity of Michelet's pantheism as a physical reciprocity between bird and nest, an Emersonian physical fact of bi-directional influence. The corporeal act of nest-building may then be argued to imply the continuity of an organism and its environment.

Self-expression is the representative activity of the poet, and the result of such expenditure, as Ralph Waldo Emerson tells us, is that "[t]he man is only half himself, the other half is his expression" (448). This aphorism, drawn from the essay, "The Poet," is directly preceded by the statement "…we study to utter our painful secret" (448). The palpitations of Michelet's bird suggest not only pain, but a pathological suffering that is here vented muscularly, at the chest from whence originates the agent of poesis—the breath. Suffering expressed through the rhythms of song and intensified in the singing is a time-honored poetic modus, but the ramifications of nest-building to the dynamics of poem-making suggest affinities linking these pursuits that enrich the simple association of birds with the afflicted poet-singer. As Henry David Thoreau intuits during his experiment in self-reliant simplicity at Walden Pond, poetic value inheres in the very act of building one's house:

> There is some of the same fitness in a man's building his own house that there is in a bird's building its own nest. Who knows but if men constructed their own dwellings with their own hands…, the poetic faculty would be universally developed, as birds universally sing when they are so engaged? But alas! We do like cowbirds and cuckoos, which lay their eggs in nests which other birds have built, and cheer no traveler with their chattering and unmusical notes. Shall we forever resign the pleasure of construction to the carpenter? What does architecture amount to in the experience of the mass of men? I never in all my walks came across a man engaged in so simple and natural an occupation as building his house. (300–301)

Thoreau's wisdom insists that the simple and the mundane part company as the home-made is elevated to the level of the poetic, and the mass-produced is concurrently devalued. As he points out, singing also conveys the pleasure of home construction, and, in fact, suffering and rejoicing give rise to polar lyric moods that are nevertheless intimately intertwined. The bird, spent at last in palpitation, is at length attenuated; poetic self-expression is achieved only at a cost. Yet, the bird also has reason to celebrate its creative enlargement achieved via the affiliated tasks of singing and building. There is something about the strenuously self-expressive and local act of providing shelter—the metaphoric feat of home-making—that is, as these two passages suggest, intrinsically poetic.

The spatial dimension of lyric poetry is an implicit presence, something sensed as it were, part of the *mythos* of the form. Poems, as the legends of poets would have it, are houses. Conceived of by custom as an architectonic entity, the poem is constructed of the overlay of rooms, of the elaborate formation of *stanzas*—the intricate bejeweled salons of the Renaissance sonnet or the "pretty" chambers Donne set out in earnest to erect. Northrop Frye, in fact, attributes the effect of lyricality to the stanzaic unit that he contends "may impart a lyrical quality even to a long continuous poem: *The Fairie Queene* seems 'lyrical' in a way that *Paradise Lost* does not" (34). What is perhaps a central clue to lyric spatiality is lodged within the term "verse," heir to the Latin *versus*, the turning (or the turning back) that permits the tilling of a field, an alternative unit of apportioned domesticity. Charles Olson's mid-twentieth-century poetics of "field composition" recalls the etymology in order to renovate the form by bursting out of stanzaic constraints to reclaim the field as the fundamental compositional unit. According to the conceit, the poet marks off a plot of ground, traverses it in order to cultivate, that is, to manipulate it to his own ends, an aim the bird achieves via the tool of the breast pressing on raw material. The turning back at the edges of the evolving structure recapitulates the bird's rotational movements, but here the (poetic) foot is the organ and implement of pressure.

The partitioned unity given by the metaphors of "stanza" and "field" reflects the lyric reversion from the linear thrust of language and the resultant dimensionality that characterizes the lyric poem. For present purposes, "room" and "field" will be regarded as more or less interchangeable tropes: the domesticating activities of cultivation and building function as overarching metaphors for human action into and within the environment. In its agricultural sense, cultivation "converts" the earth into a beneficent force, establishing thereby a system of interchange in which ontological flow is in fact bi-directional. It is not only that man is sustained, enlivened by this fundamental instance of barter; his environs are constituted of his effluence. The root "hum" common to "human," "humus" (soil), and also "humble" evokes within this image the consubstantiality attributed to bird and nest, suggesting that verse is built of a material exchange. It is precisely this realization that led Wallace Stevens to revise the opening declaration of "The Comedian as the Letter C" from "[m]an is the intelligence of his soil" to "his soil is man's intelligence" (CP 27, 36) and to acknowledge, thereby, that the line between mind and matter is not so clearly defined. Michelet's interpretation of the event of building likewise rejects the Western tradition that regards the space contiguous to the animal as a bloodless, geometric abstraction in favor of an embodied view of adjacency as informing, enlivening consubstantiality. In this thinking, inhabited space transcends geometry (Bachelard 47).

Further, the notion of enclosure—and thus a degree of stability or substantiality—is built into any ecology, or Thoreavian economy, as both words derive from the Greek *oikos,* or "house." Building establishes its bi-directional flow; it makes of said interchange an *establishment* that is, in Bachelard's way of thinking, deeply intimate and immediate, what he refers to as a "garment-house" (101). In describing the construction of his own dwelling, Thoreau finds refuge in a different organic metaphor:

> This frame, so slightly clad, was a sort of crystallization around me, and reacted on the builder. It was suggestive somewhat as a picture in outlines. I did not need to go outdoors to take the air, for the atmosphere within had lost none of its freshness. It was not so much within doors as behind a door where I sat, even in the rainiest weather (338).

The garment-house is in this rendering translucent and reactive, shaping the builder as it frames his view of the out-of-doors. Thoreau ensconces himself not simply within his home, but near a threshold with imminent access to what lies beyond. In his symbolism, the sheltering edifice becomes a metaphor for the other consummate medium of making—perception:

> It is something to be able to paint a particular picture or to carve a statue, and so to make a few objects beautiful; but it is far more glorious to carve and paint the very atmosphere and medium through which we look, which morally we can do. To affect the quality of the day, that is the highest of arts. Every man is tasked to make his life, even in its details, worthy of the contemplation of his most elevated and critical hour. (343)

What are most fitting to us, in other words, are our own imaginative constructions including, fundamentally, our perceptions. The insight that we render artistically the "atmosphere," the medium through which we perceive, and engage thereby in a supreme practice of making, is profound. Thoreau's pronouncement sets up *Walden*'s famous mandate to live "deliberately" by "front[ing] only the essential facts of life" (343), which is directed specifically at the process of constructing one's house: "It would be worth the while to build still more deliberately than I did, considering, for instance, what foundation a door, a window, a cellar, a garret, have in the nature of man, and perchance never raising any superstructure until we found a better reason for it than our temporal necessities even" (300). By "temporal," Thoreau means both transitory and earthly; anticipating pragmatism, he prods his audience to evaluate the long-term returns of both physical and spiritual actions so that they may be compared on a kind of balance sheet to the effort expended in their execution.[2] The urgency for such evaluation is extended to imaginative effort, which must be "worthy of the contemplation of [our] most elevated and critical hour," and it is with this gesture that Thoreau uncovers the artistic or poetic value of constructing the house of perception. The house built deliberately, economically is—symbolically and actually—"the very medium through which we look," necessarily erected at and establishing the border between self and environment. For such a "garment-house" to fit, it must be stitched conscientiously of meet actions, of carefully weighed decisions. It must conform to the builder if it is to serve its function to be sturdy yet permeable.

To probe both the native spatiality of lyric poetry and the innately poetical quality of the house, to grasp the significance of the poem's peculiar method of imparting a sense of transit, of inscribed demarcation, dimensionality and enclosure, one must conceive of space as the emergent consequence of the lyric's deep investment in perception and action, the creative wellsprings and structuring dynamics evoked and engaged in the experience of the lyric poem. The poem's sense of apportioned space reflects the dynamics in play at the immediate juncture at which an organism actively accommodates itself to an environment using perceptual and motor tactics to engage in the cognitive processes implicated in the function of inhabiting and the habitat it constructs. To fully comprehend the poetic idea of the garment house, it is necessary to visit the fundamental faculty of perception.

FEELING SPACE

To account for spatial apprehension within his proto-phenomenological treatise, *The Principles of Psychology,* William James grounds the availability of spatial knowledge in perception. He begins "The Perception of Space," the chapter he dedicates to the topic, "with the direct observation that a sense of space accompanies acts of perception within most sense modalities. All spatial knowledge," he observes, "is at bottom sensorial" (152). The range of each of the sensory systems, from the limits of taste in interiority to vision's terminus at the horizon, then, modifies corporeal reach in evoking spatial awareness. The first thing that bears noting about lyric space in light of this simple observation is that it is not necessary to make an abstract or theoretical argument for its existence, because an inchoate spatial quality may be said to accompany the derivative perceptual experience of the mental images poetry occasions.[3]

James next posits that the perceptual experience of space yields, to varying degrees of exactitude, the quality of voluminousness or vastness. Vastness is in fact the primary sensation within the experience of space, the quality that makes all others possible (135), and yet, in itself vastness yields an impression that is void of order (145).[4] To become subject to our grasp, space must first be demarcated. The primordial expanses yielded by sensation must "be *measured and subdivided* by consciousness, and *added* together, before they can form by their synthesis what we know as the real Space of the objective world" (145).[5] The modality most capable of intricate subdivision, of "perceiving space to be composed of lesser portions simultaneously coexisting alongside of each other" and within one another, is vision (136). For James, the visual nesting of spatial units within larger ones imparts "the very rudiment of order" (147).[6]

The transition from a vague feeling of capaciousness to a precise specification of space is then the transition to understanding:

[The] entrance [of the idea] into the mind is equivalent to a more detailed subdivision, cognizance, and measurement of the space considered. *The bringing of subdivisions to consciousness constitutes, then, the entire process by which we pass from our first vague feeling of a total vastness to a cognition of the vastness in detail.* The more numerous the subdivisions are, the more elaborate and perfect the cognition becomes. (152)

James emphasizes the way in which a backdrop of spatial ambiguity—some melodious Keatsian plot—foregrounds the partitioning that permits the apprehension of one's surroundings. In the first stanza of Poem 783 quoted in the epigraph, Emily Dickinson uses the adjective "numerous" to modify the nouns "music" and, by virtue of comparison, "space," eschewing the expected "voluminous." Although volume is the appropriate concept for measuring space with objective accuracy, she instead asserts the fact of the divisibility of space and enacts, rather than denotes, its division into component units. The word "numerous," of course, entails the notion of number, of poetic foot and musical measure, but it also acknowledges that vacant space may be quantified, lent divisibility and rendered graspable. Notably, James qualifies hearing as a sense capable of evoking relative vastness but particularly resistant to subdivision. Dickinson goes one step further in recognizing that scission is among the functions of the medium of song and that the divisions of poems and homes permit the apprehension of the spaces they delimit.

James's analysis of spatial apprehension is qualitative, not only in its focus, but also in its origin. Remarkably, his far-reaching work is based in great part on introspection. Reconciling qualitative experience with the incommensurate realm of physical reality (and especially the brain) is, of course, one of the major tasks facing present-day philosophy. To broach the problem, Gerald Edelman begins by maintaining that it is reasonable to assume that the brain must be capable of generating the features of consciousness. Writing with Giulio Tononi, he postulates that the physical substrate must share the structural and dynamic qualities of consciousness, including integrity and differentiation, if it is to be productive of them (143, 146–52).[7] The function of differentiation upon which subdivision depends is in fact salient in the early phase of visual perception, in which information is processed in parallel; once triggering stimuli in the form of electro-magnetic radiation have been selected from the environment and received by the neurons in the retina, they are isolated and processed on parallel optic tracks that do not initially interact.[8] At this level, and henceforth, the brain engages in a series of contrast mechanisms that accord significance to the divisions the sensory systems have created. Differentiation is a scalar process: as discrete information is eventually associated and merged into neuronal networks, progressively larger assemblies of neurons are contrasted through oscillating rhythms until the brain is able to distinguish a neural correlate of the self from a neural correlate of the non-self (*Brains* 56). The function of the sensory systems is first—though not exclusively—to articulate into meaningful divisions the input it has selected from the environment and to differentiate it into features by means of neuronal contrast mechanisms.[9]

PERCEIVING SPACE

Perception is also an original, constructive faculty, but if its revelations were uncon-
nected to the world, it would be quite literally maladaptive. Logically, survival depends
on a degree of correlation between the environment and the percept that specifies it. The
perceptual significance of environmental information was first explored by psychologist
James J. Gibson ini his 1979 study, *The Ecological Approach to Visual Perception*. In this
landmark text, Gibson challenges the then-current experimental model by liberating
the subject from his restrained, quiescent posture in the laboratory chair in order to
make possible the study of *ambient vision,* enabled by looking around, and *ambulatory
vision,* enabled by walking around. With an attention to first-hand perceptual experience reminiscent of James, Gibson replaces the physical understanding of a world constituted of matter with an ecological understanding of world made up of *media* affording
the transmission of information and *substances,* environmental constituents with properties, especially surfaces, that are potentially available to perception. It is this ecological, cognitive definition of substance that is relevant herein.

Gibson begins with the observation that the minimal viscosity of air, the medium in
which birds and animals subsist, both facilitates their movement and permits the transmission of light, which bounces off surfaces and reverberates until the medium achieves
a saturation point in ambience (50). The study of what he names "ecological optics" is
concerned with the information that is available for perception as a result of the reflection of light off the surfaces of substances (16–18, 47, 50). As surfaces variously absorb,
reflect, transmit, or project light (30–31), these heterogeneous facades that comprise
objects and separate them from the medium and from one another become the aspects
of an environment available to perception (22, 94). Surfaces enable perception because
they feature textural differences within themselves and may be differentiated from other
surfaces by virtue of their borders (23, 52). Gibson refers to the layouts of relative opacity,
translucency, and transparency they enable as the *ambient optic array:* the environing
field of view consisting of visual angles formed by light reflecting off surfaces and con-
verging at the eye, and thus existing only relative to the viewer (53–54).

Movement is critical to Gibson's understanding of perception, for by moving, an
organism disturbs the ambient optic array in altering its structure (103) and determines
thereby which aspects of the array are more or less invariant (73). What remains stable through movement specifies a structural layout (89), while instability may specify
either the motion of the perceiver or the motion of substances in the environment (73).
Perception functions by extracting invariants from the flux and ascertaining the structure that persists in the way that the revolutionary motion of the bird confirms the familiar contours of the nest. It gives access to *affordances*—what the environment offers the
organism for its use as determined by both the environment and the animal cognizing it.
Affordances are not subjective properties of the environment, then, but rather those that
are significant relative to the organism (Turvey and Shaw 97).

The visual heterogeneity that in Gibson's model affords an understanding of the environment is constituted of borders, edges, corners, and brinks—sites of distinction that

are consequential to the organism. They furnish contact, as by grasping, or avoidance, as not falling off a cliff and into the vague (29). Analogously, discontinuity is an affordance—perhaps the defining affordance—of lyric, a genre characterized by the use of lineation. By means of its tendency to disjoin its unit structures, lyric poetry registers and exploits the innate structuring tendencies an environment offers and a mind enacts. Within the various metaphorical conceptions of lyric space, the brink that is the poetic line break becomes the wall, the periphery of the field or nest, beyond which is the unknown from which one reverts necessarily upon the withdrawal into interiority, upon perceiving. The brink at line's end is the edge of the fertile, or the negotiable, of positive affordance. It marks the limits of the terrain in which one is at home while simultaneously exposing one to the ambiguity of the undefined, or the vague, afforded by the use of, for example, enjambment.

What is it that Dickinson's Birds "begun" at "Four o'clock"? At the limit of this, the poem's first line, possibility is vented and meaning is undetermined. With the shift of viewpoint onto line two, the information that the object of the past participle "begun" (oddly deprived of an auxiliary verb) is "Their period for Dawn—" becomes available and meaning is recovered. The fact that this second line is demarcated allows us to the grasp the idea that the period was begun "for" or "on behalf of" Dawn. Yet it is necessary to re-orient ourselves only slightly to see that beyond this self-contained and cohesive unit lies further possibility if we take "for Dawn" to mean "because Dawn" and in so doing to initiate a new clause. The potential vista opened as the clause is curtailed at line's end is then occluded (yet still present to knowledge) by the entrance of an object appositional to "Their period": "A Music numerous as space—" with which the Birds (have/had) begun to define and to fill their Period.

Gibson further observes that surfaces available for perception are characteristically disposed in a continuous, nested hierarchy.[10] Visual nesting occurs because nearer surfaces occlude more distant ones. Occluding surfaces are visual clues for "depth" as the effect of nesting gives rise to a sense of behindness (Gibson 77); they purvey the knowledge of behindness which one might access if one were to venture around an entity, analogously by troping, or turning to examine its anterior surfaces, its poetic depth or interpretive possibility—the meaning beyond. Lyric poetry's ability to nest "episodes within episodes, subordinate ones and superordinate ones," to use Gibson's language (101) does not effect occlusion literally. Yet, by virtue of its propensity to embed lines within sentences, sentences and phrases within lines and stanzas and to foreground words (and the word is heftier and more prominent within poetry) salient subunits may indeed obscure the meaning of their contexts at the same time they fit into them as into a picture. Truncated as it is, the subordinate clause "for Dawn" is nested within the line in which it appears as a prepositional phrase: focusing on the former usage obscures the fact that the period is intended for dawn, as a gift. In addition, the alternate meaning one might assign to the word "period" of sentence-ending punctuation mark allows us to interpret these first lines to mean that the birds "begun" to confirm the conclusion of dawn by punctuating it. A paradox inheres in the co-extensiveness of the past and present given by the two meanings of "period" that render an extent of time that is just beginning even as its ending is signaled. The paradox is recapitulated by the use of the verb form "begun": the replacement of the expected imperfect "began" by the lone past participle indicates that the action has been completed in the past, if we infer the helping verb "had," or that it has only just begun, if we prefer the auxiliary "have." Surfaces and brinks may afford mutually exclusive usages, as a cliff may offer protection, as from an enemy, or death, as from falling. Entertaining alternate and at times mutually exclusive affordances, bringing them forward into our grasp while maintaining knowledge of what lies behind, provides us with an understanding of the poem that accommodates potential perspectives and is thereby richly conceptual. The line structure of a poem allows one to make various uses of the poem while not foreclosing upon the possibility in which Dickinson wished to dwell.[11]

The act of perceiving, then, assumes three co-extensive orders: the qualitative distinctions of James's psychology; their corresponding enaction at the neurological level; and the analogue of both: the borders affording perception within Gibson's environment. Perceptual attention distinguishes space and in so doing abstracts the lighted structure of the world around us in order to build percepts. A cognitive propensity to distinguish is adapted to a landscape of difference.

ENACTING SPACE

The liberation of the viewer into action permits the definition of cognitive environment as that which is perceptually available to an organism; in Gibson's words, the "surroundings of those organisms that perceive and behave" (7). What the organism is afforded by its surroundings are possibilities for behavior (Gibson 96, Turvey and Shaw 97). (Likewise, linguistic objects and events afford potential interpretative behavior to one conversant with and liberated within a language.) In this theory, behavior (movement) enables perception by changing the ambient optic array. The recuperation of movement as a necessary agent within perception has also been adopted within constructivist models of the faculty that entwine it with action in a single, indivisible activity. The most radical of these, Francisco Varela's Buddhist-inspired "enactionism," is built on two premises: the first and most relevant herein is that "Perception consists in perceptually guided action" (Varela, Thompson, and Rosch 173). With this claim, Varela merges perception and action into a single process and in so doing gives prominence to embodied sensory-motor structures in the shaping of the exterior world. In his own words:

> [T]he point of departure for the enactive approach is the study of how the perceiver can guide his actions in his local situation. Since these local situations constantly change as a part of the perceiver's activity, the reference point for understanding perception is no longer a pregiven, perceiver-independent world but rather the sensorimotor structure of the perceiver (the way in which the nervous systems link sensory and motor surfaces). This structure—*the manner in which the perceiver is embodied*—rather than some pregiven world determines how the perceiver can act and be modulated by environmental events. (173)

The emphasis in this quotation is Varela's, but the passage emphasized could apply to Michelet's interpretation of nest-building. In the parable of the bird, the shape of the breast allows the organism to act upon and shape environmental events (the natural ingredients of the nest) and to be "modulated" by them on a perceptual level. Action shapes perception, the tailoring of environmental events to the perceiver, and perception serves action. This connection is forged within the neurobiology of the organism as well.

> Thus the overall concern of an enactive approach to perception is not to determine how some perceiver-independent world is to be recovered; it is, rather, to determine the common principles or lawful linkages between sensory and motor systems that explain how action can be perceptually guided in a perceiver-dependent world. (Varela, Thompson, and Rosch 173)

A representative mechanism of sensory-motor connection has been theorized by neuroscientist Walter Freeman, who disturbs the longstanding linear, cause-to-effect trajectory that saw the percept's terminus in action in order to prioritize the constructive role the body plays in shaping its perceptual grasp of the world. Redefining analytic intentionality—the concept of the "aboutness" of mental contents or their relationship to the objects in the outer world at which they are directed—he conceives intentionality as rather the means by which organisms proactively position themselves to perceive. Intentionality is relocated from the organismic action into the environment that constructs the perception. At the neurological level, it is "[t]he process by which goal-directed actions are generated in the brains of humans and other animals" (*Brains* 8). Using the past results of similar actions as a guide, the brain predicts the perceptual result of an intended action and acts—or does not act—accordingly. An intentional action may be as simple as the turning of the head to confirm the source of a noise visually. The bird's incremental adjustment of its position within the nest is intentional in this sense. As action determines perception, the directionality of the perceptual process is in its full sense an outward directionality. The problem of the passivity of the observer was perhaps the central flaw of Locke's epistemology, and it is one Freeman remedies by inverting the ingrained understanding of the agent/patient relationship within perception so that the outside, the environment, also exhibits the feminine quality of pliancy: "The form of the nest is commanded by the inside" (Bachelard 101).

The long-standing prioritizing of perception in relation to action assumed that the mind represents the world as it is and subsequently acts upon its representation. The prioritizing of action assumes that a representation of the world is co-constructed by the organism of its past experience (memory), the parameters of its capacity for action (the limits of its body), and perceptual input (its environment). On a neurological level, intentionality is enabled by the phenomenon Freeman names "preafference," which involves a corollary discharge of the plan of action: "When a motor plan is sent to the motor systems in preparation for innervation of the spinal column, a 'copy' of the plan is simultaneously relayed to the sensory cortices to enable them to predict the sensory consequences of the intended action" ("Consciousness" 151). Through preafference, the organism "imagines" how its projected actions might alter the position of the sense organs (the eyes, the ears, the fingertips, the breast) within their environment (Freeman 2000 33). The senses are thereby primed to anticipate particular stimulation, and such expectation shapes the percept on a neurological level. Percepts have been implicitly acted into: they have been actively (whether voluntarily or not) sought and constructed. To integrate Thoreau into this theory, deliberate action leads to a most fitting carving of the air. Living deliberately is living with an eye to the selection of an action that constructs a best perception and in so doing affects the quality of the day.

We have before us two divergent philosophies that privilege action in the construction of the perception of space. Varela's enactionism and Freeman's neurodynamics focus on the way specific embodiedness shapes percepts, while Gibson's ecological optics provides a justification for a cognitive continuity between organism and environment in a search for a realistic basis for perception in optical structures. The work of Varela and Freeman stresses the constructivist function of perception, the way that input is reassembled under the constraints of organismic history and physical embodiment to form percepts that remake the world as it is. A notorious example is the qualitative experience of color, which does not necessarily correspond to the physical definition of color as a wavelength range of electro-magnetic radiation. It is this kind of example that leads Freeman into an epistemological solipsism: the idea, shared by Wallace Stevens, that we cannot know the world objectively because it eludes our capabilities to do so. I am suggesting that this view is not incompatible with Gibson's claim that the concept of the affordance is evidence of a kind of realism, or of the connectedness of perception and environment. We couldn't grasp an object, for example, if its edges were not where we suppose them to be. The variegation or array of sites of distinction within the layout of a cognitive environment are the points of connection between the two. The marking off, the surveying of a homestead implicit within the notion of verse is enabled by, and gives rise to, the fitting structures that establish the complementarity of the expandable organism and its environment.

Each of these theories concedes that the perceiving body moves in space and, as a result, perceives differently. Spatial apprehension is shaped by movement, which constructs perception (and thus the perception of space) both neurologically and by shifting the vantage point of the observer in order to confirm transience and relative permanence, per Gibson. Traversing involves a repositioning, which for the bird-poet takes the form of turning or troping, where troping—figuration—becomes the revised vantage point enabled by verbal action. The movement of the builder/farmer demands that an understanding of lyric space be forged in terms of the organism's changing experience.[12] In the lyric poem and in Michelet's nest, space is an experiential and not an abstract phenomenon. The poem is a nest of shifting orientation that inscribes one's position, or more properly *disposition*—one's tone, or indeed attitude (in at once a kinaesthetic and a moral or emotional sense); it is a space created by the breath-driven revolutions of the bird, a home that at all points makes reference to the body of its inhabitant. What the poet encloses with the end of understanding, are its own limits—the limits of its bodily self, which are at times narrow and defined and at times extend into unanticipated vistas. The house and the field and their poetic counterparts are then transitional spaces in which an exterior is actively made interior, and an interior refashions what is outside in order to comprehend it. A home is a space tailored with reference to the body and grasped as it is disposed. It is an expressed composition of the outside; the manipulated space of positive affordance; the way a speaker delimits and apportions for comprehension the perceptually extended borders of its self.

Varela's second principle for enactionism, that cognitive structures emerge from "the recurrent sensorimotor patterns that enable action to be perceptually guided," is also applicable herein (Varela, Thompson, and Rosch 173). His idea that conception emerges from the more fundamental activity of perception and action is an insight shared by Gibson and Freeman, and it allows one to read a poem comprised of concept-laden language as a perceptual act. There is, appropriately, a mythos surrounding poetic language that invests it with the dual powers of agency and acute perceptual awareness. Poetic words are actors: the term "utterance" itself bespeaks an expressive or outward gesturing in which the expulsion of the breath is emblematic of poetic action. "Words and deeds are quite indifferent modes of the divine energy" observes Emerson (290). This notion of the word as efficacious actor, as disembodied mover, the word of the *fiat lux* or the decree to the stately pleasure dome is an idea deeply rooted in the Western tradition.

Equally tenacious within Western poetics is the idea that the poetic word is situated on, or directly informed by, an irrepressible perceptual stream. The notion that lyric poetry inscribes an attention to perception and both registers and prompts its processes subtends radically dissimilar poetry and poetics and has instigated the spilling of much critical ink. For example, Coleridge bases the dynamic of his creative, secondary imagination in the perceptual dynamic driving the primary imagination (263). The idea is also germinal and constitutive for the figure who is perhaps the Romantics' best critic, Charles Olson, who prescribes that the momentum of the faculty be enacted in the poem where "[o]ne perception must flow instanter on the other" (17). Each poetics seeks to tap into the current of unreflective (that is, unconscious or marginally conscious) perception, presumably in order to preserve it in its essence. As lyric poetry imagines the word as an enactor or creator of a world and as a constructed image of a world, its spatial sense may be seen to inhere in the lexical interplay of perceived and enacted space.

NUMEROUS MUSIC

Given the insights offered by Michelet, Thoreau, and James, it is perhaps inevitable to explain this last assertion by turning to the principal experimental poetics of the nineteenth century. It goes without saying that the poems of Emily Dickinson and Walt Whitman evoke divergent senses of space. In the light of biography in particular, it is easy to read Dickinson as a poet of enclosure, of bounded domesticity and withdrawal, and all the more so when her warren-like compositions are set against the foil of Whitmanian illimitability. The latter's near-contemporaneous technique, in which one long line pulls the reader around to the next, and lists are all-inclusive and presume, with every entry, their own continuation, stands in strong opposition to the former's poetics of concision.[13] If the lyric repertoire features means of subdivision, the poetry of Emily Dickinson is exemplary in its lyricism: its bent toward scission is amplified by the veer of her pervasive dash, which also serves to foreground the units it segregates, producing, at times, a nesting effect of occlusion. The curtailed extension of line effected by the punctuation mark heightens the poem's propensity to fold back in upon itself and to refer internally, creating thereby an architectonics. The presentation of the poems suggests containment, stability, graspability at the same time it allows for many changes of perspective. Hers is a poetics of disjunction, and, per James, it should and does render conceptual complexity.

Yet, Dickinson's structural pretensions to sequestering domesticity belie the penetrability of her domiciles by the undomesticated. On the one hand labyrinthine structures housing oddly-shaped Quasimodos, her poems are yet Thoreauvian frameworks letting in the air. Every disjunction provokes (as it records) a moment of disorientation, an imbalance that is acknowledged and intensified by the use of off-rhyme and marks the necessity and the opportunity for re-orientation. The wide-open doors and windows letting in spring breezes to aerate the home allow for the leakage of what is often named the pre-conceptual. Each brink or caesura is a threshold to the uncognizable: at her line breaks, one both encounters and reverts from the unknown (as Thoreau situates himself behind a door and not *within* doors). In Dickinson, this tension between the Jamesian vague, recurrent in her poetry, for example, as notions of eternity and as lack, and the subtly constructed means of their reconceptualization, is extreme. The dash is also a kind of joinery, the ur-mark of continuity across discontinuity, at once an intensification and a mitigation of the brink it spans. In Gibson's lexicon, it affords the disjunction and continuity of the edge of a surface or signifying division within contiguity. And as the divisions are unexpected, the architecture novel, one must work to comprehend their significance. What Dickinson chooses to select and to construct of the world allows for the uncognizeable to co-habit with the cognized in an open-air edifice resembling a nest. She maintains a space for the ambulant, thinking self that is intimate, yet infinitely capable of admitting the unknown, the outside, without pretense to understanding it as it is. In Poem 1084, a single, singing bird "propounds" a melody and, at length, creates place:

> At Half past Three, a single Bird
> Unto a silent Sky
> Propounded but a single term
> Of cautious melody.
>
> At Half past Four, Experiment
> Had subjugated test
> And lo, her silver Principle
> Supplanted all the rest.
>
> At Half past Seven, Element
> Nor Implement, be seen—
> And Place was where the Presence was
> Circumference between. (491)

Through the articulation of song, "Experiment" or risk-taking, the willing negotiation of the unknown, subjugates "test," the evaluation of demonstrated knowledge, and by poem's end, presence is place-bound. Place, in the common usage of the term, is space that has been sufficiently demarcated as to be coherent—it is fitted to the presence of the perceiver. However, the syntax here inverts the role of the divisive preposition "between" as the terms it distinguishes are ambiguously its objects. As a result, circumference may be seen to intervene between place, where presence is, and non-place/non-presence, what the speaker calls the "silent Sky," or, alternatively, it may be interpreted to separate presence from place, thrusting it into a vastness without anchor.

"Circumference" is a recurring term in Dickinson's lexicon, one that often marks sensory limits. Unattainable and horizon-like, it is "Beyond the Dip of Bell" in Poem 378 where "Dip" is taken to mean aural diminishment (180). In Poem 633, circumference is available only upon the cessation of the rotation of a "Cog," a metaphor for the "cognitive" apparatus that puts circumference in motion and blurs it (313). (Only upon the cessation of thought does the ultimate become definable.) Finally, Poem 1620 suggests that circumference is unreachable, "possessing," that is, striking only in the future if one could but arrive there; otherwise it is available only as a courtly ideal, as the "Bride of Awe" (667). In each of these examples, Dickinson's horizon-like notion of circumference allows the indefinite to seep into the place it surrounds without being assimilated into that place. Her use of the term is an admission that there is a beyond, an unreachable Stevensian reality, and with it, she gestures toward an ecological definition of place as an *unlimited* extension of surfaces nested in a relationship of inclusion. Because place is unstable and comprised of nesting surfaces that entail "mutual embeddings and mutual separations" (Gibson 57), its units may not be counted and are potentially "as numerous as space." Place, in the ecological sense, is not locatable with the aid of Cartesian coordinates; that is, it cannot be identified in relation to other, stabilized places. Enclosed by the horizon that is the contingent and temporary limit of the perceiver in relation to its environs, forming and deforming as it coheres around the presence of the perceiver, place is finally, like Dickinson's poems, unbounded and vulnerable (Turvey and Shaw 96).

This poetic understanding of the relationship between an organism and the place it specifies is reflected in the ecological doctrine of "animal-environment mutuality and reciprocity" (Turvey and Shaw 99). The concept of mutuality assumes commensurability and thus symmetry of relation (as numbers may be added to one another), while reciprocity refers to difference that is complementary. The difference between an organism and its environment confers an asymmetry of relation without sacrificing the commensurability of the terms. Gibson's theory, as elaborated and quantified by M. T. Turvey and Robert E. Shaw, assumes a level of analysis at which elements are "complementary duals" in the sense that they complete one another (99). In tandem, mutuality and reciprocity are the conditions of an epistemic ecosystem providing that "[t]he knower (animal) and the known (environment) are not rigidly separable components, they are not definable

independently of each other, and knowing cannot be isolated from these components"
(Turvey and Shaw 100).

> For a synergy of animal and environment, the asymmetry of dualism (where ani-
> mals and environments are merely incommensurate kinds) must give way to the
> symmetry notion of duality (where the two are commensurate kinds). The ecologi-
> cal counter to the traditional doctrine of animal environment dualism is, therefore,
> animal-environment duality. (Shaw 99)

Ecological analysis then obviates the dualism of mind and matter in defining a cognitive
environment as that which is available to be perceived.[14] The reciprocal alignment of the
distended breast with the nest's inner curvature is emblematic of an animal-environment
relationship of duality in which the raw materials are the environment shaped and perceived, and the nest is a present *structure* of perception. What poetry does is to preserve
the hypothetical structure that is evidence of the cognitive contiguity of organism and
environment as well as their "consubstantial flexibility." The divisions the mind creates
are complementary to the surface disjunctions in the environment, and the poem is the
point at which their complementarity is manifest; song is "neighboring, like noon" (a
border that has no extension, but divides and secures the complementary contingents
morning and afternoon). The poem is a kind of cognitive hinge referring in both directions, outwardly to an apprehended cognitive environment and inwardly to the cognitive process by which it apprehends.

PLACE AVAILS NOT

Reflecting, in the late essay "Democratic Vistas," on his life-long project of answering
Emerson's call for a national poet of America, Walt Whitman also expresses a metaphorical understanding of the poet's vocation as the erection of a vesture house:

> ...we have again pointedly to confess that all the objective grandeurs of the world,
> for highest purposes, yield themselves up, and depend on mentality alone. Here,
> and here only, all balances, all rests. For the mind, which alone builds the perma-
> nent edifice, haughtily builds it to itself. By it, with what follows it, are convey'd to
> mortal sense the culminations of the materialistic, the known, and a prophecy of the
> unknown. (994)

At times, Whitman's prideful "I" seems something more or less than organismic, timeless, roving and unrestrained by the gravity that binds mere creatures to the earth. His
sense of space is often conceived of as spaceless because it is relatively uninterrupted by
perceptual and conceptual distinction: percept and concept for him aspire to inclusiv-
ity. His use of anaphoric repetition, for instance, brings one back to the same space and
enlarges, rather than subdividing and defining space. His lists may be said to have the
same effect: in embracing the grand scale, they supersede place. Particularly, in relation

to Dickinson, Whitman is a non-pronominal poet who eludes finite situation. The girth of his "I," unconstrained as against an opposing "you," instead assumes every "you" and with it the environment each "you" entrains. Note the progression of the first five lines of "Crossing Brooklyn Ferry":

> Flood-tide below me! I see you face to face!
> Clouds of the west—sun there half an hour high—I see you also face to face.
> Crowds of men and women attired in the usual costumes, how curious you are to me!
> On the ferry-boats the hundreds and hundreds that cross, returning home, are more
>   curious to me than you suppose,
> And you that shall cross from shore to shore years hence are more to me, and more in my
>   meditations, than you might suppose. (307–8)

There is, of course, division within Whitman's poetry; it is, after all, composed of words and lines, and place is rendered as a result (the East River on which Brooklyn Ferry sails and the New York Harbor beyond it). Yet, there is always an overwhelming counter-tension that seeks to eradicate the local by distending it—present-day Brooklyn Ferry encompasses Brooklyn Ferry of yesteryear. This is Whitman's manner of rendering the visionary mode of lyric, freeing body from physical constraints and yet subjecting it to a perceptual dynamic. The resultant expansion of perspective enables his poetry to become vatic. The irony is of course that Whitman is avowedly a poet of embodiment, championing the singular, unidealized, and even putrid ashes-to-ashes body of earth. For Dickinson, the two modes cohabit in tension, the unknown beyond leaking in to the substantive structure, but for Whitman, their co-presence is simply unparadoxical. Place is placeless because the eye is liberated. It avails not.

In Ovid's version of the Orpheus myth, the mournful tones uttered by the poet grieving the loss of his bride Eurydice summon to himself an apparently exhaustive host of species. Trees in particular are uprooted unnaturally, drawn to the poet and catalogued in a Whitman-like listing (if one will pardon the inversion of historical priority). In aspiring to include all tree species, the recitation of the list lends the idea that the poet evokes not just a local, but a full sense of environment with his song by calling it into perceptual range and expressing it. Orpheus is here the exemplary, visionary ur-poet. Built into the vatic mode is the sense that one can transcend bodily, human limits without transcending the dynamics of the body. (Orpheus's descent into Hades and his consummate poeticizing in the realm of the afterlife from which he returns is indicative of this paradox.) The poet therefore must remain at all times attentive to an environment, expressing it by building a cognitive edifice that preserves its structures. The construction of the nest is supplied by outings (utterances) into the environs for sticks, straw, and blades of grass, ventures abroad that domesticate the outside, bringing pertinent potential structure into the space one occupies, and in occupying, structures. It is the structural commonality and complementarity of the two terms that allows the garment to be cut and re-cut to fit. Wallace Stevens posits just such a structural common ground in expressing the possibility for representation within a schema in which reality includes the mind: "The accuracy of accurate letters is an accuracy with respect to the structure of reality" (*NA* 71). The poem as it stands is both a structural, linguistic replication of the environment's tendency to nest and to disjoin, and an emergent act of perception inscribing a new environment available to be perceived by the reader. An ecological, constructivist *poeisis* of space presumes fresh perception to rule out the reflexive and the automatic and their end in the pre-fabricated and the mass-produced, which is antithetical to the poetic tradition of making. The poem is a new nest, verse a converse—a conversation and a reversal or bidirectionality of predication emergent as a "dwelling together."

Notes

1. Michelet's original French text reads:

    "Et au dedans, l'instrument qui imprime au nid la forme circulair en'est encore autre que le corps de l'oiseau. C'est en se tournant constamment et refoulant le mur de tous côtés, qu'il arrive à former ce cercle.

    Donc, la maison, c'est la personne même, sa forme et son effort le plus immédiat; je dirai sa souffrance. Le résultat n'est obtenu que par un expression constamment répétée de la poitrine. Pas un de ces brins d'herbe qui, pour prendre et garder la courbe, n'ait été mille et mille fois poussé du sein, du coeur, certainement avec trouble de la respiration, avec palpitation peut-être." (208–9)

2. It will remain, of course, for Charles Sanders Peirce and William James to give full-development and efficacy to this idea.
3. Neurologically, the experience of mental imagery activates sense-motor representations; in other words, it utilizes the same neural pathways as perceptual experience.
4. James had introduced his analogous idea of "the vague" in the earlier, 1884 article, "The Stream of Consciousness," in which he argues for its import to cognition and underscores the need to attend to it (Vol. 1, 254).
5. The significance of this move will be amplified by James's later radical empiricism and its emphasis on relation, which he argues is apprehended directly.
6. The experience given by the other sense modalities is more difficult, but not impossible to subdivide. Hearing, the sense literally engaged by poetry, also permits distinction-making and a sense of nesting as one sound may occlude another.
7. The work of James himself, who foresaw many of the advances of cognitive science, vindicates this idea. His identification of discrimination, association, and selection as decisive, qualitative methods affording the apprehension of space through its subdivision (135) predicted analogous propensities that have since been identified within the neurological dynamics of perception.
8. An example may be drawn from color vision. The retina consists of three types of color receptor neurons processed separately on three optic tracks. The brain contrasts the input of two of them, sums the difference between them and then contrasts the result with the input provided by the third in order to interpret color.
9. The existence of specialized receptor neurons (the notion of a receptive field) alone justifies this claim. Discrete bits of potential information are selected from the environment based on their compatibility with a particular receptor.

10. It would be too easy to make a connection between the phenomenon of the nesting of smaller units within larger ones that describes poems and the environment as it is available to vision and the structures built by birds.

11. See Poem 657.

12. Hugo notes that for Quasimodo, the cathedral had been in succession "egg, nest, house, country and universe" (Bachelard 91).

13. This is literally the case. The poet cut lines of verse into strips and sewed them together.

14. The material basis for organism-environment continuity at the level of analysis of physics, for example the exchange of oxygen and carbon dioxide, is not available to perception.

WORKS CITED

Bachelard, Gaston. *The Poetics of Space. 1958.* Trans. Maria Jolas. Boston: Beacon, 1994.

Coleridge, Samuel Taylor. *The Selected Poetry and Prose of Samuel Taylor Coleridge.* Ed. Donald A. Stauffer. New York: Random House, 1951.

Dickinson, Emily. *The Complete Poems of Emily Dickinson.* Ed. Thomas H. Johnson. Boston: Little, Brown, 1960.

Edelman, Gerald and Guilio Tononi. *A Universe of Consciousness: How Matter Becomes Imagination.* New York: Basic Books, 2000.

Emerson, Ralph Waldo. "The Poet." *Ralph Waldo Emerson: Essays and Lectures.* New York: The Library of America, 1983. 445–68.

Freeman, Walter J. "Consciousness, Intentionality and Causality." *Reclaiming Cognition: The Primacy of Action Intention and Emotion.* Eds. Rafael Núñez and Walter J. Freeman. Thorverton, UK: Imprint, 1999. 95–110.

——. *How Brains Make Up Their Minds.* New York: Columbia UP, 2000.

Frye, Northrop. "Approaching the Lyric." *Lyric Poetry: Beyond New Criticism.* Eds. Chaviva Hosek and Patricia Parker. Ithaca: Cornell UP, 1985. 31–37.

Gibson, James J. *The Ecological Approach to Visual Perception. 1979.* Hillsdale, NJ: Lawrence Erlbaum, 1986.

James, William. "The Stream of Thought." *The Principles of Psychology.* Vol. 1. 1890. New York: Dover, 1950. 224–90.

——. "The Perception of Space." *The Principles of Psychology.* Vol. 2. 1890. New York: Dover, 1950. 134–282.

Michelet, Jules. *L'Oiseau. 1861.* Paris: Elibron Classics, 2006.

Olson, Charles. "Projective Verse." *Charles Olson: Selected Writings.* Ed. Robert Creeley. New York: New Directions, 1951. 15–26.

Ovid. *Metamorphoses: Books IX–XV.* Cambridge: Harvard UP, 1884.

Stevens, Wallace. *The Necessary Angel.* New York: Vintage Books, 1942.

——. *Wallace Stevens: The Collected Poems. 1954.* New York: Vintage Books, 1990.

Thoreau, Henry David. *Walden, 1854. The Portable Thoreau.* Ed. Carl Bode. New York: Penguin, 1947. 258–572.

Turvey, M. T. and Robert E. Shaw. "Ecological Foundations of Cognition: I. Symmetry and Specificity of Animal-Environment Systems." *Reclaiming Cognition: The Primacy of Action Intention and Emotion.* Eds. Rafael Núñez and Walter J. Freeman. Thorverton, UK: Imprint, 1999. 95–110.

Varela, Francisco J., Evan Thompson, and Eleanor Rosch. *The Embodied Mind: Cognitive Science and Human Experience*. Cambridge: MIT Press, 1991.

Whitman, Walt. "Crossing Brooklyn Ferry." *Whitman: Poetry and Prose*. New York: Library of America: 1996. 307–13.

——. "Democratic Vistas." *Whitman: Poetry and Prose*. New York: Library of America: 1996. 953–1018.

CHAPTER 26

··

RETHINKING ECO-FILM STUDIES

··

DAVID INGRAM

OVER the last decade, ecocritics have insightfully addressed the representation of ecological issues in film and have also begun a vital environmentalist critique of the political economy of the audio-visual media by assessing the ecological effects of their production. The field now has its own Ecomedia Wiki and an extensive bibliography, and is sufficiently developed to garner retrospective scrutiny. Adrian Ivakhiv's 2008 essay in *ISLE*, "Green Film Criticism and Its Future," is an excellent assessment of the state of what he calls "eco-cinecriticism" at the end of its first ten years. What have not always been explicitly addressed in such works are questions of film theory and methodology. This essay is therefore concerned with the theoretical and methodological assumptions which inevitably shape all ecocritical writings on film, and seeks to identify possible future directions for research in the subject.

As Steven Cohan shows in his case study of *Singin' in the Rain* (1952), the meaning of a film changes according to the different interpretive frameworks applied to it. "This is not to suggest that a film can mean just about anything," he observes, "but that its meanings are determined through interaction with a critical theory" (Cohan 2000: 53). Important questions for ecocriticism are whether one theoretical framework is better than another, and what criteria, philosophical, political or aesthetic, should be used to judge this. Is one theory more valid, or more pragmatically useful, for eco-film criticism, than another? What are the strengths and weaknesses of the various theories and methods that have been employed by ecocritics working in film studies?

The rise of contemporary film theory in the late 1960s was part of the wider political turn in the humanities out of which ecocriticism itself eventually emerged from literary studies two decades later. In the early 1970s, "psycho-semiotic" or "screen" theory, derived from Althusserian Marxism and Lacanian psychoanalysis, became the main critical orthodoxy, under the general approach of so-called "Continental" philosophy. This paradigm continues today in a revised form in the work of Slavoj Žižek and Todd McGowan, who has recently applied it to an ecocritical study of film, as we shall see in this essay.

A major challenge to the psycho-semiotic paradigm came in the 1990s from advocates of analytical philosophy and cognitive psychology such as David Bordwell and Noël Carroll and now Torben Grodal has added evolutionary psychology to this new paradigm. Bordwell and Carroll's *Post-Theory* (1996) made a significant break in film studies by calling for the subject to concentrate on small, low-level theories of film (or "historical poetics") to replace the search for a single grand, unified Theory (with a capital 'T'). However, although Bordwell and Carroll view cognitivism as a combination of low-level theories, rather than a grand theory in its own right, Grodal plausibly argues that the new psychological approaches do effectively constitute a new grand theory of film, which he calls "evolutionary bioculturalism" (Grodal 2009: 4).

Although these different film theories sometimes use shared terms and explore the same problematics, they work from different philosophical assumptions. Many of these concern questions central to ecocriticism, such as the epistemological status of science and rationality, the relationship between conscious and unconscious motivations in human subjectivity and the relative philosophical merits of social constructionism and biological naturalism. As we shall see, overlaps also exist between the different theories, so it is misleading to view them as entirely polarized and incompatible. This essay concentrates on how the two main competing paradigms, the psychological and the psychoanalytic, have shaped the conceptualisation of ideological analysis in eco-film criticism.

Looking back over fifty years of "screen theory" in 2009, Annette Kuhn maintained that "theorizing" itself, as "an activity that is open and continuing rather than closed off and static," remains "essential" to screen studies. Nevertheless, she argued that the era of "militant theory" is over, and that screen studies today "seems increasingly to comprise a concatenation of subdisciplines, in which a focus on the historical, the local and the specific flourishes and any ambitions to create a totalizing theory are eschewed" (Kuhn 2009: 4–5). Ecocriticism, on the other hand, remains attracted to metanarratives, or overarching theories, as it necessarily moves beyond the humanities into the natural sciences, especially ecology and biology. What are the theoretical bases of this move towards interdisciplinarity in ecocriticism?

Successful interdisciplinary research in ecocriticism depends on an understanding of the methodological differences between the humanities and the natural sciences. As a humanities subject, film studies is, like literary criticism, a non-foundational discipline, so that, as philosopher Richard W. Miller puts it, "a situation in which different explanatory frameworks are in the field, attributing contrary explanations to the phenomena, is no crisis. For accepting a theory, approach, or explanation only requires belief in its adequacy to cope with the phenomena" (Miller 1987: 501). Film studies is in this way more theoretically and methodologically permissive than a scientific discipline. Judgments of artworks, Joseph Margolis writes, are not subject to criteria of truth and falsity, but of "critical plausibility—which entail (a) compatibility with the describable features of given artworks and (b) conformability with relativized canons of interpretation that themselves fall within the tolerance of an historically continuous tradition of interpretation" (Margolis 1980: 163).

Scientific disciplines, in contrast, are foundational, in the sense that, as Miller puts it, "investigators should require the true description of underlying causes" (503). In the sciences, therefore, the incompatibility of different theories is a crucial issue, in that "when frameworks for explanation posit incompatible causes of observable phenomena, this is taken as a crisis demanding resolution, not a healthy diversity of models" (499). In geology, for example, rival theories as to whether the Earth's continents drift or are static cannot both be correct, and require testing against empirical evidence. However, the interdisciplinary nature of both film studies and ecocriticism means that when film theorists draw on psychoanalysis or cognitive and evolutionary psychology for their explanation of texts, and ecocritics draw on scientific ecology and biology, such philosophical and empirical questions come into consideration after all.

The "philosophical turn" in film studies which opens up this investigation of foundational principles has been heavily contested. However, the methods of analytical philosophy provide for film studies an effective means of discriminating between different theories and methodologies at this meta-theoretical level. Richard Allen and Murray Smith describe analytical philosophy as a "style or approach, rather than a doctrine or body of knowledge," which aims to encourage open-minded inquiry through a self-reflexive and rigorous questioning of fundamental methodological assumptions (Allen and Smith 1997: 4). Analytical modes of inquiry in film studies include conceptual analysis, by means of which the critic, as Carroll puts it, "tries to clarify the concepts that make activities within the relevant domains possible" (Carroll 1999: 4).

Allen and Smith make a convincing case for the superiority of analytical philosophy over Continental philosophy, which they argue is based on two dubious assumptions: "First, the primary purpose of philosophy is taken to be the critique of epistemology; the task of philosophy is to demonstrate that the apparent justification of our beliefs have no objective grounding. Second, the critique of epistemology is identified with the ethical critique of modernity, conceived as a capitalist, scientific culture that apparently enhances, but in fact devalues and degrades, human existence" (Allen and Smith 1997: 10). Continental philosophy is central to the approach of several ecocritics, such as Patrick Curry and Verena Conley, among others (Curry 2003; Conley 1997).

For Allen and Smith, Continental philosophy takes an "opportunistic" or "on-again, off-again adherence to the standards of careful argument" (Allen and Smith 1997: 6, 9). Bordwell also criticizes the assumption made by film critics influenced by Continental philosophy that merely "applying" theories is seen as a justification for them, even in the absence of "confirmatory evidence" (Bordwell and Carroll 1996: 24). Theoretical authority for this approach is often found in Gilles Deleuze, for whom, following Friedrich Nietzsche, philosophy "does not consist in knowing and is not inspired by truth. Rather, it is categories like Interesting, Remarkable, or Important that determine success or failure" (Deleuze and Guattari 1994: 82).

Advocates of Continental philosophy in film studies, such as Robert Sinnerbrink, argue that the analytical approach is too "exclusionary" of other approaches, such as psychoanalysis (Sinnerbrink 2010: 182). However, what analytical philosophy is really trying to exclude is an uncritical pluralism which fails to provide justification for why one critical reading might be preferred to any other, and therefore risks authoritarianism by placing interpretation beyond critical scrutiny. Allen and Smith thus endorse analytical philosophy because it "strives to avoid the pitfalls of both dogmatism (the subordination of argumentative rigour and consistency to the defence of a particular doctrine) and uncritical pluralism (the acceptance of a range of positions with little interest in argument about their relative and particular merits, or attention to inconsistencies among them)" (2).

"Continental philosophy" is a broad area, and is not necessarily always in opposition to analytical philosophy. However, beyond the straw man arguments into which both sides can descend, the issue is important because philosophical choices at this level of abstraction inform everyday practices of eco-film criticism, as we shall see in the following pages.

Eco-film Criticism and the Implied Audience

Every piece of film criticism includes implicit assumptions about audience reception which can be framed by the different theoretical paradigms outlined above. Such assumptions have also informed the various ways in which ecocritics have practiced the ideological analysis of individual films. For example, in her analysis of monster movies, Stacy Alaimo writes that "representations have material consequences" and "shape contemporary responses to environmentalism" (Alaimo 2001: 279). Monster movies "vilify nature, justifying the slaughter of creatures we construct as repulsive" (280). However, Alaimo provides no evidence for a direct causal link between horror movies and the unwarranted killing of egrets in Carrollton, Texas, the real-life case of the mistreatment of wildlife that she mentions. In her essay on *Happy Feet* (2006) and *Over the Hedge* (2006), Sarah McFarland similarly makes assumptions about the audience reception of children's animal movies with no evidence to back them up, and no theoretical claims to account for them. The way films represent animals, she asserts, "have real consequences for the actual living and breathing beings" (McFarland 2009: 90).

In such ecocritical writings, assumptions about audience reception are often conflated with ones about narrative form. In her textual analysis of popular animal movies, McFarland asserts that their happy endings discourage the development of environmental agency or activism in the audience. She writes that the "movie industry's desire for 'happy endings' precludes the kind of ending that a genuinely environmental film would have—one that makes us rise and leave the theatre with a sense of urgency, a clearly defined action plan, and a desire to make a difference" (103). The aesthetic and ethical assumptions implied here, that films should be agitation-propaganda for a political cause, move beyond the scope of this essay, except in the way that they imply a particular notion of reception that accords the end of a movie decisive ideological significance.

In contrast to McFarland, Pat Brereton draws on the aesthetics of humanist Marxist Ernst Bloch to propose that happy endings in eco-films are a utopian prefiguration of a more benign relationship between human beings and the rest of the natural world (Brereton 2005: 11). What unites Brereton and McFarland is the idea that the ending of a film plays the key role in creating meaning for its viewers. Alaimo, on the other hand, proposes an alternative mode of reception, according to which the endings of monster movies may not be ultimately determinate of their meaning. As her essay demonstrates, many monster movies end by containing the symbolic threat that the monster had made to the ontological boundaries between human beings and animals earlier in the narrative. However, Alaimo suggests that the viewer can nevertheless interpret these films in a way that transcends these predictably conservative endings. The most memorable images, she proposes, may be the more pro-ecological ones in the middle of the narrative. "As these creatures run, rampage, and scheme," she writes, "they dramatize nature as an active, purposeful force—neither a being-landscape for quiet contemplation nor a passive, empty resource for human consumption" (Alaimo 2001: 293).

Let us test these modes of interpretation against *The Simpsons Movie* (2007). At the end of the film, Lisa Simpson gives up being an environmental activist, preferring instead to go for an ice cream with her new boyfriend, an ending that may be deemed politically conservative since it undermines the environmental protest politics she displayed earlier in the story. For Sarah McFarland, such an anti-environmentalist ending would presumably defuse any activist energies roused in the audience by Lisa's actions earlier in the film. However, another interpretation is possible, in which Homer's comments on his silo of pig shit early in the film—"it's not leaking, it's overflowing!"—is the most memorable pro-environmentalist moment in the film (it was quoted by at least two speakers at the ASLE conference at the University of Bath in 2010 in this regard). The silo disposal sequence would then carry a warning about environmental risks that is not contained by the film's happy ending. As Kim Newman wrote in his review of the film, Homer Simpson is "always more convincing as the 21st century ugly American, so concerned with his immediate trivial comforts that he is literally willing to drown the rest of the world in his own shit, than he is as the reformed man of the fade-out" (Newman 2007: 71).

A parallel case for this mode of interpretation are the endings of 1940s *film noir* movies, which appear tame from a feminist point-of-view, but nevertheless fail to stifle the rebellious energies performed by actresses such as Barbara Stanwyck or Joan Crawford in their starring roles. Janey Place wrote of female protagonists in *film noir* that it is "not their inevitable demise we remember but rather their strong, dangerous, and above all, exciting sexuality [...] The final 'lesson' of the myth often fades into the background and we retain the image of the erotic, strong, unrepressed (if destructive) woman" (Place 1998: 36). The general point here, as Janet Staiger notes, is that the critical assumption that textuality wholly determines audience reception is dubious (Staiger 2000: 29). Interpretation for her depends more on the social and cultural context than on the text itself. Yet the relative weighting between text and context is debatable. As Jim Collins argues, the production of textual meaning is a dialectical process: "A given text will inevitably be met with different reactions, but it does not necessarily follow that variation of reception means the text does not try somehow to control its eventual reception" (Collins 1989: 85). Film-makers will thus cue their films to create intended responses in their audience, but this does not guarantee that such intentions are always clear to the audience. Audiences are relatively free to interpret film texts against the intentions of their creators, and, as we have seen, ecocritics sometimes make over-deterministic and speculative assumptions about textual effects based on a notion of an "ideal spectator" which does not actually exist in reality (Staiger 2000: 39). The hunches about media effects made by the ecocritics quoted above may be correct, but in the absence of empirical or ethnographic audience studies, they remain hunches. Yet such research poses practical problems for film theorists working in humanities' departments who are untrained in the relevant methods; nor are quantified or empirical methods necessarily neutral or value-free (Hall 1999: 252–3). Nevertheless, Thomas Austin's study of television wildlife documentaries, for the way it combines empirical, theoretical and textual analysis, provides an exemplary way ahead for eco-film studies in this regard (Austin 2007: 122–77).

Eco-film Criticism and Ideological Analysis: The Psycho-semiotic Paradigm

Alaimo quotes Cary Wolfe and Jonathan Elmer on horror films as the source of her theory of audience reception: "What horror suggests for ideological critique, then, is that the ideological 'point' of fictions may lie not so exclusively with the reimposition of ideological norms in the fiction's ending but rather with its complicated and contradictory middle, where identificatory energies are released and invested" (Alaimo 2001: 293). As we shall see, by identifying ideological fissures within the text, and arguing that narratives contain an "excess" which undermines their own ideology, Wolfe and Elmer apply a revised version of subject positioning theory to the film they are discussing (Maltby 1995: 395–99).

The psycho-semiotic theory of subject positioning extrapolates Louis Althusser's Marxist concept of "interpellation" to the cinema. For Althusserian film theory, so-called dominant cinema is an Ideological State Apparatus which tends to reinforce capitalist ideology. The theory draws on Lacanian psychoanalysis for its notion that the subject's delusory misrecognition of itself as a unitary and autonomous ego gives support to the capitalist status quo. According to the theory, the formal structures of a film are inherently ideological: the techniques of continuity editing used in "classical" Hollywood cinema, such as reverse angles, analytical cutting and point-of-view shots, "suture" the viewer to capitalist subjectivity (Heath 1981: 101–7).

RETHINKING ECO-FILM STUDIES   465

Subject positioning theory can be crudely deterministic in its account of how films actually work on their audiences. By the late 1970s, the theory had been revised to make interpellation by cinema a less deterministic process. The control that media institutions exercise over the means of production, wrote Jim Collins in 1989, "does not entail control over the creation of meaning or the mode of consumption" (Collins 1989: 40). He added that the "larger and more sophisticated culture industries become, the more diversified they are in regard to institutions, discourses, and audiences, and the less they tend to produce homogeneous modes of textuality and unified forms of subjectivity" (42). According to the revised theory, film "texts" are thus polysemous and contradictory at the level of both production and reception. "Reading against the grain" can therefore reveal fissures in the overt ideological position of a film, which become possible points of ideological resistance for the viewer. It is this theoretical position that is implied in Alaimo's analysis of monster movies, quoted above.

Even though the earlier crude model of cinema spectatorship as a form of brainwashing has been replaced by a more nuanced version, subject positioning theory still tends to be simplistic and over-generalizing when applied to real cinema audiences. The conceptual gap between an abstract notion of a film viewer as "subject" and as a real, complex "person" remains a problem. Moreover, in *Mystifying Movies*, Carroll carefully refuted the claim that elements of mainstream cinema such as "the cinematic image, narrative construction, film editing, sound, and so forth" have been used "to facilitate subject construction, or, more specifically, the construction of the kinds of subjects with attributes congenial to the continuation of capitalism" (Carroll 1988: 59). His pragmatist view of film frees the theorist from such an over-deterministic and overly prescriptive approach to cinema.

Althusserian-Lacanian theoretical models are nevertheless still active in film criticism. Indeed, Todd McGowan's 2010 essay "Maternity Divided: *Avatar* and the enjoyment of nature" applies the revised paradigm to ecocriticism. His main claim is that James Cameron's films partly question the dominant patriarchal ideology on which capitalism is based. However, in line with Lacanian theory and the Continental philosophy that underpins it, McGowan conflates these political assertions about gender inequality with philosophical questions about the relationship between language and reality. "Modernity as an epoch calls into question the ground of the social order and thus the paternal side of ideology," he writes. "The linguistic turn in philosophy completes this revolution as it locates meaning and truth in language, unmoored from any ultimate ground" (McGowan 2010: 2).

McGowan here repeats the linguistic determinism of Lacan's use of Saussurean structural linguistics, which he extrapolated into large metaphysical and epistemological assumptions about the nature of language and reality. According to Lacan, patients under psychoanalysis resist symbolizing the trauma that is the cause of their neurosis or psychosis. Lacan expanded this notion from clinical practice to all attempts to know reality through language. As Žižek puts it, there is an "irreducible gap separating the real from the modes of its symbolization" (Žižek 1992a: 36).

Lacan became the dominant theorist for literary and cultural critics in the 1980s in part because of his interest in Saussurean structural linguistics. However, this theory of language is limited because of its lack of interest in the empirical status of the referent. As Carroll points out, "for language to begin and for it to be taught requires some fixed relations between some words and their referents. Thus, the Saussurean theory under Lacan's dispensation fails to explain such basic facts about language as language learning" (Carroll 1988: 70). Critical realist philosopher Christopher Norris writes that Saussurean linguistics is "inadequate to account for certain strictly ineliminable features of language, among them its referential capacity and its expressive (that is to say, its motivated) aspect as a bearer of speaker's intentions" (Norris 1997: 9).

McGowan's argument reflects the extreme cultural relativism of some post-structuralist and radical feminist theories of epistemology, which have been effectively critiqued by feminists such as Janet Radcliffe Richards and others (Richards 1997: 385–412). "It is true," writes Kate Soper, "that we can make no distinction between the 'reality' of nature and its cultural representation that is not itself conceptual, but that does not justify the conclusion that there is no ontological distinction between the ideas we have of nature and that which the ideas are about" (Soper 1995: 151). For critical realists such as Soper, the epistemological issue of language's referential capacity is determined by neither modernity nor gender difference.

Biosemiotics provides an alternative theory of semiotics, based on Charles Peirce's tripartite model of the sign, that is more promising for both film studies and ecocriticism than the Saussurean model. This new field is both better at accounting for the referential capacity of language and more compatible with empirical scientific inquiry than Saussurean linguistics (Solomon 1988: 205). Peircean semiotics is beginning to make headway in film theory, and is an area which deserves to be explored more in the future (Ehrat 2005).

The ecocritical aspects of McGowan's essay on *Avatar* include a provocative critique of deep ecology. For McGowan, "the most intransigent illusion of contemporary ideology" is "maternal or natural plenitude." Eywa, the planetary goddess or Gaia figure in *Avatar*, questions this conservative ideological position by being "divided" and "incomplete." The myth that "our world is complete and balanced" is thus effectively challenged (McGowan 2010: 10). McGowan's critique of deep ecology and Gaian mysticism has two implicit contexts: Lacan's critique of ego psychology and Žižek's critique of "New Age obscurantism." Žižek has questioned the commonplace assumption about the supposed "balance of nature." "The very notion of man as an 'excess' with respect to nature's balance circuit," he writes, "has finally to be abandoned. The image of nature as a balanced circuit is nothing but a retroactive projection of man" (Žižek 1992: 38). Accordingly, we should come to terms with our alienation from nature, rather than harbour impossible fantasies about going back there.

Significantly, Žižek cites scientific sources (James Gleick and Ian Stewart) for this rejection of the concept of natural balance. Unlike earlier claims based on Saussurean linguistics, then, the plausibility of this interpretation is helped by its grounding in fallibilistic science. Nevertheless, Žižek's attitude to science remains ambiguous. While he rightly distances himself from the extreme epistemological relativism he attributes to Cultural Studies, he is unclear and inconsistent over the issue of scientific realism. Lacan, he writes, believed that modern science "is resolutely *not* one of the 'narratives' comparable in principle to other modes of 'cognitive mapping.' Modern science touches the Real in a way totally absent in premodern discourses" (Žižek 2005: 94). Žižek goes on to endorse Thomas Kuhn's argument in *The Structure of Scientific Revolutions* that "the shift in a scientific paradigm is *more* than a mere shift in our (external) perspective of reality, but nonetheless *less* than our effectively 'creating' another new reality" (95). Yet Žižek's use of brackets in this sentence is particularly obscure. Critical realism shows more clearly that a scientific paradigm shift is precisely a shift in our perspective of an external reality, no more or less. Moreover, its emphasis on fallibilist knowledge of an extra-discursive reality is a more defensible notion, and therefore more useful for eco-criticism, than Žižek's prevarication (Soper 1996).

The general methodological problem here is that psychoanalytic critics like McGowan and Žižek tend to ignore both the logical flaws and the absence of empirical testability of their theories. From the approach of analytical method discussed earlier, Lacanian psychoanalysis is methodologically weak. Lacanians do not supply clear grounds and warrants for their arguments, nor do they properly take on possible rebuttals and counter-arguments. Instead, they tend to argue by verbal association, homology and fiat (O'Neill 2001).

Before addressing the overall issue of methodology in film studies at the conclusion of this essay, cognitivism, the main competing theoretical paradigm to psycho-semiotics, needs to be explored in detail, as it can produce a very different way of doing eco-film criticism.

ECO-FILM CRITICISM AND IDEOLOGICAL ANALYSIS: COGNITIVIST FILM THEORY

From an ecocritical perspective, Althusserian Marxism is anthropocentric and perpetuates pre-environmentalist assumptions about the benefits of unlimited economic growth (Eckersley 1992). Moreover, as Bordwell notes, psycho-semiotic theory is "very reluctant to grant the existence of a priori factors, particularly those which might be biologically innate, since some positions of this sort have led to theories of biological determinism and to repressive political programs" (Bordwell 1989: 6). In contrast, cognitivists reject such extreme cultural relativism which denies the relevance of universal, bodily determinants on film viewing. When the concept of "nature" has been discussed in film studies at all, it has tended to be mostly in terms of "naturalization"; that is, the cultural processes according to which values and ideas that are socially and historically constructed, and therefore potentially changeable, are passed off as "natural" and therefore inevitable and uncontestable. This issue is of great importance to ecocriticism, as can be seen in Cynthia Chris' analysis of wildlife television (Chris 2006: xix). However, exclusive concentration on the concept of naturalization has tended to draw attention away from a discussion of what Bordwell calls "good naturalization," which is the focus of cognitivism (Bordwell 1989: 2).

Cognitivist film theory provides a more empirical theory of audience reception, and therefore has different implications for ecocriticism, than subject positioning theory. Noël Carroll has rehabilitated the "images of women" approach of the 1970s, which proposed that films that reinforce stereotypical views of women can contribute to the perpetuation of social domination in real-life situations, for example when women attend job interviews. Drawing on cognitive psychology, Carroll thus proposes that films can shape the mental maps within which people frame reality. "When confronted with situations," he writes, "we will often grasp for whatever heuristics—such as commonplace generalizations—are available to us for the purpose of rendering the situation intelligible. That a film reinforces one of these heuristics with respect to some fictional behavior may then have some spill-over effect in the sense that when searching for a heuristic to apply to real circumstances, the heuristic in question is one whose availability is attractive because it has succeeded in the past in rendering some stretch of phenomena, albeit fictional, intelligible" (Carroll 1996: 285).

Carroll here develops cognitive psychology into a theory of ideology that recalls the Marxist notion of "false consciousness." "To show that a proposition with its corresponding belief is ideological," he writes, "one must show that it is epistemically defective and that its continued invocation plays a role in practices of social domination" (279). He gives two examples. The statement "2 + 2 = 1492" is not ideological, because even though it is epistemically defective (i.e., false), it is not linked to social domination. "The unemployed are lazy," on the other hand, *is* ideological, because it is both epistemically "defective" and can be deployed within a context of social domination.

Philosophically, Carroll's theory of ideology is based on two realist assumptions which tend to be rejected by post-structuralist or Continental philosophies of film: that it is possible to distinguish epistemologically between true and false claims about the world, and that films can represent a knowable extra-filmic reality. This approach may be attractive to ecocritics aware of the importance of making truth-claims about how ecosystems actually function in the real world. It presupposes a fallibilist, critical realist epistemology that is able to distinguish in principle between facts and value judgments. Consequently, Carroll's theory of ideology works best when there is a scientific issue involved in the film in question. In such cases, it can be applied convincingly to ecocriticism.

Let us take *Jaws: The Revenge* (1987) for example. The movie was promoted with the tag line, "This time it's personal": a shark follows the Brody family to the Bahamas, seeking revenge for the killing of its mate. Applying Carroll's cognitivist model to the film, the idea that sharks behave according to motives of personal revenge can be tested against current knowledge in marine biology, in line with a fallibilist conception of science. If, according to the current state of scientific expertise, the film thereby presents ideas about shark behaviour that are inaccurate, then the film is epistemically defective, and fulfils the first of Carroll's criteria for ideology. If these ideas have potential consequences for real sharks, then the movie's representation of sharks is ideological in

Carroll's sense: it is false and could be used in social domination (if we ethically extend our notion of the "social" to include animals). Moreover, there is anecdotal evidence of a rise in shark hunting after the release of *Jaws*, though this claim has been disputed, including by the book's author Peter Benchley (Alaimo 2001: 279).

A major strength of Carroll's cognitivist theory of ideology is that it is not overly deterministic, in that it seeks, as he puts it, to "explain how films dispose audiences toward various ideological stances, while also admitting that viewers do not always succumb to them" (289). It therefore avoids the simplistic determinism of Althusserian subject positioning theory, according to which, as we have seen, films are assumed to have a conditioning effect on their spectators which is built into their very formal structure.

Nevertheless, there are possible objections to Carroll's cognitivist theory of ideology. Its main weakness is that not all epistemological cases present the clear choice between truth and falsity that the theory requires. Many real-life social and environmental issues appear to be closer to matters of opinion than to facts, and are therefore fuzzy, vague or contested. Indeed, Carroll's chosen example, "the unemployed are lazy," is a different kind of truth claim from a mathematical formula, and is not self-evidently false in the same way that $2 + 2 = 5$ is. Testing cognitivist film theory against a harder case than *Jaws: The Revenge* may thus be fruitful. Returning to *The Simpsons Movie*, the narrative represents the Environmental Protection Agency as a ruthless, totalitarian organisation. After Homer Simpson has caused an environmental catastrophe in Springfield by polluting the lake with sewage, Russ Cargill, head of the EPA, proposes to detonate a nuclear bomb to eradicate the city. Taking comic exaggeration into consideration, does the idea that the EPA is a government bureaucracy working against the interests of the American people make the film ideological in Carroll's sense? One may object that the film constructs Russ Cargill as a fictional trope, rather than as a proposition about the EPA. Tropes are matters of opinion, and therefore not necessarily epistemically defective. Nevertheless, the idea that the EPA is villainous could still become a psychological "heuristic" in Carroll's cognitivist sense. Such an interpretation of *The Simpsons Movie*, like those of the monster and animal movies discussed earlier in this essay, assumes its own ideal viewer and particular kind of audience reception. Yet the empirical side of cognitive psychology allows for the testing of this ideal type or hypothetical viewer against evidence about whether real people actually do act and think in such a way. Even though the empirical side of cognitivism is open to critical scrutiny, such an approach adds an important dimension to audience reception studies that subject positioning theory tends to rule out in advance.

CONCLUSION: SOME FUTURE DEVELOPMENTS IN ECO-FILM CRITICISM

Can a "both-and" approach, which reconciles psycho-semiotic theory and cognitivism, be justified? Considering the *Jaws* cycle again, psychoanalytic criticism has been more interested in the symbolic role of the shark than in actual sharks. When Stephen Heath wrote of *Jaws* (1975) that "the evil is something else ... call it a shark," the shark was for him merely an arbitrary sign in a narrative which for the psychoanalytic critic is really about threats to patriarchal control (Ingram 2000: 72). Similarly, when Žižek discusses Hitchcock's *The Birds* (1963), the film is about the fantasies of the film spectator, rather than birds attacking a coastal town (Žižek 1992: 236–37). Yet an ecocritical reading could bring psychoanalysis and cognitivism together, by investigating the role played by sharks or birds in both our fantasies and in the real ecosystems of which we are a part, and how the two interrelate.

Yet a "both-and" approach should be aware of points of conceptual incompatibility between the two theories. In some respects the two paradigms are not completely polarized. Like Carroll, Žižek's psychoanalytical approach rejects the crude "top-down" thesis of ideological manipulation favoured by subject positioning theory. However, his theories imply a radically different conception of subjectivity and ideology. For Žižek, ideology is not a false consciousness that can simply be unmasked to reveal an objective reality underneath. "The function of ideology," he writes, "is not to offer us a point of escape from our reality but to offer us the social reality itself as an escape from some traumatic, real kernel" (Žižek 1989: 45).

Žižek's notion of ideology thus questions the search for empirical truth in Carroll's version of cognitivism. However, notions of ideology as false consciousness, as proposed by cognitivist film theory, cannot easily be dismissed as simplistic. Ideology, writes Terry Eagleton, "does not consist primarily in a set of propositions about the world; and many of the propositions it *does* advance are actually true. None of this, however, need be denied by those who hold that ideology often or typically involves falsity, distortion, and mystification. Even if ideology is largely a matter of 'lived relations,' those relations, at least in certain conditions, would often seem to involve claims or beliefs which are untrue" (Eagleton 1991: 26).

That cognitivism and psycho-semiotics assume such radically differing conceptions of the self makes a "both-and" approach difficult to conceive. The Lacanian notion of ideology assumes the divided self of psychoanalysis, rather than the more unitary self on which cognitive psychology is based. These differences have profound implications for eco-film theory. For Žižek, popular attitudes to ecology and the environment are characterized by disavowal: "I know very well (that things are deadly serious, that what is at stake is our very survival), but just the same... (I don't really believe it, I'm not really prepared to integrate it into my symbolic universe, and that is why I continue to act as if ecology is of no lasting consequence for my everyday life)" (Žižek 1992a: 35). Yet Žižek's assumption that people "know very well" the seriousness of ecological issues is merely an assertion that derives from the application of fundamental Freudian-Lacanian psychoanalytical principles, rather than a claim backed up with evidence. Indeed, the social sciences provide much evidence to the contrary, suggesting that people's perceptions of environmental risk, such as that of anthropogenic climate change, are complex and varied. As environmental scientist Mike Hulme puts it, risk perceptions are "socially constructed, with different groups prone to take notice of, fear and amplify some risks, while ignoring, discounting or attenuating others" (Hulme 2009: 199). Environmental psychology may be beginning to account for such popular attitudes to the environment in a more empirical way than a dogmatic, over-generalizing application of Lacanianism (Bonnes et al. 2003).

It is for such reasons that Carroll rejects a "both-and" approach, arguing that the onus of proof should be on psychoanalytic critics to show that their theories are necessary to explain behaviour that cannot be explained by cognitive assumptions alone. He takes this position because psychoanalysis lacks an empirical basis, and consequently is open to neither verification nor falsification. It thereby fails to construct arguments that pass analytical tests of rigour and coherence (Carroll 1996: 260–72).

It may be that Carroll's cognitivist approach does not itself adequately account for audience reception either. His essay on the pleasures of reading "junk" fiction, for example, concentrates on the formal techniques of such fiction, but does not adequately explain why people are attracted to the seemingly unpleasant or disturbing content of some of the stories he mentions (Carroll 2001: 335–47). Torben Grodal's biocultural model of evolutionary psychology, on the other hand, expands on cognitivism to provide an alternative explanation to psychoanalytic criticism of the deep or hidden motivations in a viewer's aesthetic appreciation of cinema (Grodal 2009). As Cynthia Chris observes, evolutionary psychology risks being reductive in its application of neo-Darwinist models to culture, and can also itself lack a firm grounding in empirical evidence (Chris 2006: 137). Nevertheless, cognitivist and evolutionary psychology are developing in a self-reflexive and intellectually sophisticated way that has great potential for the future development of eco-film studies.

A more radical methodology for film studies than a "both/and" approach has been proposed by Thomas Elsaesser and Warren Buckland. Influenced by Deleuze's concept of the "fold" (Deleuze 2010), they explore a method that does not view "theories and the methods derived from them as incompatibly juxtaposed." In their analysis of *The Silence of the Lambs* (1991), they write that the theories they deploy construct "conflicting viewing positions" which have "been resolved not by adopting an either/or, or both... and stance, but by a kind of theoretical layering, appealing to a reconceptualization at another level, which allowed us to see this particular film [...] presenting us with different worlds, and several ways of conceiving their protagonists' and antagonists' identities" (Elsaesser and Buckland 2002: 282). The problem with this model of non-linear multiplicity and multiple "worlds," however, is that it risks being the sort of uncritical pluralism addressed at the start of this essay. Analytical methods, as practiced by Bordwell and Carroll, have the advantage of being both more rigorous and more comprehensible. What exactly is a stance that is neither "either-or" nor "both-and"? To be convincing, such a difficult concept at least requires more clarification and justification than that presented by Elsaesser and Buckland.

Analytical eco-film studies will avoid both uncritical pluralism and dogmatism. In this regard, the biocultural paradigm may be preferable to psycho-semiotics, and cognitivism preferable to psychoanalysis. However, there are several psychoanalytic theories of the unconscious which have yet to be fully explored in both film studies and ecocriticism, and may constitute important counter-arguments to cognitivism. Jung and Winnicott, for example, have occasionally been applied to film analysis without becoming favoured authorities like Lacan or Žižek. John Bowlby, as a psychoanalyist interested in evolutionary psychology, has recently been adopted for film criticism by Grodal, and is a promising possibility for future research. Within ecocriticism, ecopsychology is another growing field that promises a productive overlap with eco-film studies. Lacan dismissed American ego psychology as a conservative ideology that merely affirmed the capitalist status quo, or, as he put it, made "good employees" (Lacan 2008: 19). Yet its revision as ecopsychology, whatever its philosophical flaws, at least shows how notions of personal and social health can be based on a notion of unified subjectivity and still be socially radical, and not merely a reinforcement of liberal capitalist subjectivity, as in the straw-man version criticized by Lacan. Such research into the nature of subjectivity remains open and unresolved. Indeed, the object of research in eco-film studies as a whole should be opened up further, as the search for better theories, and even a grand unifying theory of film, goes on.

WORKS CITED

Alaimo, Stacy. "Discomforting Creatures: Monstrous Natures in Recent Films." In Armbruster, Karla and Kathleen R. Wallace (eds). *Beyond Nature Writing: Expanding the Boundaries of Ecocriticism*. Charlottesville and London: University Press of Virginia, 2001, 279–296.

Allen, Richard and Murray Smith. Eds. *Film Theory and Philosophy*. Oxford: Clarendon Press, 1997.

Austin, Thomas. *Watching the World: Screen Documentary and Audiences*. Manchester: Manchester University Press, 2007.

Bonnes, Mirilia, Terence Lee and Marino Bonaiuto (eds). *Psychological Theories for Environmental Issues*. (Aldershot: Ashgate, 2003).

Bordwell, David. *Making Meaning: Inference and Rhetoric in the Interpretation of Cinema*. Cambridge and London: Harvard University Press, 1989.

———. "Contemporary Film Studies and the Vicissitudes of Grand Theory." In Bordwell, David and Noël Carroll, eds. *Post-Theory: Reconstructing Film Studies. 1996*. Madison and London: University of Wisconsin Press, 1996, 3–36.

Brereton, Pat. *Hollywood Utopia: Ecology in Contemporary American Cinema*. Bristol: Intellect, 2005.

Carroll, Noël. *Theorizing the Moving Image*. Cambridge: Cambridge University Press, 1996.

Carroll, Noël. *Mystifying Movies: Fads and Fallacies in Contemporary Film Theory*. New York: Columbia University Press, 1988.

Carroll, Noël. *The Philosophy of Art: A Contemporary Introduction*. London and New York: Routledge, 1999.

Carroll, Noël. *Beyond Aesthetics: Philosophical Essays*. Cambridge: Cambridge University Press, 2001.

Chris, Cynthia. *Watching Wildlife*. Minneapolis and London: University of Minnesota Press, 2006.

Cohan, Steve. "Case study: interpreting *Singin' in the Rain*." In Gledhill, Christine and Williams, Linda (eds). *Reinventing Film Studies*. New York: Oxford University Press, 2000, 53–75.

Collins, Jim. *Uncommon Cultures: Popular Culture and Post-Modernism*. Routledge: New York and London, 1989.

Conley, VerenaAndermatt. *Ecopolitics: The Environment in Poststructuralist Thought*. London and New York: Routledge, 1997.

Curry, Patrick. "Re-Thinking Nature: Towards an Eco-Pluralism. *Environmental Values*. 12:3 (2003), 337–60.

Deleuze, Gilles. The Fold: Leibniz and the Baroque. London and New York: Continuum, 2001.

Deleuze, Gilles and Félix Guattari. 1994. *What Is Philosophy?* Trans. H. Tomlinson and G. Burchell. New York: Columbia University Press.

Eagleton, Terry. *Ideology*. London and New York: Verso, 1991.

Eckersley, Robyn. *Environmentalism and Political Theory: Toward an Ecocentric Approach*. London: UCL Press, 1992.

Ehrat, Johannes. *Cinema and Semiotic: Peirce and Film Aesthetics, Narration, and Representation*. Toronto, Buffalo and London: University of Toronto Press, 2005.

Elsaesser and Buckland. *Studying Contemporary American Film: A Guide to Movie Analysis*. London: Hodder, 2002.

Grodal, Torben. *Embodied Visions: Evolution, Emotion, Culture, and Film*. Oxford: Oxford University Press, 2009.

Hall, John R. *Cultures of Inquiry: From Epistemology to Discourse in Sociohistorical Research*. Cambridge: Cambridge University Press, 1999.

Heath, Stephen. *Questions of Cinema*. London and Basingstoke: Macmillan Press, 1981.

Hulme, Mike. *Why We Disagree About Climate Change: Understanding Controversy, Inaction and Opportunity*. Cambridge: Cambridge University Press, 2009.

Ingram, David. *Green Screen: Environmentalism and Hollywood Cinema*. Exeter: University of Exeter Press, 2000.

Ivakhiv, Adrian. "Green Film Criticism and Its Future." *Interdisciplinary Studies in Literature and Environment*, 15:2 (Summer 2008): 1–28.

Kuhn, Annette. "Screen and Screen Theorizing Today." *Screen*, 50:1 (2009): 1–12. http://screen.oxfordjournals.org/cgi/content/full/50/1/1

Lacan, Jacques. *My Teaching*. London: Verso, 2008.

Maltby, Richard and Ian Craven. *Hollywood Cinema*. Oxford and Cambridge: Blackwell, 1995.

Margolis, Joseph. *Art and Philosophy*. Atlantic Highlands, NJ: Humanities Press, 1980.

McFarland, Sarah. "Dancing Penguins and a Pretentious Raccoon": Animated Animals and 21st Century Environmentalism." In Sarah E. McFarland and Ryan Hediger. *Animals and Agency: An Interdisciplinary Exploration* (Leiden and Boston: Brill, 2009), 89–103.

McGowan, Todd. "Maternity Divided: Avatar and the Enjoyment of Nature." *Jump Cut: A Review of Contemporary Media*, 52 (Summer 2010): 1–13.

Miller, Richard W. *Fact and Method: Explanation, Confirmation and Reality in the Natural and the Social Sciences*. Princeton: Princeton University Press, 1987.

Newman, Kim. Review of *The Simpsons Movie*. *Sight and Sound*, 17:10 (October 2007): 70–71.

Norris, Christopher. *Against Relativism: Philosophy of Science, Deconstruction, and Critical Theory*. Malden, MA: Blackwell, 1997.

O'Neill, Edward R. "The Last Analysis of Slavoj Žižek." *Film-Philosophy* 5:17 (June 2001).

Place, Janey. "Women in Film Noir." In E. Ann Kaplan (ed.). *Women in Film Noir*. London: BFI Publishing, 1998.

Richards, Janet Radcliffe. "Why Feminist Epistemology Isn't." In Paul R. Gross, Norman Levitt, and Martin W. Lewis. *The Flight from Science and Reason*. New York: New York Academy of Science, 1997, 385–412.

Sinnerbrink, Robert. "Disenfranchising Film? On the Analytic-Cognitivist Turn in Film Theory." In Jack Reynolds, James Chase, Jack Williams, and Edwin Mares. *Postanalytic and Metacontinental: Crossing Philosophical Divides*. New York and London: Continuum, 2010, 173–188.

Solomon, J. Fisher. *Discourse and Reference in the Nuclear Age*. Norman and London: University of Oklahoma Press, 1988.

Soper, Kate. *What is Nature? Culture, Politics and the Non-Human*. Oxford and Cambridge: Blackwell, 1996.

Staiger, Janet. *Perverse Spectators: The Practices of Film Reception*. New York and London: New York University Press, 2000.

Žižek, Slavoj. *The Sublime Object of Ideology*. London and New York: Verso, 1989.

——. *Looking Awry: An Introduction to Jacques Lacan through Popular Culture*. Cambridge, Mass. and London: MIT Press, 1992a.

——. "In His Bold Gaze My Ruin Is Writ Large." In Slavoj Žižek (ed). *Everything You Always Wanted to Know about Lacan (But Were Afraid to Ask Hitchcock*. London and New York: Verso, 1992, 211–272.

——. *Interrogating the Real*. Rex Butler and Scott Stephens (eds). London: Continuum, 2005.

——. *The Parallax View*. Cambridge, MA: MIT Press, 2006.

FILMS CITED

Avatar. 2009. Dir. James Cameron. Twentieth Century Fox.

Happy Feet. 2006. Dir. George Miller. Warner Bros.

Jaws. 1975. Dir. Stephen Spielberg. Universal.

Jaws: The Revenge. 1987. Dir. Joseph Sargent. Universal.

Over the Hedge. 2006. Dir. Tim Johnson. DreamWorks.

The Simpsons Movie. 2007. Dir. David Silverman. Twentieth Century Fox.

CHAPTER 27

···

GREEN BANJO

The Ecoformalism of Old-Time Music[1]

···

SCOTT KNICKERBOCKER

INSOFAR as the modern environmental movement originated in the 1960s with progressive activists from cities (even if some of them went "back to the land"), country music and all it stands for may seem to be the anathema of environmental enlightenment. As a reader of one of Rebecca Solnit's recent books wrote:

> The country music parts of the US you love so much are also home of the most racist, reactionary, religiously authoritarian (i.e., Dominionist) people in the country. You don't have to go far: just look at voting patterns among rednecks (descendants of the white yeomanry, if you wish to be polite) in the Central Valley. They love Bush and are very backward people by the standards of the Enlightenment. The question might be, what is the correlation between country music and political backwardness, if any? (55)

As Solnit argues, however, this urban, leftist, and often environmentalist scorn toward "rednecks" and country music reveals an attitude that is elitist at best and virulently classist at worst. Such an attitude is also politically counterproductive, as it only reinforces cultural stereotypes associated with polarized positions in the culture wars: city vs. country, tofu vs. steak, yoga vs. hunting, Prius vs. pickup, Cabernet vs. Coors. For better or worse, such cultural markers and images not only reflect but also subtly shape one's identity, worldview, and voting patterns. From a pragmatic point of view, the most substantive and enduring societal progress—including our treatment of the nonhuman world—comes from moving past caricature and instead building coalitions between seemingly conflicting stakeholders. For example, some ranchers and environmentalists in the American West have, in recent years, collaborated to oppose suburban sprawl into open spaces. As the cowboy song "Home on the Range" implies, the "deer and the antelope play" in and require such open space as much as cattle do (which is not to ignore the serious impacts ranching has had and often continues to have on the land).

The simplistic reaction against country music also begs the question, "which country music" (Solnit 55)? To be sure, corporate country stars like Toby Keith herded his fans toward supporting our so-called "war on terror," but alternative country musician (and quasi-Marxist) Steve Earle galloped in the opposite direction, and even pop country stars the Dixie Chicks famously derided fellow Texan President Bush (and were subsequently vilified by other country music stars and DJs, especially in Texas). Johnny Cash, a self-proclaimed "dove with claws," spoke out against the Vietnam War and in favor of Native American rights. "Outlaw country" stars Willie Nelson, Merle Haggard, and others have taken socially and politically progressive positions that do not fit the "redneck" stereotype. Willie Nelson's Farm Aid, a musical fundraiser for the benefit of small family farms (rather than environmentally and socially destructive corporate agribusiness) reclaims the Jeffersonian agrarian ideal and demonstrates "the populist power of countering economic conservatism from culturally conservative positions... In this way reclaiming traditions can be seen as radical—literally, a return to the roots—setting history against capitalism's attempts to deny continuity and against pop's timeless present of consumption" (Webster 169). As R. Serge Denisoff cautions in his study of the protest tradition in American music, it is misleading of northern writers to paint country music as entirely reactionary when it also partly an expression of the American populist tradition. Indeed, to the extent that progressive concerns coincide with populism, then country music and those it represents—the rural working class—complicates any careless, casual categorization of red and blue states. Populism, that is, takes on a purplish hue.

Environmentalism, like country music and populism, also exists in a complex political ecotone, especially when we consider its nineteenth-century conservationist roots, strains of which persist today in sportsman organizations like Ducks Unlimited or the agrarian philosophy of Wendell Berry, for whom (unlike wilderness preservationist John Muir) an ethical relationship with the land involves mindful human *use* of it. Nature in country music is most often a worked landscape and rarely a pristine wilderness, a fact that touches on class-based environmental justice in terms of the exploited coal miners of Appalachia. As Merle Travis sings in "Dark as a Dungeon": "Come and listen, you fellers, so young and so fine / And seek not your fortune in the dark dreary mine / It'll form as a habit and seep in your soul / Till the stream of your blood runs as black as the coal." The ravaged coal landscapes of Appalachia include the ravaged body of the miner who "owe[s] [his] soul to the company store" (Travis, "Sixteen Tons"). Travis's "Dark as a Dungeon" became a rallying song among unionized miners fighting for improved working conditions.

Country music, especially in its traditional and alternative forms (as opposed to its commercial "Top 40" forms) offers rich soil for the growth of environmentalist sensibilities that transcend stereotypes of style and taste that we habitually associate with political positions. Ted Olson helpfully organizes environmentally themed country music into five categories: "songs possessing nature references as pure metaphor; protest songs; complaint songs; nostalgic 'sense of place' songs; songs expressing humans' connections with the natural world and animals" (189). In addition to Merle Travis's "Dark as a Dungeon," another good example of environmental protest in country music is Johnny Darrell's 1969 song "The Coming of the Roads": "We used to hunt the cool caverns deep in our forest of green / Then came the road and the tavern, and you found a new love it seems / Once I had you and the wildwood, now it's just dusty roads." John Anderson even more pointedly lambasts reclamation efforts in his 1992 "Seminole Wind": "Progress came and took its toll / And in the name of flood control / They made their plans and they drained the land / Now the glades are going dry."

Contemporary Idaho cowboy poet and songwriter Wayne Nelson, a former rancher, wrote a powerful country song entitled "Scatter My Ashes" that thoughtfully engages with the land. Here are the first two verses and the chorus:

> What I'd like you to do, when my time has run out,
> Take me out by the Big Butte, and just lay me down,
> Let the coyotes have me, but the Feds might complain,
> So scatter my ashes, 'cross the Snake River Plains.
>
> Tell the Indians I'm sorry, for my people's greed,
> It's always our custom, to take more than we need.
> Where they once rode their ponies, is all spuds and grain.
> But we can't steal the sunsets, on the Snake River Plains.
>
> It's a plowbustin' desert, where volcanoes once roared
> In a time before memory, when the lava rock poured.
> It's a God awful waste land, but it still calls my name.
> So scatter my ashes, on the Snake River Plains.

The song is environmental in at least three ways: as elegy for a once wild landscape converted into large monocultures of "spuds and grain," as apology to Native Americans for white greed over natural resources, and as love song to the "God awful waste land" of the Snake River Plains. Indeed, the speaker not only loves the Snake River Plains, he intends to become physically at one with it in his death; he wants his ashes, reminiscent of the land's volcanic ash, to be incorporated by the landscape, although he would prefer to be literally ingested by the coyotes.[2] He also perceives the land in terms of geologic time, rather than just a human time scale: the land's power and agency, depicted in its geologically violent past of roaring volcanoes and flowing lava rock, still offers real resistance to human control in its present-day "plow bustin'" desert soil.

Traditional country music grew out of older musical forms, including what people today term "old-time." Old-time—one form of American roots music[3]—describes traditional Appalachian mountain music that pre-dated the radio but is still played today. It is sometimes confused with its offspring bluegrass, which evolved in the 1940s, after the dawn of radio; bluegrass is therefore more commercial and performance-oriented. Old-time, on the other hand, has always emphasized participation and downplayed celebrity. Traditionally, old-time musicians provided music for square and contra dances; therefore, the music often has a hard-driving rhythm. Most often the fiddle is the lead instrument in old-time, accompanied by a banjo played in the clawhammer (or "frailing") style (rather than the three-finger bluegrass style as pioneered by Earl Scruggs). The clawhammer style of playing the banjo came from western Africa with the banjo itself, originally a gourd instrument. A full old-time stringband today typically includes fiddle, banjo, most likely rhythm guitar and upright bass, and sometimes mandolin. Old-time evolved in isolated watersheds of southern Appalachia when predominantly Scottish and Irish immigrants brought their fiddles and old-world tunes and ballads there beginning in the eighteenth century. Because of the geographical isolation of communities in this rugged landscape (roads and railroads and other infrastructure developed more slowly here than elsewhere), each watershed contained its own style of playing the fiddle or banjo and its own variations of tunes. If a person hiked up over a ridge and down to an adjacent watershed, he or she would suddenly inhabit a different aural atmosphere. The dawn of radio in the early twentieth century, for all of its benefits, also partly ironed out this rich diversity in old-time music, as more people in remote locations emulated fewer musicians on the airwaves, and bluegrass began to catch on in the 1940s.

Old-time music, however, including the attitudes and values that accompany it, did not die out; in fact, it is currently experiencing (another) robust resurgence among many young people across the United States and beyond in search of what it has to offer.[4] Musicians of varying age groups and skill levels flock to annual old-time festivals where hundreds of attendees camp in tents and stay up playing furiously until dawn. The participatory element, the feeling of authenticity and tradition, the do-it-yourself ethic (punk rock shares this "DIY" attitude), and the pure infectious joy and energy of the music draw many people in reaction against the commercialism of mainstream society. One will find in these gatherings, therefore, a fascinating mix of generations and styles, ranging from elderly rural conservatives to young anarcho-punk neo-hobos with piercings and tattoos. If old-time music is a powerful uniter across differences of age and style, perhaps it can also facilitate bridge-building across political divides.

Old-time music, like much of country music, exudes a sense of place, long considered an important starting place in thinking and behaving ecologically. Indeed, perhaps the most environmentally powerful aspect of roots music in general is its uncanny ability to plant one in a place, at least imaginatively. Contemporary Americans find their ties to specific places increasingly threatened by both the transformation of once unique places into paved-over, homogenous spaces dominated by franchises and big-box stores and by how often they are uprooted for job-related or other reasons. As a result, they often crave the feeling of immediacy, intimacy, and authenticity that place-based roots music seems to embody. Ginny Hawker, who sings traditional country, gospel, and old-time mountain music with her husband Tracy Schwarz (of the old-time band New Lost City Ramblers) and others, was born and raised in West Virginia—the heart of Appalachia—and grew up singing in a Primitive Baptist Church. When asked what she thinks attracts so many folks beyond Appalachia—from cities, both US coasts, even beyond US borders—to Appalachian mountain music, Hawker replied,

> It's close to the bone. It puts them in a place, and I think a lot of what they feel is that connection to a place. They feel the connection; the song that we're singing will put them there. It's not so much a time as it is a place [She prefers the lococentric term "rural music" to the temporal terms "old-time" and "traditional"]. If I were going to

learn some other music from another completely different culture, I would want to go there, but if I couldn't go there, I would want to hear somebody play that music who was very grounded in that place. (Personal interview)

This music therefore goes beyond feeding one's modern craving for place-rootedness; like literature and other arts, music gives one an artistic, emotional, and metaphorical sense of a place and people unlike one's own. Roots music especially increases one's cultural empathy and historical and geographical understanding, since curiosity drives many contemporary players of old-time to research the origins—sometimes quite mysterious—of songs and the historical context surrounding them.

Some words in old-time music express environmental sentiments, such as in the old call-and-response song (anonymously and collectively "written" over time as it passed from musician to musician) "Mole in the Ground," which was possibly African American in origin. Here are just some of the words:

> I wish I was a mole in the ground.
> I wish I was a mole in the ground
> If I was a mole in the ground,
> I'd root that mountain down.
> I wish I was a mole in the ground.
>
> I wish I was a lizard in the spring ...
> If I was a lizard in the spring, I'd hear my true love sing ...
>
> I wish I was a bird with wings to fly ...

In Charles Frazier's 1997 novel *Cold Mountain*, set in southern Appalachia during the Civil War, one of the main characters Ada reflects on this strange song while camped in the woods with mountain woman Ruby, whose father Stobrod is a talented fiddler:

> The fire threw patterns of light and shadow on the pitched roof stone, and Ada found that if she watched long enough the fire would form the shapes of things in the world. A bird. A bear. A snake. A fox. Or perhaps it was a wolf. The fire seemed to have no interests other than animals.
>
> The pictures put Ada in mind of a song, one of Stobrod's. It had particularly stuck in her mind. She had noted it for the oddity of its lyric and for Stobrod's singing, which had been of an intensity that Ada could only assume represented deep personal expression. It took as subject the imagined behavior of its speaker, what he would do had he the power to become one of a variety of brute creature. A lizard in the spring—hear his darling sing. A bird with wings to fly—go back to his darling weep and moan till he dies. A mole in the ground—root a mountain down.
>
> Ada worried over the song. The animals seemed wonderful and horrible in their desires, especially the mole, a little powerless hermit blind thing propelled by lonesomeness and resentment to bring the world falling around him. More wonderful and horrible still was the human voice speaking the song's words, wishing away its humanity to ease the pain inflicted by lost love, love betrayed, love left unexpressed, wasted love. (379–380)

In Ada's experience of "Mole in the Ground," not only are nonhuman creatures personified, but in a striking chiasm, the human speaker experiences species envy and wishes to naturalize himself, albeit from a painful sense of self-erasure. Furthermore, if the song is indeed African American in origin, the speaker could be wishing away its humanity as a response to slavery and other racial injustice, despite Ada's unsurprising—given her experience in the novel—projection of "lost love" onto the song. That the speaker would wish he could, as a powerful mole, "root the mountain down," also possibly suggests the resentment that a miner in Appalachia would likely feel as a response to his life-threatening labor and harsh working conditions, thus reminding us why nature-worship was more common among the leisure than the working class. Is a mountain still beautiful, after all—and does its beauty even matter—when you have to descend beneath it, inhale its coal dust, and possibly be buried there? On the other hand, the song could easily be much older than the beginning of large-scale mining in the United States, so the mole and mountain verse may express a deeper and stranger resentment toward the mountain. As Marjorie Nicolson argues, before the eighteenth century, Europeans and Americans commonly perceived mountains to be ugly protuberances on the land, and it was only later that mountains began to be perceived as sublime.

It is hardly difficult, therefore, to locate environmental themes in country music (especially in its alternative and traditional forms) but for several reasons explained below, old-time asks to be pondered at a deeper level than the thematic. While most modern country songs conform to the same conventions we find in other popular music, old-time music, one of country music's most important fountainheads, provides rich ground for ecoformalist analysis.

Old-time is a markedly different form of American folk music than the topical protest folk music of the 1950s and 1960s, famously embodied by Pete Seeger in such songs as the anti–Vietnam War "Waist Deep in the Big Muddy." As David Ingram explains, the overt political motivations in protest music often resulted in proletarian realism as a mode of expression, and such expression demanded clarity of message. Music that is meant to improve society through its overt message avoids ambiguity in its song lyrics and foregrounds the singing voice (from which the rallying call comes) while pushing the instrumentation somewhat into the background, sometimes at an aesthetic cost. Seeger's half-brother Mike Seeger (of the New Lost City Ramblers, one of the first old-time stringbands comprised of young urban people) and other young mid-twentieth-century musicians who discovered old-time music through Harry Smith's 1952 *Anthology of American Folk Music* (musicians recorded in the late 1920s and early 1930s) recognized a different, stranger, form of folk music than the topical protest music of their peers. As Bob Dylan put it, "What folk music is... the main body of it is just based on myth and the Bible and plague and famine and all kinds of things like that which are nothing but mystery and you can see it in all the songs. Roses growing right up out of people's hearts and naked cats in bed with spears growing right out of their backs and seven years of this and eight years of that and it's all really something that nobody can really touch" (qtd. in Marcus 29–30). Partly as a result of steeping himself in this mysterious tradition, Bob Dylan moved away from the topical songs of his early career; he wanted to be an artist rather than activist. Greil Marcus terms this strain of American roots music "Old Weird America," in which "nature is sublime and uncanny, an enchanted world that includes miraculous transformations between human beings and other living organisms" (Ingram 115).

The dark, enchanted world of Old Weird America may seem to resemble, from literary history, medieval and Romantic works, but the way old-time creates and shapes meaning is actually similar to the experimental poetics of high modernism: mostly nonreferential (in the plenitude of wordless fiddle tunes, with the exception of a few tunes like "Cluck Old Hen" in which a pluck of the fiddle string is meant to echo the cluck of the hen); often absurdist in imagery ("She opened her mouth so big and wide/ She swallowed the barber and all" in the anonymous song "Letter From Down the Road"); and lyrically often fragmentary rather than linear (with the exception of ballads, of course). This song fragmentation Marcus terms the "folk-lyric," "made up of verbal fragments that had no direct or logical relationship to each other, but were drawn from a floating pool of thousands of disconnected verses, couplets, one-liners, pieces of eight" (115–116). Of course, T. S. Eliot's "The Wasteland" and the old-time standard "Liza Jane" are fragmentary for very different reasons, but collage and pastiche exist nonetheless in both.

There is one way that old-time music is even more aesthetically radical than modernism (albeit, again, unintentionally): old-time has always been mostly a nonrecorded and noncommercial activity. For every recorded musician of old-time (whether in the 1920s or today) and for every live performer of old-time, there are legions of unrecorded musicians, many of them quite skilled, who play their fiddles and banjos at home, in informal jam sessions at old-time festival campgrounds, and often just for themselves. The art of old-time music is thus mostly experiential, participatory, and not solely or even mainly the CD one buys, the MP3 one downloads or the concert one attends; the art is in its production. It would be as if one identified Eliot's "The Wasteland" neither as the printed poem on the page nor as the oral recitation of it but rather in the very act of Eliot writing and revising it—and then, if he were an old-time musician and his poem were a tune, it got passed on to someone else who revised it further before passing it along again, gathering and shedding layers like soil. Paradoxically, then, roots music is simultaneously deeply traditional and aesthetically radical (though again, the fact that *roots* music should be *radical* makes sense at an underlying etymological level, since these two words are related), in the sense of working against our habitual ways of understanding art as reified objects created by individual artists.

The aesthetics of old-time music does not, therefore, lend itself to direct political (including environmental) message-making the way the proletarian realism of Pete Seeger and his musical heirs does. Old-time does, however, provide rich ground for eco-formalist study. That is, instead of asking what old-time says about nature, we can ask how it formally enacts ecological ways of knowing, how it reiterates natural processes, and how it envelops its musicians in an aural environment often coextensive with an outdoor environment.

To return to the same section of *Cold Mountain*, the novel shifts from the theme of the song "Mole in the Ground" to the form it and similar fiddle tunes take over time:

> Ada could hear in Ruby's breathing that she was yet awake, and so she said, Do you remember that song of your father's about the mole in the ground? Ruby said that she did, and Ada asked if Ruby thought Stobrod had written the song. Ruby said there were many songs that you could not say anybody in particular made by himself. A song went around from fiddler to fiddler and each one added something and took something away so that in time the song became a different thing from what it had been, barely recognizable in either tune or lyric. But you could not say the song had been improved, for as was true of all human effort, there was never advancement. Everything added meant something lost, and about as often as not the thing lost was preferable to the thing gained, so that over time we'd be lucky if we just broke even. Any thought otherwise was empty pride. (Frazier 380)

The idea that the old-time song is communally experienced, modified, and passed down resonates with ecological interrelation over competition and individualism. In a jam circle of musicians at an old-time festival, generally a fiddler will choose a tune and lead it, but he or she is not soloing, per se. Unlike bluegrass, rock, jazz, and other popular music, old-time musicians don't take turns soloing in the spotlight. Rather, they play in tight formation with each other, the guitars supplying a steady rhythm of strummed chords while the banjos and fiddles share the melody. These musicians, perhaps just having met each other, lean in close to each other and listen attentively, working hard to recall melodies others propose, or they pick them up on the spot. The result is an intricate and interwoven tapestry of sound; ideally no one instrument dominates, even if a fiddler leads a particular tune. Similarly, square dancing emphasizes group collaboration over solo showmanship. The dance caller proclaims various commands, and each square of people follows to the rhythm of an old-time stringband.

In addition to interrelation, old-time embodies at a formal level a combination of chance and order similar to that of the natural world. Traditional fiddle tunes are, on one hand, tight little structures of sound, most often made up of two repeating parts in the melody; these tunes might sound highly repetitive to the unaccustomed ear. Close and practiced listening reveals, however, that not only does a tune vary according to each fiddler that plays it, but even within one tune that a fiddler plays, he or she will make slight variations in emphasis or bowing each time through the melody. Similarly, each square of folks in a square dance will vary slightly in their fulfillment of the dance caller's commands. Like good metrical or rhymed poetry, repetition with a difference is the happy consequence in old-time music and dance, and this balance resembles the close association of chance and order in the natural world, the stuff of chaos theory (sometimes more accurately termed "anti-chaos" or complexity theory). Indeed, when viewed from above, a square dance resembles the ever shifting fractal patterns chaos theorists observe in leaves, shells, and other natural phenomena.

In an old-time jam circle, moreover, the musicians create an environment in a very real sense, an intimate atmosphere of sound that envelops the players and anyone nearby. This aural environment is similar to what Timothy Morton terms "ambient poetics" and what some musicologists and composers call "immersive sound" that requires "immersive listening," which can facilitate ecological thinking: "The link between immersive listening and ecological thought focuses on the idea of music as a vibration that works on the unconscious or intuitive parts of the human mind-brain" (Ingram 60). Old-time musicians often speak of the trance-like state that they fall into while playing a tune in a group. Partly this is the effect of repetition—playing a repetitive tune many times over, sometimes up to thirty minutes of one tune in a jam circle or square dance—as well as the droning effect of double-stopped fiddle strings and the unfretted fifth string of the banjo. But the old-time trance occurs also as a result of the music prying one out of oneself into a relational, ecological mode of being; that is, one's musical self in such experiences becomes closely integrated with the others in the circle. The goal is never the elimination of distinct individuality, even at an acoustical level— each player adds something different—but instead the overall cohesive sound, more than the sum of its parts.

Some modern composers take their music outside for deliberately environmental reasons, such as "the Canadian composer and 'acoustic ecologist' R. Murray Schafer, who performs pieces such as his opera *Princess of the Stars* (1985) outdoors, rather than in concert halls, in order to reconnect his listeners with living environments" (Ingram 14). But old-time musicians, even if not for overtly environmentalist reasons, have always brought their music outdoors. It is music that not only instills a sense of place, but literally takes place in specific environments that shape its production and reception. That is, the aural environment old-time musicians create when they play outside exists inside a larger, often nonhuman, environment, and the border between these environments is quite porous. Some contemporary musicians who play old-time reproduce this experience through various media. For example, Dirk Powell's 2009 album *Time Again* includes a live recording of Powell and Riley Baugus playing "When Sorrows Encompass Me Round" late at night on a porch. The throb of cicadas pulses behind, inside, and around the song. Tim Eriksen (mostly a solo musician these days but also the front man of the "hardcore Americana" or roots-punk band Cordelia's Dad) has posted on YouTube many amateur but beautiful short films of himself playing old-time music outdoors on fiddle, banjo, and guitar: singing and picking a gentle version of "Careless Love" as meditative as the creek next to him (his repetitive, arpeggio picking on the guitar set to the trickling "brook rhythm," as he puts it in the video description); singing the sad ballad "Frozen Girl" while standing in the falling snow; singing and fiddling a stark "O Death" up in the bare, bone-like limbs of a tree, and so forth. The natural environment in these short films tends to be much more than just a pleasant backdrop to the music. Rather, Eriksen incorporates nature into the overall visual and aural aesthetic of the film; he wants to play with and not merely in nature. In one video, entitled "Tom Dooley—Tim Eriksen and Frogs" (suggesting a collaborative relationship, even if the frogs had no say in the matter), Eriksen plays a fretless banjo and sings the familiar old murder ballad[5] while sitting cross-legged in the Plum Brook Swamp outside Amherst, Massachusetts. For the first thirty-five seconds and last twenty-two seconds of the film, the camera offers us no music and no image of Eriksen, just a shot of the sun-filled swamp and the sound of chirruping frogs, which are quite audible throughout Eriksen's playing as well. By bookending his performance this way, Eriksen respectfully lets nature have the first and last word; his music is a temporary aural addition to nature's preexisting sound patterns. We hear the swamp inside the song and the song inside the swamp.

Eriksen's DIY films express how old-time music is often experienced, particularly for the musicians themselves (even if few people play fiddle up in a tree like Eriksen): as coextensive with its environment rather than abstracted from it. Of course, one could play jazz, classical, and other "unplugged" music in a swamp, and even the most seemingly primitive, natural, and authentic art is mediated in various ways.[6] Indeed, one of the fascinating things about Eriksen is the way he relies on technological mediation—the video camera, YouTube, Facebook—to construct a sense of immediacy and authenticity. But the mediation of art exists on a spectrum; old-time music—particularly in its common experiential, participatory aspects—is only lightly packaged by technological, commercial, and other layers. For example, contemporary recordings of old-time music are typically minimally produced (usually no over-dubbing and never any auto-tuning), a form of voluntary simplicity given all of the technological options in today's recording studios. For current members of the old-time music community, the phrase "old-time music" does not likely bring to mind a particular CD, celebrity, or concert venue. To these folks "old-time" refers partly to a particular sound associated with southern Appalachia but perhaps more importantly to a set of qualities associated with that sound: communitarian, place-based, experiential, process- rather than product-oriented, mostly noncommercial, and, as this essay has claimed, deeply ecological in its form. The ecoformalism of old-time reveals much about the various and complex ways art and nature may conjoin.

Notes

1. Ecocriticism has only recently turned its attention to music. Examples include Ingram, Olson (both cited in this essay) and Volume 15 (Autumn 2011) of *Green Letters: Studies in Ecocriticism*, which focuses entirely on music.

2. By positioning the speaker against the "Feds," the song evokes antigovernment sentiments common among conservative westerners, and so the song's potentially libertarian environmentalism is thus another complex example of "purplish" politics.

3. I use the term "roots music" to describe traditional American folk music that began before the radio, was originally and is often still non-commercial, and was and is most often played acoustically. Roots music includes old-time, traditional country, blues, and Cajun.

4. Old-time has most often emphasized live playing over recording. Still, some very skilled contemporary players of old-time music have put out excellent recordings: Dirk Powell, Bruce Molsky, Rayna Gellert, Tim Eriksen, Foghorn Stringband, the Carolina Chocolate Drops, and The Freight Hoppers are just a few. One can also find them and many other old-time musicians on YouTube.

5. Based on a true story, the Appalachian murder ballad "Tom Dooley" (first recorded in 1929 but likely written in the late nineteenth century) was made famous to a wide audience by the Kingston Trio's polished pop-folk version recorded in 1958, but in his YouTube film Tim Eriksen instead plays a version in the style of Frank Proffitt (1913–1965), an old-time musician from North Carolina.

6. Benjamin Filene offers a thorough and mostly persuasive account of the way American roots music has always passed through significant filters on its way to mainstream culture. He examines the

> cultural "middlemen" who move between folk and popular culture. These folklorists, record company executives, producers, radio programmers, and publicists "discovered" folk musicians, recorded them, arranged concert dates for them, and, usually, promoted them as the exemplars of America's musical roots. In doing so, they did more than deliver "pure" music: they made judgments about what constituted America's true musical traditions, helped shape what "mainstream" audiences recognized as authentic, and, inevitably, transformed the music that the folk performers offered…they "romanced" the folk, in the sense both of wooing them as intimates and of sentimentalizing them as Other. (5)

> Despite the undeniable mediation involved in the transmission of roots music from musician to audience, I argue that old-time music is still relatively less packaged than popular music.

References

Anderson, John. "Seminole Wind." *Seminole Wind*. BNA Records, 1992.

Darrell, Johnny with Anita Carter. "The Coming of the Roads." 1969. Single.

Denisoff, R. Serge. *Sing a Song of Social Significance*. Bowling Green, OH: Bowling Green University Popular Press, 1972.

Filene, Benjamin. *Romancing the Folk: Public Memory & American Roots Music*. Chapel Hill: University of North Carolina Press, 2000.

Frazier, Charles. *Cold Mountain*. New York: Vintage Contemporaries, 1997.

Hawker, Ginny. Personal Interview. 1 August 2009.

Ingram, David. *The Jukebox in the Garden: Ecocriticism and American Popular Music Since 1960*. New York: Rodopi, 2010.

Marcus, Greil. *The Old Weird America: The World of Bob Dylan's Basement Tapes*. New York: Picador, 1997.

"Mole in the Ground." Perf. Dirk Powell, Tim O'Brien and John Herrmann. *Songs From the Mountain*. Sugarhill, 2002.

Morton, Timothy. *Ecology Without Nature: Rethinking Environmental Aesthetics*. Cambridge: Harvard University Press, 2007.

Nelson, Wayne. "Scatter My Ashes." *Dadburned Guitar*. Home recording, 2005.

Nicolson, Marjorie. *Mountain Gloom and Mountain Glory: The Development of the Aesthetics of the Infinite*. Seattle: University of Washington Press, 2011.

Olson, Ted. "'Pass It On Down': Environmental Themes in Country Songs." *Shenandoah* 56.2 (Fall 2006).

Solnit, Rebecca. "One Nation Under Elvis: An Environmentalism for Us All." *Orion* 27.2 (March/April 2008).

Travis, Merle. "Dark as a Dungeon." *Folk Songs of the Hills*. Bear Family Records, 1993.

——. "Sixteen Tons." *Folk Songs of the Hills*. Bear Family Records, 1993.

Webster, Duncan. *Looka Yonder! The Imaginary America of Populist Culture*. New York: Routledge, 1988.

CHAPTER 28

MEDIA MORALIA

Reflections on Damaged Environments and Digital Life

ANDREW MCMURRY

Johnny Head-in-Air. Ecocriticism has never not been a crisis discipline. Anyone who thought, "Aha!, here is an academic *Green Zone* for safe and wholesome discussions about birds in texts and their counterparts at my feeder" missed the point altogether. Ecocriticism is a conversation in a trench along a collapsing front, and ecocritics must shout over the roar of the tanks, bulldozers, and flamethrowers. *Blood-on-the-ground* is the ur-trope for the ecoliterate text: nothing praiseworthy can be registered without the deep foreboding of its pending annihilation. Behind every paean or even casual nod to nature is the dreadful knowledge: "there is no longer beauty or consolation except in the gaze falling on horror, withstanding it, and in unalleviated consciousness of negativity holding fast to the possibility of what is better" (Adorno 25). In this perverse realism, textual signifiers refer not to the things themselves but to the void where things once stood. One cannot fall back to the old salients of *formal autonomy* or *well-wrought urn* because such concepts have been blasted to pieces: they no longer hold water, let alone calm the panicking imagination. We would love to keep the beautiful objects apart from the rest of the shite, but the poem cracked and in oozed a greasy leachate from the chemical plant upriver. The blackbirds have scattered from the trees or, rather, stumps; the jar in Tennessee was removed, along with the mountaintop upon which it was placed. All ecocritical interventions are eulogies to the dead and the doomed: places, species, cultures, natures.

The planet on the table. Elizabeth Kolbert throws up her hands at the end of her *Field Notes on a Catastrophe*, which investigates the whys and wherefores of global warming: "It may seem impossible to imagine that a technological society could choose, in essence, to destroy itself, but that is what we are now in the process of doing" (187). That we would choose self-destruction is a datum in great need of explanation by anyone who styles himself an ecocritic. *Literature*, the lodestar of ecocriticism from its inception, helps us understand what sort of creatures we are to knowingly immolate ourselves and the planet. Amongst many other functions it serves as a medium of storage: poems, though they cannot take the place of a mountain, bear "some lineament or character, / Some affluence, if only half-perceived, / In the poverty of their words, / Of the planet of which they were part" (Stevens 532). Literature, taken as a whole, is the human pageant distilled—and equally the transhistorical rap-sheet of a sad and furious primate. Passed through the interpretive lens of ecocritical theory, literature reveals instance after instance of our utter failure to project, limit, and abate our inborn corrosive effect on the ecosystems in which we live. In simple terms, the price we have paid for the complexity of our lifeways is the decomplexity of Earth's. As a species, we have the power to modify our surroundings to suit our needs but not the wisdom to suit our needs to our surroundings.

Let us drink a toast to literature's magnificent rendition of our tortured history while casting a cool ecocritical eye toward the future. Though literature has ploughed long and truly the broad fields of human ignorance and conceit, ecocritics must now look to our newer mediums of record: television, film, computer-based media and, more broadly, the digital *datasphere* (first imagined in Dan Simmons's science fiction novel of 1989, *Hyperion*) that is growing over the earth like a new mantel. Making predictions about the future of digital media is a mug's game because tomorrow seldom unfolds as the present believes it must. But what seems safe to say is that if the world as we know it survives a little longer, the mature datasphere will allow us to query the air and have answers whispered into our ears, or make gestures and cause holograms to fill the room. Our lives will be led in this thick broth of information and we will drink from it deeply. Billions of us will be telepresent around the same virtual campfire sharing stories, the apotheosis of Walter Ong's secondary orality. Via ubiquitous computing, this planetary information cloud (or fog) will connect every human with every human artifact; it will link us to natural geophysical structures using GIS [Global Information Systems], to animals equipped with RFID tags [Radio-Frequency Identification], and to sections of the atmosphere and oceans seeded with various monitoring instruments. The whole earth will be able to observe itself and track its vital signs: summer/winter cycles of CO_2 inhalation and exhalation, rising sea levels and temperature spikes, crashing of waves and glaciers, songs of birds and groans of whales. Data is everywhere, just waiting to be mined. From our listening posts we planetary (mis)managers will be able to monitor the life and death of Gaia in this, our terminal epoch, the Anthropocene.

Goodbye Maldives, it's been nice. NASA's *Eyes on the Earth 3D* is a desktop tool that allows users to access the latest telemetry from a host of Earth observation satellites. Jason 2, for example, keeps track of ocean heights using a microwave radiometer, which bounces a beam off the surface of the water and measures its return time. This altimetric record is one of the most precise ways to follow sea-level fluctuations, which occur for many reasons, including planetary wobble, ocean circulation, thermal expansion, wind and storm surges, seasonal runoff, El Niño and La Niña events, seiches, tsunamis, tides, a great many bathers entering the sea all at once, and polar ice-cap melting.

Where's my noosphere? Are new media adding yet more layers of distraction and diversion to our already thick-coated sensorium? Sometimes these new media seem to provide merely sexier packaging for the same old bad news, like the doctor on *The Simpsons* who tells Homer's worried family, "we can't fix his heart, but we can tell you exactly how damaged it is"—to which Homer replies "What an age we live in!" ("Homer's."). On the other hand, perhaps the playgrounds and battlefields of cyberspace will provide healthier outlets for our restless energies, which in the real world continue to go to work on the planet as if it were an endless frontier and business opportunity. Might there even be ways that new media can revive our fading connection to the Old Holocene?

Well, there are a few hopeful notes. Some ecocritics argue that digital media technologies are qualitatively different from earlier technologies that ran on or were made from petroleum. They think that the information gusher is lighter than the old crude, that the datasphere will substitute wireless for pipelines, information highways for asphalt, knowledge commons for the tragedy of the commons. They hope the datasphere will outmode and replace so much of that dirty, energy-hogging infrastructure that we will be ushered out of the industrial into a new ecotechnic (Greer) or ecocosmopolitan age (Heise 10). Digital media appear frictionless, as though causing things to happen through the application of *thought*, not *energy*. Perhaps they can help us live on the planet *smartly*. Thus, with respect to ecopsychological health ecocritics hope that digital media are to the mind what wind power is to the atmosphere: carbon neutral. They hope, as well, that the integrative propensities of the datasphere will not draw us into a social media echo chamber but, indeed, will restore (or perhaps for the first time *create*) a healthy rapport with the natural world. In this view, new media could foster awareness, transparency, compassion; they could put us in touch with the unseen things; they could show us the way the world is ending and empower us to save it. For ecocritics, the immediate task is straightforward: "it behooves us to discover what imaginative and conceptual resources we need to construct ethical and healthy relationships between digital and material worlds, just as ecocritics have been working to establish such relationships between textual and material worlds" (Ulman 345).

Operation Frog. Puslinch, Ontario. Summer, 1995: they were housed in a converted barn at the back of the pasture. There were six of them, barely out of college, the leader a precocious high school dropout, and they were writing code to make Earth a safer place for *Ranacatesbeiana*. That worthy amphibian, to the tune of millions a year, was being pickled in formalin for biology students to dissect. Digital Frog International would make that classic lab activity obsolete: using its CD-ROM-based, virtual anatomy lesson, a student could tease apart the lungs, heart, and kidneys of a frog without ever leaving the desk-station; with a mouse click she could spark its dead thigh muscle to life, so to speak, just as Galvani had done 200 years before. Moreover, the disk would contain enough leftover space for other items of educational value: lessons on ecology and frog distributions; a dictionary of terms; self-tests and quizzes.

If one pages through a lab supplies wholesaler's catalog, one comes away wondering where all those preserved bullfrogs—4–6 inches, 6–8 inches, in bulk bags or pails, as you wish—come from. And given that all over the world frogs are dying off like … frogs? … one could rightly suppose that in the near future the digital frog will be the only anatomy kit practically obtainable. But, in the absence of the real animal, will savvy about amphibian anatomy still have cash value? Or will it be like knowing that the diplodocus possessed eighty tail vertebrae? In point of fact, such knowledge is, like most knowledge of low creatures, usually just scaffolding to an understanding of the mammalian anatomies—of the rat, the fetal pig, the rhesus monkey—that are closer to the human. Indeed, biological education sometimes seems designed merely to move students stepwise toward that question of singular importance at least since Francis Bacon: *How can nature be made to divulge her secrets so that we humans may live longer and healthier lives?* That this question has been answered in part through ongoing violence toward our animal cousins is exactly what the programmers at DFI were trying to address: by rendering obsolete animal sacrifice for the purposes of education, they were pointing toward a future in which science and medicine could be modeled and extended by digital means rather than animal suffering.

Disruptive technologies. The most powerful moment in Kubrick's oeuvre occurs in *2001: A Space Odyssey* when the first killer hominid *weaponizes* a thigh bone to the strains of Strauss's *Also Sprach Zarathustra.* This scene symbolizes the fortunate fall: the *first* man exteriorizing his mind into a tool and so initiating the technology-assisted ecocide that is leading to the *last*. In "Why I am Not Going to Buy a Computer," Wendell Berry avers that any new tool should be demonstrably superior to the tool it succeeds. In his view a benign tool is one that does "not replace or disrupt anything good that already exists" (172), a standard to which we can all bow our heads. Yet this is not the way we killer apes have ever *done things.* Like chimps puffing up their fur before battle, we feel bigger and safer inside our technological swaddling. Artifact evolution is driven by the desire to get ever more power quicker to hand. The ideal tool would be a titanium magic wand or perhaps a death-ray with a built-in Pez dispenser. We want godlike power in a slick package. The concentration of many digital capabilities into a single mobile device is exemplary: apps for all contingencies—and heavy on the fun-factor. The switch from continuous (analog media) to discontinuous information representation (via the digital computer that Berry rejects) makes this matter-symbol convergence possible. Digitalization permits our representational systems—speaking, writing, telephony, recording, broadcasting, and so on—to manifest anywhere and everywhere across the screens and portals that connect us to the ethereal infrastructure of our world. Already wearable, very soon computers will be embeddable, etched into our very bones, silent, invisible, potent. We will radiate tool-power; indeed, we will *be* the tools we wish to use. But the question must be asked: Has there ever been a tool that did not lead to an increase in human pride and arrogance?

Fish in water. Marshall McLuhan liked to say that he didn't know who invented water but he knew it wasn't a fish. Literary critics, after spending a couple decades gasping on the shores of digital media and imagining they were evolving into something else, are soon to become fish again, and when they do they will, thankfully, stop obsessing about digital media. For the same reasons that few bother to theorize the word processor or the hypertext novel anymore, literary critics will stop noticing new media: the latter will just be the water in which they swim. The gnashing of teeth over the death of the paper-based book or the virtualization of the library—this too shall pass. As Katherine Hayles points out, "So essential is digitality to contemporary processes of composition, storage, and production that print should properly be considered a particular form of output for digital files rather than a medium separate from digital instantiation" (*Electronic Literature* 159). But while paper books are now digital media's stepchildren, content is still king for literary critics. The text, not the delivery mechanism, bears the important secrets.

One group that might linger a bit longer on the beach are ecocritics, whose relationship to media has always been dicey. Ecocritics are ever mindful that prior to any medium are the mediated entities themselves—the moose, the sandpiper, the toxic event, the white squall of reality. Not to say that other critics do not find so-called nature compelling as well, but ecocritics claim a special regard for the premediated world. They are less likely to insist (if anyone ever has) *there is nothing outside the text*. Some even wish to hold a place in the queue for this nothing. Although they hope otherwise, they fear the digital ecology will become too seductive, its pictures of virtual entities too vivid, for the rest of us dullards to maintain our already feeble grip on the environmental real.

Ecocritics should probably come clean: they have a *reality bias*, which is only to say they believe the red-cockaded woodpeckers in the pine forests of southeastern North America are realer than the characters in *Super Mario Galaxy 2*. Gamers could rightly reply that there are hundreds of millions of copies of *Mario* and fewer than 15,000 copies of the woodpecker; Mario himself is a character beloved worldwide, but most of us will never see the red-cockaded. Still, there is something about flesh-and-blood fauna that to ecocritics remain more compelling than software entities. Gamers, deep down, probably feel the same. Yet they might be correct in a certain way were they to opine, "The human world would be more diminished by the deletion of Mario than the extinction of one little-known, maladaptive species." No doubt this formulation proposes a false choice, one we need not make, as false as claiming Stone Age man had to pick either the Irish elk or the cave paintings of Lascaux. But in this regard there are significant differences between old media and new, differences that help explain why ecocritics prefer their students to read more Emily Dickinson (e.g., "His bill an auger is, / His head, a cap and frill. / He laboreth at every tree,—/ A worm his utmost goal") and play fewer video games. The poem, ecocritics would say, points back to the bird; Mario points only to more Mario.

Our growing alienation from the environmental real is partly the result of *radical dematerialization*, which owes its early theorization to Dr. McCoy on the old *Star Trek* series, who said of the ship's matter transporter, "I signed aboard this ship to practice medicine, not to have my atoms scattered back and forth across space by this gadget" ("Space Seed"). But more to the point is the extraordinary degree to which everyday life is being incrementally disembodied, the mind hurled into cyberspace and the meat left behind to keep the chair warm. "However incompletely the new media have been implanted, however faltering is their present state of interconnection, the modal conversion of the human has sensibly begun" (Massumi 132). What does the conversion bode for our relationships to that which, like the woodpecker, is not "beamed up"? Granted, we have long been creatures of media and, as McLuhan argued in his summation, *Laws of Media*, what any medium—any technology, any idea, in fact—gives by *enhancement* it eventually takes back through *reversal*. The automobile heralded unprecedented mobility and *Fahrvergnügen* but its very success resulted in traffic jams and road rage. Yet for McLuhan media were more or less discrete entities and so could be *understood from within as if from without*. It seemed to him that "if we keep our cool during the descent into the maelstrom, studying the process as it happens to us and what we can do about it, we can come through" (268). (To which McCoy might reply, "How do you study a process at the very moment it is rendering you a collection of particles in a pattern buffer?") There was, too, McLuhan's deep and abiding humanism: "I expect to see the coming decades transform the planet into an art form; the new man, linked in a cosmic harmony that transcends time and pace, will sensuously caress and mold and pattern every facet of the terrestrial artifact as if it were a work of art, and man himself will become an organic art form." It is *exactly* this knee-jerk faith in our cognitive virtuosity, in mind over media, that has some ecocritics worried. Conventional literary humanists want to view biophysical reality as a toy boat on a sea of discursive regimes, tossed about by waves of ideology, mass media distortion, hackneyed scripts, bureaucratese. We can get the vessel to safe harbor by learning to *speak the storm*. Ecocritics, by contrast, believe the real storm will fill our throats with brine.

Pharmakon. Ecocritics should recall that theories of media determinism all find their backstory in Plato's *Phaedrus*, in which the god of writing, Theuth, champions his gift as an *aide-mémoire* while the Egyptian king, Thamus, scorns writing as a *pharmakon* that will actually destroy memory by anchoring it outside the mind in written characters. *True truths* can be known only by committing them to onboard, living memory (*anamnesis*); writing is the realm of falsity, rhetoric, and dead memory (*hypomnesis*). Every new medium puts us on the horns of the same dilemma: what part of our mental life shall be outsourced this time? For ecocritics, the digital dilemma can be posed this way: does the hyperimmediacy of the digital environment poison or enhance our relationship with the natural one? More baldly: if a boy spends much of his waking life inside Facebook or the *World of WarCraft*, how fares his nascent attachment to the *non-virtual*, that portion of existence unresponsive to mouse clicks?

The Unenlightenment. Bill McKibben developed one answer to the digital dilemma through an experiment in comparative phenomenology. He watched over 1,000 hours of the television programming from one day in 1990. He then spent twenty-four hours outdoors hiking, swimming, making supper, and stargazing. McKibben discovered what most ecocritics will have suspected: a media ecology that features *The Simpsons* and The Shopping Channel as keystone species is stunningly impoverished. Notwithstanding the density of information in this ecology, McKibben believes our era is one of "deep ignorance, when vital knowledge that humans have always possessed about who we are and where we live seems beyond our reach. An Unenlightenment" (*Age* 9). In McKibben's view, a duck paddling in a pond is a far richer source of quality information than television because it links us to "A realer world, maybe—certainly an older one" (248). "Each day," as ducks and other organisms are extinguished or are replaced in our consciousnesses by screen-based entities, "information leaks away—some branch of life that evolved for millions of years is gone, and the next day two more, and six the day after that. The world grows stupider, less substantial" (85). The new media ecology roars in to fill the void left as old nature exits. If McKibben revised his book to account for the rise of what Mark Bauerline dubs the Dumbest Generation, that is, the info-saturated youth of today who are "fabulously autonomized by digital technology" (234), he might be forced to pronounce the world now effectively brain-dead. (On the other hand, perhaps not. Later in his career, McKibben used the power of the internet to mobilize climate actions and applauded the democratizing effects of digital media and digital networks: "The Internet may be precisely the tool we need; it's as if it came along just in time, a deus ex machina to make our next evolution bearable," [*Eaarth* 196]).

Of course, the "missing information" argument has been dismissed on a variety of grounds, not least of which are its unfashionable, rather icky sentimentalism and high-culture bias. John Parham complains that "there is a damaging discrepancy between McKibben's impressive relaying of 'information' about the natural world and threats to it and his ill-tempered, lamentably researched media criticism" (118). H. Lewis Ulman provides further corrective by noting that virtual spaces are simply another type of mental modelling, and if they are "leading us into unhealthy relationships with our environment, then we need to change those models, not fantasize about abandoning virtuality" (355). Hypermediation should not be construed as unique to the digital era but rather as the latest moment in a long technological continuum (which includes books and television, for example, but equally clothes, farm implements, cannons, and chewing gum) that has always blended matter and information. For time out of mind humans have lived in richly composed *semioscapes*, retoolings, and retellings of the unadorned earth that preceded them, and "the virtual is always embodied in the real, just as the real is always mediated for us by the virtual" (348).

In this view, highly immersive spaces like 3-D movies and computer games stretch us in ways that are different in scale but not in kind from, say, cooking in a medieval castle kitchen or attending an opera in Vienna in 1913. We are always already working not just with things but with information about things, moving effortlessly between data patterns and data sources. What digital media do, then, is extend our capacities to compile, separate, sort, and reintegrate data in fruitful new directions. Steven Johnson posits a "Sleeper Curve" (after the future envisaged by the Woody Allen film in which cigarettes are considered healthy), whereby oft-derided media forms such as television shows and video games turn out to be good for us, part of a "progressive story: mass culture growing more sophisticated, demanding more cognitive engagement with each passing year. Think of it as a kind of positive brainwashing: the popular media steadily, but almost imperceptibly, making our minds sharper, as we soak in entertainment usually dismissed as so much lowbrow stuff" (xv). Moreover, as Hayles puts it, "today's media have tended to move out of the box and overlay virtual information and functionalities onto physical locations and actual objects," thus creating "environments in which physical and virtual realms merge in fluid and seamless ways" ("Cybernetics" 148). This emergent *mixed reality* promises to its users (which will eventually include almost everyone, if only by default) no less than *enhanced consciousness*, for what appears to be in play is not just the Sleeper Curve but a bona fide "coevolutionary dynamics in which computational media and humans mutually modify, influence, and help to constitute one another in a phenomenon known as technogenesis" (154). McKibben's diatribe against information smacks not only of Luddism but looks downright antievolutionary.

However, what confounds those who wish to satisfyingly refute McKibben's crude experiment is the fact that it is repeatable and verifiable. One needs only inspect one's own experiences to confirm McKibben's thesis. These days, all but the most committed *media ignoramus* can claim to know more facts about ducks than *la famille Simpson*. The pharmakon of *always-on, ever-present media* poisons—or, if one prefers, cures—the human relationship with so-called nature (and much else besides), sending the ducks packing and replacing them with the dried husks of media-manufactured memories: streets of San Francisco and Coronation Street, Mr. Whipple and Colonel Klink, the morning zoo and what's behind door number three. For many children in the media-narcotized West, the only extant ducks are Donald and Daffy. On a happier note: because this process of estrangement has been going on a long time—long before the advent of digital media—at least the bitter pill has been well-coated for easier swallowing. Ernst Cassirer memorably stated what many others, from Plato onward, had already noticed: "Physical reality seems to recede in proportion as man's symbolic activity advances. Instead of dealing with the things themselves man is in a sense constantly conversing with himself" (25).

That we are dealing with an age-old problematic, however, does not negate but rather confirms its continuing relevance. And the new, distinctive feature of the datasphere is that it will have the genuine capacity to at last replace *in a sense* with *in fact*. With media penetration complete, the virtual will become the default, and whatever information might have transited unmediated from the environmental real will now have to pass through digital *codecs*. Those moments of startling rawness, when the tang of unprepared experience hangs in the air, will be fewer and far between, and difficult to recognize when they are offered. Anne Dillard's much-anthologized essay, "Living Like Weasels," epitomizes this rerouting of all experience, even that of untrammeled nature, through media. "I tell you I've been in that weasel's brain for sixty seconds, and he was in mine. Brains are private places, muttering through unique and secret tapes—but the weasel and I both plugged into another tape simultaneously, for a sweet and shocking time. Can I help it if it was a blank?" (124). In locking eyes with the weasel, Dillard encounters the absolute Other, a pure wildness immensely attractive precisely because it smacks of nothing human—yet to cognize the experience she requires the metaphorical intervention of a recording technology.

From new transmitters came the old stupidities. The boys were at the Brecht Creek Nature Centre, and the naturalist explained the game. "Each team will be assigned one GPS handheld. Press the menu button, then cycle through to the stations you must find. Once the screen gives you a distance and direction, you can start walking. It should beep when you're close but keep looking around because we find these devices are accurate to only about five meters. When you get to the station, search for the sign and copy down the symbol you see on it. You need to be out from under the trees for best results because you want at least three satellites to triangulate on your position. You can try the digital compass if you want but you probably won't need it, and keep in mind it points in the direction you're going, not north." Then they were off, and there was a lot of shrieking and general fun; we could hear them all the way back at the firepit where we were getting the marshmallows ready. As it turned out, my son's team completed the circuit first. I asked the boys if they had seen any wildlife during the geocaching activity. "Wildlife?" one of them said, puzzled. "Were we supposed to look for animals?"

Quintessence of dust. Conventional literary and cultural critics—humanists, for the most part—have yet to appreciate the debilitating nature of their anthropocentricism when it comes to confronting environmental challenges like climate change and species loss. They are insensate to all but that which warms them to their favorite subject, *man,* as though in viewing the Arcimboldo portraits they did not notice the faces were composed of fruits, vegetables, and creatures. The critiques they are wont to produce are rooted in the powerful conviction that all reality, insofar as that reality is filtered through discursive and cultural systems, is best understood as a social construction. "Yes, yes," they seem to say, echoing Wallace Stevens' solipsistic Hoon, "we are the world in which we walk, and what we see or hear or feel comes not but from ourselves" (65). Their fixation on humankind's lavishly constructed *Umwelt* insulates them from its dodgy footings. True, every organism lives in its own world, and the rest, for good or ill, is of no account. (The fly, according to Von Uexküll, specifies a fly-world, though this is no defense against the intersecting reality of a fly-swatter.) It is as if these critics have planted themselves at a peephole in a tall hoarding; squinting through they see a titanic building site where workers, overseers, craftsmen, machines, tools, and materials are all being mobilized to erect a grand, rambling edifice. Architects and engineers race around shouting directions, often contradicting one another, calling for Byzantine structures built one minute to be demolished in the next. Mesmerized by this glorious crazed intricacy, the critics fail to notice that beneath everything are the rotten pilings and black, sucking mire that will soon swallow the entire folly, including the ground beneath their feet.

I don't understand. Why aren't more humanists tearing out their hair over the passing of their subject, as if their own lives hung in the balance, which maybe they do? Could the answer be that ecocide looks to be the business of the other professions (e.g., "Sure, I know the oceans are dying but my gig's Shakespeare.") Or maybe it's because this niggling detail, *the crash of man,* if considered too closely, overshadows *the triumph of man,* which is the controlling motif, as though by institutional fiat, of every humanist analysis of every human production. Therefore, constant forgetting and comfy provincialism are required to keep the talking points on the *human pageant* forever fresh and spritely. What are humanists, after all, if not the tribunes of culture? And who needs them if they can't stick to the script? Not only are they disinclined to talk about collapse but they have been superbly *incentivized* not to.

Perhaps such conventional critics have learned all-too well the lesson that the medium is the message and so assumed they could dispense with the message altogether. It is all very well to yammer on about *ecological catastrophe,* they seem to say, but its *representation* is what we are here to discuss! Unfortunately, the cataclysm is not waiting on the minutes from this colloquy: it moves forward without our consent—though, of course, with our full participation. Rush Limbaugh, declaiming against global warming on the basis of selective evidence and outright lies, does scarcely more damage to our future prospects by active malevolence than does the flimsy constructivism of cultural critics who wish to make warming a metonym for other controversies that hold more human interest. Andrew Ross, in his early 1990s take on the matter, wrote "These theories [of climate change] draw their power in the world from an elite culture peopled by those accustomed, by education and an inherited sense of entitlement, to see the globe as part of their dominion, a territory that exists to be rationally surveyed, itemized in a cost-benefit analysis, and protected by political action that further regulates its natural economy" (219). While his criticisms bear eerie similarity to the pungent right-wing rhetoric used against high-value enviro-targets like Al Gore, Ross did not necessarily deny global warming, instead cagily keeping to the constructivist high ground that cultural studies folk like to occupy. But he did spot opportunity in the "crisis" (his scare quotes) to expose the aggrandizing machinations of those wielding expert power and knowledge. In retrospect, his sublimation of the climate emergency into an object lesson in global class struggle reads like yet another example of the arrogance of humanism. What one prefers of critics is to first get the *facts on the ground* before looking down at them from 10,000 feet.

The forecast calls for rain. "Media determine our situation" (xxxix). Do they? So says Friedrich Kittler in the catchiest bit of media phrasemaking since the Northern Magus himself. But it depends on what is meant by *situation*. In situ, in place, on the ground, media determine nothing about record rainfall or brushfires in the canyon. Yet media shape the constraints and affordances of our psychic and social systems, and when we speak of rain and fire we do so from within the extant media programs that run on those systems. Kittler writes, "What remains of people is what media can store and communicate. What counts are not the messages or the content with which they equip so-called souls for the direction of a technological era, but rather (and in strict accordance with McLuhan) their circuits, the very schematism of perceptibility" (xli). Another way to put this is to say that although at one time our brains were attuned to the cycles of moon and season, planting and harvest, more recently they were grooved by phonograph needles and cathode rays. Currently, according to Bernard Stiegler, we possess a cinematic consciousness, tutored by the moving picture to perceive the flow of reality as a montage of flickering, disposable images, with predictable corollaries: "Controlling the temporal flow of mass consciousness allows the culture industry to control behavior, for instance, to guarantee the consumption of products that the process of permanent innovation (the principle underlying industrial production) constantly releases into the global market" (76–77). What looks to come on the heels of the cinematic consciousness is the fragmented, saccadic drift of the Internet mind, open to the lure of personalized Google ads and one-click ordering buttons. Broadcast gives way to narrowcast just as the assembly line gives way to neo-bespoke production, flexible labor, and on-time delivery. So-called nature, correspondingly, is now all about patchworks and fluxes, variable resilience regimes, and adaptive cycles. The climax ecosystem is a thing of the past; only succession is permanent.

Well, what of it? We are all Heracliteans now. The old networks die, the new ones are born. Departmental colleagues who have never spoken by phone have exchanged hundreds of emails. Students once daydreamed and doodled in class, and now they text and tweet. *Plus ça change, plus c'est la même chose.* The crux for ecocritics is, again, the dematerialization of everyday life. The social network fills all space and time. Yesterday, the solitary daydreamer gazed out the classroom window at passing clouds; today, the screen-based student is jacked into his device, whether indoors or out, clutching it like a talisman, alert to distant events and urgent communiqués, such as *WRU@?* The clouds: they are passé. And crossing bare common is the interval between wi-fi hot-spots. This is not to suggest that the content of the alfresco experience ever mattered much: like all animals, humans have no pressing stake in any particular feature of their environment unless it threatens or is of use to them. (The fact that many humans do exhibit a sustained biophilic response to natural environments and entities seems a wonderful aberration.) Instead, the issue is medial: our frames of reference are now almost fully interiorized, anchored in built environments and, increasingly, virtual ones. The external world, the one over which human command and control is minimal, coarse, and *clunky*—that world is now obscure, mostly irrelevant, and, when sensed at all, sensed remotely. Reality, the original heads-up display, is off behind a screen. (For some—what a relief! If you don't like the show, the footage of killer mudslide or oil-drenched pelican, turn the channel.)

But ecocritics cannot go too far along the road with Kittler or Stiegler toward the media-determined situation. That is, they can go along the road until it slams into a brick wall: biophysical reality. They must continue to insist that biophysical reality forms the most profound determination of all. "True," they say, "the Earth is now cloaked in layers of virtuality—but it is not armour!" For them, to adopt a Kittlerian perspective would mean conceding that a mental infrastructure acclimatized to tv weather reports is more determinant than the weather itself. It would mean conceding that media are where humans live—not on a planet but on a represented planet. Instead, ecocritics maintain that massively intransigent, frequently punitive biophysical reality will not yield pride of place to any media technology or cultural wrapping, however vigorously applied. For instance, not climate change but the politics of climate change is currently consuming most of the oxygen in the room. But ecocritics believe that even politics must bend at last to the environmental real, for we cannot grow food without water, cannot breathe superheated air, cannot live on a planet with soda-pop oceans. Always privileging the facts on the ground, ecocritics are willing to take the linguistic turn but not the relativist off-ramp. Ecocritics, to remain ecocritics, must place their bets on the determining force of so-called nature, knowing full-well that they may be accused of naive realism.

The fix. Digital media are the veils between us and an environmental real already well veiled *and at the same time* the means by which to observe and understand that environmental real all the better. We live at a moment of lucid myopia, when our optics, our sensors, our means to create and disseminate representations of the natural world are overwhelming our Paleolithic brains. The passionate eye sees how massively our *techne* has eroded that natural world. But the retina cannot hold the image for long.

Like forensic pathologists at a global crime scene, we have found our DNA everywhere but we just *know* it wasn't us that did the deed. One would think that the more media technology revealed the truth, the more our social system would be outraged by the damage technology has caused. Yet more information does not necessarily lead to effective action. In fact, the opposite may occur. Paul Virilio describes this state of affairs as "dromospheric pollution," by which the planet recedes in direct proportion to the media prostheses that enhance its visibility and our sense of control. "*Has Mother Earth become humanity's phantom limb*" (66; italics in original)? Media zoom us in close and give the illusion of mastery, but at the same time they distance us, making their subjects ever more peripheral to our quotidian frames. We see the Patagonian glaciers melting—so exotic, so remote—yet right alongside are the reporters and the scientists, documenting everything, apparently taking charge—we are reassured that something is being done (Doyle 294). The equipment itself engenders the false conclusion on which we have pinned all our hopes: that what technology has broken *more* technology will fix. It is a feature of observing systems that they cannot observe their own observational distinctions: the price of insight is blindness to insight's conditions of production. What you must keep in mind, in other words, is that when at long last you capture the flitting red-cockaded on your Sony HD video camera, what *the bird* sees are *your* wings, spread out to infinity behind you, the human horde harrying it to extinction.

Allegory of the CAVE. In another experiment in comparative phenomenology, Lee Rozelle spent many hours playing *Oddworld*, a video game in which a benign alien "ecoactivist" named Abe is pitted against a ruthless industrial opponent in a dangerous, predator-filled gamescape. The challenge is to guide Abe on a quest to save his "green friends" before he is killed—as, of course, he is, frequently and graphically (110). The question hovering over his experiment was simple: "Can video games like *Oddworld* in any useful way permeate simulation and provide the player with a genuine sense of agency? Can manipulating virtual place bring one any closer to environmental action for the millennial planet?" One fear is that such games are little more than enormous time sinks. But the greater fear is that MOOs, MUDs, automatic virtual environments, synthetic worlds, and the like will eventually become so alluring, and come to absorb so much time and effort from so many people, that by comparison the real world will seem cheap and tedious. Human agency emigrates from the real world to take up residence in the game world, where quests and challenges are more captivating and, in certain respects, personally uplifting. Edward Castronova writes "if all crew members are in the holodeck no one will be running the ship. If you put a holodeck on every starship, no starship would ever report back to base; indeed, *no starship would do anything at all*" (Exodus 4). The holodeck, claims Castronova, has effectively arrived in the form of the massive multiplayer online environments, like *WarCraft* and *Second Life*, where players pursue entire parallel fantasy lives, often more uplifting and purpose-driven than their offline counterparts.

While Castronova, an economist, believes that to *compete* with the virtual the real world will have to become more gamelike, socially conscious game designers argue that immersive games have the potential to *save the world*. They believe positive behaviors and problem-solving strategies learned in virtual worlds can migrate across the digital divide, empowering individuals and collectives to apply those game skills to real-world issues. To be sure, billions of man-hours are spent in video game environments, and it would be of some comfort to know that all that time was not going to waste. In *Reality is Broken*, Jane McGonigal writes that in fact *more*, not less, of our time must be invested these fledgling holodecks. While some see alternate reality games as entertainment, McGonigal believes they provide all the ingredients of productive, satisfying, and meaningful *work*. In part her argument depends on a certain interpretation of Herodotus's history of the ancient Lydians, who rode out a decades-long famine by linking fast-days to dice play, thus fostering social cohesion and shared risk in the face of scarcity. More importantly, her claim is based on research derived from analysis of games like *World of WarCraft* ("without a doubt one of the most satisfying work systems ever engineered" [60]) and her own games, *World Without Oil, Superstruct*, and *Evoke*, which challenge players to take on real-world problems and *game* the solutions. Extending this model, she envisions a pan-national, pan-generational, universally subscribed "Long Game," in which the stakes are no less than the salvation of Earth. As with the Lydians, our real-world and game-world goals would align, with moves in the game space leveraging positive actions in normal space. The upshot of this extraordinary "new scale of cooperation, coordination, and cocreation" (342) might be "humanity's next epic win" (353) Would it not be pretty to think so? Rozelle, however, gets the last word:

> Players ... experience the vague heaviness of history and experience reenactments of cultural struggle, but the cloying disquiet of information never surfaces to make Abe's fatality the ground for reprieve. This is the awe and terror of simulacrum, the absurd waste of the media age; the simulated life suppresses human desire for ecological contact and offers glittering images that divert as they bore. Activists who spend hours inside, designing green games and websites (not to mention writing scholarly books), often fail to differentiate the language and image that seek to provide environmental education and the outdoor teaching-in-action that supersedes discourse. (111)

My ape nature ran off. The report to the academy should note that the world is teeming with hybrids, material-semiotic actors, quasi-objects, assemblages, and, soon, synthetic lives and intelligences. Translation: there are bears rooting in the dumpster and they are wearing radio collars. First nature and second nature combined, and tertiarily fused with information. Disclaimer: nature actually ended; it died, kind of. (But never fear: there can be *ecology without nature*, just as blood still circulates even if pumped by the Jarvik-7 heart.)

Well, whatever we are dealing with, it looks unruly: lots of scraps, cast-offs, and loose ends. The tools we carried didn't stay in our pockets. We hoped they would help us, and *voilà* they did. But they also messed things up. Profoundly. Probably they are going to keep messing things up because we cannot put them away. They changed us, too. We are the *artificial ape*: "Not only have we invented all technology, from the stone tools to the wheeled wagon, from spectacles to genetic engineering, but that technology, within a framework of some 2 to 3 million years, has, physically and mentally, made us. The result is a new, symbiont form of life" (Taylor 198).

The answers we seek are beyond us, but the questions are simple: Can the chainsaw also raise a tree? Can the girl touch a flower through the screen?

References

Adorno, Theodor. *Minima Moralia*. 1951. London: Verso, 2005.

Bauerline, Mark. *The Dumbest Generation*. New York: Tarcher/Penguin, 2009.

Berry, Wendell. *What Are People For?* San Francisco: North Point Press, 1990.

Cassirer, Ernst. *An Essay on Man*. New Haven: Yale University Press, 1944.

Castronova, Edward. *Exodus to the Virtual World: How Online Fun Is Changing Reality*. New York: Palgrave Macmillan, 2008.

Dickinson, Emily. "The Woodpecker. III, XVIII" *Poems, Series Three*. Project Gutenberg. Web. Accessed 1 April 2011.

Dillard, Anne, "Living Like Weasels." *The Annie Dillard Reader*. New York: HarperCollins, 1994.

Doyle, Julie. "Seeing the Climate? The Problematic Status of Visual Evidence in Climate Change Campaigning." In *Ecosee*. Eds. Sidney Dobrin and Sean Morey. Albany: SUNY Press, 2009. 279–298.

Greer, John Michael. *The Ecotechnic Future*. Gabriola Island, British Columbia: New Society Publishers, 2009.

Hayles, N. Katherine. *Electronic Literature*. Notre Dame: University of Notre Dame Press, 2008.

Hayles, N. Katherine. "Cybernetics." In *Critical Terms for Media Studies*. Eds. W. J. T. Mitchell and Mark B. N. Hansen. Chicago: University of Chicago Press, 2010. 145–156.

Heise, Ursula. *Sense of Place and Sense of Planet*. Oxford: Oxford University Press, 2008.

"Homer's Triple Bypass." *The Simpsons: The Complete Fourth Season*. Fox Video, 2004. DVD

Johnson, Steven. *Everything Bad Is Good for You: How Today's Popular Culture is Actually Making Us Smarter*. New York: Riverhead/Berkeley/Penguin, 2005.

Kittler, Friedrich. *Gramophone, Film. Typewriter*. 1986. Trans. Geoffrey Winthrop-Young and Michael Wutz. Stanford: Stanford University Press, 1999.

Kolbert, Elizabeth. *Field Notes from a Catastrophe*. New York: Bloomsbury, 2006.

Massumi, Brian. *Parables for the Virtual*. Durham: Duke University Press, 2002.

McGonigal, Jane. *Reality Is Broken*. London: Penguin, 2011.

McKibben, Bill. *The Age of Missing Information*. New York: Random House, 1992.

McKibben, Bill. *Eaarth*. Toronto: Alfred A. Knopf Canada, 2010.

McLuhan, Marshall. *Laws of Media*. Toronto: University of Toronto Press, 1988.

——. "The Playboy Interview." *Essential McLuhan*. Ed. Eric McLuhan and Frank Zingrone. Concord, Ontario: Anansi Press, 1995.

Parham, John. "Academic Values: Why Environmentalists Loathe the Media." *Interdisciplinary Studies in Literature and Environment*. 13.1 (Winter 2006): 113–133.

Plato. *Phaedrus*. Trans. Benjamin Jowett. Project Gutenberg. Web. Accessed 1 April 2011.

Ross, Andrew. *Strange Weather*. New York: Verso, 1991.

Rozelle, Lee. *Ecosublime: Environmental Awe and Terror from New World to Oddworld*. Tuscaloosa: University of Alabama Press, 2006.

Simmons, Dan. *Hyperion*. New York: Doubleday, 1989.

"Space Seed." *Star Trek the Original Series*. Paramount, 2008. DVD.

Stevens, Wallace. *The Collected Poems*. 1954. New York: Alfred A. Knopf, 1987.

Stiegler, Bernard. "Memory." In *Critical Terms for Media Studies*. Eds. W. J. T. Mitchell and Mark B. N. Hansen. Chicago: University of Chicago Press, 2010. 64–87.

Taylor, Timothy. *The Artificial Ape*. New York: Palgrave Macmillan, 2010.

Ulman, H. Lewis. "Beyond Nature/Writing: Virtual Landscapes Online, in Print, and in 'Real Life.'" In *Beyond Nature Writing: Expanding the Boundaries of Ecocriticism*. Eds. Karla Armbruster and Kathleen R. Wallace. Charlottesville: University of Virginia Press, 2001. 341–356.

Virilio, Paul. *Open Sky*. Trans. Julie Rose. London: Verso, 1997.

Von Uexküll, Jakob. *A Foray into the Worlds of Animals and Humans*. 1934. Trans. Joseph. D. O'Neil. Minneapolis: University of Minnesota Press, 2010.

CHAPTER 29

TALKING ABOUT CLIMATE CHANGE

The Ecological Crisis and Narrative Form

URSULA KLUWICK

PREVENTION and mitigation—these are the keywords that tend to dominate climate change debates, at least where they focus on ways to encounter and deal with the eco-logical crisis. International climate change conferences, global environmental and pub-lic policy meetings, world economic forums—all of these seem to invest, nowadays, in finding strategies of averting the worst effects of climate change, and of preserving the planet as we know it—in short, into finding solutions to the crisis. But as Mike Hulme has pointed out, "climate change is not a problem that can be solved" (326). Rather, cli-mate change is a "wicked problem" (Hulme 334), a concept "planning theorist Horst Rittel proposed ... to describe a category of public policy concerns that defied rational and optimal solutions" and which can be viewed as "symptoms of yet other problems" (Hulme 334). Wicked problems are fundamentally complex, and are themselves the symptoms of closely interconnected systems. This, of course, affects attempts to solve them: "Solutions to wicked problems are difficult to recognise because of complex inter-dependencies in the system affected; a solution to one aspect of a wicked problem often reveals or creates other, even more complex, problems demanding further solutions" (Hulme 334).

In this essay, I start with the assumption that climate change was, for a long time, and to some extent still is, regarded as a predominantly scientific problem. For my analy-sis, this has two important implications: On the one hand, the construction of climate change as a fundamentally scientific problem means that its intricacies, its complexi-ties, and its logic are understood to be only accessible to the select few. Members of the nonspecialist public—that is, the majority of the world population—have to rely on mediators to translate scientific models and data into a language more readily compre-hensible. But this simultaneously turns climate change into a problem of communi-cation and hence an intrinsically social problem. On the other hand, the overarching "'problem-solution' framing of climate change" (Hulme 328) means that in engaging with climate change, we have tended to concentrate on the search for scientific, techno-logical, and, increasingly, economic solutions.

In the following essay, I analyze some of the narrative forms employed in the mediation of climate change science. I focus on the narrative strategies used by mediators who are not themselves scientists in the transmission of scientific information to a non-specialist readership or audience. In addition, I am interested in the extent to which the problem-solution paradigm is active in the stories told about climate change, and in whether an awareness of climate change as a wicked problem can be identified in climate change discourses. My data mainly comes from four texts, all of which combine the communication of scientific theories and facts with pedagogical and motivational impulses. I analyze one climate change documentary (David Guggenheimer's *An Inconvenient Truth*), one popular science book (*The Last Generation: How Nature Will Take Her Revenge for Climate Change* by Fred Pearce), and two climate change manuals (*The Live Earth Global Warming Survival Handbook* and the Greenpeace *How to Save the Climate* booklet). Produced by nonscientists with (generally self-pronounced) claims to higher scientific expertise for a nonscientific audience, these works clearly betray the effects of mediation in which I am interested. As products of the selection and interpretation of scientific facts and reports which in themselves are already the outcome of particular choices, the texts that form the basis of my analysis demonstrate the processes of multiple mediation that characterize the communication of climate change science. What these processes show is that public perceptions of climate change are intrinsically tied to narrative strategies; whether or not we are aware of it, when we read and hear about climate change, we are offered not just facts and models but stories.

Increasingly, it seems that the stories we have been offered have not been able to prompt reactions to an extent adequate to the crisis. If the stories we have been told were intended to raise awareness of climate change, evoke concern and, as a result, provoke action, they have not yet fulfilled their purpose, at least in this last respect. Admittedly, given the urgent time factor that dominates climate change scenarios, and given the wickedness of the problem, it is doubtful how much could have been achieved even if climate change discourse had been undivided and led to policy changes immediately. Energy infrastructures and the world economy are hugely complex apparatuses that need time to alter, and political and technological barriers to the type of dramatic action needed to mitigate climate change have been overwhelming. In the face of the powerful anti-environmentalist narratives that have also developed, as well as the massive imaginative effort involved in attempting to grasp the threats to our own species, one needs to be careful when evaluating what has or has not been achieved. The reality of the environmental crisis appears to have become more accepted of recent years, though with such a global and globally complex issue, generalizations are necessarily fraught with dangers.[1]

But where recognition lags behind, this is hardly the fault of a lack of stories about climate change. Environmental issues and climate change have gained a conspicuous media presence, though to what extent the media respond to or shape public anxieties or indifference seems inconclusive. The newspaper coverage of the 2009 Copenhagen climate summit, for instance, was extensive, even hyped. But the summit was not merely a news item in itself; instead, it triggered a flood of feature articles related to the science and politics of climate change in all kinds of newsprint publications, hence providing the opportunity for a repetition and reaffirmation of the relevant mainstream climate change science on a public stage. And climate change is not just conspicuously present in the newsprint arena either; the environmental crisis has already spawned an impressive number of literary engagements with climate change,[2] and the film industry has now also discovered climate change as a subject.[3] As one of the overarching problems facing humanity today, it is not surprising that climate change has also been co-opted by the entertainment industry. As a social problem, it naturally infiltrates all kinds of social discourses. Put more radically, climate change is in itself turning into one of our dominant discourses: Rayner contends that it has become "the key narrative within which political issues from the local to the global are framed" (xxiii). But interestingly, the gap between public awareness of climate change and not only large-scale mitigating action but also individual social *reaction* remains in place, regardless of the ubiquitousness of climate change as a discourse. In the case of climate change, discursive reach and power do not seem related to its (in)effectiveness in influencing behavioural patterns and choices.

Climate change rhetoric can remain curiously ineffective even when there seems to be a decidedly pedagogic component involved in it. Mike Hulme, for instance, cites the active commitment professed by the producers of *The Day After Tomorrow* (2004) to affecting their audience's behavior in relation to climate change:

> Although the film makers acknowledged their exaggeration and sensationalisation of the science, they nevertheless claimed that their portrayal of dramatic climate events could have a major influence on the behaviour of society. They suggested that it might motivate people to do something about climate change before it "became too late." (Hulme 212)

And in an article on climate change-inspired disaster movies in *The Guardian Online*, journalist Ryan Gilbey voices similar sentiments:

> It will be interesting to see how our ongoing struggle with climate change, which can't be moved so easily to the back-burner, is reflected in the stories we tell on film. Even if carbon emissions were to be reduced to zero tomorrow, our need to contemplate our own extinction would still remain. For all their sobriety, the latest dystopian visions fill the same need within us as the cheesiest disaster movie, but with one important difference. When we see *The Road*, we can't discard the fears provoked by the film once the lights come up. Instead, we take them home with us and, if we're smart, act on them.

What is noticeable in both these statements is the profound vagueness that surrounds possible reactions to climate change. The producers of *The Day After Tomorrow* hope that their audiences will be induced to "do something about climate change," but what this "something" would entail remains speculatively open. And Gilbey's hope that we will learn to "act on" our fears is similarly unspecified, while the link to climate change is revealingly inaccurate given that *The Road* constructs a scenario that seems much closer to the aftermath of nuclear war.

Hulme cites reports on the effect of *The Day After Tomorrow* which suggest that "any increase in concern about climate change induced by the film appeared short lived, with most viewers treating the film purely as entertainment" (213), and while this lack of impact is, perhaps, not overly surprising, it nevertheless reveals how the paradox described above operates: climate change discourse permeates our culture, but it tends to circulate through it without offering concrete docking points to normal citizens, who continue to remain unclear about the relation between climate change and their own lives, and, specifically, about the impact of their own actions and choices on global climate change. The conclusions drawn by the reports Hulme discusses are hence indicative of one of the main problems in the communication of climate change: the difficulty—for specialists, as well as for laypersons—of translating information and knowledge about climate change into action. But information is never innocent, and its impact is related to the narrative strategies employed in its transmission. In the case of climate change, the narrative forms in which climate change scenarios are presented are, arguably, in conflict with many of our most cherished narratives of advancement and fulfilment—career success, parenting, travel and conspicuous consumption—and these conflicts can function as powerful barriers to mental, let alone behavioural, adaptation.

As its rhetorical context and make-up elucidate, this difficulty is glaringly obvious in David Guggenheimer's documentary film *An Inconvenient Truth*. The film has a very explicit mission, a mission already signalled by its title: its primary aim is to convince its audience of the reality of climate change, or, as it is referred to in the documentary, global warming. Thus the film "adopts a generally serious and at times earnestly moralizing tone to communicate the message that, contrary to the U.S. government's official position, climate change is a scientifically proven phenomenon" (Spoel, Goforth, Cheu, and Pearson 55). Those who challenge what Al Gore presents in the film as evidence of climate change are dismissed as "so-called skeptics," whose counternarratives *An Inconvenient Truth* sets out to dismantle. To this end, the film focuses on the transmission of information and what Gore calls "hard facts," which are mainly presented in the form of Powerpoint graphs and corroborated with visual evidence, such as photographs or short film sequences of melting glaciers and other ice sheets, scientific models, and cartoons, for instance of polar bears searching for firm ground.[4] In tune with his mission of enlightening and convincing the public, Gore repeatedly emphasizes the scientific consensus on climate change, silently passing over conflicting data and scientific controversies in order to avoid the impression of uncertainty.[5] While he concedes the "complexity" of much of the information and many of the data he presents, there is no room for doubt in a documentary which seeks to persuade; *An Inconvenient Truth* hence clearly bears the mark of its intended audience, a U.S. public characterized by strong resistance to the reality of climate change and hence still in need of convincing. As a result, *An Inconvenient Truth* stops short of what other audiences, already less hostile to the idea of climate change as a given, might expect of a film about climate change; simultaneously, it bears witness to the core problem of climate change communication

I have singled out above. For once Gore has rushed his audience through a variety of statistics, figures, models, and graphs—once he has added emotional and moral appeals (visually and rhetorically),[6] when he has, in short, presented his main evidence—he basically just stops. Once all the "hard facts" are on the table, energy seems to seep out of the performance, and pedagogical persuasion is not followed by any convincing call to action. "You are going to hear a lot more about this," Gore promises when alluding to the importance of individual action, but at least in the documentary, "a lot more" never comes. Nordhaus and Shellenberger laconically comment on the inadequacy of the behavioral tips included in the film:

> And that's the way the film ends. Apparently as an afterthought, the film's producers decided they needed to offer viewers something that they could actually do. So as the film credits roll, a list of "simple things" flashes on the screen.... (106)

The suggestions for behavioural changes which the credits provide are indeed half-hearted, as if half-aware of the inadequacy of "simple" solutions for a wicked problem. There seems to be a promise of more concrete advice on individual contribution in the reference to a website viewers are invited to visit, but this, in fact, merely sums up the tips already included in the credits sequence.[7] *An Inconvenient Truth*, then, presents itself as informative, educational, and persuasive, but it stops short of being practically or politically, motivational. The essential dilemma of climate change communication, namely the challenge of forging a connection between knowledge and behavior, is not something the film sets out to address.

Essentially, this omission points to a break in the perception of reality, a widespread discrepancy between a passive kind of knowledge which accepts climate change as a theoretical fact, and a more active form of awareness which entails the realization of how climate change relates to individual lives. It is in this gap that the resistance arises to the fundamental recognition of how the individual is affected by but also implicated in the environmental crisis. Intellectual does not equal emotional acceptance.

Already in 1998, Richard Kerridge drew attention to the failures of both environmentalists and politicians in rendering the environmental crisis palpable for the general public, and concluded that the environmental crisis "is also a cultural crisis, a crisis of representation" (4). More than a decade later, the question of how to make the crisis tangible in a manner that simultaneously fosters productive reactions remains open. Indeed, as Hulme elucidates, climate, and hence climate change, are always and by their very nature, bound to remain intangible:

> Climate cannot be experienced directly through our senses. Unlike the wind which we feel on our face or a raindrop that wets our hair, climate is a constructed idea that takes these sensory encounters and builds them into something more abstract. Neither can climate be measured directly by our instruments. (4)

This surreal quality of climate change facilitates the erection of a firm emotional barrier to its reality. After all, the prospect of what the full effect of climate change might entail is so daunting that it is a lot easier to ignore and distance oneself from its reality than to face its inevitable impact on one's lifestyle and indeed one's life.[8] Such distancing techniques are varied but ubiquitous, reaching from jokes about the term "global warming" when summers are cold and rainy, to the sheer comfort people take in the thought that all cannot be as bad as scientists claim while things still *appear* to be pretty normal. And while floods such as the one that devastated Pakistan in the late summer of 2010 are uncomfortable reminders of the likelihood that things are anything but "pretty normal," for most first-world citizens, at least, such natural disasters, though shocking, merely scratch the complacent surface momentarily. Too far removed to impinge on their own lives in any serious way, they can quickly be ignored, seeping out of first-world consciousnesses as swiftly as they have entered them. It is not surprising that one of the first comments included in the voice-over which accompanies pictures of the disaster wrought by hurricane Katrina in *An Inconvenient Truth* is Gore's question, "How could this have happened here, in America?" Giving voice to the disbelief and shock felt by US audiences at the effects of Katrina, he performs a reality check for his audience by vocalising his incredulity at the very moment when the perceptual barrier to the destructive potential of nature is challenged. Rhetorically, the semantic ambiguity of "this" in Gore's phrase is crucial. In the voice of a citizen of this hurricane-tested country, "this" is not just a hurricane, but refers to the disturbing fact that a hurricane can wreak such havoc *here*, that it can effectively destroy a city such as New Orleans, that it can actually kill *Americans*; simultaneously, "this" also expresses shock at the unbelievable ineffectiveness of the Bush administration in the face of a natural state of emergency.

As reactions to potentially anthropogenic "natural disasters" reveal and as scientists have had to acknowledge, the production, publication, and circulation of data, models, and scientific predictions alone does not—or only very rarely—prompt public or even political acceptance. Data and predictions might suggest frightening developments, but as long as catastrophe is not imminent in any directly perceptible way, it is as tempting as it is easy to ignore them. As Gore emphasizes, climatologists have long been warning the world of the increasing frequency and ferocity of natural disasters, but preventive action has been slow in coming. To some extent and for some countries, this might not seem so surprising, since regional data suggest that in specific parts of the world, such as the United States, adaptation to climate change will pose fewer problems and costs will be relatively low. But in our highly globalized world, the question remains of how the massive changes and destruction that scenarios predict for geographically and economically disadvantaged parts of the planet will impact on regions likely to be less severely affected. And even for privileged areas such as parts of North America, the fourth Intergovernmental Panel on Climate Change (IPCC) report warns that the "vulnerability of North America depends on the effectiveness of adaptation and the distribution of coping capacity, both of which are currently uneven and have not always protected vulnerable groups from adverse impacts of climate variability and extreme weather events" (Field, Mortsch, Brklacich, Forbes, Kovacs, Patz, Running and Scott 639). The report also highlights the fact that "[i]ndigenous peoples of North America and those who are socially and economically disadvantaged are disproportionately vulnerable to climate change" (Field et al. 639). The desperately uneven geographical and demographic distribution of the benefits and risks of inaction is perhaps the most fundamental political challenge posed by climate change. Even so, a discursive analysis remains useful for elucidating the peculiar public apathy which we find expressed in so many people's decision to basically continue as if nothing was amiss—alongside a dreadful sense of urgency that flares up at periodic moments. I therefore turn now to texts which actively focus on individual contribution and action in their approach to climate change, scrutinizing the techniques of mediation and narratization they employ in order to instigate action in their readership.

Efforts to package information about the ecological crisis in a manner which spurs action take many forms, ranging from attempts to create a mindset for behavioral change to direct and concrete calls to action. Among the long-established textual genres employed to this end are popular science books, which aim at translating scientific research into readily intelligible information for the layperson, hence subscribing to a deficit-transmission model of science communication. *The Last Generation* by Fred Pearce clearly falls into this category. As one of Britain's best-known popular science writers and scientific journalists, Pearce can rely on a certain *ethos*. As Aristotle remarks, the credibility enjoyed by "good men" is particularly important "where exact certainty is impossible and opinions are divided" (25), a situation which clearly applies to climate change. But while Aristotle posits that ethos should not be an effect of preconceptions, reader expectations clearly come into play in Pearce's case.[9] In fact, for readers solely familiar with *The Last Generation*, appraisal of his ethos might be considerably affected by the particular narrative tradition he activates.

Much that is noteworthy about his narrative strategies is already encapsulated in the striking, but not necessarily untypical, title of Pearce's book—*The Last Generation: How Nature Will Take Her Revenge for Climate Change*,[10] a title that is already very suggestive with its apocalyptic tinge and personification of nature as a victim of climate change, but a victim ready to fight back. The impression created here is corroborated by the back cover, which contains the message of the book in a nutshell and gives a good taste of its rhetorical style:

> In the past, Europe's climate has switched from Arctic to tropical in three to five years. It can happen again. So forget what environmentalists have told you about nature being a helpless victim of human excess. The truth is the opposite. She is a wild and resourceful beast given to fits of rage. And now that we are provoking her beyond endurance, she is starting to seek her revenge. (Pearce, back cover)

This reads like the voiceover of a trailer for an ecological disaster movie. Nature is depicted as something comparable to a Godzilla-like monster, a dangerous beast the more lethal the more it is provoked. Indeed, the thinly disguised antagonism Pearce constructs here is emphasized in the book by his repeated depiction of nature as an anthropomorphic monster:

> Now our most feared global Armageddon is climate change. One reason we have to fear its consequences lurks in the frozen bogs of western Siberia. There, beneath

a largely uninhabited wasteland of permafrost, lies what might reasonably be described as nature's own doomsday device. It is primed to be triggered not by a nuclear bomb but by global warming. The device consists of thick layers of frozen peat containing tens of billions of tonnes of carbon. (134)

Fully equipped with destructive devices, nature emerges as a combative agent, a vengeful creature who has it in for humanity. Hence one story is substituted for another: the story of nature-as-victim makes place for an apocalyptic narrative of nature as a dangerous threat. And this is by no means the only familiar story which is changed; since nature for Pearce is female, while he himself and most of the scientists on whose research *The Last Generation* rests are male, the narrative of nature as a benign mother is substituted by a vision of nature as a capricious and dangerous femme-fatale-cum-combat-girl. Nature, in Pearce's construction, does not easily suit the role of nurturing mother; indeed, she might prefer to kill rather than care for her children. But not only does the gender aspect loom large here; the role reversal taking place in this tale also affects the position of humanity as such. From victimizer it is turned into a victim of both nature and of its own hubris, thus occupying a position that veers between activity and passivity. The role reversal Pearce accomplishes hence complicates visions of the interaction between humanity and nature, leaving the question of agency fundamentally unclear. Simultaneously, it also entails a decisive reinforcement of the humanity–nature dichotomy. Humanity and nature are placed in a firmly antagonistic relationship, characterized by division rather than unity.

The value of Pearce's book partly lies in the fact that it draws attention to the existence of alternatives to the climate change scenarios projected by the IPCC, though he exclusively discusses scenarios worse than the IPCC consensus. As such, Pearce challenges the master narrative of climate change discourse and gives its lay readership access to climate change models not as readily available. But in the communication of the possibility of more radical, faster, and dramatic changes, Pearce's style fails to trigger anything but panic. This is precisely what Hulme criticises when he attacks current climate change discourse for its emphasis on "fear and terror," claiming that it "operates 'as an ever-weakening vehicle for effective communication or inducement to behavioural change'" (qtd. in Risbey 32). Risbey counters this claim, arguing that the discourse Hulme blames for being "alarmist" constitutes, in fact, an accurate rendition of the state of scientific research. Rather than being judged alarmist, he contends, current climate change discourse should be regarded as "alarming," since it seeks to alert people to the seriousness of the crisis while simultaneously offering alternative behavioural strategies in order to mitigate climate change. Yet just as with *An Inconvenient Truth*, such strategies are largely absent from Pearce's account, which focuses on drawing the worst-possible climate change scenario rather than on how we might meet it. Accordingly, Pearce ends the main part of his account with the following bleak outlook: "Migration has always been one of our species' great survival strategies. Now we have nowhere else to go. No new frontier. We have only one atmosphere; only one planet" (350). It is only in the appendix that Pearce briefly turns to attempts to mitigate climate change, discussing various models such as the "contraction and convergence" formula for the reduction of global emissions (358–359) or the "wedges" model of technological development (361–362). But even though these provide useful insights, due to their positioning in the appendix they only slightly alleviate the atmosphere of despair characteristic of the rest of the book. As a whole, even though Pearce's book might be intended to mobilize a passive public, it is more likely to elicit fear, helplessness and antagonism than productive attempts to mitigate climate change. Solutions and alternative scenarios just do not fit into the combative revenge narrative he constructs. As Ted Nordhaus and Michael Shellenberger point out, however, while fear might be unavoidable in the face of the ecological crisis, "despair is a choice" (17).[11]

This is precisely the starting point for the climate change manuals I have sampled. These manuals constitute a more recent genre which has sprung up in response to the necessity to communicate what can and should be done about climate change. Geared towards an audience prepared to invest in instructions for self-help, the rationale on which these "manuals" are based is emphatically different from the one behind Pearce's book. Their basic aim is the instigation of behavioural together with attitudinal change, and they seek to facilitate this by highlighting both individual responsibility and impact. Most strikingly, they destigmatize climate change, defusing its overwhelming and disempowering character by offering people easy strategies of addressing it in their daily lives. As such, they address one of the core aims of endeavours to alleviate climate change—the targeting of the individual. As the Stern Report makes clear:

> In the case of climate change, individual preferences play a very important role. High-level international agreements alone are not going to stop dangerous climate change; it will need behavioural change by individuals and communities, especially with regard to their housing, transport, and food consumption preferences. (Stern Report qtd. in Greenpeace 11)

Climate change manuals tend to turn this necessity into a positive appeal, as in the introduction to *The Live Earth Global Warming Survival Handbook*: "The good news is that each of us can take action to solve this crisis. All of us have a role to play and none of us bears the burden alone" (Reiner 6). Conjuring up a sense of community, this plea for individual action combines the appeal to personal responsibility with a reminder of the status of climate change as a common challenge. In the same vein, *The Live Earth Global Warming Survival Handbook* is anxious to address and defuse one of the most destructive emotional reactions to climate change, the feeling of helplessness:

> Live Earth is the start of a global environmental movement, one that harnesses the power of everyone working together. So let us not be overwhelmed by the size of the problem. The positive sum of small actions, multiplied by millions of people, can lead to dramatic effects. You are part of this movement and the small changes you make will add up. (Reiner 6)

The rationale behind this appeal is psychological empowerment, based on the conviction that recognition of individual impact elicits productive reactions. To this end, climate change needs to be presented as an if not simple, at least a solvable problem, which can be influenced by "small actions." Thus *The Live Earth Global Warming Survival Handbook* offers its readers "77 skills" designed to alleviate the impact of serious climate change. And so climate change is turned from a threat into a challenge, with everybody able to practice and acquire useful behavior. Most importantly, the required changes are not even overly dramatic; at least, they are not presented as such. Greenpeace, for instance, promote its own climate change manual with the promise that it will show readers how to save energy by singing in the shower. Inside the *How to Save the Climate* booklet, what sounds like a rather astonishing magic trick is revealed to be fairly practical advice: Greenpeace recommends that readers use a short song in order to time their shower, thus significantly reducing the amount of water and energy wasted (16). The message conveyed here is that climate change is manageable without requiring major changes to the everyday. Hence the manuals clearly signal their dissent from what Nordhaus and Shellenberger have identified as one of the overarching environmentalist discourses, the discourse of "sacrifice" (124–125). Instead, the manuals suggest that major changes are unnecessary and that an environmental lifestyle need not be limiting. Indeed, as my discussion of their discursive strategies in the remainder of this essay shows, rather than activating a discourse of sacrifice, they seek to endow environmentalism with a certain coolness factor, employing a partly flippant style in order to signal hipness.[12] Thus, the manuals attempt to mobilize an audience different from the one normally reached by environmentalism and its discourses of sacrifice, austerity and doom. Simultaneously, the different narrative strategies favored by the manuals betray a strong desire to de-dramatize climate change, and to forestall hopelessness.

The Live Earth Global Warming Survival Handbook in particular exhibits a humorous style of narration, as evident, for instance, in the skills dealing with the reduction of the amount of energy wasted on heating. Skill 14 ("Green your Home") refers to better insulation, skill 16 ("Pick Your Power") discusses various power options, skill 33 ("Harvest the Sun") promotes solar power, Skill 51 ("Dig a Very Deep Hole") deals with geothermal heating systems. And then there is Skill 20, "Put on a Jumper." That it is more ecologically responsible to dress warmly than to turn up the heating is no secret, though it is a simple form of ecological behavior easily overlooked. But whether we really need a step-by-step instruction to putting on a jumper is another matter. De Rothschild follows this instruction with hard facts, claiming that wearing warmer clothes and simultaneously lowering your thermostat by 1°C can save 225kg of CO_2/year. Thus the scientific basis to this skill is present, but successfully leavened by the humorous tone. Though this casualness might appeal to an audience for whom environmental behavior is "cool," the mixture of humor and scientific fact displayed here is also indicative of the difficulty of choosing a discursively satisfying environmentalist form. As Richard Kerridge has observed, one of the factors that renders environmentalism discursively unproductive is the fact that it does not have a stable narrative form.[13]

The situation is slightly different with the Greenpeace brochure. Though also aiming at a light rather than an alarmist tone, the brochure still follows an intensely practical program; in addition, and most strikingly, it seems to have a clear and clearly identifiable agenda. This is no random collection of possible forms of encountering the crisis; rather, the precise agenda of the Greenpeace manual also endows it with a recognizable and stable narrative form: a fusion of science fiction and utopia. As with the other texts I have analyzed, scientific information forms the basis for everything else. The chapter on heating, for instance, contains sections on healthy temperatures, insulation, airing, passive houses, and on the energy efficiency of various heating systems. In general, Greenpeace provide very clear-cut and straightforward information and advice, and though the style employed is not scientific in itself, the strategies they suggest are obviously built on scientific research. But, and this is where the Greenpeace booklet differs from the other texts discussed, the strongest narrative thread here is constituted by a utopian projection of the available science onto the future as ecological scenarios for future suburbs, cities, and villages are introduced.

Hence the Greenpeace manual embodies a utopian drive which distinguishes it from the other, more dystopian, texts on climate change analysed here. By conjuring up a sustainable future through the power of words these visions offer the strongest assurance to the reader that such a future is possible and worth fighting for. What is noticeable here is that the first section of each of these projections uses the future tense while most of the rest of the depiction has already subtly shifted to the present tense, thus discursively including these visions in the present and rendering them real. The same, incidentally, is true of *Global Warming*, an introduction to climate change by Mark Maslin, Co-Director of UCL's Environment Institute. At the end of his book, as well, a vision of the future is provided in the present tense, suggesting very strongly that this utopian scenario is feasible. This impression is strengthened by the fact that the narrative structure employed activates familiar reading paradigms, as we are used to reading about the future in typical epilogue fashion. The narrative gap between present and future might well be constituted by the necessary period of mourning prescribed in Clive Hamilton's Requiem for a Species, but it remains a blank in both the Greenpeace manual and Maslin's book, both of which silently ignore the fact that the earth's climate will have changed and continue to change in the utopian visions they construct.

By demonstrating how contemporary science and concerted individual action hold the key to a utopian rather than dystopian future, the tales that Maslin and Greenpeace tell subtly fuse a narrative of progress with a narrative of sustainability. That nature continues to be regarded as a source for human exploitation in their narratives is clear; efforts are directed at showing how it can be a sustainable source of exploitation rather than at generating new ideologies. Climate change itself is represented not so much as complex and "wicked" but as manageable, a challenge easily met if humans rely on their faculties of intelligence and creativity. Indeed, the point about climate change that the Greenpeace booklet emphasizes most consistently is that we already have all the technology necessary to tackling it successfully. Hence environmentalism is co-opted by a utopian narrative which seeks to fuse visions of intellectual, technological, and economic progress in what is essentially a typical Enlightenment discourse. Nordhaus and Shellenberger's evaluation of developments in the alternative energy sector is symptomatic of this narrative of progress: "these are the makings of a new dream, and a new story, about America and the world" (11).

Contrary to this enthusiastic appraisal, I would argue that the problem with the narrative of progress is that this discourse, this "dream," is anything but new. Rather, it is precisely a story about deliberate human advancement, also characteristic of discourses of economic and technological progress implicated in the environmental crisis, that is here employed to suggest solutions to the present situation. Whether such narratives can lead to long-term changes and whether they can motivate people to engage productively with the vision of a changed climate is doubtful.

The greatest challenge for climate change stories is how to transport the message that climate change is inevitable and already happening without crippling our power to imagine a future worth changing for. For literary scholars and teachers, a related challenge is constituted by the dilemma of how to determine which stories might function in this manner. Ultimately, what my discussion of the narrative forms of climate change suggests is that ecocriticism needs to develop tools for determining the effects of narrative strategies and structures on readers and their behavior. Traditionally, ecocriticism has assumed that reading about nature changes people's attitudes towards the environment, but this is by no means certain. What is required is an empirical reader-response theory that allows conclusions to be drawn about the effect of environmental stories on readers. We have seen that people fall back on a variety of different narrative formula when they talk and write about climate change. It would be interesting to see which of them actually work to what purpose.

Notes

1. A poll conducted in 2007 by GobeScan in cooperation with the Program on International Policy Attitudes at the University of Maryland for BBC World Service indicates that awareness of climate change is, nowadays, significant in the twenty-one countries included in the survey: "Asked how much they have heard about climate change or global warming, seven in ten overall say that they have heard a great deal (35 percent) or some (35 percent). A majority in 16 countries—including many developing countries—say that they have heard at least something about the issue" (2), and percentages for individual countries are much higher. Nevertheless, numbers vary significantly. While in France and South Korea, 92 percent and 94 percent, respectively, claim to have heard "a great deal" or "some" about climate change, in Russia (35 percent) and Indonesia (28 percent), the numbers are considerably lower (8). For the United States, Corfee-Morlot, Maslin, and Burgess cite a survey which "showed public awareness of global climate change had doubled since 1981 when compared with 1989: 79 percent of Americans had heard of the greenhouse effect by 1989 when compared with 38 percent in 1981" (2760).
2. For the treatment of climate change in creative fiction, see Adam Trexler's essay in this volume.
3. Examples are *The Day After Tomorrow* (2004), *Waterworld* (1995), and the *Ice Age* films. Francis Lawrence's *The Day the Earth Stood Still* (2008) is arguably also influenced by a climate change imaginary when compared with the 1951 original, which is a product of

the Cold War nuclear arms race. In the remake, Klaatu comes to punish humans for their destruction of the environment.

4. For a reading of visual apocalypticism in Gore, see Johnson 35.

5. One example of this strategy is Gore's misrepresentation of the consensus position on sea level rises. For more details, see Spoel et al. 68–73.

6. Gore very skilfully invokes personal tragedies in order to evoke the individual as well as the communal emotional loss a changed climate will bring. These narratives have allegorical functions: Gore's son, who nearly died in a car accident as a child, becomes representative of all children under threat through climate change, while in the story of Gore's sister, a smoker who eventually died of lung cancer, the tobacco industry comes to stand for the carbon industry as well as climate change sceptics (Gore's father, who only stops growing tobacco once his daughter is fatally ill), while the addiction metaphor equates smokers' nicotine needs with developed countries' carbon addiction.

7. Although the website provides a carbon-footprint calculator, and promises suggestions of how the reader's carbon footprint, once calculated, might be reduced, these devices are specifically geared towards a US audience, as clear from the fact that the calculator can only be used by US residents.

8. I would argue that even *The Age of Stupid*, which is set in a future in which humanity has destroyed itself by not preventing climate change, fails to break through this barrier. Our present here becomes a distant past. The film juxtaposes a bleak future with present-day documentary footage depicting people from across the globe, blindly heading towards self-inflicted doom in their failure to grasp the reality of climate change. The dystopian narrative strategies and rhetoric of disaster make the film resemble Pearce's book, discussed below, though *The Age of Stupid* combines its dystopian discourse with an ample dose of nostalgia, most notably through close-ups of its solitary protagonist's sorrowful face. While the direct confrontation of real documentary with a fictional future is intended to function as a mirror and wake-up call to the audience, the familiar dystopian narrative strategies seem to facilitate the maintainance of the audience's mental distance from the events depicted.

9. As they do in Gore's when he consciously activates such preconceptions by introducing himself as the man who "used to be the next President of the United States of America," thus invoking his reputation as the basis of the ethos he needs in his fight against climate change scepticism and complacency.

10. Similar titles are Alastair McIntosh's *Hell and High Water* (2008), or Lovelock's *The Revenge of Gaia: Why the Earth Is Fighting Back—and How We Can Still Save Humanity*.

11. Clive Hamilton does not agree. For him, hopefulness is "a means of forestalling the future" (211) when it comes to climate change. He argues that we need to enter a new phase of acceptance which entails mourning: "we must respond and that means allowing ourselves to enter a phase of desolation and hopelessness, in short, to grieve" (211). Grief, for him, is an essential stage in the process of bringing our dreams, ideas and expectations of the world into tune with the external reality of a changed climate (211). According to this logic, it is only by allowing ourselves to mourn our lost future that we can detach ourselves from what can no longer be and become ready to embrace a radically changed version of the future with renewed emotional and cognitive investment (213).

12. Killingsworth and Palmer have drawn attention to the manner in which environmental "how-to" books endorse green consumerism, hereby strengthening rather than refuting

dominant, non-environmentalist, ideologies, concluding that green consumerism "is all too open to be appropriated by forces whose long term interests are anything but environmentalist." They further argue that the foregrounding of "small scale actions or personal agendas that ignore public causes may function ideologically, blinding the general public to the need for massive shifts in government policy and curtailments of large scale industrial activity" (qtd. in Herndl and Brown 7). While this is valid and necessary criticism, one also needs to acknowledge that more radical discourses and movements have not yet been able to initiate the more drastic ideological changes they promote. In the face of the undeniable time pressure, therefore, less fundamental personal action should be recognised as having its own value, though one should distinguish between action promoted to—illusorily—prevent climate change, and action intended to accommodate climate change, offering strategies of living in and with a changed climate.

13. Richard Kerridge. "Environmentalism and Literary Genre."

References

Age of Stupid, The. Dir. Franny Armstrong. Spanner Films, 2009.

Aristotle. *Rhetoric and Poetics. Rhetoric* trans. W. Rhys Roberts. *Poetics* trans. Ingram Bywater. Intro. Friedrich Solmsen. New York: Modern Library, 1954.

Corfee-Morlot, Jan, Mark Maslin, and Jacquelin Burgess. "Global Warming in the Public Sphere." *Philosophical Transactions of the Royal Society: Mathematical, Physical and Engineering Sciences.* 365:1860 (2007), 2741–2776.

Day After Tomorrow, The. Dir. Roland Emmerich. 20th Century Fox, 2004.

Day the Earth Stood Still, The. Dir. Robert Wise. 20th Century Fox, 1951.

Day the Earth Stood Still, The. Dir. Scott Derrickson. 20th Century Fox, 2008.

Field, Christopher B., Linda D. Mortsch, Michael Brklacich, Donald L. Forbes, Paul Kovacs, Jonathan A. Patz, Steven W. Running and Michael J. Scott, "North America." In Climate Change 2007: Impacts, Adaptation and Vulnerability. *Contribution of Working Group II to the Fourth Assessment Report of the Intergovernmental Panel on Climate Change.* Ed. Martin Parry, Ozvaldo Canziani, Jean Palukitof and Co-authors, Cambridge: Cambridge University Press, 2007. 617–652.

Gilbey, Ryan. "Climate change is inspiring the ultimate scary movies." *The Guardian Online.* 1 January 2010. Web, 20 August 2010.

GlobeScan. "All Countries Need to Take Major Steps on Climate Change: Global Poll." *BBC News.* BBC World Service, 25 September 2007. Web. 20 February 2012.<http://news.bbc.cbo.uk/2/shared/bsp/hi/pdfs/25_09_07climatepoll.pdf>.

Greenpeace International. *How to Save the Climate, Join the Energy [R]evolution.* Web, 25 August 2010. <http://www.greenpeace.org.uk/files/pdfs/climate/howtosavetheclimatepers.pdf>.

Hamilton, Clive. *Requiem for a Species: Why We Resist the Truth About Climate Change.* London: Earthscan, 2010.

Herndl, Carl G. and Stuart C. Brown. "Introduction." *Green Culture: Environmental Rhetoric in Contemporary America.* Ed. Carl G. Herndl and Stuart C. Brown. Madison, Wisconsin: University of Wisconsin Press, 1996. 3–20.

Hulme, Mike. *Why We Disagree About Climate Change: Understanding Controversy, Inaction and Opportunity.* Cambridge: Cambridge University Press, 2009.

Ice Age. Dir. Chris Wedge and Carlos Saldanha. 20th Century Fox, 2002.

Inconvenient Truth, An. Dir. David Guggenheim. Paramount Pictures, 2006.

Johnson, Laura. "(Environmental) Rhetorics of Tempered Apocalypticism in *An Inconvenient Truth.*" *Rhetoric Review* 28:1 (2009), 29–46.

Kerridge, Richard. "Introduction." *Writing the Environment: Ecocriticism and Literature.* Ed. Richard Kerridge and Neil Sammells. London, New York: Zed Books, 1998. 1–9.

——. "Environmentalism and Literary Genre." Environmental Change—Cultural Change. Sixth Biennial ASLE-UK and Fourth Biennial EASLCE Conference. University of Bath. 2 September 2010.

Maslin, Mark. *Global Warming: A Very Short Introduction.* 2nd ed. Oxford: Oxford University Press, 2009.

Nordhaus, Ted and Michael Shellenberger. *Break Through: From the Death of Environmentalism to the Politics of Possibility.* Boston, New York: Houghton Mifflin, 2007.

Pearce, Fred. *The Last Generation: How Nature Will Take Her Revenge for Climate Change.* London: Transworld, 2007.

Rayner, Steve. "Foreword." *Why We Disagree About Climate Change: Understanding Controversy, Inaction and Opportunity.* Mike Hulme. Cambridge: Cambridge University Press, 2009. xxi–xxiv.

Reiner, Rob. "Foreword." *The Live Earth Global Warming Survival Handbook.* David de Rothschild. London: Virgin Books, 2007.

Rothschild, David de. *The Live Earth Global Warming Survival Handbook.* London: Virgin Books, 2007.

Spoel, Philippa, David Goforth, Hoi Cheu, and David Pearson. "Public Communication of Climate Change Science: Engaging Citizens Through Apocalyptic Narrative Explanation." *Technical Communication Quarterly* 18:1, 49–81.

Waterworld. Dir. Kevin Reynolds. Perf. Kevin Costner, Jeanne Tripplehorn, and Dennis Hopper. Universal Pictures, 1995.

PART IV

THE VIEWS FROM
HERE

CHAPTER 30

....

ECOCRITICISM IN JAPAN

....

YUKI MASAMI

OVERVIEW

....

"'Ecocriticism'? That doesn't sound entirely new. In Japan, there is more than a thousand-year-old literary tradition of paying attention to nature. Take a look at tanka, haiku, or any of the many sorts of literary works in this country—there are few that do not touch upon something about nature." Such a reaction was, and to some extent still is, commonly encountered in Japan when you talk about ecocriticism to those who haven't heard of it. An association between literature and nature is so deeply imprinted in the Japanese mind that "ecocriticism" may not sound entirely foreign to those who share such a cultural upbringing. But although literary interest in nature and ecocriticism may have some similarities, they are actually radically different: ecocriticism characteristically accompanies a concern about environmental crises, while literary study of nature does not necessarily imply such awareness. Perhaps because the distinction between ecocriticism and thematic literary studies concerning nature has not been clearly perceived, it has taken a long time for ecocriticism to spread its roots deeply in Japan's literary and cultural soil.

With the exception of a few self-driven literary studies which encompass environmental awareness (e.g., Takahashi 1978), environmentally oriented literary criticism did not exist in Japan until it was imported from the United States in the mid-1990s.[1]

In the nearly two decades since ecocriticism was introduced to Japan, its process can roughly be divided into three stages. The first phase (early 1990s to2000) focuses on the introduction of the literary movement, mainly by means of translation. The second phase (the 2000s) sees the development of a comparative approach, mostly practiced by scholars of American and British literature who attempted to apply an ecocritical approach to Japanese literature. The third, overlapping, phase (the late 2000s to the present) is characterized by a cross-fertilization between ecocriticism and Japanese literary studies. This last stage marks a major shift in Japan's academic landscape of literary environmentalism, with the emergence of Japanese ecocriticism. I will give an outline of each of the three stages and show how ecocriticism was initiated and has been developing in Japan.

The First Phase: Translation

The idea of "ecocriticism" was brought into Japan's academic arena around 1993 when the leading American ecocritic Scott Slovic gave lectures on nature writing and ecocriticism throughout the country during a one-year stay as a Fulbright visiting scholar. Not only promoting a new literary approach, Slovic also helped form a community of interested individuals, a community that quickly developed into the Association for the Study of Literature and Environment in Japan (ASLE-Japan) founded in May 1994. The majority of the initial sixty-one members (including five graduate students) of the organization were literary scholars, mostly Americanists (ASLE-Japan Newsletter 1).

Around the same period of time or even earlier, in the country's environmental zeitgeist, there was a period of intensive publication of American nature writing in Japanese translation. For instance, in 1993 and 1994, under the series title of "A Naturalist's Bookshelf," Tokyo Shoseki, one of Japan's major publishers, issued translations of seven works such as Edward Abbey's *Desert Solitaire*, Gretel Ehrlich's *The Solace of Open Spaces*, and Gary Snyder's *The Practice of the Wild*. Another major publisher, Takarajimasha, had eight works including John Muir's *My First Summer in the Sierra*, Henry Thoreau's *Faith in a Seed*, and Terry Tempest Williams's *Refuge*, translated and published in its "American Nature Library" series, which continued from 1993 through 1995. Likewise, in 1994 and 1995, Hakusuisha's *Collection of the Best American Naturalist Writing* brought out translations of six works such as Rick Bass's "Wild to the Heart" and Gary Nabhan's "Desert Smells Like Rain." There are a number of other works published in translation during that time, such as Barry Lopez's *Arctic Dreams* and Robert Finch's *Common Ground*. Some other works including Peter Matthiessen's *The Snow Leopard*, Annie Dillard's *Pilgrim at Tinker Creek*, and Lauren Eiseley's *The Night Country* were made available in translation even earlier in the late 1980s and the early 1990s. In addition, literary periodicals and journals had special issues of literature and environment, offering major literary and scholarly works—again, mostly from the United States—in translation to an interested public. For instance, the literary journal *Folio A* featured American nature writing in 1993, and a nationwide literary periodical *Eureka* highlighted nature writing in March 1996; both journals provide translations of literary works as well as seminal scholarly articles. The growing trend towards introducing ecocritical theory and practice in translation is evident in many other publications as well (cf. Slovic and Ken-Ichi 1996; Ito et al. 1998). Such a boom of translation in the 1990s played a significant role in publicizing ideas of nature writing and ecocriticism, by making a number of landmark works in the field of literature and environment accessible for a Japanese-speaking audience. (For more detailed information regarding related publication movements in the mid and late 1990s, see Ikuta 1998, 279.)

Not content with merely bringing in the literary movement, the emerging ecocritical communities such as ASLE-Japan recognized the importance of collaboration with eco-critics in other countries and regions. The 1996 publication of Environmental Approaches to American Literature, a collection of essays by fourteen scholars from Japan and five from the United States, is perhaps the prototype of the now increasingly common attempts to create transnational ecocritical networks. Another example is the international sympo-sium of ASLE (U.S.) and ASLE-Japan, which was held in Hawai'i in August, 1996. Some fifteen participants from each organization gathered to discuss American and Japanese environmental literary works by such writers as Gary Snyder, Miyazawa Kenji, and Ishimure Michiko and as well to talk about the agendas of the then newly born ecocriti-cism, such as issues of communication by means of journals, newsletters, and translation.

The introductory phase seems to have been completed with the publication of a nature-writing guidebook compiled by ASLE-Japan (2000). The guidebook, which pro-vides concise yet informative descriptions of one hundred and twenty works from the United States, the United Kingdom, and Japan, helped facilitate the discussion of norms for nature writing in Japan.[2] It should be noted that a majority of the works presented in the guidebook are from the United States and the United Kingdom, with one-sixth of the collected works being from Japan. Perhaps this apparent disproportion reflects the country's scholarly situations of ecocriticism in the late 1990s in two ways. On the one hand, the inclusion of a small number of Japanese works illustrates the simple fact that there were few Japanologists who worked on ecocriticism at that time: the guidebook was planned, written, and edited mostly by ecocritics of American and British literature in Japan, who were not necessarily familiar with literary environmentalism in Japan. On the other hand, presenting twenty works of "Japanese" nature writing reflects those literary scholars' intention of going beyond their specialties to explore internal issues of literary environmentalism as well.

THE SECOND PHASE: A COMPARATIVE STUDY

As previously mentioned, the majority of those who initially worked on ecocriticism in Japan specialized in American or British literature, but their interests were not necessar-ily focused on the movements within the United States or the United Kingdom alone. In fact, the very nature of environmental issues led their attention to where they live, urging them to open up a path where the foreign-born idea of ecocriticism could meet the local culture and literature. Scholars who had learned ecocriticism via the move-ments abroad groped for ways to apply ecocritical concepts and methodology within a Japanese context. The attempt, however, to employ such imported concepts as "sense of place" and "land ethic" was rather hesitantly made in reading Japanese literature, simply because those scholars were not necessarily well versed in Japanese literature, which was considered the domain of traditional literary scholarship. It will take a while yet to see how successful the efforts to apply ecocritical concepts to Japanese literature has been, for the key concepts as well as theoretical dimensions of ecocriticism have just started to be discussed in the established scholarly communities of Japanese literature.³ What is clear is that the non-Japanologists' struggle to explore ways in which to apply ecocriticism to Japanese literary studies demonstrates the inception of a comparative approach, which would characterize the second phase of the development of ecocriticism in Japan.

The increasing interest in a comparative approach can be observed in two tendencies: creating dialogue with ecocritics in other East Asian countries, and a more committed effort to apply ecocriticism to the interpretation of Japanese literature. As mentioned above, for the first decade of its development, ecocriticism was examined and practiced mostly by scholars of American and British literature and, to a much lesser degree, attracted the interests of Japanologists. Eager to find a way of developing ecocriticism in an East Asian context while continuing to work on collaboration with Japanologists, interested communities and individuals sought out intellectual exchanges with ecocritics in East Asia. The 2003 international symposium in Okinawa hosted by ASLE-Japan demonstrated such an inclination to ecocriticism as practiced in East Asia, seeking out dialogues among writers and scholars from Korea, Taiwan, the United States, and Japan. This direction was further endorsed at the first ASLE Japan-Korea joint symposium that was held in Kanazawa, Japan, in August of 2007, in which scholars discussed literary environmentalism in Japan and Korea.⁴ What was significant about this joint symposium is that, instead of using English as an official language, it provided an interpreter-supported multilingual environment, in which the English-, Korean-, and Japanese-speaking participants could use their first language, in order to facilitate truly intercultural exchanges of ideas and visions. Those two cross-cultural scholarly events were developed into publications: *Dialogue between Nature and Literature* (Yamazato et al. 2004) is based on the Okinawa symposium, and *Poetics of Place* (Ikuta et al. 2008) the joint symposium in Kanazawa.

Unlike the first-phase ecocriticism that almost exclusively focused on American and British literature of the environment, the publications of the second phase demonstrate a subtle yet increasing tendency to use a comparative ecocritical approach towards Japanese literature. This inclination is most clearly represented in monographs written by ecocritics specializing in American literature.⁵ In his book on American nature writing from Henry Thoreau to Annie Dillard, Noda Ken-ichi includes a chapter on Japanese nature writing, in which he examines the discourse of the wild in a story written by Japanese photographer and writer Fujiwara Shinya. Comparing Fujiwara's artistic approach to the wild to that of Annie Dillard's literary representation of the wild, Noda shows a critical hesitation in using the term "Japanese nature writing," asking what "Japanese" implies in a literary and historical imagination of the environment. Noda says:

> The idea of "Japanese nature writing" brings about many questions. For instance, is there any original cognitive mode, rhetoric, style, or thought pattern that can be characterized as "Japanese" in what can be defined as Japanese nature writing? The truth is that modernity has oppressed a variety of modes which had operated actively, replacing them with a dominant, homogenized mode. We are all located

in modernity, which is so complex that it cannot be approached with general conceptual categorizations such as East, West, Asian, and so forth. (Noda 2003 203; my translation)

Hinting at the danger of a nationalistic, ideological attitude regarding Japanese-ness, Noda's analytical observation draws attention to the issue of modernity as an imperative topic to be addressed in ecocriticism in Japan and beyond.

Another pioneer work in comparative ecocritical practices is Yamazato Katsunori's 2006 book titled *Poetics of Place: Reading Gary Snyder.* In one chapter, Yamazato discusses the work of Miyazawa Kenji, internationally renowned Japanese poet and writer of the early twentieth century, in comparison with Gary Snyder, examining the writers' representations of sense of place and their literary and cultural implications. Noda and Yamazato are both Americanists by profession, contributing to Japan's development of ecocriticism (they served as the first and second president of ASLE-Japan respectively); their modest yet deliberate inclusion of ecocritical interpretations of Japanese literature suggest that a comparative approach to ecocriticism had finally started to take shape. Yuki Masami (2010), who also started her career as an Americanist, published *Remembering the Sound of Water,* which is more distinctively comparative in scope, examining the theme of relationships between language and perception of the environment in the works by American and Japanese writers such as Gretel Ehrlich, Terry Tempest Williams, Ishimure Michiko, and Morisaki Kazue.

THE THIRD PHASE: ECOCRITICAL
INTERVENTIONS IN JAPANESE LITERATURE

As demonstrated by Karen Colligan-Taylor's 1990 book titled *The Emergence of Environmental Literature in Japan,* discussions regarding literary environmentalism in Japan began outside the country as early as 1990. Domestically, however, ecocriticism did not really begin to be discussed by scholars of Japanese literature until the late 2000s. Perhaps it was ignored as an ephemeral literary trend in tandem with the environmental movement, or perhaps Japanese scholars did not care for the seemingly political stance of ecocriticism. Whatever the reason, it took more than a decade for ecocriticism to be perceived by domestic Japanologists as a possible critical tool for literary studies in the age of the environment. In 2008, the Association for the Modern Japanese Literary Studies, an academic organization with over one thousand members, held a symposium on representations of the environment. It was interdisciplinary in approach with panelists including an ecocritic (Americanist) and a philosopher in addition to scholars of modern Japanese literature. Another notable event was the two-day international symposium on ecocriticism and Japanese literary studies, which was hosted by Rikkyo Univerity in Japan in collaboration with Columbia University in the United States and held in Tokyo in January of 2010. It was probably the first large-scale scholarly meeting in which Japanese literary works were ecocritically approached by a number of domestic and overseas Japanologists as well as ecocritics and scholars in related fields. Some thirty presentations examined a wide variety of Japanese literature which included Manyōshu, the oldest existing collection of poetry compiled in the middle of eighth century; *The Tale of Genji*, an eleventh-century Japanese classic regarded as the world's first novel; literary and cultural legacies of the Edo period; and works by contemporary writers such as Oe Kenzaburo, Hino Keizo, and Kato Yukiko.

The direction of comparative and collaborative studies of environmental implications in Japanese literature can also be observed in published works. One example is the special issue of ecocriticism in the journal 'Suisei Tsūshin' (2010), to which twenty-one scholars of Japanese, American, and British literature as well as from other fields such as linguistics, contributed essays on ecocritical practice and theory. Another example is a book titled *Kankyo to iushiza* [Views of the Environment: Japanese Literature and Ecocriticism] (2011), which collects twenty-three essays—mostly written by scholars of Japanese literature—which were delivered at the international symposium in Tokyo the previous year, as I have mentioned. The book has four sections: Second Nature and Wild Nature, The Modern and the Pre-modern in Descriptions of Nature, Environment as Cultural Representations, and Center and Periphery. They represent the major framework of the emerging field of Japanese ecocriticism. It is important to notice that those themes are not so different from considered central in ecocritical arenas in the rest of the world. In fact, as the transcript of the keynote roundtable at the opening of the book emphasizes, ecocriticism has finally started to be perceived among Japanologists as a powerful tool to deconstruct urban-born, hierarchical, and ideological views of nature that have fashioned Japanese literary tradition (Shirane, et al. 18–33). Perhaps Views of the Environment signals the birth of Japanese ecocriticism; ecocriticism that could be expected to shift scholarly interests as well as the theoretical matrix in directions that are yet to be clearly defined.

At the crossroad between ecocriticism and Japanese literary studies, there are quite a few issues which should be examined. For instance, at the roundtable in *Views of the Environment*, Haruo Shirane claims the importance of paying greater attention to literary representations of coded nature, or "second nature" as he calls it, whose ideological elements have not been fully discussed (Shirane et al. 18). Coded nature dominates Japanese literary traditions including haiku; therefore, Shirane's remark can be an allusion to the danger of the West's idealization of an Eastern literary imagination. Responding to Shirane, Noda Ken-ichi mentions that the issue of coded nature, especially that of Romanticism, has continued to be critical in American and British ecocriticism, the observation of which implies that theoretical approaches developed in American and British ecocriticism will provide a helpful framework within which to ecocritically examine Japanese literature (Shirane et al. 21). This is just an example, but it is also evidence of the fact that exchanges between literary scholars of different fields with shared interest in literature and environment bring about a cross-fertilizing intellectual matrix of literary environmentalism.

If the burgeoning Japanese ecocriticism can promote a revisionist examination of conceptually appropriated ideas such as East and West, monotheism and animism, or Christianity and Buddhism, it will operate as a disturbing yet creative force in the field of ecocritical theory and practice, helping remap a conceptual terrain of human relationships with the environment.

NOTES

Throughout this essay, name order follows the cultural convention of the country where the named person is originally from. For instance, Japanese are referred to with a family-name given-name order, and Americans are mentioned with a given-name family name order.

1. The direction of influence may not be one-sided. Shirane et al. discuss Japanese literary influence on the American movement of nature writing as well, pointing out that writers such as Gary Snyder were inspired by haiku and other Japanese literature (Shirane et al. 16–17).
2. While in the United States "environmental literature" started to replace "nature writing" by the late 1990s, there has been a tendency that "nature writing" is preferably used in Japan. Perhaps the term "environmental" is so politically charged that, whether consciously or not, scholars as well as writers may try to bypass the word.
3. As one of the early cases of a Japanologist recognizing an applicability of ecocriticism, Hojo Katsutaka in his 2007 article suggests the theoretical usefulness of ecocriticism in the field of Japanese history studies (Hojo 40).
4. Interestingly, it was in the United States that the importance of a scholarly network of eco-critics in East Asia and the idea of a joint symposium in East Asia were first discussed. The root of an East Asian ecocritical network can be traced back to a series of gatherings at the ASLE biennial conference in Eugene, Oregon, in 2005. For details regarding how an East Asian scholarly network in ecocriticism was developed, see Yuki 2008.
5. In addition to monographs, there are some notable collections of essays which attempted a comparative approach, such as Noda Ken-ichi and Yuki Masami, eds., *Ekkyosurutoposu* [Topoi Crossing Borders: Critical Essays on Environmental Literature] (Tokyo: Sairyusha, 2004), and Scott Slovic, Ito Shoko, Yoshida Mitsu, Yukota Yuri, eds., *Ecotopia to kankyo-seigi no bungaku* [Literature of Ecotopia and Environmental Justice: From Hiroshima to Yucca Mountain] (Tokyo: Kouyo Publishing, 2008).

WORKS CITED

ASLE-Japan. Newsletter 1. 1 September 1994.
——, ed. *Tanoshikuyomeru nature writing [Introduction to Nature Writing: 120 Selected Works].* Kyoto: Minerva, 2000.
Colligan-Taylor, Karen. *The Emergence of Environmental Literature in Japan.* New York: Garland, 1990.
Hojo, Katsutaka. "Shutai o tou, Jitsuzon o kataru [Questioning a Subject, Narrating Existence]" *Kokubungaku* 52.5 (2007): 34–43.

Ikuta, Shogo. "Modern Japanese Nature Writing: An Overview." *Literature of Nature: An International Sourcebook.* Ed. Patrick D. Murphy. Chicago: Fitzroy Dearborn, 1998: 277–80.

——,Murakami Kiyotoshi, and Yuki Masami, eds. *Basho no shigaku [Poetics of Place: Ecocritical Essays].* Tokyo: Fujiwara, 2008.

Ito, Shoko, Yokota Yuri, Yoshida Mitsu, Harold Fromm and Lawrence Buell, eds. *Midori no bungakuhihyo [Green Literary Criticism: Ecocriticism].* Tokyo: Shohakusha, 1998.

Noda, Ken-ichi. *Kōkan to hyōsho [Correspondence and Representation: Essays on Nature Writing].* Tokyo: Shohakusha, 2003.

Shirane, Haruo, Komine Kazuaki, Watanabe Kenji, and Noda Ken-ichi. "Zadankai: Kankyo to iushiza [Roundtable Discussion: Views of the Environment]" *Asia Yugaku 143 Kankyo to iushiza [Views of the Environment: Japanese Literature and Ecocriticism].* Eds. Kenji Watanabe, Noda Ken-ichi, Komine Kazuaki and Haruo Shirane. Tokyo: Benseishuppan, 2011:13–33.

Slovic, Scott, and Noda Ken-ichi, eds. *Amerikabungaku no shizen o yomu [Environmental Approaches to American Literature: Towards the World of Nature Writing].* Kyoto: Minerva, 1996.

Special issue in ecocriticism. *Suisei Tsūshin 33* (Tokyo: Suiseisha, 2010): 85–281.

Takahashi, Kazuo. *Nihon bungaku to kishō [Japanese Literature and Meteorology].* Tokyo: Chuōkōronsha, 1978.

Yamazato, Katsunori. *Basho o ikiru [Poetics of Place: Reading Gary Snyder].* Tokyo: Yamatokeikokusha, 2006.

——, Noda Ken-Ichi, Takahashi Tsutomu, Takada Ken-Ichi and Scott Slovic (eds). *Sizen to bungaku no daiarōgu [Dialogue between Nature and Literature: Urban, Rural, Wild].* Tokyo: Sairyusha, 2004.

Yuki, Masami. "Towards the East Asian Network of Ecocriticism." Plenary speech. The International Conference on Literature and Environment, Wuhan, China, November 8, 2008. http://www.asle-japan.org/english/2008/11/joint_plenary_speech_at_intern. html#more

Yuki, Masami. *Mizu no oto no kioku [Remembering the Sound of Water: Essays in Ecocriticism].* Tokyo: Suiseisha, 2010.

CHAPTER 31

ENGAGING WITH *PRAKRITI*

A Survey of Ecocritical Praxis in India

SWARNALATHA RANGARAJAN

What is at issue now is the very nature of our democracy. Who owns this land? Who owns its rivers? Its forests? Its fish? These are huge questions. (Roy 2001:50)

IN a recent study conducted by the University of Adelaide's Environment Institute, India figured seventh among the world's top ten pollutant countries of the world. Home to an array of ecologies and a population of more than a billion people, the diverse ecological endowment of India has significant implications in any environmental audit. With factors like rapid urban growth, industrialization, and population boom, environmental conflicts have become more pronounced and revolve around competing claims. Sites of struggle range from forests, unethical mines, dam projects, and displacement of tribals and agriculture-dependent poor people to land and resource depletion, pollution, decimation of biodiversity, and species threat. The history of exploitation in India's colonial past and the capital-intensive process of development which jettisoned her from agrarianism into industrialization are reckoning factors which lend a distinct socio-ecological basis to her environmental conflicts. Classifying the entire population into three categories—the omnivores, the ecosystem people, and ecological refugees—Madhav Gadgil and Ramachandra Guha classify environmental issues in India as the "environmentalism of the poor," which, unlike the "environmentalism of the rich," engages mainly with question of subsistence and survival (2007:424).

The environment debate has added a new facet to Indian civil society, not only in the socio-economic spheres of development, but also in the cultural categories of society, religion, art, and literature where these debates have remained partially obscured and marginalized. Ecocriticism in the Indian context, therefore, has a unique "advocacy function" both with regard to the reality of the world that it inhabits and "the imaginary spaces it opens up for contemplation of how the real world might be transformed" (Huggan and Tiffin 2010:13).

In addition to this ecosocial critique there is a pressing need in the Indian ecocritical context for what David Barnhill refers to as "ecosocial ideals" that "concern speculations about positive alternatives to our contemporary problems, turning our attention to behaviors, values, ideologies, cultures and social structures that might constitute a wiser and healthier relationship with the earth and each other" (2010:282). An alternative pattern of social and ecological harmony with well-formulated dharmic injunctions for environmental protection that uphold a vision of all living beings in the universe as members of the earth family (*vasudhaiva kutumbakam*), can be found in ancient Indian literature, polity, philosophy and cosmologies. S. Murali, president of ASLE-India, calls for a rereading of India's cultural inheritance that must accompany the introduction and teaching of scientific curricula in India since "the ultimate historical foundations of nature preservation are aesthetic" (2008:12).

India's hoary civilization faces the danger of losing its traditional oikonomics—the traditional household wisdom of living harmoniously with the world. The ancient Vedic vision of geopiety envisaged a cosmos governed by *ṛta*, the impersonal underlying order and regulator of all life on earth. In this world view, man does not stand apart but is yoked by *ṛta* in a relationship of interdependence and interrelationship with nature. The integral bond between humans and nature, embedded in agricultural cycles, the flux of seasons, the alternating wet and dry spells, and regularity of the cosmic order, is celebrated and emphasized through sacred ritual, art and architecture in the geographically diverse subcontinent which offered all types of ecosystems (see Caley and Rangarajan 2009). Conservation, therefore would mean "a state of harmony (*ṛtam*) with land, forest, waters and natural environment" (Khanna 1995:111). Furthermore, the balance of the five primary elements was considered indispensible for maintaining ecological balance. *Ṛta*, which literally meant "the course of things," spelt out the right path for all things from the natural to the moral order and laid the foundation for the concept of *dharma*, a multivalent term of great importance in Indian religions and philosophy, usually translated as the integral law: "that which upholds or supports" the whole creation from the microcosm to the macrocosm. The epistemic worldview of the different literary traditions in Sanskrit literature gives importance to the notion of a dharmic individual whose code of conduct is characterized by environmental wisdom (See Rukmani 2000:110–11).

A brief look at ancient Sanskrit texts on polity provides an overview of responsible stewardship measures that were taken by state governments. Kautilya's *Arthasastra* (4th century BCE), a treatise on politics that is often compared with Plato's *Republic*, presents an ideal society run on sound principles of environmental management. Described as a "geographical web of interconnections" and an "extraordinary ecological fresco" by Francis Zimmerman (1987:50), the text illustrates the ruler's exercise of power over space that is conceived to be ecologically complete since it included diverse ecosystems and ideas regarding spatial organizations, divisions, and decentralization.

The *Arthasastra* gives extensive evidence on mining, agricultural and forestry practices in ancient India, strictly forbids the overuse of a resource base and prescribes severe punitive laws for polluting the public domain. Though inspired by pragmatic concerns, its politics of environment was inextricably connected to the awareness of man's dependence on nature. Therefore enjoyment as well as protection became the moral duty (*dharma*) of the king and also the common law (*samanya dharma*) for all citizens. This concept of *dharma* was lacking in the colonial model, which altered the ecosystem by viewing it as private property. The moral imperative becomes equally nebulous in the modern Indian state where it is projected as a national ideal but not enforced.

Different from the Western conceptions in their outlook, the theories of nature in Indian philosophical schools of thought, both theistic and non-theistic (though with the exception of Charvaka and other schools of materialism), "conceive nature as the stage for moral beings, constituted and guided by moral needs" (Datta 1936:223). Nature is widely revered as *Prakriti*, "the primordial vastness, the inexhaustible, the source of abundance" (Shiva 1996:281). A vibrant definition of nature is provided by the theory of the five elements, the *Panchamahabhutas*, which postulates that "Nature and the environment are not outside us; they are not alien and hostile to us. They are an inseparable part of our existence" (Rao 2000:26). According to this, the five primary elements of fire, earth, water, air, and space, which co-constitute all forms of matter, are evolutes of *prakriti*, the matrix of all material creation. Though distinct in form and function, the *panchamahabhutas* are interdependent. The *bhuta* theory provides an integral framework that connects all phenomena and recognizes the dialectical unity between the microcosm with the macrocosm.

The two great Indian epics, the *Ramayana* and the *Mahabharata*, offer rich insights into the ethnoecology of the terrestrial ecosystems of India. The epics contain "forest texts" in which the city is contrasted with the epic forests teeming with an overabundance of diverse plant and animal species indigenous to the varied ecosystems of the land. The *Aranyakas*, or the forest texts of the Upanishadic period, establish the forest as a place of transcendence where it is possible to go beyond human limitations and establish a vital connection with the cosmos. The warrior-king heroes of these epics become complete men only after they have learnt to temper the consumerist tendencies in their lifestyle in the forest (see Lutgendorf 2000:284). An alternative reading of the forest episodes of these epics through an ecological lens reveals debates relating to the forest commons and rights of forest-dwellers who were facing an enormous pressure due to the growth of towns. Forced migration to the Indo-Gangetic plain and war over resources form the subtext of these epics. In his alternative reading of the *Mahabharata*, Aiyer argues that *dharma*, the central concern for which the great war was fought, came to be established "as a result of a conflict over social policies in response to on-going environmental crises" (2009:50). Similarly, the absence or disguised presence of the aboriginal people in the vast forest landscapes in the *Ramayana* is emblematic of the ambiguous relationship between Adivasis and the orthodox Hindus.

An intrinsic sense of order characterizes Sangam literature, the earliest extant literature of the Tamils (300 BCE—200 CE), which stems from a culture deeply rooted in the soil where place is the first principle of literary representation. This relational web "integrating the human, nature and the spiritual realm" is known as *tinai* (Selvamony

2008:153) in which human beings do not occupy a central place. For instance, the *Natrinai*—a collection of four hundred poems relating to the five landscapes of Sangam literature—casts trees in the role of principal presences and identifies them as close kith and kin. The poetic tradition of *Sangam* literature was grounded through metaphor and content in the socio-economic activities of the five physiographical zones namely *Kurinji* (Mountains), *Mullai* (Forests), *Marutam* (Pastoral Fields), *Neidhal* (the littoral zones), and *Paalai* (parched zones or deserts). The earliest known theoretical account of the *tinai* theory can be found in the *Tolkappiayam*. Today there is a revival of *tinai* studies in Indian academia, pioneered by Nirmal Selvamony, president of OSLE-India. The research focuses on the contemporary relevance of *tinai* studies and the ways it can benefit from comparison with related theories from other fields like anthropogeography, human ecology, social ecology, biogeography, bioregionalism, and nativism that study the earth's human communities in relation to their natural environment (see Selvamony 2004:13).

The creation myths and way of life of tribal cultures also emphasize the human–nature continuum. The oral traditions of the hunter-gatherers, fishers, farmers, and the pastoral transhuman envisage the seamless view of man and nature as an inseparable whole (Saraswati 1995:4). Many tribal traditions debunk the notion of human superiority by attributing primordial knowledge to birds and animals. Folk tales and lore also reveal this sense of co-partnership with nature. The speaking animals in the *Jataka* tales and the *Panchatantra* exhibit human qualities, and sometimes these animals are shown as possessing superior qualities of wisdom lacking in human beings. *Dharma* and *ṛta*, therefore, are two important ecocritical principles to consider when we talk about India, which was a cultural entity for over two millennia before it was politically constituted as a state under the British colonial regime.

The changing contours of ecological changes impacting cultural spaces as a result of the clash between industrial and preindustrial cultures can be represented in terms of what Gadgil and Guha refer to as "the closure and creation of niches" (1992:242). The British government declared community control illegitimate and put wood lots and grazing lands to commercial use to maximize revenue yield. Tribal lands were converted into tea plantations and monoculture of commercially valued trees like teak and deodhar was encouraged. Moreover the colonial administration alienated the peasants, herders, fisher folk, artisanal groups, and other ecosystem people who formed a large part of the population. The resource processors of the British colony caused the ecosystem to dwindle into rapidly shrinking niche spaces. Writers like Rabindranath Tagore expressed their concern about the mindless mechanization that brought in its wake a reductive, use-oriented worldview. In plays like *Red Oleander* (1950, f.p.1924), Tagore uses the metaphor of the mine to critique capitalism and "to condemn the ways of thinking and knowing that lead to capitalist exploitation in the first place" (Crowley 2009:24). *Muktadhara* (1922) has a visionary apocalyptic message about the damming of rivers and its ecological disruptions. The principal characters in this play are ecowarriors who are fully aware of the penalty that their revolutionary act of breaking the dam would bring about. The play anticipates the adverse impacts on the ecosystems and displacement of tribal lands in the wake of projects like the Narmada Valley Development Project, which Arundhati Roy, the activist-writer, refers to as "India's Greatest Planned Environmental Disaster" (2001:86).

The post-independence development model aggressively focused on the urban-industrial sector and its bureaucratic apparatus ignored the needs of the ecosystem people in the process. A telling example is the construction of large dams, which involved displacing poor people and laying to waste the traditional systems of small village tanks. The alternative Gandhian paradigm of development based on the principles of sustainability and agrarian self-sufficiency through economic decentralization was not implemented. Gandhi's ideas of trusteeship, sustainability, and conservation are natural corollaries of his belief in dharmic practice both in social and political life. The Gandhian model offers a nuanced understanding of ownership in which the owning of resources is seen as "primarily a responsibility and not a freedom for unconstrained action" (Baindur and Sarukkai 2010:18).

The erosion of values in India's developmental philosophy arises from the conflict of approaches between what Vandana Shiva refers to as "market paradigms" and "ecological paradigms" (Shiva 2002:14). The former are scarcity paradigms, which are created by ecologically blind market assumptions, generate value by depleting resources and impact the poor and the environment in significant ways. Guha points out that the ongoing struggle between the peasant and industrial modes of resource use in both the colonial as well as post colonial stages of the country's development has resulted in "a fissured land, ecologically and socially fragmented beyond belief" (1992:245).

The ability of the *bhutas* (primary elements) to reflect the fissured scapes of India is the subject of Ruchir Joshi's *The Last Jet-Engine Laugh* (2002). The crisis of water, represented through the image of blood on water, epitomizes the violence that will be at the centre of water wars in contemporary India. The novel evokes the economic, social, and political dispensations which that are instrumental in the structural poverty and eco-apartheid that accompanies the water crisis. Similarly, the toxic discourses that followed the aftermath of the ghastly Bhopal Gas Tragedy of 1984, one of the worst industrial disasters in human history, bring into question the glaring aporias in international frameworks of law and human rights. Indra Sinha's *Animal's People* (2007), a fictional recreation of the Bhopal disaster, has for its chief narrator, Animal, who declares in the opening lines of the novel, "I used to be human once." This proclamation of identity by Animal who embodies both human and nonhuman qualities is a statement about the new global world order which locates the underprivileged in the lowest rung of hierarchy in such a manner that they no longer qualify to be called "human."

Continuing human inequalities and environmental abuses in this fissured land have led cultural historians and ecocritics to question the promotion of conservation ideals over human development issues. Huggan and Tiffin see the coming together of postcolonialism and ecocriticism as areas in conflict since ecocriticism as a whole tends to prioritize extra-human concerns, whereas postcolonialism has tended to be predominantly anthropocentric (2009:17). Nevertheless, deep concern about conservation has been expressed by writers like Kailash Sankhala, the chief motivating force behind

Ranthambore Wildlife Reserve Protection in Rajastan and Project Tiger, one of India's largest wildlife conservation programs. In his autobiography, *Tiger! The Story of the Indian Tiger* (1978), Sankhala describes a Leopoldian moment of epiphany when as a trigger-happy young forest cadet, he killed a tiger for sport. The dead tiger seemed to look into his eyes and question the futility of the sport. Far from being the mere story of Sankhala's life, the autobiography becomes the platform for discussing the protection of the Indian tiger's habitat. The book questions notions of the dangerous man-eating tiger, popularized in the works of Jim Corbett, and deconstructs the widely prevalent ethos of hunting—a legacy handed down by the princes of Rajasthan who organized tiger hunts (see Rangarajan 2008: 406).

On the other hand, the uneven ecological-historical nexus of blind conservation projects and sham environmentalism that is prevalent in post-independence development patterns comes in for criticism in novels like Amitav Ghosh's *The Hungry Tide* (2004). The novel delves into the empirical reality of the Sundarbans where the humans and nonhumans are pitted in opposition over scarce resources due to a postcolonial elitist agenda which criminalizes certain communities. Woven into the novel's narrative are issues of misrepresentation and the plight of the Bangladeshi refugees who were persecuted by the Left Front Government in 1978 for trespassing into the habitat of the endangered tigers at Marichjhapi. Novels like *The Hungry Tide* bring into representational space what Pablo Mukherjee refers to as "the complex but palpable continuities between human and non-human communities" (2010:113).

Arundhati Roy is another writer who records the "small voices of history" and offers striking narratives of the institutionalized marginalization of the "ecosystem people." The neocolonial global market and the postcolonial state that sanctions the continuing dispossession of people come in for stringent criticism in her works like *The Algebra of Infinite Justice* (2002). Roy's writings exhibit the vital nexus between environment, history, and culture and offer agency through counter-narratives to people who live in the margins. A committed critic of the gigantic dam projects on the river Narmada in the Indian states of Gujarat and Madhya Pradesh, Roy uses the trope of apocalypse in her writings and clearly connects environmental issues with the metastasization of democracy in India into a "predatory organism with a constricted imagination that revolves almost entirely around the idea of maximizing profit" (Roy 2009:2).

The "rhetoric of ownership society" is held up for close scrutiny by Vandana Shiva, one of India's renowned environmental activists and a vociferous critic of Western concepts of science and development that violate the integrity of organic systems. Shiva's writings encompass and record the political struggles of women, peasants, and tribals based on ecology. A similar vein of protest runs through the writings of Mahasweta Devi, a tireless crusader for the "de-notified" tribes of India—"the suffering spectators of the India that is travelling toward the twenty-first century" (Devi 1995:xi). In works like the *Chotta Munda and His Arrow* (1980) and *Imaginary Maps* (1995) Mahasweta Devi highlights the struggles of these tribes who have been systematically pauperized by the loss of forest land and mainstream government practices. Questions of identity are also closely bound with ecology in the case of tribal cultures of the eight Indian northeastern states which are marked by ethnic, linguistic, and cultural diversity. Indian English literature is a newly emerging literature of North East India and writers like Mamang Dai, Robin S. Ngangom, Temsula Ao, to name a few, are engaged in acts of environing ecology through the poetic use of tribal myths and values in ways that are both cultural and spiritual (see Chandra and Das 2007:v).

The ecofeminist discourse in India attempts to redefine the uneven patterns of development that devalue the environment as well the third world rural women's vital contributive role in sustenance economies regarding basic, vital needs. Shiva invokes the empowering sacral vision of feminine geopiety of traditional Hindu cosmologies in which person (*purusha*) and nature (*prakriti*) constitute a "duality in unity" (Shiva 1988:40)—a worldview which was lost with the advent of the industrial/developmental model. Shiva writes, "For women ... the death of Prakriti is simultaneously a beginning of their marginalization, devaluation, displacement and ultimate dispensability. The ecological crisis, at its root, is the death of the feminine principle" (Shiva 1988:42). According to Shiva, women and tribals are the traditional guardians of ecological knowledge and have played a vital role in maintaining balance in traditional Indian agriculture. The Chipko Movement of the 1970s in which women belonging to the backward classes of the Himalayan region tried to protect trees from the axes of the cutters by clinging to them is a striking example of the third world rural woman's interest in preserving the wealth of natural resources. Indian ecofeminist discourse therefore advocates a different form of knowledge and economic value. In the words of Karren Warren it, "builds on the multiple perspectives of those whose perspectives are typically omitted or undervalued in dominant discourses" (Warren 1995 as cited in Merchant 2005:195). The recovery narratives in Indian cultural ecofeminism range from the rewriting of mainstream epics to the foregrounding of oral narratives by women in folk traditions in which there is a valorization of woman's culture which includes the body, emotions, and subjective feelings. Ecofeminist fables by writers like Mahasweta Devi, Kamala Das, Ambai, Gauri Deshpande, Pratibha Ray, Sara Joseph, Arundhati Roy, and Bama focus on the invention of new stories about the sacredness of the body and about how inhabiting one's body is an important way of being at "home." These stories become very important in a culture that defines both the human female body and the land as "resource," as someone else's "property." The way a culture sees the body is intimately connected to the way it perceives the earth.

This survey indicates the emerging trends in the socio-cultural spaces of India that call for imaginative ways of engaging ecocritically with a contemporary ecological dharma. Lawrence Buell succinctly defines the objective: "Criticism worthy of the name arises from commitments deeper than professionalism" (2005:97). Ecocriticism in the present and newly evolving contexts will have to deal with what Greg Garrard refers to as "a lethal compact of ignorance, economic self-interest and the legacy of anthropocentric values" with all the "vigour, wit and critical insight of which an alternative culture is capable of" (2009:5). Scott Slovic makes a relevant point about the ecocritic's attentive gaze when he describes his own sensitization to environmental concerns relating to pollution and privatization of water sources by the Coca-Cola company's operations during a visit to India. This inspired him to begin writing a series of correspondences with representatives of the corporate giant voicing his concern about environmental stewardship. Although the responses were far from assuring, Slovic writes, "What I've learned from my communications with The Coca-Cola Company is that that the process of paying attention and speaking out is ongoing" (2008:220). The opening up of similar spaces for communication in ecocritical praxis holds the key to the act of re-imagining relationships of mutuality in an ecological democracy.

ECOCRITICISM: CONTEXTS IN INDIA

Today ecocriticism is taught in India as an independent paper in many universities and colleges and also as part of courses on literary theory and criticism. The main fora for promoting ecocriticism in India are OSLE-India (Organisation for Studies in Literature and Environment-India) and ASLE-India (Association for the Study of Literature and Environment-India).

OSLE-India (http://www.osle-india.org) provides a platform to address the pedagogical aspects of ecocriticism through its annual conferences, seminars, and ecoliteracy workshops and puts out a peer-reviewed international journal, *The Indian Journal of Ecocriticism*, annually. It also brought out *Essays in Ecocriticism* (2007), the first of its kind in India, covering the recent critical avenues explored by Indian and international scholars in ecocriticism.

ASLE-India (https://asleindia.webs.com) seeks to promote a collective understanding of the intimate relations and biological ties existing between literature, art, culture and the environment. It brought out its first book on ecological critical theory and practice: *Nature and Human Nature: Literature, Ecology and Meaning* in 2008.

WORKS CITED

Aiyer, K. R. (2009) "A Socio-Ecological Perspective on Some Episodes from The Mahabharata," *The Indian Journal of Ecocriticism* 2: 50–60.

Baindur, M. and S. Sarukkai. (2010) "The Possibility of Conservation: Some Philosophical Questions," *The Indian Journal of Ecocriticism* 3: 9–21.

Barnhill, D. L. (2010), "Surveying the Landscape: A New Approach to Nature Writing," *ISLE*,17(2), 273–90.

Buell, Lawrence. (2005) *The Future of Environmental Criticism: Environmental Crisis and Literary Imagination*, Malden: Blackwell.

Caley, M. and S. Rangarajan (eds.) (2009) "Editorial," *The Trumpeter* 25(2): 1–7. Accessed on July 1, 2010, from <http://trumpeter.athabascau.ca/index.php/trumpet>.

Crowley, Thomas. (2009) "Mine as Metaphor: Visions of Industry in Tagore and Hamsun," *The Indian Journal of Ecocriticism*, 2: 22–29.

Contents

Chandra, N. D. R. and N. Das. (2007) *Ecology, Myth and Mystery: Contemporary Poetry in English from Northeast India*, New Delhi: Sarup and Sons.

Datta, D. M. (1936) "The Moral Conception of Nature in Indian Philosophy," *International Journal of Ethics*, 46(2): 223–28.

Devi, M. (1995), *Imaginary Maps*, trans. G. C. Spivak, London: Routledge.

Gadgil, M. and R. Guha. (1992) *This Fissured Land: An Ecological History of India*, New Delhi: Oxford University Press.

——. (2000) *The Use and Abuse of Nature*, New Delhi: Oxford University Press.

Garrard, Greg. "Ecocriticism: the ability to investigate cultural artefacts from an ecological perspective," in Arran Stibbe and Heather Luna (eds) *The Handbook of Sustainability Literacy*. Accessed on August 29, 2010, from http://arts.brighton.ac.uk/stibbe-handbook-of-sustainability.

Ghosh, A. (2005) *The Hungry Tide*, New Delhi: Ravi Dayal Publisher.

Huggan, G. and H. Tiffin. (2010) *Postcolonial Ecocriticism: Literature, Animals, Environment*, Oxon: Routledge.

Joshi, R. (2002) *The Last Jet-Engine Laugh*, London: Flamingo.

Khanna, M. (1995) "Nature as Feminine: Ancient Vision of Geopiety and Goddess Ecology," in B. Saraswati (ed.) *Man in Nature*, Vol. 5, New Delhi: D. K. Print World.

Lutgendorf, P. (2000) "City, Forest, and Cosmos," C. K. Chapple and M. E. Tucker (eds) *Hinduism and Ecology: The Intersection of Earth, Sky, and Water*, Cambridge: Harvard University Press.

Merchant, C. (2005) *Radical Ecology*, New York: Routledge.

Mukherjee, U. P. (2010) *Postcolonial Environments*, London: Palgrave Macmillan.

Murali. S. (ed.) (2008) "Contextualising Literature, Ecology, and Meaning," in *Nature and Human Nature: Literature, Ecology, Meaning*. New Delhi: Prestige Books.

Rangarajan, M. (2008) "Five Nature Writers," in Arvind Krishna Mehrotra (ed.) *A Concise History of Indian Literature in English*, Ranikhet: Permanent Black.

Rao, Seshagiri K. L. (2000) "The Five great Elements (Pañcamahābhūta): An Ecological Perspective," in C. K. Chapple and M. E. Tucker (eds) *Hinduism and Ecology: The Intersection of Earth, Sky, and Water*, Cambridge: Harvard University Press.

Roy, A. (2001) *The Algebra of Infinite Justice*, New Delhi: Penguin.

——. (2009) *Field Notes on Democracy: Listening to Grasshoppers*, Chicago: Haymarket.

Rukmani, T. S. (2000) "Literary Foundations for an Ecological Aesthetic," in C. K. Chapple and M. E. Tucker (eds) *Hinduism and Ecology: The Intersection of Earth, Sky, and Water*, Cambridge: Harvard University Press.

Sankhala, K. (1978) *Tiger!: The Story of the Indian Tiger*, London: Collins.

Saraswati, B. (1995) "Introduction," in K. Vatsyayan (ed.) *Prakriti: The Integral Vision*, Vol. 1, New Delhi: D. K. Print World.

Selvamony, N. (2004) "Tinai Studies," in Nirmaldasan and Selvamony (eds) *tinai 3* Chennai: PASO.

——. (2008) "Portable Homeland: Robin Ngangom's take on the dying Tinai tradition of the Indian Northeast," *Kavya Bharati*, 20: 150–70.

Shiva, V. (1988) *Staying Alive: Women, Ecology and Survival*, London: Zed Books.

——. (1996) "Science, Nature and Gender," in A. Garry and M. Pearsall (eds) *Women, Knowledge, and Reality: Explorations in Feminist Philosophy*, London: Routledge.

——. (2002) *Water Wars: Privatization, Pollution and Profit*, Cambridge: South End Press.

Sinha, I. (2007) *Animal's People*, London and Sydney: Simon and Schuster.

Slovic, S. (2008) *Going Away to Think: Engagement, Retreat and Ecocritical Responsibility*, Reno: University of Nevada Press.

Tagore, R. (1950) *Three Plays*, trans. M. Sykes, Bombay: Oxford University Press.

Zimmerman, F. (1987) *The Jungle and the Aroma of Meats: An Ecological Theme in Hindu Medicine*, Berkeley: University of California Press.

....

CHAPTER 32

CHINESE ECOCRITICISM IN THE LAST TEN YEARS

....

QINGQI WEI

CHINESE ecocriticism came into being more than ten years ago,[1] but the last decade has definitely seen its greatest flourishing. Ironically, since Western ecocriticism was introduced to this ancient land, across which a young industry was rapidly sprawling, it has found a congenial academic reception founded on acute awareness of the deterioration of both cultural and natural ecology. Chinese academia, particularly the humanities, which had already accepted other postmodern movements, embraced green scholarship not only because critics were professionally ready to accept another useful interpretive tool but also because they felt, probably unprecedentedly, worried by the pressure looming outside their offices and classrooms. The anxiety was strengthened by the realization that the decline of their own status was somewhat connected to that of the environment. Events in the human community that threatened to push them into a hostile market was acutely perceived as having everything to do with what was occurring to the nonhuman world. Chinese ecocriticism therefore appeared from the beginning to be concerned with ecologies rather than ecology.

MAIN CHARACTERS OF CHINESE ECOCRITICISM

Familiarity: A Sense of Feeling at Home

Unlike its previous radical interpretive-critical cousins (new historicism, feminism, postcolonialism, etc.), ecocriticism encountered a place both strange and familiar: on the one hand, it was accepted merely condescendingly (not far from the condition back at its American home) as a new term that amusingly joins "eco,-" a prefix that implies a scientific rather than humanistic approach, with criticism; on the other hand, it recognized the familiar traditional Chinese ideology about nature echoed by the orientalizing elements that surged inside ecocriticism's deep ecological frameworks. It was perhaps the first time that a Western criticism, among dozens of others that had already traveled and settled here, had felt a sense of feeling at home, and this sensation was reported by both the Western and native ecocritics, the latter, for example, being pleased with the idea that Thoreau implies a shadow of Chuang Chou as his spiritual teacher. However, the familiarity was obscured by a premodern and postmodern gap, which, though generating space for interpretation, dialogue, and cross-cultural communication, ought to be soberly distinguished by Sino-Western scholars. It is as if critics were located at stages of a spiral structure that looked similar and familiar, yet was experienced differently. Only with empathy as well as rigorous critique can the sense of "kinship," while we come to terms with ecocriticism, be fully analyzed in a contemporary Chinese context.

Dialogue: A Tale of Two Cultures

Despite running the risk of essentializing cultures, for subgroups in Western communities can be as different from each other as from China—itself being more than a monoculture—I see clearly that the entrance of ecocriticism into China was a process consciously attempted by an Oriental-Occidental joint effort. It was neither a passive nor a unilateral agenda, but an interactive and dialogical one. From the very beginning, it impressed Chinese researchers with its openness to mutually informing and respectful debate. This was by no means the repetition of previous introductions of other Western critical paradigms, which appeared more or less dominant and could find few counterparts on their arrival. There were three reasons that for the duet.

First, the ideological resources such as deep ecology and environmental ethics, on which much Western ecocriticism is based, can to a large extent be matched by traditional Chinese environmentalist resources. To quote Lawrence Buell, "Chinese art and culture's inherently rich resources guarantee a significant potential for the entry of Chinese ecologists in the movement" (personal interview, 2002, 89). Though it is modest of Buell to deny expertise in Chinese philosophy, he does suggest that "you can find an understanding towards value, and broadly speaking, a relative, non-binary, earth-loving mode of thinking that Chinese intellectuals have consistently employed since ancient times when considering the relationship between man and the physical world—forming a stark contrast with the Judeo-Christian tradition, especially Christian culture" (89).

Second, when ecocriticism became established in China in the 1990s, it did not find itself alone, nor was it a wasteland where you could only (re)search relics for ancient comrades, as contemporary Chinese scholars had already been on their own way to ecological cultural studies, Yu Mouchang's *Ecological Philosophy* being one of the early trailblazers. The "spiritual ecology" posed by Lu Shuyuan and Xia Zhongyi in the mid-1990s marked the green perspective emerging in literary studies. Though exchanges scarcely took place between Lu and American ecocritics until the beginning of the new century, Chinese scholars were at least well prepared. Thus the Chinese eco-criticism we see today has two origins. Though the term itself comes from the West, it genuinely combines both native and foreign ideas.

And last but not least, the disciplinary feature of ecocriticism has always taken "cross" as its keyword: it is ambitious enough not only to cross disciplines, but to cross cultures, borders, and ideologies as well. It is not surprising to see that Scott Slovic's *Going Away to Think,* one of the first translated ecocritical works ever published in China, appeals to the readers with its title and its effort to "cross." Dialogues, therefore, have become one of the major knots of the ecocritical web that boasts diversity as the sign of its own eco-logical health.

Reconstruction: A Strategy That Leads the Way

Although all the Western critical methodologies have more or less undergone a pro-cess from acceptance to metamorphosis, ecocriticism in China is perhaps the most successful one, which has been and is being reconstructed as an open and inclusive system that conducts its critical activities on plural theoretical platforms and within a multi-cultural-textual context.

As one of the leading postmodern theorists, Wang Ning believes that "the entrance of Chinese literary art onto the global stage has become an inevitable his-toric trend; besides, Chinese literary theorists are now capable of voicing their own voices in the international arena. They, after a period of 'aphasia,' have been able to update their structure of knowledge, and pose their own theoretical proposal through dialogues with Western scholars" (*The Transcendence of Postmodernism* 366). Wang offers generous applause for the rise of ecocriticism by which he testifies to the legitimacy of his strategy of naturalizing theories from abroad. He optimisti-cally writes that "[e]cocriticism, after its introduction to China at the beginning of this century, has gradually been localized, becoming both a methodology and a theoretical perspective for literary criticism and research on ecology and the envi-ronment" ("Ecocriticism and the Construction of Literary Eco-environmental Ethics" 12). He even believes that ecocriticism has a better chance to take a main-stream position, for, with the Taoist tradition, "it is not surprising that once the term was introduced eco-criticism has quickly become one of the most prom-ising and cutting-edge critical approaches in China. It has been attracting the attention of more and more critics and literary scholars in China, although it still remains marginalized in Western academia" ("Toward a Literary Environmental Ethics: A Reflection on Eco-Criticism" 291).

In the case of the growth of ecocriticism in China, there have been two transformations that restructured literary ecological study. It is noteworthy that ecocriticism was
first introduced mainly by scholars from English departments. Early publications
include the translation of several major Anglo-American ecocritical essays, and I myself
held interviews with two important American ecocritics (Lawrence Buell in 2002 and
Scott Slovic in 2008). Detailed analysts of the American nature writing tradition include
Cheng Hong (also the translator of T. T. Williams's *Refuge*), who wrote *Return to the
Wilderness*. These efforts served as a cue as well as a clue, for with these initiatives, major
scholars from Chinese departments, more established as experts on comparative studies of Chinese and Western nature aesthetics, began to take over the agenda of creating
Chinese ecocriticism. This transformation was marked by such terms as Lu Shuyuan's
"ecological studies in literature and art" and Zeng Fanren's "eco-ontological aesthetics,"
although "ecocriticism" has proved a more general and convenient term to be applied in
Sino-Western dialogue, providing a framework that allows conceptions to be defined in
comparable and competitive way.

The second transformation that followed has concentrated on modernizing numerous traditional Chinese aesthetic categories from an ecological perspective, and thus
restructuring ecocriticism with Chinese elements. I believe this is a bi-directional construction, in that critical essays written by ancient scholars, who preferred a poetic and
metaphysical form to a theoretical and explicit pattern, are being reinscribed ecocritically so as to be accessible to contemporary readership, within and without China. What
intrigues the Chinese interpreters involved is that traditional nature-oriented works are
so "green"—it is almost as if they had been waiting for thousands of years to be rein-
stated via environmentalist discourse.

Major Chinese Ecocritics: Lu Shuyuan and Zeng Fanren

Lu Shuyuan, basing himself on locality, takes the critique of modernity as his ecocritical
starting point. Such core values as enlightenment, reason, technology, progress, market,
competition, and consumption are rendered problematic by an ecological vision and,
to him, need reconsidering, reviewing, and reintegrating. Lu takes the "Anthropocene"
era as the context in which ecocriticism is studied, with the contemplation that, since
the industrial revolution, the way human beings impact the physical environment has
tended towards accelerating harm. *Homo sapiens* on its own has been precipitately shifting the physical, chemical, and biological natures of this planet. Unlike other terms
such as Cambrian and Devonian periods, the Anthropocene is more than a geological period: it covers all the ways in which human society interacts with the nonhuman
world; it includes issues such as economy, politics, security, education, and religion; and

CHINESE ECOCRITICISM IN THE LAST TEN YEARS   541

it confronts all nations and ethnicities. In this sense, the Anthropocene is coterminous with the process of "globalization."

Lu calls for the reflection on the Anthropocene rather than the overheated propaganda for globalization. Lu points out that ecology has grown well beyond its core scientific discipline and has developed into a discursive system that shelters beliefs about life and environment, mankind and nature, society and earth, spirit and material, and so on. In the new context of the Anthropocene, ecology has developed into a counter-discipline against the industrial, and as an aspect of postmodern trend, it is revealing its subversive edge. The deconstructive and reconstructive significance of ecological thoughts has been inevitably extending into the realm of spiritual and cultural studies. Lu thus promotes "Ecological Research in Literature and Art" as a pioneer of a green era in academia.

Lu has always been attached to what he calls "spiritual ecology." As early as in 1987, he published "Land and Rainbow" in the *Journal of Literature and Art,* claiming that the art of literature takes root in the earth with its branches and leaves reaching the sky of spirit. But what is "spirit"? To human beings, what brings the existences of nature, society, and spirit together? Lu confesses:

> I pay more attention to the communication of moods and souls and the recreation of meaning in literary criticism, to insight and intuition, faith and fidelity, imagination and ingenuity, in other words, to the spiritual activities of literary world, to the way criticism marches towards a pilgrimage that provides no definite answer, instead of tracing all the way back to the flat and clear starting point of literary work. Above all, I lay focus on that beyond language and logic, text and texture, something "spiritual." ("The Spiritual Level of Literary Criticism" 80)

To him, then, ecocriticism is a "spiritual coming-home," an ontological conversion that surges with more local energy. He argues that the main cause of the deterioration of earth's ecology lies in the decline of human spirit, the improvement of which directly precedes the job of redemption. Lu's ecocritical practice is thus to represent what has been lost in human process of modernization, reveal the deep spiritual wounds cut by dualism, and call for the reshaping of "ecological spirit," which is undoubtedly of great importance.

A comrade of Lu's, albeit a more central figure, Zeng Fanren has been making every effort to use his resources to push Chinese ecocriticism forward. A theorist in aesthetics, modern and ancient, Western and Chinese, Zeng was ready to embrace ecocriticism and relocate it in a terrain overlapping its original landscape yet extending deeper into a broader field of aesthetics, thus fulfilling his hope of a Chinese renewal of ecocriticism. Having carefully investigated the evolution of Western ecocriticism, Zeng summarizes six major characters of ecocriticism. According to the fifth of these, a key effect of Western ecocriticism is to make possible, by "green reading," the "negentropy" of nature. Zeng is not the first to apply the ecological nomenclature, but he metaphorizes it to stress the very urgent function of literary criticism in an environmentally endangered world: "Changing, through ecological literature and criticism, [the] human standpoint and attitude and choosing to coexist with nature are the way[s] to the self-redemption of human beings, and are the effect[s] of literary ecocriticism" (43). Zeng suggests two patterns in ecopoetics: namely, the creation of new poetic principles and the transformation of old ones, and, on the whole, he finds it an ever progressing and open process.[2] From this point, Zeng is ready to set up his project of Chinese eco-aesthetics, and his *On Eco-ontological Aesthetics* is a grandly designed monograph that probes into the theoretical construction of eco-aesthetics.

With the proposition of "eco-ontological aesthetics," Zeng argues that the question of eco-aesthetics is in the final analysis that of the being of mankind. Western civilization, shaped by anthropocentrism, may be the fundamental cause of contemporary ecological crisis, which directly threatens the survival of human beings, and which counts as one of the major elements that contribute to "the non-aesthetical being of humans." Zeng agrees with some of his Western colleagues: to solve the environmental crisis, the most critical issue lies in developing a non-anthropocentric attitude towards physical nature, rather than finding new technologies or transforming economic relationships.

Zeng further asserts that the proposition of eco-ontological aesthetics helps make a breakthrough in contemporary Chinese discipline of aesthetics: it contests its traditional epistemological conception, anthropocentric tenets, and dualistic thinking pattern, thus realizing the transformation from epistemology to ontology. He particularly interprets, discusses, clarifies, and modernizes Taoist ecological insights, turning to Lao Tzu and Chuang Tzu, who may help modernizers to diagnose the sticking point of ecological crisis. Zeng elaborates, not without passion, that "such Taoist descriptions as 'Tao as matrix of all' (道为万物母), 'homogeneity of everything in the world' (万物齐一), 'Tao is the Law of Nature' (道法自然), 'the circulatory nature' (天倪), 'the Way of nature' (天道), profoundly explained, at so early an era, the modern deep ecological terms like 'universal symbiosis', 'biological chain', 'ecological ego', 'ecological value' and so on, in a unique way of oriental wisdom" (*On Eco-ontological Aesthetics* 142). Admittedly, an adaptive strategy has to be developed to "modernize" those ancient Chinese terms so that they may be accessed to in a contemporary ecological context. Indeed, aren't we always echoing the voices of the ancients, Western or Eastern? It is just necessary that ancient discourse be transformed in a systematic manner. For example, Zong Yongcheng has attempted to "ecologize" ancient Chinese literary concepts such as *qiyun* (the rhyme of *qi*), which he defines as a kind of "rhythm of life circle." His effort actually belongs to a grander agenda that takes as its hard task the modernization of the whole package of ancient Chinese aesthetic and philosophic categories.

As leading art-literary scholars in Chinese academia, Lu and Zeng are typical representatives of Chinese ecocritics, who have been profoundly trained in double fields of Chinese literary and art research and Western philosophies (Marxism significantly included). They have been able to direct the two into a new and harmonious development, and ought to be looked upon as Chinese voices contributing to a polyphonic "world ecocriticism."

ECOCRITICISM IN CHINA: INADEQUACY AND FUTURE

In an interview with Scott Slovic, I praise his *Going Away to Think*, translated by me and published by Beijing University Press in 2010, as one of the first three American ecocritical works for a Chinese readership (the other two being Glen Love's *Practical Ecocriticism* [trans. by Hu Zhihong] and Buell's *The Future for Environmental Criticism* [trans. by Liu Bei]). From it, I extract four important crossings, namely: "out of text—crossing the critical object" (advancing critical practice beyond literary researches); "out of genre—crossing the critical style" (namely, so-called "narrative scholarship"); "out of [the] discipline—crossing the critical theory" (taking other fields of humanities and even scientific studies into consideration); and, no doubt, "out of [the] study—crossing the critical responsibility" (appearing as activists and public intellectuals) (2). The spirit and courage of "crossing" are what many Chinese ecocritics want and have to learn from, and I agree with Hu Zhihong's criticism of Chinese ecocriticism for its current limitations.

First, though, there is an energetic effort such as Liu Bei's to evoke a multi-disciplinary context, which is to her, after all, "a universal ecological discipline" (24), Chinese ecocritics are less inclined to cross disciplines, and consequently have difficulties interpreting the kinship between man and nature or critiquing anti-ecological elements in human civilizations from a broader, more multi-disciplinary perspective. In contrast, Western ecocritical writing is often such an inclusive effort as to bring philosophy, ethics, politics, theology, psychology, law, and anthropology into its vision. Moreover, scientific disciplines like physics, modern ecology, and chemistry are also frequently referenced, partly because a number of American ecocritics have been academically trained in double fields of humanities and science.

Second, Chinese ecocriticism is supposed to be more cross-cultural in order to be more vigorous and resourceful. The "culture" here does not refer to that from abroad but also that from other aspects of domestic tradition, and yet neither should be regarded as a flat and monotonous unit. The import of foreign ecological resources might also take, for instance, Indian holism into consideration, as another oriental otherness used to deconstruct dualism. And as to Chinese traditional ideology, Taoism has been far more stressed than Confucianism, while Western sinologists have already observed how valuable the latter might be to the contemporary green movement, as illustrated in *Confucianism and Ecology* as a project of the Harvard series of "Religions of the World and Ecology," in which Tu Weiming's contributions ("Beyond the Enlightenment Mentality" and "The Continuity of Being: Chinese Visions of Nature") suggest forcefully the potential of what Confucianism can do.

Third, many an ecocritic is too ambitious to cross "theory" into the "lower" field of critical practice, which undoubtedly is the most vital activity of ecocriticism. To provide evidence I have searched the China National Knowledge Infrastructure (CNKI) for articles published from 2000 to 2009 whose titles contain the keywords "ecocriticism" and "ecocritical," and I have found eighty; the following table provides an elementary analysis.

focuses	numbers	percentages
reports and reviews of ecocriticism as a Western movement	25	31 percent
reports and reviews of ecocriticism as a Chinese movement	2	3 percent
reports and reviews of ecocriticism as a universal critical tool	26	33 percent
comparative studies of the Chinese acceptance of ecocriticism	7	8 percent
case studies on Western texts	16	20 percent
case studies on Chinese texts	3	4 percent
comparative case studies on Chinese–Western texts	1	1 percent
total	80	100.00 percent

There are other important articles not included in CNKI, and there are other ecocritical works without the two keywords in their titles, yet I argue that these sample statistics represent in general the academic interest of Chinese ecocritics. Among the possible number of conclusions, one point may demonstrate that grander descriptions and views about ecocriticism are the major interest (75 percent), while case studies on specific texts take up merely a quarter of the publications. Chinese texts draw the attention of only three articles. There is so much yet to be done, but so much that we can do in the broad prospect of the future of ecocriticism.

Finally, it is worth noting that, despite all those wise Taoist remarks about eco-philosophy and ethics, massive construction projects have been a regular feature of Chinese history. In reality, before undergoing modernization, China's ecological resources had already suffered serious damage, and the gulf between idealism and reality was widespread. How to mobilize China's relatively disconnected pieces of ecological thought into a critical force is the central task in the modernization of Chinese environmental discourse. Wang Nuo, another pioneer ecocritic, thinks it highly urgent that ecocritical studies address Chinese ecological crisis: "Ecocriticism cannot be confined to disciplinary construction and theoretical self-sufficiency, [n]or to pure scholarship and obscurity" (236). Thus, the construction of a practical and open Chinese ecocriticism will not only facilitate exchange and complementarity between China and the West, but it will also provide a green platform and a successful new paradigm in the dialogue between Chinese and Western literary theory.

Notes

1. Hu Zhihong takes Li Xinfu's "On Eco-aesthetics" (in *Nanjing Social Science*, Vol. 12) and She Zhengrong's "Philosophical Reflections on Ecological Beauty" (in *Studies of Natural Dialectics*, Vol. 8), both published in 1994, as the beginning of Chinese ecocriticism. See his *Studies of Western Ecocriticism*, Beijing: China Social Sciences Press, 2006, pp. 352–3.

2. Other important summarizations of ecocriticism include Wang Yuechuan's delineation, which I generalize as follows: 1) interaction of culture and nature; 2) revision of literary canon; 3) political correctness; 4) cross-disciplinary studies; 5) ecological cultural spirit; and 6) double visions of life and earth (138–39).

Works Cited

Cheng, Hong. *Return to the Wilderness*, Beijing: Sdxjoint Publishing Company, 2001.

Chen, Hong. *Bestiality, Animality, and Humanity*, Wuhan: Huazhong Normal University Press, 2005.

Hu, Zhihong. *Studies of Western Ecocriticism*, Beijing: China Social Sciences Press, 2006.

Liu, Bei. "Ecocriticism in a Cross-disciplinary Vision." *Jiangxi Social Sciences*, *257*, no. 4 (April 2008): 23–26.

Liu, Wenliang. *Ecocriticism: Category and Methodology*. Beijing: People's Publishing House, 2009.

Lu, Shuyuan. "Land and Rainbow." *Journal of Literature and Art*, July 11, 1987.

Lu, Shuyuan "The Spiritual Level of Literary Criticism." *Theoretical Studies of Literature and Art*, no. 3, (1996): 80.

Lu, Shuyuan. *Ecological Research in Literature and Art*. Xi'an: Shanxi People's Education Publishing House, 2000.

Lu, Shuyuan. *The Space for Ecocriticism*. Shanghai: East China Normal University Press, 2006.

Lu, Shuyuan "Meaning of 'Nature' in the Perspective of Eco-criticism." *Journal of Guangxi University for Nationalities* (Philosophy and Social Science Edition), *31*, no. 3 (May, 2009): 8–16.

Slovic, Scott. *Going away to Think*. Reno: University of Nevada Press, 2008.

Tucker, Mary Evelyn, and Berthrong, John, eds. *Confucianism and Ecology*, Cambridge, MA: Harvard University Press, 1998.

Wang, Ning. *The Transcendence of Postmodernism*. Beijing: The People's Literature Publishing House, 2002.

——. "Ecocriticism and the Construction of Literary Eco-environmental Ethics." *Journal of SJTU (Philosophy and Social Sciences)*, *17*, no. 3 (Summer 2009): 5–12.

——. "Toward a literary environmental ethics: a reflection on eco-criticism." *Neohelicon*, *36* (November 2009):289–98.

Wang, Nuo. *Euro-American Ecocriticism*, Shanghai: Xuelin Press, 2008.

Wang, Yuechuan. "The Contemporary Value of Ecological Literature and Ecological Criticism." *Journal of Beijing University* (Philosophy and Social Sciences), *46*, no. 2 (March 2009): 130–42.

Wei, Qingqi. "Opening Ecocriticism's Sino-America Dialogue: An Interview with Lawrence Buell." *Tamkang Review 36*, no. 3 (Spring 2006):76–90.

———. "Eco-critics' Responsibility: An Interview with Scott Slovic on His Going away to Think." *Foreign Literature Studies*, *31*, no. 4 (August 2009): 1–11.

Yu, Mouchang. *Ecological Philosophy*. Xi'an: Shanxi People's Education Publishing House, 2000.

Zeng, Fanren. "Western Modern Literary Ecocriticism: Generation, Growth and Basic Principles." *Journal of Yantai University* (Philosophy and Social Science), 22, no. 3 (July 2009): 39–43.

Zeng, Fanren. *On Eco-ontological Aesthetics*. Changchun: Jilin People's Publishing House, 2003.

....

CHAPTER 33

GERMAN ECOCRITICISM

An Overview[1]

....

AXEL GOODBODY

THE contrast between the largely enthusiastic response to ecocriticism in the Anglophone academy and its relative invisibility in the German-speaking world is a puzzle. Why has it yet to gain wider recognition as a field of literary study in Germany, Austria, and Switzerland, countries in whose philosophy and cultural tradition nature features so prominently, whose people are shown by international surveys of public opinion to show a high degree of environmental concern, and where environmental issues rank consistently high on the political agenda? One reason may be that German scientists, political thinkers, and philosophers have been pioneers in ecology since Alexander von Humboldt and Ernst Haeckel, and nonfiction books have served as the primary medium of public debate on environmental issues in Germany. There has been a wealth of twentieth-century ecological thinking rooted in phenomenology (from Martin Heidegger to Gernot and Hartmut Böhme), classical humanism (from Erich Fromm to Hans Jonas and Klaus Meyer-Abich) and social theory (from the Frankfurt School to Ulrich Beck). But German literary writing has had a more limited impact on environmental discourse and public attitudes, at home as well as abroad.

Although most major writers over the last forty years (including Christa Wolf, Hans Magnus Enzensberger, and the three recent Nobel prize winners Günter Grass, Herta Müller, and Elfriede Jelinek) have treated environmental issues at some point in their work, relatively few important novels (or films) have foregrounded environmental issues in Germany since a brief period in the early to mid 1980s. The one German writer whose thinking on the environment enjoys global recognition is in fact Johann Wolfgang von Goethe, who wrote during the Romantic period.[2] Even the "Culture and Climate" project launched by the Goethe Institute in 2009 as a special thematic focus of their work in representing German cultural interests abroad is mainly concerned with artists, photographers, film makers, and performance artists, rather than with writers. Nature and environment have certainly been prominent concerns in twentieth-century German art (from the artists of the Worpswede colony and Expressionism in the early

1900s to Joseph Beuys and Friedensreich Hundertwasser), and arguably also in film (if one considers German mountain films, the Heimat film, Werner Herzog's oeuvre, and the many nature documentaries and regional landscape films shown on TV in recent years).[3] However, it remains a notable fact that artists and film makers are currently considered so much better able than German writers to assist the public in reflecting on the human causes of climate change and imagining its consequences.

A second reason for the reluctance of literary scholars in Germany to engage in environmentally focused criticism has been the legacy of suspicion regarding "irrational" feeling for nature after 1945. Into the 1980s and beyond it was common for these to seek to distance themselves from the *völkisch* (i.e., racist-nationalist) thinking that emerged towards the end of the nineteenth century and culminated in the Nazis' cult of blood and soil, and to distrust the links between nature and national identity which are often encountered elsewhere. The racially inflected ideological loading of German thinking on nature that was fed by prominent literary historians and critics in the 1930s appeared to some to be echoed in core thematic concerns of ecocritics such as nature conservation and place belonging. When the environmental movement emerged in Germany in the early 1970s, about a decade later than in the United States, its blend of (sometimes oversimplified) rational arguments with emotionally charged opposition to materialist values and what were perceived as high-risk technologies, its apocalyptic rhetoric seemed to skeptical academics a potentially dangerous throwback to Romantic and turn-of-the-century forms of antimodernism.

Environmental history has, however, flourished in Germany since the 1980s. Scholars in both Europe and America have subjected shifting attitudes towards nature and conceptions of appropriate management of the environment in the German-speaking countries to extensive critical analysis.[4] More specialized studies have tended to focus on either the Heimat (homeland) and back-to-nature youth movements at the turn of the twentieth century,[5] the Third Reich,[6] or the environmental movement.[7] Environmental history has emerged as a field embracing elements of the history of ideas and cultural history alongside political and social history, and cultural geography. In some instances, literary history has been subsumed into historical accounts of German culture and society: literary and artistic representations have been drawn on in a series of monographs and collections of essays.[8] At the same time, important work has been conducted by German philosophers, reviewing shifting understandings of nature,[9] and exploring environmental ethics[10] and aesthetics.[11] Linguists, media studies specialists, psychologists, sociologists, ethnologists, and political theorists have all produced further work of relevance to ecocritics. It is not, however, possible to do justice to the contribution of these disciplines to the ecocritical cause within the scope of this chapter.[12]

The contrast is striking between this wealth of ecocritical work in the broader sense and the relatively few scholars of German literature who have, as already indicated, chosen to address environmental themes directly. (Fewer still have labelled their work "ecocritical"). A high proportion are, moreover, *Auslandsgermanisten*, or scholars working abroad (e.g., Jost Hermand, Bernhard Malkmus, Heather Sullivan, and Sabine Wilke in the United States, Kate Rigby in Australia, Axel Goodbody, and Colin Riordan in the

United Kingdom, Serenella Iovino in Italy, and Nevzat Kaya in Turkey). Germans who have made significant contributions to ecocritical studies such as Hannes Bergthaller, Catrin Gersdorf, Christa Grewe-Volpp, Sylvia Mayer, and Hubert Zapf have generally been working on American or British literature, and the first ecocritical conference in Germany, at which ASLE's European affiliate (European Association for the Study of Literature, Culture, and Environment) was founded, was hosted by the English Department of the University of Münster in 2004.

English—more precisely American—studies have then led the way in introducing literary ecocriticism in Germany. (The discipline had earlier performed a similar role with postcolonialism.) However, this should be understood as a reflection of the sedimentation of national historical experience in cultural difference, rather than as an indication that mainstream literature departments in Germany have nothing to contribute to environmentally oriented literary scholarship. The cultural difference is present on several levels. First, there are the differences between the linguistic repertoires and the resonances that individual terms such as 'environment' possess. Then there are discrepancies between the relative importance of literary writing on particular themes and in particular genres: for instance, depictions of wilderness are less common than those of "cultural landscape," and nature writing plays a much less significant role in German than in American cultural tradition. Indeed, it is not recognized as a genre. Last but not least, there are asymmetries in academic discourse and its philosophical underpinning, in the constellation of schools of thought and rival theoretical approaches, and in the emergence of concepts, categorizations, research questions and approaches. All these factors have led to the pursuit of different trends in cultural theory.

However, the fact that Ansgar Nünning's influential *Metzler Lexikon Literatur- und Kulturtheorie* has contained an entry on "Ecocriticism" since its second edition (Heise 2001) may be seen as an indication that the approach is no longer entirely unknown to German students of literary theory. Indeed, German ecocriticism has slowly begun to gain international recognition. German contributions to nature philosophy, ecological thinking, and the study of the investment of nature with symbolic meaning in popular culture have been widely acknowledged abroad (see Worster 1977, Harrison 1992, Schama 1995), and Timothy Clark's recent introduction to literature and the environment (Clark 2011) discusses (for the first time in an English book of its kind) a work of German environmental writing and cites German ecocritics. As well as presenting Wilhelm Raabe's novella *Pfister's Mill* (1884) as a pioneering work of ecojustice (pp. 96–98), Clark examines Heidegger's critique of modern technology (pp. 55–60), Gernot Böhme's aesthetics (pp. 81–82), and Hubert Zapf's theory of literature as cultural ecology (pp. 153–155).

Without conceiving of themselves as ecocritics, German literary scholars have long explored the rich field of German literary, artistic, and cultural representations of our relationship with the natural environment; asked what contribution novelists, essayists, dramatists and poets, film directors and artists have made to reconceiving it and imagining alternatives; and analyzed their modes of production and adaptation of cultural tradition. This work includes articles and books which appeared already in the

1960s and 1970s on Baroque idylls (Garber 1974), physico-theology, and its reflection in eighteenth-century nature poetry (Ketelsen 1974), Goethe's conception of nature (Zimmermann 1969), Romantic nature imagery (von Bormann 1968), and modern nature poetry (Hans Dieter Schäfer 1969). Then in the late 1970s the first anthologies of environmental literature appeared, and with them pioneering articles approaching texts in the literary canon from a position of environmentalist concern: Leo Kreutzer called for a new reading of Goethe's nature poems (1978), and Horst Denkler drew attention to Raabe's aforementioned *Pfister's Mill* as an early example of reflection on the social and cultural consequences of industrial pollution (Denkler 1980). From the early 1980s onwards a range of studies followed, such as Herles's account of the human/nature relationship in novels since 1945 (1982), Haupt's study of twentieth-century German nature poetry (1982), and Knabe's (1985) and Mallinckrodt's (1987) article and book on representations of the impact of industrialization in East German novels.[13]

A list of genuinely ecocritical titles, in the stricter sense of being substantially focused on either German literature or literary theory and driven by concern for the environment, would be confined to a dozen monographs and a roughly equal number of edited volumes. The first of these might be seen as Reinhold Grimm and Jost Hermand's collection of essays on literary representations of nature and naturalness (1981). Hermand followed this with a ground-breaking monograph, *Grüne Utopien in Deutschland* (1991), a paperback written for a general readership, which reviewed Green thinking in Germany since Rousseau from an ecosocialist standpoint. Discussing canonical fiction and poetry, and many forgotten authors, alongside essays and political manifestos, Hermand revealed the richness of the intellectual tradition on which contemporary writers associated with the environmental movement could draw.

The first scholar working in Germany to publish a book-length study of ecocriticism, this time from the perspective of literary tradition rather than the history of ideas, was Gerhard Kaiser. *Mutter Natur und die Dampfmaschine* (1991) examined the idealization of nature which accompanied the growing scientific objectivization and technological domination of the natural world as a complementary phenomenon in the early nineteenth century, and argued that literary texts (by Goethe, Keller, and Raabe) played a key role in promoting the influential figure of "mother nature." The first significant publication in English was a collection of essays *Green Thought in German Culture*, edited by Colin Riordan in 1997, which resulted from a conference of British Germanists in Swansea. This volume combined a historical overview with contributions on the environmental movement in the early twentieth century, ecological dimensions of critical theory, new age religiosity and right wing politics, and essays on West and East German writing, Swiss literature, and art and film. The literary production of the Bavarian novelist, cultural commentator and Green thinker and activist Carl Amery was the principal focus of a further multidisciplinary essay volume, *The Culture of German Environmentalism* (Goodbody 2002). This juxtaposed accounts of the history, sociological make-up, and theoretical foundations of the environmental movement since the 1970s with contributions on German journalism, literature and film.

The Australian Germanist and Comparativist Kate Rigby had meanwhile presented a masterly comparative account of the German and English Romantics' understanding of humanity's place in the natural world in *Topographies of the Sacred* (2004). Rigby showed how Goethe, Novalis, Tieck, and Eichendorff registered and reflected on the dual impoverishment of humanity which resulted from the demand we close off our imagination and capacity for empathy with natural others, and from relegation of the corporeal aspect of the self to mechanical nature. Their work is placed in the context of continental Romantic philosophers and their English contemporaries. Building on Jonathan Bate's *Song of the Earth* and informed by post-Heideggerian readings, Rigby confirms the importance of conceptions of dwelling for ecocritical analysis, while introducing significant modifications.[14]

The years 2005 and 2006 saw the publication of two significant volumes of papers from the first conference on ecocriticism in Germany. *Natur—Kultur—Text* (Gersdorf/Mayer 2005) and *Nature in Literary and Cultural Studies* (Gersdorf/Mayer 2006) combined explorations of ecocritical theory with textual analysis. The former contained an introduction to ecocritical theory for German-speaking readers, and essays (in German) on cultural theory, environmental communication and German authors since Kleist. The English language volume opened with an introduction to ecocriticism foregrounding the theory of cultural ecology. The essays which followed are mainly on American literature, but contributions from Riordan, Meacher, Griffiths, and Goodbody address German texts.[15] Stefan Hofer's exposition of an ecocritical systems theory, a longer study published in 2007, drew on Niklas Luhmann to provide a theoretical grounding in the social function of literature that was lacking in previous ecocritical scholarship. Luhmann's insistence on the separateness of the political, economic, legal, and cultural systems in society, and their relative inability to influence each other, is conceived as a way of avoiding normative arguments and the trap of relying on moral exhortation to solve environmental problems. Bergthaller (2011) has recently presented an English language version of this systems theory approach.

Axel Goodbody's book *Nature, Technology and Cultural Change in 20th-Century German Literature* (2007) opens with an introduction on nature and environment in German culture, and American, British and German ecocritical approaches, followed by a chapter on Goethe's legacy. The book then traces the shifts in attitudes towards the environment over the course of the twentieth century through comparative studies of works on four themes: technological disasters, dwelling, hunting, and the city. A more recent collection, *Ökologische Transformationen und literarische Repräsentationen* (Ermisch 2010) contains essays originating in a symposium held by German literature specialists (with the support of environmental historians) at the University of Göttingen. It may be seen as marking the final acceptance of ecocriticism in mainstream German literary studies.[16] The volume brings together closely argued contributions on classical, early modern, and contemporary authors, and on genres ranging from poetry and nature writing to children's literature and ecofiction.[17]

In Germany as elsewhere, pastoral and apocalypse have served as key modes of cultural production in representations of the environment. The *Heimat* (or homeland) was redefined and local belonging rehabilitated in the 1970s in the context of the environ-mental movement. Novels and films such as Edgar Reitz's *Heimat* (which has developed into a fifty-three-hour epic since its first series in 1984, tracing life in a rural village from 1919 through to 2000) have reflected this process. Critical studies of Heimat and its liter-ary and visual representation[18] have increasingly included reflection on the role played by place-belonging in the motivation to lead a sustainable way of life.[19] Literary topog-raphy has emerged as a related focus for German contributions to ecology-oriented research. Representations of landscape as a repository of historical experience (the emphasis being normally on political violence and destruction of the environment) in the work of Wolf and Sebald, and of the Austrian writers Bachmann, Bernhard, Handke, and Jelinek, have for instance been subjected to critical analysis.[20]

Studies of literature in the apocalyptic mode since the 1980s have focused increas-ingly on the representation of environmental catastrophes.[21] Climate change has led to an upsurge of interest in the topic in the last few years (see Dürbeck 2012 and Mauch/ Mayer 2012). Climate change in German literature is also an area of interest of the "Climate Culture" group led by Claus Leggewie at the Institute for Advanced Studies in the Humanities in Essen, and a strand of the Environmental Humanities Transatlantic Research Network funded by the Humboldt Foundation and led by Sabine Wilke in Seattle.

Representations of and reflections on natural disasters, instances of human destruc-tion, and natural processes of decay have been a feature of German writing since the Second World War from Arno Schmidt to W.G. Sebald, and Sebald's richly complex work (especially his long poem *After Nature* and account of a walking tour in Sussex, *The Rings of Saturn*) has served as a nexus of interest for ecocritics, scholars of cultural mem-ory, travel writing, autobiography, and Holocaust literature.[22] Environmental justice and environmental racism issues have been addressed obliquely in Germany through depic-tions of the deterritorialization and dispossession of the Jews, resulting in an ecocritical dimension to some work in the field of Holocaust studies. In Sebald, there is a further link between the two subjects: the narrator's distinctive position on the margins, seek-ing tactful identification with his Jewish protagonists, is echoed in the way Sebald gives voice to animals and nature as victims of wanton human destruction. In one of the most thought-provoking ecocritically oriented contributions to the body of Sebald scholar-ship that has grown so rapidly since the author's untimely death in 2001, *On Creaturely Life* (2006), Eric Santner takes up Agamben's redefinition of the theological concept of the "creature" as a biopolitical category, where the human is reduced to a state of passiv-ity, of being perpetually created, under the traumatic conditions of arbitrary sovereign rule and institutional violence in modernity. Santner reads Sebald's prose as a site for exploration of the realm of creaturely suffering in the aftermath of the Holocaust.

An overview of this kind would not be complete without seeking to give a more general picture of developments in ecocritical theory in Germany and to identify the German contribution. In the spread of the approach from the Anglophone world to other countries and academic communities over the past decade, German scholars have, like those elsewhere, frequently drawn on locally predominant traditions, diversifying and enriching the ecological approach in the process. German theoretical debates in the 1970s and 1980s were dominated less by postmodernism and poststructuralism than by hermeneutics, drawing on Gadamer, Frankfurt School Neo-Marxist approaches indebted to Adorno and Benjamin, and cultural anthropology (especially Wolfgang Iser's reception theory and Jan and Aleida Assmann's work on cultural memory). It is only natural that German ecocriticism should have been influenced by these currents of thought.

Timo Müller has recently (2011) argued that two of the principal models of German ecocritical theory today have their roots in literary anthropology.[23] In the 1980s, Wolfgang Iser developed a conception of the function of literary texts as lying in their potential to contrast everyday experiences with possible fictional alternatives, permitting readers to develop and modify their self-understanding in a process of imaginative boundary-crossing. Gernot and Hartmut Böhme subsequently thought through the ecological consequences of this approach. Their "aesthetics of nature" is grounded in traditional liberal humanism, but inflects it by the idea of a special sensibility allowing human beings to reconnect to nature.

In order to establish new, nonhierarchical relations with nature, the Böhmes argue, we need to revisit premodern, symbiotic conceptions of the human being in its natural environment, such as Paracelsus's idea of a symbolic "language of nature." This may have been superseded in the natural sciences, but it has remained a productive force in the history of ideas, contributing to both literature (Novalis, Baudelaire, and much twentieth-century nature poetry), and philosophy (Kant, Benjamin, Adorno, and Blumenberg). Moreover, they claim that it is through our bodily feelings and reactions to the environment that we enter into communication with the objective world.[24] Traces of bodily experience are present in all language, but most palpable in poetic texts working with metaphors and images, hence literature's special role as a medium facilitating reconnection with nature. In an age of environmental destruction, the cultural archive of literary texts is a resource whose potential should not be overlooked in strategies of renaturalization. Literature records and stores information about how societies position themselves within nature, giving voice to aspects of culture which are otherwise excluded and silenced, such as women, "uncivilized" peoples, and the physical world. The survival of the human race depends on the reinstitution of threatened sensibilities as a high priority. Hartmut Böhme links this role of literature, art and aesthetics in facilitating human survival with a conception of nature as a "cultural project" (Böhme/Matussek/Müller 2000, 118–131). We must accept responsibility for shaping it, in the knowledge that our control over it is not unlimited. Works of art can both serve as aesthetic models of human interaction with nature, and imagine and represent utopian alternatives to contemporary patterns of behavior.

The second significant contribution to ecocritical theory, Hubert Zapf's fusion of cultural ecology and textual criticism, regards literary texts as capable of revitalizing the cultural system, by condensing and transforming elements of public discourse in nodal constructs such as symbols and metaphors. Whereas Böhme remains subject-centered in his attempt to overcome the problems associated with anthropocentrism, Zapf adopts a systemic approach, asking what function culture performs within society. He distinguishes between three equally important discursive functions of literature in his model of literature as a medium of cultural ecology: a culture-critical, an imaginative, and a reintegrative function (Zapf 2002, 33–39). First, literature draws attention to oppressive structures of the cultural system. Second, it gives voice to what these structures suppress, and provides a testing-ground for alternative forms of cultural organization. And finally, it has a unique capacity to address the whole person and cross boundaries between otherwise divided social systems and discourses. The cultural impact of literary texts derives above all from their symbolic and metaphorical condensation of information.

How then might the achievements and contribution of German ecocriticism to date be summed up? Perhaps by saying that it has drawn on and explicated a body of thought which shares much with American and British culture, but nevertheless differs in possibly instructive ways. Through theoretically informed interdisciplinarity and intercultural comparisons, it has also added to the range of perspectives and methodologies in the toolkit of the international community of scholars. My starting point was the fact that literary criticism appears to have played a less prominent role in humanities debates on sustainability in Germany than in the United States, and that this may be a reflection of the dominance of philosophical, ethical, historical, political and social discourses, and the relatively modest volume and status of German literary writing on the environment. Must eco-thinking necessarily be centered on literature? Perhaps there are special historical and cultural reasons why this is so in the United States, and it should be regarded as the exception rather than the rule.

Notes

1. My thanks go to Gabriele Dürbeck, Agnes Kneitz, Bernhard Malkmus, Ute Seiderer, Berbeli Wanning, and Evi Zemanek, who commented on a draft of this essay. Without their help it would have been considerably less well informed.
2. See for instance Seamon/Zajonc 1998, which brings together essays on the "ecological" views in Goethe's science, and its contemporary use (see especially Nigel Hoffmann's essay, "The Unity of Science and Art: Goethean Phenomenology as a New Ecological Discipline," pp. 129–176). Peter Smith's work is also relevant in this context (e.g., Smith 2000).
3. Studies of German environmental and landscape art include Finlay 1997 and Jael Lehmann 2012. Relevant work on German film includes studies of the mountain film (Rentschler 1990), the rural Heimat film (Palfreyman 2002, von Moltke 2005), and the films of Werner Herzog (Gandy 1996).
4. E.g., Lekan 2004, Mauch 2004, Blackbourn 2006.
5. Rollins 1997.
6. Biehl/Staudenmaier 1995, Brüggemeier/Cioc/Zeller 2005.
7. Dominick 1992, Radkau 2011.
8. Sieferle 1984, Groh/Groh 1991 and 1996, Kirchhoff/Trepl 2009.
9. Rapp 1981, Gernot Böhme 1992, Lothar Schäfer 1993, Wilke 1993.
10. Krebs 1999.

11. Gernot Böhme 1989, Vietta 1995, Seel 1997.
12. The institutional context is a factor in literary ecocriticism's emergence in Germany as a branch of cultural studies, rather than as an autonomous field of literary enquiry, and its strong links with other humanities disciplines. The Rachel Carson Centre in Munich is a key site of interdisciplinary ecocritical study today. Founded in 2009 as a joint initiative of the University of Munich and the Deutsches Museum (Germany's national museum of technology), the RCC is concerned with all aspects of interaction between human agents and nature. Seeking to strengthen the role of the humanities in current political and scientific debates about the environment, it is led by historians, but includes among its affiliates scholars of literature and film such as Sylvia Mayer, Agnes Kneitz, and Alexa Weik.
13. Programmatic statements on the necessity of examining literary representations of the natural environment followed in the late eighties and nineties (Hartmut Böhme 1988 and 1994, Hermand 1997).
14. Heather Sullivan is responsible for further innovative ecocritical work on Goethe and the Romantics—see Sullivan 2003 and 2010.
15. Unpublished doctoral theses by Hope, Meacher, and Griffiths, and Andrew Liston's book study of contemporary Swiss writing (2011) are further examples of British Germanist ecocriticism. The Swiss literary tradition, in which Alpine landscapes have served as a focus for reflections on the sublime, the simple life and the detrimental impact of modernisation, has also been the subject of studies including Barkhoff 1997 and Ireton/Schaumann 2012.
16. Principal organiser of the symposium was Heinrich Detering, whose longstanding interest in the subtleties of literary reflection of environmental issues is evidenced by Detering 1992 and 2008.
17. Genres of popular prose writing which have attracted critical attention include the eco-thriller (Wanning 2008), science fiction (Stapleton 1993), and risk narratives (Heise 2008, Zemanek 2012).
18. Blickle 1992, Boa/Palfreyman 2000.
19. Goodbody 2013.
20. Key studies of German literary topography include Weigel 1996, Hartmut Böhme 2005, and Webber 2008.
21. For instance Groh/Kemper/Mauleshagen 2003 and Rigby 2008.
22. Publications on nature in Sebald's writing include Fuchs 2007 and Malkmus 2011.
23. This is not to deny that other aspects of literary theory widely engaged with by German scholars (e.g., Marxism and psychoanalysis) possess an ecocritical dimension. However, there has been a notable absence of ecofeminist contributions, and while Heidegger remains a key point of reference for international ecocritics, his critique of technology is rarely cited as a model by German literary critics.
24. Gernot Böhme's theory of "atmospheres" (see Rigby 2011) is the principal form in which phenomenology is present in German ecocritical theory.

REFERENCES

Barkhoff, Jürgen, "Green Thought in Modern Swiss Literature," in Riordan 1997, 223–241.
Bergthaller, Hannes, "Cybernetics and Social Systems Theory," in Goodbody and Rigby 2011, 217–229.

Biehl, Janet and Peter Staudenmaier, *Ecofascism. Lessons from the German Experience*, Edinburgh and San Francisco: AK Press 1995.

Blackbourn, David, *The Conquest of Nature. Water, Landscape, and the Making of Modern Germany*, London: Jonathan Cape 2006.

Blickle, Peter, *Heimat. A Critical Theory of the German Idea of Homeland*, Rochester, NY: Camden House 1992.

Boa, Elizabeth and Rachel Palfreyman, *Heimat. A German Dream. Regional Loyalties and National Identity in German Culture 1890–1990*, Oxford: Oxford University Press 2000.

Böhme, Gernot, *Für eine ökologische Naturästhetik*, Frankfurt am Main: Suhrkamp 1989.

—— *Natürlich Natur. Über Natur im Zeitalter ihrer technischen Reproduzierbarkeit*, Frankfurt am Main: Suhrkamp 1992.

Böhme, Hartmut (ed.), *Kulturgeschichte des Wassers*, Frankfurt: Suhrkamp 1988.

—— "Literaturwissenschaft in der Herausforderung der technischen und ökologischen Welt," in Ludwig Jäger and Bernd Switalla (eds.), *Germanistik in der Mediengesellschaft*, Munich: Fink 1994, 63–79.

—— (ed.), *Topographien der Literatur: Deutsche Literatur im transnationalen Kontext*, Stuttgart: Metzler 2005.

Böhme, Hartmut, Peter Matussek, and Lothar Müller, *Orientierung Kulturwissenschaft. Was sie kann, was sie will*, Reinbek bei Hamburg: Rowohlt 2000.

Brüggemeier, Franz-Josef, Mark Cioc, and Thomas Zeller (ed.), *How Green Were the Nazis? Nature, Environment, and Nation in the Third Reich*, Athens, GA: Ohio University Press 2005.

Clark, Timothy, *The Cambridge Introduction to Literature and the Environment*, Cambridge: Cambridge University Press 2011.

Denkler, Horst, "Nachwort," in *Wilhelm Raabe. Pfisters Mühle. Ein Sommerferienheft*, Stuttgart: Reclam 1980, 225–251.

Detering, Heinrich, "Ökologische Krise und ästhetische Innovation im Werk Wilhelm Raabes," *Jahrbuch der Raabe-Gesellschaft* 1992, 1–27.

—— "'So könnte die Welt untergehen': Ökologie und Literatur im 18. Jahrhundert,'" *Lichtenberg-Jahrbuch* 2008, 7–20.

Dominick, Raymond H., *The Environmental Movement in Germany. Prophets and Pioneers, 1871–1971*, Bloomington; Indianapolis: Indiana University Press 1992.

Dürbeck, Gabriele, "Popular Science and Apocalyptic Narrative in Frank Schätzing's The Swarm," *Ecozon@ 3:1* Spring 2012: 20–30.

Ermisch, Maren, Ulrike Kruse, and Urte Stobbe (eds.), *Ökologische Repräsentationen und literarische Repräsentationen. Veröffentlichungen des Graduiertenkollegs Interdisziplinäre Umweltgeschichte*, Göttingen: Universitätsverlag Göttingen 2010.

Finlay, Frank, "Joseph Beuys' Eco-Aesthetics," in Riordan 1997, 245–258.

Fuchs, Anne, "'Ein Hauptkapitel der Geschichte der Unterwerfung': Representations of Nature in W.G. Sebald's *Die Ringe des Saturn*,'" in Anne Fuchs and J. J. Long (ed.), *W.G. Sebald and the Writing of History*. Würzburg: Königshausen and Neumann 2007, 121–138.

Gandy, Matthew, "Visions of Darkness: The Representation of Nature in the Films of Werner Herzog," *Ecumene 3:1* (1996), 1–21.

Garber, Klaus, *Der locus amoenus und der locus terribilis. Bild und Funktion der Natur in der deutschen Schäfer- und Landlebendichtung des 17. Jahrhunderts*, Cologne and Vienna: Böhlau 1974.

Gersdorf, Catrin and Sylvia Mayer (ed.), *Natur—Kultur—Text. Beiträge zu Ökologie und Literaturwissenschaft*, Heidelberg: Universitätsverlag Winter 2005.

—— (ed.), *Nature in Literary and Cultural Studies. Transatlantic Conversations on Ecocriticism*, Amsterdam and New York: Rodopi 2006.

Goodbody, Axel (ed.), *The Culture of German Environmentalism. Anxieties, Visions, Realities*, New York and Oxford: Berghahn 2002.

—— *Nature, Technology and Cultural Change in Twentieth-Century German Literature. The Challenge of Ecocriticism*. Basingstoke: Palgrave Macmillan 2007.

—— "Heimat als Identität und ökologisches Bewusstsein stiftender Faktor: Zu Ansätzen in Romanen um 1900 von Bruno Wille, Hermann Hesse und Josef Ponten," in Adam Paulsen and Anna Sandberg (eds.), *Natur und Moderne um 1900*, Bielefeld: Transcript 2013.

Goodbody, Axel and Kate Rigby (ed.), *Ecocritical Theory: New European Contributions*. Charlottesville and London: University of Virginia Press 2011.

Grimm, Reinhold and Jost Hermand (ed.), *Natur und Natürlichkeit. Stationen des Grünen in der deutschen Literatur*, Königstein im Taunus: Athenäum 1981.

Groh, Dieter, Michael Kempe, and Franz Mauleshagen (eds.), *Naturkatastrophen: Beiträge zu ihrer Deutung, Wahrnehmung und Darstellung in Text und Bild von der Antike bis ins 20. Jahrhundert*, Tübingen: Gunter Narr 2003.

Groh, Ruth and Dieter Groh, *ZurKulturgeschichte der Natur* (2 vols), Frankfurt am Main: Suhrkamp 1991 and 1996.

Harrison, Robert Pogue, *Forests. The Shadow of Civilization*, Chicago and London: University of Chicago Press, 1992.

Haupt, Jürgen, *Natur und Lyrik. Naturbeziehungen im 20. Jahrhundert*, Stuttgart: Metzler 1982.

Heise, Ursula, "Ecocriticism/Ökokritik," in Ansgar Nünning (ed.), *Metzler Lexikon Literatur- und Kulturtheorie*, Stuttgart and Weimar: Metzler, 2nd ed. 2001, 128–129.

—— *Sense of Place and Sense of Planet: The Environmental Imagination of the Global*, Oxford: Oxford University Press 2008.

Herles, Wolfgang, *Der Beziehungswandel zwischen Mensch und Natur im Spiegel der deutschen Literatur seit 1945*, Stuttgart: Heinz 1982.

Hermand, Jost, *Grüne Utopien in Deutschland. Zur Geschichte des ökologischen Bewusstseins*, Frankfurt am Main: Fischer 1991.

—— "Literaturwissenschaft und ökologisches Bewußtsein. Eine mühsame Verflechtung," in Anne Bentfeld and Walter Delabar (ed.), *Perspektiven der Germanistik. Neueste Ansichten zu einem alten Problem*, Opladen: Westdeutscher Verlag 1997, 106–125.

Hofer, Stefan, *Die Ökologie der Literatur. Eine systemtheoretische Annäherung. Mit einer Studie zu Werken Peter Handkes*, Bielefeld: Transcript 2007.

Ireton, Sean and Caroline Schaumann (ed.), *Heights of Reflection. Mountains in the German Imagination from the Middle Ages to the Twenty-First Century*, Rochester, NY: Camden House 2012.

Jael Lehmann, Annette, *Environments: Künste Medien Umwelt. Facetten der künstlerischen Auseinandersetzung mit Landschaft und Natur*, Bielefeld: transcript 2012.

Kaiser, Gerhard, *Mutter Natur und die Dampfmaschine. Ein literarischer Mythos im Rückbezug auf Antike und Christentum*, Freiburg im Breisgau: Rombach 1991.

Ketelsen, Uwe-Karsten, *Die Naturpoesie der norddeutschen Frühaufklärung. Poesie als Sprache der Versöhnung, alter Universalismus und neues Weltbild*, Stuttgart: Metzler 1974.

Kirchhoff, Thomas and Ludwig Trepl (ed.), *Vieldeutige Natur: Landschaft, Wildnis und Ökosystem als kulturgeschichtliche Phänomene*, Bielefeld: transcript 2009.

Knabe, Hubertus, "Zweifel an der Industriegesellschaft. Ökologische Kritik in der erzählenden DDR-Literatur," in Redaktion Deutschland Archiv (ed.), *Umweltprobleme und Umweltbewußtsein in der DDR*, Cologne: Verlag Wissenschaft und Politik 1985, 201–250.

Krebs, Angelika, *Ethics of Nature*, Berlin and New York: de Gruyter 1999.

Kreutzer, Leo, "Wie herrlich leuchtet uns die Natur?" *Akzente 25*:4 (1978), 381–390.

Lekan, Thomas M., *Imagining the Nation in Nature: Landscape Preservation and German Identity, 1885–1945*, Cambridge, MA, and London: Harvard University Press 2004.

Liston, Andrew, *The Ecological Voice in Recent German-Swiss Prose*, Oxford: Peter Lang 2011.

Malkmus, Bernhard, "Das Naturtheater des W.G. Sebald: Die ökologischen Aporien eines poeta doctus," in Paul Michael Lützeler and Erin McGlothlin (eds.), *Gegenwartsliteratur. A German Studies Yearbook 10*, Tübingen: Stauffenburg 2011, 210–233.

Mallinckrodt, Anita, *The Environmental Dialogue in the GDR. Literature, Church, Party and Interest Groups in their Socio-Political Context. A Research Concept and Case Study*, Lanham, MD: University Press of America 1987.

Mauch, Christoph (ed.), *Nature in German History*, New York and Oxford: Berghahn 2004.

Mayer, Sylvia and Christoph Mauch (ed.), *American Environments: Climate, Cultures, Catastrophe*, Heidelberg: Universitätsverlag Winter 2012.

Meyer-Abich, Klaus Michael, *Revolution for Nature. From the Environment to the Connatural World*, Cambridge: White Horse Press 1993

Müller, Timo, "From Literary Anthropology to Cultural Ecology: German Ecocritical Theory since Wolfgang Iser," in Goodbody and Rigby 2011, 71–83.

Palfreyman, Rachel, "Green Strands on the Silver Screen? Heimat and Environment in the German Cinema," in Goodbody 2002, 171–186.

Radkau, Joachim, *Die Ära der Ökologie*, Munich: Beck 2011.

Rapp, Friedrich (ed.), *Naturverständnis und Naturbeherrschung. Philosophiegeschichtliche Entwicklung und gegenwärtiger Kontext*, Munich: Fink 1981.

Rentschler, Eric, "Mountains and Modernity: Relocating the Bergfilm," *New German Critique 51* (Autumn 1990), 137–161.

Rigby, Kate, *Topographies of the Sacred. The Poetics of Place in European Romanticism*, Charlottesville and London: University of Virginia Press 2004.

—— "Discoursing on Disaster: The Hermeneutics of Environmental Catastrophe," *Tamkang Review 39*:1 (2008), 19–40.

—— "Gernot Böhme's Ecological Aesthetics of Atmosphere," in Goodbody/Rigby 2011, 139–152.

Riordan, Colin (ed.), *Green Thought in German Culture. Historical and Contemporary Perspectives*, Cardiff: University of Wales Press, 1997.

Rollins, William H., *A Greener Vision of Home. Cultural Politics and Environmental Reform in the German Heimatschutz Movement, 1904–1918*, Michigan: University of Michigan Press 1997.

Santner, Eric, *On Creaturely Life. Rilke, Benjamin, Sebald*, Chicago: University of Chicago Press 2006.

Schäfer, Hans Dieter, *Wilhelm Lehmann. Studien zu seinem Leben und Werk*, Bonn: Bouvier 1969.

Schäfer, Lothar, *Das Bacon-Projekt. Von der Erkenntnis, Nutzung und Schonung der Natur*, Frankfurt am Main: Suhrkamp 1993.

Schama, Simon, *Landscape and Memory*, London: HarperCollins 1995.

Seamon, David and Arthur Zajonc (ed.), *Goethe's Way of Science. A Phenomenology of Nature*, New York: State University of New York Press 1998.

Seel, Martin, *Eine Ästhetik der Natur*, Frankfurt am Main: Suhrkamp 1991.

Sieferle, Rolf Peter (ed.), *Fortschrittsfeinde?Opposition gegen Technik und Industrie von der Romantik bis zur Gegenwart*, Munich: Beck 1984.

Smith, Peter D., *Metaphor and Materiality: German Literature and the Worldview of Science: 1780–1955*, Oxford: Legenda 2000.

Stapleton, Amy, *Utopias for a Dying World. Contemporary German Science Fiction's Plea for a New Ecological Awareness*, New York: Peter Lang 1993.

Sullivan, Heather, "Organic and Inorganic Bodies in the Age of Goethe: An Ecocritical Reading of Ludwig Tieck's Rune Mountain and the Earth Sciences," *ISLE* 10:2 (2003), 21–46.

—— "Ecocriticism, the Elements, and the Ascent/Descent into Weather in Goethe's Faust," *Goethe Yearbook* 2010, 55–72.

Vietta, Silvio, *Die vollendete Speculation führt zur Natur zurück. Natur und Ästhetik*, Leipzig: Reclam 1995.

von Bormann, Alexander, *Natura Loquitur. Naturpoesie und emblematische Formel bei Joseph von Eichendorff*, Tübingen: Niemeyer 1968.

von Moltke, Johannes, *No Place Like Home: Locations of Heimat in German Cinema*, Berkeley and Los Angeles: University of California Press 2005.

Wanning, Berbeli, "Yrrsinn oder die Auflehnung der Natur—Kulturökologische Betrachtungen zu Der Schwarm von Frank Schätzing," in Hubert Zapf (ed.), *Kulturökologie und Literatur. Beiträge zu einem neuen Paradigma der Literaturwissenschaft*, Würzburg: Königshausen and Neumann 2008, 339–357.

Webber, Andrew, *Berlin in the Twentieth Century. A Cultural Topography*, Cambridge, Cambridge University Press 2008.

Weigel, Sigrid, *Body- and Image-Space. Re-reading Walter Benjamin*, transl. by Georgina Paul, Rachel McNicholl, and Jeremy Gaines, London: Routledge 1996.

Wilke, Joachim (ed.), *Zum Naturbegriff der Gegenwart. Kongressdokumentation zum Projekt "Natur im Kopf"*, 2 vols, Stuttgart, Bad Cannstatt: Frommann-Holzboog 1993.

Worster, Donald, *Nature's Economy: A History of Ecological Ideas*, San Francisco: Sierra Club 1977.

Zapf, Hubert, *Literatur als kulturelle Ökologie: Zur kulturellen Funktion imaginativer Texte an Beispielen des amerikanischen Romans*, Tübingen: Niemeyer 2002.

Zemanek, Evi, "Unkalkulierbare Risiken und ihre Nebenwirkungen. Zu literarischen Reaktionen auf ökologische Transformationen und den Chancen des Ecocriticism," in Georg Braungart et al. (eds.), *Literatur als Wagnis/Literature as Risk*, Berlin and New York: de Gruyter, 2011.

Zimmermann, Rolf Christian, *Das Weltbild des jungen Goethe*, Munich: Fink 1969.

CHAPTER 34

....

BARRIER BEACH

....

ROB NIXON

TOUCH is our most primal, our most amniotic sense. It offers us our first knowledge of what the poet, Joy Harjo, calls "the weather in the womb." At six weeks—when we're one-inch embryos—we're already developing a sense of touch. Long before our ears, our eyes, and our noses have begun to absorb information from the world, we have started leading sensuous lives through our porous, excreting, breathing skins. Touch endures: it guides us from fetal vulnerability to the frailties of old age. Touch persists even when sight and hearing have fallen into ruin and our powers of taste and smell are shadows of themselves.

We can shut our eyes and mouths, hold our noses, block our ears. But our skin is always on the *qui vive*, surrounding us in constant readiness—informing, warning, pleasing. Our skin is twenty square feet of pure receptivity: the largest and (after the brain) the most versatile of our organs. The skin serves as the self's sheath, sealing and concealing us, holding us together, keeping us apart.

In memory, touch begins for me not with an outstretched hand but inside childhood's tidal pools. My brother and I are immersed—peering, poking, hesitantly handling the creatures the sea delivers, then withdraws from the water that some days rises above our waists, other days lies ankle shallow. The pools are alive with revelations that we cannot name but try, with four small hands, to grasp.

A few yards up the sand, a blue beach umbrella shelters my parents, grandmother, and three sisters. Behind them in turn, where the dune grass begins, a tall, one-legged wooden sign declares in English and Afrikaans: "Whites Only. Blankes Alleen." "Only" was a decisive environmental word along the sixty-mile bay that the Indian Ocean has scythed out of South Africa's Eastern Cape. If your body was deemed to be the wrong color it wasn't safe to bathe here, only over there; access to the water was policed into the sand. A phenomenology of touch must necessarily include the following signs that between them divided up the shore: "Whites Only," "Blacks Only," "Coloureds Only," "Indians Only," "Malays Only."

I experienced environmental change before I understood the tides of history. Environment, history, tides are adult words that, back then, were unavailable to me: the change that touched me first was salt water's movement back and forth across the skin as I stood immersed beside my brother, toes curled for balance into the sand, my whole being awash with curiosity. The Indian Ocean was warm, but didn't yet have a name. For all childhoods are provincial: they start from me, from us, from here. In the absence of a social analysis, where we are becomes the center of everything. When you're a child you live life close up, so close that life's shaping fundamentals, for a time, stay hidden.

To that segregated tide pool scene I should add this: we went to the beach because it was "free." We were somewhat inter-tidal ourselves, lower middle class with middle-class aspirations. My father was earning, in today's money, about $40,000, as sole bread-winner for our sprawling nine-person, four-generation outfit—five children, two parents, one grandmother, one great-grandfather—ranging in age from three years old to ninety-nine, all crammed under one roof in an atmosphere of frugal scarcity. From the perspective of the Xhosa township across the veld, we were rich beyond belief. But nobody on either side of the family had ever made it to university; my father alone had finished high school. So my parents shaped their lives around an unwavering goal: to get their children the college education they had been denied. That I'm writing this essay as a middle-class professional owes everything to their fiscal severity in tandem with apartheid's atrociously inequitable school system.

We never once, during my childhood and adolescence, ate in a restaurant or stayed in a hotel or motel; the cinema was off limits as too pricey. All those things would belong to the future, to my middle class American life. But our family could partake of apartheid Nature—for beach trips, bush walks, mountain climbs—without paying, without jeop-ardizing my parents' educational hopes for us. We were a family that only went places where there was no entrance fee.

Nadine Gordimer has written of "falling, falling through the South African way of life." After my fall into politics the landscape seemed illusory, warped by an unethical geography. By the time I got to college, Nature itself had become a toxic discourse. For a decade-and-a-half into adulthood—long into my exile to America—if I thought at all about my Nature-saturated childhood I would focus on the politics in the view and leave childhood's tactile body behind, an uninhabited exhibit of injustice to be opposed. I was certainly not inclined to reach for anything as complex as a segregationist phenomenol-ogy of those tidal pools on that skin-entitled beach.

What I know is that that contrapuntal scene—oceanic and societal, a body immersed, a body apart—shaped the reader I became, of books and landscapes alike. I can trace to that pooled water and divided sand my passion for environmental justice, above all for all issues of access—whether under apartheid or the Washington Consensus, as in the name of freeing markets the rich carve up the commons, and the gated mindset and pri-vate security detail spread like kudzu across the globe. That tidal scene—and others like it—turned me into a reader who parses literature and landscapes for who is present, who is missing, for the forced removals, physical and imaginative, from the permitted view; a reader alive to who precisely (in the cropped photo, the selective story, the seemingly seamless landscape) has been driven off the beach.

II

African Americans are three times as likely as their white compatriots to declare US national parks "uncomfortable places." A 2009 survey found that less than one percent of Yosemite visitors were black. Mountains? A nineteen-year old Denver woman knows why she stays away: "My granddaddy told me the K.K.K. hangs out up in the mountains. Why would I want to go?" Trees? The poet Ed Roberson puts the matter bluntly: "American trees had ropes in them."

For the parks to become a viable commons—the "nation's playground" they purport to be—America's dominant culture of nature must undergo a radical overhaul. Decades after official segregation was outlawed, many African Americans feel shadowed by a history of rural ambush, violence, and terror that retains a visceral, bodily tenacity. Historically, the great outdoors were not so great. Shelton Johnson is working to turn that race memory around. Johnson is an anomaly: one of the few African American park rangers anywhere, he worked for seven years in Yellowstone before moving to Yosemite where, since 1994, he has been active as an interpretive specialist. One of his specialties, it turns out, is reinterpreting history.

In 2001, Johnson stumbled across an archival photograph—dated 1899—of five US Army cavalry troopers patrolling Yosemite's backcountry on horseback. The troopers were black: Buffalo Soldiers from the 9th cavalry who, it emerged, had been assigned to safeguard the park from poaching, illicit grazing, logging, and forest fires shortly after Yosemite's creation.[1] After Johnson unearthed a trove of letters by Buffalo Soldiers who had served in Yosemite and Sequoia National Park, he felt emboldened by precedent: his discovery eased his sense of being a pioneering oddity and intensified his determination to make the parks more culturally available to African Americans by publicizing their foundational role as environmental stewards.

For now, Johnson quips, black visitors to Yosemite remain real "sightings." He is more likely to encounter a tourist from Finland or Israel than an African American. To tackle this imbalance, Johnson has added to his daily interpretive work a three-pronged strategy: archive, celebrity, and fiction. An imploring letter persuaded Oprah Winfrey to devote two shows—and a personal road trip—to race and the national park system. And Johnson, who holds a creative writing MFA from the University of Michigan, in 2009 published a novel, *Gloryland*, which takes the form of a buffalo soldier's fictional memoir. "Race is the core of this history," he observes. "It shows that the national parks are as much a cultural as a natural resource."

Like many heroic counternarratives, Johnson's racial salvage story is not without its contradictions. The buffalo soldiers stationed at Yosemite had just returned from fighting an imperial war in the Philippines. And Johnson—whose mother was half Cherokee and father part Seminole—would be alive to the violence against Native peoples behind Yosemite's invention as exemplary, untouched American sublime. In order to create the park that the buffalo soldiers patrolled, the Ahwahneechee had been evicted from their historic lands. But Johnson also knows, from the inside, the role the military has long played as a channel of racial uplift—his own father, James O. Johnson Jr., had enlisted in flight from the Jim Crow South.

Johnson's story is not reducible to a patriotic, Ken Burns–style national frame. His commitment to challenging America's dominant culture of nature arose, in large part, from his ability to see that culture from the outside looking in. Two international experiences—one an unsettling revelation, the other a childhood epiphany—fired his resolve to make America's park system more fully representative, something closer to a national commons. After graduating from college, Johnson spent two years in Liberia with the Peace Corps, where he was astonished by the casual fluency with which everyone, even children, could name the birds, animals, flowers, and trees surrounding them. This brought home to him the environmental alienation inflicted by the Middle Passage and by the long, layered violence against African Americans that ensued. It became his goal to help turn that culture of alienation around.

Yet his historical insight in Liberia would have been insufficient without the animating force of an early childhood encounter. In 1961, Johnson's mother and his staff sergeant father, stationed with the US military in Germany, had taken him to the Berchtesgaden National Park in the Bavarian Alps. Berchtesgaden may not have been as remote as the Swiss hamlet that James Baldwin portrayed as a "white wilderness" in his classic 1953 essay, "Stranger in the Village," a village where children felt at liberty to trail their fingers through his unprecedented hair and where in Baldwin's words, he remained "a sight," "a living wonder." Still, it must have taken some initiative, some fortitude for Johnson's parents to venture into that fiercely conservative Bavarian redoubt. As it happens, the mountains moved the five-year old Shelton indelibly—the sensation of being so high, so intimate with big sky that he could touch it—lived on in him. Growing up thereafter in inner city Detroit, his encounter with the Alpine sublime remained lodged in his urban body's tissue memory. That brief, boyhood thrill shook up a life, quickening his adult commitment to opening up the outdoors early to African American children: "I can't not think of the other kids, just like me—in Detroit, Oakland, Watts, Anacostia—today. How do I get them here? How do I let them know about the buffalo soldier history, to let them know that we, too, have a place here?"

III

The early passions that shape our neural pathways—on an Alpine trail or in an Indian Ocean tidal pool—are inseparable from history's undertow. My history travels with me: when a Cape Cod marine ecologist utters the phrase "barrier beach" it passes through my body with a jolt. I cannot hear those words as merely topographical.

Ever since Nelson Mandela's release, I have started to return each year—usually around Christmas—to childhood's provincial city to visit my ailing mother and my brother who tends to her. Most days I drive the ten minutes to the beaches that ring what's now called Mandela Bay. The "only" signs have long since disappeared, sinking into what W. G. Sebald once called "the lagoon of oblivion." But the desegregated path down through the dune grass still crosses for me a shadow beach, where childhood's vast emotions first gathered around my feet, a place where history's tides and the tuggings of the moon remain conjoined. Here, there, where memory began to pool before memory was known to me.

I'm reading on this beach Camille Dungy's powerful anthology of African American poetry, *Black Nature*. In an introductory essay, she revisits her immersed early years in Southern California: "When I was a child on Bluff View, the dogs we call bloodhounds, the slave trackers' tool, were nothing I knew to remember. I was a girl-child in that kingdom of open space, and all the land I could see and name and touch was mine to love." Her adult, writer self wrestles with the gap between that intense, tactile innocence and the plummet into collective trauma: "How do I write a poem about the land and my place in it without these memories: the runaway with the hounds at her heels; the complaint of the poplar at the man-cry of its load; land a thing to work but not to own?"

For a time, after Mandela's release, it was if black South Africans had to work at owning the beaches in my hometown. In the first year or two, people trickled back to the prime seaside spots, but in groups not crowds, as if still hesitant in their reclamation, as if still mentally looking over their shoulders for hostile signposts and police. But today, by noon, the shoreline is filled to bursting. It's Boxing Day, which, alongside Tweede Nuwe Jaar (January 2) is the biggest beach day of the year: hundreds of High-Ace mini-van taxis disgorge their pleasure seekers, until the beaches throng with 300,000 people. Corpulent middle-aged ladies step out with umbrellas to fend off the blatant heat; young women twirl gold-lamé high-heels from ruby fingernails; ghetto blaster rivalries are staked out, kwaito over here while, a few towels away, Irene Mawela gives it her all with gospel jive. Music markers in place, the young men jog off for a close-range football game of flamboyant ball control. Down by the water's edge a wedding party gathers in a ring while a white-robed man whisks his knife across a bleating throat. Soon, the aroma of whole goat on the braai, the barbecue, mingles with the sea's low-tide mineral smell.

In this place of casual plenitude, class divisions still register, though in a minor key. Fully half the bathers are in their underwear, while the better off flaunt their sheeny bathing suits, the men in those taut speedos that Australians call "budgie smugglers." Older women venture in gingerly, skirts hoist to the knee, as they bend to fill bottles with sea water to send as a curative to relatives inland.

Leisure may seem a surface thing, in a country beset by deeper challenges: a mismanaged AIDS crisis, rural destitution, car jacking, thwarted land claims, unserviced, unmanaged sprawl, tenacious unemployment, and xenophobia. Just this morning, I was talking to a boardwalk vendor who, bent beneath sacks of carved giraffes, told me that in Malawi he'd dreamed "Johannesburg, every day," but when he got there he'd soon fled south, here to Mandela Bay. For him, South Africa's city of gold was paved with nothing but problems.

In the broad journey from dispossession to self-possession, this beach may be a modest thing. But it still seems—this roiling place, this commonage restored—in every sense phenomenal. It's the children in the water who most interest me. The tiny body surfer, who times his push just right, as he trusts the break and feels the ocean fold over him, angling into the slide, the full forward flow of him perfectly balanced between submission and control. And there, just below the sandpipers that scissor through the tidal wrack in pale, skittish flocks, the rock pool children, crouching, wet-bottomed, eyes down, hands alive. The children rise in concert each time a small wave floods their world, stirring the sand, fogging the water which will slowly clarify again, revealing whatever will be revealed: turbaned whelks perhaps, sea squirts, crimson and yellow anemones that close their fronds around a finger, translucent pipe fish, keyhole limpets, spiny crabs, bulb-eyed fish that press their mouths indiscriminately against seaweed strands and toes, seahorses that jerk like marionettes as they fly through the fronded canopy that sways in the underwater breeze. Here the children make their stand, in clustered curiosity, inside the salt warmth that recalibrates the body's electromagnetic fields; here, where apartheid's systemic segregations once appeared as unchanging, as resilient as the rocks themselves.

I swim out beyond the breaker line and dangle, rising and falling with the swells. Out here I feel what I've always felt: that in water I'm more secure, more upheld than on dry land. Out here being at sea means the opposite of loss, means being alive to the life of the skin, trading anxiety for some deep flow of necessary breath. I peer back, like the visitor I now am, at the shoreline of this town. A young Xhosa woman, further out than the rest, glides by with easy limbs, with a freedom of movement (crawl, breaststroke, backstroke) in history's desegregated sea.

NOTE

1. The 9th Cavalry was one of four African American regiments of the US Army formed in 1866. Members of these regiments were dubbed Buffalo Soldiers by the Native American tribes they fought against.

INDEX

A Sand County Almanac (Leopold), 149, 341, 399–400, 406

Abbey, Edward, 222n26, 383, 387–389, 520

abduction, 133

aboriginals, 88, 349, 529
    Australian, 244, 248, 418

Abram, David, 268, 279–283, 285, 287, 292, 296, 366

Abrams, M.H, 71

Adams, Richard, 409, 411

Adorno, Theodor, 63, 105, 107, 487, 553

AEC (Atomic Energy Commission), 329–330

aesthetic atmospheres, 280

affect, 130, 135, 166, 329, 364–365, 368
    ecoglobalist, 325

affordances, 446, 448, 496; *see also Umwelt*

African Americans, 118–130, 143, 194, 413; *see also* race
    and old-time music, 479–480
    and urban nature, 128–130
    and wilderness, 118–119, 122–127, 562–564

After the Fire (Rule), 306, 311–313, 315–317

Against Women Unconstant (attr.Chaucer), 30

Agamben, Giorgio, 243, 253, 552

Alaimo, Stacy, 103, 136, 151, 159, 162, 166, 176–177, 236n9, 306, 363, 366, 402, 469; *see* trans-corporeality
    and eco-film theory, 462–465

Alan of Lille, 28

alienation, 63, 283, 286, 424, 466, 491, 563
    critique of romantic theory of, 160–161, 165–166

Aliens of the Deep (Nouvian), 193–195, 202

allegory, 29, 44, 251, 373, 498

Allen, Richard, 461–462

allomorphism, 66, 304; *see also* alterity

Almanac of the Dead (Silko), 11, 172, 175–184

alterity, 70, 106–107, 126
    animal, 66–67, 255

postcolonial, 321, 325–327, 329, 331–334, 339n54

Althusser, Louis, 464

An Inconvenient Truth (film), 20, 503, 505–507, 509, 516

Anderson, Jill, 308

animal culture, 229, 231–232, 236–237, 239

Animal Liberation (Singer), 52

animal rights, 13, 51, 66, 263, 412, 418
    and conservation, 242, 244–245

animal studies, 29, 226–227, 236n9, 397
    and ecocriticism, 242–244, 253

animal trans, 306, 318

Animal, Vegetable, Miracle (Kingsolver), 403–405

animals, 81, 85, 122, 132, 157–158, 179–180, 207, 209, 212, 215, 217–218, 221n19, 229–235, 241, 250, 252, 291, 298, 301, 314, 341, 343–345, 351–352, 367, 377, 397, 409, 411–414, 446, 449, 454, 462–463, 469, 476, 479, 488, 495, 497, 530, 552, 563
    in children's stories, 411–414
    feral, 243–245, 247–248, 254–255
    marine, 194–195, 198–201
    in middle ages, 29, 33
    and modernism, 100, 104, 109, 111
    phenomenology and, 280–281, 284
    queer, 306–307
    Renaissance, 45, 50–56
    and romanticism, 66–67, 70
    zoosemiotics and, 261–264

animism, 280–281, 525

Antarctica, 155, 322, 331–334, 339

Anthropocene era, 226, 276, 285–289, 488, 540–541

anthropocentrism, 42, 103–104, 108, 145, 201, 207, 227, 232–233, 247–248, 253, 279, 424–425, 467, 531, 533, 542, 553

anthropodenial, 232, 235

anthropomorphism, 58, 73, 126, 182, 235, 238n23, 248, 252, 263, 280, 284, 332, 411, 508
    animalcentric and anthropocentric, 232
ants, 183–184, 186, 229–230, 247
Anzaldúa, Gloria, 175, 177
apartheid (S African racial segregation) 560–561
Apollo space missions, 327–328, 333, 337–339
Appalachia, 476, 478–480, 484
Armbruster, Karla, 396, 425
Armstrong, Philip, 243–244, 248, 256
Arnold, David, 80, 83–84
Arthasastra (Kautilya), 528
'As Birds Bring Forth the Sun' (Macleod), 250
ASLE (Association for the Study of Literature and the Environment), ix, 2, 4, 20–21, 417, 463, 549
    ASLE-India, 528, 534
    ASLE-Japan, 20, 520–523
Attridge, Derek, 242
Augé, Marc, 139, 143
Australia, 60, 88, 244–246, 330, 419

Bachelard, Gaston, 440–441, 443, 449
Bacon, Francis, 53, 63, 490
Bakhtin, Mikhail, 45, 390
Ballard, Robert D., 191
Ballets Russes, 104
Barad, Karen, 164, 189, 192, 307, 314, 317n2, 366; *see also* intra-action
Barkawi, Tarak, 328, 331, 338–339
Bass, Rick, 385, 520
Bate, Jonathan, 5, 62, 69, 106, 114, 135, 207, 551
Beck, Ulrich, 158, 161–162, 547
Beckett, Samuel, 105–106, 111
Behn, Aphra, 345
Bekoff, Marc, 238n23, 252
Bennett, Jane, 103, 367–368
Bennett, Michael, 426–427
Bentham, Jeremy, 66
Berlant, Laurent, 305, 310
Berlin, Isaiah, 62
Bernstein, Charles, 132, 135–136
Berry, Wendell, 383, 388, 476, 490
Between the Acts (Woolf), 107
Bible (Christian), 53, 54

bio-power, 2, 7, 88, 236n8, 244, 253, 305, 310; *see also* Foucault, Michel
biophilia, 43, 413–414, 416, 497
biosemiotics, 18, 133, 138, 142, 184, 253, 260–269, 367; *see also* animal culture
    contrasted with Saussurean semiology, 13, 260–261, 466
Black Beauty (Sewell), 409, 412–413, 420, 422
Boethius, 28, 37
Böhme, Gernot, 14, 279–280, 282–283, 285, 547, 549, 553
Böhme, Hartmut, 283, 547, 553
Bök, Christian, 133, 135–136, 140–141, 144–145
Bonnie, Kristin E., 232
Borderlands/La Frontera (Anzaldúa), 174–177
Bordwell, David, 460–461, 467–468, 471
Botkin, Daniel, 65, 312
Bradshaw, Gay, 12, 230
Bravo (nuclear test), 330, 333
Brown, Gillian R., 231, 233
Bryld, Mette, 188, 193
Buckland, Warren, 471
Buddhism, 294, 525
Buell, Lawrence, 1–2, 8, 21, 113n6, 139, 165, 174–176, 208, 322–324, 327, 363, 393–394, 399–400, 435, 437n16, 533, 538, 540, 543
Buonarroti, Michelangelo, 50
Burnett, Frances Hodgson, 409, 415
Butler, Marilyn, 1, 73
Butler, Robert, 377
Byrd, William, 381
Byron, Alfred Lord, 61, 66, 73–74

Callicott, J. Baird, 245, 247
Calvin, John, 56, 59
Calvinism, 52, 54–55
Cameron, James, 193–196, 201, 465
canon, 3, 60, 62, 100–102, 206–207, 220, 322–323, 460, 550
    climate, 206–207
    ecocritical, 16, 210, 393–394, 398, 423–425
Cantrell, Carol, 100–101, 107
Caribbean, 320, 341–354
Carroll, Noël, 460–461, 465–466, 468–471
Carson, Rachel, 161–162, 165, 391, 393, 400–403, 417

Cartesian philosophy, 42, 107–108, 110, 226, 307, 453
  critiques of, 45, 100, 113n27, 244, 366
  dualism in, 67
Castronova, Edward, 498
chaos theory, 482
Chaucer, 30, 32–34, 37–38
children, writing for, 408–419
Childs, Peter, 430
China, 155–156, 219, 222n30
  ecocriticism in, 4, 22, 537–544
cholera, 81–91, 93–97
Christianity, 6, 35–36, 72–73, 525
  and animals, 52–55
  Lynn White thesis on, 28, 33
Clare, John, 62, 270, 273, 435
Clarke, Stephen, 29
Clements, Frederick, 65
climate change, 3–4, 19–20, 22, 44, 166, 190, 194, 196, 201, 241, 287, 320, 323, 333, 377, 396, 398, 401, 403, 470, 502–516, 548, 552
  and crisis of representation, 276, 424–425, 502–516
  and literature, 205–220, 361–373, 431–434
  as spectacle, 155–156, 163
  Cochabamba Conference on, 172, 175, 180, 186
  scepticism, 47–48, 161, 299, 495–497
Cloud Atlas (Mitchell), 429–431, 436n8
co-evolution, 248, 253, 255, 367
coexistentialism, 70, 300–301
cognitive, 18, 42, 45, 48, 230, 263–264, 279, 460–461, 467–471, 492–493, 522
  film theory, 460–461, 467–471
  poetics, 18, 440–456
Cold Mountain (Frazier), 479, 482
Coleridge, S.T., 60–61, 66–67, 70–71, 110, 451
Collins, Jim, 464–465
colonialism, 41, 127, 165–166, 188, 194–195, 212–213, 244, 324–331, 339, 381, 409, 415
  and conservation, 210, 324
  and disease, 80, 85, 93–95
  environmental harms of, 230, 341, 346, 348–350, 352–354, 429, 527, 529–531
  homogenization of space, 321
commodity fetishism, 156, 158–159
Condé, Maryse, 347

consilience, 242
Continental philosophy, 459, 461–462, 465, 468, 551
Cooper, David E., 276–278, 280–281, 286–288
Coppinger, Raymond, 249, 257n8
Cosgrove, Denis, 324–325, 327, 332–334
cosmovisions, 175, 181–185
country music, 475–478, 480; see also old-time music
Coupland, Douglas, 155–156, 161, 163, 165, 167
Cowley, Jason, 402
Cracking the Ocean Code (TV documentary), 195, 198
creole pig, 348, 352–354
Cronon, William, 9, 103, 160, 395–396, 398
cultural biology, 229, 232, 234–235; see also animal culture
cultural ecology, 549, 551, 553–554
cyberspace, 489, 491

Darkwater (Du Bois), 118–120, 122, 129
Darwin, Charles, 45, 108–109, 195, 257, 295–296, 307, 393, 411
datasphere, 488–489, 494
DDT, 10, 134, 158–159, 164, 170, 405, 428
De Beauvoir, Simone, 276, 285
De Waal, Frans, 228–229, 231–233
deconstruction, 14–15, 74, 291–302, 325
deep ecology, 5, 21, 29, 37, 41, 103–104, 368–370, 538, 542
  critiques of, 58, 165, 173, 288, 325, 337n26, 466
Deleuze, Gilles, 110, 137, 307, 461, 471
DeLoughrey, Elizabeth, 2–4, 15–16, 21, 81
democracy, 120, 127, 387, 527, 532, 534
  earth, 326
  science and, 157, 165
Dennis, John, 388
Derksen, Jeff, 139
Derrida, Jacques, 14, 70, 227, 236n8, 283, 294–297, 300–302; see also deconstruction
Descartes, René, 50, 63; see Cartesian philosophy
Desert Solitaire (Abbey), 17, 388, 520; see Abbey, Edward
Devi, Mahasweta, 21, 532–533
dharma, 528–530, 533

Dickinson, Emily, 440, 445, 447–448, 451–453, 455, 491
différance, 14, 295, 298, 300
disease, 7, 46, 74, 121, 221n18, 343–344, 401, 431
  colonialism and, 80–87, 89–95
DNA, 13–14, 140, 151, 162, 195–196, 235, 291–295, 301, 498
Dodds, Joseph, 364, 367
Dog Boy (Hornung), 252–255
dogs, 245–249, 252–259, 346, 564
double consciousness, 118–119, 122, 124; *see also* African Americans
Du Bois, W.E.B., 118–131
Dungy, Camille, 564

eco-cosmopolitanism, 113n8, 175, 322, 489
eco-film, 459–465, 467, 469–473
ecocriticism, 42–43, 48, 225, 260, 262, 302, 378, 383–384, 408, 459, 487, 513; *see also* postcolonial ecocriticism
  and animal studies, 227, 242–246, 285
  and deconstruction, 291–302
  divergent tendencies within, 2–3, 7–10, 363–368, 395–398, 424–425, 434–436, 464–472
  and environmental justice, 172–186
  feminist, 321, 335, 363, 365–366, 378, 396, 533, 555
  and genre, 16, 368–373, 392–394, 503–513
  histories of, 1–2, 320–321, 335n4, 325
  and modernism, 98–112, 118–130
  and phenomenology, 276–288, 296–297
  and queer theory, 305–317
  postmodern, 132–148
  and romanticism, 60–75
  and science, 133–136, 163–165, 188–192, 208–209, 226–235, 246–248, 286, 295, 306–308, 361–362, 460–461, 502
  urban, 426–429
ecofeminism, 2, 5, 14, 321, 335n4, 363, 365–366, 378, 396–396, 533, 555n23
ecoglobalism, 322–323, 334–335
Ecological Indian, 11, 172–174, 181, 185
ecology, 45, 70, 100–101, 104, 132, 162, 192–193, 210–211, 242, 244, 260, 288, 296, 328–329, 391, 427, 443, 470, 530, 532–533, 537, 543, 547, 549, 552; *see also* cultural ecology;

deep ecology; modernist ecology; postequilibrium ecology; queer ecology; romantic ecology
  and environmentalism, 27, 47–48
  Augustan, 65
  ecocriticism and, 1–2, 36, 65, 156–159, 208, 278, 460–461, 541
  negative, 106,114n27
  scientific, 109, 225, 288, 323–324, 329, 400, 489
  without nature, 111, 391, 499; *see* Morton, Timothy
ecophenomenology, 14, 278, 284, 288–290, 296
ecopoetics, 102, 135–136, 143, 148, 542; *see also* negative ecopoetics
  Heideggerian, 106
Edelman, Lee, 15, 308–309, 317n4, 445
Eden, 43, 54, 303, 420
Eeckhout, Bart, 103–104
Eichendorff, Joseph von, 60–61, 71, 551
Elder, John, 102, 396, 398–399
Eliot, T.S., 102, 283, 481
Elsaesser, Thomas, 471
embeddedness, 10, 163, 226, 234, 266, 284, 296
embodiment, 73, 93, 104, 226, 234, 305–306, 308, 450, 455
  phenomenology and, 280–282, 368
Emerson, Ralph Waldo, 382, 441, 451, 454
empire, 320–327, 346; *see also* imperialism
  American, 323, 327, 334
  British, 81, 83–84, 87, 89, 93–95, 325
enactionism, 448, 450–451
Enlightenment, 1, 63, 105, 111, 157, 226–227, 278, 280, 283, 381, 408–409, 475, 512
  critiques of, 50, 106–109, 198, 321, 324, 333, 540
entanglement, 11–12, 188–189, 191–193, 195–196, 199, 201, 214, 220, 307; *see also* science studies
environmental fascism, 245
'environmentalism of the poor' (Gadgil and Guha), 179, 527
environmental justice, 11, 100, 120, 207, 218–219, 321, 396, 418, 476, 552, 561
  and indigenous literature, 172–177, 181, 184, 186
  movement, 165, 174, 190–191, 309

environmental nonfiction, 16–18, 20, 113, 279, 394

environmental racism, 174–176, 552

EPA (Environmental Protection Agency), 469

Erasmus, Desiderius, 56

Erickson, Bruc, 309

Eriksen, Tim, 483–484

Essay on Man (Pope), 65, 74

Etter, Ron J., 192

Evernden, Neil, 28–30, 36

evolutionary psychology, 238, 263, 460–461, 471–472

Exploits & Opinions of Dr. Faustroll, Pataphysician (Jarry), 133

extinction, 173, 182, 201, 246, 367, 491, 498, 504
    of Caribbean fauna, 341–344, 346, 348–354

false consciousness, 468, 470; *see also* ideology

Fanren, Zeng, 540–542

Farr, Moira, 396

feminism, 2, 5, 11–12, 16, 63, 166, 198, 242, 285, 393, 463, 466; *see also* ecofeminism
    and phenomenology 285
    and science studies 188–190

ferality, 242–257

Figueres, Christiana, 362

film noir, 463, 473

fire, ecology of, 311–316

Foucault, Michel, 2, 9–10, 162–164, 305, 310; *see also* bio-power

Foxe, John, 51

Franklin, Adrian, 244

Frazier, Charles, 479, 482

Freedom, romantic conception of, 62–64, 67, 125, 233

Freeman, Walter, 449–451

Frye, Northrop, 442

Gadgil, Madhav, 527, 530

Gaia, 45, 48, 70, 300, 369, 376, 466, 488, 514

Galef, Bennett G., 232

Gandhi, 531

Garrard, Greg, 41, 47, 62, 66, 172–174, 207, 424, 432, 435, 533

gender, 2, 32, 60, 89, 162, 182, 188, 191, 241, 285, 306, 320, 324, 391, 465–466, 509

George, James, 331–334

German, 21–22, 43, 244, 261, 265, 277, 297, 345
    ecocriticism, 547–559
    romanticism, 43, 60, 62, 65, 70–73, 118, 128

Gessner, David, 380, 384

Gheyn, Jacques De , 49–51

Ghosh, Amitav, 12, 21, 210–218, 532

Gibson, James J., 265, 446–448, 450–453

Gilbert, Daniel, 241

Gilbey, Ryan, 504

Glissant, Édouard, 21, 101, 326–327, 331

global warming, 17, 49, 205–207, 210, 219–220, 241, 298–299, 344, 361, 369, 377–378, 395, 417, 487, 496, 503, 505, 507, 509–513; *see* climate change

Glotfelty, Cheryll, 234, 426

Goethe, J.W. von, 60–61, 65, 68, 280, 547, 550–551

Goodbody, Axel, 21–22, 78–79, 432–433

Google, 299, 373, 496

Gordimer, Nadine, 561

Gordon, Deborah, 184

Gore, Al, 496, 505–506

gothic, 20, 61, 158
    imperial, 82, 87, 89, 92–93, 95

Grahame, Kenneth, 409, 416–417

Grand Canyon, 118–119, 121–127, 129–131

Green, James, 430

Greenpeace, 192, 503, 511–512

Grodal, Torben, 460, 471–472

Grove, Richard, 323–324

Grusin, Richard, 120

Guha, Ramachandra, 179, 325, 527, 530–531

Haddock, Steven, 200–201

Haiti, 342–343, 348, 350–357

Halberstam, Judith, 305

Handley, George, 2–3, 81, 326, 339

Hansen, James, 48

Haraway, Donna, 9–10, 101, 110, 112, 195, 200
    and dogs, 247–248, 255
    and science studies, 108, 110, 163, 188–189, 247–248, 255

Having Faith (Steingraber), 402

Hawker, Ginny, 478

Head, Dominic, 424, 431

Hegeman, Susan, 101

Heidegger, Martin, 103, 105–107, 295, 299,
    301–302, 549, 551
  and phenomenology, 276–277, 279–280,
    285, 289, 292, 547
Heimat, 70, 548, 551–552
Heinämaa, Sara, 285
Heine, Heinrich, 7, 60, 73
Heise, Ursula, 15, 113n8, 172, 174–175, 184, 322,
    329, 368–369, 372–373, 397, 489
heteronormativity, 9, 15, 90, 103, 111, 305,
    308, 310–313, 315–316, 418; see also queer
    ecology
Hird, Myra, 306–307
Hoffmeyer, Jesper, 133, 144, 184, 260–261, 264;
    see biosemiotics
Hornung, Eva, 252–253, 255
Huggan, Graham, 326, 328, 397, 528, 531
Hulme, Mike, 470, 502, 504–506, 509
Humboldt, Alexander von, 65, 547
humor, 17, 364, 377–390, 404, 511
Husserl, Edmund, 276–277, 292, 302
Hutchings, Kevin, 62, 70

ideology, 80–81, 161, 208, 211–212, 215, 299, 368,
    416, 492, 538, 543
  and film criticism, 464–466, 468–470, 472
  critique of, 161, 167, 228, 363, 387–388
If Nobody Speaks of Remarkable Things
    (McGregor), 426–429, 431
Imanishi, Kinji, 229, 231–232, 237n14
imperialism, 7, 15, 70, 80–95, 214, 329, 348, 409,
    414, 562
  ecological, 81, 323–324, 397
In the Palm of Darkness (Montero), 348,
    350–351
India, 4, 7, 21, 210, 219, 326, 349
  and ecocriticism, 210, 219, 222–223, 527–535
  colonial representation of, 80–93
indigenous ecological wisdom, 172
indigenous peoples, 9, 73, 80, 172–186, 218,
    281–282, 324, 329, 345–346, 348–350,
    355n4, 419, 529
  writing for children by 418
  political movements of, 11, 172–173, 175, 178,
    182
Ingram, David, 480–481, 483
interpellation, 464–465

intra-action, 151, 164, 189, 193, 252
IPCC (Intergovernmental Panel on Climate
    Change), 163, 219, 507, 509
Iser, Wolfgang, 293, 553

James, William, 108, 110, 444–446, 448,
    451–452, 456nn2,4,7
Jameson, Frederic, 155–156
Japan, 21, 229, 330
  ecocriticism in, 519–525
Jaws: The Revenge (film), 468–470
Jim Crow (racial segregation laws), 118–119,
    121, 123–125, 127, 130, 563
Johnson, Shelton, 562–563
JPod (Coupland), 155–156, 161, 165, 167–168

Kac, Edouardo, 140–141, 145
Kadir, Djelal, 327
Kant, Immanuel, 68, 162
Katrina, 383, 507
Keith Thomas, 52, 58, 411
Kempe, Margery, 29
Kerridge, Richard, 12, 16–17, 19–20, 22, 421,
    424, 430, 432–433, 506, 511
Kingsolver, Barbara, 403–405
Kipling, Rudyard, 81–85, 87, 89–95, 409, 415
Kiser, Lisa, 29
Kittler, Friedrich, 496–497
Kolbert, Elizabeth, 403, 487
Kolodny, Annette, 11, 185
Kroeber, Karl, 62, 67, 69
Krutch, Joseph Wood, 392–394

Labat, Père, 342–343, 346–347
Lacan, Jacques, 9, 296, 300, 459
  critique of, 464–467, 470–472
Laclau, Ernesto, 166
Laland, Kevin N., 228, 231–233
Lanchester, John, 364–365, 367, 433
Langland, William, 28
Latour, Bruno, 9–12, 21, 103, 108, 114n24,
    163–164, 188–189, 191, 196, 211, 221n9, 325;
    see also science studies
Lawrence, D.H., 100, 108–110, 225, 348, 384
Leopold, Aldo, 102, 341, 391, 399–401
Levertov, Denise, 292
Lewis, Wyndham , 99

Lewontin, Richard, 238n26, 253
Limbaugh, Rush, 496
'Lines Composed a Few Miles Above Tintern
    Abbey' (Wordsworth), 72
'Lines Written in Early Spring' (Wordsworth),
    63, 68
Linnaeus, 243, 324
London, Jack, 246–247, 249–250, 254
Lopez, Barry, 393, 411–413, 520
Love, Glen, 114n24, 236n9, 363
Lovelock, James, 70, 369–370, 372
Luther, Martin, 53, 55
Lykke, Nina, 188, 193
Lynas, Mark, 362
Lyon, Thomas J., 393–394, 396, 402

Machinal, Hélène, 431
Macleod, Alistair, 250–251
Mao, Douglas, 100, 106–107
Marcus, Greil, 481
Margolis, Joseph, 460
Margulis, Lynn, 144–145, 307, 317n2
Martin, James Ranald, 83, 86, 88
Marx, Karl, 156, 158–160, 167, 181
Marxism, 156, 210, 221n9, 242, 321, 371, 459,
    464, 467, 542
masculinity, 89, 91–92, 120–121
Mbembe, Achille, 236
McCarthy, Cormac, 206, 373–374
McEwan, Ian, 18, 206, 242, 373, 424,
    431–433
McFarland, Sarah, 462–463
McGonigal, Jane, 499
McGowan, Todd, 459, 465–467
McGregor, John, 18, 426–427
McIlvanney, Liam, 425
McKay, Don, 145
McKibben, Bill, 362, 366, 395–396, 428,
    492–494
McKusick, James, 62, 74
McLuhan, Marshall, 490–492, 496
Meeker, Joseph, 383
men of 1914, 7, 98
Merleau-Ponty, Maurice, 105, 107–108, 276,
    280–281, 284–285, 292, 366
Meyer, Steven, 110
Michelet, Jules, 440–442, 449–451

Midsummer Night's Dream (Shakespeare),
    44–46, 58
Miklòsi, Adam, 247–248, 253, 255, 258
militarism, 177, 320, 322, 325, 327–334
Miller, Richard W., 460–461
modernism, 98–109, 111–112, 297, 368–370, 373,
    481
    African American, 119, 123, 128–130
modernist ecology, 101, 105–106, 108–110
'Mole in the Ground' (song), 479–480, 482
monk seal, Caribbean, 341–343, 354
Monroe, Harriet, 98–101, 103, 112
Montero, Mayra, 348, 350–352, 355n8
Morton, Timothy, 13–14, 17–19, 62, 65, 67, 70,
    103, 113n22, 135–138, 144, 147–148, 165, 207,
    255, 287–288, 367, 373, 396, 483
Mouffe, Chantal, 166, 170
Muffet, Thomas, 46, 52
Muir, John, 98, 103, 112n3, 413, 476, 520
    and race, 119–122, 124, 126
multinaturalism, 12
multiple chemical sensitivity, 202
Murphy, Patrick, 335, 394, 425

NAACP (National Association for the
    Advancement of Colored People), 118
Naess, Arne, 29, 37, 103
NAFTA (North American Free Trade
    Agreement), 173, 178
Nagasaki (nuclear attack), 330–332
Naipaul, V.S., 348–350, 352
narrative, 18, 27, 68, 91–92, 130, 167, 201, 208,
    211, 216, 218, 227, 253, 264, 266, 305, 309,
    311, 346, 352, 375, 400, 411, 413, 462–467,
    532–533
    ecocritical theory of, 106–107, 139, 205, 207,
        349–350, 368–373, 424, 426–431, 503–513
    of decline, 20, 48, 283
    of progress, 89, 193, 195, 247, 321, 325, 430,
        512–513
    scholarship, 8, 22, 543
naturalization, 21, 103, 288, 306, 330, 334,
    467–468
nature writing, 104–105, 119, 123–124, 127,
    129, 157, 265–266, 268, 372, 374, 383–384,
    391–404, 424–425, 429, 434, 520–522, 534,
    540, 549, 551

nature writing (*Cont.*)
    critiques of, 112n3, 136, 160, 291, 380, 386,
        395–398
nature, end of, 391, 395, 428; *see* McKibben, Bill
negative ecopoetics, 110
neoliberalism, 160, 178, 311, 321, 323, 327, 329
neopastoral, 64, 69–70, 110–111; *see also*
        post-pastoral
Nicolar, Joseph, 11, 185
Ning, Wang, 539, 544
Nixon, Rob, 168, 172, 176–177, 179, 181, 226, 321,
        323, 328, 338, 352
No Future (Edelman), 15, 308
'No Ordinary Sun' (Tuwhare), 330
Nordhaus, Ted, 398, 506, 510–512
Nouvian, Claire, 199–200

O'Brien, Susie, 323, 326
Oates, Joyce Carol, 380
Ober, Frederick, 347
object oriented ontology, 292
ocean conservation, 191–194, 196, 198
Ocean Roads (George), 331–334
Odum, Eugene, 329
Oerlemans, Onno, 62, 66, 70–71
Oken, Lorenz, 67
Old Weird America, 481, 485
old-time music, 477–485
Olson, Charles, 442, 451
Olson, Ted, 476
'Only a Subaltern' (Kipling), 84, 90–91
On Religion (Schleiermacher), 72–73
Oppermann, Serpil, 137, 424–425
Origin of Species (Darwin), 139, 226, 294, 411
Oroonoko (Behn), 345
Our National Parks (Muir), 120–121
outbreak narratives, 83, 89
Outka, Paul, 121–122, 130n1

Pacific Islands, 329–330
palliative imperialism, 82, 85, 89, 94
pastoral, 40, 61, 115, 122, 127–128, 158, 378, 384,
        394–395, 417, 530, 551
    critiques of 43, 44, 69, 397, 417, 434–437; *see
        also* post-pastoral
pataphysics, 133–135, 137, 139, 142, 146–148
Pater, Walter, 107

Paul E. More, 392
Pearce, Fred, 344, 503, 508–510, 514
Peiffer, Katrina Schimmoeller, 383
Peirce, Charles Sanders, 133, 260–261,
        265–266, 466; *see* semiotics
PETA (People for the Ethical Treatment of
        Animals), 245
phenomenology, vi, 14–15, 22, 72, 105, 107, 262,
        268, 276–290, 296, 298, 302, 441, 492, 498,
        547, 554–555, 558, 560–561
Phillips, Dana, 17, 34, 36, 114n24, 135–136, 149,
        207–209, 396–397, 401, 434–435
Pickering, Andrew, 189, 195, 211–212, 217
Plumwood, Val, 233–234, 339, 366
poetics, 14, 71, 103, 264, 268, 287, 372, 441–442,
        451, 530, 540, 553; *see also* cognitive
        poetics; ecopoetics; poetry, lyric;
    eco-formalist 18, 102, 369, 442–443, 447, 481,
        pataphysical 133–148, 149n28
poetry, lyric, 370, 373, 442, 444, 447, 451, 457
Polanyi, Karl, 159
politicization, 156–157, 303
Politics of Nature (Latour), 10, 46–49, 137
Pollan, Michael, 247, 403
Ponting, Clive, 245
population pressure (human), 15, 22, 83, 181,
        212, 278, 309, 345, 350, 527
post-pastoral, 69, 76, 115, 131, 435, 437n16
postcolonial ecocriticism, 81, 320–324,
        341–354, 530–533, 560–565
postequilibrium ecology, 7, 15, 65, 466; *see also*
        Botkin, Daniel; Pyne, Stephen
posthumanism, 13, 14, 17, 20, 105, 109, 147–148,
        200, 235, 255, 306, 314, 397
    definitions of, 225–227, 235n6
postmodernism, 10, 14, 162, 165, 167, 189,
        208, 296, 398, 537–539, 541, 553; *see also*
        ecocriticism, postmodern
Potter, Beatrix, 409–411
Pound, Ezra, 98, 102
Pratt, Mary Louise, 324
preafference, 449
Price, Jenny, 397, 402
Protestantism, 41–42, 49, 51–53, 55–56, 72
psychoanalysis, 296, 364, 459, 461, 464–465,
        467, 470–472
Pyne, Stephen, 314–315

queer ecology, 109–111, 297, 305–319, 371, 397

race, 7, 16, 60, 67, 101, 118–130, 143, 179, 186, 188,
        320–321, 562–563
    colonialism and 88, 94,
    in Tolkien 299
Rees, Martin, 27–28
relativism, 2, 10, 163–164, 466–467, 473
Renaissance, 30, 40–58, 61, 69, 298, 442; see
        also animals, Renaissance
    Harlem 127–128
Rex, Michael A., 192
Rigby, Kate, 106, 112nn5,21,23, 548, 551
risk society, 158, 161, 169; see Beck, Ulrich
Ritter, J.W., 66
Robertson, Lisa, 135
Robisch, S.K., 246, 249–250
romanticism, 1, 17–18, 40–41, 60–75, 99, 101,
        105, 112n5, 119–121, 125, 216, 283, 393,
        395–396, 399, 451, 524; see also animals
        and romanticism; German romanticism;
        romantic ecology;
    as response to Enlightenment 43, 65,
        107–111,
romantic ecology, 5, 17, 62, 65, 106, 297
Roosevelt, Theodor, 119–120, 124, 127, 195–196
Rose, Stephen, 242
Ross, Andrew, 180, 436n6, 496
Roy, Arundhati, 101, 379, 527, 531–533
Rozelle, Lee, 498–499
RSPCA (Royal Society for the Prevention of
        Cruelty to Animals), 245
Rule, Jane, 306, 311–313, 315–316
Ryan, Ray, 425

S*PeRM**K*T (Mullen), 140, 142–143
Sandilands, Catriona, 14–15, 110–111, 168n10,
        366, 368
Sankhala, Kailash, 531–532
Santner, Eric, 552
satire, 73, 386, 388, 432–434
satisficing, 293, 302n8
Saunders, Paul, 105–107
Schelling, F.W.J., 67–68
Schlegel, Friedrich, 61, 67
Schleiermacher, Friedrich, 72–73
Schneider, Richard, 249, 257n8

Schulze, Robin, 109
science fiction, 68, 369, 372, 488, 512
science studies, 9, 11–13, 105, 108, 110, 163–165,
        208, 211; see also feminism and science
        studies
scientification, 20, 47
scientism, 208, 217, 220, 276, 278
Sebald, W.G., 552, 564
Sebeok, Thomas, 132–133, 260–261, 264; see
        biosemiotics
Seidl, 403–404
semiotics, 135, 144, 260–262, 265–266, 268,
        466–467, 470–471; see also biosemiotics
Seuss, Dr., 416–417
Sewell, Anna, 409, 412
sex, 66, 144, 162, 164, 241, 305–309, 311, 379,
        404, 432
Seymour, Nicole, 309, 363–365, 367
Shakespeare, Williams, 41–42, 44–46, 56, 295,
        378, 495
Shellenberger, Michael, 398, 506, 510–513
Shelley, Percy, 66
Shiva, Vandana, 326, 531–533
Shuyuan, Lu, 539–542
Siewers, Alfred, 29
Silent Spring (Carson), 27, 134, 156–158, 323, 327,
        400, 412
Silko, Leslie Marmon, 172–187
Simon, Bart, 226
Singer, Peter, 52, 58, 244–245
Sinha, Indra, 166–167, 531
Sir Gawain and the Green Knight (anon.), 27,
        33, 35–37
Slovic, Scott, 21, 363, 397, 401, 433, 520, 533–534,
        539, 543
slow violence, 126, 168, 176–177, 179, 181,
        183–184, 328, 352, 354; see Nixon, Rob
Snyder, Gary, 9, 103, 283, 286–287, 383, 520–521,
        523
social ecology, 427, 530
Solar (McEwan), 18, 206, 373, 426, 431–434
Solnit, Rebecca, 475–476
Soper, Kate, 7–8, 75, 466–467
Spiegelman, Sol, 295
Spinoza, Baruch, 64
Spivak, Gayatri Chakravorty, 125, 323, 326–327,
        331, 334

Sprackland, Jean, 374–375
St. Francis, 29
Stables, Andrew, 268
Stegner, Wallace, 416
Steingraber, Sandra, 17, 161, 402–404
Stevens, Wallace, 102–103, 442, 450, 455, 495
Stiegler, Bernard, 496–497
Strands (Strackland), 374–375
sublime, 48, 130, 144, 206, 375, 562–563
    romantic 41, 71–73, 121–122, 480–481
    Kantian 124–127
Sullivan, Heather, 68, 548
surveillance, 2, 163, 334
Swampy, 1, 24
symbiosis, 8, 43, 52, 194, 248, 301, 355n5, 367,
    500, 542, 553
    transgenic, 135, 137–138, 141, 144–145, 148

Tagore, Rabindranath, 530
Tarlo, Harriet, 369, 373
technogenesis, 494
technoscience, 103, 108, 169, 190
The Call of the Wild (London), 249–250, 258
'The Daughter of the Regiment' (Kipling), 84,
    90
The Day After Tomorrow (film), 504–505, 513
The Deep: Extraordinary Creatures of the Abyss
    (Nouvian), 199–201
The Ecological Thought (Morton), 65, 137, 144,
    147, 255
The Hungry Tide (Ghosh), 205, 210–212, 215,
    217–219, 221–224, 532, 535
The Last Generation (Pearce), 503, 508–509
The Live Earth Global Warming Survival
    Handbook (Greenpeace), 503, 510–511
The Lorax (Suess), 416–417, 419
The Lord of the Rings (Tolkein), 296, 299, 303
The Natural History and Antiquities of
    Selbourne (White), 65
theriomorphism, 46; *see also* zoomorphism
The Road (McCarthy), 206, 373–374, 403–404
The Secret Garden (Burnett), 409–410, 414, 416
The Simpsons Movie (film), 463, 469
The Spell of the Sensuous (Abram), 280–283,
    302, 366
'The Strange Ride of Morrowbie Jukes'
    (Kipling), 84, 92

The Tale of Peter Rabbit (Potter), 409–412
The Tempest (Shakespeare), 55
The Well of Loneliness (Hall), 110–111
The Wind in the Willows (Grahame), 409,
    416–417
The Xenotext Experiment (Bök), 135, 140–141,
    144–145
Thoreau, Henry David, 98, 382–384, 391–393,
    397, 399–401, 413, 441-443, 450–452, 520,
    522, 538
Tiffin, Helen, 328, 397, 528, 531
Tilt, Edward John, 83, 85–87
tinai, 529–530
Titus Andronicus (Shakespeare), 57
Toadvine, Ted, 278, 284–285
Tolkien. J.R.R., 14, 29, 33, 36, 38–39, 296–299,
    303
Tononi, Guilio, 445
trans-corporeality, 190, 402
Tsing, Anna Lowenhaupt, 326
Tuwhare, Honi, 330–331
Twain, Mark, 380, 382, 384–385, 388–389,
    410
Twelfth Night (Shakespeare), 52–53
Twining, William, 83, 87

UDRME (Universal Declaration of the Rights
    of Mother Earth), 172, 175, 178, 180–182,
    184
Uexküll, Jakob von, 132–133, 253, 261, 267, 300,
    495; *see also* biosemiotics
Umwelt, 18, 132–134, 137, 144, 147, 253, 258n12,
    261–262, 267, 495; *see* biosemiotics
unconscious, the 67–68, 295, 471, 483
UNDRIP (Universal Declaration of the
    Rights of Indigenous Peoples), 172,
    175, 178
Unenlightenment, 492

Varela, Francisco, 110, 448–451
vegetarianism, 52–54
Venter, Craig, 195–196, 201, 225, 234
Villard, Oswald Garrison, 129–130
Virilio, Paul, 330, 498
vitalism, 56
Vogel, Steven, 160–161
Voros, Gyorgi, 103–104, 106

Wald, Priscilla, 83

Walden (Thoreau), 322, 382–383, 399, 401, 441, 443

Wallace, Jeff, 108–109

Wallace, Jennifer, 1

Wallace, Kathleen, 396, 425

Warner, Michael, 305, 310

Watership Down (Adams), 409, 411

We Have Never Been Modern (Latour), 182, 208–209, 213–214

Welling, Bart, 198

Westling, Louise, 107–108

Wheeler, Wendy, 133, 264, 367

White Fang (London), 246

White, Lynn, 5–6, 28, 33, 35

Whitman, Walt, 225, 235n4, 388, 451, 454–455, 458

Wilde, Oscar, 107

wilderness, 1, 3, 43, 111, 189, 193, 195, 252, 299, 302, 321, 384, 403, 434, 549,
  fetishization of, 73, 160, 325, 374, 395, 398,

preservation, 98–99, 119–122, 388, 414, 476
  race and 119, 122, 124–125, 129–130, 563

Williams, Raymond, 9, 64, 69, 160, 229–230, 395, 416

Williams, William Carlos, 99

Wilson, E.O., 233, 238n22, 242

Wither, George, 54

Wolfe, Cary, 145, 227, 464

Woodstock (cartoon character), 293

Woolf, Virginia, 99–100, 107–109

Wordsworth, William , 60, 70

World Ocean Census: A Global Survey of Marine Life (Crist et al), 197, 200–201

Worster, Donald, 329

Zapatista movement, 178, 184, 418

Zapf, Hubert, 369, 549, 553–554

Žižek, Slavoj, 155–156, 167, 365, 367, 459, 465–467, 470, 472

zoomorphism, 253–254, 257–258
  racial 125